THE LETTERS OF MARSILIO FICINO

Volume 10

(*Liber XI*)

The Letters of
MARSILIO FICINO

Translated from the Latin by members of the Language Department of the School of Economic Science, London

VOLUME 10

being a translation of
Liber XI

SHEPHEARD-WALWYN

This translation first published in 2015 by
Shepheard-Walwyn (Publishers) Ltd
107 Parkway House, Sheen Lane,
London SW14 8LS
www.shepheard-walwyn.co.uk

Publisher's Note:

The beehive motif shown on the title page appears on a number of Ficino Manuscripts which were illuminated for Lorenzo de' Medici's library. The end-papers show two pages in Ficino's own hand from a manuscript containing Book 1 of his *Letters*. This is now in the Biblioteca Nazionale Centrale, Florence (Cod. Naz. II IX 2)

British Library Cataloguing in Publication Data
A catalogue record for this book
is available from the British Library

ISBN: 978-0-85683-500-1

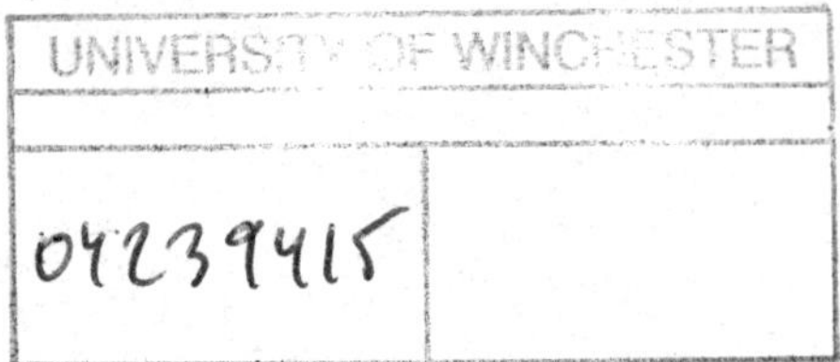

Typeset by Alacrity, Chesterfield, Sandford, Somerset
Printed and bound through
s|s|media limited, Rickmansworth, Hertfordshire

For
Clement Salaman
amico inseparabili

Contents

	Page
Acknowledgements	viii
Letter Titles	ix
Introduction	xiii
Translators' Note	xix
The Letters	1
Appendix Letters	53
Notes to the Letters	59
Note on the Latin Text	89
The Latin Text	93
Biographical Notes	117
German correspondents	117
Correspondents in Italy	120
Names from Letter 28	125
Bibliography	137
Index	145

Acknowledgements

DURHAM University Library Archives and Special Collections generously allowed the translators to use their copy of the Venice edition of Ficino's *Epistolae* with its valuable annotations. This is once again reproduced as the Latin text.

The Bayerische Staatsbibliothek, Munich, kindly supplied a copy of its manuscript, MS Lat. 10781, which provides important extra material, especially for the Appendix Letters.

Thanks are due to the Biblioteca Medicea Laurenziana, Florence, for permission to use the jacket illustration, from MS Acquisti e Doni 665, p.1 recto.

The translators wish to express their gratitude for suggestions and help from a number of scholars on individual points; in particular, their thanks go to Mr Geoffrey Pearce for carefully considering the astrological passages in this volume. Their indebtedness to the wider community of scholars is acknowledged, with gratitude, through the Bibliography.

Letter Titles

1 Epistola in dono argentei calicis
A letter accompanying the gift of a silver chalice

2 Responsio pro dono argentei calicis
Response to the gift of a silver chalice

3 Quomodo aliquis sub aliena persona cogitanti sibimet occurrat
How a person in reflection meets himself under the guise of another

4 Ad magnos pertinet beneficia conferre etiam non merentibus
It befits great men to bestow kindness even on the undeserving

5 Charitas et pietas potissimum est sapientis officium
Love and devotion are particularly incumbent on the wise man

6 Purgatio de litteris non redditis
Apology for letters not delivered

7 Pro adolescentibus e Suevia missis ad Academiam Florentinam
Concerning the young men sent from Swabia to the Academy in Florence

8 De quattuor speciebus divini furoris. Item laudes Medicis Laurentii verae.
On the four kinds of divine frenzy; and true praises of Lorenzo de' Medici

9 Vera laus Marci cardinalis sancti viri
True praise of Cardinal Marco, a holy man

10 Rationes negotiorum suorum amico reddendae
Accounts of all one's activities should be given to a friend

11 De simplicitate et integritate morum
On simplicity and integrity of character

12 Procemium in Platonicas institutiones
Preface to the 'Principles of the Platonic Teachings'

13 Gratiarum actio
An expression of thanks

14 In librum de vita dono datum
Concerning the 'Book on Life' offered as a gift

15 Philosophica ingenia ad Christum perveniunt per Platonem, ut Augustino Aurelio contigit
Philosophical minds come to Christ through Plato, as happened to St Augustine

16 Commendatio
A commendation

17 Commendatio
A commendation

18 Actio gratiarum. Item de ostentis in obitu principis.
An expression of thanks, and thoughts on the portents accompanying the death of a ruler

19 Actio gratiarum
Giving thanks

20 Causae prodigiorum in obitu principis contingentium
The causes of portents attendant upon the death of a prince

21 De vita solitaria, et quanti facienda sit fama
On the solitary life and the value to be placed on fame

22 Laudes amici scilicet Bindacii Recasolani
In praise of a friend, Bindaccio da Ricasoli

23 Laudes legitimi principis
In praise of a true prince

24 Qui futuris praedicendis incumbunt infortunati sunt
Those who are given to predicting the future encounter misfortune

25 Opiniones non temere divulgandae Item Orphei carmina
Beliefs should not be rashly promulgated, nor should the 'Hymns of Orpheus'

26 Exhortatur amicos ut Plotino foras prodeunti faveant
Urging friends to act in support of Plotinus as he comes forth

27 In librum de Vita missum ad amicum
Concerning the book 'On Life' sent to a friend

28 Catalogus familiarium atque auditorum
A list of my friends and students

29 Procemium in compendium Proculi
Preface to a selection from the writings of Proclus

30 De Daemonibus
On daemons

31 Philosophia cum fortuna et divitiis non coniungitur
Philosophy is not linked with fortune or wealth

32 Ubi plus fortunae, ibi sapientiae minus, atque vicissim
Where there is more fortune, there is less wisdom, and vice versa

33 Procemium in comparationem Solis ad Deum
Preface to 'A Comparison of the Sun to God'

34 Laudes saeculi nostri tanquam aurei ab ingeniis aureis
Praises of our age as golden on account of its golden minds

Appendix Letters

A Sortes humanae vitae et cura Dei erga Medices
The lots apportioned to human life, and God's care for the Medici

B Laudes Petri Medicis
In praise of Piero de' Medici

C De fortuna Platonis et miraculis in obitu Laurentii
On Plato's fortunes and the marvels attendant upon Lorenzo's death

D Primo de daemonibus communiter, secundo de daemonibus familiaribus, tertio de daemone Socratis
First, on daemons in general; secondly, on familiar spirits; thirdly, on the daemon of Socrates

Introduction

THE LETTERS in this volume span the seventeen months from 13th April, 1491 to 13th September, 1492. This is a crucial period for Marsilio Ficino and for the whole of Florence, for it witnesses the death of Lorenzo the Magnificent, whom Ficino praises in Letter 18 as 'the great and god-like Lorenzo'.

It may be something of a shock to realise that Lorenzo was only forty-three at his death, for his association with Ficino seems to have been of immense duration. The first letter we have to him from Ficino (Letter 17 of Volume 1) is undated, but it would have been written almost twenty years prior to the letters of the present volume. Ficino's first sentence in this early letter praises Lorenzo's actions: 'Almost all other rich men support servants of pleasure, but you support priests of the Muses.' This is immediately followed by an exhortation and a prediction: 'I pray you, continue, my Lorenzo, for those others will end up as the slaves of pleasure whereas you will become the delight of the Muses.' Now, two decades later, Ficino speaks of Lorenzo's continuing support. In Letter 7 he writes to two eminent lawyers in Germany about the care that is being given to the young men who have been sent to Florence for the furtherance of their education: 'Let your princes know that the magnanimous Lorenzo de' Medici, on whose support we depend, has most generously undertaken to provide for the young men.' Of Lorenzo as the delight of the Muses, Ficino proclaims in Letter 8: 'Truly inspired from on high, he pours forth upon mankind celestial songs in elegant form, whose profound thoughts no one may ever penetrate unless his spirit has been seized by a similar frenzy.' In Letter 11 Ficino applies to Lorenzo the appellation that many would ascribe to Ficino himself: 'restorer of the Platonic teachings'. 'I believe,' Ficino writes to Martin Prenninger in the autumn of 1491, 'that the printing of the books of Plotinus will be completed by next March, in princely style and at great expense on the part of Lorenzo de' Medici.'

It is little wonder, then, that Lorenzo's death on 8th April, 1492, made a great impact upon Marsilio, who seventeen days later, in a letter to Filippo Valori (Letter 20), calls Lorenzo 'protector of his native Florence' and writes, with reference to the unusual occurrences that took place in the sky and on the earth at the time of the death: 'Bereft of her father, unhappy Florence thus grieves and shudders at these portents.' Three nights before Lorenzo's death, news was brought that two lions caged in the Signoria as symbols of liberty had fought each other to the death. On the same night lightning had struck the lantern atop Brunelleschi's dome and one of the marble balls had shattered on striking the piazza. When Lorenzo heard of this, he was anxious to know where the ball had fallen. Learning that it was on the side nearest to his house, he exclaimed that this was a sure sign of his impending death. Other portents were reported: of she-wolves howling in the night and of strange lights appearing in the sky.

Lorenzo's body was taken from Careggi to San Marco, and from there to the old sacristy of San Lorenzo, to be buried next to his brother, Giuliano. In 1559 his coffin was moved to the new sacristy designed by Michelangelo, where it lies in a vault under the statue of the Madonna.[1]

Of the thirty-four letters in this volume, as many as five are addressed to Martin Prenninger, Professor of Ecclesiastical Law at Tübingen University and counsellor to Count Eberhard. To Martin's name Marsilio often adds 'Uranius', which he construes in Letter 33, written to Eberhard, as the 'heavenly one', adding 'and he really is a contemplator of the heavens'. An earlier letter, also addressed to Eberhard, refers to Martin as 'a most reliable witness and surety in our midst and a herald of your praises most worthy of everyone's trust'. In three letters Marsilio calls Martin his 'unique friend', and in the other two 'his especial friend' and 'his most beloved brother'. In Letter 17 he declares 'how often I speak of Martin as my second self', and Letter 22 confirms this.

Letter 29, also written to Martin Prenninger, is the longest in the volume. It consists mainly of extracts selected by Ficino from the commentaries by Proclus on Plato's *Republic.* The letter has a short introduction by Ficino, who speaks of the recent arrival in Florence of many books from Greece, among which are Proclus' commentaries to the first six books of the *Republic* and the beginning of the seventh book. Ficino points out to Prenninger, whom he here calls 'a man noted for his religious faith', that the letter contains specially chosen passages, or 'little flowers', which are 'more fragrant with holy religion than the rest'. The first passage states that the three attributes of every divinity are goodness, power, and knowledge. The second – and much longer – extract expatiates on the proposition that a god causes no evil, never changes form, and never deceives anyone. The third declares that souls separated from the body have three states or dispositions: the contemplative, the active, and the pleasure-seeking. Prenninger is then offered a brief consideration of the three lives of the soul – divine, human, and bestial – before being introduced to a fourfold division of creation, to the crucial and perennially controversial proposal that the Good is above being and essence, and, finally, to Plato's view that the Good has a threefold location: within us, within Ideas, and above Ideas.

It is from his words to Prenninger that we are kept abreast of Ficino's scholarly undertakings in this period. Letter 10 informs us of his current work with the *Divine Names* of Dionysius, the copy of the *Philebus* commentary that is being made for Martin, and the re-printing, in Venice, of his translations of Plato's dialogues, together with the *Platonic Theology*. Letter 16 commends Martin's excellent qualities to Francesco Soderini, Bishop of Volterra; and the following letter reveals that 'he even named his son Marsilio after me and organised a celebration of my birthday'.

The Germanic element is notable throughout the book, which indeed begins with a letter from Georg Herivart of Augsburg, praising Ficino's 'exceptional abilities', 'outstanding virtues' and 'sweet-flowing eloquence'. Letter 2 constitutes Ficino's reply, in which he declares that ever since his childhood he has felt a natural goodwill towards the Germanic peoples. He commends Martin Prenninger to Georg with the highest praise; and he closes the letter by stating that the whole of this book will be a token of his delight with Georg's letter and the accompanying gift of a silver chalice. Letter 7, addressed to the two German lawyers and mentioned earlier with reference to Lorenzo, proclaims that 'you, men of great modesty, follow Socrates and disclaim what is your own' and that 'you pursue the heavenly splendour of wisdom among all nations.'

For some readers, Letter 28 will prove the most interesting and the most intriguing. It is an answer to Martin's frequent request to receive a list of Marsilio's friends. The list that is given is preceded by an expression of Marsilio's hope that no one will be offended by thinking that he is drawing comparisons among the names listed or by wrongly evaluating the order in which they are given. The plan he follows is to put the members of the Medici family first as his patrons, beginning with Cosimo de' Medici. He then identifies two groups of friends. The first group are 'friends through close association, conversation-partners so to speak, those who share in to-and-fro discussions and liberal studies.' The second group 'have sometimes listened to us reading and, as it were, teaching.' The first group is then subdivided according to three phases of Marsilio's life: his earliest years (only Naldo Naldi is given here); his youth (Cristoforo Landino, Leon Battista Alberti, and Giovanni Cavalcanti are three of the twenty-two listed); and his mature years (Angelo Poliziano, Pier Leone, and Giovanni Pico della Mirandola appear in a list of fourteen). The letter ends, somewhat abruptly, with a straightforward list of the second group, totalling thirty-four, which includes Piero Soderini, Filippo and Niccolò Valori, and Bindaccio da Ricasoli.

Letter 28, however, is not the only one to reveal fascinating aspects of Ficino's life, thought, and experience. In Letter 3 he expresses his high view of Dionysius the Areopagite: 'No form of knowledge is more beloved than the Platonic, and nowhere is this form to be more revered than in Dionysius. Indeed, I love Plato in Iamblichus, I am full of admiration for him in Plotinus, I stand in awe of him in Dionysius.' He follows this statement with the conjecture that 'Platonists prior to Plotinus, such as Ammonius and Numenius, or perhaps earlier ones than these, read the books of Dionysius before they vanished in some calamity of the Church; and from them the truly Platonic sparks of Dionysius were transferred to Plotinus and Iamblichus: whence such a great blaze has been kindled.'[2]

Letter 6 shows that Ficino, like a good businessman, kept a copy of his correspondence. On being accused by Cristoforo Marsuppini of failing to write to Cardinal Raffaele Riario, he is able to open his file and show Cristoforo the originals of at least four letters which have been sent to the Cardinal but which have been 'truly ill-fated' in not reaching their destination. With regard to another cardinal, Cardinal Marco Barbo, Ficino, writing to Antonio Calderini in Letter 9, records his indebtedness to Calderini because 'long ago you gave me as a friend that holy man, Cardinal Marco of St Mark's, and on many occasions when I was in danger you provided me with his protection.'

In the following letter, Ficino uncharacteristically discloses something of his own state when he writes, 'For my part, I am well, as far as my condition, my age, the summer heat, and unremitting scholarly studies allow.' Letter 22 connects his protracted illness with that of Lorenzo and refers to the tedium that Ficino experienced during this time. He affirms that 'by the grace of God I have now recovered fairly well from that long period of infirmity.'

In drawing a comparison between himself and Pier Leone in Letter 11, Ficino points to the qualities of honesty and straightforwardness when he writes, 'Neither of us knows how to pretend or deceive.' The next letter speaks of 'the first-fruits of my studies', which Ficino says were four books related to the Platonic teaching which he started to produce when he was twenty-three. Cristoforo Landino and Cosimo de' Medici approved of these works but advised the young man to keep them to himself until he had learned Greek and could 'imbibe the Platonic teachings from their sources.'

Ficino's sense of humour, which is never deeply hidden, becomes obvious in Letter 14, when he declares that he has good reason to entrust his *Three Books on Life* to the distinguished physician Mazzingo, 'for I long ago entrusted to you the care of my own life and that of my dependants.' The humour surfaces again in Letter 19, where Ficino is seeking to outdo the grammarians by going beyond the superlative! 'I have been accustomed for some time,' he writes to Francesco Soderini, Bishop of Volterra, 'to give you the greatest possible thanks for your many kindnesses towards me. Now I give you more than the greatest thanks and I acknowledge myself to be more than most devoted to you.'

Letter 34, addressed to 'Paul of Middelburg, the eminent scientist and astronomer', fittingly brings this volume to a close with a paean of praise to an age which has 'brought back into the light the liberal arts, which were almost extinct: grammar, poetry, rhetoric, painting, sculpture, architecture, music, and the ancient art of singing to the Orphic lyre', an age which 'has united wisdom with eloquence, and prudence with martial prowess'. Perhaps we can forgive Ficino his patriotic exuberance in proclaiming with a flourish, 'And all this in Florence.'

Arthur Farndell
Editor

NOTES

1 For information in this and the previous paragraph, the following publications are gratefully acknowledged: J. R. Hale, *Florence and the Medici*, London, 1977, repr. 1983 and 2011; Vincent Cronin, *The Florentine Renaissance*, London, 1967, repr. 1972, 1992; Christopher Hibbert, *The Rise and Fall of the House of Medici*, London, 1974, repr. 1979, 1999.

2 For a discussion of the changing views regarding the dating and authorship of the writings attributed to Dionysius, see note 6 to Letter 3 (pp. 60-1).

Translators' Note

THIS volume contains Ficino's eleventh book of letters, comprising letters written from April 1491 to September 1492. There is no separate preface or dedicatory letter, as this book was dedicated jointly with the previous book to Niccolò Valori. The Latin text of these letters is printed on pages 93 to 116, with notes below expanding unusual abbreviations and showing significant variant readings.

Textual Sources

The 1495 printed edition of Ficino's Letters was published in Venice by Matteo Capcasa of Parma. The copy in the library of the University of Durham, used here, shows some corrections in the hand of Ficino Ficini, Ficino's nephew. These may be regarded as corrections authorised by Ficino himself.

Besides the printed edition, there is only one manuscript for the letters in this volume, siglum Mo2, Munich, Bayerische Staatsbibliothek, MS lat. 10781, fols. $54v^{o}$ to $57v^{o}$. This was a composite manuscript compiled in November, 1492 for Filippo Carducci to whom two letters in this volume are addressed. This manuscript also contains the letters of Books IX and X and the first few of Book XII. It is the source for all the Appendix letters in this volume.

The Latin texts of the Appendix letters are already reproduced: Appendix A and Appendix B in Kristeller, *Supplementum Ficinianum*, I, pp. 62-64; Appendix C in Ficino, *Opera omnia* (Basle, 1576), p. 1538 as a dedicatory letter to his Plotinus commentary; Appendix D as a section within Proclus, *De anima et daemone* in Ficino's 1497 volume of translations of later Platonists (without pagination) and in *Opera*, p. 1912.

The Letters

I

Epistola in dono argentei calicis

A letter accompanying the gift of a silver chalice

Georg Herivart of Augsburg to Marsilio Ficino the Platonist: greetings.

WHENEVER I call to mind, as I do every day and, to speak more truthfully, every hour, that auspicious and joyful day which brought me the beginning of your sweet acquaintance and friendship, I am pleased to consider it worthy of that celebration with which a birthday is usually honoured and, as the custom was in ancient times, to observe it with a white pebble.[1] For that was the day which also brought me your exceptional abilities, your outstanding virtues and that familiar sweet-flowing eloquence which flourishes abundantly in you. I value all these qualities so much that I have given myself, even devoted my whole self, to you, who are thus endowed. I would like nothing more, should the opportunity present itself, than to be able, wherever I may be, to please you in all matters and for you to be happy to use my services, diligence and talents, however insignificant they are. Again and again I fervently ask you to do this.

I am now sending to you a silver cup or rather, I should say, a very trifling little cup, a small childish gift.[2] Your virtues are such, of course, that they deserve to be requited with greater gifts, but as you are very kind, you will call this not a gift but in some way a token and evidence of our friendship, recently begun, and of your kindness to me. And so you will consider that I am sending it to you in the same spirit.

Farewell, and love me.

Venice.
13th April, 1491.[3]

2

Responsio pro dono argentei calicis

Response to the gift of a silver chalice

Marsilio Ficino of Florence to Georg Herivart the German: greetings.

EVER since my childhood, my dear Georg, I have felt a natural goodwill towards Germans. This is brought about by some hidden connection. So the allies of the Florentines in San Miniato, who are of Germanic stock, are our especial friends,[1] and the Pico and Cavalcanti families, who draw their origins from German lands, hold us very dear.[2] Therefore if Germans in general are all my own brothers, what should I say about the distinguished men and friends amongst you? About my heavenly friend Martin Uranius? And about you, my dearest Georg? Clearly, whoever is more than a brother to me is beyond question a second self, so that if what is your own is most dear to you, it will be no surprise if what is mine gives you special pleasure, as if it were your own.[3] If only I were as great in virtue in my own eyes as I am in yours, my friends!

Certainly in my goodwill towards you I am like that chalice you have just given me: silver on the outside but gold within.[4] I perceive that your nature, too, under an outward appearance of silver, possesses that gold which Socrates in the *Phaedrus* humbly seeks from God,[5] and which in the *Republic* he recognises within heroic natures.[6]

Finally, the witness of how much your letter and the gift I have received have pleased me will be the eleventh book of our letters, which begins by including your letter first and then this reply of mine.

Farewell, fortunate man. And if you love Marsilio, love Martin surnamed Prenninger. If you wish to embrace me with heavenly love, embrace my beloved Uranius with your whole heart.

29th April, 1491.

3

Quomodo aliquis sub aliena persona cogitanti sibimet occurrat

How a person in reflection meets himself under the guise of another

Marsilio Ficino to his fellow Platonist, Pier Leone: greetings.

I HAVE received your letter, Pier Leone, full of love and kindness and truly, if I may praise it with a single word, Platonic. In it you plainly write that Marsilio runs to help you as soon as you meet something Platonic; but take care that the outer appearance does not perhaps deceive you. I really think that Pier Leone himself lies hidden in the guise of Marsilio,[1] for if any human form presents itself to you when you are considering Platonic matters, it is probably a very Platonic form that shows itself first. But in human affairs what is more Platonic than great Leo, the abode of the Platonic sun?[2] Therefore, perhaps, just like Narcissus, when you gaze at yourself you think that you are gazing at someone else, and especially at Marsilio, with whose image you are clothed by burning love.[3] But whereas we are taken in by the image, you really know that reason is the intermediary between imagination and intellect, and into it from the imagination on one side flow the images of nature but on the other side, from the intellect, stream in the forms of things divine.[4] For this reason it often happens that a divine form in the presence of human reason assumes a natural image, and therefore that which is inwardly divine often appears natural to the eyes of reason. So why should Pier Leone not meet himself frequently in the form of Marsilio? But no more on these matters.

You seem to me to have formed a correct view of Dionysius the Areopagite:[5] certainly to me no form of knowledge is more beloved than the Platonic, and nowhere is this form to be more revered than in Dionysius. Indeed, I love Plato in Iamblichus, I am full of admiration for him in Plotinus, I stand in awe of him in Dionysius; but I often conjecture that Platonists prior to Plotinus, such as Ammonius and Numenius, or perhaps earlier ones than these, read the books of Dionysius before they vanished in some calamity of the Church;[6] and from them to Plotinus and Iamblichus were transferred the truly Platonic sparks of Dionysius, whence such a great blaze has been kindled.[7] Enough on Dionysius. I shall be grateful for Galen's *On the teachings of Hippocrates and Plato.*[8]

You are frequently spoken of at the home of Lorenzo de' Medici. Certainly he loves you in a wonderful way, as always, and he honours you fully, as is fitting.

12th May, 1491.
In the countryside, at Careggi.

4

Ad magnos pertinet beneficia conferre etiam non merentibus

It befits great men to bestow kindness even on the undeserving

Marsilio Ficino humbly commends himself to his Reverend Father in Christ, his Lord Raffaele Riario, Cardinal of San Giorgio.

EVEN if there are perhaps no merits by which I might obtain something from you, I shall venture, however, to ask for something as a favour, not indeed trusting in any merits, but relying both on my respect for you and on your mercy towards all. It is indeed just, yet human, to show kindness to the deserving, but it is most merciful and God-like to give generously even to the undeserving. Certainly great and divine things are especially fitting for a great and holy priest.[1]

5

Charitas et pietas potissimum est sapientis officium

Love and devotion are particularly incumbent on the wise man

Marsilio Ficino to his most beloved brother, Martin Uranius: greetings.

IF only I had sufficient wisdom to fulfil what you have promised on my behalf and to satisfy the expectations of others! But I have already fulfilled my office to the best of my ability, for I have welcomed with great pleasure the young men whom you have recently sent to us to be educated.[1] I entrusted them immediately to one of our devout hosts.[2] Every day I will take care that they flourish and that they are educated and instructed as well as possible. With regard to this at least, my most excellent Martin, please give assurance of my special care to the young men's parents and your rulers, to whom you have promised wisdom.

To this extent you will be a truthful guarantor, I hope, and I will perhaps have given satisfaction, if in return for the expectation of wisdom I shall have especially fulfilled the office of love and devotion, for devotion is the highest wisdom in the sight of God.

1st June, 1491.

6

Purgatio de litteris non redditis

Apology for letters not delivered

Marsilio Ficino humbly commends himself to his Reverend Father in Christ, his Lord Raffaele Riario, Cardinal of San Giorgio.

OUR close friend Cristoforo Marsuppini, having recently returned to Florence from Rome, immediately after the first words of greeting told me how dearly you hold me in your kind esteem.[1] Nothing could have been more welcome to my ear than that.

What troubled me, however, was that soon afterwards he began to accuse me of negligence, as if I had written no letters to you after your departure. But immediately upon opening the collection of my original letters to show Cristoforo, I read at least four that were sent to you at that time.[2] There is no doubt that on their way to Rome they were truly ill-fated, for they do not appear to have reached you yet. Nevertheless, there are letters that have long since flown elsewhere supported by better fortune, not only throughout Italy, but even into Spain, France, Germany, and Hungary.[3] These letters bear witness to my regard and reverence toward you everywhere but in Rome. Therefore I was rightly to blame, not because I sent you no letters, but because I sent you only a few. But may those letters which seemed ill-fated at their first birth be at least reborn more fortunate today! Then, profiting from this better fate, they may reach their happy patron and commend your humble servant.

4th June, 1491.

7

Pro adolescentibus e Suevia missis ad Academiam Florentinam

Concerning the young men sent from Swabia[1] to the Academy in Florence

Marsilio Ficino to the distinguished German lawyers Ludwig Nauclerus and Johannes of Pforzheim:[2] greetings.

YOU write to us, in your own name, that German princes are sending their young men to Florence for their education, as if to an Academy.[3] Yet at the same time you write with such elegance that you appear to be sending their sons not to an Academy but from an Academy, and to be looking abroad for learning you already have at home, which is the wrong way round.

Just as very many arrogant people, in the manner of the Sophists, rashly claim what is not theirs,[4] so do you, men of great modesty, follow Socrates and disclaim what is your own; and you are to be admired above all for this, that, just as many search out gem-stones hidden in the bowels of the earth,[5] so with equal care do you pursue the heavenly splendour of wisdom among all nations. For this reason, moved by an extraordinary love for you, we took on the guidance of your young men in a spirit of devotion, and first we entrusted them to a host distinguished for his devoted care;[6] and we shall make it our concern day by day to ensure that the naturally fertile field will in due course bring forth fruit in abundance.

So be of good cheer and in our name let your princes know that the magnanimous Lorenzo de' Medici, on whose support we depend, has most generously undertaken to provide for the young men.

5th June, 1491.
In the countryside, at Careggi.

8

De quattuor speciebus divini furoris. Item laudes Medicis Laurentii verae.

On the four kinds of divine frenzy; and true praises of Lorenzo de' Medici

Marsilio Ficino to Piero Dovizi, a man most distinguished in learning and conduct: greetings.

WHEN long ago you had heard our Plato discoursing extensively on love in the *Symposium* and wished, moreover, for a concise summary of his views on love, I produced a little work for us to read on this subject, composed in my youth for Peregrino Agli, a young man renowned for his skill in poetry.[1] Indeed, I remember how exceedingly delighted you were to hear that love itself is in truth not sensual desire, but a certain kind of frenzy divinely aroused in lofty spirits by divine influence; and that divine frenzy, like a genus, contains four species: love, poetry, prophecy and the sacred Mysteries.

You heard that love is from Venus and poetry from the Muses, but that prophecy proceeds from Apollo and the sacred Mysteries from Dionysus. In this way, the varying natures within men are moved mostly by one divinity or another through the different frenzies.

It remained, most gifted Piero, to enquire diligently whether a single nature, stirred by different frenzies, may be inspired simultaneously by several gods, if I may put it like that.[2]

Now the enquiry about love, and also about poetry, does not seem to be too difficult. For we do not doubt that Homer, Pindar, Callimachus, Sappho, and Virgil were deeply moved by poetic inspiration and simultaneously by love;[3] or Epimenides and the Sibyl by prophecy as well;[4] but it is said that only those born of the gods were able to be inspired by the sacred Mysteries in addition to the other three frenzies. Such were Orpheus in the ancient tradition[5] and David in our own;[6] and we ourselves have come to know in our time a most fortunate man who has attained these four gifts of the frenzies in equal measure from the four divinities.[7]

Long ago, in the very flower of his youth, he received the spirit of poetry from the Muses and the spirit of love from celestial Venus, as his sweet songs and wonderful poems proclaim everywhere; but when riper in years, he drew prophecy from Apollo. By means of prophecy, indeed, once a wonderful keenness of mind has been implanted from heaven, he frequently divines future crises in both private and public affairs, offers a healing hand in times of danger, and immediately provides a remedy through the power of Phoebus. Now close to full maturity, he has succeeded in acquiring the mystical frenzy from Dionysus.[8]

The ancient theologians explained Dionysian intoxication as the withdrawal of the mind when it is separated from earthly things but penetrates the hidden mysteries of the divine. 'Bacchus loves the hills.'[9] In the hills of Ambra and the valley of the Agnano, the Phoebean Lorenzo, intoxicated with the nectar of Dionysus, revels wildly far and wide.[10] Then, being truly inspired from on high, he pours forth upon mankind celestial songs in elegant form, whose profound thoughts no one may ever penetrate unless his spirit has been seized by a similar frenzy. At times that patron of ours carries along with him quite a few who are listening more attentively and to better purpose, pouring especially upon them from the abundance of his frenzy.

How he himself, wonderfully moved by divine will, has the power to stir up others in almost the same way, is explained by our Plato in the book entitled *Ion*, where he places a small iron ring beneath a powerful Herculean stone,[11] to be instantly caught up. To this first ring he immediately hangs a second; a third to the second, and after that a fourth. He forms a chain of rings suspended one after the other from the magnet, through which the power of attraction is rapidly transmitted from one to the next. He considers that in the same way the Muse is seized by Phoebus, the poet is seized by the Muse, and likewise the hearers are seized by the poet.

Perhaps Virgil is giving expression to this mystery in these lines: 'Those things which the Father Almighty made known to Phoebus, and Phoebus Apollo made known to me, I, eldest of the Furies, unfold to you.'[12]

But I would not wish to name the Furies at present, while we are discussing a frenzy which is not of the Furies but of the Graces.[13] Overflowing with this, our patron at once touches you and me equally, O most fortunate Piero, and the rest of those who attend upon him. Those touched he seizes; those seized he possesses; those possessed he soon showers with incomparable delight. Therefore, being touched by the great blessing arising from this, let us continue steadfastly in our most ardent love for him. In loving like this, each one of us daily regains divine inspiration.

8th June, 1491.

9

Vera laus Marci cardinalis sancti viri

True praise of Cardinal Marco, a holy man

Marsilio Ficino to his most beloved Antonio Calderini: greetings.

YESTERDAY our Pietro Fanni,[1] a learned and honest man, gave many examples in proof of your singular goodwill towards me, which has long been confirmed by your countless acts of kindness. Although there are, in fact, many reasons why I am much in your debt, my Calderini, I am indebted most of all because long ago you gave me as a friend that holy man, Cardinal Marco of St Mark's,[2] and on many occasions when I was in danger you provided me with his protection. We could not but grieve deeply at his death, unless we hoped that from heaven, where he leads a blessed life, he would favour us with a still surer patronage in days to come.

Both in life and in death, this man, as you well know, is certainly seen to have followed the words of David: 'My soul is continually in my hand'[3] and also to have realised the words of the Gospel: 'I have the power to lay down my life.'[4] For he foretold the hour of his death and departed from the body happily and as if by his own will, in such a manner that he seemed not even to die but to journey forth of his own accord, or rather to return to the homeland he longed for, ready to give an example of immortal life to mortals and to become a new light among the lights in the heavens. Blessed indeed, my Antonio, is our friendship, for it has been confirmed under the protection of the most blessed patron of all.

Farewell, prosper, and, as you always do, love me who especially love you.

29th June, 1491.

10

Rationes negotiorum suorum amico reddendae[1]

Accounts of all one's activities should be given to a friend

Marsilio Ficino to his especial friend, Martin Uranius Prenninger: greetings.

SINCE there is no one dearer to me than you, my most beloved Martin, no one has a greater right than you to be sent regular accounts of our activities.

For my part, I am well, as far as my condition, my age, the summer heat, and unremitting scholarly studies allow. As I wrote long ago, I am proceeding with the *Divine Names* of Dionysius.[2] At the same time, I am renewing my acquaintance with Plotinus as he comes from the printers; he will, I judge, be published four or, at most, five months hence.[3] Our commentary on *Philebus* is being copied out for you.[4] I am sending part of it now, eight quinternions, and the rest later. In Venice the books of Plato and the *Theology* are currently being printed again, and printed with greater accuracy, so they say.[5]

The young men entrusted to us are thriving and day by day are making good progress in their learning and the way they conduct themselves.[6]

Our singular love requires a very detailed account of every single activity, but circumstances prevent this. So, content with these words, fare well, and may all prosperity attend you.

20th July, 1491.

II

De simplicitate et integritate morum

On simplicity and integrity of character

Marsilio Ficino to Pier Leone, his fellow Platonist: greetings.

GREETINGS, Pier Leone, most worthy as you are of whole-hearted greetings,[1] being a man of the greatest integrity, or, rather, of the greatest simplicity. Yet our Plato in the *Symposium* thinks that in our time no one is born whole, but divided,[2] and in the *Timaeus* and the *Phaedrus* he affirms that all men are twofold.[3] Therefore, when I call you whole and simple, I am judging you to be a child not of this age but of another, in which, as Plato says, men used to be born both whole and simple, as long as a certain divinity reigned within humanity.[4] For in the divine realm integrity is the same as simplicity; natural things, however, have an integrity that is manifold; finally, unnatural things fall away from both integrity and simplicity.[5] Yet a letter hardly accommodates mysteries, but it can accommodate destinies.

Therefore see, Pier Leone, my second self, how similar a destiny we have obtained in most things, as well as the same indicator in the stars for the pursuit of learning. As I understand it, we have Saturn as our guide, as well as Plato, and we also have the same patron, Lorenzo de' Medici, restorer of the Platonic teachings. In fact, we have the same friends, but no enemies, for we love everyone. Perhaps the only person we would not love would be someone discovered to love only himself.

Besides, who would say that our characters are not similar? For neither of us knows how to pretend or deceive. Pretenders and deceivers alike deceive each other, but let them deceive again and again as much as they like, provided that they themselves, being already false, do not at any time change our characters and make us false, too.

Farewell and prosper in your integrity and simplicity. Even with an unfavourable destiny you will prevail in life.[6]

20th August, 1491.[7]

12

Procemium in Platonicas institutiones

Preface to the 'Principles of the Platonic Teachings'

Marsilio Ficino to his most beloved Filippo Valori: greetings.

IN the year of our Saviour 1456, when I was in the twenty-third year of my life and you were born, I started to produce the first-fruits of my studies with four books of *Principles* related to the Platonic teaching.[1] Cristoforo Landino, a most learned man and a great friend to me, encouraged me to write them.

However, when he and Cosimo de' Medici had read them through, they approved, but advised me to keep them to myself until such time as I had learned Greek and could imbibe the Platonic teachings from their sources. For in producing those *Principles* I had been helped partly by a chance discovery[2] and partly through reading some of the Latin Platonists.[3]

Thereafter, having applied myself to Plato and the Greek Platonists,[4] I gradually revised those *Principles* in the books that followed. Yet it did not feel right to destroy the book itself that was, so to speak, my firstborn child, fathered in the year you were born – you who are certainly a son to me by virtue of your respect and also a patron through your continuing favour.

Therefore, Valori, my most beloved son,[5] I call upon you to embrace with brotherly love this brother of yours, who will live and flourish as I would wish in the home of the Valori, which has been a home to me from an early age.[6]

Farewell.
5th November, 1491.

13

Gratiarum actio

An expression of thanks

Marsilio Ficino to his unique friend, Martin Uranius Prenninger: greetings.

YOUR Johann Streler, who is now ours also, today read me part of your letter to him. It was full of most ardent love for me, and it further showed that you had celebrated my birthday at great expense in a gathering of learned men.[1] It follows that I cannot satisfy such great devotion to me unless I love you as much as I love myself. But the proofs of my incomparable love towards you, my dearest Martin, will be not only my letters but also certain books due to be published hereafter.[2] So live happily, Martin, never less dear to me than my own life.

I am sending you the remaining four quinternions of my commentary on the *Philebus*.[3] I believe that the printing of the books of

Plotinus will be completed by next March, in princely style and at great expense on the part of Lorenzo de' Medici.[4] He has also resolved that the books of our Plato should be published soon afterwards to the same standard.[5] But I shall take all possible care that this second printing will be more accurate than the first.[6] I shall also divide each book into a number of chapters and sections and introduce them with unambiguous headings as guides.

On account of my occupation with this, the books of Dionysius, which I began long ago, will be completed somewhat later.[7]

Farewell.
24th November, 1491.
Florence.

14

In librum de vita dono datum

Concerning the 'Book on Life' offered as a gift

Marsilio Ficino to the distinguished physician Mazzingo, his inseparable friend: greetings.

GREETINGS, God-sent guardian of our health and truly inseparable friend.[1] You may initially wonder why I have chosen to call you an inseparable friend. It is, of course, because Earth cannot separate those whom Heaven has joined. For how will Earth, the lowest in the cosmos, be able to separate our souls by physical distance when the highest of the planets has joined them in his house by love? Such love is as lasting as Saturn himself is constant.[2]

Now let this *Life* of mine be a pledge to you of my unshakeable goodwill. I have good reason to entrust this *Life* to you for you to test and put into practice, for I long ago entrusted to you the care of my own life and that of my dependants.[3]

15

Philosophica ingenia ad Christum perveniunt per Platonem, ut Augustino Aurelio contigit

Philosophical minds come to Christ through Plato, as happened to St Augustine[1]

Marsilio Ficino of Florence to Giovanni Pico della Mirandola, his fellow philosopher: greetings.

MY excellent friend, you write (which itself is most pleasing to me) that you are urging many people every day, and have already convinced some, to leave the irreligion of Epicurus or lay aside certain beliefs of Averroes and to follow the sacred view of our Plato concerning the soul and God.[2] Indeed, through this view, as if through a middle way, they will finally attain to Christian piety.

Greetings, therefore, true fisher of men. For those who persuade common minds seem to catch fish, or rather little fish, but those who persuade eminent minds are judged to be fishers of men. The Gospel, perhaps, calls these 'great fishes', and what is more, in taking them the net is not broken.[3] Of course, our net now, Mirandola, is Platonic reason, which, provided it is drawn correctly, under Christian truth, does not break, but remains intact all the time it is being filled.

You have read that in the past none of the philosophers apart from the followers of Plato have accepted the Christian religion.[4] You are right, therefore, to fish for the greatest minds for Christ with Platonic nets, if I may call them that. Would that there were at least three such fishermen for religion so that there would be no big fish left in the sea! How pitiable we are, or rather, unfortunate! 'The harvest truly is great but the labourers are few.'[5] Therefore, my Mirandola, the fewer we are the more constantly and the more vigorously we must work.[6]

Farewell.

16

Commendatio

A commendation

Marsilio Ficino to Francesco Soderini, Bishop of Volterra: greetings.

MARTIN Uranius has come to Rome from Germany to carry out his prince's commands to the best of his ability; and he will fulfil them if, as I hope, you make available your guidance and assistance.[1] Indeed, I desire so strongly that they be made available that there is nothing I now want more. If you get to know this man, his excellent qualities will commend him to you. So while he is not yet known to you, let my great friendship with him commend him to you. For this man is so dear to me that I can describe him in no other way than to say that he is my second self.

Since I have so far commended none of my friends to you in vain – such is your remarkable humanity and compassion – I now hope, indeed, I know for certain, that Martin, or rather Marsilio, has been successfully commended to you.

1st April, 1492.

17

Commendatio

A commendation

Marsilio Ficino to his own Filippo Valori: many greetings.[1]

YOU remember, my Valori, how ardently our Martin Uranius loves me, so much so that he even named his son Marsilio after me and organised a celebration of my birthday.[2] Therefore I have no doubt that he is very dearly loved by you. He is about to call on you, to explain his purpose, and to ask for your assistance.[3]

If you remember how often I speak of Martin as my second self, I have no doubt that you will hold him wonderfully commended in every way.

I have written in the same vein to our esteemed Soderini. To him, therefore, commend Marsilio's twin, as you now know him to be, with entreaties that are twinned with mine.

18

Actio gratiarum. Item de ostentis in obitu principis.

An expression of thanks, and thoughts on the portents accompanying the death of a ruler

Marsilio Ficino humbly commends himself to his lord and Most Reverend Father in Christ, Cardinal Giovanni de' Medici.

SINCE medics consider the fourth stage to be the most important,[1] and you are my fourth patron from the noble Medici family beginning with Cosimo, you are without doubt the most important.[2] I am keenly aware of this from the fact that you are giving me, not something belonging to another, but something of your own. Some time ago you conferred on me your own canonry.[3] Now you have unexpectedly given me the Martiana church which had been bestowed on you as a benefice.[4]

So, on the death of our magnanimous Lorenzo it is not right for me to bewail my lot, because by succession I see myself especially entrusted to so great a patron; nor should I feel pity for Lorenzo's fate, since we know by many clear signs that he has been conveyed to the realms above.[5]

I believe you have read in Hesiod that, throughout the upper air, thirty thousand benevolent daemons look after human affairs.[6] These the ancients call the guides and examiners of mankind. Moreover, the most distinguished leaders among men migrate after death to become hereafter their fellows, as it were, in directing human affairs.[7] The Platonists hold that the guides welcome the happy souls flying towards them, but give signs of their welcome that are portents astonishing to mankind: thunder, lightning, flames, structures collapsing, prophecies, and dreams.[8]

Such portents sometimes appear to indicate the greatness of the departing soul; sometimes the loss to the bereft people; sometimes the passing of ancient power to their heirs. This is what is said to have happened, without doubt, on the death of Romulus and of Caesar.[9]

This has even now been shown to almost everyone in Florence on the death of the great and god-like Lorenzo.[10] Therefore live happily, my most important patron, accepting the will of God, rejoicing in your father's happiness, and trusting in God's help.

25th April, 1492.
In the countryside, at Careggi.

19

Actio gratiarum

Giving thanks

Marsilio Ficino to his Most Reverend Father in Christ, his lord Francesco Soderini, Bishop of Volterra: especial greetings.

GRAMMARIANS hold that there is nothing beyond the superlative, but orators and poets add something.[1] Perhaps the well-known line of Virgil, 'O thrice and four times blessed', tends this way.[2] The thrice blessed are indeed most blessed, but the four times blessed are beyond the most blessed.

Until now I have clearly perceived myself to be most dear to you, and I thought that I could never be dearer. But now I see without doubt that I am more than most dear. For you rob those who are dearest to you in order to clothe me.[3] I have been accustomed for some time to give you the greatest possible thanks for your many kindnesses towards me. Now I give you more than the greatest thanks and I acknowledge myself to be more than most devoted to you, or rather, I am immensely indebted to that dear friend of yours,[4] for I hear that at your entreaty he yielded promptly and willingly to us.

25th April, 1492.
In the countryside, at Careggi.

20

Causae prodigiorum in obitu principis contingentium

The causes of portents attendant upon the death of a prince

Marsilio Ficino to Filippo Valori of Florence, ambassador at the papal court: greetings.

WHILE I was reflecting on the causes of portents attendant upon the deaths of outstanding men, and especially of princes, it first came to mind that these things do not happen by chance, as there is a pattern to them, nor do they arise naturally, for they are at variance one with another, so that they cannot be attributed to a natural course of events proceeding in one particular way; they also contain mysteries which wholly transcend nature.[1] Then it occurred to me that if such signs come neither from chance nor from nature, they undoubtedly come from some divinity, that is, from a sublime intelligence which transcends the powers of nature. But let us not refer every small detail to the first mind without some intermediate steps.

It seems that these things (if I may speak as a Platonist) should be ascribed chiefly to three divine powers. For there is the spirit attendant upon the individual, that is, the daemon accompanying the human being, which our theologians call the guardian angel; there is also the spirit of a place, guardian of a home, a city, a kingdom, and this theologians call a Principality; and thirdly there is a sublime company of divine powers, be they daemons or angels, into whose number and order an outstanding soul, because of the similarity of his function, will ascend as if to his own star, and, performing the same function there, he will become as one of that company.[2]

Just as there are three originators of portents, so also there seem to be three types of portent. That sublime company sets comets ablaze, stirs up thunder, and hurls flashes of lightning, flames, and shooting stars. The presiding spirit of a place shakes and topples buildings, pours forth prophecies, prompts auguries and auspices, and indicates storms, while the guardian spirit inspires dreams and omens and incites dogs to bark as if warding off an evil spirit.[3]

Furthermore, it seems to me that you will require an explanation for these portents. The first ones signify that the most outstanding souls are not extinguished or forgotten, but that after death they reign with the higher beings. The second ones proclaim the misfortune of a people deprived of such a great man and warn them to beware henceforth of imminent dangers. The third ones both remind the dying man and indicate to his people that when he dies the goodwill of heaven does not die but will be favourable to his family after him.

Some Platonists add that between these sublime imperishable daemons and men, whose lives are short, there are some intermediate daemons of great longevity: the more powerful men have therefore been entrusted to the more powerful of these daemons.[4] And they say that, when one of these daemons dies after many ages, at the same time the great prince who has been entrusted to that particular daemon immediately falls ill and departs from life.[5] They say that the atmosphere is stirred up, and strange and wonderful things occur, both when the airy bodies of great daemons are dissolved and when fellow daemons feel distress at the fate of the great daemon and also of the prince.[6]

(All these types of portent occurred recently on the death of the great Lorenzo de' Medici, protector of his native Florence. Bereft of her father, unhappy Florence thus grieves and shudders at these portents, but at the same time the hero's strength of that Hercules, Piero de' Medici, consoles her.)[7]

Farewell.[8]
25th April, 1492.
In the countryside, at Careggi.[9]

21

De vita solitaria, et quanti facienda sit fama

On the solitary life and the value to be placed on fame

Marsilio Ficino to Giovanni Pico della Mirandola:[1] greetings.

Do you ever hope to be out of the public eye, my dear Mirandola? The small and dull can easily lie hidden, but the great and brilliant cannot. In order to live well, you are always eager to be well hidden.[2] But, at the same time, the more extraordinary you appear to the people, the greater your fame. Hence, whatever you try, different rumours immediately spring up.[3] So what are you going to do? Will you always be looking to the general public and what they will say? As you look to the future, will you be their slave? Or rather, being content with your way of life, will you place no value on the judgement of the crowd?

For my part, I know what you are like and so I think I can see what you will do. You will not value such things at nought: you will value them a little, but you will place the greatest value on the judgements of the wise. But enough of this.

My beloved Giovanni, I grieved all the more at your departure because you suddenly deserted me when I was beset by overwhelming sorrow at the death of two friends together.[4] I was hoping that you would be my sole comforter and physician. I hope still that you will return soon. Relying on this hope, I too shall comfort our friends.

Farewell, prosper, and return.

28th April.[5]
In the countryside, at Careggi.

22

Laudes amici scilicet Bindacii Recasolani

In praise of a friend, Bindaccio da Ricasoli

Marsilio Ficino to Filippo Valori, Florentine ambassador:[1] greetings.

THE extended illness of Lorenzo de' Medici, together with the adversity of the times, was, I believe, the reason that I also was quite ill. But by the grace of God I have now recovered fairly well from that long period of infirmity.[2]

Nobody relieved me of the tedium of my protracted illness more than our close friend Bindaccio da Ricasoli,[3] assuredly a man most noble by nature, most esteemed in virtue, and most attentive in service. He often called on me of his own accord and just as frequently on your behalf. He also indicated that he is greatly indebted to you. So above all, my Valori, love this man, for he loves you dearly and is of all men the worthiest of love.

Martin Uranius, my second self, returned to us today and told us how you welcomed him with both friendship and generosity. You acted as you always do, and you could not have done anything to please me more in the present circumstances.[4]

26th June, 1492.

23

Laudes legitimi principis

In praise of a true prince

Marsilio Ficino[1] to Eberard, Duke of Württemberg and Seigneur of Mount Peligard:[2] especial greetings.

FOR a long time now we have been hearing a great deal from many quarters about the special excellence of your virtues. More recently we have heard much from our Martin Uranius, a most reliable witness and guarantor in our midst and a herald of your praises most worthy of everyone's trust. For this reason, the great brilliance of your wonderful virtues, shining even as far as us like the brilliance of the stars, has already fired us with an extraordinary desire to show you great love and the highest respect and reverence.[3]

I have long been wanting what our Plato also said he would like: to find a prince in whom wisdom would combine equally with power, just as it does in Pallas Athene,[4] and, of course, nobility of spirit would join with clemency, as in Caesar,[5] and severity with kindness, as in Scipio.[6] Furthermore, in this prince the justice of Minos[7] and the religion of Numa[8] would both flourish; under him the peace of Augustus[9] would return; he would place the pursuit of peace above the machinations of war; he would establish temples and create seats of learning; his subjects would not so much fear as love, honour, and admire him.[10]

Such is the model[11] of a true prince, longed for by Plato in the past and now desired above all by us. And, as your enduring reputation has already shown, this model is particularly strong in you, so that it is no wonder that I and all my Platonic friends are lit up by the rays of your abundant virtues, and that we honour and revere you above other princes as a heavenly power. But more than this, we are compelled by some incredible love to beseech you to love us who have a singular love for you; and to continue always to hold in mind, as you do now, that just as every light derives from on high, so the brilliance of your virtues derives from God Himself, the Father of lights.[12] And so, for the future, may the supreme Author of all good strengthen your integrity and happiness alike and magnify what He has made strong.

28th June, 1492.

24

Qui futuris praedicendis incumbunt infortunati sunt

Those who are given to predicting the future encounter misfortune

Marsilio Ficino to his very close friend Bindaccio da Ricasoli: greetings.

DO proceed with the study of astronomy, which you began some time ago, where you consider the present disposition of the spheres and the daily cycles and aspects of the heavenly bodies. I do indeed approve of this, my best beloved Bindaccio. But if ever you undertake that astrology by which over-confident predictions of the future are vainly promised, that I will certainly not approve.[1] For I desire that the man who is closest of all to me should also be the most fortunate. But we find that all those who give too much gaping curiosity to telling the future are, or become, the most unfortunate of all.

We think that there are two kinds of causes for this affliction: apparent and hidden. The apparent causes are undoubtedly that such people are compelled by their endless and quite futile pursuit of the future to constantly neglect their own affairs. Trusting in the promises of imminent fate or frightened by its threats – both of these being unavoidable, in their opinion – they themselves for the most part do nothing, for they are all dependent on fate.

The hidden causes for this affliction are, I think, that divine providence, to which nature, fate, and fortune are subject, does not give everything to everyone but justly apportions to each his own. So those who are granted things to come, in accordance with their wishes, are rightly denied things present. For things present are very few and trivial if you compare them with things to come. So if you lack them yet somehow possess very many substantial things to come, you should not complain to providence of your lot.

Perhaps fortune seems opposed to fate in this respect at least, that fate maintains an inescapable order in the creation, whereas fortune rejects order of this kind: so no wonder fortune turns hostile and averse to those who foretell things to come as though they were advocates and prophets of fate.[2] Perhaps also those who brazenly grasp in advance the things that are to come, which the heavenly

Father has placed in His own authority, arrogantly usurp what belongs to God Himself. So Jupiter, in his wrath, blasts them like those giants of old when they were carried away by their own arrogance.[3]

At this point I need hardly mention the astrological implications which occur to me, namely, that those who peer into what lies hidden and far distant from the present fall headlong into Saturn, who holds all that is most concealed and remote, being content with the mysteries of the distant future, since he has conceded to Jupiter the present benefits of fortune.[4]

Therefore, to sum everything up, my dearest Bindaccio, as we fall far short of handling the present and are even less able to meet the needs of the future, we should always remember to hold in mind Paul's divine precept: Seek not to know more than you ought to know, but seek to know wisely.[5]

Farewell.

25

Opiniones non temere divulgandae
Item Orphei carmina

Beliefs should not be rashly promulgated, nor should the 'Hymns of Orpheus'[1]

Marsilio Ficino of Florence to his unique friend Martin Uranius: greetings.

It never seemed a good idea to publish the *Argonautica*, the hymns of Orpheus, of Homer or Proclus, or the *Theology* of Hesiod,[2] which, as you saw when you were recently a guest in my house, I had translated, word for word, just for myself in my youth (I know not how).[3] I was afraid I might seem to be calling readers back to an ancient worship of gods and daemons that was justly condemned long ago. Just as the Pythagoreans of old took care not to reveal divine secrets to the multitude, I too have always been so careful not to spread impieties abroad that I did not spare the little commentaries on

Lucretius which I composed while yet a boy (again I know not how).[4] Indeed, I gave these to Vulcan just as Plato did his tragedies and elegies.[5] For a riper age and a more attentive consideration often condemns, as Plato says, those things which the inexperience of youth either rashly believed or at least did not know it should reject.[6] But, as Plato also says, it is more dangerous to imbibe harmful beliefs than to spread the worst poison.[7] For just as the good is more divine the more widespread it is, so the most widespread evil is the most pernicious. But I promised to send you some of the more acceptable songs of Orpheus. Here they are.

From the 'Hymns of Orpheus' on God[8]

Eusebius of Caesarea,[9] in Book XIII of his *Preparation for the Gospel*, says, 'But even Orpheus, in the hymns which he wrote on the holy word, declares that all things are governed by a divine power and that everything is brought forth from God in this way, as we read in the book which Aristobulus wrote for Ptolemy.[10]

'You who cherish virtue, pray incline your ears
And fix your minds upon my words alone.
But all you unholy wretches, who despise the sacred laws,
Get you hence and flee far away.
But you, Musaeus,[11] who gaze upon the divine utterances
And take them deep into your mind,
Seeing them with consecrated eyes, embrace them
And hold them in your heart.
Having embarked on this journey,
Look up to that one alone,
The one great immortal Creator of the world.

'With the words we now speak we declare who he is.
One and perfect is God, who has created all things;
Cherishing all, he yet transcends them all,
Apprised by mind alone, perceived by mind alone.
No evil does he ever bring upon the mortal race.
There is none else but he.

'Look at all things, the better to see him here on earth.
For here I see his footprints, here I see his mighty hand,

But to perceive him as he is, in no way am I able,
For he is seated high upon the clouds.
None save one born of Chaldean blood[12] can see him
Whom heaven's high and golden throne supports;
His right hand stretches forth to the ends of Ocean;
At him the mountains tremble, shaken to their deepest roots,
Nor can they withstand him, however mighty their mass.
He who dwells in the heights of heaven is yet never absent from earth.
He is unchanging: the beginning, the middle, and the end.'

Also from the 'Hymns of Orpheus'[13]

In the third book Eusebius also gives the following words of Porphyry:[14] 'Wonderful is the wisdom of the Greeks; they considered Jupiter as cosmic mind which, holding the cosmos in itself, brought it forth. Proceeding in this way from the theology of Orpheus, they passed on this teaching about Jupiter:

'He is the king of the starry realm, Jupiter himself,
The beginning and the source of creation,
The one force, the one all-powerful God.
In his royal body all things have their place:
The earth, the sea, fire and air, night and day.
Wisdom and the first cause and delightful love
Are in this great body of Jupiter, the king on high.
For you will see his neck as you raise your eyes
To the great vaults of heaven that stand in awe of him;
And then his head with its golden tresses.
The golden rays of the stars brighten his locks.
Then his head puts forth twin horns of gold.
They are just like the horns of a bull. One is the east, the other the west.
His two eyes are Phoebus, resplendent with intense light,
And the Moon, wreathed in the radiant hue of Phoebus.
His prescient mind is the royal firmament,
And no uproar, violence, rumour, or secret can lie hidden from it.
It pervades all, in victory.
His body, indestructible, extends without limit or measure:
His broad shoulders and expansive chest are the air,

He has wings of air and flies to the ends of the earth,
Faster than the east wind itself.
His sacred belly swells from ancient Mother Earth
And rises in its vastness from the high mountains.
The roaring waters duly gird his waist.
Lastly, they say that the uttermost bounds of the earth,
And the foundations of the broad globe, and raging Tartarus[15]
Are the soles of the feet of the mighty ruler of Olympus.[16]
He it was who hid all things under the earth,
Then drew them back out from the depths
And brought them forth into the bounteous light.'

Porphyry's exposition of this image of Jupiter[17]

'So Jupiter is the whole cosmos, a living being composed of living beings and a god formed of all gods. But he is Jupiter to the extent that he is highest mind. From him all creation is brought forth, and he creates all things through the action of mind.

'Given that theologians think of Jupiter in this way, it is not possible to make an image such as the hymns have described.

'So we should think of Jupiter as a bountiful and life-giving power, which they represent with a sphere and rounded shapes; they ascribe to him the likeness of a man, for he is the mind which brings forth all things by the seed of reason. He is portrayed as seated, so as to represent a constant and unchanging power. His upper body is naked and revealed, for he is visible to the intelligences and higher beings; but his lower half is covered, because he is hidden from the lower creatures.

'He holds a sceptre in his left hand because on this side of the body is found, as it were, the dwelling-place of the very breath of life. For the Creator is ruler of the highest mind and is the life-giving breath of the cosmos.

'In his outstretched right hand he holds an eagle or a figure of Victory: the eagle, because Jupiter is lord of the other gods, just as the eagle is of the other birds; Victory, because all things are subject to him.'

This is what Porphyry says.

9th June, 1492.

26

Exhortatur amicos ut Plotino foras prodeunti faveant

Urging friends to act in support of Plotinus as he comes forth[1]

Marsilio Ficino to his beloved Filippo Carducci: greetings.

GREETINGS, my Carducci, most attentive supporter of the Academy.[2] See how true is the well-known proverb, 'The nature of all things is change':[3] our divine Plato long ago begat the great Plotinus; Plotinus, now pregnant with Plato, is about to give birth very soon.[4] Plato gave light to Plotinus; Plotinus will give back light to Plato as soon as he himself comes forth into the light.

I have already been in labour with Plotinus, but somehow he is still lingering on the threshold.[5] Arise and act, Carducci, most spirited of all our friends! Move the lingering Plotinus forward and encourage all our friends, and anyone else, to grasp him eagerly with their hands so that, moving forward immediately into the light, he may in turn give out light to all who behold him.[6]

12th July, 1492.

27

In librum de Vita missum ad amicum

Concerning the book 'On Life' sent to a friend

Marsilio Ficino to his beloved friends Giovanni Canacci and Bindaccio da Ricasoli: especial greetings.

IF any of my friends can read my mind, surely you, the closest of all my friends, know it perfectly. So you are not unaware of the counsel

I took and the hope and faith that supported me when I wrote the books *On Life* to be of use to all gifted men, but much more to my friends amongst them, and most of all to those citizens on whom the health of our state primarily depends. For my part, I never doubted that I would at any time help as many people as possible, or rather everyone, if I took especial care of any who look after the welfare of the people. Until now it has been my task to write these books with this intention and with all care; from now on it is your task to give the work your close attention in case I have been misled and have laboured so hard in vain.[1]

Therefore whenever you pay your respects to our Paolantonio Soderini,[2] a man most worthy of continual respect and of lasting good health, do remember always to remind him before all else to read again and heed the books *On Life.* For we earnestly wish him in particular a long life and constant good health, since he is, after all, an exceptionally able man and the best of friends and he is bound to our great Medici patrons not by the bond of nature, which is weak, but by that bond of goodwill which is surely the strongest of all. In fact, he is fully committed to the welfare of the people. If that man were as robust in health as he is superior in judgement, he would not need the remedies of doctors for good health, just as now he does not need anyone's advice for a good life. Indeed, if he were ever to pay as much attention to his health as he gives every day to looking after what has to be done, as well as the interests of his friends and the prosperity of the state, I would not press you at all to remind him to care for the health of his own body.

And so, fare well. And, as you usually do, pay your respects frequently to our Paolantonio, advising him every day to take more care of his health, so that he too may live at least as long for his son Tommaso, a brilliant young man, as his own father, Tommaso, that most illustrious knight, lived for him.[3]

22nd July, 1492.

28

Catalogus familiarium atque auditorum

A list of my friends and students

Marsilio Ficino of Florence to his unique friend, Martin Uranius: greetings.

YOU could not ask me for anything more right and fitting than what you have already been frequently requesting through your fellow countryman Johann Streler,[1] namely a list of our friends – not those who happen to come together through any business or social contact but those who come together only in the communion of liberal studies.[2] For since I never ought and never want to be without the presence of my friends, and since I myself am not only in myself in Italy but also in you in Germany, it is only right to want my friends here to be with me there as well.

Know that they are all, in fact, tried and tested in character and conduct. For I decided never to have any friends without first determining that they had united learning with integrity of conduct, as if uniting Mercury with Jupiter.[3] For our Plato says in his letters that true integrity of life is philosophy; learning, however, he calls an outer embellishment of philosophy.[4] He also says in his letters that philosophical communion is more excellent and more stable than any other bond of goodwill or friendship.[5]

But to come directly to the list, receive all my friends together as thus commended. For if I wished to sing fitting praises of each one I would be embarking on a very lengthy task; if I were to pass over any without equal praise, it would be thoroughly invidious. It would be quite absurd, moreover, if, in trying to list friends in order, I were meanwhile to throw everything into disorder by making comparisons, causing offence in the end instead of goodwill.[6]

The first and foremost place among our friends is quite rightly claimed by our patrons: the great Cosimo; his two sons, Piero and Giovanni, both outstanding men; also Piero's two sons, the great Lorenzo and the illustrious Giuliano; Lorenzo's three sons, the magnanimous Piero, the most reverend Cardinal Giovanni, and the outstandingly talented Giuliano. But to avoid praising each at length, let me include all the Medici in one common praise: a line of heroes.

Besides patrons, we have two groups of friends. The first group are not all students and are not in any way disciples, but are friends through close association, conversation-partners so to speak, those who share in to-and-fro discussions and liberal studies. The second group, in addition to what I have said, have sometimes listened to us reading and, as it were, teaching. Although they are like pupils, they are not in fact pupils, for I do not claim to have taught or to teach anyone, but, more in the manner of Socrates, I question and encourage everyone and I am continually summoning to birth the abundant talents of my friends.

In the first group are Naldo Naldi, a friend of mine from my earliest years; then, in our youth, Peregrino Agli, Cristoforo Landino, Leon Battista Alberti, Piero de' Pazzi, Benedetto Accolti of Arezzo, Bartolomeo Valori, Antonio Canigiani; a little later, Giovanni Cavalcanti, Domenico Galletti, Antonio Calderini, Girolamo Rossi, Amerigo and Tommaso Benci, Cherubino Quarquagli of San Gimignano, Antonio Serafico and Michele Mercati, both of San Miniato, Francesco Bandini, Lorenzo Lippi of Colle, Bernardo Nuzzi, Comando Comandi, Baccio Ugolini, and Pietro Fanni the priest. Very many of these, with the exception of Landino, Leon Battista, and Benedetto Accolti, heard our first readings from time to time.

But now in my more mature years, as close friends rather than students, are Antonio degli Agli, Riccardo Angiolieri, Bartolomeo Platina, Oliviero Arduini, our cousin Sebastiano Salvini, Lorenzo Buonincontri, Benedetto Bigliotti, Giorgio Antonio Vespucci, Giovanni Battista Buoninsegni, Demetrius of Byzantium, Giovanni Vittorio Soderini, Angelo Poliziano, Pier Leone of Spoleto, and Giovanni Pico della Mirandola.

In the second group, that is, in the rank of students, are Carlo Marsuppini; five named Piero: del Nero, Guicciardini, Soderini, Compagni, Parenti; two named Filippo: Valori and Carducci; four named Giovanni: Canacci, Nesi, Guicciardini, Rosato; four named Bernardo: Vittorio,[7] de' Medici, Canigiani, Michelozzi; four named Francesco: Berlinghieri, Rinuccini, Gaddi, Pietrasanta; Amerigo Corsini; Antonio Lanfredini; Bindaccio da Ricasoli; Niccolò Michelozzi; Matteo Rabatta; Alessandro degli Albizzi; Fortuna Ebreo; Sebastiano the priest; Angelo Carducci; Andrea Corsi; Alessandro Borsi; Blasio of Bibbiena; Francesco da Diacceto; and Niccolò Valori.

29

Procemium in compendium Proculi

Preface to a selection from the writings of Proclus

Marsilio Ficino to his special friend, Martin Uranius: greetings.

SOON after your departure from Italy, many books were brought from Greece to the magnanimous Piero de' Medici. These had been selected shortly before from a much larger number by Lascaris, a Greek of exceptionally fine judgement, for that princely library so successfully established much earlier by the great Lorenzo.[1]

Moreover, I read the Platonic texts first, as I always do, and first among these the commentaries of Proclus on six books of Plato's *Republic* and on the beginning of the seventh.[2]

And so, as I ranged far and wide, I picked from the most delightful meadows of the commentaries these little flowers, which are more fragrant with holy religion than the rest,[3] to send to you, a man noted for his religious faith.[4]

3rd August, 1492.[5]

Excerpta ex Proculo in Rempublicam Platonis a Marsilio Ficino

Extracts taken by Marsilio Ficino from the commentaries of Proclus on Plato's 'Republic'

The three attributes of every deity

In the *Laws*, Plato defines the essential nature of a god through three attributes, that is, through goodness, power, and knowledge; and in the *Republic* through three similar ones: goodness, immutability, and truth.[6] In fact, immutability is characteristic of power, while truth is the culmination of knowledge. Moreover, any god is truly said to be good, because no evil is mixed with his goodness and because the goodness in him is not a state of being which is added to his essential nature, but is itself his very essence. He is not a god first and subsequently good. For by that same essence of his he is, in form, equally both a god and good. Therefore any god is said to be good in himself, in his very nature, just as the first God in himself is the Good.[7]

(Proclus proves precisely this point in the *Elements of Theology*: any god is in his form a certain essential goodness, just as the first God is the Good itself that is above essence. And likewise, he shows that these three attributes belong in form to the godhead: pure goodness, unlimited power, and absolute knowledge.)[8]

A god causes no evil; he never changes form; he deceives none[9]

In the *Republic* Plato states three theological principles. The first is that if every god is, by his own nature, truly good, he is indeed always the cause of good things, but never of anything evil. The second is that if he is truly powerful, he is not subject to any change whatever. The third is that if unchanging power, truth, and goodness belong to a god, he never deceives anyone with any deceptions or lies.[10]

Concerning the first principle, there is a question as to where evils originate, if a god gives no impulse to evil. Concerning the second, if no deity undergoes any change, how do the deities show themselves of their own accord, sometimes with forms and sometimes without? If we do not accept such things, we will have completely done away with all knowledge of sacred matters and the works of the priests, as well as those very visions in which the gods spontaneously reveal themselves in different forms at different times. Concerning the third, how is it that false answers are sometimes given, for many false statements can now be detected in the oracles?[11]

In relation to the first, the answer is that it is not from a god or from any other cause that evil makes its appearance among things that exist. It is not possible either to propose an Idea of evils or to say that matter is the cause of evils; for all Ideas are like intellectual and divine archetypes, and they exist as models both of essences and of the perfections pertaining to essence. But matter has been brought forth from God as being necessary for the world, and it is not productive of evil; for in fact it contributes to the generation of the universe; and it is not good either, since it is the lowest of all, yet it has its place among the necessary constituents of creation. For whatever exists is as it is for the sake of something else.[12]

Therefore it is not lawful to propose any special or material cause of evils or any single cause whatever. But, as Plato says, it should be stated that particular and scattered influences bring in evils: 'particular' because none of the universals, such as the intellect, the soul, or the body, is the cause of evils; and 'scattered' because no one thing is the cause of evils.[13] But, as he himself says, other explanations of evils must be sought. In the body, evil, that is, illness, occurs on account of various influences flowing together without due measure while one thing in particular strives to dominate. In the soul, evil also occurs on account of different and opposing kinds of life fighting amongst themselves. When they fight, evil occurs from some to others, with each one doing what is in its own interests. But it was necessary for the body to be like this, made of opposing and mutually hostile elements, so that there might also be something transient in the world. And thus the world is completed, being constituted of all things.[14]

It was also necessary for souls here to have a mixed nature, for these regions of the world should not be devoid of rational beings, but rational lives should not be implanted in bodies without an intermediary: they should engage in action and suffer the conditions of irrational beings also, and mortals do indeed desire, feel, and imagine such things, which they need if they are going to survive in these regions even for a short time. Therefore, as long as anything whatsoever does what is in its own interests, evils consequently occur on account of nothing but the good.

The universe undoubtedly makes use of these occurrences in an appropriate way, and these things turn out for the good through the very power of the users. Therefore nothing anywhere is pure evil but in some way participates in the good. And so evil can also be said to depend in some way on heaven, as if it were in some way good. But at the same time it can be said to occur through very many other particular agencies, like something accidental, happening, I mean, through these many different agencies.[15]

To the doubt concerning apparitions we shall reply next in the following way.[16] While the gods above remain unchanging and neither gain nor lose anything, divine appearances spring forth from them and manifest in the space around us. For since observers use bodies, while the gods are without bodies, the visions emanating from heaven in the presence of those worthy of the sight have indeed something from the gods above who are bringing them forth but also something related in all respects to the observers. This is why they appear, but not to everyone. And those to whom they appear catch sight of nothing more than some very bright coverings of the souls.[17] And for that reason they are frequently observed when the eyes are closed. Therefore, insofar as they have dimension and appear in the air, which also has dimension, they become recognisable to those who are watching. But insofar as they are full of divine light and have power and represent the strength of the gods through their image by means of these very clear symbols or signs, they depend continuously, as if suspended, on the divinities producing them. So their ineffable rites and mysteries are represented through such symbols or signs, while they show various forms to those looking on.

This is attested by the sacred words which address the priest in the following way: 'All divine things are without bodies. But bodies are given to them for your sake, because you are not able, on account of that bodily nature in which you have been enclosed, to perceive in a non-bodily way things which have no bodies.'[18] This is what is said.

Therefore these apparitions appear and disappear by the will of the gods, though they themselves are hidden; in the meantime the gods are by nature permanent, neither gaining nor losing anything through these manifestations. In the same way, those intellectual forms, that is, Ideas, do not become corporeal, either as composites or as whole forms, while such apparitions are being brought forth by them, that is, by those Ideas, which are of a quite different nature. Every god, therefore, remains without a form, although of his own volition he may present himself as if having a form. For any such form is not within him, but is from him, while the observer does not have the power to see without a form that which is without a form, but in his own way discerns the formless beneath the form.

To the third question we give the following answer.[19] Falseness is not in the gods who answer but in those men who receive the answers, taking the words of the oracle in a perverted manner on account of their weakness. Indeed, this very deception does not occur against the will of the divine powers, who wish only the worthy to attain the fulfilment of their prayer. There are also some for whom it is not proper to know the pure truth that abides with the gods, but it is proper for them to suffer something through the deception occurring within themselves. Therefore the gods are not ignorant of the truth and they do not obscure it, yet they use the confusion happening to us on account of our lack of judgement for our benefit. The very history of the oracles already bears witness that it is on account of the place, the time, the manner, or some other error made by the enquirer, that falsehood arises in the answers.

When Plato says in the *Republic* that not only every divine statement but also every daemonic statement is always truthful and does not lie,[20] it is to be understood that he is speaking of the true, natural daemon and not of the familiar spirit called a daemon on account of its ways, which undergoes very many changes and misleads those it has befriended. However, in essence it is a familiar spirit, and when it is rational it is wholly truthful, but when it is irrational it is without truth, it is deceived and it deceives as something false. It is considered to be of a deceitful kind which, history relates, often deceives when it gets close to the oracles, overhears the invocations, or accosts people of its own accord. And all of that occurs, not through their nature as daemons, but through the way they behave.

All religion, the office of the priests, all history, and the common report of mankind are agreed that the gods appear to the senses and present many forms and various guises, and that at some times they put forth light without form and at other times light with form, now in human form, now in another form, while clearly the godhead abides everywhere, unmoving.[21] For indeed the very simplicity of the gods appears manifold to the beholders, certainly not through change or deception on the part of the godhead but because of the condition of nature, which defines the properties of the gods according to the limitations of the participants. For although the god himself who is experienced is one and single within himself, the intellect experiences him in one way, the intellectual soul in another way, the imagination in yet another way, and likewise the senses. For the intellect experiences without division, the intellectual soul experiences in circular fashion,[22] and the imagination experiences through forms, while the senses experience passively.

That which is experienced is uniform in its substance, but becomes multiform in experience. It is unchangeable, but appears changeable on account of our weakness. And although it has no weight, it seems to weigh down what it occupies, as the poets say of Pallas,[23] for what is received must necessarily appear with the quality of what receives it. When, therefore, some of the gods meet us as guests or in some other form, it should not be thought that the apparent change is in them but that varying images come about in different recipients. And this is one way in which poetry presents the gods, which are unchangeable in themselves but which are, as it were, changeable to us.

And there is a second way, as when the divine itself, having many powers within itself and being full of all forms, proffers various intelligible visions to the contemplative person.[24] For the poets then tell us that the divine itself, containing these powers within itself, changes the variety of the powers that has been demonstrated into various forms, bringing forth one in one place and another in another place, always acting in conformity with all the forms, yet always appearing to the conductive intelligences of souls as one thing or another, on account of the multitude of forms which it contains within itself.

In this way the celebrated Proteus is said to completely change his own form, appearing as one thing after another before the eyes of those watching.[25] Proteus is a divine intellect, who is full of all powers and forms and is numbered within the lineage of Neptune.[26] Particular souls, who within the same lineage are named Phocae,[27] continuously contemplate him and look upon some of his forms at one time and other forms at other times, and attaching the succession of their thoughts to Proteus, they infer that the change of forms is within Proteus. And so, to the beholders, Proteus himself 'seems to become all things whatsoever that inhabit earth, water, air, or fire'.[28] For the number of forms he contains within himself, or rather the number of forms he himself is throughout all eternity, seems to be the same number of forms that are being successively produced through the perpetually changing perception of the observers.

The third way in which appearance differs is when various visions of the same god appear, not on account of the perceptions of the subjects or the variety of divine powers, but when the same god issues forth in accordance with the different ranks, and he descends, as it were, to the furthest limits, multiplying himself in number and sinking down into the lower orders.[29]

Then again, the myths relate that that divinity is changed into the very appearance into which he has issued forth from on high. So, on this principle, they say that Minerva presented herself in the likeness of Mentor,[30] Mercury presented himself as a garrulous sea-bird,[31] and Apollo as a hawk,[32] thus displaying the nobler of their ranks, into which they have come forth from universals. Therefore, when the myths describe divine apparitions, they strive to keep them without shape or form, as when Pallas showed herself to Achilles alone but not to the army that was there.[33] Yet when the myths present apparitions as angels, they are showing the gods dressed in forms other than their own, but these are still universal. They relate how they have come down into the appearance of a human being, an appearance common to both man and woman but not characteristic of anyone in particular.

However, when they talk of apparitions as daemons, they are not afraid to present transformations into particular individual people and things, and even a descent into brutes. For the lowest of the orders which follow the gods are revealed through figures of this kind.

Now it is worth considering how closely such things agree with the natural order. For the simple accords with the divine, the universal with the angelic, and the particular with the daemonic; what is intellectual, too, is in harmony with the divine, the rational with the angelic, and the irrational with the daemonic. For the irrational life is closely bound up with the order of daemons.[34]

The three dispositions and states of souls after separation from the body: the contemplative, the active, and the pleasure-seeking[35]

The dispositions of souls are different even when separated from the body. Similarly, the places they inhabit in the universe are different. Therefore souls that have been so separated from their mortal instruments that they have no habitual recourse to inferior matters and are not filled with the disturbances and trivia of mortal existence need to take with them their original bright, clear coverings, which are still pure, just as they were before, unruffled by the vapours of materiality and not hardened by earthly nature.

Souls, however, that are not yet perfectly purified by philosophy, but are inclined towards feelings of attachment for a gross body and are still striving to obtain a life in common with it, also need to show, to those able to see, those conveyances of their own which are attached to them,[36] that is, shadowy, material conveyances falling backwards under their own weight and carrying with them most of the hardened mortal nature. This is clearly recounted in the *Phaedo*.[37] There are many differences also among these souls which are still inclined towards this life. For these souls have led more of an active life, have not yet desisted from a life of this kind, and naturally choose an instrument capable of practical action. Aggrieved at having been separated from it, they earnestly desire connection with it. They prefer this life of ours to the life of separation, as they cannot lead such a life, being plainly more suited to the active life.

It is fitting, however, that those souls which cling to a transient body for the sake of a dissolute life and think that with it nothing will be different from the life they led in it, are taken down into the darkest and lowest place in the universe.

Both Homer and Plato distinguish the soul from its image,[38] and the intellect from those things which belong to the soul. They say that the soul makes use of the image, while the intellect is more divine than both. They say that the image and the soul are known in some degree even in this body, caring and providing for it while within it and away from it, and naturally longing for it, but the intellect is not understood by the movements of our imagination and sense-impressions.[39]

Accordingly, the instruments of souls ascending into heaven utter a harmonious sound and display pleasing motion, whereas the sound of those going down under the earth, and now possessed of less reason, is like a lament,[40] carrying as it were the impression of a life of empty attachments and fantasies.[41]

Furthermore, it should not be thought that the regions of the underworld, places of judgement under the earth, and the rivers, all of which Homer and Plato describe, are meaningless imaginings and merely fictitious horrors.[42] On the contrary, just as there are different places allocated according to the merits of the souls seeking to return to the heavens, so it should be thought that places under the earth are allocated to the souls which are in need of punishment and purification, places receiving down-flows from the elements surrounding the earth; and these down-flows they call rivers.

Finally, they say that there are different orders of daemons put in charge of this process: some are avengers, some are correctors, some are purifiers, and some are servants of the judges. It is fitting for the souls there, in accordance with their deserts and qualities, to be utterly terrified by their mental image of the daemons in charge, and by their own changing and confused state, which is cut off from the celestial rays of the sun.

The three lives of the soul: divine, human, bestial[43]

We can set out the threefold life of the soul briefly as follows. The first life, indeed the best and most perfect, is that by which the soul is joined to the gods, and in their company leads a life most closely related to the celestial beings. Through a very great similarity, the life is now united with them, not under its own control, but under the control of the gods. While the soul is still subject to its own intellect, at the same time it calls forth the ineffable gift and mark of that uniform substance of the celestial beings;[44] and, uniting like with like, its own light with that divine light which is the One itself that stands above all being and life, it joins that single light as closely as possible to its own being and life.[45]

We put in second place that life in which the soul has come down from the divine life into itself, and establishes mind, together with knowledge, as the ruler of action, where it evolves a great number of principles, surveys the manifold differences of all appearances, and gathers into itself as one both that which perceives and that which is perceived, and re-presents them. Comprehending intelligible nature, as it were, in one, it expresses the intellectual essence as if through an image.

Finally, we judge the third life to be the one that now enters into dealings with the inferior powers, acts with them, employs the imaginings and the senses, which are devoid of reason, and is completely filled with what is inferior.

Division of created things into four classes; also concerning images and shadows[46]

Plato, in the seventh book of the *Republic*, compares the order of created things to a line, on account of their unbroken connection which, in fact, springs from their mutual likeness.[47] But the likeness is a kind of unity within creation arising from pure unity itself, the beginning of everything. Indeed, this unity, wishing to make everything most like itself, but not simply one, made everything as unified as possible. The very goodness of the beginning also contributes to that union. For since it is the nature of the Good to diffuse itself, as it were, by issuing forth through everything and conversely to call everything back to itself, the One, by natural appetite, it consequently makes the universe fully united.[48]

Now the universal line, according to Plato, is divided into two main parts: the category of the insensible and that of the sensible. The first category is greater by far than the second, embracing the second within itself. The former is further divided into the intelligible and the cogitable, that is, into divine and mathematical forms, while the latter is divided into substantial things and semblances. Substantial things are bodies, but the semblances are images and shadows of bodies. The images and mirror-like reflections of bodies require a foundation which has three conditions: density, smoothness, and lustre. Density is in fact necessary lest the appearance, if it falls upon too insubstantial a foundation, might at once disperse and so the image would fail to be single on account of its manifold dispersal. Smoothness is needed lest roughness, due to some of its parts being raised and some sunken, be the cause of unevenness for the image which is to be composed. A shining lustre is also needed so that the image, which would otherwise have a dim form, becomes clearly visible. For thus even the tiniest particles in the air are often revealed to the eyes in the rays penetrating through small openings and chinks in a house; otherwise they are hidden from us because of their insubstantial nature.[49]

Therefore it should be said that, according to Plato's thought in the *Sophist*, visible images are the substances of likenesses, substances fashioned by daemonic contrivance.[50]

The shadows, too, which he mentions with images as if they are related, have a similar nature, for they are themselves images of bodies and of forms and are very much in sympathy, that is, they have fellow-feeling and correspondence, with those things from which they fall. They therefore show that however many things the magic arts promise and undertake to perform, these are accomplished in relation to apparitions and shadows.

But what shall I say of the powers of images and shadows, powers whereby many things surpassing all reason often occur within living beings devoid of reason? For they say that the hyena, trampling on the shadow of a dog sitting above, immediately brings him tumbling down and devours him.[51] Also Aristotle says that a woman while going through the purging of her menstrual flow defiles with blood the mirror opposite and her image.[52]

Finally, Plato confirms that images are substances when he says: Just as the cogitable are related to the intelligible, so images are related to visible bodies. Indeed, the cogitable, that is, the mathematical, are in themselves objects and have specific natures.[53] In the same way, since images are natural effluences from natural objects, they also have their own natures.

How the Good is above essence; and how it may be known[54]

Plato, in the sixth book of the *Republic*, compares divine things in this way: he likens the Sun to the Good itself, the light of the Sun to the truth flowing from the Good, and the colours dependent on the light to the formative and ideal principles of all things, principles suspended under the truth that proceeds from the Good.[55] Moreover, he compares the eyes, which are brought into being by the Sun and are lit by it, to the intelligences related to the Good in the same way.

He further adds that just as the Sun exists above the creation of the lower visible world, so the Good is above being and essence. Again, just as the Sun and its light are above colours and appearances, so the Good and the truth (which is the light of the Good) are above Ideas, beings, and minds.

Finally, just as the Sun is the cause of activity and fulfilment for the things that we see and for our eyes, as well as the cause of their generation, their nature, and their power, so the Good is the originator of all things for the intelligible and for intellects, and thus is higher than all these. Therefore, as the Good itself is higher than the intelligible, the intellect, and truth, it cannot be known in the same way as the intelligible, but it is known through a divine insight and perception transcending intelligence, which Plato calls an illumination of the soul, when the soul is divinely illuminated, having by a process of negation separated from the Good all things which are beneath the Good and having duly evaluated them in relation to the Good. By this process the soul, turning back and raising itself towards the Good, is now made to face upwards, as it were, whilst hitherto it had been inclining downwards.

It appears that, of all cosmic entities, the Sun alone is self-existent,[56] for it loses none of its own attributes and receives none of another's. Everything else, however, constantly receives fresh rays of light from the Sun, while the Sun revolves around its own particular centre, thus lighting up the heavenly bodies around it as well as everything below it. Therefore the Sun, being of such a nature, rules over all cosmic beings, but inasmuch as it is a body and is changeable it is subject to something, namely, the highest sphere, which is said to hold the circle of sameness.[57] For even the Sun itself is moved and is taken back again by that sphere to the wisest circle of all, that is, the mind.

In all this, remember that within things divisible there is something indivisible, such as unity or a point, and likewise within things corruptible there is something incorruptible.

The threefold Good: within us, within Idea, and above Idea[58]

Plato considers that the Good, which is worthy of reverence, has three levels. One is within us, as a certain condition of life blended aright from intelligence and pleasure; another is in the realm of Ideas; and the final one is above Ideas.

Now among Ideas some constitute and define the essences of things, while others bring to the essences their perfections. Of the former group, the first Idea is being and essence. This is the archetype for all other essential Ideas, that is, those which pertain to the formation of essences, as, for instance, living being, man, horse. But of Ideas pertaining to the perfections of all things, the first is not the simple Good itself but the ideal good, which likewise is the archetype of all Ideas relating in any way whatever to the perfections of all created things. Such Ideas are the beautiful, the just, the wise, and so forth. Accordingly, just as the essences of all created things precede their perfections through their origin, for 'to be' naturally comes before 'to be well', so being and essence, in the very sequence of Ideas, immediately precede the ideal good. Ultimately, however, the simple Good is higher than being, and also it cannot be participated in. For the good within Ideas also cannot be participated in, but it is nevertheless with essence or below being. Finally, the good within us is both below essence and can be participated in.

Now indeed the common view of all in defining the Good, for whose sake everything seeks the Good, seems to indicate that the Good does not exist for the sake of anything else and does not, in truth, seek another. Therefore that Good is neither any being nor any particular good within being. For every essence seeks the Good, that is, it seeks to be in accordance with nature and to be fully and perfectly itself. Also the good within essence is sought for the sake of that substance itself so that it may be in perfect accord with nature. It is not the simple Good, but no more or less than the good of something and the good in something. Finally, to speak briefly: that ideal good has been placed as if it were part of something and within something, for the sake of the whole. And so, above that ideal good is the simple Good itself.

30

De Daemonibus

On daemons

Marsilio Ficino to his most beloved Filippo Carducci: greetings.

WHILE I was translating the Commentary of Proclus the Platonist on Plato's *Alcibiades*, from Greek into Latin, not word for word but according to the meaning, I remembered that you wanted an outline of the Platonic view concerning daemons. Finding one there, I have decided to send it to you.

May you profit from reading it.[1]

31

Philosophia cum fortuna et divitiis non coniungitur

Philosophy is not linked with fortune or wealth

Marsilio Ficino to Filippo Valori, Florentine ambassador to the Pope: greetings.

'A MAN'S enemies are the members of his own household.'[1] The members of my household are many and are very troublesome because they are not philosophers and are therefore not content with the food and furnishings of philosophy. They frequently complain that all the other dependants of the house of Medici, even the lesser ones, have received a great deal from them in just a few years, while I, by far the most intimate and, dare I say, most loyal dependant, have brought back very little over many years.[2]

But hear for a moment, my Valori, how I answer my household. The other friends of the Medici have not yet received as much as they wanted, while I, had I but asked, would have received as much as I wanted. And I certainly have all I want. They receive mostly by begging, but I receive freely. Again, to others the Medici have given the property of others, but to me they have given their own.[3] So this is how I neatly prove my case to my household. But they do not prove theirs, which I find very troublesome. For, with hindsight, either my household should have become philosophers with me at some time or I should not have been a philosopher. For it seems to have been ordained from the beginning of time that no philosophers will ever be rich and that rich men cannot easily become philosophers. For it is said that Minerva has never had any dealings with Juno; nor do Jupiter, Phoebus, and Venus favour the same men as Mercury and Saturn;[4] and Fortune, who governs events, does not readily agree with Wisdom, who contemplates them.

One thing, then, is essential: where you direct your energies, your ability grows stronger. Ability and fortune thus hold divided rule within us, the former chiefly in the cultivation of the soul, the latter mainly in external matters. So we speak of the blessings of fortune, although perhaps natural abilities have equal power over the body. But this letter cannot philosophise any further at the moment, for other business is already pressing.[5]

32

Ubi plus fortunae, ibi sapientiae minus, atque vicissim

Where there is more fortune, there is less wisdom, and vice versa

Marsilio Ficino to that outstanding citizen, his beloved Bindaccio da Ricasoli: especial greetings.

THOSE words of Aristotle, 'Where there is more intelligence, there is less fortune; and, conversely, where there is more fortune, there is less intelligence' will be taken by most people to mean that all truly wise men and all philosophers are anything but fortunate.[1] The hymns of Pythagoras acknowledge this, experience confirms this,[2] and so does astrology, which holds that philosophy is indicated principally by Mercury and Saturn and that these have no dealings with Jupiter, the Sun, or Venus, which signify abundance of material things.[3] Again, genuine contemplators of truth disregard the blessings of Fortune and are themselves disregarded by those who are most fortunate: they neither please princes nor win the approval of the people. So it is no wonder that they have very little fortune. On the other hand, the most fortunate are those who commonly neglect wisdom and generally live without due thought or care, relying as they do on the winds of fortune.

Although I do not reject the above interpretation, I would like to offer a more useful and more spiritual interpretation of Aristotle's words. For we have found that the more prudent men are, the less haphazardly they live and fewer things in their families and affairs are driven by chance. We can therefore conclude beyond any doubt that to God, the most wise Creator of all things, nothing ever happens by chance, but everything has been arranged by providence. And in turn, since we see that all things in the heavens and in the natural world are arranged in a definite order beyond the reach of fortune, we may conclude that supreme wisdom governs all these things.[4]

33

Procemium in comparationem Solis ad Deum

Preface to 'A Comparison of the Sun to God'

Marsilio Ficino to Eberhard, illustrious Duke of Württemberg[1] and Seigneur of Mount Peligard: greetings.

OUR Martin 'Uranius', which means 'heavenly one' – and he really is a contemplator of the heavens – discussed with me in a long exchange the indisputable fact that, as the Sun is among the stars, so are you among all the princes of Germany. Fired by praises of this kind, as if by rays from your virtue, I gave you a short letter a long time ago[2] which was indeed a pledge of my great love for you, though the pledge fell far short of the love.

Therefore, so that I might do rather more justice both to your supreme dignity and to my desire, I am now sending to the Sun of Germany the Sun of Plato and of Dionysius, which through its splendour will let our remarkable love for you be known far and wide. Just as Mercury brings the gifts of Phoebus to the minds of men, so Johann Streler, like a second Mercury to us, will bring this Phoebean gift of ours to you.[3] Therefore, O Phoebean Prince, you will be happy to read what Plato and Dionysius the Areopagite said on the comparison of the Sun to God, combined with my explanation and commentary.[4]

Live happily in this shadow of life, after which you will at length enjoy the everlasting Sun.

Farewell.

34

Laudes saeculi nostri tanquam aurei ab ingeniis aureis

Praises of our age as golden on account of its golden minds[1]

Marsilio Ficino to Paul of Middelburg, the eminent scientist and astronomer: especial greetings.

IN former times poets sang of four ages: lead, iron, silver, and gold.[2] In the *Republic* Plato applies this to the four natures of human beings. He argues that lead is naturally implanted in the minds of some, iron in others, and likewise in others silver or gold.[3] Therefore, if we are to call any age golden, it is undoubtedly one that brings forth golden minds everywhere.[4] Whoever chooses to consider the splendid discoveries of these times will have no doubt that this age of ours is such an age. For, as if golden, this age has brought back into the light the liberal arts, which were almost extinct: grammar, poetry, rhetoric, painting, sculpture, architecture, music, and the ancient art of singing to the Orphic lyre. And all this in Florence.[5]

Similarly, this age has united wisdom with eloquence,[6] and prudence with martial prowess,[7] as in Pallas, unions once honoured among the ancients but now almost obliterated. It revealed this most remarkably in Federico, Duke of Urbino, and it has made his son and brother heirs to his manly spirit.[8]

In you too, dear Paul, this age seems to have perfected astronomy,[9] and in Florence it has brought back the Platonic teaching from darkness into the light.[10] In Germany devices have been invented in our own times for printing books.[11] There are also tables by which in a single hour, as it were, the whole face of the heavens for a complete century is revealed;[12] and may I just mention the Florentine device which reproduces the daily movements of the heavenly bodies.[13]

But now our Michelozzi is bringing you some carefully printed German tables, as an offering to your distinguished duke, a celestial gift worthy of a celestial prince, worthy, as I judge, of being approved even by you, a contemplator of the heavens, and worthy indeed of being recommended to you by us.[14]

Farewell.
13th September, 1492.

Appendix Letters

A[1]

Sortes humanae vitae et cura Dei erga Medices

The lots apportioned to human life, and God's care for the Medici

Marsilio Ficino to Filippo Valori, Florentine ambassador: greetings.

POETS of old picture two large urns standing in front of Jupiter: one full of goods, the other full of evils; for each person at birth, Jupiter blends both kinds of lot.[2] Plato confirms this in the tenth book of the *Republic.*[3] The goods and evils relate to soul, body, and fortune. Thus to the noble family of the Medici are given from heaven very substantial goods of soul and of fortune, but sometimes less substantial goods of body. However, God balances this weakness with the wonderful strength of the other goods. In weighing this out, He considers the Medici as His sons, since, as parents do, He chastises their bodies but cherishes their souls and increases their fortunes. But He does not suffer them to be chastised by their enemies and He destroys those who strike them, so that with this family, just as with the family of Abram, almighty God seems to have made His covenant: 'I will bless them that bless thee.'[4] Often therefore, when they seem to be cast down from the heights, they rise up again even higher, so that they seem not so much to be subjected to fortune as to command it, with the help of virtue, of course, and certainly by the will of God.

28th April, 1492.
In the countryside, at Careggi.

B[1]

Laudes Petri Medicis

In praise of Piero de' Medici

Marsilio Ficino to Filippo Valori, Florentine ambassador: greetings.

I HAVE touched upon the causes of the portents in my usual philosophical way as briefly as possible, while our Poliziano has described those unnatural events and the death of Lorenzo more fully and elegantly.[2] However, I should not wish us to overlook this one thing, a very great and widely known miracle: in Pythagorean terms, Lorenzo's own soul has poured itself completely into the body of his son Piero;[3] or, in more theological terms, just as any star breathes upon earthly things merely by casting down its rays without forsaking its place in the heavens, so the great hero breathes from heaven into his son and shapes him to his own form so completely that you may recognise the whole essence of the father in the son.[4]

In Piero, Lorenzo's ideas, plans, intentions, judgements, words, gestures, and even his features, make this plain, so that he seems not so much to resemble his father as to be him. As a result he can openly declare: 'He that sees me, sees my father also. For all things belonging to him have been delivered unto me of my father.'[5] This is surely why they all hang upon the words of Piero, and it is undoubtedly why they honour, admire, and revere him.

I have mentioned this to you, my Valori, so that the measure of the grief you have been feeling since Lorenzo's death may now be matched by your joy at his rebirth.

26th June, 1492.

C[1]

De fortuna Platonis et miraculis in obitu Laurentii

On Plato's fortunes and the marvels attendant upon Lorenzo's death

Marsilio Ficino to the Magnanimous Piero de' Medici: greetings.

ON the Ides of November, whilst I was strolling with the great Lorenzo de' Medici in the countryside at Careggi, and we were expounding to each other Plato's numerous mysteries, I happened, during the discussion, to fall from wisdom and alight upon fortune; and I began to complain somewhat bitterly that she had for many centuries thwarted Plato's attempts to reach the light. Then Lorenzo said, 'Marsilio, do not call our Plato unfortunate, unless perhaps you think that I shall be unfortunate.' In fact, we then ended our conversation with these words.

Yet it would not be right, would it, to think that Lorenzo was unfortunate because he subsequently died, and that Plato's fortune collapsed at the same time? Far be it from me to consider as unhappy that soul whom the joyous heavens welcomed with exceptional acclaim when he broke free from the shackles of the body and when a star of some magnitude fell upon the Laurentian abode and extraordinary flames flared down upon the countryside of Careggi for three days.[2] But two days prior to Lorenzo's death, Jupiter struck at the sacred citadels with his reddened right hand.[3] He smote terror into the land which was soon to be deprived of such a great father, and he terrified enemies into not making any serious move against the unconquered House of Medici.[4]

Thus neither the hero Lorenzo nor his heroic son Piero should be deemed unhappy as a result of recent events; and our Plato is not unfortunate. Until now, his head has been protected by the wholesome shade of the Laurel; his feet now stand upon an immovable Rock.[5] At last, now that you are holding Plotinus in your hands, he will carry his father Plato on his pious shoulders, and will bring him out into the light, with you leading the way.[6]

D[1]

Primo de daemonibus communiter, secundo de daemonibus familiaribus, tertio de daemone Socratis

First, on daemons in general; secondly, on familiar spirits; thirdly, on the daemon of Socrates

WE should speak about daemons in proper sequence: first, in general; then about those which are allotted to us and guide us; and thirdly, about the daemon of Socrates.[2] When the daemons have been allotted a first substance by the life-giving goddess,[3] they flow from this, as if from a source, and obtain a soul-essence. Those who have a greater and more perfect substance have a more intellectual essence, while those who have a medium substance obtain an essence that is less intellectual but is rational. Those of the third order of daemons, holding the last place, have a nature that is changeable, irrational,[4] and material. Being composed of this kind of substance, they are divided in the same way as the gods are divided, as one might expect for those who function as ministers to the gods. For they respond to and serve in one way the gods who are wholly unattached and who lay the warp and weft prior to the cosmos, but they serve in quite another way the cosmic gods who are directly in charge of the different parts of the cosmos. The first daemons are also allotted as followers of the twelve supercelestial gods[5], but the other daemons have been distributed in accordance with all the characteristics of the cosmic gods. For every cosmic god rules over a rank of daemons and directly imparts to each a share of his own power. For the creator god generously bestows the creative force; the unchangeable god displays a capacity that cannot be defiled; the god who perfects likewise displays the capacity to perfect. What is more, around each and every god is an innumerable multitude of daemons, and they carry the same names as their leader-gods. They really rejoice[6] when they are called Apollos, Jupiters, or Mercuries, because they are expressing the characteristic of their own gods in themselves.

Accordingly, mortal things obtain divine influences through these daemons, and thus plants and animals are fashioned that bear the images of one god or another. The daemons directly bestow upon them the gifts of their own leaders but the gods, being superior, control the daemons from above. For this reason, the very last things are in sympathy[7] with the very first. For the imprints of the first things are present in the last, and the causes of the last things are held within the first. Of course, the middle classes of the daemons fill everything out and at the same time bind everything together, and they themselves maintain the communion[8] of all. They are participants in the gods, whereas mortal things also participate in them. So if anyone says that God, the creator of the universe, has established the pivotal points[9] of the whole order on the daemons, he will not stray far from the truth, since Diotima also attributes to them this rank, which binds together the divine and the mortal, draws down the streams[10] flowing from above, and links to the gods all that follows: in a word, this rank completes everything through the binding power of the mean.[11]

Notes to the Letters

1

1 The ancient Roman custom of marking a birthday with a white pebble is described by the poet Martial in *Epigrams*, IX, 58. White marks on a calendar were also used to indicate auspicious days and, following an ancient Thracian custom, white pebbles were thrown into an urn to record days that had passed favourably. Pliny, *Natural History*, VII, 41; Martial, *Epigrams*, XII, 34.

2 No mention is made of any cup of high value in Ficino's will, but a silver drinking cup would more likely have been a common domestic item. In *De vita*, I, x, 32 Ficino advises people to drink from gold or silver vessels when possible. Silver wine cups were believed until recent times to be especially hygienic.

3 In MS Mo2 this letter is dated 9th April rather than 13th.

2

1 There were two communities called San Miniato: that better known today is San Miniato al Monte, comprising a beautiful church and an Olivetan convent on a hill immediately overlooking Florence. San Miniato al Tedesco, referred to here, lies some 35 miles west of Florence. (The soubriquet 'al Tedesco' was dropped in 1918.) San Miniato occupied a strategic location on the Via Francigena as it passes through the valley of the Arno, on the main route between Northern Europe and Rome. A castle was established on the site of an existing village, San Genesio, by the Emperor Frederick Barbarossa in 1160. Subsequent emperors maintained it as an outpost of imperial rule, but eventually imperial authority in Italy declined. From 1347 San Miniato al Tedesco was closely allied with Florence.

2 Pico's family was of Lombard origin and held lands in northern Italy: the Duchy of Mirandola lay adjacent to the territories of Modena, Ferrara, and Mantua. The Lombards had entered Italy in the sixth century, from their original homeland in Swabia. Augsburg, home of Georg Herivart, was the capital of Swabia. The Cavalcanti were a Florentine family whose nobility dated back to the thirteenth century but whose origins were in trade and support for the Guelf party. Perhaps Ficino is still considering Guelf support as a German connection. The house of Welf, to whom the Guelfs looked in the great controversy between Pope and Emperor, was associated with the region of Bavaria, of which Swabia formed part. The rival Ghibellines (associated with the house of Waiblingen) also had their roots in Swabia, but as supporters of the Emperor. Over and above any possible reflection of this kind, in the background to any comments Ficino makes on 'Germans' we should

remember his fondness for associated meanings, such as *germanus*, a full brother, or even a twin-brother. Certainly Giovanni Pico and Giovanni Cavalcanti were both close friends of Ficino's.

On Ficino's connections in Germany, and the significance of '*germanus*', see Michael J.B. Allen, 'Ocean Blue: *Epistolae teutonicis complatonicis tribus*,' in E. Kessler and H.C. Kuhn, *Germania latina, Latinitas teutonica: Politik, Wissenschaft, humanistische Kultur vom späten Mittelalter bis in unsere Zeit*, 2 vols. (Munich; Fink, 2003), vol.1, pp. 143-56.

3 'What is your own is most dear to you' is an expression Ficino has used a number of times. See, for example, *Letters*, **7**, 39 and 72; Letters 18 and 31 in this volume; *Platonic Theology*, XVIII, viii, 38. Several variants of this proverb were in common use. A classical source may be Cicero's saying '*suum cuique pulchrum est*' (To each, his own is beautiful), *Tusculan Disputations*, V, 22 (63) and it re-appears in the collection of proverbs or *Adages* made by Erasmus, the first edition of which was published in 1500.

4 Cf. the Silenus figure to whom Socrates is likened, which is ugly on the outside, but shining and golden on the inside (Plato, *Symposium*, 215b and 216d-217a). On a more practical level, there are many examples of drinking cups that were silver on the outside and gold inside.

5 In *Phaedrus*, 279, Plato says 'Beloved Pan, and all you other gods who haunt this place, give me beauty in the inward soul; and may the outward and inward man be at one.'

6 In *Republic*, III, 415a, Socrates links gold to the qualities of the rulers, and silver to their auxiliaries. See note 3 to Letter 34.

3

1 Ficino uses this figure of speech, of one person hidden in the guise of another, on several occasions. See especially *Letters*, **9**, 9. Cf. **8**, 6 and 19; **9**, 7, and (arguably) **5**, 41.

2 Plato's Sun is especially associated with the constellation Leo, and the lion (*leo*) is regarded as a solar animal. (See *De vita*, III, xiv, where Ficino uses material he drew from Proclus's commentary on the first *Alcibiades* and another extract he translated under the title *On sacrifice and Magic*.)

3 For the Narcissus myth of delusion in love, see *Letters*, **6**, 4 and *De amore*, IV, 17. The story was familiar to his readers from Ovid, *Metamorphoses*, III, 344-510.

4 Cf. *Platonic Theology*, VIII, i, and Letter 29 in this volume where he discusses the different manners in which imagination and intellect operate (see p.39 above). As in many other places, Ficino locates human powers of reason midway between nature and divinity.

5 By 1491, Ficino had made considerable progress on his translation of the *Divine Names* from Greek and had started on the *Mystical Theology*. Ambrogio Traversari had already produced new Latin versions of the Dionysian works, improving on earlier medieval translations. The other two main treatises were the *Celestial Hierarchy* and the *Ecclesiastical Hierarchy*, accompanied by ten letters. Ficino sent early versions of his translations to particular friends for their comments before publication. See *Letters*, **9**, 26, 27 and 28.

6 Note the relative importance Ficino accords to each of these authors who drew inspiration from Plato. Iamblichus (250-325 AD), whom Ficino 'loves', adapted

Platonism to the context of Greek religious life; Plotinus (203-262), whom Ficino 'admires', was the key interpreter of Plato and originator of the entire Neoplatonic tradition; Dionysius, whom he 'revered', was assumed to have lived even earlier, and he therefore thought Dionysius must have exerted an influence on them. Ammonius Saccas was Plotinus' teacher in Alexandria. According to tradition Ammonius was raised as a Christian although he later devoted himself wholly to philosophy. Numenius of Apamaea was a great teacher in the second century AD of Pythagorean and Platonic philosophy. In a letter to Jacobo Rondoni, Bishop of Rimini (*Epistolae*, XII, 25) Ficino notes that these authors acknowledged the Gospel of St John and considered it as important in the transmission of Platonic ideas as the work of Dionysius that he assumed to be in circulation at the time. Certainly Greek philosophy of that period accepted the influence of Chaldean and Judaic ideas.

In suggesting that Dionysius's works subsequently disappeared in 'some calamity of the Church' Ficino is trying to account for an apparent problem in the transmission of the writings of Dionysius now known to be unreal. The problem centres on the apparent disappearance of those works between the first century AD when they were presumed to have been written by Dionysius, St Paul's convert on the Areopagus in Athens, and the sixth century when they start to be mentioned by other writers. By the ninth century they had acquired a great reputation, and began to be associated with the first Bishop of Paris, a third-century martyr, who shared the name Dionysius (St Denis). In fact, the writings had not disappeared at all. They were not written until the early sixth-century, by a follower of Proclus in Syria, invoking the authority of Dionysius the Areopagite, with whom he may or may not have shared a name, by attributing the work to him – but this was not known until long after Ficino's day. Even though a few individual scholars, before and after Ficino, suspected the Dionysian writings were of later date (e.g. Peter Abelard, Lorenzo Valla and Desiderius Erasmus), for Ficino and nearly all his contemporaries these Platonic texts carried special authority because of their supposed link with the Apostle Paul.

The identity of the real author remains unknown, and he is therefore sometimes referred to nowadays as Pseudo-Dionysius.

7 The figure of sparks of light kindling a blaze of intelligence and/or love comes from Plato (*Epistles*, VII, 341CD and cf. *Symposium*, 210E-211A on the sudden revelation of truth and beauty) and is used frequently in Ficino's writings. [See, for example, *Platonic Theology*, VIII, iii, 5; XII, i, 10; XIV, x, 12; *Commentary on St Paul*, chapters VI and XXVI; *Letters*, **4**, 7.].

8 *On the Doctrines of Hippocrates and Plato* (*De placitis Hippocratis et Platonis*) was one of the major works of Galen, the first-century physician, writing in Greek in late Imperial Rome. It stresses the similarities between the physician and the philosopher regarding the tripartite functions of the soul.

Ficino read a copy of Galen's *De placitis* between 1491 and 1499 – possibly Pier Leone's. (See Vivian Nutton in *Le opere Psicologiche di Galeno,* ed. Paola Manuli and Mario Vegetti, Naples, 1989, pp. 281-309, at pp. 299-4.) He had long been aware of Galen's Platonism (e.g. *Letters*, **4**, 7); he continued to study and discuss the *De placitis* with Giorgio Ciprio during the 1490s and he reports his reactions to Galen's critique of Plato in his commentary on *Timaeus*, (*Opera*, p. 1465; ed. Farndell, pp. 98-101).

4

1 After Riario left Florence in 1478, he was appointed to a position of influence in Rome (see Biographical Notes). It is not known what favour Ficino was requesting in this undated letter. It may have followed in the copy sent to the cardinal but it has not been preserved. The fact that he refers to the intended recipient of the favour as 'undeserving' suggests that it is for himself (following the custom of assuming humility). See Letter 6 for the history of a lapse in their communications between 1478 and the time of this volume (1491).

5

1 The young men referred to in this letter are Dionysius Reuchlin and Johann Streler. See Letter 7 and the Biographical Notes for the full background.

2 The boys were lodged with Giorgio Antonio Vespucci. See Armando Verde, *Studio Fiorentino*, vol. 3.1, p. 240.

6

1 The nature of Marsuppini's visit to Rome is not known but it did allow Ficino the pretext to resume his connection with Riario.

2 The lost letters to which he refers are *Letters*, **4**, 39 and **5**, 3, 5 and 33, all written between Riario's departure from Florence in June 1478 and the summer of 1480. They may have failed to reach Riario or, more likely, he may have simply chosen not to reply. In *Letters,* **5**, 4 Ficino charges Giovanni Niccolini with handing over the preceding letter to Riario in person. Ficino consistently refuses to be deterred by Riario's silence.
Other letters to Riario (*Letters*, **4**, 26, 27, 28 and Appendix B) were written before Riario's departure. *Letters,* **4**, 34 on the uses of adversity may also belong with this earlier group.
It is not now thought that there were any further letters to Riario beyond the ones mentioned above. (Kristeller, *Sup. Fic.*, I, CVI, corrects the earlier view of Della Torre, *Storia dell'Accademia Platonica di Firenze*, p. 93f.)

3 Ficino's correspondence with the Hungarian court is now well known and is documented in *Letters*, **2**, **3** and **7**). *Letters,* **8**, **9** and the current volume record his correspondence with Germany. Most of his letters to France belong to Book XII, although he had contact earlier with French representatives in Florence and Florentine ambassadors to the French court. For his connections with Spain, see Susan Byrne, *Ficino in Spain* (Toronto: University of Toronto Press, forthcoming 2015). His works were known in Spain, very likely through Spanish visitors to Italy, amongst whom was the Catholic reformer Francisco Jiménez de Cisneros (later Cardinal Cisneros) who spent the years 1459 to 1465 in Rome. There is more to be discovered about Ficino's Spanish connections.

7

1 Johannes Reuchlin, who was born in Pforzheim, see Biographical Notes.

2 Swabia had been a large independent duchy in the Middle Ages; its capital was Augsburg. The duchy later fragmented into several principalities, and in 1491 the section of former Swabia that was of greatest interest to Ficino was the principality of Württemberg ruled by Count Eberhard. In 1495, Württemberg regained the status of a duchy. (See Biographical Notes.)

3 Ludwig Vergenhans, who took the Latin name of Nauclerus, and Johannes Reuchlin of Pforzheim were both in the service of Count Eberhard, with particular responsibility for the newly founded University of Tübingen. In the following sentence Ficino is praising their achievements. Since one of the young men in Florence was Reuchlin's brother, he is perhaps also suggesting that Reuchlin himself is of princely character. Alternatively, it may be read as suggesting a continuing flow of further students. There had been a small but steady flow of German students to some of the universities of northern Italy, especially the university of Padua, and the nobleman Johann van Dalberg, who later became Prince Bishop of Worms, had studied Greek at Ferrara, and founded a chair of Greek at the University of Heidelberg in 1484. That chair was first occupied by his friend Rudolph Agricola (1444-1485), who had also studied in Pavia and Ferrara.

4 Socrates speaks of the false claims of the Sophists in the *Apology*, 21A-23C. He also reiterates there his own claim that he possesses no wisdom save that of knowing he knows nothing. Cf. *Sophist*, 229CD. For the contrast between finding gold in the earth and finding real knowledge, cf. Plato, *Euthydemus*, 228E-229A.

5 The reference to searching out gem-stones hidden in the earth may be intended to refer to the mining operations undertaken by notable merchants and bankers of the same region (e.g. the Fuggers of Augsburg).

6 Giorgio Antonio Vespucci was the host; see letter 5.

8

1 Ficino's letter to Peregrino Agli is *Letters*, **1**, 7, written in 1457 but clearly reused later. It circulated widely in manuscript. Ficino returned to expand on the themes of love and divine rapture many times, especially in his commentary on *Phaedrus*, 265B, in *De amore*, VII, 14; *Philebus* commentary I, 34 and *Platonic Theology*, much of Book XIII, and XVII, ii. See also *Letters*, **1**, 52.

2 In *Letters*, **7**, 5 and Appendix F, Ficino conducted a conversation with 'Callimachus' (Filippo Buonaccorsi) on the simultaneous operation of different daemons. Here the question is extended to the simultaneous influence of different gods. He has already discussed the simultaneous operation of Apollo, Jupiter/Mercury and Venus acting together as the three Graces in *Letters*, **6**, 10 to Lorenzo di Pierfrancesco de' Medici. *Letters*, **4**, 46 to the same also specifies ways in which aspects of human nature may be turned towards and receive qualities from the various gods. (cf. *De vita*, III, xi.)

3 Homer's *Iliad* and *Odyssey* were the great epics of ancient Greece; Pindar (520-445 BC) wrote lyric poetry in the form of odes; Sappho (c.600 BC) is known for her lyric

love poetry; Callimachus of Alexandria (c. 300-245 BC) introduced a new freedom and emotional range into Greek epic verse, leading to the style known as elegiac (much favoured by Roman writers Ovid, Propertius, and Catullus). Virgil wrote in several styles, from his great epic, the *Aeneid*, with its famous love story centred on Dido, to his pastoral *Eclogues* and his inventively didactic *Georgics*. All poetry owes its inspiration to the Muses and ultimately to their leader, Apollo. Venus also presides over the work of these poets.

4 Ficino places Epimenides and the Sibyls in a different category, though also inspired by Apollo, because they really belong to a priestly tradition. Epimenides is thought to have lived around 600 BC and is reputed to have been one of the seven wise men of the ancient world. The Sibyls, according to Roman myth, held knowledge recorded on leaves. When mankind failed to value their wisdom they allowed the leaves to be scattered by the wind. Apollo is also the god of prophecy.

5 The Thracian Orpheus, whose divinely inspired music moved the rocks and charmed the wild beasts, was revered by the Greeks and inspired a religious cult based on the mysteries: see the last section of Virgil's *Georgics*, (IV, 453-566). Poliziano wrote a pastoral drama in vernacular verse while he was in Mantua, between 1478 and 1480, *Fabula di Orfeo*, in which Baccio Ugolini sang the principal part. Ficino refers frequently to Orpheus and the Orphic tradition. See *Letters*, **1**, 52 and especially Letter 25 in this volume.

6 David, whose music healed King Saul and who was also known for divinely inspired song and dance, is credited as author of many of the biblical Psalms. Clement of Alexandria had famously compared the two musicians in the opening of his *Exhortation to the Heathen* (*Protrepicus*). In this letter, Ficino associates the inspiration or mystical frenzy exemplified in them both with the divine power represented by the Greek god Dionysus. The followers of Dionysus in the ancient world were known for their uninhibited, ecstatic rites and revels. See Michael J. B. Allen, 'Eurydice in Hades: Florentine Platonism and an Orphic Mystery', *Ingenium*, 17 (2012) pp. 19-40; also *The Platonism of Marsilio Ficino*, ch 2, 'Poetic Madness,' p. 44ff.; D.P. Walker, *The Ancient Theology* (London: 1972) pp. 23-24.

7 Ficino is alluding to Lorenzo de' Medici, for whom Piero Dovizi had been first tutor, then principal secretary.

8 At the time of this letter, Lorenzo was 42 years old. He died the following year on 9th April, aged 43. See Letters 18 and 20.

9 'Bacchus loves the hills': Virgil, *Georgics*, II, 113. The Roman god Bacchus was identified with the Greek Dionysus, son of Zeus, and god of wine, intoxication and ecstasies. See Ficino's preface to *De vita*, *Letters*, **8**, Appendix A and the notes on Bacchus in that volume (pp. 77-78).

Like Bacchus, Lorenzo had a great fondness for his estates in the hills and valleys around Florence. In 1479 he had acquired a villa at Poggio a Caiano, by the river Ombrone and near a rocky island. He appointed Giuliano di Sangallo as architect to rebuild it in perfect classical form and it became a favourite residence, commanding views over the surrounding plains. It is now known as the Villa Medici, but he named it Villa Ambra after the nymph associated with the location, who was pursued by the river god of the Ombrone. Lorenzo's poem *Ambra* recounts the myth. (See bibliography for details of English translation.) Poliziano also wrote a Latin poem entitled *Ambra* as an introduction to his lectures on Homer; in the preface he connects the villa with the nymph of that name.

Villa Agnano was another favourite retreat, constructed as a hunting lodge and retreat on the fertile slopes of Monte Pisano, near San Giuliano Terme. The land was acquired from the Olivetans (who held it in tenure from the Knights Hospitallers) in 1486, and work was advanced enough for Lorenzo to stay there several times in 1491, even though the building was not regarded as complete when he died in 1492.

10 Likening Lorenzo to a revelling Bacchante, Ficino affirms divine inspiration for Lorenzo's poetry.

11 The 'stone of Hercules' is the lodestone, a naturally occurring magnet. The analogy of magnetic rings is found in Plato, *Ion*, 533D ff. Plato asserts that lyric poetry is written only in a state of frenzy or possession: *Ion*, 534.

12 Virgil, *Aeneid*, III, 251-2. Traditionally the Furies were Alecto, Tisiphone and Megaera, but Virgil is speaking here principally of harpies, and uses the term Furies generically for avenging gods.

13 The Furies also bring madness but of a different kind. They avenge unnatural crimes.

9

1 For Pietro Fanni, probably in Rome where Calderini also was, see Biographical Notes.

2 Marco Barbo had defended Ficino's reputation in Rome. It is interesting that Ficino here says he protected him 'on many occasions'. Ficino's long-standing friend Calderini was Barbo's secretary. Barbo had died on 2nd March 1491, but this letter, written towards the end of June, seems to be the first letter to Calderini since Barbo's death. It is possible they had already met in Florence earlier in the year. See Biographical Notes.

3 Psalm 119:109. It refers to a life lived in constant danger.

4 St John 10:18.

10

1 '*Rationes negotiorum*' carries the suggestion of a set of business accounts, but here it is simply an account of all the tasks that have kept him so fully occupied.

2 Ficino wrote of his progress with Dionysius in *Letters*, **9**, 26, 27 and 45 which may have been copied also to Prenninger.

3 The Plotinus was finally published on 9th May, 1492 by Antonio Miscomini in Florence.

4 Ficino revised his *Philebus* commentary substantially. The first version was written in 1469. It was thoroughly revised for publication with the Plato translations in 1484, and a third version appeared in his 1496 volume of commentaries on Plato. See Michael J. B. Allen, *Marsilio Ficino. The Philebus Commentary* (Los Angeles: University of California Press, 1975, repr. MRTS, 2000), pp. 48-58. The remainder of the work was sent in November: see Letter 13.

5 Ficino's Plato translations were published first in Florence by Lorenzo Veneto in 1484, then again in Venice on 13th August, 1491 by Bernardino de Choris and Simone da Lovere. The *Platonic Theology*, which had been published separately in Florence by Miscomini in November 1482, was included in the Venice edition of Plato.

6 See Letters 5 and 7.

11

1 Ficino uses the phrase *salute dignissime*, to describe Pier Leone. This implies that he is worthy of health and wholeness as well as greetings.
2 See the opening of Aristophanes's speech in Plato, *Symposium*, 189E-193A.
3 *Timaeus*, 42A; *Phaedrus*, 237E-238A.
4 *Symposium*, 189E-190A. Cf. *Statesman*, 271E-272B, *Laws*, IV, 713A-E.
5 Wholeness and integrity are two aspects of the single word *integer* and both should be understood in this paragraph.
6 Sadly this was not to be the case. When Lorenzo died the following spring, Pier Leone's body was found at the bottom of a well. Whether he was murdered, in reprisal for failing to preserve the life of his patient, or whether he committed suicide, in despair, has never been unravelled.
7 MS Mo2 adds Florence as the place where this letter was written.

12

1 Ficino's *Institutionum ad Platonicam disciplinam libri quattuor* of 1456, which is no longer extant, predated his mastery of the Greek language by several years. It was based on his study of the traces to be found in Roman writers (Cicero, Apuleius, Seneca, Boethius, Macrobius), in the Church Fathers Lactantius, Eusebius (already translated into Latin) and St Augustine and in the Latin commentator Calcidius. He was also able to draw on earlier translations by Uberto Decembrio (*The Republic*) and Leonardo Bruni's versions of *Gorgias* and *Phaedrus*. A number of other dialogues had been translated into Latin in the first decades of the fifteenth century, but it is not clear whether Ficino had access to them. For the details, see James Hankins and Ada Palmer, *The Recovery of Ancient Philosophy in the Renaissance: A Brief Guide,* Florence: Leo S. Olschki, 2008, pp. 10-12. See also note 3 below.
2 'Chance discovery': Ficino uses the phrase *fortuita quadam inventione*, which has rich associations ranging from a random discovery to a highly imaginative idea, or even a happy juxtaposition of arguments. It is possible that he is referring to his own early use of William of Moerbecke's 13th-century Latin translations in manuscript of certain texts of Proclus, made for Thomas Aquinas.
3 See note 1 above and *Letters*, **8**, 12 to Martin Prenninger for a list of Latin Platonists.
4 Ficino included among 'Platonists' Theophrastus, Plotinus, and all the later Neoplatonists, some of whose work he studied again intensively in the 1480s: Proclus, Porphyry, Iamblichus, Synesius, Olympiodorus, Hermias, Synesius and the medieval Psellus.
5 Since Filippo was so much younger than Ficino, he felt justified in using a phrase with overtones from the Gospels.
6 Ficino was frequently a guest in the Valori villa at Maiano. Local tradition also associates him with 'Villa Marsilio Ficino', a house the Valori family owned on the edge of Fiesole (via del Salviatino 11), with a panoramic view over the valley.

13

1 'Gathering of learned men' (*doctorum coetu*). A custom of celebrating birthdays of famous men may be seen in Ficino's own celebrations of Plato's birthday described in his *De amore*. This custom soon spread in Germany, actively promoted by the poet Conrad Celtis, who founded several groups or *sodalitates* in different cities from 1488 onwards.

2 Besides the letters he wrote to Martin Prenninger, Ficino also dedicated to him the entire ninth book (see *Letters*, **8**, Preface).

3 Eight quinternions of this work had been sent with Letter 10 on 20th July. This second instalment completed the work.

4 The publication of Plotinus suffered some further delay, perhaps on account of Lorenzo's death in April 1492 and Ficino's own illness, but it appeared in May of that year, from the publishing house of Antonio Miscomini in a fine printed edition.

5 The plan to republish all Ficino's Plato translations with the full collection of commentaries in a version superior to that of 1484 was never realised. The commentaries alone were finally published in 1496. However in August 1491, i.e. shortly before this letter was written, a second edition of the Plato translations, together with the *Platonic Theology*, had been published by de Choris and da Lovere in Venice.

6 Ficino complained about the printers in *Letters*, **7**, 20. That edition lacked his chapter divisions, omitted most of his commentaries, and contained so many typographical errors that he insisted on the inclusion of fourteen folios of *errata* at the end of the second volume.

7 His translation of and commentary on Dionysius's *Mystical Theology* and *Divine Names* was eventually published by Lorenzo Veneto in Florence in 1496 or 1497, although the preface is dated 1492.

14

1 Ficino writes in very warm tones to his physician, Mazzingo, both here and in Book XII (Letters 10 and 22). The idea of heaven joining two people inseparably is reflected in the marriage service but was also applied more widely to the bond between friends. Cicero's *On Friendship* was a key text, especially sections 21-24. In his commentary on Plato's *Lysis*, Ficino says that friendships between men are images of friendship reflecting God, who is loved first and causes all else to be loved. (See *Gardens of Philosophy*, p. 33.)

This letter confirms that Ficino's intention for the *De vita* was that it be of practical use in caring for the health of others.

2 Saturn's constancy is stressed here, and by implication his great age and long orbit. For his other qualities, see Letter 24, note 4 and Letter 31, note 4.

3 Ficino's dependants had included his elderly mother. See also *Letters*, **7**, 24 and Letter 31 in this volume.

15

1 In *Letters*, 7, 19 Ficino discussed at some length the need to engage philosophical minds through philosophy in order to bring them to an understanding of and love for religion.

2 The rediscovery of Lucretius, *De rerum natura* by Poggio Bracciolini in 1417 had led to a resurgence of interest in a text which challenged the irrationality of religion. The emergence of a group of politically disaffected Florentines in a 'Lucretian network' has been charted by Alison Brown, *The Return of Lucretius to Renaissance Florence*, Cambridge, MA, 2010. Great importance was ascribed to the text in Stephen Greenblatt, *The Swerve*, London, 2011; a more nuanced account is given by Gerard Passannante, *The Lucretian Renaissance*, Chicago, 2011.

Averroism was mainly a problem in the universities, where it reinforced Aristotelian thinking of a particular kind, and posed a threat to Christian doctrines on the immortality of the individual soul. Ficino dedicated Book XV of the *Platonic Theology* to the refutation of contemporary Averroism and he also deals with Epicurean ideas, especially in *Platonic Theology*, VIII, iv and XIV, x. Pico had these problems in mind too: his *900 Theses* contains 41 points for discussion drawn from Averroes. Pico appears to have been more interested in the atomist Democritus than in either Epicurus or Lucretius who reflected some of his theories (see *Letters*, **8**, 20). Elsewhere Pico does not often refer to Averroes or the Epicureans by name, but many of his arguments contribute clearly to a refutation of their views. Some examples that do explicitly name them are *Heptaplus*, V, 3 and VII, proem; *De ente et uno*, 5.

3 St Matthew 4:18-22; St Mark 1:16-20; for the 'great fishes' and unbroken net, St John 21:11.

4 Augustine, *City of God*, VIII, 5; *Confessions*, VIII, 2; *On True Religion*, iv, 7.

5 St Matthew 9:37; St Luke 10:2.

6 Ficino ends the letter with a strong reminder of unity and a common task. This would argue against the hypothesis sometimes advanced of a deep rift developing between the two men, despite critical comments often made by Pico.

16

1 In this first of the two letters Ficino writes to assist his friend Martin Prenninger during his Italian journey, he draws on his long-standing friendship with Francesco Soderini in Rome. Soderini held the important position in the papal *curia* of Apostolic Secretary. He was therefore influential and could make sure that any requests or petitions would be heard. The precise purpose of Prenninger's visit to Rome is not known, but the aim was to see the pope on behalf of Count Eberhard. He used the opportunity of being there to visit libraries, but it is thought he did not manage to see Pope Innocent VIII, who was already very ill. Prenninger left Rome shortly before the election of Alexander VI.

17

1 This second letter of introduction is addressed to Filippo Valori, who was also in Rome at the time, as an ambassador from Florence. MS Mo2 adds the words *oratori Romae* ('ambassador in Rome') to the opening address.

2 Martin Prenninger's first child was born c.1484, and was named after Marsilio. On the celebration of Ficino's birthday in Germany, see Letter 13.

3 Such explanations were not recorded. See W. Zeller, *Der Jurist und Humanist Martin Prenninger gen. Uranius (1450–1501)*, Tübingen, 1973, p. 38.

18

1 Hippocrates and Galen both identified four stages to any disease: onset, increase, climax or crisis, and declination. The fourth stage therefore indicates recovery (fatal cases had only three stages).

2 Ficino's relationship with four generations of the Medici family is spelled out in an earlier letter to Giovanni, *Letters*, **8**, 9.

3 Giovanni relinquished his place as cathedral canon in Ficino's favour on 4 April, 1487 (see Kristeller, *Marsilio Ficino and His Work after 500 Years*, pp. 33-34). The letters acknowledging this gift were not included in the first printed edition of the *Letters* (printed while the Medici were in exile from Florence) but were included in early manuscript versions and are restored in our translated volumes. See *Letters*, **7**, 38-40.

4 '*Aedes martiana*': G. B. Picotti, in his *La Giovinezza di Leone X* (1928), suggested that this letter refers to the gift of the position of prior among the Augustinian Canons of San Marco in Mantua. This seems questionable, although Leandro Alberti's *Descrizione d'Italia* (Bologna, 1550) includes a fine account of that church, which attracted the attention of French kings and Italian dukes. In 1958, Raymond Marcel conjectured that the benefice in question related to the Church of St Michael at Monte Marciano, 18km southeast of Figline, in the hills above the Val d'Arno near Montevarchi (see Marcel, *Marsile Ficin,* p.514, fn. 1). Kristeller felt unable to identify the benefice in his 1985 article 'Marsilio Ficino and the Roman Curia', (*Roma Humanistica*, ed. by Josef Ijsewijn, *Humanistica Lovaniensia*, 34A, 1985, pp. 83-98, reprinted in *Studies in Renaissance Thought and Letters*, vol. IV, Rome, 1996, pp. 265-280 at p. 275).

An undated letter from Ficino to Gentile Becchi (*Letters*, **9**, 32) refers to Monte Marciano, which almost certainly indicates the same place as *aedes martiana*, given the variations in spelling that were common in the period. In the notes to that letter, we considered the most likely reference was to certain grain revenues which are mentioned in Ficino's will, in the parishes of Santa Maria and Santa Lucia of Monte Marciano (which could be in the Monte Marciano identified by Marcel). However, in the absence of conclusive documentation, other possibilities should not be ruled out: there is a Monte Martano close to Spoleto, in the Papal States, Montemartano near Perugia and a Montemarciano near Ancona.

The spelling *martiana* used on this occasion has suggested to some a church of St Martin, a suggestion which gains weight from a possible reference to St Martin in

Letter 19 (see note 5 to that letter). There were churches of St Martin in and around Florence: within the city, San Martino del Vescovo was home to the charitable society Buonomini of San Martino. However, there is no known connection between Ficino and that institution, and, more importantly, the expected form of a name derived from San Martino would be *aedes martiniana*.

Whatever the gift, it came at a time of great changes in Giovanni's status and needs. Giovanni was formally invested as cardinal at Fiesole on 9th March, 1492 and soon after left Florence for Rome, arriving two weeks later. Giovanni then returned to Florence on his father's death but found it better to spend most of his time outside the city, in the Medici villas and religious houses rather than be too closely involved with his brother's erratic leadership in the city. However, apart from a journey for the conclave of August 1492, he stayed close to Florence for the next two years, until the overthrow of Medici rule in 1494.

5 For the signs, see note 9 below.

6 Hesiod, *Works and Days*, lines 122-5 and 250-255. Plato discusses Hesiod's suggestions in *Cratylus*, 398B and incorporates them in the Myth of Er (*Republic*, X). See also *Laws*, IV, 713D.

7 The idea that just rulers join the gods and have an influence on human affairs from heaven is echoed in Macrobius's *Commentary on the Dream of Scipio*, I, 4. Plato in *Gorgias*, 523A, speaks only of a special place for them in the Isles of the Blest, but in the elaborate allegory of the *Phaedrus* dialogue, he speaks of their further exploits in the heavenly cavalcade (*Phaedrus*, 248). Alcinous (Albinus), interpreting this passage, explains that they become companions of the gods and journey with them. (*The Handbook of Platonism*, 27, 3.)

8 For the arrival of souls among the spirit guides, cf. Plato, *Phaedrus*, 246E-247E and Proclus, *Commentary on Parmenides*, I, 666-7; for the intermediate role of daemons between gods and mankind, *Symposium*, 202E; for the involvement of daemons in producing atmospheric effects, see Porphryry, *De abstinentia*, II, 38ff., translated by Ficino for Braccio Martelli in 1486 (*Letters*, 7, 29). On daemons in general, see Ficino's translation of Iamblichus, *De mysteriis*, dedicated to Giovanni de' Medici in 1489; of Proclus's *Commentary on Alcibiades*, 71ff. (Letter 29 below) and of Psellus, *On the operation of Daemons*, dedicated to Piero de' Medici in 1488.

9 For the portents on the deaths of Romulus, see Livy, *Histories*, I, 16; Cicero, *Oration against Catiline*, III, 1; Plutarch, *Life of Romulus*, XXVII; St Augustine, *City of God*, III, 15. On that of Caesar, Plutarch, *Lives*, Caesar, 63; Suetonius, *The Twelve Caesars*, 81, 88, 95, 96. Cf. Shakespeare, *Julius Caesar*, II, 2: 'When beggars die, there are no comets seen; The heavens themselves blaze forth the death of princes.'

10 For portents in Florence, on Lorenzo's death on 8th April, see Letter 20 and Appendix C. Also, Poliziano's letter to Jacopo Antiquari, dated 18th May, 1492, *Angelo Poliziano: Letters* (ed. Shane Butler, I Tatti Renaissance Library, Cambridge, 2006) vol. 1, IV, 2, sections 18-20. Some of these portents are also recorded in the journal of the apothecary Luca Landucci. (*Diario fiorentino dal 1450-1516*, ed. G.C. Sansoni, Florence, 1883). For an interesting parallel, compare Shakespeare's account of Duncan's death in *Macbeth*, Act II, scene 3:

> The night has been unruly: where we lay,
> Our chimneys were blown down; and, as they say,
> Lamentings heard i' the air; strange screams of death,
> And prophesying with accents terrible

Of dire combustion and confused events
New hatch'd to the woeful time: the obscure bird
Clamour'd the livelong night: some say, the earth
Was feverous and did shake.

19

1 In grammar there are three degrees available for adjectival and adverbial expressions: positive, comparative, and superlative.

2 Virgil, *Aeneid*, I, 94.

3 There is no evidence to show what favour Ficino has received, but the dating of this letter, coinciding with that of Letter 18, suggests it may have to do with the same benefice. It would appear here to have brought a welcome addition to Ficino's income. The holding of multiple benefices required permission from the papal *curia*, and Soderini, as papal protonotary, would have been the person to grant this. However, it sounds as if Soderini may also have been involved in persuading Giovanni to assist Ficino. In saying that Soderini is robbing his dearest in order to clothe Ficino, there is perhaps a hint of the legend of St Martin (who gave his own cloak to clothe a beggar), but no clear evidence enables us to identify the benefice concerned, and the name *aedes martiana* (see notes to Letter 18) remains difficult to interpret.

4 '*That dear friend of yours*': the Latin, *familiari tuo*, may indicate a close friend, household member, or a kinsman. The Soderini family had been close supporters of the Medici, and through marriage alliances came within their wider family circle.

20

1 'Chance' and 'nature': in this letter Ficino uses the terms *fortuna*, here translated as 'chance', as opposed to *natura*, by which he means a law that operates inevitably. 'Fortune', on the other hand, with her wheel, was always regarded as capricious and unpredictable. Cf. *Letters*, **2**, 61 and Letters 31 and 32 in the current volume.

2 Having dismissed chance and nature, Ficino follows the tradition of the later Platonists in ascribing the supernatural origin of portents to three different classes of intermediary divine powers, be they daemons or angels. In this letter he enumerates the spirit attendant on the individual, that of a place, and celestial spirit bands in general, and he seems to have Dionysian angel categories in mind (guardian angels, principalities and cherubim or seraphim). In Appendix D, describing daemons, he enumerates spirits in general, the individual spirit and one particular individual spirit, that of Socrates. Ficino summarises views on daemons in his commentary on Plato's *Apology of Socrates*, see Farndell, *Gardens of Philosophy*, pp. 122-126. He suggests that airy daemons govern the active life, watery daemons the life of pleasure and fiery daemons rule over contemplation. Further divisions of spirits can be found in Iamblichus, De *mysteriis*, V, 24ff.; Proclus, *Commentary on Alcibiades I*, 71-73, *Commentary on Cratylus,* and *Commentary on Timaeus*, 155.30-156.1. For the soul being appointed to a particular star, see Plato, *Timaeus*, 41DE and *Commentary on Alcibiades I*, 72. Cf. Plotinus, *Enneads*, III, 4, 'On our allotted Guardian Spirit'.

3 The three classes of intermediary beings govern three types of portent. The celestial bands give rise to cosmic portents, those of place bring local disturbances and prophecies, while the guardian spirits appear to operate through the mind of the individual, in dreams or individual omens. The portents listed in this letter were also observed in Florence following Lorenzo's death. See note 10 to Letter 18 above.
4 Iamblichus adds a class of heroes between mankind and the divine beings. Iamblichus, *On the Mysteries*, II, 3.
5 Proclus and Plotinus differ on the status of daemons: for Plotinus they are virtually part of the human soul. For Ficino, following Proclus, they exist in a hierarchy of supernatural beings. See Proclus, Commentary on *Timaeus*, 165.3-167.31. Plutarch discusses the death of daemons in his *Failure of Oracles*, 16-19. For the internal action of the daemon on the individual's behaviour, see Plutarch, *On the Daemon of Socrates*, esp. XXII.
6 Plutarch (45-120 AD) describes atmospheric disturbances that accompany the death of daemons in *On the Failure of Oracles*, 419E-420.
7 For the portents on Lorenzo's death, see also Appendix C. This final paragraph of the letter appears only in MS Mo2. Ficino removed it, as he removed a number of other passages relating to the Medici, perhaps in this case after Piero proved such a disappointment to the city.
8 'Farewell' appears only in the printed edition.
9 Only in MS Mo2.

21

1 MS Mo2 adds 'a true philosopher'.
2 Pico had been living relatively quietly in Fiesole, under the terms of an agreement made between Lorenzo and the papal authorities, after the condemnation incurred by his earlier philosophical writings, and the further punishment provoked by his inflammatory *Apologia*. His official pardon was not granted until 1493.
3 During the year just past, Pico had completed *De ente et uno* (On Being and the One), intended as the first part of a reconciliation of Platonist and Aristotelian interpretations of the first principles of philosophy. He dedicated it to Angelo Poliziano. He was also working on a commentary on the Psalms.
4 Pico had been in Florence when Lorenzo died, on 8th April, 1492. Their close friend Pier Leone was found dead the next day. It is not clear how soon Pico left the city, but by May he was in Ferrara for a Dominican convention and to study some oriental manuscripts.
5 MS Mo2 gives the year as 1492. The printed editions give only the day and month.

22

1 Although Valori was a close friend, he was away from Florence during this period as ambassador in Rome.
2 This letter is the first that Ficino has written since 28th April. He was absent from the group that gathered around Lorenzo's deathbed on account of his own illness, about which no further information is available than is given in this letter. Ficino's

illness had kept him away from the Medici household during the time that Lorenzo was dying. This is why Ficino's name occurs only in Poliziano's famous account of Lorenzo's death in relation to a meeting held shortly before his final days (Poliziano, *Letters*, IV, ii, 14).

3 On Ricasoli, see Biographical Notes.

4 Uranius, Martin Prenninger, had visited Ficino on his way to Rome in the spring and has now returned, on his way back to Germany, visiting Ficino on June 25th. Valori had evidently been able to help Martin Uranius on his recent visit. Ficino loses no time in writing.

23

1 MS Mo2 adds 'of Florence'.

2 Ficino uses the title *dux* in the printed edition of the letters (published in the spring of 1495) although in 1492 Eberhard was still Count (*Graf*). No title is given here in the sole surviving manuscript (MS Mo2), but see Letter 33, note 1. In Latin usage the term *dux* is used for a duke, but can also mean chieftain, leader or guide, a great general or commander, or even an emperor. The title of Duke was not conferred on Eberhard until 21st July 1495 by Maximilian, who held him in high regard. Mount Peligard (Mömpelgard) is nowadays within the French region of Franche-Comté, very near the Swiss border and just 45 miles west of Basel. It belonged to the rulers of Württemberg (see Biographical Notes, under Eberhard).

3 Following Martin Prenninger's visit, Ficino was moved to write to Count Eberhard as a likely protector of Platonic studies. On Eberhard's death in 1496, Maximilian declared, 'Here lies a prince who has left no equal in the German empire in princely virtues, and whose advice I have frequently followed with advantage.'

4 See Plato, *Republic*, 473D. In *Cratylus*, 407, Plato confirms the dual nature of Athene's powers, based on both might and wisdom.

5 On Caesar, see Suetonius, *The Twelve Caesars*, I, 75; Augustine, *City of God*, III, 30.

6 Scipio the Elder, also called Scipio Africanus (236-183 BC), led the Roman troops in their great victory over Hannibal in the Battle of Zama (202 BC) which ended the Second Punic War. He became the heroic model of courage, restraint and dignity, see Livy, *History of Rome*, especially books 29-30; St Augustine, *City of God*, III, 21. Augustine also discusses Scipio in *City of God*, II, 21, based on Cicero's *De re publica*, only part of which was known in the Renaissance (the important metaphysical passage known as the *Dream of Scipio* preserved through Macrobius's commentary). Scipio's importance as a character model, however, was well established and can be seen, for example, in Petrarch, especially in his epic poem *Africa*.

7 Minos, the legendary lawgiver of Crete, features in Plato, *Laws*, I, 624; Homer, *Odyssey*, XIX, 178ff; Virgil, *Aeneid*, VI, 430-433.

8 On Numa, lawgiver of Rome, and inaugurator of religious rites, see Livy, *History of Rome*, I, 17-21; Augustine, *City of God*, III, 9.

9 The reign of Augustus (27 BC-14 AD) marked the end of a long period of turbulence and civil war and was praised by all contemporary writers. See, for example, Virgil, *Aeneid*, VI, 847-853. See also Tacitus, *Annals*, I, end of ch. 3; Pliny, *Natural History*, XXVII, 1.

10 Following the sequence given by Ficino, Eberhard had pursued peace at home, reuniting the ancestral territories of the divided Duchy of Württemberg (1482);

he had visited the Holy Land (1468) and established several new collegiate churches, introduced ecclesiastical and other reforms at home, and founded the University of Tübingen (1477). Johannes Nauclerus records all these activities in his Chronicle, published in 1516.

11 Ficino uses the term '*idea*' here, referring to the Platonic ideal or archetypal model.

12 Cf. James 1:17.

13 MS Mo2 provides the date for this letter.

24

1 The study of astronomy was not controversial in Ficino's time. However, this letter alludes to its close links with predictive astrology. In 1477, Ficino had written a *Disputatio contra iudicium astrologorum* which was not published but formed a basis for his comments on astrology in other works (for its text, see *Sup. Fic.*, II, pp. 11-76). See also *Marsilio Ficino: Scritti sull'Astrologia*, ed. O.P. Faracovi, Milan, 1999. For recent scholarship, see Faracovi, *Lo Specchio Alto. Astrologia e filosofia fra Medioevo e Prima età moderna*, Pisa, 2012; *Nello Specchio del cielo,* ed. M. Bertozzi, Florence, 2008. The topic will be discussed in more detail in the next book of Ficino's letters.

2 For Ficino, divine Providence stands far above the operations of fortune, fate or nature. Fate is also granted an important status, but fortune, ever fickle, appears to defy established order. In his *Disputatio* of 1477 Ficino explains that the stars produce fate and have their influence on the body and the senses, but can be resisted by will and reason, which flow not from any astral source but directly from Providence and God. In a letter of 1482 to the Duke of Urbino, also based on the *Disputatio*, Ficino suggests that reading heavenly signs requires a deeper understanding than the science of astrology can provide (*Letters*, **6**, 17, esp. pp. 26-27).

3 For the wars of the giants and the Titans against the Olympian gods, often depicted on temple friezes in the ancient world, see Apollodorus, *The Library*, I, 1-6; Hesiod, *Theogony*, 617-735; Ovid, *Metamorphoses*, I, 151-162. See also Plato, *Sophist*, 246A-C.

4 On Saturn, mentioned frequently as a force for contemplation, see especially, *Letters*, **2**, 24; **8**, 18 and p. 62; *Platonic Theology*, XII, ii, 2-3; *De vita*, I, 4. See also Michael J.B. Allen, 'Life as a Dead Platonist' and 'Marsilio Ficino on Saturn, the Plotinian Mind and the Monster of Averroes' (publication details in Bibliography). On Jupiter, see *De vita*, III, 4-6. Saturn (as Cronos) ruled the earth in a golden age, far in the past, but was compelled to give up his rule to Jupiter, who still holds sway. Ficino is suggesting that Saturn's rule, one of deeper wisdom, might be re-established at some time in the future – in this life or the next.

5 Romans 12:3. It has been translated here following the Latin closely and using 'wisely' for *ad sobrietatem*. The translation chosen by the translators of the Bible under King James casts it in a different direction, relating it principally to self-esteem: 'not to think of himself more highly than he ought to think; but to think soberly'. Ficino is using it in a wider sense, which in a way sums up his opinion on astrology that has been so keenly debated.

25

1 The *Orphic Hymns*, regarded as an ancient philosophical theology dating from before Pythagoras and Plato, circulated in manuscript among Greek scholars in Italy from 1423. They were published in a Greek printed edition in Florence in 1500. This indicated considerable interest in their contents. Ficino was reluctant to publish his Latin version as they are ritual hymns to the Greek gods, but he was clearly very interested in them. Two Latin translations were made, one being published later, in 1540, but now generally attributed to Janus Lascaris, also greatly interested in writers of the later Platonic tradition.

A favourite hymn that Ficino ascribes to Orpheus is actually not found in the surviving Orphic collections but is known only through the *De mundo* ascribed to Aristotle (401a), which was considered a safe source (*Hymn to Zeus*, quoted by Ficino, *Letters* 1, 7 and *Philebus* Commentary, XXX, ed. Allen, p. 292). Apart from the current letter, other hymns are only paraphrased or quoted in short fragments. In this letter, however, Ficino uses the entire text of two genuine Orphic hymns already published. They could be considered 'safe' by their inclusion in the *Praeparatio Evangelica* (Preparation for the Gospel) of the fourth-century Church Father, Eusebius. Ficino sends not his own translation but a transcription of the published Latin edition of Eusebius – translated for Pope Nicholas V in 1470 by George of Trebizond, an adversary of Platonism often castigated for his poor translations. However, his translation of Eusebius was generally well attested. While Ficino presents the whole text of George of Trebizond's version, George himself had omitted some lines from the beginning and the end of the original Greek fragments quoted by Eusebius. For Ficino's wider use of Eusebius, see John Monfasani, 'Marsilio Ficino and Eusebius of Caesarea's *Praeparatio Evangelica*', *Rinascimento*, XLIX (2009), pp. 3-13.

2 The *Argonautica* tells the story of Jason and the golden fleece. There were at least two versions known in the Renaissance: the more famous narrative poem by Apollonius of Rhodes and one attributed to Orpheus, which is more likely to be the one Ficino means here. For the hymns of Orpheus, see note 1. The first Renaissance translation of Homer was by Poliziano, who translated Book II of the *Iliad* while still in his teens, in 1469, and Books II-V a few years later. However, no one translated the Homeric hymns, a collection of 33 hymns to the gods that were associated with Homer only by virtue of the metre they employ. Some are very ancient (7th century BC) but others may come from a later period. They begin with invocations and the longer ones include narratives. The *Hymns of Proclus,* ascribed to the fifth-century AD Neoplatonist philosopher, include hymns to the Sun, Aphrodite, Musaeus, and other gods. Hesiod's *Theogony* (called here by Ficino *Theology*), an epic poem of the 8th century BC, gives an account of the birth of all the Greek gods and the rise of Zeus to supremacy. Earlier Italian writers had explored these themes, especially Giovanni Boccaccio in his influential *Genealogy of the Gods* (written between 1360 and 1374, published in print in 1472) and were interested in Porphyry's allegorical guide to Homer, *The Cave of the Nymphs*, but Ficino hesitated to become fully involved in this field even though fully committed to the idea that philosophy and poetry overlap in deeply rewarding ways, as is shown in his consistently high estimation of Virgil, Dante and the commentaries of Cristoforo Landino, and his appreciation

of poetic qualities in Plato. See especially *Letters*, **2**, 3; Ficino's own translations of the Orphic hymns did not survive, apart from a short unpublished section sent to Cosimo de' Medici in 1462 (*Sup. Fic.*, II, pp. 87-88) and fifteen brief extracts, mostly single lines, quoted in the *Platonic Theology* (see Klutstein, *Marsilio Ficino et la Théologie Ancienne*, pp. 40-41). A few lines of translation from the opening of the Orphic *Argonautica* and from the Homeric hymns in MS Riccardiana 62 were attributed to Ficino by B. Kieszkowski (*Studi sul Platonismo del Rinascimento in Italia*, Florence, 1936, Appendix, p. 156). Greek copies of some hymns of Proclus and Orpheus in Ficino's hand are in MS Ricc. 92.

3 Prenninger must have visited Ficino on his way to Rome in the spring of 1492.

4 The *De rerum natura* of Lucretius, lost after the fall of Rome, is a didactic poem presenting the philosophy of Epicurus. It was rediscovered by Poggio Bracciolini in 1417. Ficino's *De voluptate* (On Pleasure) does survive and was published in his *Opera omnia*. It was written quite early, in 1457, and even if he burned a more complete commentary he did learn and retain much from what he read. His short work on the *Four Schools of Philosophers* also reflects those early interests. In 1473, Lucretius appeared in print and two further editions followed in 1486 and 1495, but it was still regarded by many as a dangerous work. For arguments against Lucretius, see *Platonic Theology*, *passim* and esp. II, xiii and XIV, x.

5 See Diogenes Laertius, *Lives of the Philosophers*, III, 5, though he is quoting from a satirist. In *Phaedo*, 96A-C Socrates speaks of his youthful interest in natural science, later replaced by interest in the mind.

6 Plato, *Laws*, X, 888A-C.

7 The effects of harmful beliefs are discussed in Plato, *Republic*, II, 378 and III, 386-7 and were taken up by Proclus in his Commentary on the *Republic* which Ficino was reading at this time.

8 This first poem is sometimes known as the 'Palinode', a song of Orphic recantation, in that Orpheus is urging Musaeus to replace his previous devotion to a multitude of gods with devotion to one supreme God. Ancient and Renaissance scholars argued about this: if all the gods are to be interpreted as aspects of the One, no recantation would be needed. Ficino seems to support that view. In selecting this hymn he is at least presenting the idea that the gods of the pagan tradition co-existed with and could be incorporated within principles of monotheism, even in the ancient Greek world.

9 Eusebius lived in the late third and early fourth centuries of the Christian era. He was deeply immersed in philosophy and literature and became Bishop of Caesarea, on the Mediterranean coast (now northern Israel). He wrote the *Preparation for the Gospel* in support of Christian learning, but is better known for his influential history of the early Church. He wrote in Greek. For the Latin translation of the *Preparation*, see note 1. The quotation that follows is from Book XII, chapter 9.

10 Aristobulus was a Jewish priest of the second century BC in Alexandria, and tutor of one of the Ptolemies, probably Ptolemy VI (186-145 BC). Few of his writings survive, but he is credited by Clement (2nd-century Church Father) and Eusebius with presenting the idea that the books of Moses (see note 11) were a significant source for Pythagoras, Socrates, and Plato.

11 Musaeus is thought to have lived in pre-Homeric times in Attica. He is associated with priestly poetry and the Eleusinian mysteries, and is named in the Orphic

hymns as a follower of Orpheus. Several Greek and Hebrew writers of the second century identified him with Moses.

12 'Chaldean blood' here refers to the Hebrew lineage from Abraham (born in Ur of the Chaldees) rather than to the *Chaldean Oracles* attributed to Zoroaster. The point of the allusion here is to the monotheistic vision of the Hebrew tradition. The only prophet said to have 'seen' God is Moses (Exodus 33:19-23). In his earlier book *On the Christian Religion*, 26, Ficino suggests that these lines refer to Abraham or Enoch or Moses, though the Platonists claim it was Zoroaster.

13 Porphyry (232-305 AD) was responsible for preserving the works of his teacher Plotinus, and for his explanations of poetic allegory (*The Cave of the Nymphs*). His other works, including those quoted here, have survived only in fragments. They included a work on *Philosophy from Oracles* (*De Philosophia ex Oraculis Haurienda*), and a major polemic against Christianity. Eusebius is quoting from Porphyry's *Concerning Images*, which only survived later in the fragments preserved in the *Anthology* of the fifth-century scholar, Stobaeus, I, 2, 23.

14 The second Orphic hymn is also from the extract of Porphyry (Eusebius, *Preparation for the Gospel*, III, 9; Porphyry *On Images*, fragment 3).

15 Tartarus is the region of the underworld reserved for judgement and for the punishment of the most serious offenders, including the giants who threatened Olympus. Later writers saw it as the place of imprisonment of the fallen angels. It is called 'raging' perhaps because of Phlegethon, the flaming river of boiling blood that flowed into it.

16 The ruler of Olympus, home of the principal Greek deities, is Zeus, being presented here as the lord of Creation, embodying within himself all the other gods.

17 Porphyry's *On Images*, fragment 3, continues with this commentary, relating conventions used by sculptors of religious imagery to the Orphic verse.

26

1 Ficino spent several years revising and polishing his translation of the *Enneads* of Plotinus, and writing commentaries on its various sections, some longer, some shorter. The work finally issued from Antonio Miscomini's press in Florence, after two further months of delay (see Letter 13), on 7th May, 1492. This letter is therefore amongst those aiming to promote its dissemination.

2 The nature of the Platonic Academy of Florence has been much discussed. See *Letters*, **9**, 16 and note 2 to that letter. See also the circle of his fellow students of philosophy, in Letter 28 in this volume.

3 A proverb quoted by Terence, *The Eunuch*, II, 2, 44 and discussed later by Erasmus, *Adages*, I, vii, 63.

4 Plotinus (203-262 AD) famously insisted that all teaching should be oral, but his lectures were recorded and written out by his pupil Porphyry, and became known as *The Enneads* of Plotinus. Plotinus' whole enterprise was conceived as an exposition of Plato, but in fact his system marked a further development of Plato's ideas and provided the foundation for what became known as Neoplatonism (a name only introduced by historians of philosophy in the eighteenth century).

5 Ficino's metaphor of Plotinus giving birth to Plato, some 600 years his senior, is now transferred to Ficino giving birth to Plotinus. Cf. *Letters*, **6**, 34. The image

is modelled on that of Socrates as midwife (*Plato, Theaetetus*, 149-151). The process implies that Plato or Plotinus only come to life again when contemporary readers revive their teachings.

6 Carducci is being called upon to act in July. Although the book was officially published on 7th May, Lorenzo had died just a few weeks before that, and Ficino himself had been ill (see Letter 22). Valori, to whom he often turned for support, was away in Rome. In a letter in Book XII, dated 14 November 1492 Ficino shows his close connection with Carducci, and a copy of the three most recent books of letters (IX, X and XI) is written out for him, including also the first five letters of XII. This is the Munich manuscript Mo2 that has been so useful in the preparation of this volume and the two previous ones. The same manuscript contains earlier letters by Bartolommeo Scala, chancellor of the city of Florence.
The idea that an important philosophical work can diffuse light is characteristic of Ficino. The power of divine light is discussed in many places, from his earliest commentaries onwards. See, for example, *De amore*, IV, 4 and *Platonic Theology*, XVIII, viii, 10 and 18. Three months after the date of this letter he sends out part of his revised work on the Sun and its light (see Letter 33).

27

1 For the care Ficino took to avert opposition prior to the publication of his *Three Books on Life* (*De vita*), see *Letters*, **8**, Introduction, Letters, and Appendices. Three years later he is still concerned that his writings should not be misunderstood, and therefore stresses their link to truly medical considerations of health rather than the more mysterious aspects of astral influence, magic, and talismans that were also discussed. Canacci and Ricasoli were both from patrician families and were active in the political life of the city.

2 The concern he expresses for the health of Paolantonio Soderini may be more than physical. After the death of Lorenzo de' Medici, to whom he was related, in April of 1492, Paolantonio's support for Lorenzo's son, Piero, wavered and he was increasingly attracted towards the party of Savonarola. In fact, there were political divisions within the Soderini family, all of whom were highly active in the city.

3 Paolantonio's son, Tommaso Soderini (1470-1531), named after his grandfather (1403-1485), also played his part in political life. He assisted in his father's attempt to hold opposing factions together during 1498. Later he went on various embassies to Rome.

28

1 On Johann Streler, see Biographical Notes. Ficino here calls him *congermanus*, a rarely used word meaning a person with whom one has grown up or become united, but as with the word *germanus*, meaning 'full brother' (as opposed to half-brother) Ficino exploits its other meaning, 'German'. (See Letter 2.)

2 As Ficino states, the list he will give does not contain everyone in his circle, but those committed to the pursuit of philosophy. Even amongst those, not all are listed. Some had died by this time, a few others are inexplicably omitted. See Biographical Notes

on pp. 135-6. As so often, in Ficino's letters, it is hard to distinguish between what he regards as 'my' and what he regards as 'our' as the possessive pronouns sometimes seem interchangeable.

3 Mercury embodies the spirit of inquiry and imparts skill in interpretation and expression to his followers; Jupiter conveys powers of governing and ruling. (See, for example, *De amore*, VI, 4 where Ficino summarises the gifts conveyed by each of the ancient planetary gods.) See also note 3 to Letter 32.

4 Plato, *Epistles*, X and Ficino's commentary on it (translated in A. Farndell, *Gardens of Philosophy*, p.173). Cf. Ficino, *Letters*, 1, 20.

5 Plato, *Epistles*, VI and VII, 340C-341D.

6 On all the names mentioned below, see Section III of Biographical Notes.

7 Bernardo Vittorio is likely to be Bernardo Vettori, about whom relatively little is known. (See Biographical Notes.) But it is surprising that Bernardo Rucellai, who opened his gardens to those in pursuit of philosophy, is omitted.

29

1 Uranius had been in Florence at the end of June. (See Letter 22.) Janus Lascaris made two journeys to Greece for Lorenzo, in search of manuscripts in monastic and other libraries, one in the autumn of 1490 to Thessalonika, Macedonia and Mount Athos, the second from the spring of 1491 to the summer of 1492, reaching Constantinople before returning via Mount Athos again and Crete. He returned in 1492 with 200 manuscripts. He also reported on sensitive diplomatic matters.

2 MS Laur. 80.9 is the first half of a codex from the ninth or tenth century that contained the whole of Proclus's commentary on Plato's *Republic*. The second half was not known to Ficino, and was only rediscovered in the Vatican Library in the nineteenth century. Laur. 80.9 contains the first twelve of the original seventeen dissertations by Proclus. Ficino borrowed the manuscript on 7th July, 1492 (see library loan note, *Catalogo*, p. 189) and had produced the digest that follows by 3rd August.

3 The figure of distilling knowledge from a variety of flowers, culled even among non-Christian works, goes back to St Basil, *Homilia ad adolescentes*, 7-8.

4 Martin had no official place within the church, and was a married man, but he had served as Chancellor of the important religious centre of Konstanz and may well have had religious leanings which would have been known to Ficino through their personal contact in Florence.

5 MS Mo2 gives no date.

6 Plato, *Laws*, X, 900-902; *Republic*, II, 379-382.

7 This paragraph is a summary of the opening of Proclus's 4th Dissertation on Plato's *Republic*, referring to Plato's second book, where the discussion centres on how the gods should be represented in literature. Sections of Proclus's text are numbered according to page and line numbers in the standard edition by Kroll (1901), followed by later editors.

8 The paragraph in brackets is Ficino's own addition. The reference is to propositions 119 and 121 of Proclus, *Elements of Theology*.

9 All the subheadings are Ficino's and are not found in the Proclus text.

10 Plato, *Republic*, II, 379-382. (Proclus, section 28.9-33.7). Proclus subsequently

clarifies Plato's discussion with formal argumentation from logic; Ficino takes from Proclus the essence of the syllogisms and principles presented.

11 Proclus, 37.3-22.

12 Summarising Proclus, 37.23-39.1.

13 Plato, *Republic*, II, 379C. Plato is keen to ascribe evils to causes other than divine will. Proclus, 38.8ff.

14 Proclus, 38.17.

15 Proclus, 38.15 – 31.

16 The next three paragraphs summarise Proclus, 39.1-40.5.

17 *Perfulgida quaedam animarum involucra,* 'Bright coverings of the soul'. In this case Mo2's reading of *divinarum* in place of *animarum* is almost certainly incorrect.

18 *Chaldean Oracles*: 'But bodies are applied to them on your account because ...'; fragment of a lost part of the *Oracles* quoted in Proclus, *Commentary on Plato's Statesman,* 359. Fragment 142 in Edouard des Places, *Oracles Chaldaïques*, Paris, 1971.

19 This paragraph follows most of Proclus, 40.5-41.2.

20 Plato, *Republic*, II, 382E. In this paragraph, Ficino uses the extra note on daemons added to the end of the fourth dissertation by Proclus, 41.12-29.

21 Ficino here moves to the sixth dissertation of Proclus, which develops the earlier argument about apparitions in support of claims that Socrates is in full agreement with Homer, and that theurgy is an important aspect of religion. The opening sentence of this paragraph summarises 110.21-27; thereafter Ficino follows Proclus's text more closely (110.27-112.12).

22 The Greek word used by Proclus for 'in circular fashion' is an unusual one: *aneiligmenōs*. It is also used by Hermias in his *Phaedrus* commentary, where it has been translated as 'explicitly'. Festugière and Robert Lamberton, in their editions of Proclus's Commentary on the *Republic*, both translate it as 'discursively'. Ficino discusses the circular motion of the activity of understanding in *Platonic Theology* VIII, xvi, 1-4. See also IV, ii, 8-10, VI, xii, 14-15 on circular motion of the soul.

23 Homer, *Iliad*, V, 838.

24 This paragraph and the following one deal with Proclus's *Commentary on the Republic*, 112.13-113.19.

25 The tale of Proteus is told in Homer, *Odyssey*, IV, 384-569, with the dramatic shape-shifting episode occurring at lines 453-461. A great favourite, it was retold by Virgil, in *Georgics*, 387-529; see also Ovid, *Metamorphoses*, XI, 221-256.

26 *Odyssey*, IV, 404.

27 The 'Phocae' are seals.

28 *Odyssey*, IV, 417: 'For try he will and will assume all shapes of all things that move upon the earth and of water and of wondrous blazing fire.' (tr. A. T. Murray). Air is not mentioned.

29 This paragraph and the three which follow cover 113.20-114.29 in Proclus.

30 *Odyssey*, I, 105.

31 *Odyssey*, V, 51.

32 *Odyssey*, XV, 525-6, though Homer presents the hawk as Apollo's messenger. Eusebius quotes, in his *Preparation for the Gospel*, I, 10, a Chaldean image of the supreme God with the head of a hawk.

33 *Iliad*, I, 188-222.

34 Proclus's commentary on Plato's *Alcibiades* is a major source on daemons, both rational and irrational (which may roughly correspond to Christian ideas of angels

and demons). Ficino was translating a small section of it around the same time as he produced this extract from the *Republic* commentary. See Appendix D, which includes a formulation of how the daemons derive their powers from the gods under whom they are classed in what are elsewhere called '*serai*' (ropes or chains).

35 This section presents a summary of very detailed material in Proclus from 119.5 to 122.20, omitting the many literary examples.

36 This refers to the ethereal body or *ochema*, the presence of which is important to both Plato and Proclus as one of the stages involved in linking the pure eternal soul to a corrupt and mortal body.

37 *Phaedo*, 81D. See also *Platonic Theology*, XVIII, iv, 4.

38 The image of the soul is the *eidolon* (or Latin, *idolum*) discussed by Ficino in his *Platonic Theology*, see for example, XIII, ii, 11 and his commentary on the *Sophist*. See Michael J.B. Allen, *Icastes: Marsilio Ficino's Interpretation of Plato's Sophist*, Berkeley, 1989, pp. 200-204. Plotinus discusses it in *Enneads*, I, i, 12; IV, iii, 10, 12, 29-30, and VI, iv, 16. See also Plethon's *Chaldean Oralces*, 15 (= fragment 158). The function of the *idolum* is to make images and to connect the higher functions of soul with body. According to Homer, it may have an existence separate from the soul after death (*Odyssey*, XI, 602-4).

39 To Aristotle, imagination (*phantasia*) consisted in movement of the mind generated ultimately by sensation but not through direct impressions of things immediately present. See *On the Soul*, III, 3. For Plato, imagination works with opinion (*doxa*) as well as with sensation. See *Sophist*, 264A. See also Plutarch, *On Nature*, IV, 12. Proclus is emphasising the fact that imagination cannot understand intellect.

40 Plato, *Republic*, III, 386C-387B, quoting Homer, *Iliad*, XVI, 856 and XXIII, 100. Other classic references to the noises of the souls under the earth are *Odyssey*, XXIV, 6-10, Virgil, *Aeneid*, VI, 417-27.

41 'empty attachments and fantasies' (*affectuosae phantasticaeque vitae dumtaxat imaginem*): Figliucci's Italian translation of 1546-8 renders this rather harshly as 'a hateful and brutish life'.

42 Epicurus (whose teachings were preserved mainly by Lucretius) taught that the gods and the underworld with all its regions and rivers were figments of the imagination. Proclus is here rejecting Epicurus, favouring an allegorical interpretation of real suffering, with the traditional 'rivers' as some kind of 'downflow'. In *Republic*, III, 387 BC, Plato refers to the river Cocytus as lamentation and Styx as hatred; *Phaedo*, 112A-115A describes the mysterious courses of the four rivers in some detail, as well as their part in the punishment and purification of souls. See also *Republic*, X, 614ff., the myth of Er, and the description of the underworld in *Odyssey*, XI.

43 Ficino has omitted a large section on the meaning of various allegories in Homer, and resumes at section 177.15 of Proclus's commentary.

44 Reading *uniforme* with MS Mo2.

45 The proposition here, in Proclus, is that the soul brings about union. Elsewhere Ficino accepts that only God can bring it about.

46 Ficino now moves to the 12th dissertation of Proclus, on the Divided Line (287.20-290.29).

47 The main discussion of the Divided Line occurs in *Republic*, VI, not VII, at 509D ff., but it is alluded to in connection with the Cave allegory again at VII, 517A and 533E.

48 This is the characteristic feature of the metaphysics of Proclus, traditionally described as the three stages of 'procession', 'conversion', and 'return'. These became

technical terms. 'Procession' has been rendered here as 'issuing forth', which seems to give a clearer idea of the process of emanation which is being described.

49 Ficino is referring to particles that appear only when lit up by a ray of light amid darkened surroundings.

50 Plato, *Sophist*, 266B.

51 This takes the hyena's actions a little further than Aelian, *De natura animalium*, VI, 14, for whom the dog is paralysed and can be carried off (but is not eaten); Aelian's version is itself an elaboration of a version attributed to Aristotle, *On marvellous things heard*, section 145 (845a, 24-27) – where the dog is only paralysed (but human beings can also be affected).

52 Aristotle, *On dreams*, 459b-460a, and cited earlier by Ficino in *De amore*, VII, 4 and *De vita*, III, 16.

53 Plato, *Republic*, VII, 534A. Ficino's term *cogitabilia* is here translated with its simple English derivative 'cogitable'. The meaning is 'what can be grasped by the mind'. In this short passage Ficino paraphrases both Proclus and the lines he refers to in Plato. In Plato, there is a simple pair of equations, summarising the figure of the Divided Line: 'being' is to 'becoming' as 'intellect' is to 'opinion'. Similarly, as 'intellect' is to 'opinion', so is 'knowledge' to 'belief' and 'understanding' to the 'perception of shadows'.

54 This section goes back to the eleventh dissertation in Proclus's text, starting at 276.23-282.11. Ficino skips lightly over the detailed explanations given here of the allegory of the Sun and the Cave, which he has dealt with in so many other places, even before he had access to this particular text. See, for example, *Letters*, 5, 48. The process of separating all things from the Good by a process of negation, evaluating them in relation to it, and facing deliberately back towards the good, so that illumination can be received, becomes a central practice he commends in his last written works. It is reminiscent of the *via negativa* commended by Dionysius, and also of the separation he urges in his Commentary on St Paul.

55 Truth is presented as flowing from the Good, not as the Good itself. The 'formative and ideal principles' are the Platonic Forms, or Ideas held in divine Mind, sometimes also known as 'Reason Principles'. For more on the Ideas, see *Letters*, I, 43.

56 'Self-existent': Ficino's Latin term is *ingenitus*, 'implanted by nature' or, in a Christian context, 'unbegotten'.

57 On the circle of sameness, in the construction of the cosmic soul, see Plato, *Timaeus*, 36B-37C.

58 For his final section, Ficino goes back to 272.8 in Proclus, where the terms used were clarified and defined. The manuscript of the Commentary that Ficino was using ended at 296.16, breaking off just after the Cave Allegory.

30

1 Ficino translated an extract from Proclus's *Alcibiades* commentary in 1488. His recent work on Proclus evidently put him in mind of it, and of Carducci's earlier request for it. The entire extract, entitled *On the Soul and Daemons*, was subsequently published in the volume of 1497 with Iamblichus's *De mysteriis* (Venice, Aldus Manutius). See also *Opera Omnia*, pp. 1908-1928. In MS Mo2 Ficino's translation of the 'summary' follows, consisting of one short section of that work. See Appendix D.

31

1 Micah 7:6; St Matthew 10:36. Cf. *Letters*, **7**, 24.
2 Ficino's household seems to have included his brothers' children and those of his housekeeper. One of his nephews, Ficino Ficini, stayed with him for many years as an amanuensis. He was also obliged to provide dowries for the daughters. Meanwhile, he regards himself in a similar way as a dependant of the Medici household.
3 Ficino is still conscious of the Medici family's gift of the canonry of Florence Cathedral in 1487, vacated in his favour by Giovanni de' Medici. See also letter 18.
4 Minerva, wisdom, is traditionally at odds with Juno, ambition. Jupiter, Phoebus (Apollo) and Venus represent the three Graces, whereas Mercury is the god of eloquence and also of merchants and moneylenders, while harsh Saturn governs scholarly life, contemplation and withdrawal from society. Fortune was characterised by her wheel, whereby men are lifted high or cast down, in endless cycles. In the following letter, 32, Ficino connects Mercury and Saturn with philosophy, while Jupiter, Apollo, and Venus signify abundance of physical things – though he clearly regards these interpretations as somewhat superficial.
5 According to Kristeller, there may have been further material in this letter personal to Valori, since there is no formal ending to the letter (*Sup. Fic.*, vol. II, pp. lxxxix-xc). Ficino describes his own approach to letter-writing in *Letters*, **1**, 16, suggesting that each one was intended to be fully considered and shaped. However, it is also possible to take Ficino at his word here, and visualise him breaking off writing to attend to something else.

32

1 The quotation is from Aristotle, *Magna Moralia*, II, 8 (1207a, 4-6). In a letter to Cavalcanti near the end of the twelfth book, Ficino resumes this topic in response to current adversities.
2 Pythagoras, *Golden Verses*, 16-20 (Ficino, *Opera*, p. 1979).
3 In *De amore*, VI, 4, Ficino lists the gifts of the planets. Saturn gives contemplation, Mercury's gift is in speech and interpretation; Venus inspires love, Jupiter the qualities appropriate to governing and ruling and the sun conveys clarity of the senses and of opinion, whence also comes prophecy.
4 Ficino's interpretation places wisdom above providence and providence above fate or fortune. See also Letter 24.

33

1 In Mo2 Ficino here addresses Eberhard as Count (not Duke). See Letter 23, note 2.
2 Ficino is referring to Letter 23.
3 This is Mercury in his role as intelligent messenger of the gods and close companion of the Sun, cf. *Letters*, **6**, 14. On Johann Streler, see Biographical Notes.
4 This is the dedication letter to Ficino's *De sole* in its initial form, as sent to the Count. It represents a considerable expansion of themes he had treated earlier on the Sun

(as for example in his Orphic comparison of the Sun to God, *Letters*, 5, 27). In Ms Mo2, this dedication is immediately followed by several chapters of *De sole* itself. It is hoped that a translation of these chapters will be included in the next volume of Ficino's *Letters*, as we find in the twelfth book of Ficino's letters a further chapter written for Count Eberhard the following year.

Having added further material, Ficino published his *De sole* in a composite volume with his *De lumine* (On light), a work foreshadowed by a letter on light to Febo Capella (*Epistolae*, II, 9) composed around 1476. The two together were then dedicated to Piero de' Medici and published on 1st February 1493 by Antonio Miscomini in Florence. Two later editions of this double work were published in Germany (Leipzig, 1502 and Strasbourg, 1508) as well as a Venetian edition of 1503 and it was included in the *Opera omnia* (1561 and 1576).

There is also an extremely rare edition of the original version of *De sole*, which was published in 1547 in Tübingen by Ulrich Morhard, with a prefatory letter from Kaspar Volland (Vollandius); this is based on Count Eberhard's manuscript (Württembergische Landesbibliothek Stuttgart, MS HB XV 65).

34

1 Ficino uses the word *ingenium* with great frequency to denote various ideas always connected with inner qualities of a positive kind. It is notoriously difficult to translate, as it covers aspects of character, spirit and ability, besides 'mind' and intelligence.

2 Hesiod, *Works and Days*, 109-210; Ovid, *Metamorphoses*, I, 89-150. (Hesiod adds a Heroic age between those of bronze and iron).

3 Plato, *Republic*, III, 415A-C. While the four metals symbolise four successive ages for Hesiod and Ovid, Ficino notes that Plato ascribes to them qualities, or functions, within any age: gold for those fit to rule, silver for the auxiliaries, iron and brass for craftsmen and farmers. See his commentary on the end of *Republic* III, Ficino, *Opera*, p.1402; Farndell, *When Philosophers Rule*, p. 16.

4 Previous golden ages in which public life, literature and architecture flourished would include fifth-century BC Athens (the age of Pericles) and late Republican Rome (the age of Virgil, Horace, Cicero etc). For discussion of Ficino's ideas on 'golden minds', see Michael J. B. Allen, *Synoptic Art* (Florence, 1998), pp. 1-49. See also, Ficino, *Platonic Theology*, XIII, iii for an extended discussion of the arts.

5 On the revival of ancient learning, cf. *Letters*, 7, 19. The renewal of classical norms, first in grammar and poetry, then in rhetoric, painting, sculpture, architecture and music, is the story of the Renaissance in Italy, in which Florence played a leading part. For a recent overview of the earliest stages in literature, from Lovato dei Lovati in 1268 to Dante, Petrarch and Boccaccio, Salutati and Bruni, see Ronald Witt, *In the Footsteps of the Ancients* (Leiden: Brill 2000). In architecture, leading figures include Brunelleschi and Alberti; among sculptors Ghiberti, Desiderio da Settignano, Donatello, Mino da Fiesole, the Rossellino brothers and the della Robbia family. Outstanding Florentine painters of this period are numerous, including Fra Angelico, Masaccio, Andrea del Castagno, Botticelli, Filippino Lippi, and Verrocchio, to name but a few, and famous illuminators include Attavante degli Attavanti and Antonio di Chierico. Of the musicians active in Florence in Ficino's

day, many of the most outstanding were of Flemish origin (Dufay, Josquin des Prés, Heinrich Isaac) or from Northern Italy. Antonio Squarcialupi (1416-1480), organist of the cathedral of Santa Maria del Fiore, enjoyed great fame, and is buried there, as is Ficino. Squarcialupi owned an impressive codex of earlier Florentine secular music (MS Laur. Mediceo-Palatinus 87), including numerous pieces by Landino's great-uncle, the innovative composer, poet and instrument designer, Francesco Landini 'degli Organi' (1335-1397). Ficino contributed to this codex a short verse epitaph honouring Squarcialupi, whose music continued to resound from the organ pipes of the cathedral (*Sup. Fic.*, I, p. 97). Ficino himself was an accomplished musician and references to music abound in his letters. See especially *Letters*, **1**, 92 and **7**, 76. Ficino is often credited, both by scholars and his own contemporaries, with reviving the tradition of singing hymns to the lyre. Poliziano, Callimachus and Janus Pannonius all called him a second Orpheus. For his connection with the Orphic body of hymns, see notes to Letter 25. However, the Orphic lyre may also stand for the whole tradition of lyric poetry, in which Poliziano and Lorenzo de' Medici excelled. This was a golden age for lute music, too. Names of instruments are ambivalent in this period: the lyre may refer to the lute or the *lyra da braccio*, a bowed stringed instrument.

6 Ficino is perhaps thinking of the work of the earlier chancellors, Bruni, Salutati, Carlo Marsuppini and Bartolommeo Scala or of the professors at the Florentine *Studio*, Marsuppini, Landino and Poliziano.

7 Following Plato's comment on the need for wisdom in government, Ficino tried to inspire various rulers during the 1480s to bring about the vision ascribed to Socrates in *Republic*, V, 473: 'Until philosophers are kings, or the kings and princes of this world have the spirit and power of philosophy, and political greatness and wisdom meet in one, and those commoner natures who pursue either to the exclusion of the other are compelled to stand aside, cities will never have rest from their evils – no, nor the human race, as I believe.' He placed great hope in Federico, Duke of Urbino, who was an outstanding military commander and a great patron of the arts. Ficino says in the preface to his translations of Plato that he met Federico in Florence in 1482, when he undertook to lead the Florentine forces against the papacy and Venice in the war of Ferrara. However, Federico died later the same year. Paul of Middelburg, to whom this letter is addressed, had been an adviser to him from 1480, the year in which he also took up a post at the University of Padua.

8 Federico's heir was his son Guidobaldo, who had an exemplary education. Federico's half-brother had preceded him in the dukedom of Urbino. Another ruler Ficino regarded in the same Platonic light was Matthias Corvinus of Hungary.

9 Paul wrote important studies of the astronomical conjunction of 1484, and several works on corrections to the calendar. The latter were particularly valued within the Church.

10 This modest reference is to his own work, as well as that of his predecessors. It was no accident that Ficino made sure his Plato translations were published in 1484, the year of the grand conjunction.

11 The invention of movable type is credited to Gutenberg in Mainz around 1454. The German printers Arnold Pannartz from Mainz and Konrad Sweynheim from Prague set up the first Italian printing press at Subiaco near Rome in 1464. Other printing houses soon followed, both German and Italian.

12 Regiomontanus (Johannes Müller of Königsberg) used his consummate knowledge of mathematics and astronomy to produce a greatly improved set of astronomical tables, the *Ephemerides*, which he printed on his own press in Nuremberg in 1474. These tables were of immense benefit to navigators, especially those venturing to the New World, enabling them to calculate their longitudinal positions with accuracy.

13 Lorenzo della Volpaia, a goldsmith and mathematician, from a family of clock and scientific instrument makers possibly originating in Nuremberg, constructed an astronomical clock with moving parts that showed the movement of the planets. This was intended as a gift from Lorenzo de' Medici to King Matthias of Hungary. Ficino mentions in his unpublished *Disputatio contra iudicium astrologorum* of 1477, and in *Platonic Theology*, II, xiii, the maker of a very clever automaton with animals that he had seen in 1475. In *De Vita*, III, 19 he describes a working model of the universe made by della Volpaia. This model was also described by Poliziano in 1484, in a letter to Francesco della Casa (Poliziano, *Letters*, IV, 8. See Stéphane Toussaint, 'Ficino, Archimedes and the Celestial Arts' in *Marsilio Ficino: his Theology, his Philosophy, his Legacy*, eds. Allen and Rees, pp. 307-326.) A second version of this clock was made in 1510, and a modern reconstruction exists in the Museum of the History of Science in Florence.

14 Bernardo Michelozzi was a former student of Ficino's, now engaged as secretary to Lorenzo. The tables referred to could have been the latest version of those of Regiomontanus, which were regularly updated. Four publishers brought out new editions in 1492. The duke referred to is almost certainly Guidobaldo in Urbino. The abbey of Castel Durante now in Paul's care was within his territories. Paul's other great friend and benefactor, Maximilian, was now Holy Roman Emperor, so the title *dux* would be insufficient.

15 Mo2 gives 14th September.

Notes to Appendix Letters

A

1 This letter, written to Valori in Rome very soon after Lorenzo's death, appears in MS Mo2 but not in the published versions of the Letters.

2 Homer, *Iliad*, XXIV, 527-532 (and criticised by Plato in *Republic,* 379d). In Hesiod, *Works and Days*, 55-105 Pandora opens Zeus's cask of evils which are then let loose all over the world.

3 Plato, *Republic*, X, 618-620.

4 Genesis 12:3. After the covenant Abram's name is changed to Abraham (Genesis 17:5).

B

1 Like the previous letter, this appears only in Mo2. By the time of the first printed edition the Medici had been expelled from Florence, and a number of letters relating to them were removed.

2 Ficino refers to the portents accompanying the death of Lorenzo in Letter 20. See also Letter 18. Poliziano's more detailed account of Lorenzo's death is in his letter to Jacopo Antiquari of 18 May, 1492 (Poliziano, *Letters*, IV, ii, 18-19).

3 Pythagoras proposed the notion of reincarnation, discussed but never fully accepted by Ficino or other Platonic philosophers. Plato's discussion of it takes the form of a myth. Ficino is using it here to express an idea he returns to quite frequently, that the qualities of one person may be found in another. In the context of the death of Lorenzo, it may also offer consolation.

4 For the stars and their rays, see *Letters*, **8**, Appendix B. For divine breath shaping man, see Genesis 2:7; Job 33:4 and John 14:11-12.

5 Matthew 11:27.

C

1 This letter is included in MS Mo2, but not in printed editions of the letters. It was, however, printed as a dedicatory letter before the preface to the Plotinus commentary (*Opera*, p. 1538 (misprinted as 1528 in Basle edition of 1576).

2 Poliziano describes the portents in detail in his *Letters*, IV, ii, 20.

3 Horace, *Odes*, I, ii, 3.

4 It was significant that no enemies took advantage of Lorenzo's death to mount an attack on Florence, although there had been earlier instances, and war would resume in 1494 with the arrival of French troops.

5 The laurel is Lorenzo's symbol; *petrus*, 'rock', signifies Piero.

6 The image is that of Aeneas carrying his elderly father Anchises on his shoulders out of the burning city of Troy. His traditional epithet is *pius*, 'pious' or 'dutiful'. As presented in Virgil's *Aeneid*, II, 707 ff., he carries his father out of destruction to a new life elsewhere, and he holds his child Ascanius by the hand. It must have been a great disappointment to Ficino to lose his main patron just as the Plotinus was ready, and before the project of publishing a revised edition of Plato with all the commentaries could be completed.

D

1 This extract appears in MS Mo2 as part of a letter to Filippo Carducci (Letter 30). It consists of one section of the longer work, excerpting the Commentary on Plato's *Alcibiades* by Proclus. Ficino's version was published in 1497 in the volume of Platonic writings, *Iamblichus de mysteriis* ... (Venice: Aldus Manutius, 1497).
The section sent to Carducci represents one page of that text, which runs to 44 pages in all. Cf. *Opera Omnia* (Basle, 1576), pp. 1908-1928, where it occupies half of p. 1912. It corresponds to pp. 68-69 of the Greek of the Creuzer edition (1820)

of Proclus' text, which can be followed in the later edition of L. G. Westerink and W. O'Neill (*Proclus: Alcibiades I*, Leiden, 1965; repr. Prometheus Trust, 2011). Our translation follows Ficino's Latin rather than Proclus' Greek.

2 The second and third topics are only indicated in this short passage, and are discussed only in the full extract published later.

3 The life-giving goddess is generally Rhea, the earth. In the *Chaldean Oracles* she is also named as Hecate (Fragments 32, 51 and 56, ed. Des Places). Hecate is also the goddess of magic and moonlight, guardian of the barrier between earth and the underworld, who helps Demeter find her lost daughter Persephone.

4 Reading *irrationalem* with Mo2 (and in conformity with Proclus's Greek).

5 Proclus has a very complex division of the gods which Ficino appreciated but sought on several occasions to simplify. Twelve 'divine souls' or supercelestial gods (six male and six female) are listed by Ficino in *De amore*, V, 13 and *Platonic Theology*, IV, i, 15-16 as presiding over the celestial Zodiac: Pallas, Venus, Apollo, Mercury, Jupiter, Ceres (Demeter), Vulcan, Mars, Diana, Vesta, Juno and Neptune. In Ficino's commentary (*Epitome*) on Plato's *Laws*, 5 they also preside over different parts of the human anatomy. These are the twelve Olympian gods of the Roman Pantheon. Yet Saturn, who rules over the highest part of the mind, over contemplation, and over the supercelestial world, is not included in those lists. Ficino discusses the different ways of enumerating the gods in his *Phaedrus* commentary, chapters X-XI, when speaking of the heavenly cavalcade of Plato's *Phaedrus*, 247A-C. For a full discussion of this problem, and one that includes Saturn as the leader of the supercelestial twelve, see Michael J. B. Allen, *The Platonism of Marsilio Ficino*, Berkeley, 1984, pp.117-121 and 252-3. The twelve gods that he proposes are Uranus (as the fixed stars), Saturn, Jupiter, Mars, Apollo, Venus, Mercury, Diana (representing the seven planets), and four representing the elements fire, air, water and earth: Vulcan, Juno, Neptune and Vesta. Thus Uranus and Saturn have here replaced Demeter and Athene of the traditional Olympian twelve. On the gods of the cosmic spheres, see also *Timaeus*, 34B-41A and *Epinomis,* 986AB, 987B-D.

6 Reading *gratulantur,* with the printed editions.

7 'In sympathy', an idea pervading the metaphysics of Proclus. Ficino translated this as '*in passione consentiunt*' (lit. 'agree in emotion') but the meaning clearly refers to the concept of sympathy.

8 Reading *communionemque* with Mo2.

9 Reading *centra*, with Mo2 (as opposed to *contra* in both printed texts). The Greek of Proclus confirms this reading.

10 'Streams': seems to indicate finally the Forms or Ideas which spring from the First Intellect and flow forth into the creation: as fountains, springs, or finally streams that connect with bodies. See Proclus, *Commentary on Parmenides*, III, 801, quoting *Chaldean Oracles*, 37.

11 *Medietas* suggests the whole area between two extremes, here rendered as 'the mean'. Diotima speaks of the power of love as an intermediary spirit which binds the universe together in Plato, *Symposium*, 202D-E.

Note on the Latin Text

A copy of the 1495 Venice edition has been used for the Latin text. As with all early printed books, it follows a system of abbreviations, the most important of which are given below. Likewise, its punctuation and orthography differ from more modern texts, as discussed below.

The copy used is by kind permission of Durham University Library (shelf mark SR.2.C.22). It shows manuscript corrections made to the printed text by Ficino's nephew, Ficino Ficini, under Ficino's own supervision. The corrections are referred to in the annotations as Dur, to distinguish them from the simple printed version of Venice, V.

The annotations printed below the text on the following pages indicate these corrections if they are not clearly visible and show alternative readings from the one surviving manuscript of this book, MS Mo2 (Munich, Staatsbibliothek, MS lat. 10781). Any significant variant readings from the Basle printed edition of 1576 are also indicated. These sources are referred to in the annotations as MS and B respectively.

Variant forms are given at the foot of each page with a letter in the vertical margin indicating where amendment is due. This yields a reliable reader's edition of the text, even if not a full critical edition. Variations in spelling and punctuation have been recorded only if they affect the reading. In the introductory greetings to the addressee of each letter, MS Mo2 generally omits the D. of S.D. (*salutem dat*), or the P. of S.P.D. (*salutem plurimum dat*). This is a trivial change and has not been recorded.

Where a variant is too long to show in the normal way, its place has been indicated by an asterisk (*), and the variant is given below, at the foot of this note.

In general, manuscript readings are improvements to the printed text, but not invariably so. Some variants (usually from the Basle edition) have been marked as erroneous, but have been included for the record.

Abbreviations

As in previous volumes, the main abbreviations used by the printer of the Venice edition are as follows:

A slightly inclined line over what would be the penultimate letter of a word indicates omission of a final letter, usually an 'm'. Thus **quidē** for 'quidem'.

A similar line over a letter in the middle of a word indicates omission of one or more letters. The missing letters may be either side or both sides of the abbreviation mark. Thus **nūc** for 'nunc', **nr̄a** for 'nostra' **ur̄m** for 'vestrum'. Sometimes these abbreviations have been expanded in the amendments shown, especially where the marks are very faint.

Other abbreviations include:

9 for 'us' as in **conat9** for 'conatus'

A flourish from a final 't' as in **morit́** to indicate a passive, here for 'moritur'

ꝗ; as in **atꝗ;** for 'atque'

ē for 'est'

ēt for 'etiam'

ꝓ for 'pro' as in **ꝓcul** for 'procul'

ꝑ for 'per'

q̄ for 'quam'

qn̄ for 'quando'

ꝗ for 'qui'

qđ for 'quod'

ꝑꝑ for 'propter'.

Punctuation and Orthography

The Venice text uses punctuation in a way that admits of some fluidity. In general, it uses colons in place of commas, but a full stop may also sometimes indicate a break between clauses rather than between sentences. Sometimes a capital letter follows a colon, but does not necessarily indicate the start of a new sentence. Brackets are used more frequently than in the other versions.

Variations of spelling have been noted only where considered helpful to the reader. Common features to be noted are that 'u' is used for both 'u' and 'v'. The diphthong 'ae' is often printed simply as 'e'. Variant spellings of proper names and some common words have not been recorded.

In numerous places MS and B offer alternative punctuation, which is sometimes to be preferred to that of V. This is not always indicated, unless it affects the meaning; but in the poetry of Letter 25, where it is significant, some indication of the differences has been given.

In reading the Venice text, lower case 'f' and 's' may be difficult to distinguish. In general, a horizontal mark on the ascender indicates that the letter is 'f': thus **infudisse** is 'infudisse'.

Additions to the text

In both the Venice and Basle editions, the beginning of Letter 24 has been omitted as well as the date at the end of Letter 23. Ficino's 16th-century translator, Felice Figliucci, reconstructed some of the text (the omission becomes obvious), but the missing material has now been accurately restored from MS Mo2. See entry for *page clxxviiii verso* below at *v*.

For Appendix letters A-D, printed sources for the Latin texts are given in the Translators' Note on p. xvi.

Pages in the early editions are given a number which applies to both sides of the printed leaf, 'recto' (the front face of a printed page, which is a right-hand page in a bound book) and 'verso' (its back, presenting as the following left-hand page). In this volume we have adopted this standard notation in place of our earlier rubric of 'facing page' and numbered 'page'. Recto pages simply bear the number; the abbreviation *vº* is used to indicate 'verso'.

p. clxxvi *m* Dur corrections in margin are illegible, but emend as shown in *l*.

p. clxxvii vº *e* B *assimulare* for *dissimulare*

f B repeats *utrumque fallunt. Sed fallant,*

q MS adds *ipsum amen* after *quantum me* but should read *ipsum amem*

p. clxxviii *d* In MS Mo2, this letter appears later, on fol. 70, following Letter 25. It is then repeated on fol. 82, following Letter 29.

f MS on fol. 70vo *insemparabilis* (erron.).

g MS om. *est* on fol. 82.

i MS adds *Vale Die x Julii Mccccl*xxxxxij on fol. 70.

p MS has *o* superscript over *Mirandula* to indicate vocative

s B *Soderonio* (erron.)

p. clxxviiii *s* MS adds *Haec omnia prodigiorum genera nuper in obitu magni Laurentii Medicis patria servatoris Florentine contigerunt. Quamobrem orba parente suo patria maiesta gemit horretque prodigia. Sed hanc interim herculei viri Petri Medicis virtus heroice consolatur.*

u B *ama* for *fama* (erron.)

p. clxxiiii vº o MS adds *Ficinus Florentinus*, B adds *Ficinus*

p MS *Comiti vitembergensi & montis peligardi seniori*
B *Vuirtembergensi & Montis Peligardi Seniori*
Dur corrects *Senatori* to *Seniori*

v MS *xxviij Iunij mcccclxxxxij* Then new letter begins: *Qui futuris praedicendis incumbent infortunati sunt Marsilius Ficinus Bindacio Recasolano familiariss*[im]o *suo. S.*

Quod astronomie studium iamdiu inceptum: quo et presentem spherarum (dispositionem etc.)

p. clxxx *m* MS om. *Florentinus* and *D.* B has *amico suo*

p. clxxxiii *f* MS, B om. *quicquam nec amittunt*

p. clxxxiiii *i* *B separaturum* (erron.)

p. clxxxv vº e MS *Solus sol inter mundana videtur* B *Sol inter mundana videtur* (erron.)

g Dur, MS *Supremae videlicet: spherae quae* B *Supremae videlicet, quae sphaera*

l B *Oam* (erron.)

m V, B *quidem … participabile* dittograph, deleted in Dur, absent from MS.

Principium Vndecimi Libri. a

Aepiſtola in Dono argentei Calicis.

Georgius Heriuart Auguſtienſis Marſilio Ficino Platonico. S .D. b

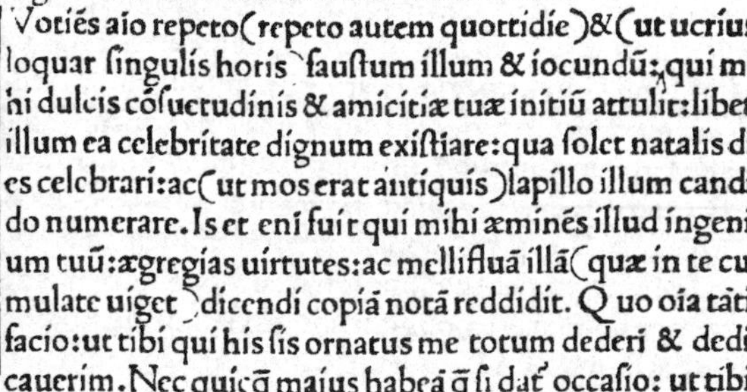

Votiés aio repeto(repeto autem quottidie)&(ut ucrius
loquar ſingulis horis) fauſtum illum & iocundũ: qui mi c
hi dulcis cõſuetudinis & amicitiæ tuæ initiũ attulit: libet
illum ea celebritate dignum exiſtiare: qua ſolet natalis di d
es celebrari: ac(ut mos erat antiquis)lapillo illum candi
do numerare. Is et enĩ fuit qui mihi æminẽs illud ingeni
um tuũ: ægregias uirtutes: ac melliflua illã(quæ in te cu
mulate uiget)dicendi copiã notã reddidit. Q uo oĩa tãti e
facio: ut tibi qui his ſis ornatus me totum dederi & dedi fg
cauerim. Nec quicq̃ maius habeã q̃ ſi dat occaſio: ut tibi hh
oibus i rebus ualeã gratificari: & ut opa mea: cura: igenio: quantulũcunq; eſt: ubi
cunq; ſim: uelis uti. Q uod ut facias uehemẽter ẽr atq; etiã rogo. Mitto nũc ad te
argenteum: uel(ut ſic loquar)potellum friuolum ſane: & puerile munuſculum. i
Q uippe ſunt uirtutes tuæ tales: quæ mereantur amplioribus muneribus condo
nari. Sed tu ita(ut es)hũaniſſimus: id non munus: ſed amicitiæ nr̃æ nup initæ &
tuæ in me humanitatis aliqua ex parte pignus & teſtimõium appellabis. Sicq; exi
ſtimabis me id ad te eo aio mittere. Vale & me ama. Dat. Venetiis. Idus Aprilis. jk
Mcccclxxxxi.

Reſponſio pro dono argentei Calicis.

Marſilius Ficinus Florentinus Georgio Heriuarti Germano. S. D.

ESt mihi a teneris ãnis mi Georgi naturalis q̃dã cum Germãis bẽiuo
lentia: Cauſis occultis cõciliata: itaq; Florentinorum ſocii Miniaten
ſes: germanũ genus præceteris hoſpites nr̃i ſunt: & familia picorum
atq; Caualcantũ a Germania ducẽs originem nobis eſt amiciſſima.
Q uãobrem ſi Germãi(cõiter oẽs)mihi ſũt germãi: quid dicã de ui
ris amiciſq; inter uos ægregiis? De Martio uranio amico cœleſti? De te inſup op
time mi Georgi? profecto qcũq; mihi pluſq̃ germanus ẽ: is extra cõtrouerſiã eſt al
ter ego: ut nõ mirũ ſit ſi ueſtra uobis cariſſima ſunt: mea quoq; uobis in primis tã
q̃ ueſtra placere. Vtinã quãtus apud uos ſum amiti: tãtus & apud me uirtute ſo l
rẽ. Beniuolẽtia certe talis erga te ſum: qualis eſt ipſe calix nup abſte mihi dono da
tus. Extra quidẽ argenteus: ſed aureus intus. Arbitror & ingeniũ tuũ: ſub argẽti
ſpecie: aurũ illud habere: quod Socrates & in phœdro ſuppliciter a Deo petit: &
in re pub. in heroicis agnoſcit ingeniis. Deniq; quantũ nobis grata fuerit epiſtola
tua: ac munus acceptũ: teſtis erit undecimus æpiſtolarũ noſtrarum liber. Ab æpi m
ſtola tua in primis aſcripta & hac reſpõſione mea ſũmẽs exordiũ. Vale fœlix. Ac ſi
Marſiliũ amas ama Martinũ cognomie p̃nyngerũ: ſi me cupis amore quodã cœle
ſti cõplecti Vraniũ amorẽ meũ tota mẽte cõplectere. xxviiii. aprilis. Mcccclxxxx. n

Q uomodo aliquis ſub aliena perſona cogitanti ſibimet occurrat.

Marſilius Ficinus Pierleono complatonico ſuo. S.D.

ACcepi lr̃as pierleõe tuas amoris & gratiæ plenas: atq;(ut uno uerbo lau
dẽ)re uera platonicas: In quibus ſane ſcribis: cũ primũ platõicũ aliquid
occurrit tibi: ſuccurrere mox tibi Marſiliũ: ſed caue ne te forſan exterior

a MS om. book and letter title; also all brackets from page **b** MS *Marsili* **c** MS *iocundum diem:* **d** *existimare* **e** MS *Quae omnia ego* **f** MS *amatus* for *ornatus* **g** *dederim* **h** *quam* **i** MS *argenteum calicem* **j** *animo* **k** MS *quinto idus* **l** MS *amici* **m** MS *mearum* for *nostrarum* **n** MS *mccccIxxxx*

a te fallat imago. Reor equidem ipsum ibi pierleonum sub Marsilii persona latere Siqua.n.humana species tibi res Platonicas contemplanti se offert: probabile est speciem maxime Platonicam præceteris se offerc. Quid autem in rebus humanis platonicum magis: q̃ leo magnus Solis Platonici domicilium. Forte igitur (quẽ admodum & narcisus) te ipsum intuens: opinaris alium intueri. Præcipue uero Marsilium Cuius imaginem ardens te induit amor. Sed q̃m incidimus in imaginem: scis profecto rationem inter imaginationem intellectumque mediam esse Atque in eam hinc quidẽ ab imaginatione confluere imagines naturalium: inde autem ab intellectu influere species diuinorum. Quamobrem sæpe contingit ut diuina quædam species apud humanã rationem imaginem quandam subeat naturalẽ. Itaq; quod intus diuinum ẽ sẹpe rationis oculis appareat naturale? Quid? si ratione simili pierleonus sub figura Marsilii sibi sæpe sit obuius? Sed de his quidem hactenus. De Dionysio Areopagita recte admodũ sentire mihi uideris: Mihi certe nec ulla scientiæ forma est gratiosior q̃ Platonica: Neque forma hæc usq̃ ma-
b gis q̃ in Dionysio ueneranda. Amo æquidem Platonem in Iamblicho: Admiror in Plotino: In Dionysio ueneror: sæpe uero suspicor antiquiores Plotino Platoni
cd cos: Ammonui atque Numenium aut his (forte priores) legisse Dionysii libros anteq̃ nescio qua Calamitate ecclesiæ delitescerent Atque illinc in Plotinum & Iamblichum Dionysii scintillas uere Platonicas fuisse transfusas: Vnde tantus sit
e ignis accensus. De Dionysio satis gratus admodum mihi erit Galienus de dogmate Hippocratis atque Platonis. Sepe de te apud Laurentium medicem uerba
fg fiunt. Amat profecto te mirifice (sicut solet) ut par est: admodum ueneratur. xii
h Maii. Mcccclxxxxi. In agro Caregio.

i Ad Magnos ptinet beneficia conferre etiam non merentibus

jkl Marsilius Ficinus: Reuerẽ. christo patri & D. Raphaeli Riario sancti Gerogii Cardinali: suppliciter Se commendat

ET si nulla forte merita sunt: quibus impetrare apud te quicq̃ debeã: audebo tamen non nihil gratia poscere: non meritis quidem confisus ullis: Sed & mea in te obseruantia: & tua in omnes clementia fræctus: Iustum quidem: sed humanum est beneficium pręstare merentibus: Clementissimũ uero
m est atque diuinum largiri etiam non merentibus. Magnum certe sacrumque Antistitem: magna imprimis diuinaque decent.

Caritas & pietas potissimum est Sapientis officium

Marsilius Ficinus Martino Vranio Germano dilectissimo Suo. S.

VTinam mihi tantum sapientię foret: ut et promissis pro me tuis: & ex pectationibus aliorum satis q̃nque facere possem: officio quidem meo ferme iam pro uiribus satis feci. Adolescentes.n.quos nuper ad nos gratia disciplinæ misistis perlibenter excepi. Pio statim apud nos hospiti commendaui. Dabo in dies opam ut bene ualeant: ut educentur erudianturq; q̃ optime. Meam saltem euismodi diligentiam optime mi Martine parentibus adolescentum uestrisque principibus quibus sapientiam promisisti: promittito. Hactenus & ipse fideiussor eris (ut spero) ueridicus: et ego satis forte fecero. si pro expectatione sa
n pientie imprimis præstitero charitatis & pietatis officium: pietas.n.summa quædam apud Deum Sapientia ẽ. Primo Iunii, Mcccclxxxxi.

a MS om. *te* b MS om. *in* c *Ammonium* d B erron. *Eunumium* e *satis.* f MS *& ut par* g MS *xiii* h Dur deletes ? i *pertinent* j MS, B *in Christo* k MS om. & l *Georgii* m MS om. *que* n MS *. Charitatis*

Purgatio de literris non redditis

Marsilius Ficinus. Reueren. In Christo patri &.D. Raphaeli Riario Sancti Georgii Cardinali suppliciter se Commendat.

CHristophorus Marsupinus familiaris noster Florentiam nuper Roma reuersus: statim post prima salutationis uerba: narrauit q̃tum me tua clementia diligas. Quo quidem nihil gratius audire poteram. Sed hoc interim molestum mihi fuit: q mox negligẽtie crimiari me cœpit quasi nullas post discessum hinc tuũ ad te litteras dederim. Sed ego statim huic Archetipũ epistolarum mearum aperiens quattuor saltẽ legi litteras ad te hoc tempore missas. Certe nimis infortunatas itinere inquã Romano. Nõdũ.n. ad te peruenisse uidẽt. Quæ tamen alibi fœliciore fortuna frete: non solum per oẽm Italiam: Sed etiam in hispaniam iãdiu Galliam. Germaniam. Pãnoniã. peruolarunt: obseruantiam & reuerentiam erga te meam ubiq; iam, præter q̃ Rome testificantes. Quamobrem non quia nullas: Sed quia paucas epistolas ad te miserim iure culpandus erã Sed utinam quæ nate semel infortunate uidentur: fortunatiores saltem hodie renascantur: ut ad fœlicem patronũ melioribꝰ usque satis quandoq; perueniant. Clientulumq; Commendent. iiii. Iunii. Mcccclxxxxi. a

Pro Adolescentibus e Sueuia missis ad Academiam Florentiam. b

Mar. F. Ludouico Nauclero & Ioãni phorcensi Germanis Iuriscõsultis. S.D. c

SCribitis ad Nos uestroq; nomine Germaniæ Principes Florentiã adolescentes erudiendos tanquã ad Academiã mittere. Sed ea interim elegãtia scribitis: ut non ad Academiam filios: immo ex Academia mittere uideamini. Atq; apud exteras natiões perquirere uobis iam domesticam disciplinam. Quæ rerũ uicissitudo est. Quantũ insolentes plæriq; more sophistarum aliena temere ꝓfitẽtur: tñ uos modestissimi uiri uel ꝓpria ritu Socratico diffitemini hoc præceteris admirandi q q̃ curiose multi lapillos terre uisceribus recõditos perscrutantur: tam accurate uos cœlestem sapientie splendorem ubiq; gentiũ ꝓsequimini. Quamobrem incredibili quodam amore erga uos affecti adolescẽtum uestrorũ curam Pia mente suscepimus. Et imprimis insigni pietate hospiti Commẽdauimus. Dabimusq; in dies operam: ut ager natura fertilis frugem quãdoq; ꝓferat fœlicissimam. Vos igitur bono animo estote: & principibus uestris nostro nomine respondere Magnanimum Laurentium Medicem: Cuius & ipsi clientes sumus: adolescẽtum prouidentiam libentissime suscepisse. v. Iunii. Mccclxxxxi. In Agro Caregio. d e fg h i j

De quattuor speciebus diuini furoris. Item laudes Medicis Laurentii uere.

Marsilius Ficinus Petro Diuitio litteris & moribus ornatissimo. S.D.

CVm iãdiu Platonem nostrum in cõuiuio audiuisses de amore latissime disputantem. Desideraresq; præterea compendiariam quandam de amore sententiam: libellum dedi legẽdum hac de re nobis in adolescẽtia poetica facultate præstantẽ ~~nra compositum ad pegrinum allium adolescentem~~. Memini equidem q̃ mirifice delectabaris audire amorẽ ipsum reuera non eẽ libidinẽ sed furorem quendam excellentibus ingeniis diuinitus instigatum. Præterea diuinum furorem tanq̃ genus quoddam quattuor in se species continere. Amorẽ poesimq; & Vaticinium: atq; mysterium. Et amorem quidem a Venere: a musis k lm n

a B *diligat* b *Florentinam* c *Marsilius Ficinus* d B om. *ad* e *plerique* f *tantum* (B *tamen* erron.) g B *diffidemini* erron. h *quod quam* i *animo estote* j *ipsi* k B *disputantes* erron. l MS, Dur *Nostra compositum ad Peregrinum allium adolescentem poetica* m * n MS om. *audire*

uero poesim: sed ab Apolline Vaticinium: a Dionysio mysteriũ proficisci. Qua
deniq; ratione alia hominum ingenia ab alio plurimum alioq; numine uariis fu
roribus agitentur. Reliquum erat ingeniosissime Petre perquirere nũquid ingenium idem a pluribus (ut ita dixerim) Diis simul afflari possit: uariis inde furori
bus concitatum. Iam uero de amore quidem atque poesi questio non admodum
difficilis eẽ uidetur. Nam Homerum pindarum Calimacum Sapphon. Maronẽ
a poetico simul amatorioque instinctu pcitos fuisse non dubitamus. Vaticinio in
super epimenidem: atque Sybillam. Sed præter hæc etiam Misteriis inspirari: soli (ut aiunt) Diis geniti potuere. Qualem gentes Orpheũ: Qualem nostri Daui
b dem fuisse tradunt. Cognouimus & nos ingenium nostro sæculo fœlicissimum
c Quattuor has æque furorum dotes a quatuor Numinibus cõsequutum. Poeti-
cum sane: Amatoriumq; spiritũ sub Musis Venereq; cœlesti iãdiu in ipo adolescẽ
tie flore concepit. Quod quidem ubiq; suauissimi cantus & miranda prorsus ei9
Carmina personant. Sed Vaticinium hausit ab Apolline iã adultus. Quo certe
mirabili quadam mentis sagacitate cœlitus insita frequẽter futura discrimina pri
uatim publiceq; præsagiens medicam periculis manum adhibet: & phœbea statĩ
uirtute medetur: Mysticum uero furorem a Dionysio prope iam maturus fœliciter est adeptus. Dionysiam ebrietatem theologi ueteres excessum mentis defi
nierũt a rebus quidem mortalibus segregate: secreta uero diuinitatis mysteria pe
d netrantis. Bacchus amat Colles. In collibus ambre Agnaneq; uallis Laurens ille
Phœbeus Dionysio nectare passim ebrius debacchatur. Tum uero afflatus ex alto cœlestia super hominem Carmina fundit ore rotundo. profunda quorum sen-
sa nullis unquam penetrare fas est: nisi ingeniis simili quodam furore correptis.
Rapit uero secum noster ille patronus: nonnullos interdum attentius atq; fœli-
cius audientes. In eos uidelicet præceteris ubertate furoris exuberans. Qua uero ratione pcitus ipse numine alios ferme similiter concitare ualeat. Docet plato noster in libro qui inscribitur Ion. Vbi ingenti cuidam Herculeo lapidi ferreũ
annulum subdit exiguum: mox facile rapiẽdũ. Primo statim annulo subnectit se
cundũ: Tertium uero secũdo: quartumq; deinceps. Catenãq; conficit annulorũ
ef a magnete subinde pendentium Per quos attrahendi uirtus a priore deinceps in
consequentem repente transfunditur. Eadem ratione putat a Phœbo Musam ra
pi: ab hac poetam a poeta corripi similiter audiẽtes. Mysterium hoc his forte car
g minibus Virgiliq; imitatur. Quæ Phœbo pater omnipotẽs: mihi phœb9 Apollo
h Prædixit: Vobis furiarum ego maxima pando. Sed furias in presentia nominas-
h se nolim. Vbi nõ de furiarum: sed de gratiarum furore tractamus. Quoquidem
i patronus noster abundans petre fœlix & te pariter atq; me: ceterosq; suos obser-
j uatores afficit protinus. Affectos corripit. Correptos occupat. Occupatos mox
incomparabili quadam uoluptate perfundit. Quamobrem tãto beneficio hinc
affecti in ardentissimo eius amore perseueremus. In quo singulariter amando di
uinum quottidie reportamus instinctum. viii. Iunii. Mcccclxxxxi.

Vera laus Marci Cardinalis Sancti Viri.

Marsilius Ficinus Antonio Calderino dilectissimo Suo. S.D.

a B *instinctum* erron. *b* B *tadunt* erron. *c* *consequuntum* *d* B *vallens*
e *per* *f* MS om. *in* *g* MS, B *Virgilius* *h* B *surias* and *suriarum* erron.
i MS *abundatis* *j* MS *patronus*

PEtrus Fannius noster uir doctus: & probus multis heri testimoniis cõprobauit singularem beniuolentiam erga me tuam: pluribus iãdiu tuis in me officiis confirmatam: cum uero multis de causis plurimũ tibi cal derine debeam: hac debeo certe q̃ plurimum: q͡ sanctum illum uirum marcum, di ui marci cardinalem & iandiu reddidisti nobis amicum: & quandoque patronũ in nostris periculis præstitisti: cuius quidem obitu non possemus grauiter nõ do lere: nisi sparemus hũc e cœlo (ubi beatã agit uitam) certiore quodam in dies pa trocinio nobis aspiraturum. Hic certe (quod te non latet) Dauidicũ illud: Aia mea in manibus meis semper: & uiuens & moriens: impleuisse uidetur: Atque il lud euangelicum attigisse: potestatem habeo deponendi animam meam. Ita eni prædixit horam ita lætus: & quasi pro arbitrio discessit e corpore: ut nõ mori qui dem: sed sponte peregrinari: immo redire in optatam patriam uideret: immorta lis uitæ mortalibus exempla daturus: nouumque lumen cœlestibus luminibus accessurus. Fœlix igitur mi Antoni ob hanc maxime causam amicitia nostra: q͡ sub patrono confirmata est omniũ fœlicissimo: Vale fœliciter: ac me (ut soles) ama singulariter te amantem, xxviiii. Iunii. Mcccclxxxxi. ab c d e

Rationes negociorum suorum amico reddende. *f*

Marsilius Ficinus Martino Vranio prænnyngero amico Vnico. S. D.

CVm neminem te perquam dilectissime mi Martine Cariorem habeam: iure nulli potiusq̃ tibi quottidianas rerum nostrarum rationes reddere debeo. Valeo æquidem bene quantum habitudo: ætas: estas: assidua lit terarum studia ferunt. Prosequor ut iampridem scripsi diuina Dionysii nomina. Recognosco Plotinum interea dum exprimitur a librariis quattuor posthac ~~ut~~ aut ad summum quinque mensibus (ut arbitror) erit expressus. Exscribitur tibi Nostrum Commentarium in philebum. Mitto nunc eius partem quinterniões octo. Alios uero reliquos Venetiis quottidie Platonis Theologiæque libri iterũ: & (ut aiunt) diligentius imprimuntur. Adolescentes cõmendati nobis prospere ualent: multumque in dies litteris moribusque proficiunt. Singularis quidẽ noster amor exactissimam singulorum rationem exigit: Sed negocia prohibeant: his ergo contentus fœlicissime Vale. xx. Iulii. Mcccclxxxxi. g h ij

De simplicitate & integritate Morum. *f*

Marsilius Ficinus Pierleono complatonico suo. S. D.

SAlue salute dignissime pierleone uir omnium integerrime: immo & oium simplicissime. Verum plato noster in symposio quidem nullos nostris sę culis nasci integros existimat. Sed diuisos. In Timeo autem atque phædro duplices affirmat omnes. Te igitur quãdo integrum simplicemque appello non huius quidem sæculi filiũ iudico: Sed alterius. In quo (ut plato inquit) homines quondam integri pariter atque simplices nascebãtur. Quamdiu uidelicet regnabat quædam in humanitate diuinitas. Diuinorũ. n. integritas eadem est: atque ipsa simplicitas. Naturalia uero multiplicem habent integritatem. Monstra denique ab integritate simul: & simplicitate degenerant. Sed mysteria uix ad k l

a quam *b quod* *c spararemus* *d* MS *quae* B *quod* *e* MS adds *die*
f Title not legible in MS *g Prosequor* *h* MS *post hoc* *i* MS, Dur *Alias* *j* B adds *brevi accipies* after *reliquos* *k* MS *integras* (erron.) *l* B om. *.Divinorum*

a mittit epistola sortes videlicet facile. Vide igitur pierleõe mi alter ego: q̃ similem
b in plerisque sortem nacti sumus disciplinæ medicẽ in cœlestibus eundem: ut coniecto Saturnum Ducem quoque Platonem: patronum rursus eundem Laurentium Medicem Platonicarum disciplinarum instauratorem. Amicos prorsus eosdem. Inimicos autem ipsi nullos. Amamus enim omnes solum forte non amaturi. Siquis denique depræhensus fuerit solum amare seipsum. Mores præterea no-
cde stros quis non similes esse dixerit. Simulare namque uel dissimulare: pariter uter
f que nescit. Simulatores dissimulatoresque similiter utrumque fallunt. Sed fallãt (utcunq; lubet) iterum: atque iterum. Modo ipsi iam falsi: quãdoque nos quoq;
g salsos mutatis moribus non efficiant. Vale fœliciter in tua integritate simplicita-
h teque in uita etiam ingrata sorte uicturus. xx. Augusti. Mcccclxxxxi.

i Prohœmium in Platonicas institutiones.

Marsilius Ficinus Philippo Valori dilectissimo Suo. S.D.

ANno salutis humane. Mcccclvi. Quo ego quidem annos ætatis agebã tres atque uiginti: Tu uero natus es primitias studiorum meorum auspicatus sum a libris quattuor institutionum ad Platonicam disciplinã. Ad quas quidem componendas adhortatus est Christophorus Landinus amicissimus mihi uir doctissimus. Cum autem ipse: & cosmus medices pellegissent eas: probauerunt quidem: Sed ut pœnes me seruarem cõsuluerunt: quoad græcis literis erudirer: platonicaque tãdem ex suis fõtibus haurirem. Eas enim partim for
j tuita quadam inuentione: partim platonicorum quorundam latinorum lectione adiutus effeceram. Platonẽ deinde platonicosque græcos aggressus: institutiões illas: paulatim libris sequentibus emendaui. Neque tamen librum ipsum placuit abolere: quem tanq̃ liberum primogenitum meum eo anno genueram quo tu natus es: mihi certe: & obseruantia filius & perpetuo quodam fauore patronus: hũc
k igitur tu mi Valor dilectissime fili fratrem tuum fraterno præcor amore comple-
l ctere: in ualorum laribus ab ineunte iam ætate mihi domesticis: optato prorsus
m ualore uicturum. Vale. v. Nouembris. Mcccclxxxxi.

Gratiarum Actio.

n Marsilius Ficinus Martino Vranio prænnyngero Amico Vnico. S.D.

o IOannes streller ille uester: ac prope iam noster legit mihi hodie partem epistolæ ad se tuæ: amoris erga nos ardentissimi plenam: qua præterea significabas te natalem nostrum: & doctorum cetu: & magnifico sumptu celebrauisse. Ego igitur tantæ huic erga nos pietati tuæ facere non aliter satis pos-
pq sum: nisi te tantum omnino quantum me. Incomparabilis autem amoris erga te mei suauissime mi martine Testes erunt non solum epistolæ nostræ: uerum etiam libri quidam in posterum nobis ædendi. Viue igitur mi martine fœlix: nõ minus mihi semper q̃ mea uita Carus. Mitto ad te reliquum commentarii nostri in Philebum: quinterniones quattuor. Plotini librorum impressio pro
r ximo huic Martio erit (ut abitror) absoluta: magnifico Medicis Laurentii sumptu: formaque Regia: cõstituit mox quoq; platonis nostri libros eadem ex-

a MS, Dur *vero* b MS *indicem* for *medicem* c B om. *esse* d *dixerit?* e * f * g MS *mutatos* h MS adds *Flor.* i B *Platonis* j MS *fortuna* k MS *hunc tu igitur tu* l B om. *ab* m MS om. *Vale* adds *Die* n MS om. *Praennyngero* o MS om. *Streller* p B *amavero* for *omnino* q * r *arbitror* primi dignitate. Ego uero curabo pro uiribus ut emendatior sit expressio secunda q̃ prima. Præterea libros singulos in Capita multa Capitulaque distinguam. Et in scriptionibus q̃ certissimis: tanquã formulis declarabo. Dionysii libri iandiu no/bis incepti propter occupationem eiusmodi aliquanto tardius absoluentur. Va/le. xxiiii. Nouembris. Mccccl xxxxi. Florentiæ. a bc

In librum De Vita dono Datum. de

Marsilius Ficinus Mazingo insigni Phisico amico inseparabili. S. D.

SAlue salutis nostræ (Deo auctore) curator ãice ,prius insepabilis. In primis forte mirabere: Cur inseparabilem amicum potiusq̃ aliter nomina/uerim. Q uia uidelicet quos cœlum coniunxit: terra minime separabit. Quo enim pacto infima mũdi terra nostros animos per locorum distãtiam disiũgere poterit: quos altissimus planetarum suis in ędibus amore coniunxit: Amore inq̃ tam durabili: q̃ stabilis est ipse saturnus. Beniuolentiæ uero tam firme pi/gnus esto uita isthæc penes te mea. Nec immerito uitam istam tibi probãdam ~~cœ~~ ~~lo dẽdãq;~~ cõmitto: cui iamprĩdẽ meã hãc meorũq; uitã cõmisi curandam. f g h i

Philosophica igenia ad christũ pueniũt p platonẽ. Vt Aũstino aut relio cõtigit. jk

Marsilius Ficinus Florentinus Ioãni pico Mirãdulæ conphilosopho suo. S. D. l

SCribis ãice q̃ optime (quod mihi oĩum est gratissimum) te multis quotidie suadere: ac iã psuasisse nõnullis: ut epicure impietate relicta uel auc roica quadam opinione posthabita: piam de anima deoque sequãt Platonis nostri sententiam. Per quam sane quasi mediam quandam uiam: Christia/nam pietatem denique consequantur. Salue igitur uere piscator hominum. Qui enim uulgaribus ingeniis persuadent: pisces uel potius pisciculos captare ~~uiden/~~ ~~ture~~ uidẽtur: Sed qui egregiis: piscatores hominum iudicãtur. Hos forte magnos pisces nuncupat euangelium. Quibus compræhendendis nec rete quidem scin/ditur: Nostrum uero mirandula rete nunc est platonica ratio. Quæquidem si modo rite trahitur sub christiana ueritate non scinditur: sed permanet integra dum impletur: Nullos legisti philosophos quendam nisi platonicos christianam susce pisse religionem. Merito igitur platonicis (ut ita dicam) rębus altissima quæque christo piscaris ingenia. Vtinam tres saltem eiusmodi religioni piscatores adessẽt Vt grandes nulli pisces pelago superessent. Sed heu miseri uel infortunati potius Messis quidem multa: operari uero pauci. Quo igitur pauciores mi Mirãdula su mus: eo frequentius nobis uehementiusque laborandum. Vale. m n o p q r p

Commendatio.

Marsilius Ficinus Francisco Soderino Episcopo Volaterrano. S. D. s

MArtinus Vranius e germania Romam uenit mandata sui principis pro uiribus effecturus: & perfecturus (ut spero) si tu consilium tuũ operãq; præstiteris. Prestari uero tam uehementer pcupio: ut nihil ardẽtius nũc affectem: hunc tibi (si noueris) uirtus eius mirifica cõmendabit. Ignotũ ergo cõmendet inges beniuolentia nostra. Hic enim mihi tam carus est: ut non aliter exprimere possim nisi dixerim: alter ego. Cum igitur amicorum meorum nullũ fi u stra tibi hactenus commendauerim: quæ tua quidem incredibilis humanitas & clementia est: spero nunc: immo certo scio: Martinum: immo uero marsilium tibi fore fœliciter commendatum. Primo Aprilis. Mcccclxxxxii. t

a B ***vobis*** (erron.) b MS adds ***Die*** c MS om. ***Florentiae*** d * e MS ***libro*** f * g * h MS, Dur ***colendamque*** i * j B ***in*** for ***ut*** k V ***aut relio*** (erron.) MS, B ***Aurelio*** l MS om. ***Florentinus*** m MS, B ***epicurea*** n MS ***pisculos*** o B ***indicantur*** (erron.) p * q ***retibus*** r MS, B ***adessent*** s * t MS ***vale***

LIBER

Commendatio.

a Marsilius Ficinus philippo Valori Suo.S.P.D.
b MEministi mi Valor q̃ ardenter nos amet Martinus noster uranius:a deo
ut & filium suum meo nomine marsilium nuncupauerit:nostrumq; na
talem instituerit celebrandum.Hunc ergo non dubito abste uehemen/
ter amari.Hic te salutabit:consilium aperiet suum:Auxilium postulabit. Si me
mineris q̃ saepe de martino dicere soleam alter ego:non dubito quin habeas hunc
in omnibus mirifice commendatum:Scripsi ferme eadem ad uenerãdũ soderinũ
nostrũ.Huic ergo tu marsiliũ ita(ut scis)geminũ:geminatis quoq; p̃cibus cõmẽ
c dato. Actio gratiarum.Item de ostentis in obitu principis.

Marsilius Ficinus Reueren.in Christo patri Domino ioanni Medici Cardina
li supliciter se commendat.

CVm quartum medici gradum maximum arbitrentur:tu uero quartus a
d cosmo i generosa medicum familia mihi sis patronus:es ꝓculdubio ma
e ximus.Quod quidem hinc plane perspicio: q̃ non aliena mihi das:sed
tua.Tuo iandiu canonicatu me ornasti:Aede nũc martiana tibi dono concessa:
subito me donasti.Quamobrem obitu magnanimi Laurentii nostri:neque for
tunam meam deflere mihi licet:qui deinceps tanto patrono me uideam maxime
commendatum:neque sortem eius commiserari.Quem multis euidentibusque
argumentis traslatum ad superos esse cognoscimus.Legisti(ut arbitror)apud he
siodum triginta beneficorum demonum milia per aerem sublimen humana cu/
rare.Quos quidem prisci rectores hominum exploratoresque cognominãt. Prae
terea excellentissimos quosque apud homines principes: post obitũ ad rectores
eiusmodi commigrare:quasi collegas eorum posthac in humana gubernatiõe fu
turos.Animis ergo foelicibus illuc aduolantibus illos congratulari Platonici pu
f tant.Congratulationes uero signa dare portenta hominibus admiranda. Toni
trus.Fulmina.Flammas.Machinarum ruinas.Oracula.Somnia.Quae quidem
g prodigia partim maiestatem transmigrantis animae:partim detrimentum orbi po
puli Partim successionem antique potestatis in heredes significare uidentur.Idq;
h in Romuli Caesarisque decessu extra cõtrouersiam afferunt:contigisse.Quod &
nunc in morte Laurentii magni propemodum diui Florentiae fuit uniuerso fer
me populo manifestum.Viue igitur foelix maxime mi patrone diuina uoluntate
ij contentus.Gaudens foelicitate paterna.Confisus ope diuina. Die.xxv.Aprilis.
Mccccxxxxii.In agro Caregio.

Actio gratiarum.

Marsilius Ficinus Reueren.in Christo Patri Domino Francisco Soderino
Episcopo Volaterrano.S.P.D.

GRãmatici quidem ultra superlatiuum nihil habent.Oratores autem at
que poetae huic aliquid addunt.Huc forsan tendit Virgilianum illud.
O ter quaterque beati. Ter quidem beati sunt beatissimi. Qua
ter uero q̃ beatissimi. Hactenus me tibi carissimum esse plane perspexi:nec un
q̃ posse cariorem fore putabam. Nunc uero q̃ carissimum esse proculdubio ui
deo. Carissimos enim tuos expolias: quo me induas. Gratias igitur quas olĩ
soleo pro multis i me beneficiis tibi maximas agere:iam q̃maxĩas ago.Ac me tibi

a MS adds *oratori Romae* b MS, B *adeo* (for V *a deo*) c MS *Primo Aprilis Mccccxxxxij* d MS *ingenerosa* e *quod* f MS, Dur *Congratulationis* g MS *orbati* h MS, Dur *asserunt* i MS om. *Die* j MS *xx*, B *xv*

q̃ deditiſſimum eſſe confiteor: Illi quin etiam familiari tuo debeo non mediocri/
ter: quem tuo rogatu: mox animo haud egro nobis audio conceſſiſſe. Die. xxv. ab
Aprilis. Mcccclxxxxii. In agro caregio.

Cauſe prodigiorum in obitu principis contingentium.

Marſilius Ficinus philippo Valori oratori apud pōtificem Florentino. S.D. c

COgitanti mihi prodigiorum cauſas in excellentium uirorum præſertim
principum obitu contigentium: primo quidem uenit ī mētē: hæc neq;
fortuna cōtingere: habent.n.ordinē: neq; natura procedere. Diuerſa.n.
inter ſe fiunt: ut ad naturalem iſluxum una quadā ꝓcedentē uia: referri nō poſſit d
Et habēt inſe myſteria natura prorſus ſupiora. Deīde ſuccurrit: ſi portenta eiuſ/
modi: neq; fortuna: neq; natura proficiſcunt a diuinitate quadā proculdubio ꝓfi ef
ciſci.i.ab itelligentia quadā ſublimi: naturę uires exſupante. Sed ne minima que
q; ad mentē primā abſq; medio quodam ordine redigamus. Vident hæc (ut pla/
tonice loquar) ad tria potiſſimum numina referenda. Eſt.n. pſone genius: Demō
familiaris hoi: quem angelum cuſtodem noſtri Theologi nominant. Eſt & loci ge
nius: Domus ciuitatis: regni cuſtos: quem cognomināt principatum. Eſt inſup
ordo ſublimis chorusq; numinum uel demonū uel angelorū: inquorum numerū g
ſortēq; pp officii ſimilitudinē: excellens animus.q. ad ſtellā ſuam migraturus ē in hi
eodem illic officio.q. collega futurus. Queadmodum ergo tres prodigiorum au/ i
ctores ſunt: ita & tria uident genera portentorum. Sublimilis quidem ille corus jk
crinitas accendit: tonitrus ciet: fulgura iaculatur. & flammas ſtellaſq; cadentes.
Præfectum prouinciæ numen quatit diruitque machinas: oracula fundit: Au/
guria & auſpicia mouet: Eſtū deſignat: Cuſtos uero familiaris ſomnia ominaque l
excitat canumq; latratus.q. malum demonium illinc arcentes. Finem pterea de
ſideraturus mihi uideris cuius hæc gr̄a fiant. Prima quidem illa ſignificant excel/ m
lentiſſimos animos non extingui non negligi: ſed poſt obitum regnare cum ſupe n
ris. Secunda calamitatem populi tanto uiro deſtituti pnunciant: & cauere iminē o
tia ſubinde pericula monent. Tertia & uirum admonent moribundum: & ſuis i
dicant cœleſtem fauorem: illo quidem moriente non mori: ſed familiæ ſuæ poſt
illū aſpiraturū. Addunt Platonici qdā iter ſublimes hæc demōes ſēpiternos atq; p
hoies uita breues: eē demōes quoſdā medios ualde longeuos: horū ergo potētio q
ribus potētiores hoies cōmēdatos. Cūq; illorū aliqs poſt multa ſæcula morit ma r
gnū ſimul pricipem ipſi cōmendatū ægrotare ꝓtinus uitaq; decedere: Turbari ue
ro aerē: nouaq; & mirāda contigere: q̄do & magnorū demonū aerea corpa diſſol
uūt: & amici demōes fatū magni tū demōis tū pricipis ęgre ferūt. Vale. xxv Apri s
lis. Mcccclxxxxii. De uita Solitaria: & quanti facienda ſit fama. tu

Marſilius Ficinus Ioanni pico Mirandulæ. S.D. v

LAtere ne unq̄ ſperas mi Mirandula? Parua quidem & obſcura latere
facile poſſunt: magna uero & præclara non poſſunt. Tu quidem ut be
ne uiuas: ſtudes ſemper latere bene. Sed interim quo populo eua/
dis admirabilior: eo notior. Hinc quicquid tentaueris: rumores uarii pro
tinus excitantur. Quid ergo? Circunſpicies ne ſemper uniuerſam plebem
& quid conſabulaturi ſint: longe proſpiciens: ſeruus eris? An tua potius pro/
feſſione contentus: uulgi iudicium nihilipendes? Noui equidem ingeniū tuum:

a aegro *b* MS om. *Die* *c* MS om. *apud pontificem* *d possint* *e* B *a fortuna* *f a natura* *g in quorum* *h propter* B *per* *i quasi* *j sublimis* *k chorus* *l* MS *esta* *m* B *huius* *n superis* *o cavere* *p* MS om. *haec* B *hos* *q* MS *quodam* *r aliquis* *s* * *t* MS *In agro Caregio* *u* * *v* MS *philosopho vero*

Videor igitur mihi uidere quid agas. Haud omnino nihilipendes hæc: sed parui-
a pendes. Plurimi uero prudentum indicia facies. Sed de his quidem satis. Ego ue
ro dilectissime mi Ioãnes eo grauius tuo discessu dolui: quod me propter duorũ
simul amicorum obitum ĩsummo mœrore constitutum repente deseruisti: sperã
bc tem mihi te solũ cõsolatorẽ medicumq; fore. Sed spo te ,ppe diẽ rediturũ: qua qdẽ
de spe fret9 aĩcos ẽt cõsolabor. Vale rediq; fœlix. Die. xxviii. Aprilis. ĩ agro Caregio.

Laudes amici scilicet Bindacii Recasolani.

Marsilius Ficinus Philippo Valori Oratori Florentino. S.D.

Diuturnus Laurentii Medicis morbus una cum iniquitate temporũ (ut arbitror) in causa fuit: ut & ego non leuiter ægrotauerim. Sed ex longa infirmitate iam satis belle conualui: uidelicet aspirante deo: Nemo uero
f lõgi lãgoris tædia magis mihi leuauit: q̃ Bindacius Recasolanus familiaris nr:
gh uir certe natura generosissimus: uirtute probatissimus: opa officiosissimus hic sæ
ij pe me sponte sua: sæpe ẽt tuo nomine salutauit: Significauit præterea se tibi debe
re q̃ plurimum. hunc igitur in primis ama mi Valor: & apprime te amantem: &
omnium amore dignissimum. Martinus uranius alter ego ad nos reuersus narra
kl uit hodie q̃ amice q̃q; magnifice eũ exceperis. Fecisti tu quidem (sicut soles) Nec
mn quicq̃ hoc tẽpore mihi gratius efficere potuisses. Die. xxvi. Iunii. Mcccclxxxxii.

Laudes legitimi principis.

op Marsilius. F. Eberardo Duci Vitebergensi & Mõtis Peligardi Sẽatori [Senori]. S.P.D.

Multa iampridem de singulari uirtutum tuarum excellentia ex multis audiuimus: Plurima nuper accepimus a Martino uranio nostro: teste quidẽ & fideiussore apud nos locupletissimo: Laudumque tuarum præcone apud omnes fide dignissimo. Quamobrẽ ingens admirabilium uirtutum tuarum: quasi stellarum splendor ad nos usq; refulgens: incredibilem in nobis iam accendit ardorem: ad te uehementer amandum & colendum in primis atque uenerandum. Desiderabam æquidem iandiu qd & Plato noster optare se prædicabat: Cognoscere principem: in quo quẽadmodum in Pallade una cum potentia: pari
q ter sapiẽtia conspiraret. Necnõ: ut in cæsare magnanimitas cum clementia: Sicut
in Scipione grauitas cũ comitate cõcurreret. In quo pterea floreret & iustitia mi
nois: & religio Nũmæ: sub quo pax illa rediret Octauiãi: Qui deniq; pacis studia
rebus bellicis anteponeret: templa fundaret: publica litterarũ Gymnasia faceret:
rs Quem subditi non tam metuant q̃ ament & obseruent atq; mirentur. Eiusmõi q
dẽ est legitimi pricipis idea: & optata quõdã a Platone: & a nobis ĩ primis deside
tu rata. Atq; (ut cõstãs iã fama phibet) ĩ te pcipue ĩgẽs: ut nõ mirũ sit me iã: meosq;
achademicos oẽs tot uirtutũ tuarũ radiis iflãmatos: te qsi cœleste numen colere
ãte alios pricipes atq; uenerari. Sed incredibili quodã aore pterea cogimur te ob
secrare (ut ipse quoq; nos ames) singulariter te amantes: sẽpq; post hac ẽt (ut iam
facis) memineris quẽadmodũ oẽ lumen pendet ex alto: ita uirtutũ tuarum splen
dorem ex ipso deo patre luminum depẽdere: ut summus ille bonorum: omnium
auctor probitatem tuam pariter atque fœlicitatem confirmet etiam in posterum
v & augeat confirmatam]dispositionem & quottidianos cœlestium cursus aspectu
w que consideras: prosequaris. Probo æquidem dilectissime mi Bandaci: Verũ
tamen si quãdo Astrologiam illam aggrediaris: qua frustra nimiũ certa futurorũ

a MS, B *iudicia* b *spero* c *propediem* d MS om. *Die* e MS adds *1492*
f *noster* g *opera* h MS . *Hic* i MS om. *Sua* j *etiam* k *quam* l *quamque*
m *quicquam* n MS om. *Die* o * p * q B *conspicaret* (erron.) r *quam*
s *quidem* t *perhibet* u Dur *est ingens* v * w MS and Dur *Bindaci*

iudicia promittuntur:id minime comprobabo. Quem enim omnium familia/
rissimum habeo:eundem & fœlicissimum fore desidero. Compertum uero habe/
mus:omnes qui prædicendis futuris curiosius inhiant omnium infortunatissi/
mos esse uel fieri. Cuius quidem aduersitatis causas:uel manifestas: uel occultas
esse putamus. Manifestæ profecto causæ sunt: ꝙ isinito:ac prorsus incerto futuro a
rũ studio sua semꝑ oia negligere compelluntur. Plerumqꝫ uero imminẽtis fati uel
promissis confisi uel minis deterriti:sua quidẽ sententia necessariis:ipsi interea ni
hil agũt:toti uidelicet ex fato pendentes. Occultas autẽ huius rei causas esse ar/
bitror. Quod ꝓuidentia diuina:Cui natura:fatum : fortuna : seruiunt:nõ dat oĩ
bus oĩa. Sed sua cuiqꝫ iuste dispensat. Quibus ergo & his quidẽ uolẽtibus futura
concessit:merito præsentia negat. Cum enim præsentia:si cum futuris compares:
paucissima minimaqꝫ sint:si rebus eiusmodi careas:dũmodo futura : quæ q̄pluri b
ma maximaqꝫ sunt quoquomodo possideas: conqueri apud prouidẽtiam dẽ tua
sorte nõ debes. Forte uero fortuna:quæ uidet᷑ in hoc saltẽ opposita fato:ꝙ illud q cde
dẽ ordinẽ rerũ asserit necessariũ:hæc uero ordinẽ eiusmodi renuit:nimirũ futuro
rũ auguratoribus tanq̄ fatidicis assertoribusqꝫ fati infensa reddit᷑ & aduersa. Forte
ẽt qui uentura audacter anticipant : quæ cœlestis ille pater in sua posuit potesta/
te:sibi ipsis quod dei ipsius est:insolenter usurpãt. His ergo Iuppiter indignatus f
eos tanq̄ gigantes illos superbia nimium elatos effulminat. Missa equidem nunc g
quæ mihi succurrunt Astrologica facio. Rerum uidelicet reconditarum longeqꝫ
a præsenti distantium perscrutatores:incidere protinus in saturnum abditissima
queque remotissimaque tenentem. Et quoniam præsentia fortunæ bona conces/
sit Ioui:rebus tandem uenturis secretissimisque contentum. Quamobrem(ut sũ
matim cuncta concludam)dilectissime mi bindaci:quoniam ad sola præsentia lõ h
ge deficimus:ne dum ad futura quoque sufficiamus:quod diuinæ præcepit pau/ ij
lus:memori semper mente tenenendum. Nolite sapere plusq̄ oportet sapere. Sed kl
sapere ad sobrietatem. Vale.

Opiniones non temere diuulgande. Item orphei carmina.

Marsilius Ficinus Florentinus Martino Vranio Amico Vnico. S.D. m

ARgonautica & hymnos orphei & homeri atque proculi Theologiamqꝫ
hesiodi:quæ adolescens(nescio quomodo)ad uerbũ mihi soli transtuli:
quemadmodum tu nuper hospes apud me uidisti:ędere nũq̄ placuit:ne
forte lectores ad priscum deorum demonumque cultum iandiu merito reproba/
tum:reuocare uiderer: quãtum enim pythagoricis quondam cure fuit ne diuina
in uulgus ędérent:tanta mihi semper cura fuit:non diuulgare prophana:adeo ut
neque commentariolis in lucretium meis quę puer ad huc(nescio quomodo)cõ
mentabar:deinde peperci. Hæc.n.sicut & Plato tragedias elegiasque suas uulcão
dedi. Maturior enim ętas exquisitiusqꝫ & examen (ut inquit Plato) sæpe damnat n
quę leuitas iuuenilis uel temere credidit:uel saltẽ(ut par erat)reprobare nesciuit
Periculosius uero est(ut & plato inquit)noxias opiniões imbibere : q̄ uenenum o
pessimum diuulgare. Sicut enim bonum:quo latius:eo diuinius:ita latissimum
malum : pestilentissimum. Promisi uero tibi tutiora quædam Orphei carmina
mittere. Ecce mitto.

Orphei Versus de Deo. p

a *quod*   *b* *quamplurima* but B *plurima*   *c* B *opposito* (erron.)   *d* *quod*
e *quidem*   *f* B *usurpent* (erron.)   *g* MS *illos quondam*   *h* MS om. *ad*
i MS *deficiemus*   *j* MS, B *divine*   *k* MS, B *tenendum*   *l* MS om. *. Sed sapere*   *m* *   *n* MS, B om. *&*   *o* B *Periculosus* (erron.)   *p* MS om. title

LIBER

a EVſebius cæſarienſis Libro.xiii.de euangelica præparatione ſic ait:ſed or
pheus ēt in carminibus quæ inſcripſit de uerbo ſacro : diuia uirtute oia
gubernari:cunctaque adeo producta hoc modo aſſerit:ut legitur in li
b bro quem Ariſtobo us ad Ptolomeum ſcripſit.

c VOs qui uirtutem colitis:uos ad mea tantum
d Dicta aures adhibete:animoſq; intendite uros.
Contra qui ſanctas leges contennitis:hinc uos
d Effugite:& procul hinc miſeri:procul ite prophani.
Tu uero qui diuinas ſpecularis & alta
d Mente capis muſce uoces:complectere:& illas.
Aſpiciens ſacris oculis ſub pectore ſerua.
Hocq; iter ingreſſus:ſolum illum ſuſpice mundi
Ingentem auctorem ſolum:interituque carentem.
e Quem nos præſenti quis ſit ſermone docemus
Vnus perfectus Deus eſt qui cuncta creauit.
Cuncta fouens:atque ipſe ſerens ſuper omnia ſeſe.
Qui capitur mente tantum:qui mente uidetur.
e Qui nullumq; malum mortalibus inuehit unq̄
e Quem præter non eſt alius:tu cuncta uideto
Hic ipſum in ter is melius quo cernere poſſis.
Hic & enim uideo ipſius ueſtigia:fortem.
df Hicq; manum uideo:uerum ipſum cernere qui ſit.
d Nequaq̄ ualeo:nam nubibus inſidet altis.
Nemo illum:niſi caldeo de ſanguine quidam.
e Progenitus uidit:quem cœlorum aurea ſedes
d Sublimiſque tenet:cuius ſe dextera tendit.
Occeani ad fines quem de radicibus imis
g Concuſſique tremunt montes: nec pondere q̄uis
Immenſo ſint:ferre queunt:qui culmina cœli
Alta colens:terris nunq̄ tamen ille ſit abſens.
Ipſe eſt principium mediumque & exitus idem.

h Item idem in tertio inducit porphyrii uerba iſta.

Admirādā eſt græcorum ſapientia:qui Iouē mūdi mētē arbitrantes:quæ ī ſe ipſa mundū continens produxit:ſic a Theologia orphei profecti de ipſo tradiderunt.

Orphei Carmina.

SIdereeq; domus Rex eſt & iuppiter ipſe
ij Principium atq; ortus ūerū uis una deuſq;
j Vnus & oipotens regali in corpore cuius
Singula ponuntur:tellus:unda:ignis:& aer.
k Nox ſimul atq; Dies:ſapientia primaq; orig.
j Ac iocundus amor magno hoc in corpore regis
Sunt iouis excelſi:ceruicem nanq; uidebis

a MS *xiii°* b *Aristobulus* c *vestros* d MS om. period after ll.2, 4, 6, 18, 19, 22 of first hymn e MS adds period at 10, 14; comma or colon at 15, 21. f B *ipse* g *quamvis* h MS *In idem* but altered illegibly i MS, Dur *rerum* j B adds comma after *ortus* (l. 2) MS after *omnipotens* (l. 3), B after *amor* (l. 6) k *origo*

Cœli suspiciens reuerentia magnaq; tecta. a
Hoc caput auricomũ: flaui de uertice crines
Stellarum rutilant radii: de hinc aurea pandit
Cornua bina caput: capitisq; simillima tauri
Vnum est ortus: ipse est occasus & aliud bc
Ast oculi fulgens: ingenti lumine phœbus
Lunaq; purpureo phœbi redimita colore.
Præscia uenturi mens constat regius æther b
Quã strepitus nullus: nec uis: nec fama latere d
Archanũ ue potest: penetratq; per oĩa uictrix b
Præterea inuictum corpus: sine fine modoq;
Pãdit. Ast humeri magni quoq; pectora lata.
Est aer: alas quoq; uento possidet ille. b
His ad cuncta uolans: euro est uelocior ipso b
Tum sacer antiqua matre ex tellure tumescit
Venter & ex altis consurgit mõtibus ingens.
Quem medio pontus subcingit rite sonorus
Vltima præterã terrarum limina & ampli e
Fundamenta globi: furibũdaq; tartara plãtas
Esse pedum magni constat rectoris olympi.
Hic dum sub terris celasset cuncta: deinde
Ex imis repetens: in lucem protulit almam.

Porphyrii expositio. Simulachrum Iouis.

VNiuersus igit mũdus Iuppiter est: aĩal ex aĩalibus: deus ex diis constitutus. Iuppiter aũt est quãtũ intellectus ẽ: a quo uniuersa ꝓducunt: & qui (f) cuncta creat intelligẽdo: hoc igit mõ theologis de Ioue sentientibus impossibile est talẽ eius imaginẽ fingere: qualẽ carmĩa descripserunt. Iouẽ igit ẽẽ ctedendũ est: uirtutẽ prouidentẽ atq; uiuificã: quã pila & rotundis figuris significãt: (g) hoĩs simulachrũ ei cõstituũt: qm̃ mens est quæ cũcta seminali rõe ꝓducit. Sedere (hij) autẽ fingitur (ut stabilis uirtus) atq; incõmutabilis exprimat. Nuda aptaq; hẽt superiora. Q m̃ cõspicuus intelligẽtiis & supioribus est: inferiora uero tegunt: qa occultat inferioribus creaturis. Sceptrũ leua tenet: qa in his corpis partibus: ceu spiritalissimũ uitæ domiciliũ inuenit. Creator. n. intellectus rerũ spiritusq; uiuificus mundi est. Dextera uero aut aquilã protẽdit: aut uictoriã: alterũ quia cæterorum deorũ dominus: quẽadmodum aliarum auium aquila est. Alterum quia omnia sibi subiecta sunt. ix. Iunii. Mcccclxxxxii. (kl) (m) (n) (opq) (rs)

Exhortatur amicos ut Plotino foras prodeunti faueant.

Marsilius Ficinus Philippo Carducio dilectissimo suo. S. D.

SAlue mi Carduci academiæ studiosissime cultor. Vide q̃ uerum sit ꝓuerbiũ illud: oĩum rerũ uicissitudo est. Diuinus Plato noster quõdã magnũ Plotinũ peperit. Plotinus Platonẽ iã parturit: ꝓpediẽ pariturus. Plato lucẽ Plotino dedit. Plotinus Platoni reddet lucẽ: Cũ ipse primũ prodibit in lucẽ. Editus ille quidẽ iã ẽ a nobis: sed adhuc (nescio quomõ) liminibus hæret. Surge age Carduci: nostrorũ oĩum ardẽtissime. Plotinũ hærẽtẽ ꝓmoue: nostrosq; oẽs & (t) (u)

&

a B *recta* (erron.) *b* MS om. period l.13; adds period ll.5, 8, 10; B period l.14 *c* B *illud*
d *vis* *e* *praeterea* *f* MS *in quantum* *g* *modo* *h* *hominis* *i* *quoniam* *j* *ratione*
k *apertaque* *l* *habet* *m* *quia* *n* MS *iis* *o* MS *creativus* *p* MS *intellectos rex*
q MS *vivificans* *r* MS *Haec Porphyrius.* *s* MS no date *t* *quam* *u* B om. *Plotinus*

cæteros cohortare ad hunc manibus alacriter cōpræhendendū: ut ipse in lucē eue
a stigio ꝓdiēs: cōuenientibus oībus: uicissim reddat lucē. xii. Inlii. Mcccclxxxxii.

In librum de Vita missum ad amicum.

Marsi. Ficinus Ioāni Canacio: & Bindacio recasolāo dilectissimis suis. S.P.D.

SI qui familiariū meorū mentē meā tenent: uos certe familiarissimi oīum
b totā prorsus hētis. Vos itaq; minime latet: quo cōsilio: usus: quaue spe
c & fiducia fretus: libros de Vita cōscripserim: ut ingeniosis quidē prodes
sem oibus: sed inter eos multomagis amicis: maxime uero ciuibus in primis salu
ti patriæ necessariis. Non dubitabā equidē me semel q̄ plurimis imo oibus ꝓfutu
rū: si quos potissimū cōseruarē: salutis publice seruatores. Meū quidē hactenus fu
d it: libros illos hac snīa: diligentiaq; cōponere. Vestrū uero deinceps operā assidue
dare ne forte me fallat opinio: frustraq; nimiū laborauerim. Quotiēs ergo paulan
toniū soderinū nostrū salutabitis. Virū & frequentissima salutatiōe: & ꝑpetua sa
lute dignissimū. Totiēs cōmemorare huic præceteris memineritis: ut libros de ui
ta relegat & obseruet. Huic. n. maxime uitā longā salutēq; perpetuā exoptamus.
e Quippe cū & ingeniosissimus amicissimusq; sit: magnisq; medicibus patrōis no/
fg stris: nō parua quidē naturæ: certe q̄maxia beniuolētiæ necessitate cōiunctus. Iō
q; saluti publice admodū necessarius. Si tantū robore uir ille ualeret: quantū con
silio præualet: ita neq; medicorū remediis indigeret ad bene ualendū: sicut nec ul
lorū iam cōsiliis æget ad bene uiuendū. Iam uero si tantū ualitudini suæ quādoq;
cōsuleret: quantum rebus agendis & amicorum cōmodis reiq; publicæ prosperi
h tati quottidie prospicit: nequaq̄ uos urgerem ut de curanda sui corporis ualitudi
de moneretis. Deniq; bene ualete. Et paulātonium nostrum (ut soletis) salutate
frequenter: de colenda diligentius ualitudine: quottidie monituri: ut ipse quoq;
tandiu saltem filio suo Tōme præclaro adolescēti uiuat: q̄diu sibi Tōmas suus pa
i ter uixit clarissimus eques. die. xxii. Iulii. Mcccclxxxxii.

j Cathalogus familiarium atq; auditorum.
k Marsilius Ficinus Florentinus Martino Vranio amico unico. S.D.

l NIhil a me iustius postulare poteras: q̄ quod per Ioannem streler conger/
manum tuum iam sæpe requiris: amicorum uidelicet nostrorum catha
logum: non ex quouis commertio uel contubernio confluētium: sed in
ipsa duntaxat liberalium disciplinarum communione conuenientium. Cū enim
absq; amicorum meorū præsentia esse nusq̄: aut debeam: aut uelim: ipseq; sim nō
in italia solum in me ipso: sed in te etiā in germania: merito amicos hic meos: istic
etiam mihi adesse desidero. Omnes quidem ingenio moribusq; probatos esse sci-
l to. Nullos enim habere unq̄ amicos statui: nisi quos iudicauerim litteras una cū
honestate morum: quasi cum Ioue Mercurium coniūxisse. Plato enim noster in
epistolis integritatem uitæ ueram inquit esse philosophiam: litteras autem quasi
externum philosophiæ nuncupat ornamentum. Idem in epistolis ait philosophi
cam communionem omni alia non solum beniuolentia: sed etiam necessitudine
præstantiorem stabilioremque existere. Sed ut mox ueniam ad cathalo/
gum: cunctos summatim amicos ita laudatos accipito. At si proprias cuiusque
laudes singulatim narrare uoluero: opus inceptauero longe prolixum: Si quos

a Iulii *b* habetis *c* MS adds *videlicet* after *ut* *d* sententia *e* B *Quippe & cum* *f* quam maxima *g* ut Ideoque B imoque *h* MS valitudine moneretis *i* MS om. *die* *j* MS, B *Catalogus* *k* MS om. *Florentinus* *l* strelerem *m* nunquam pretermisero non ęque laudatos prorsus inuidiosum. Omnino uero absurdum fuerit: si dum amicos ordine disponere tento inter in comparationibus omnia ꝑtur bauero: odium pro beniuolentia postremo reportans. Primum summūq; inter amicos locum patroni nostri medices iure optimo sibi uendicant: Magn9 cosmus Gemini cosini filii uiri prestantes petrus atq; ioannes: Gemini quoq; petri nati. Magnus laurentius & inclitus iulianus. Tres laurētii liberi. Magnanimus petrus ioannes cardinalis plurimum uenerandus. Iulianus egregia indole prædītus. Ac ne in longum singulorum laudes ꝓsequar una medices omnes communi laude complectar. Genus heroicum Præter patronos duo sunt nobis amicorum genera. Alii enim nō auditores quidē omnes: nec omnino discipuli: sed consuetudine familiares (ut ita loquar) cōfabulatores atq; ultro citroq; consiliorum disciplinarumq; liberalium cōmunicatores. Alii autem pręter hęc quę dixi nos qnq; legētes & quasi docentes audiuerūt. & si ipsi quidē quasi discipuli: nō tamē reuera discipuli: non enim tātum mihi arrogo: ut docuerim aliquos aut doceam: sed (socratico potius more) sciscitor omnes atq; hortor fœcūdaq; familiariū meorū īgenia ad partū assidue prouoco. In primo genere sunt Naldus: Naldius a tenera statim etate mihi familiaris. post hunc in adolescentia nostra peregrius allius. Christophorus Landinus. Baptista Leo: Albertus. petrus: pazius. Benedictus Accoltus Aretinus. Bartholomeus Valor. antonius canisianus. paulopost. Ioānes caualcātes. Dominicus galectus. antōius calderius. Hieronym9 Rossius. amerigus & tommas ambo bencii. Cherubinus quarqualius geminianensis. Antonius seraphicus. Michael Mercatus ambo miniatēses. Franciscus bandinus. Laurentius lippius collēsis Bernardus nuthius: cōmādus. Baccius ugolinus. Petrus fānius ꝑsbiter. Horū plurimi exceptis landino & baptista Leōe & benedicto accolto: prias lectiōes nr̄as nōnūq̄ audiuerūt. In ætate uero mea iā matura fāiliares non auditores. Antōius allius Ricciardus anglariēsis. Bartholomeus Platina. Oliuerius arduinus: Sebastianus Saluinus amitinus nr̄. Laurētius bonincōtrus. Benedictus biliottus Georgius Antōius uespucius. Ioānes Baptista bonisegnius. Demetrius bizātius. ioānes uictorius Soderius: Angelus politiāus. Pierleonus spoletinus. ioannes picus Mirandula. In secundo genere idest in ordine auditorum sunt. Carolus Marsupinus. Petri quique. Nerus. Guicjardinus. Soderinus. Compagnius. parentus. philippi duo. Valor scilicet & carducius: ioannes quattuor canacius. Nesius. Guiciardinus. Rosatus. Bernardi quatuor. Victorius Medices. Canisianus. Michelęctius. Frācisci quatuor. Berlingierius Rimicinus. Gaddus. petra sācta. Amerigus cursinus. Antonius Lanfrādinus. Bindacius Recosolanus Alamannus donatus. Nycholaus michelotius. Matheus rabatta. Alexander albitius Fortūa hebreus. Sebastianus presbiter. Angelus carduccius. Andreas cursus Alexander borsius. Blasius bibienius. Franciscus diacetus. Nycholaus ualor.

Prohœmium in compendium proculi.

Marsilius Ficinus Martino uranio amico unico. S.D.

POst discessum ex italia tuū aduecti sunt e græcia mox ad Magnanimum Petrum medicem. libri multi ex q̄plurimis electi nuper electore Lascari græco admodum elegante pro regia illa biblioteca iamprīdē a magno Laurentio fœliciter instituta. Ego autem inter multa (ut soleo) semper in primis

&ii

a MS, B *interim* b *magnanimus* c MS *heroicum.* d *disciplinarum* e B *familiarumque* f B *terrena* (erron.) g *presbiter* h B *leones* (erron.) i MS *Rinuccinus* B *Rimicinus* j *Recasolanus* k MS om. *Alamannus donatus* l MS *cursius* m MS ends at *bibienus* n B adds *Florentinus* o MS *medicem libri*

legi Platonica. primaq; inter hæc cōmētaria Procli in sex Platonis de re pu. libros principiumq; septimi. Quos igit' ex amœnissimis horum pratis flosculos passim discurrēdo collegi: religionem sanctam præceteris redolentes: ad te mitto insignē
a religione uirum. iii. Augusti. Mcccclxxxxii.
b Excerpta ex Proculo in rem publicam Platonis a Marsilio Ficino. Tres cuiusq; Dei proprietates.

Bonitas. Immutabilitas. Veritas. Bonitas. Potētia. cognitio

PLato in legibus per tres proprietates diffinit ipsam dei rationem. s. per bonitatem: potentiam: cognitionem, per tres quoq; similes in re publica. s. per bonitatem: ~~immortalitatem~~ [immutabilitatem] c : ueritatem. immutabilitas quidem ē potentiæ propria: ueritas autem cognitionis perfectio. Dicitur autē unusquisq; deus reuera bonus. Tum quia cum bono suo nullum malum est admixtū: tum quia bonitas in eo non est habitus aliquis essentię additus. Sed ipsa eius essentia. Non enim prius quidem est deus. Deinde bonus existit. Eadē enim essentia sua formaliter & deus ęque est & bonus. Sic igitur unusquisq; deus ita suapte natura dicitur
d seipse bonus sicut deus primus seipso bonū. Proculus idē in elemētis theologiæ pbat unūquenq; deū ita esse formaliter bonitatē quādā cēntialē: sicut primus ē ipsū bonū sup essentiā: Itē ad ipsam deitatē tria hæc formaliter ptinere: bonitatem puram: potentiam non impeditam: cognitionem nullius incertam.

e Deus nullius mali causa: nunq̄ mutat formas: nullum fallit.

PLato in repu. Tria dogmata theologica ponit. Primū si qsq; deus suapte natura uere bonus ē: bonorū quidē semp est cā. Mali uero alicuius nūq̄ Secūdū si uere potēs est: pœnitus imutabilis. Tertiū si ad deū & potētia imutabilis & ueritas bonitasq; ptinēt: neminē unq̄ fictionibus ullis mēdaciisq; fallit. Circa primū dubitat' unde sint mala. Si deus nihil agit ad malū. Circa secūdū
f si deus nullus ullo mō mutat': quō dii spōte apparēt? Alias quidē figurati: alias nō
g figurati: nisi. n. hæc admiserimus: oēm sacrorū disciplinā & opa sacerdotū funditus sustulerimus: & ipsa quoq; uisa ī quibus dii spōte ī figuris alias aliis sese otterunt. Circa tertiū: quō respōsa nōnūq̄ falsa reddant. Iā uero multa ī oraculis mendacia depræhendūt'. Respōdet' ad primū. Malū nec ex deo: nec ex alia cā propriū inter existentia habere processum. Neq; uero possibile est: uel malorū ideā ponere: uel materiā dicere cām eē malorū. Oēs. n. ideæ tanq̄ species quædam intellectuales sunt atq; diuinę: Extantq; exemplaria: tum essentiarum: tum perfectionum ad essentiam pertinentium. Materia uero ex deo producta est tanq̄ necessaria mundo: neq; malefica est. Quippe cū ad generationē uniuersi cōducat. Neq; ēt est bonum. Cum omnium ultima sit: sed in necessariis ordinē hēt. Quicquid enim est alicuius gratia: tale est. Nullam ergo uel specialem uel materialē malorum causā ponere fas est. Nec omnino unam eorum causam. Sed quēadmodū ipse inquit: dicendum est particularia & dispersam malum inferre. Particularia quidē. Quoniā
h nullum uniuersorum ut intellectus: anima: corpus: causa est malorum. Dispersa uero: quoniam nō res una quædam causa est malorū: sed(ut ipse inquit)aliæ malorum occasiones sunt quærendæ. In corpore quidem malum. i. morbus accidit propter diuersa quædam absq; mutua proportione inter se confluētia: Dum unū quodq; superare contendit: Malum quoq; in anima propter differentes uitæ species & contrarias inter se pugnantes. Quibus pugnantibus ex aliis malum accidit

a MS om. date but adds *vale* in margin **b** MS adds *Florentinus* **c** *immutabilitatem* **d** MS *seipso* Dur *se ipso* B *se ipse* (erron.) **e** B *mutua* (erron.) **f** MS *frequenter apparent* **g** MS replaces *figurati ... non figurati* with *tanquam lumina quaedam non figurate: aliae figurata* **h** MS, faint corr. Dur *dispersa*

aliis:unoquoq;:quod ſuum eſt:agere. Oportuit autem corpus fore tale.ſ.ex cō
trariis atq; repugnantibus(ut foret)nō nihil etiam in mundo caducum . Atq; ita
perfectus mundus:ex omnibus uidelicet conſtitutus. Animas quoq; cōmixtionē
hic habere:ne regiones iſtæ mundi:rationaliū animalium expertes forent . Neue
rationales uitæ in corporibus abſq; medio plantarent̃ ſed agerent : Paterenturq;
in rationaliū quoq; conditiones:& talia quædam appetant:ſentiāt:imaginentur. *a*
His.n.opus eſt mortalibus. Si modo uel breue tēpus in his ſunt regionibus per
manſura. Dum igitur :quod ſuū eſt :res quælibet agunt:mala ſubincidunt. Neq; *b*
propter aliud niſi propter bonum. Q uibus ſane contingentibus uniuerſum utit̃
oportune : Euaduntq; hæc in bonum per ipſam uidelicet utentiū poteſtatē. Q ua *c*
propter nullū eſt purū alicubi malū. Sed eſt boni quodāmodo particeps. Atq; ita
malū diuinitus quoq; pendere quodāmodo dici poteſt:tāq̃ quodāmodo bonum.
Sed interi ab aliis pmultis particularib9 agētibus uelut aduenticiū huic incidere: *de*
accidere inq̃ multis ipis atq; diuerſis. Ad dubiū de apparitiōibus deiceps ita reſpō
debim9. Dū ſupi pmanēt imutabiles nec admittūt qcq̃ nec amittūt diuīa q̃dā uiſa *f*
inde proſiliunt quæ generatiōem ſuam in loco nobis circunfuſo ſuſcipiunt. Cum
enim ſpectatores quidem utantur corporibus. Dii uero ſint incorporei ſpectacu *g*
la diuinitus emanantia uidelicet coram dignis aſpectu habent quidem aliquid a
ſuperis producentibus. Non nihil uero ſpectatoribus quoquomodo cognatum.
Q uapropter apparent. Neq; tamen omnibus. Et quibus apparēt aſpiciuntur dū
taxat perfulgida quædam animarum inuolucra. Et iccirco clauſis oculis frequē *h*
ter aſpiciuntur. Q uantum igitur extenſa ſunt & in alio quodam huiuſmodi .i. *i*
Aere apparent:cognata ſpectantibus euadunt. Q uantum uero diuino ſunt reſer *j*
ta lumine:& efficaciam habent:deorūq; uires imagine repræſentant: per ipſa per
ſpicua ſymbola.i.ſigna:continue uelut ſuſpenſa depēdēt a numinibus producen
tibus ea. Q uapropter & ineffabilia illorum ſacramēta myſteriaq; per talia figurā-
tur:dū formas uarias intuentibns offerunt. Teſtantur hoc eloquia ſacra:ſacerdō *k*
tem ſic alloquentia. Diuina quidē oīa incorpea ſunt. Corpora uero pp uos his ſūt *l*
adhibita. Q uippe cū incorporea icorporaliter pcipere nequeatis:pp corporeā na
turam iſtā:in quā eſtis uniuerſi. Hæc ibi. Hæc igitur & apparent & diſparent pro *m*
uolūtate deorū:ipſi uero ſūt occulti:q̃les natura ſūt̃ iterea pmanētes neq; quicq̃ p *n*
hæc oſtenta ſuſcipiētes:nec amittētes . Q uēadmodū intellectuales illæ ſpecies.i. *o*
ideæ neq; corporeæ ſiūt:uel cōpoſitæ:uel formatæ:dū p ipſas talia q̃dā efficiunt̃ p
ipſas uidelicet minime tales. Ois itaq; deus pmanet:nō formatus q̃uis ſponte .q.
formatum ſeſe offerat. Nō.n.in ipſo talis quædam forma eſt:ſed ab ipſo: dum ſpe
ctator nō ualet ſine forma:quod ē ſine forma uidere:ſed pro modo ſuo ſub forma *p*
proſpicit nō formata. Ad tertiū dubium ita reſpōdemus. Mēdaciū nō eſt in ſuperis qui reſpōdent:ſed in his qui[illegible]ſponſa ſuſcipiunt:propter infirmitatē ſuā ora *q*
culum peruerſæ ſuſcipientibus. A[illegible] hæc ipſa fallacia nō cōtingit præter numinū *rs*
uoluntatem uolentiū dignos dūtaxat uotum conſequi. Sunt & nōnulli : quibus
ueritatem ipſam puram penes deos manentem:ſcire nō conuenit. Sed pati quod
conuenit per fallaciam penes ſe contingentem. Neq; igitur ueritatem dii ignorāt
nec ipſa confundunt. Sed cōfuſione propter ineptitudinem noſtram apud nos ac *t*
cidente ad noſtram utuntur utilitatem:iam uero ipſa oraculorum teſtatur hiſto-

a ***irrationalium*** *b* B ***subscindunt*** *c* B om. ***videlicet*** *d* MS ***particularibusque*** *e* MS ***huc*** *f* * *g* MS ***incorporei:*** *h* MS ***divinarum*** for ***animarum*** *i* ***in*** *j* MS ***cognita*** B ***cognate*** *k* B ***eloquentia*** *l* B om. ***vos*** *m* MS, Dur ***immersi*** *n* ***sunt*** *o* B ***ostensa*** *p* B ***seu*** *q* ***responsa*** *r* MS, B ***perverse*** *s* ***Atque*** *t* MS ***ipsi***

ria. Propter locum uel tempus: uel modum: uel aliud interrogãtis erratũ: falsum in respõsis accidere. Quãdo Plato in repub. dicit: nõ solum omne diuinũ: sed etiam demonicum semper esse ueridicum: neq; mentiri: intelligendum est de demone uero dictum atq; naturali: nõ de demonio per habitudinem quãdam sic appellato. Quod mutationes plurimas substinet: seducitq; illos: quibus factum est
a amicum. Quod uero ſm essentiam est demonium: cum & rationale sit: est oĩo ueridicum. Irrationale uero & ipsum quidem ueritatis est impos: fallitúrq; & fallit tanq̃ falsum: existimaturq; genus fallax. Quod tradit historia sæpe decipere: dũ uel subit oracula: uel inuocationes auscultat: uel ultro aliquibus occurrit. Idq; to
b tum est nõ natura demonum: sed habitudine. Tota religio & opera sacerdotũ & historia: cõmunisq; hominũ fama consentit: deos sensibiliter apparere: multasq; offerre formas uariasq; figuras. Et alias quidem lumen proferre nõ figuratum: alias figuratum: & nũc quidem humana figura. Nunc alia. Dum uidelicet ubiq; permanet imota diuinitas. Ipsa nanq; deorum simplicitas apparet multiplex intuentibus. Non quidem per illius mutationem uel fallaciam: sed propter naturę cõditionem: quæ pro modis participantium: definit deorum proprietates. Cum enĩ
c deus ipse participatus: i se sit unus atq; simplex: aliter ipsum participat intellectus aliter intellectualis anima. Phantasia item aliter atq; sensus. Intellectus enim indiuidue. Intellectualis anima reuolubiliter. Phantasia formabiliter: sensus uero passiue. Idq; quod participat per substãtiam est uniforme. Per participationem uero sit multiforme: est immutabile. Apparet mutabile propter infirmitatem nostrã.
d Cũq; nullo modo sit graue: dumtamen implet: grauare uidet. Quéadmodum de pallade poetæ tradunt. Quale enim est quod capit: tale necesse est quod accipit: apparere. Quando igitur Deorum aliqui quasi hospites uel aliter nobis occurrũt nõ est putandum apparentem mutationẽ illis inesse: sed indifferentibus susceptaculis imaginationẽ uariam resultare. Atq; hic unus est modus: quo poesis deos in se immutabiles: tamen nobis. q. mutabiles introducunt. Est & modus secũdus quando. s. diuinum ipsum multas in se uires habens specierumq; omnium plenũ uaria contemplantibus intelligibilia spectacula profert. Tunc enim tradunt diui
e num ipsum has uires in se cõtinens demonstratam uirium uarietatem in formas
f uarias commutare. Alias aliam proferens: semper quidem secũdum omnes agens apparens tamen transitoriis animarum intelligẽtiis semper aliud atq; aliud ꝓpter formarum quas in se cõtinet multitudinem. Atq; hoc pacto proteus ille formam propriam fertur spectantibus permutare: alius deinceps aliusq; apparens. Proteum igitur qui diuinus quidam intellectus est uirium omnium specierumq; plenꝰ sub neptuni serie computatus particulares animæ quæ sub eadem serie nominan
g tur phocę assidue contemplantur: & nunc quidem alias tunc uero alias species in
h tuentur: suarumq; cogitationum progressionem proteo applicantes formarũ per
i mutationem in proteo suspicantur. Itaq; uidetur omnia fieri spectantibus ipsum
j quotcunq; terrã incolunt: uel aquam uel aerem: aut ignem. Quot enim species i se continet: immo quot species ipse semper est eterne: totidem alterne uidetur effici propter perceptionem intuetium iugiter alternantem. Tertius apparitionis uariæ modus est quando uaria unius dei uisa non proueniunt propter subiectorũ perceptiões neq; propter uarietatem uirium diuinarum: sed quando Deus idem

a B *daemonum* b MS *daemonum* B, Dur *daemonium* c *in se* d MS *implex* e MS adds *quam* or *que* after *virium* f *aliam* g MS adds *eius* before *species* h MS, Dur *Prot[h]eo* i MS adds *ut* before *in* j MS *colunt*

secũdum ordines diuersos progreditur: & usqꝫ ad ultima quasi descendit numero
se multiplicãs in ordinesqꝫ inferiores declinãs. Tũc rursus fabule tradunt diuinũ
illud permutari in hãc ipsam speciem desuper inquam processum fecit. Hac itaqꝫ
rõne Mineruam quidem mẽtori. Mercurium uero lario aui garule. Apollinẽ rur ab
sus asturi se similem reddidisse ferunt. ostendentes uidelicet pręstantiores horum c
Deorum ordines: in quos processerunt ab uniuersis. Quamobrem quãdo diuĩas
apparitiones describũt eas sine forma figuraqꝫ conseruare student. Vtpote quando pallas achilli quidem soli se declarauit exercitui uero præsenti nequaq̃. Vbi ue
ro apparitiões angelicas afferunt Deos alienis formis indutos proferunt: sed his
quidem uniuersalibus. Quemadmodum in humanam quandam speciem uiro
mulieriqꝫ communẽ nec hominis alicuius propriam deuenisse canunt. Sed quan
do demonicas narrant processiones: tunc in singula quædam particulariaqꝫ mutationes descensumqꝫ in bruta nõ uerentur afferre. Vltima enim ordinum sequẽ
tium deos per figuras huiusmodi declarantur. Iam uero consideratu dignum est
igitur apte cum ordine rerum talia congruant. Diuino namqꝫ conuenit ipsũ sim de
plex. Angelico autem uniuersale: Demonico tandem particulare. Et illi quidem
intellectuale. Isti autem rationale huic deniqꝫ genus quoddam irrationale. In ipo f
enim demonum ordine uita quoqꝫ talis est implicita. gh

Tres habitus statusqꝫ animarum separatarum. Contemplatiuus. Actiuus. Voluptuosus.

ANimarum habitus differentes sunt etiam a corpore separatarum. Simili i
ter uniuersi loca quæ inhabitant differentia sunt. Necesse est igitur aĩas
sic ab instrumentis mortalibus segregatas: ut nec ad deteriora habeant
habitudinem neqꝫ mortalium perturbationum nugarumqꝫ sint plene secũ quoqꝫ
ferre inuolucra olim lucida: adhuc pura sicut antea fuerãt: neqꝫ materialibus ua-
poribus perturbata: neqꝫ ob naturam concreta terrenam. Animas autem nondũ
per philosophiam perfecte purgatas: sed ad affectum erga crassum corpus inclia-
tas uitamqꝫ cum ipso communem adhuc affectãtes: necessarium est talia quoqꝫ
uehicula sua sibi suspensa uidere potentibus demõstrare. Vmbrosa uidelicet ma
terialiaqꝫ retroqꝫ pondere recedentia. Plurimumqꝫ secum mortalis concretęqꝫ na
turę ferentia: quod perspicue in phędone narratur. Harum præterea animarũ ad
hanc uitam se adhuc inclinantium differẽtiæ multæ sunt. Quæ enim uitam ma jkl
gis practicam duxerunt neqꝫ adhuc a uita eiusmodi destitere merito competens
diligunt practicis actionibus instrumentum segregateqꝫ ab hoc indignate com m
mertium percupiunt: Vitamqꝫ hanc nostram separate uitę præponunt: ut pote- n
qꝫ secundum uitam illam agere nequeant ad uitam uidelicet practicam aptiores o

Quæ uero ob uitam flagitiosam Caducum corpus affectant uitamqꝫ cum ipso
nihil differre putant a uita in ipso ducta conueniens est in locum uniuersi tene- p
brosum ultimumqꝫ deferri. Homerus quemadmodum & Plato animam disti
guit ab idolo suo: & intellectũ ab his quę sunt animę propria & animam quidem
idolo inquit uti intellectum uero utrisqꝫ diuiniorem esse. Atqꝫ idolum & animã
esse quodammodo nota: etiam in hoc corpore. In quo & seorsum a quo curã ꝓ
uidentiamqꝫ huius habere: Idqꝫ naturaliter concupiscere: intellectum uero phã q

a Dur *mentori* MS *Mentori* B *mencori* b MS *Laro* c B *praestantiora* d Dur illegible, MS *quam apte* B *quam aperte* e MS *tum* (erron.) f MS *ipsa* g MS *ordinatione* h B om. *est* i * j MS *inclinatum* k Dur illegible l B *magnis* m MS *indignantur* n MS *commertiumque* o MS *actiores* (erron.) p B *ipsa* q MS adds *haec* before *huius*

a tasticis formabilibusq; motibus nostris non comprehendi. Proinde quemadmodum animarum in cœlum ascendentium instrumenta harmõicam uocẽ emit
tunt: motũq; concinnum præferũt: sic sub terras descendentium: iamq; minus ra
tionalium sonus similis est lamento: ferens uidelicet affectuosæ phantasticæq; ui
tæ dũtaxat imaginem. Inferorum præterea loca & iudiciarios sub terra status
bc & flumina: quæ Homerus Platoq; describunt: non esse est putandum esse imagina-
tiones uanas fabulosaq; tantũ terriculamenta: sed quẽadmodũ animis cœlestia re
petentibus: multa uariaq; loca illic sunt pro meritis distributa: ita putandũ est pu
nitione quoq; purgatione q; indigentibus animabus: loca sub terris esse disposita
d uarios defluxus habentia ab elemẽtis circũfusis terræ. Quos sane defluxus flumi
na uocauerunt. esse deniq; differentes demonũ ordines huic præfectos operi: par
tim quidem ultores: partim castigatores: partim purgatores: partim uero iudicia
les. Perterreri uero illic animas consentaneum est imaginatione demonum præ-
ef fectorum: statuq; ꝓ meritis quidem habitibusq; uario confusoq;: & a superis solis
radiis segregato.

Tres animæ uitæ: diuina: humana: ferina.

TRiplicem animæ uitam ita summatim disponere possumus. Primã qdẽ
optimam atq; perfectissimam: qua diis coniungitur: agitq; ibi uitam su
g peris cognatissimam: ac propter summam quandam similitudinem: uitã
illis iam unitam: nec sui quidem iuris sed deorum: dũ suum quidem subit intelle
ctum: suscitat autem interim ineffabile munus caracterẽq; uniformis illius substã
tiæ superorum: copulansq; simile simili: suũ uidelicet illi lumini lumen: ipsi. s. uni
hi super oẽm essentiam uitamq; extãti: ipsum essentiæ suæ uitæq; proprie uniformæ
q̃maxime. Secundum uitæ gradum ponimus in quo animus a uita diuina de
uenit in seipsum: statuitq; mentem atq; scientiam principem actiõis: ubi euoluit
j multitudinem rationum omniformes specierum differentias contuet̃: atq; in idẽ
& quod intelligit & quod intelligitur: in se colligit: repræsentatq;: & quasi per ima
ginem exprimit intellectualem essentiam: in uno quodam uidelicet naturã intel
k ligibilem comprahendens. Vitam deniq; tertiam arbitramur quæ cum poten
l tiis deterioribus commertium iam init. Agitq; cum illis imaginatiõibus sensibus
q; ratione carentibus utitur: deterioribusq; prorsus impletur.

Distinctio rerum in genera quattuor. Item de imaginibus atq; umbris.

m PLato in septimo de re publica: rerum ordinem lineæ comparat: per con
tinuam rerum connexionem. Quæ quidem ex mutua similitudiue pro
ficiscitur. Similitudo uero est unitas quædam in rebus proueniens ex
ipsa simpliciter unitate uniuersi principio. Quæ sane totum uolens simillimum
n sibi facere: neq; tamen simpliciter unum: saltem maxime fecit unitum. Ad quam
unionem confert etiam ipsa principii bonitas. Cum enim ipsius boni natura sit:
quasi diffundere se ꝓ oĩa per processũ: uicissimq; ꝓ appetitũ ad se unũ oĩa reuocare

a B *comprehendendi* b B *ad flumina* c MS, Dur *est* d B *flumine* e B *habitusque* (erron.) f MS *solisque* g MS *hac* h B *extant* i MS *uniforme* j MS *uniformesque* (erron.) k MS *intelligibilium* (erron.) l MS *in maginationibus* (erron.) m MS *comparat: propter* n B om. *unitum* merito uniuersum summopere reddit unitum. Diuiditur autem mundana apud Platonem linea in partes præcipue duas scilicet in genus insensibile atq; sensibile. Primũ illud longe amplius est secũdo: hoc uidelicet insé continés. Illud iterum in res intelligibiles diuiditur atque cogitabiles idest in formas diuias atq; mathematicas. Hoc autem in res quasi substantiales atque imaginales. Substantiales quidem corpora sunt. Imaginales autem imagines corporum atque umbre Imagines quidem repræsentationesque corporum speculares subiecto quodam indigent tres habente conditiones: densitatem: & lenitatem: atque nitorem: Opus quidem est densitate ne influens apparitio si i subiectum inciderit nimis rarũ subito transfluat. Atque ita imago ex multis defluxibus non fiat una. Lenitate uero. Ne asperitas ipsa propter partes suas partim quidem prominentes: partim uero profundas: inequalitatis causa sit imagini componende. Nitore quoque splendido: ut imago alioquin exilem habens formam conspicua fiat. Sic enim & minutissime queque in domus ipsius aere compositiones sæpe patent oculis in radiis p fenestellas rimasque penetrãtibus. Alioquin ob tenuem naturam nobis occulte: a

Dicendum ergo secundum sententiam Platonicam in sophista apparẽtes imagines: esse substantias quasdam quorundam simulachrorum machinatiõe quadã demonica fabricatas. Iam uero & umbræ: quas cum imaginibus cõmemorat quasi cognatas: eiusmodi naturam habent: sunt enim & ipse corporum figurarumq; b imagines plurimamque sympatiam: idest compassionem consensionemque cum illis ipsis habent a quibus decidunt. Quemadmodum declarant quotcũque magorum artes pronuntiant promittuntque ad idola umbrasque conficere: Quid c uero dicam imaginum umbrarumque uires perquas fiunt in animalibus ratiõe carentibus sæpe multa: quæ omnem superant rationem. Nam hyenam ferũt calcantem canis in alto sedentis umbram: illum ex alto præcipitare statim atque deuorare. Atqui Aristoteles inquit mulierem in purgatione menstrui sanguinis constitutam fedare sanguine quodam obiectum speculum & imaginem. Imagines denique substantias quasdam esse. Plato confirmat ubi ait. Sicut cogitabilia ad intelligibilia se se habent: Sic imaginalia ad uisibilia corpora: Cogitabilia uero idest Mathematica: res in se quædam speciesque sunt. Similiter imagines: cum sint na d turales quidam ex rebus naturalibus effluxus naturam quoque suam habent.

Quomodo bonum est super essentiam: Et quomõ cognoscatur. e

PLato in sexto de repu. ita diuia comparat. Solem quidem ipsi bono. Lu f men uero solis Veritati a bono mananti. Colores ex lumine dependentes: formalibus idealibusque rerum rationibus: a bono sub ueritate pendentibus. Oculos autem & genitos & illustratos a sole cõparat intellectibus ad bonum similiter se habentibus. Subdit preterea. Quemadmodum sol sup inferiorum uisibilium generationem extat. Ita bonum super ens & essentiam. Item sicut sol lumenq; suũ colores supat atq; uisus: ita bonũ ueritasq; boni lumẽ: est sup ideas: entia: mentes. Denique sicut Sol uisibilibus nostris & oculis: nõ solũ actionis pfectionisq; causa ẽ: sed et generatiõis naturæ uirtutis: ita bonum ẽ oium tam

a B *tenuam* b *ipsae* c MS om. *que* d MS *mathematicas res* e *quomodo*
f MS *comparat solem*

intelligibilibus q̄ intellectibus auctor. His itaque omnibus est superius. Cum
a igitur ipsum bonum sit intelligibilibus: intellectu: ueritate superius non eadem
b ratione qua intelligibilia cognosci potest: sed Diuino quodam intuitu perceptio
bc neque intelligentiam excedente. Quam Plato illustrationem animæ nominat.
d Tunc uidelicet ita diuinitus illustrate postq̄ a bono p negationem segregauerit:
omnia quæ sunt post bonum: uicissimq; rite admodum comparauerit. Hac scilicet ratione reflectens erigensq; se in ipsum: quasi facta iam resupina: quæ hacte-
e nus fuerat. q. prona. Solis inter mundana uidetur ingenitus. Quoniam nihil
amittit suum Nihil alienum rursus admittit. Cætera uero omnia radios ab illo no
f uos semper accipiunt: Dum ille in proprio centro reuoluitur. Atque ita cœlestia
circum & inferiora collustrat. Sol igitur qua ratione talis est: mundanis omnibus
g dominatur: qtū uero corpus & mobile alicui subest. Supremæ uidelicet: q̄ spheræ
dicitur circuitum identitatis habere. Hinc enim & Sol ipse fertur. sphera rursus
h illa: ad circuitum refertur sapientissimum: idest mentem. Inter hæc momento si
cut in rebus diuiduis est indiuiduum uelut unitas atq; punctum: sic in rebus cor
ruptibilibus: incorruptibile aliquid esse.

Bonum triplex: scilicet in nobis: In idea: super ideam.

i PLato tres uenerandi boni cōsiderat gradus. Vnum quidem in omnibus
scilicet statū quēdam uitæ ex intelligentia & uoluptate rite permixtum.
Alium autem inter ideas. Alium denique super ideas. Inter ideas enim:
Aliæ quidem rerum essentias constituunt: atque definiunt. Aliæ uero perfectio
nes suas essentiis adhibent. Illarum præterea prima est ens & essentia. Quod qui
dem genus est ad omnes alias ideas essentiales: idest quæ ad constituendas essen-
j tias pertinent. Velut ad ipsum animal: Ipsum hominem: ipsum æqum. Idearum
uero ad perfectiones omnium pertinentium: Prima est ipsum non simpliciter bo
num sed ideale. Quod similiter genus est idearum omnium ad perfectiones rerū
quomodolibet attinentium. Quales sunt ipsum pulchrum. Ipsum iustum & sa-
piens atque similia. Sicut ergo essentiæ rerum perfectiones suas origine quadam
antecedunt: esse enim naturaliter præcedit bene esse: ita ens & essētia in ipsa idea-
k rum serie ipsum antecedit ibidem ideale bonum. Sed ipsum tādem simpliciter bo
kl num ē ente superius: simulque inparticipabile bonum. Nam bonum inter ideas
in participabile quidem est: sed ē interim cum essentia: siue sub ente. In nobis tan
m dem & sub essentia est: & participabile ~~quidem est: sed iterim cum essētia siue sub~~
m ~~ente. In nobis tandem & sub essentia est & participabile~~ bonum. Iam uero cōmu
nis omnium consensus definiens bonum: cuius gratia omnia & quod appetunt
omnia: uaticinari uidetur illud nec ullius gratia esse: nec aliud prorsus appetere.
n Illud itaque necesse ens aliquod. Nec aliquod bonum in ente. Omnis enim essen
tia bonum appetit: idest esse secundum naturam: ac bene perfecteque se se habere. Bonum quoque in essentia illius ipsius substantiæ gratia est quæsitū. ut uide
licet secundum naturam perfecte se habeat. Nec est bonum simpliciter: sed alicu
ius duntaxat & in aliquo bonum. Denique: ut summatim dicam. Illud ideale bo
op num in ipso ente essentiaque tanq̄ pars & alicuius & in aliquo totus gratia collo
catum. Itaque super illud est ipsum simpliciter bonum.

a MS *quam intellectu* b *perceptioneque* c B *nominant* d B *illustrante* e * f B om. *in* g * h MS, B *memento* i MS *nobis* for *omnibus* j MS, B *equum* k MS om. *Sed ... imparticipabile bonum* l * m * n MS *nec esse* (correct), B *necesse est esse eos* (erron.) o MS *essentiaque est tanquam pars alicuius* p MS, B *totius*

De demonibus.

Marsilius Ficinus Philippo Carducio Dilectissimo Suo. S. D.

CVm procli platonici commentarium in platonicum alcibiadem: e græca lingua in latinam non tam ad uerbum q̄ ad sensum interpætrarer: recordarerque te platonicam de demonibus sententiam summatim desiderare: hanc ibi repertam mittere ad te constitui. Lege fœliciter. a

Philosophia cum fortuna & diuitiis non coniungitur. b

Marsilius Ficinus Philippo Valori Oratori apud pontificē Florētino. S. D.

INimici hoīs domestici eius: dōestici qdē mei: q mihi sūt multi: multūq; molesti: quoniam neque philosophici: neque philosophico uictu suppellectilique contenti: frequēter obiiciunt. Cæteros medice domus cliētes atque clientulos: paucis annis inde q̄ plurimum accepisse. Me uero āplissime huius familie familiarissimum: ac (ut ita dixerim) clientissimum: multis ānis reportasse non multum. Sed audi parumper mi ualor: nostram hāc ad meos apologiā. Cæteri quidem amici medicum: non dum quantū uoluerant: acceperunt. Ego uero quantum uoluissem: si modo petissem. Et habeo certe quantū uolo. Illi plerūque præcario. Ego gratis. Medices item aliis aliena dederunt. Mihi sua: Nos igiť ita causam apud domesticos nostram perbelle probamus. At illi: quod mihi molestissimum est: non comprobāt. Oportuerat enim iandiu uel meos una mecum quandoque fore philosophos. Vel me non fuisse philosophum. Sed fatum uideť ab exordio rerum. Neque philosophos ullos unq̄ fore diuites: Neq; rursum diuites facile fore philosophos. Nullum enim fuisse fertur mineruę cum iunone commertium. Nec eisdem Iuppiter & phœbus: Venusque fauēt: quibus Mercurius simul atque Saturnus. Neque cum sapientia rerum contemplatrice: facile rerum domina fortuna consentit. Porro unum est necessarium. Vbi intenderis ingeniū ualet. Ingeniū igitur & fortuna diuisum in nobis habent imperium. Hoc quidem in animi cultum plurimum dominaņtur. Hæc uero q̄ plurimum in rebus externis. Hinc & bona fortunæ dicuntur. Sed in corpore utrumque forsitan æque potest. Verū non licet epistolæ nūc ultra philosophari. Negocium. n. iā aliud urget. de

Vbi Plus fortunæ: ibi sapientiæ minus: atque uicissim.

Marsilius Ficinus Bindacio recasolāo ciui optimo & dilectissimo suo. S. P. D.

ARistotelicum illud: ubi plus intelligentiæ: ibi fortunæ minus: atque uicissim: ubi plus fortunæ illic minus intelligentiæ. Plerique forsitan sic accipient: ut sapientissimi quique philosophique minime fortunati sint. Quod & carmina pythagorica comprobant & res ipsa confirmat: nec non Astronomica ratio: præcipue per Mercuriū atque Saturnum philosophiam significari putans. Hos uero cum Ioue: Sole: Venere: affluentiam rerum significātibus: nullum officii habere commertium. Denique legitimi ueritatis contemplatores & negligunt fortunæ bona: & ipsi a fortunatissimis negliguntur. Neque principibus placent: neque uulgo probantur. Vt nō mirum sit eos minimum habere fortunę. Vicissim uero fortunatissimi quiq; plerumq; negligunt sapientiam: plurimumq; temere & improuide uiuunt: fortunæ uidelicet afflatu cōfisi: Ego aūt & si supiorem interpętratione minime respuo: utilius tamen atque diuinius Aristotelicum illud interpætrarer. Cum enim compertum habeamus: homines f g h i

a MS *interpretarer* b B om. *non* c *philosophi* d Dur, MS *cultu* e MS om. *dominantur* Dur *dominator* f B *putant* g B om. *si* h MS *interpretationem* i MS *illum interpretarer*

quo prudentiores ſunt:eo minus caſu uiuere:paucioraque in familia rebuſque
ſuis agi fortuito : coniectare proculdubio poſſumus : deo ſapientiſſimo rerum
a omnium auctori:nihil uſq̃ caſu contingere. Sed omnia prouidenter eſſe diſpoſi-
ta:Atq; uiciſſim:cũ uideamus cæleſtia & naturalia oĩa extra fortunã ordine certo
diſpoſita:concludere licet ſummam his omnibus ſapientiam dominari.

b Prohœmium in compararionem Solis ad Deum.

c Marſilius Ficinus Eberardo inclyto Duci Virtembergenſi & montis peligardi Seniori.S.P.D.

d MArtinus noſter Vranius.i.cæleſtis:reuera cæleſtiũ contẽplator:lõgo me
e cũ ſermone tractauit:qualis ſol ẽ inter ſidera:talem:extra cõuerſia:te eẽ
f inter oẽs germaniæ pricipes. Quibus equidẽ laudibus.q.quibuſdã uir-
g tutis tuæ radiis iflãmatus:Epiſtoliũ illud iãpridẽ ad te dedi:igẽtis quidẽ i te nr̃i pi
gnus amoris. Sed non pignus(ut par fuerat) ingẽs. Quãobrẽ ut aliquãto uberi
us:& ſũme dignitati tuæ & meo ſatis deſiderio faciã ad ipſũ germaniæ ſolẽ nunc
Platonicũ & dyoniſiacũ ſolẽ mitto:mirũ in te amorẽ noſtrũ ſplendore paſſim de
claraturũ. Queadmodũ uero Mercurius phœbi mũera ad hominũ ingenia tranſ
fert:ita phœbeũ hoc munus noſtrũ ad uos feret Ioãnes ſtreler:nobis quaſi Mercurius alter. Leges ergo fœliciter phœbee priceps:quæ de cõparatiõe ſolis ad Deũ
h ptim Plato dionyſiuſq; Areopagita tractarũt:ptim ego interpretror:atq; cõmẽtor
i uiue fœlix in hac umbra uitæ poſt hanc ſole tandem perpetuo fruiturus. Vale.

jk Laudes ſæculi noſtri tanq̃ aurei ab ingeniis aueroi̊s.

l Marſilius Ficinus Paulo Middelburgenſi inſigni phyſico & Aſtronomo.S.P.D.

QVæ poetæ quõdã de ſæculis quattuor cecinerũt:plũbeo:ferreo:argẽteo
aureo. Plato noſter i libris de rep.ad quattuor hominũ igenia tranſtulit
diſputãs aliis hominũ igeniis:plũbũ quoddã:aliis ferrũ:aliis argentum.
m aliis aurũ naturaliter inſitũ. Si qd igit̃ ſæculũ appellãdũ nobis ẽ aureum:illud eſt
pculdubio tale:qd aurea paſſim ingenia profert. Id aũt eſſe noſtrũ hoc ſæculũ mi
nime dubitabit:qui præclara ſæculi huius inuẽta cõſiderare uoluerit. Hoc.n.ſæ-
culum tanq̃ aureũ liberales diſciplinas ferme iam extinctas reduxit in lucẽ. Grã-
maticã:Poeſim : Oratoriam:Picturã:Sculpturã:Architecturã:Muſicam. Anti-
quũ ad orphycã Lyram carmĩqũ cantũ. Idq; florẽtiæ:Quod ue apud priſcos fuerat uenerandum:Sed iam prope deletum. Sapientiã coniunxit cum eloquentia.
Cum arte militari prudentiam. Idq; potiſſimũ in Fœderico Vrbinate Duce: tãq̃
in pallade declarauit:filiumq; eius & fratrem uirtutis illius effecit heredes. In te
quoque mi Paule perfeciſſe uidetur Aſtronomiam:Florẽtię quin etiam Platonicam diſciplinam i lucem:e tenebris reuocauit. In Germania temporibus noſtris
imprimendorum librorum inuenta ſunt inſtrumenta. Tabule præterea : quibus
hora(ut ita dixerim)una: per omne ſæculum tota cœli facies aperitur:ut præter
mittam machinam Florentinam:quottidianos cœleſtium motus agentem. Iam
uero Germãicas tabulas Michelo ctius noſter diligenter expræſſas ad uos affert:
n inclyto Duci ur̃o dicandas:Cœleſte quidẽ munus :cœleſti pricipe dignũ: dignũ
præterea(ut arbitror)quod & abſte cœleſtium cõtemplatore probetur : dignum
o deniq; cõmendatiõe apud uos noſtra. Valete. Die.xiii. Septẽbris. Mcccclxxxxii.

Finis Vndecimi Epiſtolarum Marſilii.

a MS *providentur* b *comparationem* c *Eberardo comiti Virembergensi*
d *mecum* e *controversiam* f *quasi* g MS *a te* h MS *ergo* i MS *ac*
vive j Dur *aureis* (erron.) MS *aurei* k B *Averois* (erron.) MS *aureis* l MS
salute m *quod* n *vestro* o MS om. *Die xiiij*

Biographical Notes

The Biographical Notes for this volume have been grouped for convenience into three sets: (i) correspondents in German lands (some of whom visited Italy), (ii) correspondents in Italy, and (iii) the long list of people who are mentioned in Ficino's letter to Martin Prenninger and who formed part of Ficino's circle or could be considered members of a Platonic 'Academy'. Ficino himself divides this list into groups, and his sequence, rather than the alphabetical order, has therefore been preserved in section (iii).

Giovanni Pico della Mirandola and **Giovanni Cavalcanti** are ascribed German ancestry by Ficino in Letter 2, but their families had been established in Italy for many generations, so they have been included among the Italians. **Paul of Middelburg** has been listed here as a 'German', since his origin was in the Low Countries. However, from 1480 onwards he was resident permanently in Italy.

German correspondents

Eberhard V, Count of Württemberg (1445-1496): also known as Eberhard the Bearded, and later as Duke Eberhard I. He was educated under the supervision of Johannes Nauclerus (see below) and became fifth Count of Württemberg at the age of fourteen, inheriting the leadership of one part of a divided principality. He approached his duties with great dedication and he travelled to Jerusalem in 1468, becoming a knight of the Order of the Holy Sepulchre. To commemorate this visit he adopted the palm as his symbol. Eberhard introduced extensive administrative and ecclesiastical reforms within his patrimony. In 1477 he founded the University of Tübingen and became widely respected for his patronage of learning and education, even though at his father's specific insistence he had not been trained in Latin. In 1482, by means of a treaty with his cousin, he was able to reunite the divided principality of Württemberg, thus regaining control of Württemberg-Mompelgard, with its capital city Stuttgart. (Mompelgard, called by Ficino Mons Peligardus, is now in France, and called Montbéliard). In 1495 his state was elevated to a Duchy and he became its first Duke. Ficino is already using the title Duke rather than Count, perhaps honorifically, when he first writes to him in 1492.

In 1474 he married Barbara, daughter of Ludovico Gonzaga, Marquis of Mantua. The only child of this marriage died in infancy, and Eberhard was succeeded on his death by his cousin, former ruler of the other half of the principality, Eberhard the Younger.

Georg Herivart (Herwart) of Augsburg (1461-1508): prominent lawyer from a family of merchants in Augsburg, Herivart became a canon of the cathedral of Regensburg, the principal city of Bavaria. He also had commercial interests in Venice. He visited Ficino in Florence (Letter 1) and cherished the memory of his visit as 'the happiest days of my life'. Herivart appears to have been a friend of Martin Prenninger and, like him, an early promoter of Ficino's work in Germany. He became a member of the *Sodalitas Augustana*, a literary circle founded in 1503 by the humanist statesman Konrad Peutinger (1465-1547) along lines already established elsewhere by the German poet Conrad Celtis. He died during a further visit to Italy, at Aquapendente, between Florence and Rome, in 1508.

Ludwig (d. 1512) **and Johannes Nauclerus (Vergenhans)** (1425-1510): Swabian brothers of noble birth. Ludwig became a doctor of both civil and canon law in Italy. Johannes became a jurist, teacher, theologian and historian. They both served the divided principality of Württemberg. In the part of the principality centred on Stuttgart, Ludwig was Chancellor of the principality for Count Eberhard VI (1447-1504) and later was Provost of the Collegiate Church. After the re-unification of the principality under Eberhard V (see above), in 1485, he retained the position of Chancellor.

Johannes served Eberhard V as tutor in the 1450s. In the 1460s, he was Provost of the Collegiate Church of Stuttgart under Eberhard VI. During 1464 and 1465 Johannes taught Law at the University of Basel, and in 1466 travelled to Rome. At the foundation of the University of Tübingen in 1477, he moved back to Eberhard V's part of the principality, to teach Law. He was the first Rector of the university and from 1479 priest of the Collegiate Church. In 1483 he became the university's second Chancellor and thus had an interest in the two students entrusted to Ficino (Letter 7), although it is to his brother Ludwig that Ficino writes.

His own *World Chronicle*, covering the whole of human history from the time of Adam to the fifteenth century, was published posthumously in 1516, with a foreword by Reuchlin.

Paul of Middelburg (1446-1534): recognised as a leading mathematician of the age, Paul was born in Middelburg, capital of the province of Zeeland; he studied at Leuven (Louvain) and taught there until invited to Italy. From 1476 to 1478 he was appointed to teach Guidobaldo, son of the Duke of Urbino. He continued to serve the Duke as court astrologer, but was also appointed professor of sciences at the University of Padua.

In 1488 he was endowed with the Benedictine Abbey of S. Cristoforo in Castel Durante, and continued to enjoy the support of Guidobaldo, who succeeded his father as Duke, as well as the friendship of Maximilian, the future Holy Roman Emperor. He was appointed Bishop of Fossombrone in 1494. He thereupon destroyed some of his earlier works relating to mathematical and astronomical controversies, but he nevertheless chose an astronomical coat of arms for himself as bishop. His important works on calendar reform led to his inclusion in the Fifth Lateran Council (1512-1518), and he corresponded with Copernicus. The scholar and controversialist Julius Caesar Scaliger (1484-1558) was his godson.

Of another controversy we know only the barest facts: Paul had been awarded a canonry in Middelburg after he completed his studies at Leuven, but he was deprived of it and this 'usurpation', as he called it, left a bitterness against the country of his birth.

Martin 'Uranius' Prenninger (c.1450-1501): a leading lawyer and chancellor of the bishopric of Constance, Prenninger was a friend of Ficino's from his first visit to

Florence in 1476, while pursuing doctoral studies. He remained a friend, although they did not meet again until the period covered by this volume.

In December 1490 Prenninger had moved from Constance to the recently founded University of Tübingen, where he was Professor of Ecclesiastical Law until his death. He also served as counsellor to Count Eberhard V and travelled to Rome on his behalf in 1492. While at Tübingen he became a friend of the humanist scholar Johannes Reuchlin, and they sent two students to Ficino, mentioned in Letters 7, 10 and 32. In the current book there are six letters addressed to Prenninger (Letters 5, 10, 13, 25, 28, and 29); he is also mentioned in the letters to Count Eberhard (Letters 23 and 34).

Ficino speaks of his presence in Florence in letters 22 and 23 of this volume. More biographical details can be found in *Letters*, **8**, pp. 130-31.

Dionysius Reuchlin (b.1473): younger brother of Johannes Reuchlin and educated at his expense. After obtaining a Batchelor's degree from the university of Basel, Dionysius spent almost two years in Florence, during 1491-2. Placed in Ficino's care, he appears to have been lodged with and taught by Ficino's friend Giorgio Antonio Vespucci, even if he was in the overall care of Ficino. Dionysius also attended public lectures in the *Studio*, learning Greek from Demetrius (Dimitri) Chalcondylas, and studying with Poliziano. He subsequently returned to Tübingen, obtaining his Master's degree in 1494, and teaching Greek (though his official position was not fully recognised by the faculty). In 1498 he was appointed to teach Greek in Heidelberg, though only for a year. Later, he studied Hebrew and took holy orders.

Johannes Reuchlin (1455-1522): born in Pforzheim, in Baden, another part of the old province of Swabia, adjacent to the principality of Württemberg. Reuchlin studied Greek, Latin and Law in the universities of Freiburg, Paris and Basel. During the 1480s he was in the service of Count Eberhard V of Württemberg, and formed a friendship with Martin Prenninger. Reuchlin travelled to Italy with the count in 1482 and again in 1490, just prior to the first letters of this volume. A third visit took place in 1498.

Reuchlin was greatly influenced by his visits to Italy, where he met Ficino, Pico and other scholars. In his Hebrew grammar, *De Rudimentis hebraicis* (1506), Reuchlin refers back to having completed his studies of Greek in Florence with Demetrius Chalcondylas. When he sent his younger brother to study in Florence, accompanied by Johannes Streler, he asked Johannes to obtain for him copies of Ficino's Plato and Plotinus translations and the *Platonic Theology*, as well as works by Pico and Poliziano.

Besides his interest in Greek philosophy, Reuchlin introduced the Christian study of Hebrew and Hebrew sources into German lands. In addition to his Hebrew grammar, he wrote two books based on his Hebrew studies: *De verbo mirifico* (1494) and *De arte cabalistica* (1517). He also conducted a famous controversy with Johann Pfefferkorn and the Dominicans of Cologne, who advocated the burning of all Hebrew books. In the preface to *De arte cabbalistica* he refers to the pre-eminence of Florentine scholarship.

When Duke Eberhard I died in 1496, Reuchlin went to Heidelberg rather than serve his successor, though he returned on the latter's death. In 1498 Reuchlin paid a third visit to Rome. He later served as Imperial Judge for the Swabian Confederation (1502-1512) and as professor at Ingolstadt (1520-1521) and Tübingen (1521-1522).

After Martin Luther's challenge to the Church in 1517, Reuchlin remained loyal to Rome even though his great-nephew Philip Melanchthon was an ardent supporter of Luther.

Johann Streler or Sträler (d.1516): born in the Swabian city of Ulm, Streler was a student at the University of Tübingen and accompanied Dionysius Reuchlin to Florence to study under Ficino's guidance. He is mentioned in Letters 7, 23 and 32.

It seems that the two young men studied Greek with Demetrius Chalcondylas and Latin literature with Vespucci. They both greatly admired Pico della Mirandola. On returning to Ulm, Streler became a priest and also served with Reuchlin as one of the three judges who led the Swabian League.

On a further visit to Italy, in 1493, he obtained a copy of Ficino's Plague treatise and translated it into Latin for German readers. This survives in MS Augsburg 4° 121, folios 1-29.

Several German humanist writers dedicated works to him. Three of the letters that he wrote to Johannes Reuchlin can be found in *Illustrorum virorum eptistolae* (Hagenau, 1519).

Correspondents in Italy

Marco Barbo (1420-1491): Venetian cardinal from 1467 and Patriarch of Aquilea, Barbo resided in Rome, holding the highest office within the College of Cardinals under Pope Innocent VIII. Barbo had given protection and support to Ficino in the publication of his Plotinus commentaries, although he died on 2nd March 1491, a year before the Plotinus commentaries appeared in print, and just over one month before the first letters of this volume. For Barbo's secretary, Antonio Calderini, see below; for further details of Barbo's life, see *Letters*, **7**, pp. 191-92.

Antonio Calderini (1445-1494): trained as a notary, Calderini worked for the city and the Medici bank, both in Florence and on important missions abroad, until 1484, when he entered the service of Cardinal Marco Barbo in Rome. While there, he took holy orders and a year after the cardinal's death he asked to serve the parish of his own birth, in San Giovanni Val d'Arno. However, it is thought that he was still in Rome when he died in 1494.

In this volume, Ficino writes to Calderini following the cardinal's death (Letter 9). See also *Letters*, **1**, 106; **7**, 15, 31 and 45; and **9**, 19 and 23.

Giovanni Canacci: a close friend of Ficino and member of a patrician family, he was a *Priore* of the city in 1491. He was also a member of the society of 'Mammola' described in *Letters*, **9**.

Filippo Carducci (1449-c.1520): of noble birth, Carducci held public office in Florence, serving as *Priore* in 1485, 1493, and 1497, and later as *gonfaloniere di giustizia* (1501) and in other senior posts. He was a close friend of Ficino's and was called upon to assist when the Plotinus edition ran into problems (see Letter 26 and note 6 to that letter). Ficino also sent him his translation of Proclus on daemons, from the *Alcibiades* commentary (Letter 30).

Bernardo Dovizi of Bibbiena (1470-1520): the son of a notary, Dovizi entered the Medici household as a child in 1479, benefiting from a privileged humanist education. He entered the service of Lorenzo de' Medici in about 1488, and accompanied Piero de' Medici to Rome, undertaking important tasks that assured his place in the service of the Medici, both in the city and as a diplomat. Later he was appointed cardinal and papal treasurer to Pope Leo X. For his literary activities and further details, see *Letters*, **9**, pp. 122-3.

Piero Dovizi (1456-1514): eldest of five sons of a notary in Bibbiena, near Arezzo. He came as tutor to Lorenzo's children after Poliziano was dismissed, bringing with him his younger brother Bernardo (see above). Piero Dovizi became a secretary to Lorenzo, at first under Niccolò Michelozzi, but later acted as head of the secretariat. Much correspondence survives which shows his role in key negotiations. He was also sent on a number of diplomatic missions.

In 1494, when the Medici were expelled, Piero Dovizi left Florence as an exile, settling in Venice. In 1495 he wrote to Ficino expressing a desire to return (see *Sup. Fic.*, II, pp. 218-220), but this did not happen. However, he was able to serve the interests of Florence in Venice after the restoration of the Medici in 1513.

Cristoforo Landino (1425-1498): by 1491, Landino was a respected Professor in the University of Florence, teaching Rhetoric and Poetry. His own collection of poems, *Xandra*, was an early work (1458), but his best known writings include *Disputationes Camaldulenses*, written by 1474 but published in 1480. Ficino appears as a participant in this dialogue, together with Alberti, Lorenzo de' Medici and other leading figures. Landino's commentaries on the ancient poets included profound insights based on the interpretation of allegory. His commentary on Dante appeared in 1481 (See *Letters*, **5**, 49) and on Virgil's *Aeneid* in 1488. From 1487 Landino was writing his dialogue on the theme of 'true nobility', discussing whether it is acquired through birth or through the exercise of virtue.

His relationship with Ficino began as teacher and mentor (see Letter 12), but they became great friends and learned much from each other. There are no letters extant between Landino and Ficino, perhaps because they were in regular personal contact.

Janus Lascaris (1445-1534): born in Byzantium, of royal blood, Lascaris came with his father to Venice in 1464, under the protection of Cardinal Bessarion. He studied Latin in Padua with Demetrius Chalcondylas, who moved to Florence in 1472, and in 1489 invited Lascaris to join him. He entered the service of Lorenzo de' Medici, who sent him to Greece and the former capital of Byzantium, to acquire books and manuscripts but also to gather information on the possible reconquest of Byzantium from the Turks. Some of the manuscripts acquired are discussed in Letter 29.

In September, 1492, Lascaris succeeded Chalcondylas as professor of Greek in the Florentine *Studio,* even though his relations with Poliziano and Landino were often stormy. He set about publishing Greek literature in Florence, using new fonts for printing Greek. After the expulsion of the Medici in 1494, he was among the Greek émigrés who were attracted to the French king Charles VIII in the hopes that France would lead a reconquest of Byzantium. When Poliziano died in 1494, Lascaris was asked by the Signoria to sort out his books, but when the French returned to France in 1495 Lascaris followed, taking a number of Medici manuscripts with him. After the death of Charles, Lascaris remained under the protection of Cardinal Georges d'Amboise of Rouen and entered the service of the new King Louis XII, probably as secretary and interpreter. He accompanied Louis XII to Milan and made contact with Aldus Manutius in Venice, whom he assisted in finding new Greek and Latin texts for publication. He also promoted interest in Greek literature within the French court. During 1503 he was back in Italy, visiting Venice and Rome, and returned again in 1504 as French ambassador to Venice. He remained in Venice for several years, returning periodically to France. After the election to the papacy of Giovanni de' Medici in 1513, Lascaris went to Rome, where he was able to assist Giovanni to influence the organisation of the university, as well as continuing his own studies and representing the French king. From 1513 to his death in 1534, Lascaris divided his time between Paris and Rome.

Pier Leone of Spoleto (d.1492): little detail is known of the career of Ficino's good friend the distinguished physician, Pier Leone, because he left hardly any completed written works. However, his fame as a teacher was outstanding. He held the post of professor in the medical faculty of Pisa University with an unusually high level of pay and privileges until 1487. He seems thereafter to have spent his time between Florence, Padua and Rome, tending his noble patients and pursuing research on ancient medical and scientific texts. He was among the first to revive the medicine of Hippocrates and Galen, to replace practice based on medieval Arabic texts.

In 1487 or early 1488 Pier Leone was in Milan, at the bedside of Ludovico il Moro. During 1489 he was in Rome looking after Cardinal Marco Barbo. In June 1490 he attended Lorenzo de' Medici at a spa near Volterra. In July 1490 he was back in Rome, but was offered a prestigious and highly paid chair of practical medicine at the University of Padua, which he took up in November of that year. Pico and Poliziano joined him there in June 1491, and together they embarked on a study of mystical and philosophical works by Avempace (Ibn Bajja), Abubacer (Ibn Tufayl), Averroes (Ibn Rushd), Abraham Abulafia and Moses of Narbonne. Pier Leone had already commissioned translations of Hebrew texts in the mid-1480s, including the Kabbalistic *Sefer Yetzirah* (Book of Creation). By December of 1491 Pier Leone had decided to leave Padua. After a visit to Spoleto, he returned to Florence by February and lodged with the Martelli family while attending Lorenzo de' Medici, whose health had deteriorated sharply. For the unusual circumstances of his death the day after that of his patient, see *Letters*, 7, pp. 201-2. Ficino praises Pier Leone's penetration of the mathematics of both Plato and Aristotle in his *Timaeus* commentary (ch. 43).

Letters 3 and 11 are addressed to Pier Leone. Though their meaning is enigmatic, they may be read as encouraging Pier Leone to return to their common interests in Platonic authors.

Cristoforo Marsuppini (b. 1444, died after 1513): brother of Carlo (see List of Friends below), Marsuppini was entitled by birth to play a part in the government of Florence, but found himself continually excluded on account of undischarged debts. In 1477 Ficino had helped him obtain some measure of tax relief, but his fortunes failed to recover and in 1479 he was held in the debtors' prison for a while. By 1484 he appeared to be once again eligible for office, but was not successful in taking up any position.

In 1469 he married Lucia Acciaiuoli. A second marriage followed in which three daughters and a son were born to him. Cristoforo held lands around Prato, but was able to participate fully in the intellectual life of Ficino's circle. He was one of the speakers in Ficino's *De amore* (his commentary on Plato's *Symposium*), and in 1491 he was in Rome, as Letter 6 to Cardinal Raffaele Riario shows.

Mazzingo di Paradiso Mazzinghi (b. 1451): some time between 1475 and 1478 Mazzinghi appears to have been a pupil of Pier Leone of Spoleto, who was teaching medicine at the University of Pisa. He subsequently became a physician and was also Professor of Medicine at the University of Pisa before 1479. In this year he resigned his post, being unwilling to accept the new arrangements in the university.

Ficino and his household were among his patients (Letter 14). Little more is known about his life, beyond the fact that he came from an affluent Florentine family, and among his papers is preserved a manuscript translation of the Kabbalistic *Sefer Yetzirah* commissioned by Pier Leone (see above). Letter 14 in this volume is addressed to him, presenting the *Three Books on Life*, and there are two further letters in the twelfth book.

Cosimo de' Medici (1389-1464): first of the Medici family to figure in Ficino's life, Cosimo supported his earliest studies in Greek and appointed him to translate the works of Plato and Hermes Trismegistus. Banker, statesman and great philanthropist, Cosimo died when Ficino was 31 years old. For an account of his life, see *Letters*, **8**, p.125.

Giovanni de' Medici, later Pope Leo X (1475–1521): second son of Lorenzo, Giovanni was destined for the church from early boyhood. Among his first teachers were Poliziano, Bernardo Michelozzi, Gentile Becchi and Demetrius Chalcondylas; Ficino, too, may have played a part in his education.

His education proceeded in parallel with the accumulation of ecclesiastical benefices. At the age of thirteen, he became a Cardinal Deacon and Ficino presented him with translations of Iamblichus, Porphyry and Proclus to mark the occasion (*Letters*, **8**, 8 and 9). He lived thereafter in Rome, but after his father Lorenzo's death in 1492, he returned to assist his brother Piero in Florence. When Piero was expelled in 1494, Giovanni travelled to France, Germany and Holland, returning to Rome in 1500. There he established himself as a leading patron of culture and the arts, and after the restoration of the Medici in Florence, he was elected Pope Leo X. Further details of his life may be found in *Letters*, **8**, pp. 125-6.

Lorenzo de' Medici (1449-1492): grandson of Cosimo, son of Piero the Gouty, Lorenzo grew up under the influence of Ficino, his boyhood tutor. Their relationship became a friendship, which was under some strain after the Pazzi conspiracy in 1478, but then appears to have picked up again later. Ficino continued to dedicate his publications to him even after Lorenzo ceased to be his main financial patron. In 1487 Lorenzo arranged that his son Giovanni should transfer his place as cathedral canon to Ficino and also initiated the search for a further benefice on his behalf.

For more on his achievements, see *Letters*, **8**, pp. 126-7. In this current volume of letters, Lorenzo is praised as a poet and patron (Letter 8) and his death is recounted (Letters 18, 20 and Appendix).

Niccolò Michelozzi (1477-1527): mentioned in the final letter of this book, and recipient of several letters in *Letters*, **1** and **2**, Michelozzi was secretary to Lorenzo de' Medici for many years, to his son Piero de' Medici after him and to Piero di Lorenzo after a spell of imprisonment in 1494. From 1512 to 1527, he served as Chancellor of Florence. For further information, see *Letters*, **1**, p. 228.

Giovanni Pico della Mirandola (1463-1494): Ficino's friendship with Pico began in 1484 and survived the vicissitudes of Pico's career for the full ten years until his premature death at the age of 31. By the time of the letters in this volume, they had had several philosophical disagreements but appear to have remained on the warmest personal terms. From late 1489 Pico had been drawn into the circle of Matteo Bosso at Fiesole and then that of Girolamo Savonarola at San Marco, and his works were increasingly of an outwardly religious nature, though still deeply committed to philosophical themes. During 1491 he was working on a commentary on the Psalms, as well as his treatise *On Being and the One* which took issue with Ficino's ideas based on Plato's *Parmenides*, and was intended as part of a larger reconciliation of Platonic and Aristotelian thought.

The same year he left Florence in search of books and manuscripts in the libraries of Italy, in company with Poliziano and others. He continued to study with a view to taking holy orders, although Kabbalistic manuscripts occupied his interests. Returning to Florence, he died in the epidemic of 1494. For further details of his life and work, see *Letters,* **7**, pp. 142-147 and **8**, p. 128.

Raffaele Riario, Cardinal of S. Giorgio (1461-1521): in this volume (Letters 4 and 6), Ficino attempts to rekindle his earlier friendship with Riario, to whom he had last written in 1480. After leaving Florence in the wake of the Pazzi conspiracy (1478), Riario, a nephew of Pope Sixtus IV, received numerous benefices and embassies, as well as the post of *Camerlengo* (Chamberlain of the Holy Roman Church). He became a leading figure in papal politics, and a trusted counsellor, though never a credible candidate for the Holy See.

Letters, **4**, 26, 27, 28, 34, 39 and Appendix B reflect Ficino's close relationship with him during and immediately after the difficult period of the Pazzi conspiracy. *Letters*, **5**, 3, 5 and 33 appear all to have gone unanswered.

Bindaccio Ricasoli (c.1444-1524): a member of one of the oldest noble families in Florence, and active in the city's government from 1478, Ricasoli was a student of Ficino's from his youth and remained a lifetime friend and follower.

Although only five letters in the collection are addressed to him, he is mentioned in five further letters, and is described as closely connected to Ficino and very dear to him. He was a member of the society of 'Mammola' mentioned in *Letters*, **9** and the recipient of an important letter on Prayer in that volume (Letter 33). In this book he is the addressee of Letters 24, 27 and 32, and he features in Ficino's *De Sole* of 1493. After Ficino's death, Ricasoli was regarded as a leader of the surviving circle of Ficino's followers. Giovanni Corsi's *Life of Marsilio Ficino* was dedicated to him in 1506. For further details of his life, see *Letters*, **9**, p. 129.

Francesco Soderini (1453-1524): younger brother of Paolantonio, Francesco began his career with the study of law, but in 1478 he became Bishop of Volterra. From 1481 he was working in the Roman Curia, rising to the post of apostolic secretary under Pope Innocent VIII in 1487. In 1496 he served as ambassador to the French king, Charles VIII, and was made a cardinal in1503. For further details of his career, see *Letters*, **7**, p. 212-3.

Paolantonio Soderini (1448-1499): eldest of the four Soderini brothers, Paolantonio played an active part in the political life of the city under Lorenzo de' Medici, to whom he was a trusted adviser and ambassador. He was also a close friend of Ficino's. For further details of his career, see *Letters*, **9**, p. 131.

Filippo Valori (1456-1494): member of a leading patrician family in Florence, Filippo Valori was a close friend of Ficino's. He was himself a keen student of Plato: in his *Timaeus* commentary, Ficino calls him '*Platonicorum studiosissimus*' (end of Ch. 46, *Opera*, p. 1466). He was also a generous patron to Ficino, paying for the publication of his Plato translation in 1484 and of his *Three Books on Life* in 1489. See *Letters*, **8**, p. 133. He was also involved in the production of a Plotinus manuscript (*Letters*, **8**, 5) and three other illuminated manuscripts for King Matthias of Hungary, to whom he was expecting to go as ambassador in 1490. (*Letters*, **8**, Appendixes G, M and P).

In 1492, Filippo served as Florentine ambassador to Rome; so he was away from Florence at the time of the letters addressed to him in this volume (Letters 17 and 22; see also note 6 to Letter 26).

Names from Letter 28: a list of Ficino's friends

'Patroni'

1. **Cosimo de' Medici** (1389-1464): see Correspondents in Italy above.

2. **Piero de' Medici** (1416-1469): elder son of Cosimo, father of Lorenzo, Piero the Gouty led Florence for only five years after his father's death, before he too died.

3. **Giovanni de' Medici** (1421-1463): younger son of Cosimo, younger brother of Piero the Gouty. Best remembered as a patron of artists and poets, Giovanni worked in the Milan branch of the family bank. His only son died as a child at the age of seven. Giovanni, too, disappointed his father's hopes by an early death at the age of 42.

4. **Lorenzo de' Medici** (1449-1492): grandson of Cosimo, see Correspondents in Italy above.

5. **Giuliano de' Medici** (1453-1478): younger brother of Lorenzo, killed in the Pazzi conspiracy.

6. **Piero de' Medici** (1472-1503): elder son of Lorenzo. Despite the promise of his early years, and some successful diplomatic missions, when Piero inherited power on his father's death he soon lost the support of his fellow citizens through lack of political skill, shown especially in negotiations with the invading French king, Charles VIII. In November 1494, Piero and the entire Medici family were driven out of Florence. Piero never returned. See also *Letters*, **9**, pp. 126-7.

7. **Giovanni de' Medici** (1475–1521): second son of Lorenzo, see Correspondents in Italy above.

8. **Giuliano de' Medici** (1479-1516): third son of Lorenzo and therefore younger brother to Piero and Giovanni, he fled to Venice when his family was expelled from Florence in 1494. He returned in 1512, to rule for four years. In 1515 he married Filiberta of Savoy and was granted the title Duke of Nemours by King Francis I of France.

'Confabulatores': friends and conversation partners

From early childhood:

9. **Naldo Naldi** (1439-1513): Naldi was Ficino's earliest friend, and a notable poet. His parents died while he was still a child, and the resultant instability in his financial circumstances led him to seek employment outside Florence at times. However, from 1484 he was Professor of Poetry and Rhetoric at the university, and a prolific writer.

From youth (*adolescentia*)

10. **Peregrino (or Pellegrino) degli Agli** (1440-1469): grandson of Bernardo de' Medici and a relative of Bishop Antonio Agli (see both below), Peregrino showed early promise as a poet, but he was sent to Ferrara in 1457 to learn about banking. He returned to Florence in 1464, and subsequently visited Rome and possibly Milan. Unable to find suitable employment in a secretarial role, he took holy orders. Ficino's early letter to Peregrino on the four kinds of *furor* (*Letters*, 1, 7) is rightly famous. By June 1458, in an unpublished letter, Ficino is calling Peregrino his 'unique friend'.

11. **Cristoforo Landino** (1425-1498): see Correspondents in Italy above.

12. **Leon Battista Alberti** (1404-1472): this is the only time that Alberti is mentioned by name in Ficino's letters, but Ficino knew him personally and his influence on the cultural life of Florence was extensive. In his *Timaeus* commentary, ch. 43, Ficino praises the mathematical basis of Alberti's work *On Architecture*. Amongst Alberti's architectural commissions in Florence were the façade of Santa Maria Novella and the Palazzo Rucellai. Besides his principal literary works on painting, sculpture and architecture, he wrote a work on tranquillity of mind, a treatise *On the Family*, and the satire *Momus*. Landino included Alberti as a spokesman for Aristotelian ethics and the active life alongside Ficino as a spokesman for the contemplative life in the *Disputationes Camaldulenses*.

13. **Piero di Pazzi** (d.1464): member of a noble family who gave up their titles to take part in the political life of the city, and who became one of the leading banking families in Florence, rivals to the Medici. Piero was a *priore* in 1447, *gonfalionere di giustizia* in 1461 and led many embassies for the city. Ficino wrote a letter on justice to him and three other leading citizens (*Letters*, 1, 6) and an unpublished letter urging upon him the benefits of philosophy. Ficino appears to have been tutor to his son for a while, before 1463. *Letters*, 1, 14, written in 1473, urges Antonio Pazzi not to put off his studies.

14. **Benedetto Accolti** of Arezzo (1415-c.1464): teacher of civil law in Florence, and Chancellor of the Republic from 1458 to 1464, Accolti was also known for his poetry in both Latin and the vernacular. He was named in the letter on Law and Justice, written between January 1462 and August 1464 (*Letters*, 1, 6).

15. **Bartolomeo Valori** (1426-1477): member of a noble family, he held numerous public offices in Florence and married a daughter of Piero di Pazzi, Caterina, who

died just before her family's involvement in the conspiracy of 1478. Two of Valori's sons, Niccolò and Filippo, became loyal supporters of Ficino and generous patrons.

16. **Antonio Canigiani** (1429-1487): member of an ancient family, Canigiani played a continuous role in Florentine political life, including major offices and embassies. On the literary side, he was included among the participants in Landino's *Disputationes Camaldulenses* and Ficino dedicated to him some of his early works, composed around 1457, including a letter on music (*Letters*, **1**, 92), one on the moral virtues (*Sup. Fic.*, II, pp. 1-6), a short treatise *On the Four Schools of Philosophy*, and his work on pleasure, *De voluptate*. His own writings consist mainly of diplomatic and other letters.

'A little later'

17. **Giovanni Cavalcanti** (1444-1509): introduced to Ficino by Domenico Galletti, Giovanni was a descendant of the great poet so admired by Dante, Guido Cavalcanti (c.1255-1300). Giovanni became a lifelong friend of Ficino's. He studied in Florence under Landino and embarked on a career as diplomat. Ficino wrote more than 40 letters to him. See *Letters*, **6**, p. 98.

18. **Domenico Galletti** (1443-1501): born in Monte San Savino, near Arezzo, Domenico became a canon in Arezzo, but from 1466 worked as a *scriptor* and *abbreviator* in the Roman *curia*. He became an Apostolic Secretary after 20 years of service, in 1486. It was through Domenico that Ficino first met his great friend Giovanni Cavalcanti. Letters to Domenico include one on the folly and misery of men, addressed jointly to Galletti and two other friends from this list, Cherubino Quarquagli and Pietro Fanni (*Letters*, **1**, 58) and one on love and friendship (*Letters*, **2**, 66). In a third, on virtue as the foundation of friendship, Ficino sought assistance for his cousin, Sebastiano Salvini (*Letters*, **5**, 32).

19. **Antonio Calderini** (1445-1494): see Correspondents in Italy above.

20. **Girolamo Rossi** of Pistoia (d.1517): one of the dedicatees of Ficino's *De christiana religione* (1474), Rossi spent many years in literary circles in Venice. Book XII of Ficino's letters is also dedicated to him, and in that book, Letter 20, which names Rossi, is used as the preface of the whole printed edition of 1495. In 1504 Rossi became a Dominican monk, and Prior of San Marco in 1515. In 1517, he was appointed Vicar General of the Dominican Order.

21. **Amerigo Benci** (c.1431-c.1474): employee and later director of the Medici bank in Geneva, Benci had great success in business and banking; he also inherited a fortune on the death of his father, who had run the Geneva branch before him (1457). However, once Lorenzo came to power, Benci's interests turned from banking to the cultural and intellectual life of Florence. He became a prominent patron of scholars and artists, and a passionate collector of Latin and Greek texts. In September 1462 he presented Ficino with one of the most important Greek manuscripts of Plato's works (see *Letters*, 1, 3). In 1480, Leonardo da Vinci painted a portrait of Benci's daughter Ginevra.

22. **Tommaso Benci** (1427-c.1473): perhaps a cousin of Amerigo, he was from the branch of the family who were textile merchants. He shared the family love of literature and wrote poetry himself. With his brother Giovanni, Tommaso was an early friend of Ficino's, and both brothers were greeted, in a letter outside the collection, with the title of 'fellow-philosopher' (18th August 1462, *Sup. Fic.*, II, pp. 167-9). In 1463, Tommaso was entrusted with the translation into the Tuscan vernacular of Ficino's *Pimander* (printed only in 1548 and 1549). He was also given the part of Socrates in Ficino's *De amore*, which records the banquet in Plato's honour held in Careggi in 1468.

23. **Cherubino Quarquagli of San Gimignano**: a contemporary and friend of Domeniço Galletti (see above) and Pietro Fanni (see below), Quarquagli found employment in the service of Cosimo Orsini, Apostolic Secretary, and spent most of his adult life in Rome. A letter addressed to him *On Duties* (*Letters*, **2**, 53) was also circulated more widely by being included in an edition of Seneca's moral essays (Jacob Thanner, Leipzig, 1499), as well as being published in a Czech translation (Johannes Camp, Prague, 1500) and in a small volume of six selected letters (Thomas Wolff, Basel, 1519).

24. **Antonio Morali,** known as **Seraphico**: born c. 1433 in San Miniato, Morali was an early friend of Ficino's and a 'fellow philosopher'. Morali and Ficino studied together under Niccolò Tignosi. There are four manuscript letters to Seraphico, as well as four in the published collection (Kristeller, *Sup. Fic.*, II, pp. 82-84 and *Marsilio Ficino after 500 Years*, p. 19-20; Ficino, *Letters*, **1**, 20 and 57; **2**, 13; **7**, 33.

25. **Michele Mercati**: also of San Miniato, and another 'fellow philosopher', Mercati was a close friend from youth onwards of Antonio Seraphico (above) and of Ficino. Ficino sent some of his earliest ideas on philosophy to Mercati, including his unpublished thoughts on Lucretius and copies of his earliest translations of Plato. He dedicated to him an early copy of his *Sophist* translation and his *Dialogue between God and the Soul* (*Letters*, **1**, 4). Mercati entered a monastic order but their friendship appears to have continued. An anecdote, related later by Cardinal Cesare Baronio, tells of a promise they made to each other: the first to die would communicate to the other the truth about the afterlife. On the night of Ficino's death Mercati saw a vision of Ficino riding a white horse and exclaiming that their conclusions about the soul's immortality were true. See Michael J. B. Allen, *The Philebus Commentary* (Berkeley, 1975, repr. 2000), p. xiv.

26. **Francesco Bandini** (born 1440, died after 1490): his close friendship with Ficino and interest in Plato dates from at least 1468, and led to the exchange of numerous letters after he left Florence in 1473. In 1476 Bandini accompanied Princess Beatrice of Aragon to Hungary, for her marriage to King Matthias. Bandini remained with her, and soon became a trusted adviser and emissary of the King. For further biographical details, see *Letters*, **7**, p. 190; for letters written to him, between 1474 and 1489, see *Letters*, vols. **1**, **3**, **5**, **6**, **7** and **8**. He was also the host of the banquet described in Ficino's *De amore*.

27. **Lorenzo Lippi** of Colle in Val d'Elsa (1440/2-1485): a poet and friend of the Medici family, Lippi was appointed Professor of Poetry and Rhetoric in the newly

re-founded University of Pisa in 1473, holding this post with periodic renewals until his death in 1485. He taught regular courses in Pisa, though his salary was relatively low and his financial position precarious. He spent the summers in his home town of Colle. In 1479-80 he was unable to return for the start of the academic year due to the siege by Alfonso of Calabria, in the war that followed the Pazzi conspiracy. In the summer of 1485, Lippi, again in Colle, contracted plague and died there, leaving a wife and two sons.

28. **Bernardo Nuzzi**: details of his life are scant, although he was a *priore* of Florence in 1473 and served as one of the city's Secretaries from 1486. Nuzzi was a professor of Rhetoric and Poetry at the University of Florence. He is mentioned in *Platonic Theology*, VI.1.1, as one of those with whom Ficino discussed important matters, and he plays a major role in Ficino's *De amore.* Nuzzi was clearly a close friend of Ficino's, although no letters are addressed to him.

29. **Comando Comandi** (c.1410-after 1475): Ficino's teacher of Latin. He served for at least 45 years as a teacher of grammar. See *Sup. Fic.* II, p. 182.

30. **Baccio** or Bartolomeo **Ugolini**, (d. 1494): Baccio and his brother Taddeo were both friends of Ficino. Both were priests, and Baccio later became Bishop of Gaeta (1494) but in the 1470s and 1480s he served Lorenzo de' Medici on many diplomatic missions. He also wrote poetry.

31. **Pietro Fanni** *presbiter*: Pietro Fanni or Vanni became a priest in Florence, then entered the service of Leonardo Dati, Bishop of Massa. He is among the dedicatees of an early letter on *The folly and misery of men* (*Letters*, **1**, 59). From 1483 to 1484 he was in Rome, and from Letter 9 of this volume, where he has reported to Ficino the feelings of Antonio Calderini, we may surmise he was still based there in 1491.

In his maturity (but still *familiares* not *auditores*)

32. **Antonio Agli** or Allio (1399-1477): Bishop of Ragusa in 1465, then of Fiesole (1466) and Volterra (1470), Agli was a tutor to Pope Paul II, and a mentor to Ficino. He takes the part of Pausanias in Ficino's *De amore*. Ficino also wrote to him in *Letters*, **1**, 112 and **2**, 17.

33. **Riccardo Anglariensis** or **Angiolari** or **Angelleri** (1414-1486): a priest and theologian from Anghiari in the province of Arezzo. See *Letters,* **1**, 57 and 75; **3**, 26 and **6**, 9. He was also party to the discussions described in *Platonic Theology*, VI, 1, 8.

34. **Bartolomeo Platina,** also called **Sacchi** (1421-1481): Platina served the Gonzaga family and studied under John Argyropoulos in Florence. He moved to Rome around 1462, becoming an official in the humanist court of Pope Pius II. Under Pope Paul II he lost his position and was accused of heresy and conspiracy as a member of Pompenio Leto's Roman Academy. He was briefly imprisoned, but found favour again under Sixtus IV, becoming Prefect of the Vatican Library. His best known works are *On Right Pleasure and Good Health* (1470) and *Lives of the Popes* (1479).

35. **Oliviero Arduini** (d. 1498): an Aristotelian philosopher who also had a doctorate in theology, Arduini taught philosophy for most of his life at the University of Pisa. He assisted in the reorganisation of the university in 1475, touring Italy at the behest of Lorenzo de' Medici to find the best teachers. In 1484 the students of Pisa petitioned for his appointment as Professor of Theology, although another had already been appointed. By 1487 records show that he was teaching both physics (a branch of philosophy) and theology. In 1494 he was appointed a canon of the cathedral in Florence, although he continued to teach in Pisa until his death. By 1496 he was a keen follower of Savonarola. Amongst his pupils was Francesco Cattaneo da Diacceto, Ficino's successor. No written works survive, but Arduini appears as a participant in the discussions described in Landino's *Disputationes Camaldulenses*.

In *Letters*, **1**, 57 Arduini is addressed jointly with Angiolari and Seraphico (see above).

36. **Sebastiano Salvini** *amitinus*: Ficino's cousin is first mentioned in *Letters*, **1**, 76 where Ficino is requesting a favourable hearing for him with the Bishop of Cortona, when Salvini wished to become a deacon. There Ficino takes responsibility for him, having shared the task of educating him with Antonio degli Agli, Bishop of Volterra. Salvini helped Ficino considerably while he was writing his *De christiana religione*. In 1481 Salvini received the degree of Master of Theology and he later seems to have held a position in the Roman *curia*. By 1496 he had returned to Florence, as rector of a parish church in the diocese of Fiesole. For further details, see *Letters*, **7**, pp. 210-11.

37. **Lorenzo Bonincontri or Buonincontri** (1411-1491): philosopher, astronomer and poet from San Miniato, a close friend of Lorenzo de' Medici. Bonincontri lectured on the astronomer-poet Manilius, as well as undertaking military service for Constanzo Sforza. He spent the years 1450 to 1475 in Naples, taught in Florence from 1475 to 1478, and after serving with Sforza in northern Italy, took up residence in Rome from 1484 until his death. See *Letters*, **2**, 64; **3**, 15 and **4**, 10.

38. **Benedetto Biliotti**: a friend of Ficino's, Biliotti was, with Ficino, one of the astrologers consulted by Filippo Strozzi in July 1489 for a favourable date to lay the foundation stone of the Palazzo Strozzi. An epigram written on Biliotti's death (date uncertain but between 1489 and 1494) suggests that he may also have been a physician who failed to apply his professional knowledge and therefore perished from eating a poisonous mushroom (Michele Marullus, *Epigrams*, IV, 16).

39. **Giorgio Antonio Vespucci** (1434-1514): a close friend of Ficino and of the Medici family, Vespucci was renowned for his exemplary conduct and his wisdom. He served the city on several diplomatic missions. In 1480 he took holy orders and from 1482 was a canon of the cathedral, becoming its Dean. By 1499 he had become a Dominican friar at San Marco. His most important contribution, however, was perhaps as a teacher. His pupils included the sons of leading citizens and the two German youths mentioned in Letters 5 and 7.

Vespucci was one of the six scholars to whom Ficino had submitted his translation of Plato's dialogues in the 1470s. He was a participant in conversations on the immortality of the soul that helped to shape Ficino's *Platonic Theology*, and in conversations on health that led to the first of Ficino's three books *On Life*. He remained a close friend to the end of Ficino's life. For further details of his life, see *Letters*, **6**, p.111.

40. **Giovanni Battista Boninsegni** or **Buoninsegni** (1453-1512): a close friend of both Ficino and Poliziano, Buoninsegni was an active scholar of Greek and a participant in the political life of Florence. He was one of the six critics to whom Ficino had submitted his translation of Plato's dialogues in the 1470s, and the early version of his *De vita* in the 1480s. For further details, see Biographical Notes in *Letters*, **6** and **7**.

41. **Demetrius Bizantinus** (Chalcondylas or Chalkondyles) (c.1423-1511): born and educated in Greece, Demetrius came to Italy in 1449 and studied Plato with Theodore Gaza from 1450 to 1452. From 1455 he worked for Cardinal Bessarion and was made a professor at the University of Padua in 1463. On Gaza's death in 1475 Demetrius was appointed his successor at the Florentine *Studio*, where he had many outstanding pupils, including Giovanni de' Medici and Johannes Reuchlin.

42. **Giovanni Vittore Soderini** (1460-1528): brother of Paolantonio, Francesco and Piero; lawyer. All the Soderini brothers had their early education under Vespucci (see above) and played an active part in the political life of the city. (There is no reason to identify him with the Sienese lawyer Giovanni Vittorio of *Letters*, **7**, 60, a lawyer.)

43. **Angelo Poliziano** (1454-1494): poet, scholar and close friend. There are letters to Poliziano in *Letters*, **1**, **5** and Liber XII. For a brief account of his life, see *Letters*, **8**, pp. 129-30. His works include letters, commentaries, introductory lectures written in exquisite verse and miscellanies of literary findings.

44. **Pier Leone of Spoleto** (d.1492): see Correspondents in Italy, above.

45. **Giovanni Pico della Mirandola** (1463-1494): see Correspondents in Italy, above.

'Auditores': some of these are *quasi discipuli*, in the Socratic sense, that Ficino was simply bringing forth their own knowledge

46. **Carlo Marsuppini**: listed among the students, this would be the son of the famous Chancellor of Florence and Professor of Rhetoric (1398-1453). For the other son, Cristoforo, see Correspondents in Italy above.

47. **Pietro Nero,** or Piero del Nero (d.1512): lawyer, scholar and participant in the political life of the city, Nero was a close friend of Ficino's and financed the publication in 1493 of his *De sole et lumine*. He continued to hold political office after the expulsion of the Medici, and was *capitano* of Pisa in the year of his death. Pietro helped defend Ficino's *De vita* (*Letters*, **8**, Appendix B). Pietro's uncle Bernardo del Nero (1424-1497) is not mentioned on this occasion but was very close to Ficino, who translated several of his Latin works for him into Tuscan.

48. **Pietro Guicciardini** (1454-1513): a Medici supporter, Pietro (or Piero), son of Lorenzo's right-hand man Jacopo, served his city with distinction as *priore* in 1490 and 1497 and in other important posts during the Republican years. He was a close friend of Ficino, and was father of the famous historian Francesco Guicciardini. Pietro was the second of the three Peters called upon to defend *De vita*. See *Letters*, **8**, Appendix B and p. 124. See also *Letters*, **3**, 6.

49. **Pietro** (or Piero) **Soderini** (1451-1522): the third of the three Peters of the *De vita* defence, Soderini was one of four sons of Lorenzo's adviser and diplomat, Tommaso Soderini. His career outshone that of his brothers, as he became *Gonfaloniere* and leader of Florence from 1502 to 1512.

50. **Pietro** (di Giovanni) **Compagni**: *priore* in 1482 and 1502, a scholar and poet. Ficino adds the word *parentus*, however, which also calls to mind the local historian Piero Parenti (1450-1519). Compagni means fellow-countryman, so a confusion is possible, however Compagni was a surname: a Conte di Giovanni Compagni appears in the Florentine *catasto* (tax records) of 1427.

51. **Filippo Valori** (1456-1494): a leading patrician of Florence, Valori served as Florentine ambassador to Rome from 1492. See Correspondents in Italy above.

52. **Filippo Carducci** (1449-c.1520): Florentine nobleman and friend of Ficino who served as *priore* in 1485, 1493 and 1497 and held several government posts during the troubled years of the Republic after Ficino's death. See Correspondents in Italy above.

53. **Giovanni Canacci:** held high office during the 1490s (*priore* in 1491, 1492 and 1497) and played an important part in bringing Savonarola to account. His friendship with Ficino is clear from an appeal accompanying his *De vita* (*Quod necessaria sit*, in *Letters*, **8**, Appendix C) and the Mammola letters in *Letters*, **9**.

54. **Giovanni Nesi** (1456-1520): known mainly for a number of minor religious and philosophical writings, Nesi combined ardent support for Ficino with active engagement in Savonarola's religious reforms. The work for which he is best known is an explanation of Pythagorean sayings. He was also a *priore* in 1485, 1499 and 1503, and sat on the board of the University in 1497 and 1499.

55. **Giovanni Guicciardini:** member of an ancient Florentine merchant family with marriage links to the Strozzi and other leading families. There were two cousins with the name Giovanni in this generation, Giovanni di Michele (d. 1512) and Giovanni di Francesco (d.1516). It is not clear which cousin is referred to by Ficino. Their grandfather, an older Giovanni Guicciardini (1385-1435), was the brother of Piero (1376-1441), the grandfather of Pietro Guicciardini (1454-1513), see 47 above. Both the younger Giovannis were thus second cousins to Pietro.

56. **Giovanni** (or Johannes) **Rosato** or **Rosati**: a pupil of Ficino and of Pier Leone of Spoleto, Giovanni studied at the University of Pisa. Ficino's nephew, Sebastiano Salvini, was in correspondence with Rosato (letter of 9th September 1481), advising him and his companion Girolamo Cinozzi to be wary of undue interest in the

ancient philosophers and to inquire into the deepest causes, which are to be found in works of theology. However, Rosato became Professor of Philosophy at Pisa from 1486 to 1495 and then of Medicine from 1497 to 1502 (or possibly 1525). The two subjects were not unrelated at this time, since natural science was included under philosophy, and applicants to the higher discipline of medicine were required to have completed their studies in philosophy first.

57. **Bernardo Vettori** (Victorius): served as priore in 1494 and 1499, and later as commissioner for Pescia.

58. **Bernardo de' Medici**: a Bernardo di Alamanno de' Medici was elected as a director of the Florentine *Studio* in December 1499. The same or another Bernardo de' Medici married his daughter to Tommaso Minerbetti, with whom Ficino had influence (*Letters*, **2**, 14). Sebastiano Salvini became tutor to their children in 1476. See also 10 above.

59. **Bernardo Canigiani** (1443-1497): close friend of Ficino and politically active during the 1470s and 1480s. He was well-known as a mediator, and Ficino appealed for his help in securing the reputation of his *Three Books on Life*.

60. **Bernardo Michelozzi** (d. 1519): brother of the Medici secretary, Niccolò Michelozzi (see Correspondents in Italy above), Bernardo was both a priest and a poet. He became a canon of the cathedral in 1489. His career blossomed under Pope Leo X.

61. **Francesco Berlinghieri** (1440-1500): famous geographer, and an accomplished poet, this nobleman assisted Filippo Valori in the publication of Ficino's Plato in 1484. He became a great friend of Ficino, and was the dedicatee of the seventh book of letters. See *Letters*, **6**, Preface and p. 97.

62. **Francesco Rinuccini**: perhaps related to the famous scholar and churchman, Cino Rinuccini of Arezzo, and his grandson Alamanno Rinuccini, Ficino greets Rinuccini in a manuscript addition to *Letters*, **1** 79. Francesco later appears in Florentine public life as a member of the Buonomini of S. Martino and as a conservative supporter of Savonarola after the expulsion of the Medici (1494).

63. **Francesco Gaddi** (1441-1504): for his career in the wool trade, banking and diplomacy, see *Letters*, **7**, p. 199. His friendship with Ficino is clear from letter 74 in that volume, written in 1488.

64. **Francesco da Pietrasanta**: on the evidence available it is not possible to identify this Francesco.

65. **Amerigo Corsini** (1442-1501): poet and member of a banking family, Corsini served as an official of the *Studio* from 1482 to 1485 and a member of the Signoria in 1488. After 1494, he became a follower of Savonarola, serving the republic from 1495 to 1500, advocating moderation despite the extremes of the time. See *Letters*, **7**, pp. 197-8 and **8**, p. 123.

66. **Antonio Lanfredini**: a pupil of Giorgio Antonio Vespucci and Ficino, Lanfredini held various public offices, including that of *priore* in 1488, 1494 and 1500; he was also on the board of the University in 1492.

67. **Bindaccio da Ricasoli** (or Recasolani) (c.1444-1524): a Florentine nobleman, Bindaccio was Ficino's pupil in his youth and continued to support his work after Ficino's death as part of the continuing academy led by Diacceto (see 77 below). Diacceto's *Three Books on Love* were dedicated to him, as was Corsi's *Life of Marsilio Ficino*. See Correspondents in Italy above and *Letters*, **9**, p. 129.

68. **Alamanno Donati** (1458-1488): a friend and keen supporter of Ficino who died tragically young. See *Letters*, **8**, 2 and p. 124.

69. **Niccolò Michelozzi** (1447-1527): Lorenzo's secretary; see Correspondents in Italy above.

70. **Matteo da Rabatta**, a fellow canon at the Cathedral and a member of one of the city's banking families.

71. **Alessandro degli Albizzi** (1452-1516): little is known, except his later role as *podestà* of Bugiano in Umbria, in the service of Constanzo Sforza, Lord of Pesaro (1511). The Albizzi family was associated with shipbuilding and subsidised navigation and exploration (including the first voyage of Verazzano) from their profits in the cloth trade.

72. **Fortuna Ebreo** (or Hebreus), most likely a Jewish convert.

73. **Sebastiano** *presbiter*: this may be another reference to Ficino's cousin, Sebastiano Salvini (see 35 above).

74. **Angelo** (or Agnolo) **Carducci** (1470-1527): born into a noble family which had always supported the Medici, Carducci transferred his support in 1494 to Savonarola, and served in the republican government until 1512. After the return of the Medici he was reconciled with them and again held office.

75. **Andrea Corsi**, a canon of Pistoia.

76. **Alessandro Borsi** (born 1461): studied at the University of Florence, he became a notary of the Florentine ecclesiastical court from 1485.

77. **Blasio da Bibbiena**: wrote an *Oratio de temperantia*, dedicated to Filippo Valori.

78. **Franciscus Diacetus,** known also as **Francesco Cattani da Diacceto** (1466-1522): philosopher and orator who became Ficino's nominated successor. Diacceto studied philosophy in Pisa under Arduini (see 34 above) during 1491 and 1492, as the study-companion of Giovanni de' Medici. He did not complete his studies, being already married by this time, but became a pupil of Ficino in 1493 and remained with him until Ficino's death. From 1502 he taught philosophy at the

Florentine *Studio*. He also wrote a commentary on Plato's *Symposium* entitled *Three Books on Love*, which was published later, in 1561, by his nephew of the same name, who was Bishop of Fiesole and a theologian at the Council of Trent.

79. **Niccolò Valori** (1464-1527): younger brother of Filippo (see 50 above), Niccolò took responsibility for supporting Ficino financially after Filippo's death in 1494. Niccolò was a strong Medici supporter until their expulsion. Thereafter he supported Savonarola and held government office under the republican regime of Piero Soderini. See *Letters*, **9**, pp. 132-2.

There are some inexplicable absences from the list such as **Bernardo Rucellai** (1448-1514), **Bernardo del Nero** (1426-1497), **Francesco Valori** (1438-1498) and **Antonio Manetti** (1423-1497), with whom Ficino was in correspondence.

Four Bernardos are included, and one might wonder whether Bernardo Rucellai was intended for one of these (Bernardo Vettori is mentioned nowhere else in Ficino's works). **Bernardo Rucellai** was married to Lorenzo's older sister Lucrezia (Nannina) de' Medici, and he was sufficiently close to Ficino to be selected by Giovanni Corsi as the dedicatee of his life of Ficino in 1506. In 1478, Rucellai served as one of the *Officiales* of the Florentine *Studio*; in 1484, he was ambassador to Genoa. From 1497 to 1498, he served as *Gonfaloniere di Giustizia* under the period of the republic. After Lorenzo's death, Bernardo allowed his gardens, the *Orti Oricellari*, to become the meeting place where Ficino's circle and others could continue their philosophic and literary discussions.

Neither **Bernardo del Nero** nor **Antonio Manetti** were Latin speakers, and therefore perhaps their names would have been less useful to the Latin- and German-speaking Prenninger, for whom the list was compiled. It was for del Nero and Manetti that Ficino translated Dante's *De monarchia* into the Tuscan vernacular, as well as his own commentary on Plato's *Symposium*.

Another politically active friend who has been omitted is **Lactantio** (or **Lattanzio) Tedaldi** (d.1518), who served as the link between Callimachus (Filippo Buonaccorsi) in Poland and Ficino's circle in Florence. Lattanzio was for a time secretary to Lorenzo, but also served in the Medici bank.

A close connection was established between Ficino and the Valori family, which therefore included **Francesco Valori**, of whom he speaks warmly in *Letters*, **9**, 7, but omits him from this list. Perhaps he was never part of the group that gathered to hear Ficino's teachings. Francesco was the uncle of Filippo and Niccolò Valori, and was a leading statesman and strong supporter of Lorenzo de' Medici. He fulfilled many important roles in the government of the city and its diplomacy abroad, sometimes taking his nephews with him. Francesco accompanied Lorenzo's son Piero to Rome in 1492 and to meet the French king in 1494, but thereafter withdrew his support from him and became instrumental in Piero's expulsion from Florence. He transferred his support to Savonarola and became an architect and leading figure of the republican government. In 1497 he was largely blamed for the execution of five pro-Medici conspirators and he fell victim to an assassin on the night of 8th April, 1498, when the mob ran riot in Florence after the cancellation of Savonarola's trial by fire.

Friends named by Ficino in *Platonic Theology*, VI, 1, 1 as those with whom he discussed the soul are **Cristoforo Landino**, **Bernardo Nuzzi** and **Giorgio Antonio Vespucci**. Other friends mentioned in *Platonic Theology*, VI, 1, 8, are **Naldo Naldi**, **Bartolomeo**

della Fonte and **Giovanni Battista Boninsegni** – all described as 'highly educated men'. Pier Leone is singled out there for special mention. Of these, all except **della Fonte** (1446-1513) are also included in the list from Letter 28 given above. Della Fonte's interests were mainly literary rather than philosophical, and he spent a great deal of time out of Florence.

In the *Platonic Theology,* Ficino also mentions **Antonio Chronico** (or **Cronico**) of Venice (i.e. Giorgio Antonio Vinciguerra), **Demetrius** of Attica, (i.e. **Demetrius Chalcondylas**) both 'skilled debaters', **Riccardo Angelleri**, **Oliviero Arduini**, two Peripatetics. Apart from **Antonio Cronico**, who remained in Venice, all of this group are included in the list above.

It is also surprising that the **Martelli** family are not mentioned, although Ficino welcomes Braccio Martelli to Platonic studies in *Letters*, **7**, 7 and 29 and further encourages him in *Letters*, **9**, 39. None of the **Benivieni** family are included either, although Ficino enjoyed close relations with them: see *Letters*, **4**, 38 and **7**, 22, 68 and 76.

In short, it is important to remember that this list is compiled for the benefit of Martin Prenninger, and is not intended to be a roll of names of members of an Academy. On the nature of the 'academy' that gathered round Ficino, the most important recent articles are James Hankins, 'Humanist Academies and the "Platonic Academy of Florence"' and John Monfasani, 'Two Fifteenth-Century "Platonic Academies": Bessarion's and Ficino's', both in *From the Roman Academy to the Danish Academy in Rome*, Analecta Romana Instituti Danici Supplementum, ed. by H.R. Jensen and M. Pade, 2011.

Bibliography

Select Bibliography of works of particular use in compiling this volume.

Bibliographies

P. O. Kristeller, *Supplementum Ficinianum* (abbreviated as *Sup. Fic.*), 2 vols, Florence, 1937, I, pp. v-lxxv for primary manuscripts and editions, updated in *Ficino and his Work after Five Hundred Years*, Florence, 1987, pp. 112-44. The same volume, pp. 36-66, lists secondary works up to 1986.

T. Katinis in *Accademia. Revue de la Société Marsile Ficin*, 2 (2000), pp. 101-36, lists secondary works from 1986 to 2000; T. Katinis and S. Toussaint in *Accademia*, IV, 2003, pp. 7-17, list works from 2001 to 2003; T. Gilbhard and S. Toussaint provide updates from 2004 to 2006 in *Accademia*, VIII (2006), pp. 7-21, from 2007 to 2009 in *Accademia*, XI (2009), pp. 9-26 and to 2010 in vol. XII (2010), pp. 7-12.

Works by Ficino – Texts and Translations

Ficino, Marsilio, *Opera omnia*, 2 vols, Basel, 1576; repr. Turin, 1959, 1983; repr. Paris, 2000.

——, *Commentaire sur le Banquet de Platon*, ed. and tr. by R. Marcel, Paris, 1956.

——, *Commentary on Plato's Symposium on Love*, tr. by S. R. Jayne, Columbia, MO, 1944; 2nd edn., Dallas, TX, 1985; repr. Woodstock, VT, 1999.

——, *Commentaire sur le Banquet de Platon, de l'amour; Commentarium in convivium Platonis de amore*, ed. by Pierre Laurens, Paris, 2002. Full critical edition and French translation.

——, *Commentaries on Plato*, vol 1, *Phaedrus* and *Ion*, tr. by M. J. B. Allen (I Tatti Renaissance Library), Cambridge, MA, 2008.

——, *Commentaries on Plato*, vol. 2, *Parmenides*, parts 1 and 2, tr. Maude Vanhaelen (I Tatti Renaissance Library), Cambridge, MA, 2012.

——, *Consiglio Contro la Pestilenza,* ed. by E. Musacchio, Bologna, 1983, based on the Italian of the *editio princeps* of 1481.

——, *El Libro Dell' Amore,* ed. S. Niccoli, Florence, 1987.

——, *On Dionysius the Areopagite, Mystical Theology and The Divine Names,* ed. and tr. by Michael J. B. Allen, (I Tatti Renaissance Library), 2 vols., Cambridge, MA, 2015.

——, *Epistolae Libri XII,* Venice, 1495; Nuremberg, 1497; reprinted Paris, 2011.

——, *Iamblichus: De Mysteriis Aegyptiorum*, Venice, 1497, reprinted Paris, 2006.

——, *Lettere, I. Epistolarum familiarium liber I*, ed. by S. Gentile, Florence, 1990.

——, *Lettere, II. Epistolarum familiarium liber II*, ed. by S. Gentile, Florence, 2010.

——, *Le Divine Lettere del Gran Marsilio Ficino*, tr. F. Figliucci, Venice, 1548, Italian translation. Facsimile reprint, ed. by S. Gentile, Rome, 2001.

——, *Meditations on the Soul*, Rochester, VT, 1996. A selection of letters from vols. 1-5 of *The Letters of Marsilio Ficino*.
——, *Mercurii Trismegisti Liber de Potestate et Sapientia Dei,* Florence, 1989. Facsimile reprint of the *editio princeps* of 1471.
——, *Mercurii Trismegisti Liber de Potestate et Sapientia Dei,* ed. by Maurizio Campanelli, Turin, 2011.
——, *Liber de sole. Liber de lumine*, Florence, 1493.
——, *De sole*, tr. by G. Cornelius, D. Costello, G. Tobyn, A. Voss and V. Wells, *Sphinx. Journal of the London Convivium for Archetypal Studies*, 6 (1994), pp. 123-48.
——, *Marsilio Ficino and the Phaedran Charioteer*, text and translation by M. J. B. Allen, Berkeley & Los Angeles, 1981.
——, *Nuptial Arithmetic: Marsilio Ficino's Commentary on the Fatal Number in Book VIII of Plato's 'Republic'*, Berkeley & Los Angeles, 1994.
——, *The 'Philebus' Commentary*, ed. and tr. by M. J. B. Allen, Berkeley & Los Angeles, 1975; repr. Tempe, AZ, 2000.
——, *Platonic Theology,* tr. and ed. by Michael J. B. Allen and James Hankins (I Tatti Renaissance Library), 6 vols., Cambridge, MA, 2001-2006.
——, *Predicationes*, ed.by Daniel Conti, Turin, 2014.
——, *Théologie platonicienne de l'immortalité des âmes*, ed. and tr. by R. Marcel, 3 vols, Paris, 1964-70.
——, Plato, *Opera omnia*, tr. by M. Ficino, 2 vols, Florence, 1484.
——, Plotinus, *Opera omnia*, tr. by M. Ficino, Florence, 1492, reprinted Paris, 2005.
——, 'De Raptu Pauli', in *Prosatori latini del Quattrocento, VII*, ed. by Eugenio Garin, Turin, 1977.
——, *Three Books on Life*, ed. and tr. by C. V. Kaske and J. R. Clark, Medieval and Renaissance Texts and Studies, vol. 57, Binghamton, NY, 1989.
——, *Marsilio Ficino: The Book of Life*, English translation by C. Boer, Irving, TX, 1980.
——, *De Vita,* ed. and tr. By A. Biondi and G. Pisani, text and Italian translation, Pordenone, 1991.
——, *De vita libri tres,* ed. by Felix Klein-Franke with notes by Martin Plessner (a facsimile of the second edition of 1498, Venice), Hildesheim, 1978.
——, *Marsilio Ficino: Sulla Vita,* Italian translation by A. Tarabochia Canavero, Milan, 1995.
——, *Les Trois Livres de la Vie, translated into French by Guy Le Fèvre de la Boderie, Paris, 1582,* reprinted Paris, 2000, ed. by T. Gontier.
——, *Traktate zur Platonischen Philosophie*, ed. by E. Blum, P. R. Blum and T. Leinkauf, Berlin, 1993.
——, *Supplementum Ficinianum: Marsilii Ficini Florentini Opuscula inedita et dispersa,* ed. by P. O. Kristeller, Florence, 1937; reprinted, 1973.
Farndell, A., *Gardens of Philosophy: Ficino on Plato*, London, 2006.
——, *Ever More Shall Be So*: *Ficino on Plato's 'Parmenides',* London, 2008.
——, *When Philosophers Rule*: *Ficino on Plato's 'Republic', 'Laws' and 'Epinomis'*, London, 2009.
——, *All Things Natural. Ficino on Plato's Timaeus*, London, 2010.
Kristeller, P. O., *Studies in Renaissance Thought and Letters,* 4 vols., Rome, 1956-1996. Vols. I and II contain some early writings of Ficino not published elsewhere.
Shaw, P., 'La Versione Ficiniana della *Monarchia',* in *Studi Danteschi,* LI, 1978, pp. 289-408.

Ficino's Sources and Selected Studies

Aelian, *De natura animalium*, ed. by Valdés, Fueyo and Guillén (Bibliotheca Teubneriana), Berlin, 2009.

Alberti, L., *Descrizione d'Italia*, Bologna, 1550.

Alcinous, *Handbook of Platonism*, tr. and ed. John Dillon, Oxford, 1993, repr. 2002.

Allen, M. J. B., *Icastes: Marsilio Ficino's Interpretation of Plato's Sophist*, Berkeley, 1989.

——, *Nuptial Arithmetic*, Berkeley, 1994.

——, *Synoptic Art, Marsilio Ficino on the History of Platonic Interpretation*, Florence, 1998.

——, *The Platonism of Marsilio Ficino, A Study of his Phaedrus Commentary, its Sources and Genesis*, Berkeley, 1984.

——, 'Eurydice in Hades: Florentine Platonism and an Orphic Mystery', in *Ingenium*, 17 (2012), *Nuovi maestri e antichi testi: Umanesimo e Rinascimento alle origini del pensiero moderno*, eds. Stefano Caroti e Vittoria Perrone Compagni, pp. 19-40.

——, 'Life as a Dead Platonist' in *Marsilio Ficino: His Theology, His Philosophy, His Legacy*, eds. Allen and Rees, Leiden, 2002, pp. 159-178.

——, 'Marsilio Ficino' in *Interpreting Proclus. From Antiquity to the Renaissance*, ed. by Stephen Gersh, Cambridge, 2014, pp. 353-379.

——, 'Marsilio Ficino on Saturn, the Plotinian Mind, and the Monster of Averroes', *Bruniana et Campanelliana*, 16:1 (2010), pp. 11–29.

——, 'Ocean Blue: *Epistolae teutonicis complatonicis tribus*,' in E. Kessler E. and Kuhn, H. C., *Germania latina, Latinitas teutonica: Politik, Wissenschaft, humanistische Kultur vom späten Mittelalter bis in unsere Zeit*, 2 vols., Munich, 2003, vol.1, pp. 143-56.

——, 'Two commentaries on the Phaedrus: Ficino's indebtedness to Hermias', *Journal of the Warburg and Courtauld Institutes*, 43 (1980), pp. 110-129, repr. in Allen, *Plato's Third Eye*, Aldershot, 1995.

Allen, M. J. B. and Rees, V. R., with Davies, M. (eds.) *Marsilio Ficino: His Theology, His Philosophy, His Legacy*, Leiden, 2002.

Apollodorus, *The Library*, tr. and ed. by J.G. Frazer (Loeb Classical Library), 2 vols., Cambridge, MA, 1921.

Aquinas, St Thomas, *Summa contra gentiles*, tr. by J. F. Anderson, 4 vols., New York, 1956 and reprints.

Aristotle, *Complete Works*, ed. by J. Barnes, 2 vols., Princeton, NJ, 1984.

St Augustine, *City of God*, tr. John O'Meara, London, 1972.

——, *Confessions*, tr. Henry Chadwick, Oxford, 1991.

Bacchelli, F., *Giovanni Pico e Pier Leone da Spoleto: tra filosofia dell'amore e tradizione cabalistica*, (Quaderni di Rinascimento, 39), Florence, 2001.

Baldini, N. and Bietti, M., *Nello Splendore Mediceo*, Florence, 2013.

St Basil, *Homilia ad adolescentes*, tr. and ed. by R.J. Defarrari, vol. IV of *Letters* (Loeb Classical Library), Cambridge, MA, 1934. See also tr. and ed. by N.G. Wilson, *Saint Basil on Greek Literature*, London 1975, 2nd ed. 1998.

Bertozzi, M. (ed.), *Nello Specchio del cielo*, Florence, 2008.

Boccaccio, *Genealogia deorum gentilium*, ed. by Vincenzo Romano, Bari, 1951.

——, *Genealogy of the Gods*, vol. I., tr. by Jon Solomon (I Tatti Renaissance Library), Cambridge, MA, 2011.

Brown, A., *Medicean and Savonarolan Florence*, Turnhout, 2011.

——, *The Medici in Florence. The exercise and language of power*, Florence, 1992.

——, *The Return of Lucretius to Renaissance Florence*, Cambridge, MA, 2010

Brucker, G. A., *Renaissance Florence*, Berkeley, Los Angeles & London, 1969.
Bullard, M., *Lorenzo il Magnifico. Image and Anxiety, Politics and Finance*, Florence, 1994.
Byrne, S., *Ficino in Spain*, Toronto, forthcoming 2015.
Cambridge History of Renaissance Philosophy, ed. by C. B., Schmitt and Q. Skinner, Cambridge, 1988.
Chaldean Oracles, tr. and ed. by Ruth Majercik, Leiden 1989, repr. Westbury (Prometheus Trust), 2013.
——, *Oracles Chaldaïques,* ed. E. des Places, Paris, 1971.
——, *Oracles Chaldaïques. Recension de Georges Gémiste Pléthon* ed. and tr. by Brigitte Tambrun-Krasker, Athens, 1995.
Clement of Alexandria, *Exhortation to the Greeks* (or *Protrepicus*), tr. and ed. by G. W. Butterworth (Loeb Classical Library), Cambridge, MA, 1919.
Clucas, S., Forshaw, P., and Rees, V., *Laus Platonici Philosophi*, Leiden, 2011.
Comanducci, R. M., 'Bernardo Rucellai e l'Accademia Neoplatonica di Careggi', *Rinascimento*, 33 (1993), pp. 223-239.
Copenhaver, B. P., and Schmitt, C. B., *Renaissance Philosophy* (Series: A History of Western Philosophy, vol. 3), Oxford, 1992.
Copenhaver, B. P., 'Studied as an Oration. Readers of Pico's Letters, Ancient and Modern' in *Laus Platonici Philosophi*, eds. Clucas, Forshaw and Rees, pp. 151-98.
Cronin, V., *The Florentine Renaissance*, London, 1967, repr. 1972, 1992.
Della Torre, A., *Storia dell'Accademia Platonica di Firenze*, Florence, 1902.
Diogenes Laertius, *Lives of Eminent Philosophers*, tr. and ed. by R. D. Hicks (Loeb Classical Library), 2 vols., Cambridge, MA, 1925.
Di Napoli, G., *Giovanni Pico della Mirandola e la problematica dottrinale del suo tempo*, Rome, 1965.
Dionysius, *Pseudo-Dionysius. The Complete Works*, tr. Colm Luibheid, New York, 1987.
Dizionario Biografico degli Italiani, Rome, 1960-.
Dougherty, M. V., *New Essays on Pico della Mirandola*, Cambridge, 2007.
Eusebius, *Praeparatio Evangelica*, ed. by E. des Places, 8 vols., Paris, 1974-1991.
——, *Praeparatio Evangelica* (*Preparation for the Gospel*) tr. by E. H. Gifford, London 1903.
Fabroni, A., *Leonis X pontificis maximi vita*, Pisa, 1797.
Faracovi, O. P., *Scritti sull'Astrologia*, Milan, 1999.
——, *Lo Specchio Alto. Astrologia e Filosofia fra Medioevo e Prima Età Moderna*, (*Bruniana & Campanelliana* Supplement 32), Pisa, 2012.
Finke, K. K., *Die Professoren der Tübinger Juristenfakultät (1477-1535)* (= *Tübinger Professorenkatalog*. Vol. 1,2), Ostfildern, 2011.
Galen, *De placitis Hippocratis et Platonis*, tr. and ed. by Phillip de Lacy, Berlin, 1978.
Garin, E., *La cultura filosofica del Rinascimento italiano: ricerche e documenti,* Florence, 1961, repr. 1994.
——, *Pico della Mirandola: Vita e Dottrina*. Florence, 1937.
Gentile, S., 'Note sullo *Scrittoio* di Marsilio Ficino', *Supplementum Festivum: Studies in Honor of Paul Oskar Kristeller,* eds. J. Hankins, J. Monfasani, F. Purnell, Binghamton, N.Y., 1987, pp. 339-397.
Gentile, S., Niccoli, S., and Viti, P., *Marsilio Ficino e il ritorno di Platone: Catalogo*, Florence, 1984. (Referred to in the Letter Notes as *Catalogo*).
Gilbert, F., 'Bernardo Rucellai and the Orti Oricellari', *Journal of the Warburg and Courtauld Institutes*, XII (1949), pp. 101-131.
Gersh, S., *Interpreting Proclus. From Antiquity to the Renaissance*, Cambridge, 2014.

Grendler, P., *The Universities of the Italian Renaissance*, Baltimore, 2002.

Häberlein, M., *The Fuggers of Augsburg: Pursuing Wealth and Honor in Renaissance Germany*, Charlottesville, 2102.

Hale, J. R., *Florence and the Medici*, London, 1977, repr. 1983 and 2011.

Hankins, J., (ed.) *Cambridge Companion to Renaissance Philosophy*, New York, 2007.

——, *Plato in the Italian Renaissance*, 2 vols., Leiden, 1990, 2nd edition, 1991.

——, *Humanism and Platonism in the Italian Renaissance*, Vol. II: *Platonism*, Rome, Edizioni di storia e letteratura, 2004.

——, 'The Myth of the Platonic Academy of Florence', *Renaissance Quarterly*, 44 (1991), pp. 429-475, reprinted in *Humanism and Platonism in the Italian Renaissance*, above.

——, 'Humanist Academies and the "Platonic Academy of Florence"', in *From the Roman Academy to the Danish Academy in Rome*, Analecta Romana Instituti Danici Supplementum, ed. by H. R. Jensen and M. Pade, 2011.

Hankins, J. and Palmer, A., *The Recovery of Ancient Philosophy in the Renaissance: A Brief Guide,* Florence, 2008.

Hermias, see Allen, 'Two commentaries on the Phaedrus', above, and Sheppard, 'The influence of Hermias', below.

Hesiod, *Works and Days*, tr. M. L. West, Oxford, 1978.

——, *Theogony*, tr. by Glenn W. Most (Loeb Classical Library), Cambridge, MA, 2007.

Hibbert, C., *The Rise and Fall of the House of Medici*, London, 1974, repr. 1979, 1999.

Hurtubise, P., O. M. I., *Une Famille-témoin. Les Salviati* (Biblioteca Apostolica Vaticana. Studi e testi, 309), Città del Vaticano, 1985.

Iamblichus, *On the Mysteries*, tr. by E. C. Clarke, J. M. Dillon and J. P. Hershbell, Leiden, London and Atlanta, 2003.

——, *On the Pythagorean Life*, ed. and trans. Gillian Clark, Liverpool, 1989.

——, *On the Pythagorean Way of Life,* ed. and tr. by J. M. Dillon and J. P. Hershbell, Atlanta, 1991.

Index Nominum et Index Geographicus, ed. D. Gall, P. Riemer et al., Mainz, 2003.

Jurdjevic, M., *Guardians of Republicanism: the Valori Family in the Florentine Renaissance*, Oxford, 2008.

Katinis, T., *Medicina e Filosofia in Marsilio Ficino. Il Consiglio Contro la Pestilentia,* Rome, 2007.

Kent, F. W., *Lorenzo de' Medici and the Art of Magnificence*, Baltimore, 2004.

Kieszkowski, B., *Studi sul Platonismo del Rinascimento*, Florence, 1936.

Klutstein, I., *Marsilio Ficino et la Théologie Ancienne: Oracles Chaldaïques, Hymnes Orphiques, Hymnes de Proclus*, Florence, 1987.

Kristeller, P. O., *Marsilio Ficino and his Work after 500 Years*, Florence, 1987.

——, *Studies in Renaissance Thought and Letters*, 4 vols., Rome, 1956-1996.

——, 'Marsilio Ficino and the Roman Curia', (*Roma Humanistica*, ed. by Josef Ijsewijn, *Humanistica Lovaniensia* (34A) 1985, pp. 83-98, reprinted in *Studies in Renaissance Thought and Letters*, vol. IV, pp. 265-280.

Landino, C., *Disputationes Camaldulenses*, ed. by P. Lohe, Florence, 1980.

Landucci, L, *Diario fiorentino dal 1450-1516*, ed. G. C. Sansoni, Florence, 1883.

Lowe, K. J. P., *Church and Politics in Renaissance Italy: the Life and Career of Cardinal Francesco Soderini (1453-1524)*, Cambridge, 1993.

Lucretius, *De rerum natura*, tr. and ed. by W. H. D. Rouse and M. F. Smith (Loeb Classical Library), Cambridge, MA, 1992.

Macrobius, *Commentary on the Dream of Scipio*, tr. and ed. by William H. Stahl, New York, 1952, repr. 1990.

Marcel, R., *Marsile Ficin*, Paris, 1958, repr. 2007.

Megna, P., *Lo Ione Platonico Nella Firenze Medicea*, Messina, 1999.

Moerbecke, W., see Carlos Steel below.

Monfasani, J., 'Two Fifteenth-Century "Platonic Academies": Bessarion's and Ficino's' in *From the Roman Academy to the Danish Academy in Rome*, Analecta Romana Instituti Danici Supplementum, ed. by H. R. Jensen and M. Pade, 2011.

——, 'Marsilio Ficino and Eusebius of Caesarea's *Praeparatio Evangelica*', *Rinascimento*, XLIX (2009), pp. 3-13.

Najemy, J. M., 'Machiavelli and the Medici: The Lessons of Florentine History', *Renaissance Quarterly*, Vol. 35, No. 4 (Winter, 1982), pp. 551-76.

——, *A History of Florence*, Oxford, 2006.

North, J., *The Universal Frame: Historical Essays in Astronomy, Natural Philosophy and Scientific Method*, London, 1989.

Nutton, V., '*De placitis Hippocratis et Platonis* in the Renaissance,' in *Le opere Psicologiche di Galeno,* ed. by Paola Manuli and Mario Vegetti, Naples, 1988, pp. 281-309.

Orpheus, *Hymns* – see Klutstein above.

Passannante, G., *The Lucretian Renaissance: Philology and the Afterlife of Tradition*, Chicago, 2011.

Pico della Mirandola, G., *Apology*, ed. and tr. by B. P. Copenhaver (I Tatti Renaissance Library), Cambridge, MA, *forthcoming*.

——, *Conclusiones*, Latin and English ed. by S. A. Farmer, *Syncretism in the West: Pico's 900 Theses (1486)*, Tempe, AZ., 1998.

——, *Epistolae*, Strassburg, 1513.

——, *Heptaplus,* tr. Douglas Carmichael, in *Pico della Mirandola On the Dignity of Man*, Indianapolis, 1965.

——, *On Being and the One,* tr. Paul J. W. Miller, in *Pico della Mirandola On the Dignity of Man*, Indianapolis, 1965.

Picotti, G. B., *La Giovinezza di Leone X, Il Papa del Rinascimento*, Milan, 1927.

Plato, *The Dialogues of Plato*, tr. Benjamin Jowett, Oxford, 1892. See also Loeb editions and Oxford World Classics for individual dialogues.

Plotinus, *Enneads*, tr. A. H. Armstrong, 7 vols (Loeb Classical Library), Cambridge, MA, 1966-88.

——, tr. S. MacKenna, London, 1969.

Plutarch, *On the Daemon of Socrates*, tr. and ed.by Frank Babbitt, in *Moralia,* vol. VII (Loeb Classical Library), Cambridge, MA, 1994.

——, *On the Failure of Oracles*, tr. and ed. by Phillip De Lacy, *Moralia*, vol. V (Loeb Classical Library), Cambridge, MA, 1936.

——, *Lives*, tr. and ed. by H. Clough, London, 1957.

Poliziano., A., *Opera omnia*, Venice, 1498.

——, *Letters*, tr. by S. Butler (I Tatti Renaissance Library) Cambridge, MA, 2006.

——, *Silvae*, tr. by C. Fantazzi, (I Tatti Renaissance Library) Cambridge, MA, 2004.

——, *Lamia: Praelectio in Priora Aristotelis analytica*, ed. by A. Wesseling, Leiden, 1986.

——, *Fabula di Orfeo*, tr. by Corinna Salvadori in *Overture to the Opera*, eds. C. Salvadori, P. Brand and R. Andrews, Dublin, 2013.

——, *Lamia*, tr. and ed. by Christopher S. Celenza, Leiden, 2010.

Polizzotto, L., *The elect Nation: the Savonarolan Movement in Florence 1494-1545*, Oxford, 1994.

Polizzotto. L. and Kovesi, C., *Memorie di casa Valori*, Florence, 2007.

Porphyry, *Cave of the Nymphs*, tr. by Thomas Taylor, London, 1917.

——, *On Images*, tr. by E. H. Gifford, Internet Classics Archive, 1994.

——, *Philosophy from Oracles*, see A. Smith (ed.), *Porphyrii philosophi fragmenta*, Leipzig, 1993.

Prins, Jacomien, *Echoes of an invisible world: Marsilio Ficino and Francesco Patrizi on cosmic order and music theory*, Leiden, 2015.

Proclus, *Commentary on First Alcibiades*, tr. and ed. by L. G. Westerink and W. O'Neill, Amsterdam, 1954, repr. Prometheus Trust, 2011.

——, *Commentaire sur la République*, 3 vols., ed., tr. and notes, A. J. Festugière, Paris, 1970.

——, *Proclus the Successor on Poetics and the Homeric Poems* (Essays 5 and 6 of his Commentary on the *Republic* of Plato) tr. and ed. by Robert Lamberton, Atlanta, 2012.

——, *Commentaire sur le Timée*, tr. Festugière, 5 vols. (Bibliothèque des textes philosophiques), Paris, 1966-68.

——, *Elements of Theology*, ed. and tr. by E. R. Dodds, 2nd edition, Oxford, 1962 and reprints.

——, *Commentary on Plato's Timaeus*, 5 vols. General editor, Harold Tarrant, Cambridge, 2008-2013.

——, *Hymns*, tr. and ed. by R. M. Van den Berg, Leiden, 2001.

——, *On Plato's Cratylus*, ed. by Brian Duvick, Cornell, 2007, repr. London, 2014.

Psellus, *Dialogue on the Operation of Daemons between Timothy and a Thracian*, tr. by M. Collison, Sydney, 1843.

Rotzoll, M., *Pierleone da Spoleto: Vita e Opere di un Medico del Rinascimento*, Florence, 2000.

Safffrey, H. D., 'Florence, 1492: The Reappearance of Plotinus' in *Renaissance Quarterly*, 49 (1996), pp. 488-508.

Salvadori Lonergan, C. 'Una versione inglese in ottave dell'*Ambra* di Lorenzo de' Medici' in *Laurentia Laurus* ed. Martelli , Messina, 2004.

Sheppard, A., 'The influence of Hermias on Marsilio Ficino's doctrine of Inspiration', *Journal of the Warburg and Courtauld Institutes*, 43 (1980), pp. 97-109.

Spitz, W. ,*The Religious Renaissance of the German Humanists*, Cambridge, MA, 1963.

Steel, C., 'Ficino and Proclus. Arguments for the Platonic Doctrine of the Ideas,' in *The Rebirth of Platonic Theology*, ed. by James Hankins and Fabrizio Meroi, Florence, 2013, pp. 63-94.

——, 'William of Moerbeke, translator of Proclus' in S. Gersh, *Interpreting Proclus*, Cambridge, 2014, pp. 247-263.

Toussaint, S., 'Ficino, Archimedes and the Celestial Arts' in *Marsilio Ficino: his Theology, his Philosophy, his Legacy*, eds. Allen and Rees, pp. 307-326.

Valori, N., *La Vita di Lorenzo de' Medici*, ed. Angela Dillon-Bussi, Palermo, 1992.

Verde, A., *Lo Studio Fiorentino* 1473-1503, 6 vols., Florence, 1973-1986.

Virgil, *Eclogues, Georgics, Aeneid*, tr. H. R. Fairclough (Loeb Classical Library), Cambridge, MA, 1978.

Walker, D. P., *Spiritual and Demonic Magic from Ficino to Campanella*, London, 1958, repr. 2000.

——, *The Ancient Theology*, New York, 1972.

——, 'Orpheus the Theologian and Renaissance Platonists', *Journal of the Warburg and Courtauld Institutes*, 16 (1953), pp. 100-120.

Walter, I., *Der Prächtige, Lorenzo de Medici und seine Zeit*, Munich, 2003; Italian edition, tr. R. Zapperi, *Lorenzo il Magnifico e il suo tempo*, Rome, 2005.

Zeller, W., *Der Jurist und Humanist Martin Prenninger gen. Uranius (1450-1501)*, Tübingen, 1973.

Index

This index covers the Introduction, Letters, Appendix Letters, and main headings of the Biographical Notes. It does not include references within the Notes to the Letters.

abilities, natural 48
Abram, *see* Bible
Academy 8, 31, 136
Accolti, Benedetto 34, 126
Achilles 41
action and feelings 37, 41-2
Aelian 44
ages,
  gold, silver, lead, iron 51
Agli,
  Antonio 34, 129
  Peregrino degli 9, 34, 126
Agnano 10
Alberti, Leon Battista 34, 126
Albizzi, Alessandro 34, 134
Ambra 10
Ammonius xiv, 5
angels 21, 41
  divine powers 21
  guardian angel 21
  Principality 21
Angiolari, Riccardo 34, 129, 136
  also called Angelleri, Anglariensis
Apollo 10, 11, 41, 56
  as hawk 41
apparitions 37-8, 41, 44
architecture 51
Arduini, Oliviero 34, 130, 136
Argonautica 27
Aristobulus 28
Aristotle 44, 49
arrogance 8, 27
astrology 26, 49
astronomy 26, 51
  astronomical model 51
  astronomical tables 51
Athene 25, 40, 41, 51
Augsburg 3
Auguries 22
Augustan age, return of 25
Augustine, St 17
Averroes 17

Bacchus 10
Bandini, Francesco 34, 128
Barbo,
  Cardinal Marco xiv, 11, 12, 120
  death of 12
beliefs, wrong as poison 28
Benci,
  Amerigo 34, 127
  Tommaso 34, 128
Benefices 19
Benivieni family 136
Berlinghieri, Francesco 34, 133
Bibbiena,
  Blasio da 34, 134
  see also Dovizi brothers
Bible,
  Genesis (Abram) 53
  Matthew 54
  Psalms (David) 10, 12
  Gospels 12, 17
  Romans 27
Biliotti, Benedetto 34, 130
birthdays 3, 15, 18
Bizantinus, *see* Chalcondylas
blessings 20, 53
body,
  and soul 42, 53
  opposing elements 37
  subject to fortune 48
Bonincontri, Lorenzo 34, 130
Boninsegni, Giovanni Battista 34, 131, 136
books, purchased in Greece 35
Borsi, Alessandro 34, 134
buildings, collapse of xii, 20, 22
bull 29
Buoninsegni, *see* Boninsegni

Caesar 20, 25
Calderini xiv, 12, 120
  letter to 11
Callimachus 10
Canacci, Giovanni 34, 120, 132
  letter to 31-2
Canigiani, Bernardo 34, 127, 133
Carducci, Filippo 34, 120, 132
  letters to 31, 47
Careggi xii, 55
Cavalcanti family 4
  Giovanni 34, 117, 127
Chalcondylas, Demetrius 34, 131, 136
Chaldean blood 29
Chaldean Oracles 38
chance 21, 49
change 31, 36
Christ 17
Chronico, *see* Cronico
Church,
  Christian piety 17
  supposed calamity of 6
circles of existence, *see* existence
colours 45
Comandi, Comando 34, 129
comets 22
commendation 18
Compagni, Pietro 34, 132
contemplation 41-2, 49
Corsi,
  Andrea 34, 134
  Amerigo 34, 133
cosmos 16, 37, 56
creation xiii, 28, 29, 30, 37, 43
Cronico, Antonio 136

daemons 19, 21, 47, 56-7
  airy body 22
  as guides 56
  death of 22
  familiar spirits 39, 56-7
  fashioning images 44
  guardian spirit 21, 22
  guides and examiners of mankind 19
  intermediate 22, 57
  maintaining integrity of creation 57
  of underworld 42
  pivotal points 57
  relationship with gods 56
  soul-essence of 56
daemons—*contd*
  transmit divine influence 56-7
  truthful 39
David, *see* Bible, Psalms
De vita, *see* Ficino, works
death 20, 21, 22
  of princes 21
Diacceto, Francesco Cattani da 34, 134-5
  or Diacetus, Franciscus
Dionysius the Areopagite xiv, 5-6, 10, 50
  works, *Divine Names*
Diotima 57
'Divided Line' 43-45
divine qualities 6, 41, 43
Donati, Alamanno 34, 134
Dovizi,
  Bernardo 120
  Piero 121
    letter to 9-11
dreams 20, 22

eagle 30
Earth 16, 29, 30
Eberhard, Count of Württemberg xii, 117
  letters to 24-25, 50
Ebreo, Fortuna 34, 134
education 7
eloquence xiii, xv, 3, 51
enemies 14, 48, 53
Epicurus 17
Epimenides 10
essence(s) 36, 39, 43, 45, 46-7
Eusebius of Caesarea,
  Preparation for the Gospel 28
evil
  caused by particular, scattered influences 37
  depends on good 37
  no Idea of 36
  warding off 22
  not caused by gods 36
  no single or universal cause 37
existence, aspects of 44-6
experience, types of 39, 42

fame 23
Fanni, Pietro 11, 34, 129
fantasies 42
fate
  maintains order in creation 26
  prophets of 26

Federico, Duke of Urbino 51
heirs of 51
Ficino, letter to 3
Ficino, life,
account of activities 12, 13
birthday 15, 18
eloquence 3
friends
death of 23
list of xiii-xiv, 33-34
health xv, 13, 16, 24
household 48
offered assistance 3
personal circumstances 48
qualities of xiii, 3
requests assistance 18
sense of humour xv
working methods xiv
writing from Careggi 6, 9, 20, 21, 22, 23
writing from Florence 16
Ficino, works 13
Comparison of the Sun to God 50
De vita (On Life) 16, 31-32
Institutiones (Principles of the Platonic teachings) xv, 14-15
Letter *On Frenzy* 9
Philebus commentary xiii, 15
Platonic Theology, 2nd edition xiii, 13
Translations
Dionysius, *Divine Names* xiii
Hymns, early translations of 27
Lucretius 28
Plato xiii, 13, 16
Plotinus 13, 16, 31
Proclus,
Alcibiades commentary 47
Republic commentary 35-47
fish and fishermen 17
Florence xv, 20, 22, 32
golden age in 51
'flowers' 35
Fonte, Bartolomeo della 136
form,
changes of 40-41
divine 5, 44
mathematical 44
Fortune 26, 48, 49, 53, 55
and wisdom 48-9
France 8
frenzy,
divine xi, 10
four kinds of 9
friend, inseparable 16
friends xiii-xiv, 4, 14, 31-2,
list of 33-4, 125-136
friendship 3, 12, 18, 20, 24
token of 3
Furies 11
future, predicting the 26, 27

Gaddi, Francesco 34, 133
Galen,
On the teachings of Hippocrates and Plato 6
Galletti, Domenico 34, 127
generosity 6, 24
Germany 8, 18, 33, 51
Germans xiii, 4
German lawyers xi, xiii, 8-9, 118-120
German princes 8-9, 50, 117-8
German students 7, 13
giants 27
God 4, 6, 7, 16, 17, 20, 27, 28-9, 49, 53, 57
as the Good 36
above essence 36
as Father of lights 25
footprints of 28
hand of 28
imperceptible 29
power of 29
throne of 29
unmoving godhead 39
gods 35-6
appearing 37-8, 39
as angels 41
as daemons 41
as goodness, power, and knowledge 35-6
as goodness, immutability, and truth 35-6
change ascribed to 36
giving light 39
in poetry 40
levels of 56
life-giving goddess (Rhea) 56
nature of xiii
not false 38
perception of 39
unchanging 37
without form 38
worship of 27

gold 4, 51
 golden age 51
 golden minds 51
good and evil 28, 35-6, 53
Good, the xiii, 43, 45, 46-7
 known by divine insight 45
 participation in the 46
 three levels 46-7
goodwill 32, 33
Graces 11
grammar 51
 grammarians 20
Greek
 books 35
 learning of 14
Guicciardini,
 Giovanni 34, 132
 Pietro 34, 132
guise,
 one person in g. of another 5

health, care of 32
 see also Ficino, life
heaven (and Earth) 12, 16, 29, 42,
 heavens 50, 51
  contemplator of 50, 51
Hebreus, *see* Ebreo
Hercules 22
 stone of 11
Herivart, Georg xiii, 117
 letter from 3
 letter to 4
heroic natures 4
Hesiod 19
 Theology 27
homeland 12
Homer 10, 39-40, 41, 42, 53
 hymns of 27
horns 29
human beings 43
 after death 19, 21
Hungary 8
hyena and dog 44
hymns 27-30, 49

Iamblichus xiv, 5-6
Ideas xiii, 36, 38, 45, 46-7
 nature of 36, 46
illness 15, 24
 causes of 24, 37
 stages of 19

illumination 45
image 5, 30
images 5
 as substances 44-5
 properties of 44
imagination 5, 39, 42, 43
insight, divine 45
inspiration 10-11
integrity 13-14, 33
intellect 5, 39, 42, 43
intelligence 46, 49
 divine 21
 eyes as 45
intoxication 10
irreligion 17

Juno 48
Jupiter 27, 29-30, 33, 48, 49, 55, 56
 allotting goods and evils 53
 as cosmic mind 29-30
 as cosmos 30
 as highest mind 30
 body of 29-30
 governs the present 27
 images of 30
 material abundance 48-9
justice and religion 25

kindness 12, 20
knowledge xiii, xiv, 5, 35-6, 43

Landino, Cristoforo xv, 14, 34, 121, 135
Lanfredini, Antonio 34, 134
Lascaris, Janus 35, 121
Latin Platonists 15
Leo 5
Leone, Pier, of Spoleto xiv, xv, 122
 letters to 5-6, 13-14
letters, writing of 4, 8, 13
life,
 active 41-2
 bestial 43
 contemplative 41-2
 divine 43
 human 43
 immortal 12
light 25, 29, 30, 31, 45
 soul shares divine light 43
lightning 20
likeness 43
Lippi, Lorenzo 34, 128-9

lots, apportioning of 53
love 5, 7, 9, 10, 14, 15, 16, 24, 25
Lucretius 28

magic 44
magnet 11
Manetti, Antonio 135
Marsuppini,
  Carlo 34, 131
  Cristoforo xiv, 7-8, 122
Martelli family 136
Martiana church 19
mathematical objects 44-45
matter
  necessary for world 36
  neither evil nor good 36-7
Mazzinghi, Mazzingo xv, 16, 122-3
Medici family xiv, 53, 55
  as patrons 32, 48, 55
Medici, Bernardo de' 34, 133
Medici, Cosimo de' xiv, xv, 14 19, 33, 123
Medici, Giovanni de' 20-21, 33, 123
  letter to 19-20
Medici, Giovanni di Cosimo de' 33, 125
Medici, Giuliano di Lorenzo de' 33, 125
Medici, Giuliano di Piero de' 33, 125
Medici, Lorenzo de' xi, xii, 6, 9-11, 33, 54, 123
  as 'laurel' 55
  as patron xi, 9, 14, 16, 33
  death of xi-xii, 19, 20, 21-22, 24, 54, 55
  illness 24
  library of 35
Medici, Piero de' 22, 33, 35, 55, 125
  as rock 55
  letter to 55
  like father 54
medicine 19
Mentor 41
Mercati, Michele 34, 128
Mercury 33, 41, 48, 49, 50, 56
  as sea-bird 41
mercy 6
Michelozzi,
  Bernardo 34, 51, 133
  Niccolò 34, 123, 134
Middelburg, *see* Paul of
mind 28, 43, 45
  circle of 46
  separation of 10
  golden minds 51
mind and knowledge as rulers of action 43
Minerva 41, 48
  see also Athene
Minos 25
Mirandola, *see* Giovanni Pico
mirror, bloody 44
modesty 8
Moon 29
Morali, Antonio 34, 128
Musaeus 28
Muses xi, 10, 11
music 51
Mysteries 10, 21, 55

Naldi, Naldo 34, 126, 135
Narcissus 5
nature 21, 26, 47
Nauclerus,
  Johannes 117, 118
  Ludwig 8-9, 118
negation, process of 45
Neptune 40
Nero,
  Bernardo del 135
  Pietro del 34, 131
Nesi, Giovanni 34, 132
Numa 25
Numenius xiv, 5
Nuzzi, Bernardo 34, 129, 135

omens 22
One, the 28-9, 43, 44
oracles 36, 38, 39
orders or ranks of creation 40
Orpheus 10, 28
  Orphic Hymns 27-30
  Orphic lyre xv, 51

painting 51
papal court 21, 24, 48, 53, 54
participation in the good 46
patrons 8, 10 11, 12, 14, 15, 19
Paul of Middelburg xv, 117, 118
  letter to 51
Paul, St 27
Pazzi, Piero di 34, 126
Peligard, Mount 24, 50
perception 39, 40
Pforzheim, *see* Reuchlin

philosophers 17, 48, 49
philosophy 33, 41, 48
Phocae 40
Phoebus 10, 11, 29, 48
  gifts of 50
Pico della Mirandola, Giovanni 117, 123-4
  family of 4
  letters to 17, 23
Pierleone, *see* Leone
Pietrasanta, Francesco da 34, 133
Pindar 10
Platina, Bartolomeo 34, 129
Plato xi, xiv, xv, 5, 14, 17, 25, 31, 37, 42, 46, 51
  begat Plotinus 31
  'Divided Line' 43-45
  fortunes of 55
  on daemons 47
  reason 17
  works of 14, 35
    Ion 11
    Laws 35
    Letters 33
    Phaedo 42
    Phaedrus 4, 13
    Philebus xiii, 13, 15
    Republic 4, 25, 35-6, 39, 43-5, 51, 53
    Sophist 44
    Symposium 9, 13
    Timaeus 13
    tragedies and elegies 28
Platonists 5-6, 15, 17, 19
pleasure 41-2, 46
Plotinus xi, 5-6, 13, 31, 55
  carrying Plato on his shoulders 55
  gives birth to Plato 31
poetry 10, 51
Poliziano, Angelo 34, 54, 131
Porphyry 29-30
portents xii, 20, 21-22, 54, 55
possession 11
Prenninger,
  Martin xi-xiii, 4, 18, 24, 25, 50, 136, 118-9
  letter to 7, 12, 15, 27-30, 33-4, 35
  returns from Rome 24
  son's name xiii, 18
present and future 26-27
priests 39
princes 21, 25
Principality, *see* angels
printing 13, 15-6, 51
Proclus 35
  Commentary on Republic xii, 35
  Commentary on Alcibiades 47
  Elements of Theology 36
  Hymns of 27
prophecy 10, 16, 20, 22, 26
Proteus 40
providence 26, 49
Ptolemy 28
public life 23
public opinion 23
Pythagoras 54
  hymns of 49
Pythagoreans 27

Quarquagli, Cherubino 34, 128

Rabatta, Matteo da 34, 134
rays 25, 29, 43-5, 50, 54
reason 5
  between imagination and intellect 5
  rational and irrational 37, 41
rebirth 54
reflections 5, 44
religion xiii, 17, 25, 35, 39
Reuchlin,
  Dionysius 8-9, 119
  Johannes 119
  letter to 8-9
Rhea 56
rhetoric 51
Riario,
  Cardinal Raffaele xiv, 124
  letters to 6, 7-8
Ricasoli, Bindaccio da 24, 34, 124, 134
  letters to 26-7, 31-2, 49
Rinuccini, Francesco 34, 133
Rome 7-8, 18
  see also papal court
Romulus 20
Rosati, Giovanni 34, 132-33
Rossi, Girolamo 34, 127
Rucellai, Bernardo 135
rumour 23

Salvini, Sebastiano 34, 130
sameness, circle of 46

San Marco xii
San Miniato 4
Sappho 10
Saturn 14, 16, 27, 48, 49
Scipio 25
sculpture 51
Sebastianus *presbiter* 34, 134
second self 4, 14, 18, 19
secrets 27
senses 42-44
separation 41-2
shadow 44, 50
Sibyl 10
silver 51
  chalice xiii, 3-4
Socrates xiii
  daemon of 56-7
Soderini,
  Francesco xiii, xv, 19, 124
    letters to 18, 20
  Giovanni Vittore 34, 131
  Paolantonio 32, 124
  Pietro 134
  Tommaso 32
solitary life 23
songs 10, 28
  see also poetry
Sophists 8
soul xiii, 17, 22, 37, 41-2, 53
  conveyances of 41-2
  cultivation of 48
  dispositions of 41-2
  evil in 37
  facing the Good 45
  image of (*idolum*) 42
  sounds of 42
  three kinds of life 43
Spain 8
Stars 14, 21, 22, 25, 26, 29, 50, 54, 55
Streler, Johann 15, 33, 50, 120
substance and semblance 44
Sun 46, 49, 50
  comparison to God 50
  Plato's analogy 45, 50
  rays of 45-6
  ruled by circle of same 46
  self-existent 45
superlative 20
Swabia 8, 118-120
symbols and signs 38
sympathy in cosmos 57

Tartarus 30
Tedaldi, Lattanzio 135
theologians10, 30
Three Books on Life, see Ficino, works, *De vita*
thunder 20, 22
truth 17, 35-6, 38-9, 45-6, 49
twin 19

Ugolini, Baccio 34, 129
understanding,
  different types of 39, 42
underworld 42
unity 43, 46
  see also the One
universals 41
Uranius
  'heavenly one' 50
  see Prenninger, Martin

Valori,
  Bartolomeo 34, 126-7
  Filippo xii, 14-15, 34, 125, 132
    as Ficino's 'son' 15
    letters to 14-15, 18, 21-22, 24, 48, 53, 54
  Francesco 135
  home 15
  Niccolò 34, 135
Vanni, Pietro, *see* Fanni
Venice 3, 13
Venus 10, 48, 49
Vespucci, Giorgio Antonio 7, 34, 130-31, 135
Vettori, Bernardo 34, 133
victory 30
Virgil 10, 11, 20
virtue 25, 50
virtues 3, 24-25
  clemency 25
  devotion 7, 8-9
  friendship 24
  generosity 6, 24
  integrity 13-14, 33
  nobility 25
  prudence 51
Vulcan 28

warnings 22
wealth 48
welfare of the people 32

wings 30
wisdom 7, 8-9, 23, 48, 49
  and power 25
  with eloquence 51
world, *see* cosmos
Württemberg 24, 50, 117-9

youth, inexperience of 28

ALSO FROM SHEPHEARD-WALWYN

The Commentaries by Ficino on Plato's Writings

This four-volume series, translated from Latin by Arthur Farndell, is intended to make available for the first time all Marsilio Ficino's commentaries on Plato's Dialogues and Letters which have not previously been translated into English. As Carol Kaske of Cornell University wrote in *Renaissance Quarterly* when reviewing *Gardens of Philosophy*: '[these translations fill] a need ... Even those Anglophone scholars who know Latin still need a translation in order to read quickly through a large body of material'.

The four volumes in order of publication are:

GARDENS OF PHILOSOPHY (2006) ISBN 9780856832406 £18.95 HB

'The distilled conciseness of these writings gives us, more vividly perhaps than any other source, a sense of what Plato's wisdom meant to [Ficino] who became his apostle to the Renaissance' *Temenos Academy Review*

This volume provides a collection of short summaries of 25 dialogues and the 12 letters traditionally ascribed to Plato. The longer commentaries provide the basis for the other three volumes.

EVERMORE SHALL BE SO (2008) ISBN 9780856832567 £19.95 HB

'This is philosophy with a mystical dimension – one that is crucial to the original Socratic and Platonic teaching' *Faith and Freedom*

This volume contains the commentary to the Parmenides, in which the elderly philosopher carefully instructs the young Socrates that everything depends on the One.

WHEN PHILOSOPHERS RULE (2009) ISBN 9780856832574 £18.95 HB

'Anyone with a longing for a better world should read this book. As with Farndell's other books, this is a good, readable translation of Ficino's Latin commentary... This book should be required reading for all politicians and lawyers.' *Faith and Freedom*

This volume contains Ficino's commentaries on the Republic, Laws and Epinomis

ALL THINGS NATURAL (2010) ISBN 9780856832581 £18.95 HB

'... like previous volumes, it is gracefully translated so that one has an impression of the refined quality of Ficino's mind ... as is typical of Ficino, it is delightful to read and is imbued with a lofty love of wisdom and a dedication to divine truth that are inspiring.' *Temenos Academy Review*

This volume is a translation of Ficino's commentary on the Timaeus.

www.shepheard-walwyn.co.uk

Under the Guise of Spring

The message hidden in Botticelli's *Primavera*

EUGENE LANE-SPOLLEN

La Primavera, more than 500 years old and one of the world's most intriguing paintings, has remained an enigma despite 150 years of research and interpretation. This richly illustrated book reveals how the author's chance discovery of a disguised symbol, clearly visible in the painting, unlocks its secret message.

He explains that the painting must be understood in the context of the lives, times, customs and social currents surrounding the powerful Medici family in the tempestuous politics of late 15th century Florence. This was an age when the humbler Christian self-view of man as sinner was giving way to a new view of humanity, more god-like. Central to the revival of this classical view of man was the work of Marsilio Ficino in translating the works of Plato and the Neo-Platonists from Greek into Latin.

The owner of the painting was Lorenzo di Pierfancesco de' Medici, the nephew of Lorenzo the Magnificent. It was probably given to him to mark his strategically important wedding following the Pazzi conspiracy and the murder of Giuliano de' Medici.

La Primavera features classical gods from the classical past, but also has strong Christian overtones, typical of Botticelli's Madonna paintings, such as the church-like arches formed by the trees and the semicircle surrounding the head of the central figure, a Madonna called Venus. To avoid the risk of attracting the wrath of the medieval Church, a language of sophisticated allegory emerged: ideas were expressed by a code of symbolic pictures and little was as it seemed. The smallest detail, the author argues, had a role and the whole spoke volumes to those with insider knowledge and a classical education.

The imagery in *La Primavera* bears a close resemblance to the contents of Ficino's letter to Lorenzo the Younger (*The Letters of Marsilio Ficino*, Volume 4, letter 46).

Sepe magna est laus que brevis est. CXXII

Marsilius ficinus bartolomeo scale oratori.
legi questiones christophori Landini camaldulenses. In iis libris maronis adyta pene-
trat. ciceronis dialogos imitatur ad un-
guem. felicem virum fabricat felicissime.
Lege illos et tu. Scio mecum sentie(n)s.
Vale. Sed quare in laudando christopho-
ro tam brevis es marsili? Quia habet nescio quid, quod exprimere nequeam.
Iterum vale.

hec est [illegible] manu
scripta [illegible] a[illegible]
[illegible]
[illegible] etiam

Q[illegible] [illegible] boni sibi [illegible]. CXXIII

Marsilius ficinus laurentio medici viro
magnanimo. pax tibi. Si paci, docto
et bono sacerdoti favebis, favebis et
mihi. Cum enim viri boni et amici agitur
res, res agitur nostra: Vale.

Que sint [illegible] et commodato iusta. CXXIIII

Marsilius ficinus laurentio medici viro
magnanimo. Multi saepe digniora se
petunt. Gregorius epiphanius longe dignior
est iis que postulat. Et si nobis amicissimus est,
tamen propter eius virtutem magis quam propter amicitiam
eum tibi commendo. Nam propter virtutem est amicus.

INTERNATIONAL POLITICS OF ANTARCTICA

THE INTERNATIONAL POLITICS OF ANTARCTICA

PETER BECK

CROOM HELM
London & Sydney

Croom Helm Ltd, Provident House, Burrell Row,
Beckenham, Kent, BR3 1AT

Croom Helm Australia Pty Ltd, Suite 4, 6th Floor,
64-76 Kippax Street, Surry Hills, NSW 2010, Australia

British Library Cataloguing in Publication Data

Beck, Peter J.
The international politics of Antarctica.
1. Antarctic Regions — International
status
I. Title
320.1'2'09989 JX4084.A5

ISBN 0-7099-3239-1

Printed and bound in Great Britain by Mackays of Chatham Ltd, Kent

CONTENTS

List of Figures
Abbreviations and Acronyms Used in the Text
Preface

PART ONE
INTRODUCTION TO ANTARCTICA

1. Antarctica as an International Political Question 3

PART TWO
THE ANTARCTIC PAST

2. Exploration and Sovereignty in Antarctica 21
3. The International Geophysical Year 1957-1958: A Scientific and Political Turning-Point 46

PART THREE
THE ANTARCTIC PRESENT

4. A Continent for Peace 61
5. A Continent for Science 95
6. A Continent in Search of a Sovereign 113
7. A Continent Managed by the Antarctic Treaty System 148
8. A Continent for Limited Participation in an Open Treaty System 183
9. A Continent for the Management of Living Marine Resources in an Environmental Framework 210
10. A Continent in Search of a Minerals Regime 238
11. A Continent and its Place in the International Community 270

PART FOUR
THE ANTARCTIC FUTURE

12. Antarctica in the 1980s and 1990s 309

Select Bibliography 320

Index 323

FIGURES

4.1	Nationality of Stations visited by US Inspection Teams	75
5.1	Organisation of British Antarctic Activities	100
5.2	Organisation of Brazilian Antarctic Activities	101
6.1	Map of Territorial Claims in Antarctica	120
6.2	The Competing Antarctic Claims of Argentina, Chile and the United Kingdom	123
7.1	The Antarctic Treaty Framework	150
7.2	The Antarctic Treaty System in the International Context	151
7.3	The Antarctic Treaty Consultative Meetings	154
7.4	The Antarctic Treaty Special Consultative Meetings	161
8.1	The Antarctic Treaty Parties	188
8.2	Additions to Treaty Membership	190
9.1	Krill in the Antarctic Ecosystem	214

Figure 5.1 has been based upon a chart first published in Polar Record, vol.22, no.136 (1984), and compiled in collaboration with David Walton.
Figure 5.2 appeared as part of the Brazilian response to the UN - UNGA A/39/583 (part II), 1984, vol.2, p.9.
Figures 5.2, 7.1, 7.2 and 9.1 were designed by Barbara L. Beck.

ABBREVIATIONS AND ACRONYMS USED IN THE TEXT

Although abbreviations and acronyms prove a useful space-saving device, they constitute an everyday feature of Antarctic affairs, such as in respect to such terms as BAS and CCAMLR.

AAT	Australian Antarctic Territory.
AEIMEE	Group of Specialists on Antarctic Environmental Implications of Possible Mineral Exploration and Exploitation.
Agreed Measures	Agreed Measures for the Conservation of Antarctic Fauna and Flora.
ASOC	Antarctic and Southern Ocean Coalition.
BANZARE	British, Australian, New Zealand Antarctic Research Expedition.
BAS	The British Antarctic Survey (formerly FIDS).
BAT	British Antarctic Territory.
BIOMASS	Biological Investigation of Marine Antarctic Systems and Stocks.
CARICOM	Caribbean Community and Common Market.
CCAMLR	Convention on the Conservation of Antarctic Marine Living Resources.
CO	British Colonial Office.
CRES	Centre for Resource and Environmental Studies, Australian National University.
CSAGI	Comite Special de l'Annee Geophysique Internationale.
EAMREA	Group of Specialists on Environmental Impact Assessment of Mineral Resource Exploration and Exploitation in Antarctica.
ECOSOC	UN Economic and Social Council.
EEC	European Economic Community.
EEZ	Exclusive Economic Zone.
FAO	UN Food and Agriculture Organization.
FIBEX	First International BIOMASS expedition.
FID	The Falkland Islands Dependencies.

Abbreviations and Acronyms

FIDS	The Falkland Islands Dependencies Survey (later BAS).
FO	British Foreign Office.
FRG	Federal Republic of Germany/West Germany.
GSSOELR	Group of Specialists on Southern Oceans Ecosystem and Living Resources.
HCFAC	House of Commons Foreign Affairs Committee, Britain.
IABO	International Association for Biological Oceanography.
ICSU	International Council of Scientific Unions.
IGY	International Geophysical Year.
IIED	International Institute for Environment and Development.
ISBA	International Sea-Bed Authority.
ITU	International Telecommunications Union.
IWC	International Whaling Commission.
M	Marine Department, New Zealand.
MP	Member of British Parliament.
NERC	Natural Environment Research Council.
NIEO	New International Economic Order.
OECS	Organization of Eastern Caribbean States.
PRO	Public Record Office, Kew, London.
SCAR	Scientific (formerly Special) Committee on Antarctic Research.
SCOR	Scientific Committee on Oceanic Research.
SIBEX	Second International BIOMASS Expedition.
SPA	Specially Protected Area.
SSSI	Site of Special Scientific Interest.
UN	United Nations Organization.
UNCLOS	UN Conference (Convention) on the Law of the Sea.
UNDP	UN Development Program.
UNEP	UN Environment Program.
UNESCO	UN Educational, Scientific and Cultural Organization.
USAS	United States Antarctic Service.
WMO	World Meteorological Organization.

PREFACE

Much has been written about Antarctic science and exploration. This study is concerned with a rather different and oft-ignored problem: how Antarctica's role in international politics has developed in the past and might develop in the future. What is offered here is in the nature of a descriptive and interpretative essay designed to examine Antarctica's international political role from the perspectives of the Antarctic past, present and future through the adoption of a multi-disciplinary approach on account of the alliance of political, legal, economic, scientific, environmental and other themes characteristic of the continent's affairs. An attempt has been made to assume an international rather than a British outlook, even if its prominent and traditional role in Antarctica means that Britain figures prominently in this work.

It is perhaps appropriate that this book appears at a time (1986) when the Antarctic Treaty System is celebrating its 25th year of operation. Hopefully, the emphasis upon the international political study potential of Antarctica will enable the book to become a bridge towards international politics specialists, who have yet to integrate the region's developments into either their teaching, research or writing.

I am indebted to many officials, scholars, scientists and others both in Britain and overseas for informed advice and encouragement. A special word of thanks is due to members of BAS and SPRI in Cambridge as well as to staff at Kingston Polytechnic Library. This book has benefited also from several overseas research/lecturing visits supported by the British Council, Fundacion Perez Companc of Argentina, Kingston Polytechnic Research Fund, the Leverhulme Trust, the Law School of the University of Western Australia, the Research School of Pacific Studies at the Australian National University and the Nuffield Foundation.

Finally, I owe an immense debt of gratitude to my wife and children for their patience and understanding and for the provision of an ideal environment during the research and writing of this book. My wife's artistic abilities have served also to improve the quality of certain figures included herein.

Kingston upon Thames

<u>Note</u>:

The opportunity has been taken to provide a brief up-date at the close of the first chapter as well as to revise Figures 7.3, 7.4, 8.1 and 8.2 in the light of recent events, which occurred too late to include in the text.

PART ONE

INTRODUCTION TO ANTARCTICA

Chapter One

ANTARCTICA AS AN INTERNATIONAL POLITICAL QUESTION

At the close of 1983 one Australian academic asserted that, 'the Antarctic is likely to become a major crisis zone in the 1980s ... there is a major crisis brewing', while more recently a former British minister has pointed out that, 'there are disturbing indications that a major international dispute may be about to emerge over an important but little known area of the world's surface: the Antarctic'[1]. These predictions of impending trouble over Antarctica - some even talk of war - might seem rather over-dramatic, but they serve to reflect growing international concern and interest in the affairs of a continent treated traditionally as a marginal factor in both the geographic and political senses.

The early 1980s have demonstrated an increased tendency by governments, international organisations and non-governmental organisations to interpret Antarctica as a problem, perhaps amounting even to a crisis-point, and this trend has been paralleled by an emerging interest in academic and other circles. In addition, the past year or so has witnessed a succession of Antarctic conferences and seminars held in different parts of the world, including Chile's Antarctic base of Teniente Marsh (October 1982), Wellington (June 1983), Kiel (June 1983), the Australian National University at Canberra (March 1984), the University of Rhode Island (June 1984), the Ross Dependency in Antarctica (January 1985) and London (April 1985)[2].

It is tempting to believe that Antarctica's elevation to the international stage occurred essentially as a by-product of the 1982 Falklands War, which reminded the wider world that Antarctica was another area of Anglo-Argentine rivalry. In fact, some commentators interpreted the war as the result of their struggle for regional hegemony, while the tendency of maps describing the conflict to range southwards and to include at least part of the vast southern continent improved Antarctica's international visibility. But in reality the position is more complex, since Antarctica was emerging already as an issue prior to the Argentine invasion of the Falkland Islands and South Georgia; thus, the 1982 War merely accentuated rather than caused Antarctica's enhanced importance in the international arena, a position which derived essentially from a range of factors related to its perceived marine and mineral resource potential, changing political and legal ideas developed in the context of the New International Economic Order and the common heritage principle, the UN Law of the Sea discussions and environmental considerations. Of course, there are other reasons - for instance, commentators refer to strategic, communications and tourist roles - which have combined to impart an added emphasis to the continent's more traditional political and scientific significance. Recent developments have been evidenced not only by the number of governments taking an interest in the region for the first time but also by the manner in which Antarctica became during and after 1982 an agenda topic at such gatherings as the UN, the Non-Aligned Summit Meeting, CARICOM and the OECS, that is, at organisations which traditionally had steered clear, or rather been steered clear, of the continent's affairs. In addition, a range of non-governmental organisations, oft-connected to environmental concerns, have begun to perform a more prominent role, such as demonstrated by the activities of Greenpeace International and Friends of the Earth.

At present the continent is regulated by the 1959 Antarctic Treaty, and a notable trend has concerned the continued reinforcement of the treaty system through its extension either to undertake additional responsibilities in such spheres as those affecting resource management and environmental protection or to involve the participation of an ever-increasing range of governments in the operation of the system. Several governments joined in 1984 to boost membership to 32 governments - their numbers are reinforced by the fact that the grouping includes all the world's major states - and others appear poised to follow in the near future. Apart from this, non-signatories, of which Malaysia has proved the most prominent and articulate, have expressed more interest in the continent's future; indeed, Malaysia, supported by several other governments, has acted individually and collectively through the UN and the Non-Aligned Movement in an attempt to widen the process of Antarctic decision-making beyond the allegedly select and exclusive group of treaty powers, a demand justified upon the basis of both new political and legal concepts and the view that the affairs of the continent are too important to be left to a relatively small proportion of states in the international community, that is, to a mere 20% of the UN's membership. As a result, UN intervention in Antarctic affairs has been advocated by many treaty outsiders as one way of permitting their interests to be fed into decision-making, such as through the creation of new international mechanisms modelled upon the UNCLOS precedent to replace the Antarctic Treaty System.

In this context of international debate, Antarctica appears to be on a rising wave of interest, which will continue into the late 1980s and beyond; in fact, such a wave seems likely to gather pace rather than to disappear. This situation offers a marked contrast to earlier periods, so that Hambro, a Norwegian diplomat, could write that 'the Antarctic continent played no important part in international politics or international law before the present century'[3]. Guyer, an Argentine diplomat involved in the treaty system, has suggested that no real change in these respects occurred until after the Second World War, a view followed by others including the 1984 UN Study, which reported that 'in the middle of the 1950s, the increase in tension around the sovereignty issue, accompanied by rapidly developing activities in Antarctica, proved that the Antarctic had dramatically entered into the world of politics'[4]. However, in this book, the First World War will be presented as a more significant watershed in respect to Antarctica's international political role, especially as the whole post-1900 period has been characterised by a steady, albeit variable, growth of interest in the continent upon the part of governments as well as of explorers and others. In reality, there have been periods of intense activity - for example, the 1900s and early 1910s, the late 1940s, the late 1950s and the early 1980s - interspersed by even longer periods of disinterest and apathy, which have resulted in a general tendency to treat Antarctica as a marginal continent not only in the geographical sense but also in other respects. Over the long-term this marginal interpretation has pre-dominated, thereby submerging the impact of the more limited waves of interest, but developments during the early 1980s presage an escalating and more durable interest in a continent regarded as of higher international priority, especially as an awareness of its potential and actual material role has reinforced Antarctica's traditional scientific and wilderness qualities.

A Continent for Study

Recent events have promoted Antarctica's visibility as an international issue, and there are signs that this position will continue during the next decade or so. As a result, Antarctica, albeit oft-ignored, is becoming a more significant factor in international politics and, in this context, there is a need to promote a more informed and realistic appreciation of Antarctic questions upon the part of politicians, officials, academics and others, who are as yet unaware of the continent's characteristics and possibilities. The intrinsic interest of such a study is reinforced not only by its relevance to a range of other topics but also by Antarctica's great size.

Perhaps the key issue at present concerns the merits and future of the Antarctic Treaty System at a time of the continent's enhanced resource potential; thus, there is the question of how far the system can survive pressures emanating both from within, such as through the minerals problem, and without, such as on account of the global commons' campaign. These challenges have inspired interest and controversy, just as some might argue that the indifference characteristic of the 1960s and early 1970s was largely a product of the relative success of the treaty system in providing a multilateral geopolitical accommodation in the interests of international scientific cooperation. The absence of Antarctic crises and of a resource utility reduced the area's study attractions during the immediate post-1959 period. Scientific research and cooperation, stability and peace appeared as part of the natural order of things, thereby rendering it easier to forget also the deep-seated sovereignty problem as well as the manner in which the treaty served to contain territorial disputes. However, the situation has changed, for the treaty system is now under the international microscope, especially as the on-going debate about its merits has been accentuated by the imponderable regarding the fate of the treaty in 1991 on account of the common assumption that it expires 30 years after coming into effect in 1961. But this speculation offers a prime example of the misinformation clouding debate about Antarctica and strengthening the case for informed study, since the Antarctic Treaty possesses no termination date; in fact, the treaty can continue indefinitely - most signatories have urged its durable status - even if there exists provision for review during and after 1991.

Nevertheless, Antarctica remains still a marginal study as far as most academics are concerned, since the continent has been ignored as both an area and a topic for study by historians, international lawyers and international politics specialists, albeit perhaps with the exception of those in Latin America. One looks in vain for Antarctic references in international relations books or in imperial and international histories and, while geographers and scientists have displayed greater interest, even their publications tend to treat the region in a somewhat vague and inconsistent manner. A few books and articles have begun to fill this academic void, and gradually Antarctic publications are moving away from the usual scientific and biographical (of explorers) approach towards a more wide-ranging and inter-disciplinary political, legal, economic and scientific line centred more upon objective impersonal factors. But the pace of change has proved slow, and there remains a need to devote greater attention to Antarctica's research potential in such unexplored fields of study as history, international politics and international law, while appreciating at the same time the difficulties of treating any one aspect in isolation from scientific and geographical considerations.

In practice, Antarctic politics, law, economics and science have been, and remain, inter-connected in spite of the attempt of certain writers to separate individual spheres for the purposes of discussion. For instance, scientists like to believe that they can work unaffected by 'boring' political matters, such as evidenced by Sir Vivian Fuchs' emphasis upon the autonomy of science[5]. His argument was accentuated by an advocacy of the case for Antarctica as a 'continent for science', that is, one reserved for scientists as a kind of great laboratory kept insulated from political and other pressures. In the event, this has not proved easy, for any study of Antarctica is forced to recognise the uneasy alliance of science and politics, including the fact that scientists have been oft-exploited as political instruments. Traditionally, the interposition of politics has brought money for the Antarctic scientist, and recently Vicuna has pointed to the unrealistic efforts of scientists as well as of politicians, diplomats and jurists to isolate their work in Antarctica from other spheres[6]. In fact, this book's title is a mis-nomer in the sense that the international politics of Antarctica cannot be considered in isolation from other perspectives, a characteristic recalling Auburn's observation that scientific research has proved the currency of Antarctic politics and law[7].

The Last Continent

Therefore most academics have been rather late in discovering Antarctica as a field of study - many have yet to make the discovery - and it seems appropriate to employ the phrase 'the last continent' - the most recent continent to be discovered and now depicted as 'the site of the last great land rush on earth' - as a description of a unique region characterised by its special climate and ecosystem[8]. To some extent, more interest has been displayed in other areas oft-compared to Antarctica, namely, the Arctic and outer space. Although the southern polar regions can be compared to the Arctic, the differences are as apparent as the similarities, such as recognised by the American geographer, Isaiah Bowman, who has contrasted the Arctic as a hollow, an ice-covered ocean surrounded by continents, with Antarctica as a hump, an ice-covered continent skirted by seas[9]. Similarly, such qualities as under-utilisation, lack of population and high logistical research costs have encouraged comparisons with outer space. But, according to some, we know more about outer space, since it is possible to refer to Antarctica as an unknown continent even after a relatively long period of exploration and research. There exists still a long list of questions in need of an answer about a continent, whose territorial extent and nature remained uncertain until the early decades of this century. It was only during the 1930s that exploration established that Antarctica comprised one continent rather than a series of islands, but at this time the British government, whose explorers and scientists had proved among the most active in the region, was forced to admit that insufficient exploration, in conjunction with the difficulty of ascertaining the land limits of terrain covered predominantly by ice, rendered it impossible to determine the precise extent. Comparisons were drawn occasionally with the size of Australia, but it is now known that Antarctica is much larger and covers some 14m sq. km (circa 5.5m sq. miles), that is, about 10% of the earth's land surface. It represents the fifth largest continent, and it exceeds the combined area of say China and India or of the USA and Mexico. In turn, Antarctica's marginal character has been reinforced by its remoteness, since it is separated by a considerable expanse of ocean and ice from other southern continents, while this geographical isolation is compounded by the obstacles posed by climate and ice to all-the-year-round communications and settlement.

Although the Antarctic Treaty constitutes the crucial background factor in the sphere of international politics, it is difficult to understand either the present position or the future possibilities without some appreciation of the scientific dimension, and particularly of Antarctica's physical character. There are also the above-mentioned problems arising out of man's basic ignorance of the continent, and in the context of recent developments one of the most significant gaps in knowledge applies to an accurate assessment of Antarctica's mineral potential. Any calculations on this matter are hindered not only by an inadequate appreciation of the basic geological structures but also by a range of imponderables, including the extent, cost and availability of alternative supplies of minerals and the pace of technological development. The peculiar demands of the polar environment cannot be discounted, a point evidenced by the technological challenges posed by climate, sea depth and ice as well as by the sensitivity of the ecosystem.

The Ice Sheet

Geologically and geographically Antarctica is divided into two regions by the Trans-Antarctic Mountains, which extend from the Ross Ice Shelf in the Pacific sector to the Filchner Ice Shelf in the Atlantic sector. To the east of the mountains lies East or Greater Antarctica, a Pre-Cambrian shield covered almost entirely by an ice sheet rising to about 4,200 metres above sea level and averaging circa 2,500 metres in height. This region includes Mount Erebus (3,794 metres), one of several volcanic landforms, while west of the Transantarctic Mountains lies West or Lesser Antarctica, an area characterised by various mountain ranges, such as the Ellsworth Mountains, wherein the Vinson Massif at 4,897 metres (formerly given as 5,140 metres) represents the highest point in the continent. About 95-98% of the continent is covered by the ice sheet, even during the summer season, and the ice, which has an average thickness of 2,450 metres, exceeds 4,500 metres in places. As such, Antarctica, subject already to a range of descriptive superlatives, is the highest of all continents in terms of average elevation, while the thickness and weight of the ice sheet has depressed the bedrock surface by up to 800 metres so that in places the bedrock is below sea level. In fact, the removal of the ice sheet through melting would raise world sea-levels by some 55 to 70 metres, thereby permitting a compensatory rise in the bedrock surface as the load is relieved. Ice-loading is thought to account for the unusual depth of water (circa 400-800 metres) over the continental shelves off Antarctica as compared to the world average (100 to 200 metres), and this factor, in association with the relatively narrow shelves, exerts a further constraint upon offshore oil exploitation.

Permanent ice shelves occur where the inland ice sheet meets the coastline - the Ross Ice Shelf's area exceeds that of France - and the ice sheet acts also as the source of icebergs - some of which may be 30-40 km long and up to 200 metres thick, although bergs of 400 km in length and over have been observed - which drift northwards to melt in warmer climes. Apart from their extent and physical features, the permanent ice shelves have attracted political and legal debate regarding their legal status for the purposes of sovereignty. Are they land? Where does land end and the sea begin? Are the ice shelves included in the existing territorial claims? In addition, there is pack ice, which ranges to a thickness of 1.5 metres and builds up during the winter season (to September) to stretch a long distance away from the coastline before disappearing in the summer (to March). In this sense Antarctica can be interpreted as a 'pulsating' continent, which in effect almost doubles in size during the winter.

Clearly, the ice sheet and the related ice shelves comprise not only a kind of present-day remnant of the Ice Age but also the major feature of Antarctica, and, in the light of its extent, depth and permanence, ice constitutes an integral factor in respect to any discussion about Antarctica's status or utility. It is also a major obstacle to research, even if various developments, such as in the sphere of radio-echo sounding, have facilitated the mapping of bedrock topographical detail covered by the ice sheet. But glaciologists remain uncertain whether the ice sheet is either growing or shrinking on account of the difficulty of evaluating wastage and accumulation figures[10].

Climate

The ice sheet, in conjunction with its continental character and high average elevation, contributes to Antarctica's claim to be the coldest continent, since temperatures are low in both the relative and absolute senses. Antarctic temperatures tend to be about 10° to 30°C colder than those recorded at comparable northern latitudes, and inevitably some of the world's lowest temperatures have occurred in Antarctica, especially on the high plateau of East Antarctica, such as the Soviet Vostok station whose mean annual figure is -56°C and record low was -89.2°C. But even this was surpassed in 1983 at New Zealand's Vanda base by a low of -89.6°C. Surprisingly, most of the continent receives little snow. Most snow falls onto the coastal strip, whereas the vast interior experiences minimal precipitation (circa 5 cm per annum) - indeed it can be classified as a desert - in spite of the thickness of the ice sheet.

The other influential climatic feature is the wind, which is distinguished by its consistency, high velocity and carriage of cold air and snow. Local, katabatic winds carry very cold air and snow from the polar plateau down to the continental margins, occasionally at blizzard force, such as indicated by the title, The Home of the Blizzard, given by Douglas Mawson to the account of his 1911-14 expedition. In 1984 the Soviet Russkaya station recorded speeds of 215.65 km per hour, and Frank Debenham, a member of Scott's second expedition, has described the wind as 'the dominant, almost universal and even overwhelming feature of Antarctica'[11]. Admiral Byrd has referred to the 'extravagantly insensate' qualities and 'vindictiveness' characteristic of Antarctic blizzards, especially as a wind speed measurement fails to convey the effect upon man[12].

> You are reduced to a crawling thing on the margin of a disintegrating world; you can't see, you can't hear, you can hardly move. The lungs gasp ... the brain is shaken. Nothing in the world will so quickly isolate a man.

Man is essentially alien to such polar conditions, and arguably the combination of wind-blown snow, low temperatures and the seasonal light regime exerts the major constraint upon human activity.

Flora and Fauna

Geographical, and particularly climatic, factors render it difficult for flora and fauna to survive on the continent. Antarctica contains neither reptiles, amphibians nor mammals; thus, contrary to a popular view there are no polar bears. Terrestrial fauna comprise only a few insects, including mites, lice and midges, and a midge, Belgica antarctica, is oft-quoted as the largest terrestrial inhabitant (about 2.5-3mm in length) confined only to the Antarctic Peninsula. In addition, the continent falls south of the tree line, and the absence of trees, shrubs and other plants is basically a function of the extent of the ice sheet, low temperatures, short summers, high wind velocities and inadequate precipitation. Only a few species of flowering plants occur - for instance, a grass, Deschampsia, and a herb, Colobanthus quitensis - and then only upon the west coast of the Antarctic Peninsula, which stretches north towards South America. More common are algae, lichens and mosses, which prove relatively resistant to polar conditions, albeit vulnerable to trampling by humans.

The relative poverty of Antarctic flora and fauna contrasts vividly with not only the more temperate parts of the globe but also the Arctic, which supports a range of insects, birds and bears as well as trees and over one hundred species of flowering plants. As a result, references to Antarctic fauna tend to concentrate upon the periphery, since the relative abundant marine life of the continental margins and the Southern Ocean contrasts with the relatively lifeless terrestrial environment.

The Marine Ecosystem

The Southern Ocean encircles Antarctica, and performs a dual role both connecting the region to the Indian, Pacific and Atlantic Oceans and separating it from other southern continents. On average, Antarctica is isolated from the other continents by over 2,000km of ocean, including pack ice, and the narrowest separation is Drake Passage, where about 1,000km divides it from South America. In turn, the Southern Ocean influences the global climatic and ocean circulation, albeit in a manner as yet not fully understood. According to Llano, 'the most striking feature of the Southern Ocean is its high fertility', a feature contrasting with the poverty and desert-like conditions of the interior, and Hedgpeth has described the ocean as 'a rich, apparently productive plankton-pelagic system supporting (at least in the past) great populations of whales and millions of penguins, fishes, seals and possible abundant intermediate populations of fishes and cephalopods' (squid)[13]. The high productivity of Antarctic waters compares more than favourably with other oceans, although some experts have pointed to variations in the concentrations of nutrients and have counselled a more cautious productivity assessment[14].

The northern limit of the Southern Ocean is difficult to establish, but there exists general support for the Antarctic Convergence as the Polar Frontal zone, a ribbon of mixing water some 30 to 50 km wide located between 45°S to 60°S, where the Antarctic surface waters sink beneath the less dense and warmer sub-antarctic surface waters. Such a boundary gives the Southern Ocean an area of coverage amounting to some 10% of the total world sea area, while the 1980 Convention on the Conservation of Antarctic Marine Living Resources (CCAMLR) treated the Convergence - this was defined in article 1 to range between 45°S at 30°E and 60°S at 150°E - as the limit of the Antarctic marine ecosystem[15]. As a result, the zone between the Antarctic Convergence and Antarctica constitutes a large and semi-closed marine ecosystem - indeed, one of the largest and most important in the world - characterised by features distinguishing it from adjacent systems; in turn, it exerts a significant influence upon the climate and other aspects of the southern continents. The Antarctic ecosystem has been disturbed already by man's depletion of whales and seals, but the current and future commercial harvesting of krill, an organism at the centre of the ecosystem, will pose a more significant threat, particularly to its constituent marine mammals, fishes and birds. Although a reasonable understanding exists regarding the structure and operation of the ecosystem, further research is required in respect to such aspects as data collection and mathematical modelling, thereby providing the basis for a more informed management of the Antarctic Marine Resources Regime.

Antarctic Inter-Connections

In reality, it proves difficult to consider the continent in isolation, for just as one is forced to discuss the sub-antarctic islands with the continent when appraising the marine ecosystem, so a major cause of interest in Antarctica arises from its supposed or actual inter-relationship with other areas. For example, the South American continent is connected geologically to the Antarctic Peninsula by the Scotia Arc, and this feature, in conjunction with geographical proximity, has been utilised by Argentina and Chile to support their Antarctic territorial claims. Perhaps the most substantial link has been advanced as part of the Gondwanaland thesis, according to which geologists have re-constructed a Gondwanaland super-continent from which the existing continents, including Antarctica, were formed through a process of plate tectonics and continental drift. In fact, the hypothesis was validated to a large extent by research conducted in Antarctica, wherein fossil remains implied a historic land connection with other continents. For example, in 1967 the fossil remains of an amphibian, Lystosaurus, matched up with discoveries in India and South Africa, and subsequent research - this included the remains of a land mammal in a continent lacking mammals - served to reinforce the

Gondwanaland thesis, even if certain points require clarification.

Nevertheless, there exists now a more general acceptance of the view that some 150 to 200m years ago Antarctica drifted southwards to its present position[16]. The structural and geological continuities implicit in the Gondwanaland thesis possess a wider relevance, for pending further exploration they encourage speculation that known mineral occurrences in Australia, South Africa and South America can be extrapolated into Antarctica. At present, inaccessibility, ice cover and other factors inhibit accurate appraisals of its mineral resource potential, and hence such analogies offer one of the principal methods of filling existing gaps in knowledge.

Similarly Antarctica exerts a significant, albeit only partially understood, impact upon the global atmospheric and oceanic circulation, and thus upon the climate of the southern continents. In 1981 an Australian parliamentary report advanced the need for the country to pursue a high quality research programme because of 'the effect of the Antarctic on climate, weather and oceanic circulations in the Southern Ocean area, particularly as these relate to Australia'[17]. Similar considerations led Mrs Gandhi, the prime minister, to assert in 1982 that the Indian polar expedition's 'main objectives were to study the meteorological and other conditions of Antarctica, which are believed to control the monsoons'[18]. And there are other areas of relevance. Glaciologists are interested in the form, flow and stability of the ice sheet, partly because of its correlation to world sea levels - it is of interest to speculate how much of the globe would be covered if the ice sheet melted - and partly because ice cores as historical records of the ice sheet can yield insights into climatic change and global atmospheric pollution over long time periods. For example, the thickness of each layer of the ice sheet reveals evidence of snow accumulation and temperature change for any one year, while the analysis of the impurities held in dateable layers - these can be compared to the rings on a tree - offers a guide to changes, particularly as Antarctica itself offers a pollution-free region to serve as the base-line for the measurement of atmospheric pollution.

In addition, geospace - the term employed to describe the ionosphere and magnetosphere - can be studied most advantageously from polar regions, thereby enabling research into both fundamental and universal scientific processes and applied aspects, like radio communications. This type of work is demonstrated by the BAS' studies undertaken at the Faraday and Halley base observatories[19]. A more recent scientific concern has resulted from Antarctica's yield of meteorites in their original state upon impact - since 1969 over 3,000 have been discovered there - whereas other parts of the world provide only a few weathered specimens in any year. It has been suggested that some Antarctic meteorites may have come from Mars, while traces of amino acids found in others have fostered speculation about life other than just on earth[20].

To employ the terminology of a recent book, Antarctica has been interpreted as 'a pole apart' from the rest of the world on account of its physical isolation and of its uniqueness in respect to geographical and other factors[21]. In some respects, Antarctica remains 'a pole apart', even if both technological and communications developments, in conjunction with a growing appreciation of the continent's inter-relationship with global geophysical and geographical phenomena as well as of its resource potential, have tended to moderate this sense of isolation. The plane, helicopter and satellite communications have qualified Antarctica's remoteness, base stations may possess flush toilets, 'conference centres', and even a 'family settlement' and 'school', but serious risks and dangers persist. Three members of BAS were lost in August 1982, while the costs and difficulties of maintaining and supporting Antarctic activities are substantial, thereby serving both to limit the number of countries involved and to provide another analogy with research in outer space. Sir Hermann Bondi, chairman of the Natural Environment Research Council -the parent body of BAS - has observed that:

> In Antarctica there is of course inevitably a very high expenditure on logistics. It reminds me very much of space research in which I was previously engaged. You spend an awful lot of money to get there and that is when the science begins[22].

In particular, the remoteness and special geographical character of Antarctica necessitate a high level of logistical support, such as through the provision of ships and aircraft, and this tends to require a reasonable degree of government involvement.

An Awful Place?

During January 1912 Captain Robert Scott uttered his famous comment about the South Pole: 'Great God! This is an awful place'. Although certain developments have improved its accessibility and reduced the risks of exploration, Antarctica is still oft-regarded as an inhospitable and 'awful place'. Certainly this is true of the popular imagination, but an increasing number of governments are looking now more favourably, even acquisitively, upon the continent and its resources. Antarctica has proved of greater and more enduring interest to scientists, but even they have experienced its 'awful' qualities, including the dangers and discomforts of polar conditions.

The 1980s are likely to prove a critical decade for Antarctica's role in the international arena. In turn, the 1990s - a decade beginning in 1991 with the possibility of review of the Antarctic Treaty and closing with a period when many specialists believe that Antarctic minerals may become both worthy and capable of exploitation - promise to be even more crucial. In 1982 Sir Vivian Fuchs looked back on Antarctica's long and chequered history, and then looked forwards since 'we now stand at the brink, when the nations must take political decisions about the future' of the continent, preferably, he added, under the guidance of scientists[23]. In this context, it becomes more important to extend the frontiers of communication and dialogue upon Antarctica into a range of diverse areas, including politics, law, economics as well as science, thereby providing a more informed and integrated view of the region's position and problems as the 1980s and 1990s unfold. This need was highlighted in 1984 when the UN Study on Antarctica stressed the continent's international significance but failed to provide a clearly signed road forward. Although certain sections of the Study implied a value judgment, it was basically a bland and objective account, and failed to offer the rigorous and critical scrutiny required. This book is designed to provide a balanced and informed synthesis of the Antarctic political scene, thereby filling an existing gap in the literature on international politics.

A Late Postscript

After the completion of this manuscript in June 1985, there occurred a number of developments of relevance to the topic but impossible to incorporate into the text except as a brief postscript to the opening chapter. However, certain figures have been up-dated also. The main developments are:

1) China and Uruguay became Consultative Parties in October 1985, thereby increasing the number of Consultative Parties to 18;
2) During September-October 1985 a further session of the Antarctic mineral regime negotiations was held at Paris and was based upon a new compromise package drafted by Beeby to include an additional layer of decision-making embodied in a special conference of all parties to the regime;
3) During November-December 1985 the UN continued its discussions on Antarctica, and the passage of three resolutions (on the expulsion of South Africa from the Antarctic Treaty, the provision of information to the UN on the mineral discussions, on the application of the

common heritage and UNCLOS principles to Antarctica) highlighted the breakdown of the consensus approach characteristic of the 1983-4 debates and left the situation confused and potentially unstable, especially as the Antarctic Treaty powers have continued their objections to not only the efforts to institutionalize Antarctica but also the specific requirements of the 1985 resolutions[24].

4) a second 'Antarctic Challenge' international symposium was held at Kiel in September 1985.

Such developments reflect the continuing emergence of the Antarctic issue, and reinforce the need for dialogue and debate about problems and possibilities, such as upon the basis of the framework provided in the following chapters.

NOTES

1. Keith Suter (of University of Sydney), 'Aspects of International Environmental Law', unpublished paper delivered in Australia (November 1983); Evan Luard, 'Who Owns the Antarctic?', Foreign Affairs, vol. 62, No. 5 (1984), p. 1175. John Bechervaise, 'Imperative Need for Pax Antarctica', Pacific Defence Reporter, (July 1982), p. 28.

2. The proceedings of most of these sessions have been published, or are in press.

3. Edvard Hambro, 'Some Notes on the Future of the Antarctic Treaty Collaboration', American Journal of International Law, vol. 68, no. 2, (1974), p. 217.

4. Roberto E. Guyer, 'Antarctica's Role in International Relations' in Francisco Orrego Vicuna (ed.), Antarctic Resources Policy: Scientific, Legal and Political Issues, (Cambridge University Press, Cambridge, 1983), pp. 267-8 (UN General Assembly Records) A/39/583 (Part I), 1984, p.21.

5. Sir Vivian Fuchs, Of Ice and Men: The Story of the British Antarctic Survey, (Anthony Nelson, Oswestry, 1982), p. 250, pp. 331-343.

6. Francisco Orrego Vicuna, 'Antarctic Resources Policy: an Introduction' in Vicuna Antarctic Resources Policy, p. 2.

7. F. M. Auburn, Antarctic Law and Politics (Hurst, London, 1982), p. 93.

8. M. J. Peterson, 'Antarctica: the last great land rush on earth', International Organization, vol. 34, no. 3 (1980), p. 377; J. F. Lovering and J. R. V. Prescott, Last of Lands ... Antarctica (Melbourne University Press, Melbourne, 1979).

9. Quoted Laurence M. Gould, The Polar Regions in their Relation to Human Affairs (American Geographical Society, New York, 1958), p. 1.

10. For further details on Antarctica's physical features, see Lovering and Prescott, *Last of Lands*, pp. 1-49; H. G. R. King, *The Antarctic* (Blandford, London, 1969), pp. 22 *et seq.*

11. Frank Debenham, *Antarctica: The Story of a Continent* (Macmillan, New York, 1961), p. 126.

12. Richard E. Byrd, *Alone* (Putnam's New York, 1935), pp. 154-5.

13. George A. Llano, 'Ecology of the Southern Ocean Region', *University of Miami Law Review*, vol. 33, no. 2 (1978), p. 359; J. W. Hedgpeth, 'The Antarctic Marine Ecosystem' in G. Llano (ed.), *Adaptations Within Antarctic Ecosystems, Proceedings of the Third SCAR Symposium on Antarctic Biology* (Smithsonian Institution, Washington DC., 1977), pp. 3-10. Note also: George A. Knox, 'The Living Resources of the Southern Ocean' in Vicuna *Antarctic Resources Policy*, pp. 22 *et seq.*; Dietrich Sahrhage, 'Present Knowledge of Living Marine Resources in the Antarctic, Possibilities for their Exploitation and Scientific Perspectives' in Rüdiger Wolfrum (ed.), *Antarctic Challenge: Conflicting Interests, Cooperation, Environmental Protection, Economic Development* (Duncker and Humblot, Berlin, 1984), pp. 67-87.

14. S. Z. El-Sayed, 'Primary Productivity and Estimates of the Potential Yields of the Southern Oceans' in M. A. McWhinnie (ed.), *Polar Research in the Present and the Future* (AAAS, Boulder, Colorado, 1978), pp. 141-160.

15. *Antarctic Treaty: Handbook of Measures in Furtherance of the Principles and Objectives of the Antarctic Treaty*, 3rd edn. (Dept. of Foreign Affairs, Canberra, 1983), pp. 9501-15.

16. Lovering and Prescott, *Last of Lands*, pp. 75-9.

17. Australian Parliamentary Standing Committee on Public Works, *Redevelopment of Australian Antarctic Bases*, Parliamentary Paper 115/1981, p. 9.

18. *Indian Lok Sabha Debates*, vol. XXIV, col. 425, 19th February 1982.

19. British Antarctic Survey, *Research in the Antarctic. The Work of the British Antarctic Survey* (British Antarctic Survey, Cambridge, 1983), pp. 20-23.

20. Ursula B. Marvin, 'Extraterrestrials have landed on Antarctica', *New Scientist*, 17th March 1983, pp. 710-5.

21. Philip W. Quigg, *A Pole Apart: The Emerging Issue of Antarctica* (McGraw Hill, New York, 1983), p. 218.

22. *House of Commons Foreign Affairs Committee (HCFAC)*, Falkland Islands, Minutes of Evidence, (13th December 1982), p. 93.

23. Sir Vivian E. Fuchs, 'Antarctica: Its History and Development', in Vicuna *Antarctic Resources Policy*, p. 19.

24. Peter J. Beck, 'Antarctica at the UN, 1985: the End of Consensus?' *Polar Record*, Vol. 23, No. 143 (1986), pp. 159-66.

PART TWO

THE ANTARCTIC PAST

Chapter Two

EXPLORATION AND SOVEREIGNTY IN ANTARCTICA

The Relevance of the Historical Dimension

The central feature of international politics, law and science in Antarctica - and, it is alleged, the prime cause of the region's political stability and scientific cooperation - is the 1959 Antàrctic Treaty, and its role as a watershed is emphasised by the manner in which the events of the pre-1959 period provided an influential historical background encouraging the conclusion of such an agreement. In fact, it is difficult to understand the nature and achievements of the treaty without an appreciation of the previous events. Wyndham, an Australian diplomat, has stressed this point:

> To anyone who is of a mind to think that the present situation in the Antarctic exists independent of the Antarctic Treaty, I invite their attention to the political history of the Antarctic in the 1930s, 40s and the early 50s. I ... do not think one can really understand the success of the Treaty without being aware of this historical background[1].

Most commentators interpret the treaty as bringing stability, or rather preserving the stable state of affairs cultivated during the International Geo-physical Year (IGY) of 1957-8, to a region which had proved not only a long-standing source of international rivalry - for example, between Argentina, Britain and Chile or Britain and the USA - but also an escalating cause of inter-governmental, even super-power, tension during the decade or so preceding 1959. There was even speculation that the Cold War, having extended recently from Europe to the Far and Middle East, might reach the cold continent on account of the growing intervention of the two superpowers therein. During the 1940s the US government had assumed a closer concern for Antarctica - this succeeded the occasional periods of interest during previous decades - thereby joining the more traditional Antarctic powers, such as Britain and Norway, while after the late 1940s the Soviet government indicated an anxiety to be involved in the continent's affairs[2]. Significantly, both the American and Soviet governments supported large-scale and highly visible scientific programmes in Antarctica during the IGY.

It was perhaps inevitable that the wider context of Soviet-American relations fostered fears that Antarctica would become yet another theatre of East-West conflict; thus, 'there was genuine apprehension that the most dangerous rivalry of all time, the Cold War, might be extended to the South Pole'[3]. In addition, it was anticipated that the enhanced politicisation of Antarctica would exert unwelcome military and nuclear consequences at the expense of the cause of scientific research. However, the heightened international concern about the region should not be taken to imply that, at a time of anxiety about the Cold War, the Berlin question, the Middle East in the wake of the 1956 Suez Crisis, or the process of decolonisation, Antarctica constituted a major international topic. During the 1950s it proved still a relatively marginal area and one of the lesser international issues, albeit a matter possessing a certain significance for some governments. However, there was as yet little appreciation of Antarctica's likely international role in the future; indeed, no serious thought was devoted to the subject.

Nevertheless, Antarctica was an issue in the international arena, and memories of the tensions characteristic of the 1940s and 1950s have proved influential in moulding government attitudes in the early 1980s. Recently, at a time of challenge for the Antarctic Treaty, several governments have referred to the danger of a return to the chaos and friction of the pre-1959 period as a prime reason for the maintenance of the treaty. For instance, India, one of the recent signatories, has joined the other parties in extolling the basic virtues of the treaty, since 'any attempt to undermine the Antarctic Treaty system could lead to international discord and instability as well as the revival of conflicting territorial and other claims'[4].

In addition, the current Antarctic position of individual governments can be understood only by an appreciation of the historical perspective, according to which certain countries have acquired a polar tradition through their long-standing involvement in the region. In turn, such traditions provide an influential framework for current and future policies, and it was interesting to note the use made of tradition by many delegations during the course of the UN discussions held since 1983. For example, in November 1983, the British delegate reminded the UN First Committee of his country's Antarctic tradition, for 'the United Kingdom has been active in Antarctica since 1775', beginning with the voyages of Captain Cook and evolving during the present century into, 'a continuous British research activity', such as reflected through the work of the Discovery Investigations, the

Falkland Islands Dependencies Survey (FIDS) and now BAS[5]. Other governments shared this anxiety to prove their historical credentials in respect to Antarctica, a trend typified by Zegers, who asserted that 'by definition Chile is an Antarctic country - because of its historic mission, its geographical position, its presence there and the activities of its nationals'[6].

Academics have concentrated upon Antarctic traditions, and Bertrand's history of American exploration prompted the conclusion that:

> The Americans have played a major role. American interest is as old as the nation itself. While interest has waxed and waned, there has been no decade when at least some Americans have not been in the Antarctic[7].

Similarly, this author has oft-stressed the influence of 'Britain's historic role in Antarctic exploration, research and resource matters ... as an influence upon current British thinking'[8]. As a result, several countries, which have experienced a long-standing, albeit occasionally discontinuous, involvement in Antarctica, possess a significant Antarctic tradition, and this historical dimension provides an important foundation for present and future developments, such as highlighted also by Lord Shackleton's frequent stress upon tradition as the basis for a more active British policy towards the region[9]. In fact, the mere name of Shackleton serves as a reminder of Britain's notable polar past.

In this manner, a knowledge of Antarctic history, that is, of the Antarctic past, facilitates an understanding not only of the achievements of the Antarctic Treaty in the establishment and preservation of a zone of peace but also of the role performed by polar traditions in the formulation of policy. The relevance of the historical perspective is enhanced further by the way in which it is utilised by claimants and others in support of the view that Antarctica is already under jurisdiction, and hence ineligible for treatment as a _terra communis_.

Unveiling Antarctica

Although it emerged as a subject of substantial interest only during the present century, Antarctica had attracted speculation for about two centuries, particularly as some doubted its very existence. Controversy continues about the credit for the first sighting of Antarctica _circa_ 1820-1. Should the honour of first discovery be given to Edward Bransfield of Britain, Fabian von Bellingshausen of Russia or the American Nathaniel Palmer? National pride and sovereignty considerations have proved as influential as the quest for geographical accuracy in explaining the persistence of the controversy[10]. In any case, the absence of 'hard' evidence means that the dispute is unlikely ever to be resolved in a conclusive manner in spite of the appearance of occasional definitive statements crediting one person or the other[11].

Historically, there was considerable speculation about the existence of a Terra Australis (southern lands). For example, the ancient Greeks believed in the necessity for a southern continent in order to counter-balance the Arctic - this belief explains the origins of the term 'Antarctic' - and Maori legend postulated the existence of such lands. Mercator's 16th. century map showed a large Terra Australis occupying the southern oceans, and in 1772 Alexander Dalrymple, an Englishman, highlighted the tendency of many to dream about a vast southern continent 'larger than Asia and ... a population of 50 millions'[12]. This hypothesising took a new turn as a result of Captain James Cook's voyage of 1772-5, for this established that a southern continent, if it existed, lay south of 60°-70° South and of the ice fields barring his further progress. Although some writers feel that Cook might have seen Antarctica, this is a dubious assertion, even if he firmly believed 'that there is a track of land near the pole which is the source of most of the ice which is spread over this vast Southern Ocean'[13].

The risks and dangers of 'these unknown and icey seas' inclined Cook to the conclusion 'that no man will ever venture farther than I have done; and that the lands which may lie to the South will never be explored'[14]. But he was wrong, and the early part of the next century witnessed not only the alleged first sighting of the continent - whether by Bransfield, Bellingshausen or Palmer - but also the discovery of a range of isolated portions of Antarctica by explorers from several countries, such as James Clark Ross from Britain, Dumont D'Urville from France and Lieutenant Charles Wilkes from the USA. To some extent, these initial discoveries represented a by-product of sealing in the southern seas rather than a function of the quest for knowledge about the unknown, and geographical, cartographical and scientific knowledge remained minimal about a region which was still a blank on most maps. The period 1845-90 did little to overcome this void, or to answer the questions suggested by the recent discoveries of D'Urville, Ross and Wilkes; for instance, were their discoveries of Adélie Land and so on either of territory on the periphery of Terra Australis or of mere islands in a vast southern ocean? International interest proved relatively low, and there was little attempt to respond to such questions. This apathy was typified by the lack of response from any one of the nine governments approached in 1861 by Commander Matthew Maury, superintendant of the US Naval Observatory and Hydrographical Office, in respect to a cooperative approach towards Antarctica[15]. Although nothing materialised in the short-term, Maury has been depicted as 'probably the true father of international co-operation' in Antarctica[16]. However, in 1874 the global oceanographic expedition conducted by HMS Challenger from Britain made dredgings near the melt-line of Antarctic ice-bergs, and these samples were found to contain rocks suspected as having originated from a southern continent[17].

In the meantime, and pending further exploration, certain writers offered their own views on the subject, thereby illustrating the way in which the unknown excites the imagination. During the late 19th.century two Australian novelists gave vent to their imagination, albeit within a framework of Antarctic facts based upon the existing fragments of information. During 1888 Christopher Spotswood published a story about the voyage of an English sailor called Will Rogers, who sailed through the barrier of ice - this had been identified by Ross in the 1840s - into warm waters where he encountered an inhabited territory entitled Bencolo[18]. A few years later another book by McIver pursued the same theme and produced another interpretation of a voyage through the ice barrier; in this instance, a Captain Periwinckle encountered a fertile temperate land, Neuroomia, which supported an advanced, semi-egalitarian civilisation, comprised about 30m people and contained considerable resources, including gold[19]. But all this was hypothetical, since references to inhabited territory, temperate lands and great resources went far beyond the existing state of knowledge; in fact, the existence of the continent had still to be proved. Nevertheless, the writings of Spotswood and McIver, among others, provide an insight into man's curiosity about the south polar regions, while also offering examples of what might be described as polar-fi, a polar version of science fiction.

Another reflection of this curiosity can be found in the fact that the 1895 International Geographical Congress held in London identified Antarctica as one of the major outstanding geographical problems in urgent need of research and exploration, and during the next two decades or so a series of expeditions conducted by explorers from several nations, including Scott and Shackleton (Britain), Bruce (Scotland), de Gerlache (Belgium), Amundsen (Norway), Borchgrevink (a Norwegian resident in Australia), von Drygalski and Filchner (Germany), Charcot (France), Nordenskjöld (Sweden), Mawson (Australia) and Shirase (Japan), served not only to fill in a few blanks but also to reach the South Pole. In fact, many of the expeditions had been designed primarily as 'pole-hunts' - the concept of a race to the pole excited the popular imagination and helped to secure funds - and Amundsen's success in reaching the South Pole in 1911 paralleled the recent achievement (in 1909) of Admiral Peary (USA) in respect to the North Pole, while also preceding the arrival of Scott's ill-fated expedition, which was to give rise to an episode with heroic implications. As a result, Scott and Oates became national heroes, so that their death imparted a heroic quality to the process of Antarctic exploration and, in this instance, to Britain's role therein.

> To a nation uncertain of her values and threatened by enemies, the example of Oates' death dispelled the doubt - from these frozen regions of the South, there seems to come, like a trumpet call, a message: the greatness of England still[20].

In general, this heroic image prevails, even if a few recent publications - most notably by Huntford - have adopted a revisionist, critical view. Also one American writer has suggested an interesting, albeit debatable, analogy to the effect that Scott's story of struggle and eventual failure symbolises the rise and fall of the British Empire; thus, Quigg claims that 'the event constituted a hinge between an era of epic grandeur for the British Empire and decline to a second-ranked island nation'[21].

The Rise of Antarctic Whaling

Although exploration continued - and was inspired still by a range of research, prestige and other considerations - the period after 1904 introduced a further factor through the development of whaling, initially around the sub-Antarctic islands and then in the seas around Antarctica itself[22]. By 1914 the southern oceans supplied some two thirds of the world's whale oil, a resource utilised in the manufacture of soap, lubricants and margarine. During the First World War whale oil acquired a strategic value, particularly in Britain, where glycerine, a by-product of whale oil's use in soap manufacture, was important for the nitro-glycerine required for explosives. The British government assumed a predominant interest, a point reflected in its announcement of control over the Falkland Islands Dependencies (FID), which were defined by Letters Patent issued in 1908 and 1917 to include South Georgia, the South Sandwich and South Shetland Islands, South Orkneys and the sector of Antarctica centred upon Graham Land.

Antarctica continued to attract international interest after the First World War, especially as whaling provided the continent with an added political, commercial and scientific significance. Although the demand for whaling products fluctuated, Antarctica retained its global primacy as a whaling ground and, as the International Whaling Bureau commented in 1947, 'it is a familiar fact that operations in the Antarctic have been the most important for many years'[23]. For example, during the 1933-4 season 80.1% of the whales killed and 92.6% of whale oil production in the world came from

Antarctica, while for 1938-9 the figures were 84.1% and 94.2% respectively[24]. Whale oil production increased throughout the inter-war period, albeit with considerable fluctuations, and a range of new whaling nations, including Japan and Germany, joined the more traditional ones of Britain and Norway[25]. Usually, it proved difficult to separate economic from either scientific or political motives. The British Discovery investigations yielded valuable scientific research on whales and made significant geographical discoveries, but this overt role was complemented by political and economic contributions; thus, the investigations provided a British presence in the region in the terms used to justify 'effective occupation', while their findings provided an invaluable foundation for the whaling industry, such as in regard to the location of whaling grounds.

The 1920s and 1930s witnessed an escalation of American interest in Antarctica, although this proved less a function of whaling considerations but more the product of exploration, prestige and other factors, and particularly of the personal initiative of Richard Byrd and Lincoln Ellsworth[26]. Their expeditions served not only to provide valuable information on Antarctica - Byrd's expeditions helped to establish that it was one continent - and a further basis for US territorial claims therein but also to enhance the technology of polar exploration, such as through the use of the plane and other forms of mechanised transportation. Subsequently, the opening of the Second World War coincided with the establishment of the United States Antarctic Service (USAS) led by Byrd and intended to initiate bases in Antarctica. President Roosevelt informed Byrd that:

> The most important thing is to prove (a) that human beings can permanently occupy a portion of the Continent winter and summer; (b) that it is well worth a small annual appropriation to maintain such permanent bases because of their growing value for four purposes - national defense of the Western hemisphere, radio, meteorology and minerals. Each of these four is of approximately equal importance as far as we now know[27].

Roosevelt's rider - 'as far as we now know' - continued to act as a necessary qualification for any statement relating to the nature and utility of Antarctica, even if the pace and extent of exploration had been maintained during recent decades.

Technological advance, symbolised by the advent of the aeroplane, had enabled explorers to achieve not only an overview of the whole continent but also more rapid and extensive coverage of a given area. Byrd, Ellsworth and Wilkins pioneered the use of the plane and brought the air age to Antarctica, such as evidenced by Byrd's flight over the South Pole in 1929 and by Ellsworth's trans-continental flight of 1935-6[28]. More substantial exploration on the ground was undertaken by other expeditions, including a series of Norwegian whaling expeditions and a joint Australian, British and New Zealand BANZARE expedition of 1929-31. As a result, Antarctica proved no longer a mythical land, even if knowledge remained scanty on many aspects, a problem accentuated by the prevalence of information of dubious accuracy, such as highlighted by the continuing controversy surrounding the alleged mythical nature of the discoveries made by Wilkes in 1840. For instance, Mawson followed Scott when he accused Wilkes of having 'logged features in error' and of having mistaken distant bergs for land[29]. Even in 1939, that is, after a period characterised by the increasing scale and technological sophistication of expeditions, the British government felt unable still to state with any accuracy the continent's area 'in view of the fact that the Antarctic Continent is constantly under snow and ice, is only partly explored, and it is difficult to say with any exactitude where the land finishes and ice begins'[30].

Science, Sovereignty and International Politics

But the existence of such geographical doubts had not prevented British political interest in the control of this continent of 'great size'[31]. A sector of Antarctica (20°W-80°W) had been claimed already by Britain in 1908 and 1917 as part of the FID and, upon this foundation and in conjunction with an appreciation of strategic, resource, prestige and other motives, the British government decided in 1919-20 to aim for the acquisition of control over the whole continent through the pursuit of a gradualist strategy[32]. The adoption of such a policy gave an added political content to British Antarctic policy after 1920, and clearly various scientific activities were supported by the government either wholly or partly for political reasons. For example, the 1934-7 Rymill British Graham Land expedition undertook a range of important scientific work - for instance, it established for the first time that Graham Land, a key part of the British claim not only to sovereignty in Antarctica but also to the first-ever sighting of the continent by Bransfield, was actually part of the continent rather than an island - but depended heavily upon British government fiscal support, which was given for sovereignty rather than scientific reasons; thus, the expedition was favoured primarily as a method of reinforcing British legal title to the sector based upon Graham Land[33].

In fact, the Rymill episode typified a continuing tendency of most Antarctic publications either to ignore or to gloss over the political dimension. Studies on the expedition, including Rymill's official account entitled Southern Lights, have emphasised the primacy of geography and science, while overlooking any political motivations[34]. Obviously the geographical and scientific work of the expedition should not be under-estimated, but it is inaccurate historically to ignore politico-legal aspects, since government fiscal support proved a function of the view that the expedition was politically opportune - 'it was likely to strengthen the British position there in international law' - and offered further evidence of Britain's 'effective occupation' of the area[35]. Although many scientists prefer to ignore the political exploitation of Antarctic research, this attitude is both naive and unrealistic on account of the uneasy relationship-cum-alliance of science and politics in Antarctica. In practice, scientists, albeit oft-regarded as instruments of sovereignty, have been enabled to exploit the political motive, which has provided the money and opportunity to place them in a location - for example, Graham Land - suitable for research. The interposition of politics became more common during the inter-war period, but even explorers of the Scott-Amundsen era were influenced in part by national considerations, such as by a desire to plant their country's flag at the South Pole.

In the meantime, the adoption of a policy of Antarctic imperialism coloured British government attitudes towards the southern continent during the post-1920 period, and in 1923 resulted in the announcement of British control, albeit under New Zealand administration, over the Ross Dependency sector of Antarctica and then a decade later in the establishment of Australian Antarctic Territory (AAT). Significantly, the preceding BANZARE expedition of 1929-31 led by Mawson had been designed primarily to prepare the way for Australian claims to AAT. By 1933 the British Empire laid claim to some two-thirds of Antarctica, even if the initial British desire to control the whole continent was in the process of qualification as a result of an appreciation of international realities, since other governments not only emerged as either potential or actual claimants but also proved reluctant to acquiesce in the implementation of the British policy 'to paint the whole Antarctic red' as part of the empire upon which the sun never set[36] (See Figure 6.1).

During 1924 the French government proclaimed control over the Adélie Land sector, and then both Norway and the USA began to make difficulties for Britain. The French claim challenged the sector marked out for Australia, and the resulting complications served to delay the proclamation of AAT, while also compelling the Australian and British governments to accept a French enclave therein. Although the Norwegian government repeatedly expressed concern during the 1920s and 1930s about the nature of Britain's claims - these embraced areas discovered and named by Norwegian explorers and were felt to threaten the country's whaling interests - it was not until 1939 that Norway moved to advance a territorial claim to a sector adjacent to the FID. In the event, the Norwegian government was encouraged to act in order to pre-empt any German claim to the area. Such hesitations and vacillations also characterised the policy of the American government, which stated in 1924 that no Antarctic claim would be recognised unless satisfying a strict definition of 'effective occupation', that is, a standard well in excess of existing practice, and particularly of the British version scaled down on account of polar conditions to involve occasional visits and legislative acts[37]. This non-recognition policy caused a number of problems and irritations between London and Washington, even if the American government failed to advance any actual claims in spite of extensive rights developed through the activities of Wilkes, Byrd and Ellsworth. Upon occasions, there were signs that the US government - this was subject to pressure from explorers and others to make claims - was about to follow Britain, France and other claimants, and in 1939 it seemed that the USAS had been created for this purpose. But, in the event, the American government decided against a claim for policy reasons, partly because of the impact of the war and partly because of the relative inaccessibility and economic unattractiveness of the sector marked out for the USA, that is, the sector between the FID and the Ross Dependency[38]. Nevertheless, the continuing inconsistencies of US Antarctic policy - indeed, some have questioned whether there has ever been any real or coherent US policy - in respect to territorial claims have not prevented non-recognition and no-claims becoming consistent themes in American statements[39].

In addition, Britain's position in Antarctica, threatened already by France, Norway and the USA, was exacerbated during the early 1940s, when Argentina and Chile announced claims to Antarctic territory. These actions accentuated the international political problems of Antarctica, for not only were two more actors introduced but also the potential for conflict was enhanced on account of the overlap between Argentine, British and Chilean claims. An Antarctic perspective was added to the long-standing Anglo-Argentine dispute over the Falkland Islands, even if both Argentina and Chile assert that their formal claims advanced in the early 1940s merely reflected an Antarctic role dating back to the 1900s. During the inter-war period Argentina had begun already to challenge British claims to the sub-Antarctic part of the FID, particularly South Georgia, and the formal announcement of Argentine ambitions to mainland Antarctica provided a further dimension to the pre-existing Anglo-Argentine dispute over the Falklands. In turn, the scale of their rivalry for the same territory and the nature of their respective Antarctic activities during the early 1940s compelled the British government to take its Antarctic policy a stage further, thereby inaugurating a new chapter in the international politics and law of the region[40].

Hitherto, the territorial claims of Britain, as well as of Australia and New Zealand, had been supported by legal arguments related to prior discovery, the taking of possession and the exercise of a rather vague form of British 'administration' such as represented by the issue of whaling licences and regulations or the occasional visits of explorers and others. According to the British government, these activities constituted a form of 'effective occupation' appropriate for polar conditions, which rendered permanent settlement impossible. It was argued that a less demanding definition of 'effective occupation' was acceptable to provide legal title in Antarctica, a view encouraged by three international legal judgements announced during the inter-war period, that is, the cases centred upon the Island of Palmas (1928), Clipperton Island (1931) and Eastern Greenland (1933)[41]. In brief, these judgements suggested the need for a diluted definition of occupation when proving title to remote and uninhabited regions;for example, the Eastern Greenland case focussed attention upon a relatively inaccessible and uncolonised portion of the Arctic, and the resulting decision stressed the need merely for 'the intention and will to act as sovereign, and some actual exercise or display of such authority'[42]. By implication it seemed possible to argue that Antarctica required an undemanding version of occupation, except that in the case of rivalry the more active claimant should prevail.

Nevertheless, the situation remained cloudy, since disagreement prevailed - and still continues today - regarding such issues as the degree of effectiveness actually acceptable. The whole question was complicated by the American government's post-1924 emphasis upon a strict definition - this implied that the absence of permanent settlement ruled out the acquisition of sovereignty over polar regions - even if the validity of the Hughes' doctrine of 1924 was questioned internally in Washington, particularly at the periods when the announcement of US claims to Antarctica was under discussion[43].

The Centrality of the Anglo-Argentine-Chilean Relationship

During the period 1942-4 British concern about the escalating Antarctic activities of Argentina and Chile within the area of the FID, in conjunction with a fear that American plans in 1939 for a relatively permanent Antarctic presence - the bases were to be 'more or less continuously occupied' - to be established by the USAS offered a serious challenge to both the diluted interpretation of 'effective occupation' and Britain's position in the South West Atlantic region, resulted in the despatch of a secret naval expedition entitled Operation

Tabarin[44]. The British Foreign Office expressed anxiety about the position - 'it is evident that Argentina intends to assert title to the whole of the Falkland Islands Dependencies' - and supported positive action to protect Britain's world-wide interests, particularly in the context of the Admiralty's emphasis upon the strategic value of the Southern Oceans, including the route around Cape Horn through Drake Passage[45]. Argentina's wartime links with Germany, in conjunction with such episodes as the Battle of the River Plate of 1939 and the activities of German naval raiders against Norwegian whalers in the Southern Oceans, reinforced the impact of the Admiralty's arguments[46]. There existed also an appreciation of the vulnerability of the Panama Canal route.

Significantly, the oft-forgotten Antarctic was adjudged sufficiently important to bring before the British War Cabinet as a region worthy of a fresh policy initiative for a range of political, strategic, legal and economic reasons. On 28 January 1943 the Cabinet decided that 'all possible steps should be taken to strengthen our title to the Antarctic Dependencies of the Falkland Islands, against which the Argentines were encroaching'[47]. Action on the spot was deemed essential, and during 1944-5 Operation Tabarin established British bases in order to initiate a permanent Antarctic presence - 'a more or less continuous occupation' - and to remove Argentine and Chilean marks of sovereignty. In October 1946 the Foreign Office's legal adviser, Beckett, informed the British Polar Committee that 'international law is not static', and recent activities by Argentina and Chile had necessitated a change of course; thus:

> In these circumstances, there seemed urgent need to increase the effectiveness of our possession and control ... It was deemed necessary to establish at selected points permanent stations which should be there in actual possession if any intruders arrived[48].

Beckett employed a traffic-light analogy to warn the committee that 'the light is definitely red in the Falkland Islands Dependencies'.

After the end of the Second World War Tabarin, having begun as a secret naval expedition, was transformed into a civilian organisation, the FIDS, which was re-named BAS in the early 1960s[49]. The FIDS highlighted the alliance of politics, law and science, since - to quote from the instructions issued to the Antarctic base commander in January 1947 -

> The primary object of the Survey is to strengthen His Majesty's title to the sector of Antarctica known as the Falkland Islands Dependencies by maintaining British

> occupation parties there. There are strategic reasons for this occupation ... The secondary objective of the Survey is to continue scientific work in the Antarctic[50].

In practice, members of the FIDS tended to be scientists, who were placed by politico-legal considerations in a position to undertake a major research role in such fields as meteorology, cartography and geology. This facilitated the public presentation of the Survey as primarily a scientific body, especially as its scientific role became more important as the 1950s progressed. Nevertheless, science never overcame the priority of politics.

Operation Tabarin highlights the centrality of the Anglo-Argentine relationship in the international politics of Antarctica during the 1940s and 1950s, and, in turn, the tensions aroused by this rivalry provided one of the key background influences to the conclusion of the Antarctic Treaty, which was designed primarily to contain such sovereignty problems. The continuation of Tabarin through the FIDS illustrated the fact that the Anglo-Argentine problem not only existed after 1945 but did, if anything, become more serious, particularly as the Peronist regime in Argentina appeared to attach considerable policy significance to Antarctica such as indicated by the revival of the Antarctic Commission in 1946 and then by the despatch of a large expedition of seven ships to the South Orkneys, the South Shetlands and the Antarctic Peninsula during the 1946-7 season. Base stations were established or relieved, and the whole process was repeated by an even larger expedition the following season. Chilean activities of a similar nature, albeit on a smaller scale, complicated the situation, for base stations were located often in close proximity to each other, thereby increasing the potential for trouble. The growing post-1945 involvement of governments in Antarctic expeditions and research - many pre-1939 expeditions were private, non-governmental affairs - both caused and reflected the enhanced politicisation of Antarctica.

The acrimonious tone of the diplomatic exchanges between London on the one hand and Buenos Aires or Santiago on the other hand demonstrated the deterioration of international relations in Antarctica, and these developments were associated with the performance of various symbolic acts designed to reinforce and publicise sovereignty claims. During 1947-8 the British cruiser, HMS Nigeria. carried the Falkland Islands Governor around the FID as the symbol of British authority, while the year 1948 witnessed the visit of the Chilean president, Gabriel Videla, to his country's Antarctic bases. For a time, there was a danger that this trend would be paralleled by the militarisation of the region, such as threatened by the despatch of warships. During 1947-8 the presence of two Argentine cruisers, the Veinticinco de Mayo and the Almirante Brown, six destroyers, two transports and various support vessels around the South Shetlands was countered by the British cruiser, HMS Nigeria, and frigate, HMS Snipe. There were also Chilean warships, and in such circumstances the risk of a military incident arising out of the sovereignty dispute was intensified. However, the fear of such a confrontation, in conjunction with an appreciation of the fiscal demands, provided the background for a three-power exchange of declarations between Argentina, Britain and Chile in January 1949 in order to prevent the use of their warships south of 60°S. In turn, these tripartite declarations were renewed annually until the late 1950s, when the Antarctic Treaty effectively absorbed such a provision, albeit as part of a wider-ranging scheme.

In fact, already the British government's anxiety to avoid problems in Antarctica at a time of serious difficulties nearer home had resulted in the offer advanced in December 1947 to submit the sovereignty dispute over the FID - this excluded the Falkland Islands - to the International Court[51]. This move followed on from official appraisals regarding the legal strength of British title to the FID - the results were not very reassuring - as well as upon the desirability of a peaceful solution of the matter for policy, fiscal and other reasons. However, the British offer evoked negative responses from Argentina and Chile, and this situation was to be repeated in 1955 when Britain made yet another abortive application to the International Court. Neither Argentina nor Chile felt that there was any room for compromise or for third party arbitration on their respective claims, at least as far as their dispute with Britain was concerned. Although the two South American countries were in rivalry for the same sector of Antarctica, during the course of bilateral negotiations held in 1941 and 1947-8 their governments managed to agree upon a common line as against Britain; thus, they proclaimed the existence of a South American Antarctic to which only Argentina and Chile possessed rights of sovereignty, even if the talks had proved unable to secure a mutually acceptable definition of their respective claims. The results of these negotiations were embodied in an agreement signed in July 1947 and then in the Donoso-La Rosa declaration of March 1948:

> Until a settlement is reached by amicable agreement regarding the boundary limits in the adjacent Antarctic territories of the Argentine Republic and Chile ... both Governments will act in mutual agreement in the protection and legal defence of their rights in the South American Antarctic, lying between the meridians of 25° and 90°West, within the territories of which the

> Argentine Republic and Chile are recognised as having unquestionable sovereign rights[52].

In this manner, the demarcation of the boundary between Argentine and Chilean claims was left for some future date, partly because of the difficulties of reaching an agreed solution and partly because of an anxiety to gloss over their Antarctic rivalry in order to declare exclusive rights of sovereignty as against Britain. In effect, this situation prevails, for the concept of a South American Antarctic was reaffirmed by Argentina and Chile in the Act of Puerto Montt of February 1978[53].

The British application to the International Court in 1955 had followed a relatively serious phase in the Anglo-Argentine relationship over Antarctica, such as highlighted by the Hope Bay incident of February 1952, when Argentina attempted to prevent the reconstruction of the British base there[54]. The previous British base had been destroyed by fire in 1948, and the incident originated out of the efforts of Argentinians on-the-spot to halt the landing of supplies and stores from the British ship, John Biscoe. An initial warning, backed by the threat of force, was followed by a burst of machine-gun fire over the heads of the FIDS landing party. In turn, the Argentine station commander stated his objections to the British attempt to re-build the base hut only a few hundred metres from the Argentine base established since the destruction of the British base in 1948. In the meantime, the FIDS personnel were withdrawn, and the matter left to the two governments for resolution. But the Governor of the Falklands, Sir Miles Clifford, acting without instructions, arrived at Hope Bay on HMS Burghead Bay, which landed marines, forced the retreat of Argentine personnel and provided naval protection for the reconstruction of the British base.

The British and Argentine governments resolved the incident upon the basis of non-interference with each other's bases, while the confrontation was excused on the grounds that the local Argentine commander had exceeded his instructions. Although bilateral negotiations soon resolved the problem, apprehension continued about the future not only upon the part of the disputants but also of such third parties as the USA and India. As long as bases co-existed in close proximity to each other and as governments tried to match rivals base for base, misunderstandings seemed likely to occur, and in London fears were expressed of another Hope Bay-type incident arising out of the actions of 'trigger happy South Americans'[55]. There was no desire in London to initiate 'miniature Antarctic armaments race' - this was reflected in the enthusiastic renewal of the tripartite naval declarations - while the race for Antarctic bases was interpreted as somewhat futile. Even Clifford, a staunch upholder of British interests in the region, began to question 'to what extent we can continue this unprofitable and expensive competition with Argentina'[56]. Similarly, the members of the FIDS disliked their participation in the regular, almost automatic, exchange of protest notes and claims, and came to believe 'that it was time to end the childish games of political protest in Antarctica', especially as it interfered with scientific work and hampered international scientific cooperation[57].

Inevitably, occasional points of friction occurred; for example, in 1953 an Argentine hut on Deception Island was torn down by Britain, while two Argentines were arrested and returned to Argentina for being 'illegally' in British territory. In this context, it proved impossible to overlook the basic politico-legal motivation for Antarctic bases and research - science remained essentially a facade - and so Argentina, Britain and Chile felt the need to consolidate their respective Antarctic presences; thus, the number and location of bases were fixed more by sovereignty considerations - a desire to extend the area of 'effective occupation' - than by scientific requirements. Although this section has concentrated upon Argentina, Britain and Chile on account of the significant international political implications of their activities, it should be remembered that other claimants were equally anxious to bolster their respective legal positions, and hence the late 1940s and 1950s were characterised by an enhancement of Australian, French and New Zealand activities in Antarctica, including the establishment of permanent bases[58].

A More Visible American Role in Antarctica

The Argentine-British-Chilean impasse on sovereignty concerned the US government, which proved active during and after the late 1940s in the search for a solution to the dispute centred upon the Antarctic sector directly below the American continent. In particular, American concern was accentuated by the fact that the question involved not only its NATO ally, Britain, but also two Latin American countries linked to the USA through a form of hemispheric solidarity expressed by the 1947 Rio Treaty. The latter, known also as the Inter-American Treaty of Reciprocal Assistance, embraced a pledge of mutual support in the event of an armed attack against an American state, and the treaty area - this was defined as extending from pole to pole between 24°East and 90°West - appeared to extend to Antarctica[59]. In addition, Argentina and Chile issued declarations at the time of the conclusion of the treaty in order to reserve their Antarctic territorial rights. Certainly, the Rio Treaty provided substance for the concept of an American Antarctic; in fact, it could be interpreted as a kind of Antarctic extension of the Monroe Doctrine, thereby permitting Argentina or Chile to invoke the treaty against British moves in the Antarctic However, an American reservation was issued with the object of avoiding any commitment upon Washington to take sides, but the ambiguities of the situation, in conjunction with an appreciation of the increasing scale of the Antarctic sovereignty problem, encouraged the American government to give serious thought to the possibility of a negotiated settlement of the Anglo-Argentine-Chilean dispute, perhaps as part of a wider Antarctic agreement.

A further complication for the American government arose out of the need to balance a desire for Antarctic political stability against the pursuit of America's interests and rights in Antarctica, for these 'rights' could be interpreted to include territory within the sector already in dispute between Argentina and Britain. The USA had proved perhaps the most active nation in respect to recent exploration, and during 1946-7 Operation Highjump - the largest Antarctic expedition to date and comprising some 4,700 men, 12 ships and 9 aircraft - resumed the work commenced by the Byrd and Ellsworth expeditions during the 1930s[60]. The following season the US government sent another expedition, Operation Windmill, which was motivated, like its predecessor, by a mixture of strategic, political and scientific factors. In December 1946 the Acting Secretary of State, Acheson, indicated the predominance of the political motive, for he favoured:

> A definite policy of exploration and use of those Antarctic areas to which we already have a reasonable basis for claim ... in order that we may be in a position to advance territorial claims to those areas[61].

This political orientation was reinforced by an appreciation of the military training value of Antarctica, since its conditions were adjudged to prepare men and equipment for Arctic deployments - the Arctic was too sensitive to allow training activities. Science rated rather low in American priorities, and Admiral Richard Cruzen, the commander of the operating task force, is reputed to have stated that scientists were 'superfluous' to the Operation's requirements[62].

During the late 1940s American expeditions were authorised to deposit claims in the name of the USA - to quote Acheson - 'in order that the maximum advantage may be gained for the United States'[63]. Although the American government still hesitated to announce any formal territorial claims, the practice of depositing claim forms alarmed the British government, thereby causing occasional Anglo-American difficulties rather like those characteristic of the 1930s. For example, the British government resented the refusal of American expeditions to seek permission for exploration within 'British territory' - this was a consequence of the US non-recognition policy - and during the Finn Ronne expedition of 1946-8 there were also British complaints that there was insufficient space for two expeditions at Marguerite Bay in Graham Land. Inevitably, Ronne's arrival resulted in friction between London and Washington not only about the usual problem concerning the American failure to respect British authority over Graham Land but also about base hut locations[64]. The resultant hoisting of the Stars and stripes flag by the Ronne expedition in 'British territory' brought matters to a head. Ronne, resenting the British attitude and presence, issued a non-fraternisation decree to his expedition's members, even if only some 230 metres separated the expeditions' respective huts. One member of the Ronne expedition, Jennie Darlington - wife of the third-in-command of the expedition and one of the first women to winter in Antarctica - has highlighted this Anglo-American controversy:

> Arguments over the "facilities" took time to resolve. Although the British had set up their own hutments they still maintained a territorial toehold on the American-built camp. The Anglo-American toilet became a major issue[65].

Eventually, this particular problem was resolved in terms of the British surrendering their toilet 'toehold' and constructing their own sanitary facilities.

Although disputes over flags and toilets, along with those relating to 'post offices' and so on, are easy to dismiss as trivial, these controversies were regarded as serious by the respective Antarctic base commanders as well as by officials in both London and Washington on account of their sovereignty implications. These questions were important to Britain as a claimant, while they appeared more relevant to an American government thinking yet again of becoming an Antarctic claimant and of following up the claim forms deposited by Americans over the years. American concern was accentuated by the recent emergence of Soviet interest in Antarctica, a trend reflecting not only Moscow's reluctance to be excluded from a say in international problems but also the way in which Antarctica was being viewed as one part of the strategic perceptions of the major powers.

Hence, during the late 1940s there existed a series of possible international friction-points in Antarctica - for example, between Argentina, Britain and Chile, between Britain and the USA, and possibly between the USA and the Soviet Union - and in this context the period witnessed an American effort either to contain or to resolve the whole sovereignty problem, such as urged by a Policy Planning Staff paper in June 1948. It was argued that this:

> Is a source of embarrassment to the United States because of our close relation to Great Britain and our commitments in the Western Hemisphere. This embarrassment is susceptible of exploitation by the USSR to the further disadvantage of the United States. Our national interest requires that a settlement of this dispute be reached which will be acceptable to the three countries involved[66].

This preoccupation contributed to the American government's continuing vacillation on the subject of making territorial claims; for example, there existed the argument that a claim would serve to pre-empt any Soviet moves, such as upon the unclaimed sector, as well as to satisfy domestic opinion, whereas others claimed that any US action would merely exacerbate an already tense situation, thereby countering the American desire to contain the sovereignty problem. In any case, there was the added difficulty of deciding upon a suitable area to claim, partly because the unclaimed sector was neither materially attractive nor accessible. Any other claim would bring the USA into direct rivalry with an existing claimant.

Towards an International Solution

In these circumstances, the US government was compelled to re-consider its policies and methods, and this resulted in the advocacy of an international approach in order to resolve the sovereignty question. This period was characterised also by the usual ambivalent and hesitant attitude towards an American claim. Various modes of internationalisation were considered in Washington, such as through a UN trusteeship or a multi-nation condominium composed of interested powers. However, during the late 1940s diplomatic exchanges between the USA and the existing Antarctic powers, that is, as defined through being claimants, indicated a distinct lack of support for internationalisation; indeed, several claimants expressed strong opposition to such moves, especially as they resented outside intervention in 'their' territories. In addition, any UN role was opposed because it would enable other powers to intervene in Antarctica, and the last thing that most claimants wanted was Soviet activity in Antarctic affairs. However, the generally negative response to American proposals was qualified by the Chilean response of July 1948 - the so-called Escudero declaration - since this suggested an alternative scheme, which emphasised principles taken up in part by the 1959 Antarctic treaty[67]. Thus, Chile proposed a 5-year suspension of the sovereignty problem in order to foster scientific research and to prepare the way for an Antarctic conference.

During the late 1940s the American policy initiative failed to secure support, even if both Antarctic claimants and the USA managed to agree upon the desirability of the exclusion of the Soviet Union from Antarctic affairs, a view encouraged by an appreciation of the Cold War aspect. This awareness of wider East-West considerations was reinforced upon the part of claimants by a reluctance to face any further challenges to sovereignty, while American policy was designed to ensure 'that no occasion should be given to the Soviet Union to participate in an Antarctic settlement or administration' and also 'to forestall any Soviet attempt to become a territorial claimant'[68]. Although it was possible to argue for exclusion on the grounds of the Soviet Union's long-standing lack of interest and activity in Antarctica - there had been no real follow-up of Bellingshausen's voyage of the early 19th.century - the Soviet government began to show signs of opposition to attempts to exclude it from an area in which there was a 'historical right to participate'[69]. In essence, this attitude derived from its superpower status, and from the implicit belief regarding Soviet rights to a say in any international question. This attitude was reflected, indeed was publicised for the first time, in a resolution passed by the All-Soviet Geographical Society in February 1949, and this was succeeded by a Soviet note dated 7 June 1950 sent to the USA and the Antarctic powers, except for Chile on account of its lack of diplomatic relations with Moscow. This note gave definition to Soviet rights and interests in Antarctica - considerable emphasis was placed on Bellingshausen's alleged 'first sighting' of the continent - and asserted that the Soviet government 'cannot recognise as lawful any decision on the Antarctic regime taken without its participation'[70]. This episode served not only to re-kindle the debate about priority of discovery but also to introduce formally yet another complicating factor into the international politics of Antarctica, particularly as Soviet interest was founded upon more substantial matters arising out of the visits made since 1946 by its whaling fleets to Southern Oceans. For some Antarctic powers - most notably, Norway, the UK and the USA - Soviet moves possessed Arctic implications, such as on account of the long-standing tendency to interpret legal and other inter-connections between the two polar regions.

In fact, the anti-Soviet aspect provided one of the more consistent themes of American policy, which tended to pursue a relatively uncertain course after the internationalisation proposals had foundered upon the ambitions of the Antarctic claimants. There seemed some difficulty in defining the real nature of American interests in a continent, which still fitted uneasily into existing Cold War strategies. Nevertheless, American policy statements assumed a repetitive line in respect to a preference for the control of Antarctica by the USA and 'friendly parties', such as evidenced by a National

Security Council memorandum during 1954-5[71]. This favoured:

> Orderly progress toward a solution of the territorial problem of Antarctica, which would ensure control by the US and friendly parties ... freedom of exploration and scientific research for the United States and friendly parties ... and access by the United States and friendly parties to natural resources discovered in Antarctica.

The anti-Soviet orientation was only too apparent.

In this manner, Antarctica became the site for a range of international disputes and problems. As such, it attracted the attention of an increasing number of governments, including Britain, France and the USA. Argentina and Chile regarded Antarctica as a prime issue, while a more recent interest had been assumed by the Soviet Union. Antarctica's marginal role in the international political system was in the process of further qualification, thereby continuing trends apparent at least since the 1920s. Although the continent was rated still as of relatively minor international significance, Antarctica's value was perhaps more apparent, such as in terms of a possible strategic and resource utility - press reports oft-stressed uranium as a potential resource - or of scientific benefits. Research had continued in spite of the sovereignty troubles and had become a key aspect of Antarctic activity, and significant contributions to scientific knowledge had been made by the successive national expeditions. For example, the FIDS' political role failed to hinder the development and enhancement of its scientific work; indeed, as the 1940s and 1950s progressed it has been argued that there was a steady escalation in the relative importance of science _vis-à-vis_ politics[72]. In turn, this emphasis upon science provided a foundation for what proved a major development in Antarctica affairs, that is, the International Geophysical Year (IGY) of 1957-8.

NOTES

1. Richard Wyndham, quoted in Wolfrum, _Antarctic Challenge_, p.62.
2. Kenneth J. Bertrand, _Americans in Antarctica 1775-1948_ (American Geographical Society, New York, 1971), pp.483 _et seq_.; P.A. Toma, 'Soviet Attitude toward the Acquisition of Territorial Sovereignty in the Antarctic', _American Journal of International Law_, vol.50 (1956), pp.611 _et seq_.
3. Robert D. Hayton, 'The Nations and Antarctica', _Osterreichische Zeitschrift für Öffentliches Recht_, vol.10(1960), p.371.

4. UNGA A/39/583 (Part II), 1984, vol.2, p.89, Indian response, 16 July 1984.

5. UNGA A/C 1/38 PV 44, pp.16-18, 29 Nov.1983.

6. UNGA A/C 1/38 PV 42, p.26, 28 Nov.1983.

7. Bertrand, Americans in Antarctica, p.18.

8. Peter J. Beck, 'Britain's Antarctic Dimension', International Affairs, vol.59, no.3 (1983), p.443.

9. Hansard (Lords), vol.426, col.214, 16 Dec.1981.

10. For example, see Morton J. Rubin, 'Who Discovered Antarctica?' Polar Record, vol.21, no.134 (1983), pp.508-509; A.G.E. Jones, Antarctica Observed (Caedmon, Whitby, 1981); Quigg, A Pole Apart, pp.10-13.

11. UNGA A/39/583 (Part I), 1984, p.80 (this credits Bellingshausen).

12. Quoted Frank Debenham, Antarctica, p.39.

13. James Cook, A Voyage Towards the South Pole and Round the World (London, 1777), pp.230-1.

14. Ibid.

15. Bertrand, Americans in Antarctica, pp.198-206.

16. King, The Antarctic, p.236.

17. L.P. Kirwan, A History of Polar Exploration (Norton, New York, 1960), pp.215-8.

18. Christopher Spotswood (ed.), Voyage of Will Rogers to the South Pole (Examiner Office, Launceston, Tasmania, 1888).

19. G. McIver, Neuroomia: A New Continent; a Manuscript delivered by the Deep (Robertson, Melbourne, 1894).

20. Quoted S. Limb and P. Cordingley, Captain Oates. Soldier and Explorer (Batsford, London, 1982), p.169.

21. Quigg, A Pole Apart, p.25; see Roland Huntford, Scott and Amundsen: The Race to the South Pole (Putnam's, New York, 1980), pp.544 et seq.

22. J.N. Tønnessen and A.O. Johnsen, A History of Modern Whaling (Hurst, London, 1982), pp.157 et seq.; Peter J. Beck, 'British Policy in Antarctica in the early 20th.century', Polar Record, vol.21, no.134 (1983), pp.476-7.

23. International Whaling Statistics, vol.XVII (Oslo, 1947), p.4-5.

24. Ibid.

25. Tønnessen and Johnsen, History of Whaling, pp.414-32.

26. Bertrand, Americans in Antarctica, pp.275 et seq.; Barry M. Plott, 'The Development of United States Antarctic Policy', unpublished Ph.D. thesis, Fletcher School of Law and Diplomacy, 1969, pp.22 et seq.

27. F.D. Roosevelt to Byrd, 12 July 1939 in Elliott Roosevelt (ed.), F.D.R. His Personal Letters (Duell, Sloan and Pearce, New York, 1950), vol.2, p.906.

28. Laurence M. Gould, 'Emergence of Antarctica: The Mythical Land' in Richard S. Lewis and Philip M. Smith

(eds.), Frozen Future: A Prophetic Report from Antarctica (Quadrangle, New York, 1973), pp.20-1.

29. Douglas Mawson, The Home of the Blizzard (Heinemann, London, 1915), volume I, p.50; Robert F. Scott, The Voyage of the Discovery (Murray, London, 1905), volume II, p.391; Bertrand, Americans in Antarctica, pp.184-190.

30. Hansard (Commons), vol.345, cols.1272-3, 22 March 1939.

31. Secretary of State for Colonies to Governor-Generals of Australia and New Zealand, 6 Feb.1920, CO 532/160/1959, PRO.

32. Ibid.; see Beck, British Policy in Antarctica, p.475, pp. 479-81; Peter J. Beck, 'Securing the Dominant Place in the Wan Antarctic Sun for the British Empire: the Policy of Extending British Control over Antarctica', Australian Journal of Politics and History, vol.29, no.3 (1983-4), p.448, pp.454-8.

33. Peter J. Beck, 'Britain and Antarctica: the Historical Perspective', Fram: Journal of Polar Studies, vol.1, no.1 (1984), p.78.

34. John Rymill, Southern Lights. The Official Account of the British Graham Land Expedition 1934-1937 (Chatto and Windus, London, 1938).

35. Beck, Britain and Antarctica: the Historical Perspective, p.78.

36. Minute by R.H. Campbell, 25 August 1928, FO 371/13360/7836, PRO.

37. W. Hughes to Norwegian minister, 2 April 1924, Foreign Relations of the United States 1924 (US Government Printing Office, Washington, 1939), vol.2, pp.519-20; Plott, Development of US Antarctic Policy, pp.23-4.

38. Plott, Development of US Antarctic Policy, p.76, p.87, pp.94-5, p.111.

39. F.M. Auburn, 'United States Antarctic Policy', Marine Technology Society Journal, vol.12, no.1 (1978), pp.35-6.

40. Beck, Britain and Antarctica: the Historical Perspective, pp.78-9.

41. Auburn, Antarctic Law and Politics, pp.12-13; M.M. Whiteman, Digest of International Law (US Government Printing Office, Washington, 1963), vol.2, pp.1029-34; Ian Brownlie, Principles of Public International Law, 3rd.ed. (Oxford University Press, Oxford, 1979), pp.151-5.

42. Permanent Court of International Justice, Series A/B, no.53 (1933), pp.44-51.

43. Auburn, Antarctic Law and Politics, pp.38-9; see State Department to President Roosevelt, 6 January 1939, President's Official File, no.3673, Roosevelt Library.

44. Beck, Britain and Antarctica: the Historical Perspective, p.79; Fuchs, Of Ice and Men, pp.20-3; E.W.

Hunter Christie, The Antarctic Problem (Allen and Unwin, London, 1951), pp.247-51.

45. Peter J. Beck, 'Operation Tabarin: The Policy Background', unpublished manuscript, 1984.

46. Anon., 'German Raiders in the Antarctic During the War', Polar Record, vol.4, no.32 (1946), pp.402-3.

47. Beck, Operation Tabarin.

48. Statement by W.E. Beckett to Polar Committee, 31 Oct.1946, P(46), 2nd.meeting. This document is closed at the PRO.

49. J.M. Wordie, 'The Falkland Islands Dependencies Survey, 1943-1946', Polar Record, vol.4, no.32 (1946), pp.373-84; V.E. Fuchs, FIDS Scientific Reports:no. 1 - Organisation and Methods (HMSO, London, 1953), pp.1-10; Fuchs, Of Ice and Men, pp.54-5.

50. Beck, Britain and Antarctica: the Historical Perspective, p.79.

51. C.H.M. Waldock, 'Disputed Sovereignty in the Falkland Islands Dependencies' in British Yearbook of International Law 1948, vol.25, pp.311-53.

52. W.M. Bush (ed.), Antarctica and International Law: A Collection of Inter-State and National Documents (Oceana, New York, 1982), vol.1, pp.639-60, pp.660-2; Robert D. Hayton, 'The "American" Antarctic', American Journal of International Law, vol.50, no.3 (1956), pp.583-610.

53. Bush, Antarctica and International Law, vol.2, pp.76-82.

54. Fuchs, Of Ice and Men, pp.164-6.

55. Colonial Office to Foreign Office, 5 Feb.1952, FO 371/97375/ 15211, PRO.

56. Clifford to Colonial Office, 31 Jan.1952, FO 371/19735/15211.

57. Fuchs, Of Ice and Men, p.166.

58. See Phillip Law, Antarctic Odyssey (Heinemann, Melbourne, 1983); R.A. Swan, Australia in the Antarctic: interest, activity and endeavour (Melbourne University Press, Melbourne, 1961); French Embassy In Washington, France and the Southern and Antarctic Lands (French Embassy, Washington, 1962); John Hill, New Zealand and Antarctica (New Zealand Government, Wellington, 1983).

59. Auburn, Antarctic Law and Politics, pp.56-7; Plott, Development of US Antarctic Policy, pp.122-3; Hunter Christie, Antarctic Problem, p.284.

60. Lisle A. Rose, Assault on Eternity: Richard E. Byrd and the Exploration of Antarctica, 1946-47 (Naval Institute Press, Annapolis, 1980); UNGA A/39/583 (Part II), 1984, vol.3, p.100.

61. Acheson to Secretary of Navy, 14 Dec.1946, Foreign Relations of the United States 1946 (US Government Printing Office, Washington, 1972), vol.1, pp.1497-8; Bertrand, Americans in Antarctica, pp.483-513.

62. Paul Siple, 90° South: The Story of the American South Pole Conquest (Putnam's, New York, 1959), p.79.

63. Acheson to Secretary of Navy, 14 Dec.1946, Foreign Relations of the United States 1946, vol.1, p.1497.

64. Finn Ronne, Antarctic Conquest (Putnam's, New York, 1949), pp.58-60. The Ronne expedition was private, albeit receiving logistical support from the US Navy, but the British government interpreted it as a semi-official affair.

65. Jennie Darlington, My Antarctic Honeymoon (Muller, London, 1957), pp.87-8.

66. Memorandum of 9 June 1948, Foreign Relations of the United States 1948 (US Government Printing Office, Washington, 1980), vol.1, p.979.

67. Bush, Antarctica and International Law, vol.2, pp.382-6; Auburn, Antarctic Law and Politics, p.86.

68. Foreign Relations of the United States 1948, vol.1, p.980.

69. Resolution of All-Soviet Geographical Society, 10 Feb.1949, in Toma, Soviet Attitude towards the Acquisition of Territorial Sovereignty, pp.625-6.

70. Ibid., pp.624-5.

71. Quigg, A Pole Apart, p.137.

72. Fuchs, Of Ice and Men, pp.332-3, p.342.

Chapter Three

THE INTERNATIONAL GEOPHYSICAL YEAR OF 1957-1958: A SCIENTIFIC AND POLITICAL TURNING-POINT

The IGY and the Development of Antarctic Science

Although political and strategic motives have been stressed, science should not be forgotten, since it constituted a long-standing Antarctic interest supported on account not only of its intrinsic merits but also of its applied value, such as in regard to the provision of information on resources and to the reinforcement of claims through an 'occupation' derived from the creation of permanent scientific bases. As a result, most governments viewed Antarctic science essentially through politico-legal spectacles; thus, science per se was not a significant priority for governments, and in 1960 Phillip Law, the director of Australia's Antarctic research programme since 1949, observed that:

> For fifty years past, the main motive actuating Antarctic work has been territorial conquest. Expeditionary work was aimed primarily at discovering new territories, at establishing national sovereignty over such territories, at protecting and strengthening national claims ... Scientific work was, in general, of secondary importance. The IGY changed all this[1].

Certainly, the IGY period of intense international scientific activity coloured the thinking of such scientists as Law, who have been encouraged to interpret the IGY as a turning-point in the sphere of science. In consequence, this has fostered a general tendency to devalue pre-IGY research, such as evidenced by the Soviet delegate at the 1959 Washington Conference, where he argued that more had been learned about Antarctica during the past three to four years than in the previous 130 years or so, even if this opinion was influenced also by the recent initiation of Soviet research there[2].

Against this background, the research efforts of early 20th.century expeditions have been interpreted as contributing relatively little to the cause of scientific knowledge.

For example, the expeditions led by Scott, Amundsen and others have been oft-dismissed as mere 'pole hunts', which were dominated by a search for personal or national glory and made only a token scientific contribution. Perhaps the early explorers did display an ambivalent attitude towards science, but it would be unfair to under-estimate either the quantity or quality of their research, especially in the context of the various obstacles deriving from climatic, fiscal, logistical and other considerations. Scientific knowledge was further advanced after the First World War, such as highlighted by the British Discovery investigations, while during the inter-war period the advent of the aeroplane offered a new perspective to exploration, thereby enhancing the research contributions of Byrd, Ellsworth and others. The period during and after the Second World War witnessed further developments, including the establishment of permanent scientific bases, the enhanced scale and technological sophistication of expeditions and a more urgent emphasis upon Antarctic research.

As a result, by the 1950s a reasonable picture of Antarctica had been constructed, but significant gaps in scientific knowledge persisted in respect to both the continent and its surrounding oceans. From this perspective, the IGY episode represented merely another chapter in a long-running story of research inspired by man's intellectual curiosity about polar regions, even if many follow Law in interpreting the event as more of a discontinuity, that is, as a major scientific watershed. In turn, the wider significance of the IGY has caused it to be interpreted as a turning-point in other spheres as well, including the crucial political aspect.

The Nature of the IGY

The idea for the IGY developed initially out of proposals advanced during the early 1950s by such scientists as Dr. Lloyd Berkner of the Carnegie Institute in the USA in favour of a third polar year - the first and second polar years occurred during 1882-3 and 1932-3 respectively - as the framework for a determined scientific assault upon the poles[3]. This initiative was developed subsequently through the International Council of Scientific Unions (ICSU), which represented the world's principal scientific bodies and created a special committee, the Comité Spécial de l'Année Géophysique International (CSAGI) to plan a global, co-ordinated multi-disciplinary research programme for 1957-8, a period of intense solar activity[4]. Within this global scheme Antarctica was identified as 'a region of almost unparalleled interest in the fields of geophysics and geography', and hence worthy of a significant scientific initiative.

The scientific cooperation characteristic of the IGY was facilitated by the prior removal of the political obstacles, which hitherto had thwarted inter-state cooperation in Antarctica. There had been a few examples of international research activity - most notably the Norwegian-British-Swedish expedition of 1949-52 - but in general the sovereignty problem proved a major hindrance to scientific cooperation across frontiers[5]. In contrast, cooperative tendencies characterised the IGY in Antarctica, and this transformation was basically the product of the suspension of the sovereignty problem for its duration. This move represented a key advance in Antarctic politics and science, and was secured through a so-called, 'gentleman's agreement' in July 1955, when at the Paris Conference:

> The various governments concerned had reached a sort of gentleman's agreement not to engage in legal or political argumentation during that period in order that the scientific progress might proceed without argumentation[6].

In a sense the governments stood down for a while, pushed aside the sovereignty dispute and allowed their scientists to cooperate. This moratorium on claims, and its maintenance throughout 1957-8, was significant in the containment not only of any friction arising from the Antarctic sovereignty problem but also of tensions deriving from the wider international political context, which embraced the aftermath of such episodes as the Suez and Hungarian crises of 1956.

Upon this foundation, and in conformity with the 1955 Paris Conference's motion that the overall aims were 'exclusively scientific', the IGY has been interpreted as a 'laudable, politically innocuous event', which advanced the cause of knowledge; in turn - to quote a retrospective view of the Antarctic treaty powers -

> The encouragement provided for cooperation between scientists has enabled them to create knowledge of Antarctica at a much faster rate than would otherwise have been possible[7].

In this sense, it has been argued that the IGY reflected also in part the 'surge of internationalism' - defined in this case as a belief that 'any activity which involved international cooperation was seen as having more than ordinary virtue' - characteristic of the 1950s, since the international environment provided an encouraging atmosphere for the evolution and operation of such initiatives as the IGY[8].

The IGY commenced on 1 July 1957 and ended 18 months later on 31 December 1958. Throughout the globe some 67 nations were involved, whereas in Antarctica only twelve nations performed the research programme at 55 base stations. In essence, the episode represented the coordinated product of national scientific programmes performed by over 5,000 scientists and support personnel, and the main thrust of Antarctic investigations comprised such fields as cosmic rays, geomagnetism, glaciology, ionospheric physics, meteorology and seismology[9]. Particular emphasis was placed upon simultaneous observation of specific phenomena at varying locations, while certain participants conducted extra activities beyond the IGY brief, such as demonstrated by the Soviet Union's extensive photographic surveying and mapping activities or by the Commonwealth Trans-Antarctic Expedition led by Fuchs and Hillary[10]. The twelve countries active in Antarctica during the IGY included the seven claimants - Argentina, Australia, Chile, France, New Zealand, Norway and the UK - as well as Belgium, Japan, South Africa, the Soviet Union and the USA.

The inclusion of the Soviet Union was significant in view not only of its recent commencement of Antarctic research but also of the previous efforts of the American and other governments to exclude it from the continent's affairs. However, in practice, it proved impossible to prevent Soviet involvement in the IGY, particularly in the face of its determination to participate, such as indicated at the 1955 Paris Conference; in turn, this scientific foothold provided the foundation for its oft-expressed objective to perform a more substantial political role. This almost automatic progression was fostered by the traditional alliance of science and politics in Antarctica, so that Soviet participation in the IGY offered a scientific mode of circumventing the previous efforts of several governments to exclude it for political reasons.

In addition, the fact that it was organised by scientists ostensibly for scientific purposes encourages the suggestion that the IGY was to some extent a reaction to the increasing politicisation of Antarctica, even if - to quote one scientist - 'he naive alone will be persuaded that pure science is the sole stimulant'[11]. Although political manifestations became less frequent and overt, politics never quite disappeared from the Antarctic scene during the IGY. For example, problems occurred over the use of maps depicting territorial claims, and many base locations appeared to be a function of non-scientific considerations; thus, claimants tended not only to establish bases solely within 'their' sectors but also to indicate - much to the annoyance of the other IGY participants - a willingness to allow other nations to locate bases therein. Even non-claimants appeared to utilise the IGY for political reasons[12]. Both the Soviet Union and the USA appeared more concerned about each other, such as reflected by their substantial research programmes (the US scheme cost $500m) and choice of base locations. The establishment of the American Amundsen-Scott base at the South Pole itself was particularly significant[13].

These large-scale IGY commitments were essentially a function of superpower status, and especially of policy decisions, such as the American government's decision to maintain American rights and interests in Antarctica through the retention of a predominant status there[14]. US policy on claims remained as ambiguous as ever, and the balanced nature of the pros and cons fostered inaction as the most prudent course, since this allowed Washington to keep its options open. Similarly, Soviet policy proved a natural product of its determination to perform an Antarctic role, and this led to an announcement to continue, even to enhance, research in the continent after the IGY. Inevitably, this decision influenced the scientific and political perceptions of the other governments.

In fact, before the IGY began the Australian government had expressed consternation about the establishment of Soviet bases within its sector, and this anxiety continued during the IGY in spite of the 'gentleman's agreement', since all Soviet bases were confined to the area claimed by Australia. Already in March 1957 the American Secretary of State, Dulles, had been informed of Australia's concern that 'posts originally established under the sheep's clothing of scientific research may subsequently be revealed in their wolf reality of political and military gains'[15]. Once the IGY restraints were removed, the Australian government feared that the conversion of say the Soviet Mirny station into a submarine base would establish a strategic threat, and this encouraged certain Australians, including Mawson, to favour a claim by the USA, which should be pressed 'to thrust its finger into the Antarctic pie' in order to check Soviet moves[16]. Nevertheless, in the event the impact of such political considerations failed to hinder the international cooperation characteristic of the IGY Antarctic programme, whereas in the Arctic, an area of greater political and strategic sensitivity, IGY research was conducted in a national rather than an international framework.

The Continuation of the IGY Experience

Initially the IGY Antarctic project had been intended as an one-off scheme, but during 1956, that is, even before it commenced, there were international exchanges about subsequent possibilities[17]. This desire was accentuated by the actual IGY experience, including the resulting research output, the expansion of the horizons of scientists, the perceived benefits of cooperation and the demonstration of the need for further research on a continuing basis and within an international framework. Such considerations led to the establishment of an extension period in 1959, the International Geophysical Cooperation Year, and to CSAGI's replacement by a new body entitled SCAR - initially known as the Special

Committee for Antarctic Research, and then after 1961 as the Scientific Committee for Antarctic Research - which was intended to provide a permanent machinery for future scientific cooperation in the region.

The initial coolness of certain governments towards the continuation of the IGY episode, such as on account of fiscal, sovereignty and other factors, was qualified not only by an appreciation of the positive benefits of cooperation and of the suspension of the legal problems but also by the Soviet decision to remain in Antarctica. The scientific foothold secured by the Soviet Union during the IGY meant that it was unrealistic for the USA and the other Antarctic powers to revive their exclusion policy; thus, Soviet participation in Antarctica became an inevitable fact of future political and scientific life, and caused the other governments to seek some kind of multilateral IGY-type framework as a way of containing Soviet moves. The American government had already assumed an active Antarctic role, and in this manner the IGY confirmed the entrance of the superpowers into Antarctica; thus, for Auburn 'the Soviet Union's entry into Antarctic politics and the consolidation of its presence on the continent were the most significant effects of the IGY'[18]. This preoccupation about the political and strategic implications of Soviet involvement in Antarctic affairs served to reinforce a general appreciation of the utility of the 'gentleman's agreement' as the basis for stability in Antarctic politics and science, thereby fostering a general desire to transform this _ad hoc_ legal arrangement into a more permanent form as 'a firm foundation for the continuation and development of cooperation'[19].

Clearly the positive will for continued scientific cooperation acted as one ingredient to link together the IGY and the Antarctic Treaty, but there existed also negative reasons, which were based largely upon the fear of international clashes arising within Antarctica out of either the wider East-West confrontation or the Anglo-Argentine-Chilean dispute. During 1957 an American study-group gave expression to some of these anxieties when it described Antarctica as:

> A strategic center from which air and naval fleets may control vital seaways ... the world does not need another strategic area to be struggled for, and such a struggle between the United States and the Soviet Union would appear to be inevitable if the continent is to be divided up as Africa once was[20].

The escalating Antarctic role of the Soviet Union gave substance to such fears, which were articulated by the Indian government through the UN during the course of its abortive efforts to place the topic on the UN's agenda between 1956-8.

In May 1958 President Nehru informed the Indian Parliament of his desire to prevent Antarctica becoming 'the scene of chaos', especially as the wider context of the Cold War rendered the continent a potential site for nuclear weapons and tests[21]. The Indian government advocated the peaceful utilisation of Antarctica to ensure that it 'shall not be used in any manner that would create or accentuate world tensions, or extend to this area the influence and effects of existing tensions'[22].

Although the spread of the Cold War to the cold continent as part of the global hegemony equation excited such anxieties, it is possible that most concern derived from pre-existing disputes, which would become active again upon the expiration of the IGY and of the associated 'gentleman's agreement'. Memories of the conflicts and controversies of the 1940s and 1950s offered a potent motive for progress, particularly as the cooperative tendencies of the IGY period strengthened the general reluctance to return to a situation likely to be characterised by a recurrence of Hope Bay-type incidents and of a race for bases. In fact, since the late 1940s the US government had been attempting to remove, or at least to alleviate, the sovereignty problem, and a perennial influence upon American policy was the view that:

> While it seems unlikely that war could break out over disputed claims in Antarctica, it cannot be denied that wars in the past have grown out of disputes of even more trivial nature[23].

During the late 1940s and 1950s the British government gradually became alarmed at the conflict potential as well as the fiscal and diplomatic costs of the Antarctic sovereignty dispute, and this awareness, in conjunction with the failure of its efforts to submit the matter to the International Court, provided a further stimulus to work for a more permanent arrangement. Heap, a British diplomat, has stressed the priority of negative factors, most notably the 'fear of chaos', over other considerations[24]. Similarly, Guyer, an Argentine involved in the Antarctic diplomacy of the late 1950s, has observed that the governments involved in the region, especially in the South American sector, were at that time 'on the threshold of a conflict'[25]. In this context, most governments believed that a political and legal accommodation was imperative for a Pax Antarctica, and - to quote Heap again - the fact that the cause of science was a beneficiary of the 1959 treaty:

> Should lead no one to believe that such altruism was in the minds of the negotiators; it was not. The parties gained little from it but what they all, variously, have stood to lose without it made the exercise worthwhile[26].

The IGY and the Antarctic Treaty

Although it is somewhat naive to interpret the IGY and the Antarctic Treaty as cause and effect - the treaty's origins proved rather more complex and wide-ranging - the two events were inter-connected, a point acknowledged explicitly in the American note of May 1958 used to initiate the treaty negotiations as well as in the treaty's preamble[27]. Similarly, articles II-IV of the treaty developed the basic principles of the IGY, including freedom of scientific research, the exchange of scientific information and the suspension of sovereignty questions, thereby reinforcing the views of those who cite the IGY as the model for the treaty[28].

The IGY had the effect of calling the international community's attention to Antarctica as an object worthy of research and interest, and also made some kind of institutional framework desirable and possible. Fuchs, who crossed Antarctica during the IGY, has suggested that it 'provided the climate for discussions to begin about negotiations for an Antarctic Treaty'[29]. In this sense, the atmosphere created during the IGY helped to break the impasse characteristic of Antarctic politics in the 1950s, and hence to clear the way for movement in the political, legal and scientific spheres. The IGY, albeit presented as a scientific event, was not entirely apolitical, and the political manifestations prompted Auburn's observation that it reaffirmed scientific research as 'the currency of Antarctic politics'[30]. However, Auburn has approached the IGY-treaty connection from an alternative direction, for he has argued that the linkage merely perpetuated the weaknesses of the former event.

> Frozen into the Antarctic Treaty, the defects of the IGY as a permanent fixture became apparent ... Sovereignty issues could be avoided for a short period, but became inevitable in the long term. The basic defects of the Antarctic Treaty can to a large degree be traced to the IGY[31].

This is a debatable point, and it is perhaps unfair to blame long term problems upon an event designed to last for only 18 months. In addition, some would argue that there were advantages in pushing sovereignty questions into the distant future, such as on account of the insoluble nature of the problem.

Nevertheless, the IGY and the 1959 treaty were partially inter-connected in a significant manner, while in retrospect they can be viewed also as combining to constitute a major watershed in Antarctic politics and science; thus, the late 1950s serve as the divide between the 'Antarctic past' and the 'Antarctic present' which led the Antarctic treaty powers into an extended period of international cooperation in Antarctic affairs.

Antarctica and International Politics

To date, Guyer has been one of the few writers to consider Antarctica as an international political problem, and his thesis concentrated upon the view that the continent failed to become an international issue until 1945, when it was interpreted for the first time as a geopolitical unity on account of the involvement of the Soviet Union and the USA[32]. Prior to this period, Guyer claimed that Antarctica constituted a minor international question of limited concern, partly because the interest of governments was confined only to small parts of the continent. According to Guyer, this limited political approach, which amounted to Antarctica's non-role in the sphere of international relations, was paralleled by the partial application of the principles of international law employed to support sovereignty claims, since polar conditions rendered it difficult to satisfy the normal 'permanent occupation' criterion.

Although this account provides a correct appraisal of the legal situation as it stood before the Second World War, it can be argued that the evidence challenges Guyer's view on the other aspect, since from 1919-20 the British government at least perceived Antarctica as a geopolitical unit. This was demonstrated by Britain's adoption and pursuit of a policy to annex the whole continent through a process of Antarctic imperialism, and the resulting tendency to treat the continent as a unit affected Britain's relations with such governments as those in France, Norway and the USA, while also possessing implications for Australia and New Zealand. Eventually, the British government scaled down its Antarctic objectives, such as on account of an appreciation of international political realities, and paradoxically this reversion to a more limited political approach was accompanied by actions, including Operation Tabarin, designed to satisfy the normal legal requirements for effective occupation. Subsequently, the post-1945 period witnessed an escalation of Antarctica's pre-existing international role, since the introduction of the superpowers supplemented and sharpened the territorial and legal controversies already dividing the governments involved therein. In particular, the enhancement of American interest and the emergence of Soviet activity in Antarctica meant that the Cold War came to provide a backcloth for Antarctic politics, and an appreciation of the international political implications of this development, in conjunction with the conflict potential of the Argentine-British-Chilean dispute, offered the foundation for the IGY and the Antarctic treaty.

The Contribution of History

This book is concerned principally with Antarctica's present and future, but it has proved necessary to preface the analysis of these aspects with a lengthy, albeit selective, discussion of the 'Antarctic past'. This approach facilitates an understanding of the manner in which the 'Antarctic present' has developed out of the past, while it is also clear that the 'Antarctic future' will be influenced to a considerable extent by factors derived from the past as well as from the present. The key fact of the 'Antarctic present' is the 1959 Antarctic Treaty, and hence the 'Antarctic past' is most conveniently defined as the pre-1959 period, that is, the years covered in the previous two chapters, even if in a sense the events of the early 1980s are history now. The historical dimension explains how the current framework of the Antarctic Treaty System evolved out of and partially codified the pre-1959 experience, such as of exploration, scientific research, cooperation and confrontation. Although the IGY has been oft-interpreted as the crucial background factor for the treaty, one should not ignore other developments, including the constant interplay of science and politics, the establishment of permanent Antarctic presences, the Escudero declaration, the tripartite naval decalarations and the gentleman's agreement, which also helped to inspire and mould the Antarctic Treaty.

In turn, an understanding of the past promotes an informed appraisal of future possibilities, such as by indicating potential problems - for example, the political exploitation of science, the impasse over sovereignty, the ambivalent attitudes of the Soviet Union and the USA towards claims - and opportunities, which include the applied value of Antarctic research, possible marine and mineral resource benefits and the ability of Antarctic affairs to bring together diverse groups of governments in an effective cooperative arrangement. Another historical influence upon the future results from the long-standing involvement of certain countries in Antarctica, since their respective polar traditions provides an additional policy input. For example, a study of the past highlights the strength of Britain's stake in Antarctica, and especially why:

> Britain has exerted traditionally a prominent role in the area ... why Britain is there ... Insofar as the future is conditioned by the past and present, it is clear that Britain's Antarctic future rests upon a long-standing tradition as well as upon a fairly strong current position[33].

The events of the pre-1959 period offer an insight into the reasons why such governments as Argentina and Chile will continue to attach considerable importance to Antarctica, wherein their claims are regarded as an integral part of their metropolitan territories. Antarctica constitutes 'an emotional chapter' in their respective national histories, and thus a subject capable of causing a serious international situation[34].

The past may condition the future in other ways, and recently the impact of Antarctic tradition has been employed by various people to support an enhancement of their respective countries' Antarctic programmes. In December 1981 Lord Shackleton adopted this approach in respect to Britain, while more recently Quigg referred to history as a crucial part of his case for a reinforcement of US Antarctic policy[35].

> Despite lapses in attention ... and inconsistencies of policy, the United States has in the broader span of time played a constructive role in the Antarctic ... Many believe that, without an enlarged effort, the United States will lose its ability to influence the treaty system.

Therefore, the 'Antarctic past' offers an important foundation and framework of reference for this study, and the historical perspective - defined here as the period preceding the 1959 treaty - must be integrated into any appraisal of the international politics of Antarctica and also considered in conjunction with contemporary factors.

NOTES

1. Phillip Law, Australia and the Antarctic, The Macrossan Memorial Lecture 1960 (Queensland University Press, Brisbane, 1962), p.21.
2. V. Kuznetsov, 15 Oct.1959, in The Conference on Antarctica (US Government, Washington DC, 1960), p.23.
3. Albert Crary, 'International Geophysical Year: Its Evolution and U.S. Participation', Antarctic Journal, vol.XVII, no.4 (1982), pp.1-4; Harold S. Jones, 'The Inception and Development of the International Geophysical Year', in Annals of the International Geophysical Year (Pergamon, London, 1959), vol.1, p.393; Walter Sullivan, 'The International Geophysical Year', International Conciliation, no.521 (1959), pp.259-283; M.O. de Trevisan, 'El Año Geofisico Internacional Como Antecedente Immediato del Tratado Antartico', Revista de Derecho Internacional y Ciencias Diplomático, vol.XXVII-XXVIII, nos.48-9 (1979-80), pp.35-38.
4. Sullivan, The International Geophysical Year, pp.278-83; Walter L. Sullivan, Assault on the Unknown: The International Geophysical Year (McGraw Hill, New York, 1961).
5. John Giaever, The White Desert. The Official Account of the Norwegian-British-Swedish Antarctic Expedition (Chatto and Windus, London, 1954), pp.11-18.

6. Paul C. Daniels, 'The Antarctic Treaty' in Lewis and Smith, Frozen Future, p.35; Whiteman, Digest of International Law, vol.2, pp.1242-3.

7. Whiteman, Digest of International Law, vol.2, p.1242; Statement made by the Antarctic treaty powers on the 20th. anniversary of the entry into force of the treaty, 1981 in The Antarctic Treaty, British Command paper, Cmnd.8652 (1982), p.51.

8. John A. Heap 'Antarctic Cooperation a quarter of a century's experience', in Vicuna, Antarctic Resources Policy, p.104; Lincoln P. Bloomfield, 'The Arctic: Last Unmanaged Frontier', Foreign Affairs, vol.60, no.1 (1982), p.87.

9. King, The Antarctic, pp.234-50.

10. Vivian Fuchs and Edmund Hillary, The Crossing of Antarctica (Cassell, London, 1958).

11. G.C.L. Bertram, 'Antarctic Prospect', International Affairs, vol.33, no.2 (1957), p.143.

12. Auburn, Antarctic Law and Politics, pp.89-93.

13. Crary, International Geophysical Year, pp.2-4.

14. Quigg, A Pole Apart, pp.138-40; Henry M. Dater, 'Organizational Developments in the United States Antarctic Program, 1954-1965', Antarctic Journal, vol.1, no.1 (1966), p.23; Joseph R. Morgan, 'Strategy of the United States in Antarctica During and After the 30 Year Freeze', unpublished dissertation, Naval War College, Newport, Rhode Island, 1965, pp.32-3, p.52.

15. L.F. Goldie, 'International Relations in Antarctica', Australian Quarterly, vol.30 (1958), pp.23-9; Walter Sullivan, 'Antarctica in a Two-Power World', Foreign Affairs, vol.36, no.1 (1957), pp.161-3.

16. Sullivan, Antarctica in a Two-Power World, p.165.

17. Crary, International Geophysical Year, p.5.

18. Auburn, Antarctic Law and Politics, p.89.

19. The Antarctic Treaty, Cmnd.8652, p.51.

20. Report of the Commission to Study the Organization of Peace, Strengthening the United Nations (Harper, New York, 1957), p.214.

21. Hindustan Times, 16 May 1958; K. Ahluwalia, 'The Antarctic Treaty: Should India become a party to it?', Indian Journal of International Law, vol.1 (1960-1), pp.473-5.

22. UNGA A/3118/Add.II, 17 Oct.1956; UNGA A/3852, 15 July 1958.

23. PPS 31, 9 June 1948, Foreign Relations of the United States 1948, vol.1, pp.981.

24. Heap, Antarctic Cooperation, p.105; UNGA A/39/583 (Part I), 1984, p.20.

25. Guyer, Antarctica's Role in International Relations, p.270.

26. Heap, Antarctic Cooperation, p.105.

27. New York Times, 4 May 1958.

28. The Antarctic Treaty, Cmnd.8652, p.51.

29. Fuchs, Antarctica: Its History and Development, p.18.

30. Auburn, Antarctic Law and Politics, p.93; Finn Sollie, 'The Development of the Antarctic Treaty System-Trends and Issues', in Wolfrum, Antarctic Challenge, pp.29-30; Gordon de Q. Robin, 'Curtain Up on Polar Research', New Scientist, 16 Sept.1982, p.756.

31. Auburn, Antarctic Law and Politics, p.93.

32. Guyer, Antarctica's Role in International Relations, pp.267-9.

33. Beck, Britain and Antarctica: the Historical Perspective, pp.68-9, p.80; Vicuna, Antarctic Resources Policy, p.2.

34. Quigg, A Pole Apart, p.218.

35. Hansard (Lords), vol.426, col.214, 16 Dec.1981; Quigg, A Pole Apart, p.218.

PART THREE

THE ANTARCTIC PRESENT

Chapter Four

THE ANTARCTIC TREATY: A CONTINENT FOR PEACE

The central feature of international politics, law and science in Antarctica is the Antarctic Treaty of 1959, since when it has been supplemented by further arrangements, such as in 1964 by the Agreed Measures for the Conservation of Antarctic Fauna and Flora or in 1980 by CCAMLR. At present, a minerals regime agreement is under negotiation. Collectively, these measures, in conjunction with recommendations emanating from the meetings of the treaty powers, comprise the so-called Antarctic Treaty System, which serves not only to link together the original twelve parties and a number of additional signatories but also to provide the framework for the management of the continent's affairs by the treaty powers. The Antarctic Treaty itself is oft-regarded as one of the most successful international treaties, such as evidenced by the fact that it has been in force for nearly 25 years and by frequent claims that it has achieved its basic objectives. This view still prevails in treaty circles, although recently outside governments have indicated a more critical attitude, which moves occasionally in favour of the treaty's replacement.

Towards the Treaty

A vital foundation for the Antarctic Treaty was the IGY of 1957-8 since this brought together the original twelve signatories in an Antarctic programme of international scientific cooperation facilitated by the suspension of the sovereignty problem for its duration. Previous chapters have highlighted the manner in which - to quote the 1981 treaty Consultative Meeting - 'prior to the Antarctic Treaty the Antarctic had been more the subject of international competition than co-operation'[1]. Against this background, the IGY indicated a way forward from the existing impasse on sovereignty, and several governments proved anxious to perpetuate the stable and amicable relationship characteristic of this episode, especially at a time when the pre-existing tensions were in danger of being exacerbated by the introduction of new rivalries linked to the Cold War. The period was characterised by policy re-evaluations in many countries, including the USA, where a former ambassador, Paul Daniels, was appointed special adviser on Antarctic affairs, and the UK, whose prime minister, Harold Macmillan, used a visit to Australia and New Zealand in February 1958 to exchange views with his counterparts, Menzies and Nash respectively[2].

> Antarctica was one of the subjects which arose in the course of my talks ... we had a general exchange of views and discussed ways and means of ensuring that Antarctica did not remain a potential source of friction and conflict. I agreed with my colleagues on certain basic principles. These were the free development of science in Antarctica and the need to ensure that the area should not be used for military purposes.

Obviously, the Australian, British and New Zealand governments were coming to advocate a new framework for Antarctica, although their agreed line failed to go as far as the internationalisation solution - possibly linked to the UN - suggested by Nash during the mid-1950s.

On 2 May 1958 the US government addressed a note to the other eleven governments which had expressed 'a direct interest' in Antarctica through participation in the IGY[3]. In the light of the forthcoming end of the IGY, the note proposed that the governments should 'join together in the conduct of a treaty ... in the interests of mankind ... in consonance with the high ideals of the Charter of the United Nations' in order to ensure that Antarctica should 'be used only for peaceful purposes' through the encouragement of international scientific cooperation and the containment of politico-legal problems. There was an attempt to reassure the claimants.

> It is believed that such a treaty can be concluded without requiring any participating nation to renounce whatever basic historic rights it may have in Antarctica, or whatever claim of sovereignty it may have asserted. It could be specifically provided that such basic rights and such claims would remain unaffected while the treaty is in force, and that no new rights would be acquired and no new claims made by any country during the duration of the treaty.

Such a formula protected the positions of non-claimants with rights, like the Soviet Union and the USA, although the need to reassure domestic opinion led the note to include the usual reference to the USA's 'direct and substantial rights in

Antarctica ... my government reserves all of the rights of the United States with respect to the Antarctic region, including the right to assert a territorial claim or claims'.

Within one month all eleven invitations were accepted, and during June 1958 representatives from the twelve governments commenced secret and informal preparatory negotiations in Washington DC, wherein most meetings were held at the National Academy of Sciences building[4]. It was adjudged desirable not to convene a conference without serious consultations designed to facilitate an agreed approach towards the various novel and controversial issues involved. For example, would the treaty have a national or international emphasis? Would it be open for signature by all members of the international community? How would the treaty area be defined? How would the sovereignty problem be covered? In the event the negotiations proved somewhat prolonged and were continued over more than 60 meetings until May 1959.

The length of the preparatory talks was partly a function of the need to reconcile a range of national viewpoints on the matters under debate, although there is evidence that the Soviet government exerted a holding influence for about nine months or so, thereby delaying the pace and completion of the proceedings. The Soviet delegate, Andrei Ledovski, attempted repeatedly to confine the discussions to the time, place and procedure of a conference rather than to allow any consideration of matters of substance, while arguing also for universal participation in the talks. In addition, Ledovski asserted that the treaty should be confined to aspects relating to scientific cooperation and peaceful use, thereby avoiding matters of sovereignty. On such questions the Soviet approach, whether assumed for either tactical or policy reasons, placed the delegation on a collision course with other governments, which favoured preparatory work on substantive matters and proceeded to discuss draft articles in spite of Ledovski's opposition; in fact, on 18 November 1958 Daniels, the head of the US delegation, submitted drafts of the twelve articles that were to form the basis of the eventual treaty. However, the Soviet delegation refused to acquiesce, and it was not until March and April 1959 that a more flexible and conciliatory Soviet line enabled an agreed approach, which facilitated the conclusion of the negotiations in May 1959 and the preparation of working papers for the conference scheduled to assemble at Washington during October.

The eventual success of the preparatory negotiations in preparing the way for the conference should not obscure the obstacles that had to be surmounted, for, as Richard Casey, the Australian foreign minister, pointed out in 1959:

> When the informal negotiations began over a year ago, the Australian government was not optimistic that a

> satisfactory basis of agreement could be found ... to provide the basis for an Antarctic treaty[5].

However, in practice, a general search for consensus, albeit based upon the lowest common denominator of agreement and thwarted for a while by the Soviet delegation, helped to secure an eventual basis for agreement. The US government, and especially Daniels, performed a significant initiating, guiding and moving role, such as evidenced by the US note of May 1958 and by the draft articles submitted in November 1958. Credit should be given to individual delegates, who were given a certain amount of discretion in pushing the talks forward, as well as to contributions made by those behind-the-scenes, such as Brian Roberts of the British Foreign Office[6]. Formal negotiations commenced at Washington on 15 October 1959, and the twelve governments concerned signed the Antarctic Treaty on 1 December 1959. The subsequent ratification of the agreement by all of the signatories meant that the treaty came into force on 23 June 1961.

The Treaty in the Context of International Politics

One of the significant influences upon the negotiations derived from the policies of the two super-powers, which proved anxious to prevent the other from acquiring hegemony over Antarctica. The eventual success of the talks was encouraged by what Kuznetsov, the Soviet delegate at the Washington Conference, described as 'favourable conditions', that is, by the improved East-West relations prevalent during 1958-9 and reflected in such events as progress in the Geneva nuclear weapons talks or as Khrushchev's visit to the USA[7]. It was perhaps fortunate that the treaty was signed some five months before the rift consequent upon the U-2 spy plane affair. Even so, Cold War perspectives caused occasional difficulties. The holding approach assumed by the Soviet delegation appeared a product of this matter, particularly as it felt somewhat isolated among the twelve governments. Similarly, American officials oft-employed phrases like the 'United States and friendly nations' and referred to the wider significance of the question; for example, in July 1959 Henry Dater of the State Department stressed the Cold War framework of American policy.

> Because of its position of leadership in the Free World, it is evident that the United States could not now withdraw from the Antarctic ... national prestige has been committed. Our technical capabilities so frequently challenged in recent years are on trial in the Antarctic questions quite as much as in space ... Our capacity for sustaining and leading an international endeavour there that will benefit all mankind is being watched not only

> by those nations with us in the Antarctic but also by non-committed nations everywhere. Antarctica simply cannot be separated from the global matrix. Science is the shield behind which these activities are carried out[8].

At the time, the treaty was welcomed by many commentators as a significant development in the sphere of international politics, an episode given added emphasis not only by its novel features relating to peaceful use of Antarctica but also by the fact that it was signed by both the Soviet and American governments, even if the treaty negotiations took advantage of an 'easing of the international situation', that is, a short-term period of improved East-West relations[9]. The inclusion of the Soviet Union and the USA - and, to a lesser extent, of Argentina, Chile and the UK - in the same treaty was an achievement, especially as signatories were bound by various de-militarisation, inspection and cooperative obligations; indeed, some contemporaries interpreted the treaty as a precedent-setting agreement relevant to other topics, including disarmament in general, the Arctic and outer space[10]. Upon this foundation, the treaty was oft-presented as the product of a 'new stage in international relations' and as 'a contribution to the further improvement of relations between states'[11].

The Scope of the Treaty

Naturally, the treaty as signed proved less ambitious than some parties would have liked, and this has led some to dismiss it as a relatively modest achievement, which merely codified the existing situation. Any appreciation of the terms must be qualified by a knowledge of what had not been included, since the treaty represented the inevitable outcome of any discussions between nations with varying interests, that is, the lowest common denominator of agreement. From this perspective, it did little more than to preserve the *status quo* of the late 1950s, and particularly of the IGY period, a point confirmed by the Argentine delegation at the Washington conference in the statement that their purpose was 'not to institute regimes or to create structures. It is not its mission to change or alter anything'[12].

As a result, the 1959 treaty could be interpreted as a lost opportunity, such as in terms of either internationalising the region or resolving the sovereignty problem. In effect, it evaded the claims question through a non-solution and, while this appeared untidy and unsatisfactory, it was justified as realistic on account of the insoluble nature of the problem; thus, any attempt to resolve the issue would have meant no treaty. Some parties favoured a more ambitious institutional structure than that which emerged. For example,

> It was originally the view of the United Kingdom that some organization, vested with more effective and comprehensive powers than that which is now contemplated, would have been desirable, but in deference to the views of others we are prepared to subscribe to a less far-reaching scheme in the interests of general agreement[13].

Similarly, the Soviet Union indicated its preference for wider international participation in the treaty. However, these limitations in the scope of the treaty were compensated by its capacity for development, such as in respect to the possibility for interpretation or to the ability to fill in the gaps, most notably in the sphere of environmental protection and resource management.

Therefore, the Antarctic Treaty embodied both static and dynamic qualities, and this combination has enabled it not only to perpetuate the relative international stability prevailing in Antarctica during the late 1950s but also to permit the accommodation of the Antarctic situation to the demands imposed upon it by a changing world. Nevertheless, the evolution of the treaty has been constrained by the need for consensus, which tends to mean moving forward at the pace of the slowest; thus, sovereignty preoccupations, among other factors, restrained attempts to develop Antarctic resource regimes and it was not until the late 1970s that significant progress became possible. In the meantime, the Antarctic Treaty was, and remains, the principal source of international law applicable to Antarctica, and since 1959 its significance as the nucleus of the Antarctic Treaty System has been accentuated through the extension of the system's responsibilities into new areas and an almost three-fold expansion of membership. In turn, an understanding of the treaty, and especially of its central role in Antarctic politics, science and law, facilitates an evaluation of future developments, such as in the context of recent challenges to the validity and international acceptability of the Antarctic Treaty System.

The Treaty's Basic Objectives

Basically the treaty was designed as a limited-purpose agreement confined to a specific territorial area. A primary concern was to provide for the continent's use for peaceful purposes only, a point secured through the prohibition of military and nuclear activities and the provision of inspection and observation facilities to ensure compliance. This cleared the way for science, which was promoted by an emphasis upon freedom of scientific investigation and the exchange of information and personnel. In addition, the thorny sovereignty problem was placed 'on ice' through the suspension of disputes and the maintenance of the legal *status quo*. The management of the continent's affairs was vested in the original twelve parties meeting periodically, although a two-tier system of membership enabled the participation of other governments in these regular meetings. The treaty possesses no time-limit, and in theory these provisions can apply indefinitely, unless amended, such as at the review conference allowable during and after 1991.

The treaty preamble and article IX (1a-f) provide some insight into the way in which the parties approached the treaty, or at least into the manner in which they wished to present it to a wider audience. The fundamental stress was placed upon the view that:

> It is in the interest of all mankind that Antarctica should continue forever to be used exclusively for peaceful purposes and shall not become the scene or object of international discord.

The preamble developed this point further in order to claim that the treaty 'will further the purposes and principles embodied in the Charter of the United Nations'. The cause of science figured prominently, for it was argued that international scientific cooperation in Antarctica would make 'substantial contributions to scientific knowledge' and accord with 'the interest of science and the progress of all mankind', especially if freedom of scientific investigation could be established upon 'a firm foundation' in conformity with the experience of the IGY. Clearly there was a general desire to acknowledge the inspiration provided by the IGY episode as the basis for moving onto an international framework aimed to promote peace, prevent discord and encourage science in Antarctica. These aims were repeated in article IX (1a-f), which also mentioned a concern for 'the preservation and conservation of living resources in Antarctica'.

Area of Coverage

On the surface, the geographical coverage of Antarctica appears a relatively straightforward matter, but during the preparatory negotiations of 1958-9 a range of possibilities were considered in order to take account of such aspects as the ice shelves, island groups and the seas around the continent, and the boundary of the Antarctic ecosystem. Initial moves towards a definition of Antarctica were reversed in favour of stating the area of coverage, since it was feared that a treaty definition would provide scope for conflict with a scientific definition[14]. In the event, the Antarctic Treaty was made applicable to a specific part of the globe, which was described in article VI as 'the area south of 60°South Latitude, including all ice shelves'. In effect, this treaty zone was separated from the international political system and placed under a specific, even unique, treaty regime.

Obviously, there was a certain simplicity and clarity in regard to the choice of 60°South, even if this line of latitude possesses no real geographical or scientific relevance, such as compared to either the Antarctic Circle (66° 33'S) or the Antarctic Convergence (*circa* 45°S-60°S). In practice, politico-legal rather than geographical-scientific considerations prevailed, since many of the Antarctic territorial claims were bounded by 60°S as the northern limit. The exceptions were the Chilean and Norwegian claims, for which no northern boundaries had been announced, and the British claim to the FID, which were delimited at either 50°S or 58°S; in fact, during 1961-2 the British government acted to reconcile its claims to the treaty area through the separation of the part covered by the treaty - to be named the British Antarctic Territory (BAT) - from that outside the treaty area, which was known still as the FID. The significance of 60°S had been enhanced also by its employment in the pre-1959 Anglo-Argentine-Chilean naval declarations as the limit beyond which no warships would be sent. For these reasons, 60°S soon emerged as a relatively acceptable limit, and the early meetings were guided by British and Chilean proposals drafted along these lines, in spite of a Soviet preference for the Antarctic Convergence.

During the negotiations the phrase 'area' was preferred to anything more specific, such as 'land and waters', on account of the need to avoid the legal complications surrounding the status of 'ice', even if 'ice shelves' were specifically mentioned[15]. Although doubts continued regarding their legal status as 'land', there was a general desire to include ice shelves within the area of coverage, particularly as several research stations were located thereupon. The position of the high seas raised further problems, and hence it was stipulated that article VI was not designed to prejudice, 'the rights, or the exercise of the rights, of any State under international law with regard to the high seas within that area'. The precise meaning of this assertion remains uncertain and a continuing area of controversy, such as on account of the confused position of territorial waters in the context of the sovereignty problem[16]. However, over the years the treaty powers have tended to adopt a relatively wide definition of article VI as a crucial part of their strategy to control Antarctic affairs, and this trend has encouraged a claim to competence over the oceans south of 60°S in order to avoid external interference in questions relating to offshore resources[17]. In a sense, this objective was expressed in subsequent arrangements, most notably the CCAMLR of 1980, although the ecosystem approach meant that this convention extended north of 60°S.

Inevitably, there has been considerable discussion of the relationship between the UNCLOS and the Antarctic Treaty, with particular reference to the role of the International Sea-Bed Authority (ISBA) in the oceans south of 60°S. This debate raises matters of substance, which are considered later, but in general the Antarctic treaty powers concede that the ISBA will be involved in matters regarding the sea-bed proper, albeit without infringing their basic treaty responsibilities[18]. Further questions surround the UNCLOS-related development of Exclusive Economic Zones (EEZs) based upon a 200 mile territorial sea. For example, will the declaration of an EEZ by an Antarctic claimant be interpreted as either a natural attribute of sovereignty over an adjacent territorial sea or an extension of sovereignty in breach of the legal freeze imposed by the treaty? Therefore, a number of uncertainties relate to the area of coverage, and will continue to excite debate. However, in practice, no serious problems have occurred, and doubts about coverage have not prevented the frequent employment of the term 'Antarctic Treaty area', and in a manner designed to emphasise not only the relative specificity of the area but also an anxiety to avoid outside interference in Antarctica. Examples of the use of the phrase 'Antarctic Treaty area' include article I (1-2) of the Agreed Measures for the Conservation of Antarctic Fauna and Flora (1964), article III of the CCAMLR (1980) and various recommendations emanating from the regular Consultative Meetings, such as recommendations III-1 (1964), VI-14 (1970) and IX-1 (1977).

A Demilitarised and Nuclear-Free Zone

According to the treaty, Antarctica was established as a demilitarised and nuclear-free zone, a zone protected by rights of international observation and inspection. These points contributed to the pace-setting and unique qualities of the treaty, which represented the first nuclear test-ban agreement and made Antarctica the first nuclear-free region[19].

The preamble's hope that 'Antarctica shall continue forever to be used exclusively for peaceful purposes' was given partial effect in article I (1); thus,

> Antarctica shall be used for peaceful purposes only. There shall be prohibited, inter alia, any measures of a military nature, such as the establishment of military bases and fortifications, the carrying out of military manoeuvres, as well as the testing of any type of weapons.

This non-militarisation aspect was reinforced by article V (i), which created a nuclear-free zone, since 'any nuclear explosions in Antarctica and the disposal there of radioactive waste material shall be prohibited'. From the start of the preparatory negotiations, the 'peaceful use' of Antarctica constituted the fundamental objective - it proved a central feature of the US note of May 1958 used to initiate the talks - and the fifth meeting held on 15 July 1958 considered a draft article on this point suggested by the New Zealand delegation to the effect that 'Antarctica shall be used for peaceful purposes only'[20]. The various military qualifications were added during the course of subsequent discussions, which were motivated by a desire to retain Antarctica's non-militarised status in the context of the fear about the spread of the Cold War and the escalation of the Antarctic sovereignty problem. The advent of the superpowers prompted concern about the continent's use as the site for either nuclear weapons or tests, and the various strategic, environmental and other dangers associated with this trend began to preoccupy the Antarctic powers located in the southern hemisphere on account of their relative geographical proximity to Antarctica. In the event, the isolation of the continent from nuclear activities was not really raised until the Washington Conference, where it was introduced as article V. However, article V (2) made one exception, since the peaceful use of nuclear energy was permitted, a provision taken advantage of by the USA in 1962, when it began operating a nuclear power reactor - entitled Nukey Poo - in the hope of providing a more convenient source of energy. But the experiment was marred by the uneconomic and unreliable character of the reactor, which was closed in 1972, thereby reinforcing the traditional reliance upon petroleum products[21].

In many respects, the general tendency to employ the word 'demilitarisation' as a description of the effect of the treaty is mistaken, since the continent was not in a militarised state in the late 1950s, partly on account of the tripartite naval declarations. In such circumstances, a more appropriate interpretation would appear to be the preservation of its non-militarised state. At the time the concept of the peaceful utilisation of a whole continent represented a significant development in the sphere of international politics, although in 1959 the phrase 'peaceful purposes' was clouded in ambiguity, especially as the preparatory talks devoted little time to its precise meaning; for example, was resource exploitation allowable as a peaceful use of Antarctica? Nevertheless, this rather uncritical acceptance of the term 'peaceful purposes' did not prevent a discussion of the difficulties of separating 'peaceful' from 'military' purposes. The exact line of separation was difficult to establish, since certain 'peaceful' activities, even of the scientific nature fostered by the treaty, possessed possible military implications; thus, Admiral Tyree pointed out during the American Congressional hearings on the treaty that 'it is awfully hard ... to say what potentially can be used for military purposes'[22]. In this context, one is reminded of the manner in which certain expeditions during the 1940s and 1950s - most notably Operation Highjump - were motivated by overt military objectives, such as to train personnel or to test equipment and techniques under polar conditions relevant to the Arctic.

Obviously, current research activities may yield applied results of military value. Antarctica can serve as a testing-ground for a range of technological developments, including ice-breaking and the use of runways and aircraft under ice conditions. Similarly, scientific investigation of the upper atmosphere may prove beneficial to military communications. Many other examples could be given in order to confirm the practical difficulties of insulating the 'peaceful' use of Antarctica from military exploitation, thereby qualifying the force of the treaty's prohibitions on various military activities. The resulting ambiguity is compounded by the fact that certain Antarctic research stations and programmes are characterised by a predomoninance of military as compared to civilian personnel. During the 1960s American Antarctic stations were staffed primarily by the military, and this remains true of other countries including Argentina and Chile, where the military presence tends to be a function of the manner in which Antarctic research is organised and supported; in particular, the miltary provide logistical support even in countries whose Antarctic bases are staffed by civilian scientists.

In fact, this feature was taken into account at the time of the treaty negotiations, and article I (2) records that 'the present Treaty shall not prevent the use of military personnel or equipment for scientific research or for any other peaceful purpose'. As a result, the indeterminate nature of the boundary between scientific and military activities is reflected in the use of the military in various Antarctic programmes, such as to provide logistical support or even to perform 'research'. During the 1970s the USA corrected the military imbalance characteristic of its Antarctic presence in the 1960s - thus, during 1968-9 there were 213 military personnel as compared to 30 scientists - in a move designed partly to respond to Soviet criticism and partly to reflect changes in the organisation of the USA's Antarctic research effort, which was placed under the control of the National Science Foundation. However, Argentine research stations remain to be characterised by a predominance of the military, and during 1981-2 there were 132 military personnel as compared to 55 civilians. Although this type of military presence can be interpreted as being in conformity with the treaty, there is evidence to suggest that the military's prime role may be in conflict with the spirit, if not the letter, of the treaty. During a parliamentary inquiry in Britain one MP asked Dr. Richard Laws, director of the BAS, about the large numbers of Argentine military in Antarctica[23]. 'Would you like to hazard a guess as to what these people are doing if they are not doing scientific research? What are they up to?'. Laws responded that 'they also have claims to that sector of the Antarctic and most of their stations are manned by military personnel'. In fact, in March 1982 Laws had visited the Argentine base at San Martín, where he discovered that 'there were 23 personnel who were all military. Two of them were doing meteorological observations and no other science was being conducted'. The non-scientific emphasis of Argentina's Antarctic presence is reinforced allegedly by a relatively low scientific output of research papers and publications. A similar criticism has been directed against Chile, and figures derived from the 1982 exchange of information by the SCAR indicate that over the previous four years the average number of scientific papers produced was 14 for Chile, 18 for Argentina and 151 for the UK, a quantitative differential paralleled in part by a qualitative contrast[24]. Obviously, this British interpretation of the evidence needs to be balanced by Argentina's claim that it has performed a significant and continuous scientific role in Antarctica, which is not fairly represented in such figures[25].

Nevertheless, a range of question marks remain about article I, and some commentators have returned to the wolf in sheep's clothing theme expressed in the 1950s in order to suggest that certain research stations may be de facto military bases maintained for sovereignty or strategic reasons. In particular, the manner in which Soviet bases ring the continent and face such points as the Cape of Good Hope has invited speculation about the true nature of Soviet intentions; thus, Lord Buxton, one of Britain's Antarctic experts, has observed that:

> Russian bases in the Antarctic are not sited, like everyone else's, at the most convenient points for easy access or economical approach, but are strategically ringed around the Antarctic continent. One is certainly nearly opposite the Cape in South Africa[26].

Naturally, such views may represent an incorrect and unfair perception of Soviet policy, but their existence casts light upon possible tensions in the treaty relationship. Although it does not represent a serious problem, the comments about article I do imply the existence of a difficulty, since it remains a matter of debate as to what extent the apparent military orientation of certain Antarctic research constitutes either an actual or potential threat to the Antarctic Treaty System.

In a sense the military problem proves a function of Antarctica's strategic utility - this will be discussed later in the chapter - and the basic difficulty of defining this role tends to confuse the situation. However, problems may arise in the future, and hence a close watch should be kept upon the military presence in Antarctica. In the meantime, any analysis of possible weaknesses needs to be balanced by an appreciation of the achievements of this section of the treaty, since articles I and V provide comprehensive disarmament measures in the spheres of conventional and nuclear weapons and - to quote the recent UN Study -

> The Antarctic Treaty represented the only post-war international agreement for the complete demilitarisation of a sizeable geographical region ... the Antarctic continent and its surrounding maritime areas became a forerunner of nuclear-weapon-free zones[27].

Numerous governments made representations to guide the UN Study, and significantly 'no one challenged the fact that two and a half decades of peace in Antarctica were attributable to the achievements of the Parties to the Treaty in implementing effectively the far-reaching disarmament measures of the Treaty'[28]. As a result, the intrinsic value of Antarctica's neutralisation has been reinforced by wider benefits relating not only to international stability but also to the example of the treaty as a precedent for regional disarmament schemes. The force of such arguments is accentuated by the manner in which articles 1 and V are supplemented by a verification system of inspection and observation.

Treaty Observation and Inspection

An interesting facet of the treaty from the point of view of novel and imitative aspects concerns the inclusion of relatively extensive rights of observation and inspection, which are of interest also in offering an insight into the operation of international inspection systems in general[29]. For the first time unlimited rights of inspection were introduced for a specific region, and the mere acceptance of the principle, albeit in a relatively unimportant part of the world, by twelve governments was a significant international development, a point accentuated by the composition of the treaty parties, such as in regard to the inclusion of both the Soviet Union and the USA.

At one stage during the preparatory negotiations, inspection procedures were discussed in association with the non-militarisation proposals, but under Daniels' prompting there developed a preference to provide for inspection in another part of the treaty. This approach was followed when Daniels submitted his draft treaty articles to the meeting in

November 1958, and eventually his proposed draft article VI provided the substance for article VII of the final treaty[30]. According to article VII (1) inspection was designed 'to promote the objectives and ensure the observance of the provisions of the present Treaty', a form of words implying a check upon such aspects as the continent's non-militarised and non-nuclearised status, the facilitation of scientific research and of international scientific cooperation and the protection of living resources. An ambitious interpretation of article VII might be regarded as bringing both Consultative Meeting recommendations and other Antarctic agreements under the umbrella of the inspection system[31]. Article VII (3) states that:

> All areas of Antarctica, including all stations, installations and equipment within those areas, and all ships and aircraft at points of discharging or embarking cargoes or personnel in Antarctica, shall be open at all times to any inspection by any observers designated (in the appropriate manner by the parties).

In addition, 'aerial observation may be carried out at any time over any or all areas of Antarctica by any of the Contracting Parties' (article VII (4)).

Inevitably, during the late 1950s many governments interpreted these provisions as a major precedent in the whole sphere of international relations, especially as both the Soviet Union and the USA were signatories. It was anticipated that in time the Antarctic experience might spread to other parts of the world, even if the precedent possessed weaknesses as well as strengths. For example, neither of the two superpowers claimed Antarctic territory, and hence inspection did not apply to 'American' and 'Soviet' territory as such or raise security problems. In fact, in 1960 one Soviet writer highlighted this weakness, since the Soviet government could accept unlimited inspection in Antarctica 'where inspection cannot be used against national security'[32]. By implication, the inspection scheme could be seen as a relatively modest achievement in the global context, especially as inspections were to be conducted by national rather than international teams of observers. However, the general tendency is to stress that the principle of inspection had been conceded, and to point to the fact that the inspection provisions have been operated, thereby contributing to the effectiveness of the Antarctic Treaty System.

Although the first-ever inspection was performed by New Zealand in 1963, the dominant role has been performed by the American government, which has conducted seven inspections, that is, in 1964, 1967, 1971, 1975, 1977, 1980 and 1983 (as shown in Table 4.1)[33]. The first American inspection occurred in January 1964, and since then the periodic

Table 4.1: Nationality of Stations Visited by US Inspection Teams

Year	Argentina	Australia	Chile	France	Japan	New Zealand	Poland	South Africa	Soviet Union	UK	West Germany	Total
1964	2		2	1		1			2	2		10
1967	1	2		1	1			1	1	1		8*
1971		2		1					1			4*
1975	1		1						1	1		4
1977	1		1			1			2			5
1980	2		1				1		1	1		6
1983	2	3		1	1			1	4	1	1	14
Total	9	7	5	4	2	2	1	2	12	6	1	51*

*The 1967 and 1971 inspections also included a visit to a Danish ship, thereby making the annual totals for these years 9 and 5 respectively and the cumulative total 53.

exercise of inspection rights has proved an important element of US Antarctic policy; in fact, a separate agency, the US Arms Control and Disarmament Agency, has assumed responsibility for the performance of American inspections. For instance, in 1975 Argentine, British, Chilean and Soviet bases were inspected by a five-person team led by R. Tucker Scully, director of the Division of Oceans and Polar Affairs in the State Department, while between January and March 1983 a four-person team undertook a 47-day trip to inspect 14 stations operated by eight nations[34]. The 1983 inspection visited four Soviet - Leningradskaya, Mirny, Molodezhnaya, and Novolazarevskaya - three Australian, two Argentine as well as British, French, Japanese, South African and West German bases.

In this manner, the US government has proved important in giving effect to article VII, just as the US delegation performed an influential role in proposing the type of inspection scheme embodied in the treaty. However, the early years of the treaty were characterised by divisions within the USA regarding the prudence of inspection, for the State Department's anxiety not only to implement the principle of inspection _per se_ but also to meet commitments made to the Senate during the treaty ratification hearings was countered by the reservations expressed by the American scientific community about the external interference implicit in inspections[35]. In the event, President Kennedy resolved the impasse in favour of inspections, and subsequently this decision paved the way for the prime US role in the initiation and development of the inspection scheme[36].

Since the mid-1960s the US government has proved the most enthusiastic, indeed virtually the sole, practitioner of inspection, a point reflecting the impact of policy factors. According to Scully, the 'regular exercise of the right of inspection is an important element of United States Antarctic policy'[37]. This view has proved a function of the belief in the utility of inspection as a means of ensuring the observance of the treaty, and particularly of articles I and V, although the American government has demonstrated also an awareness of the 'precedent-setting' nature of inspection for arms control purposes; thus, it was fearful lest the right fell into disuse, and - to quote a British observer - 'in order to keep that article (_ie._VII) of the treaty open it is desirable that inspection should be carried out occasionally'[38]. A further element of US policy recalls Secretary of State Rusk's instructions delivered in November 1963 to the nine-member inspection team appointed for 1964; thus, he emphasised the need to act in conformity more with the policy to preserve and enhance 'friendly and cooperative' relations with the USA's treaty partners rather than with one to ensure strict observance of the treaty provisions[39]. In this context, Scully's experience of participation in inspection visits has caused him to refer to the 'representational function' of inspection teams, which serve to exchange ideas with other national groups in Antarctica, to break down barriers and to exercise certain support functions for other nations, such as in respect to the delivery of mail[40].

Nevertheless, the emphasis upon the bridge-building qualities inherent in the inspection scheme has not prevented the argument that:

> The inspections carried out by the United States observers are designed to verify compliance with the provisions of the Treaty, as well as with agreed recommendations developed pursuant to article IX of the Treaty. By promoting public assurance that these provisions are being followed, they promote the objectives and purposes of the Treaty[41].

The schedule of inspection visits (see Table 4.1) indicates an attempt over the years to visit the base stations of as many treaty powers as possible, partly as a means of making contact in the sense identified by Rusk and Scully and partly as a means of acting in a fair and balanced manner. As a result, 51 base visits were undertaken between 1964-83, while the desire to stress the extensive rights inherent in article VII explains why the base inspections were supplemented upon two occasions by visits to the Danish ships, M/S Thala Dan and M/S Nella Dan, in 1967 and 1971 respectively. The visits made to bases established by Poland and West Germany occurred relatively soon after both nations became full members of the treaty system, thereby suggesting that the inspections were motivated in part by a desire to check upon their respective Antarctic credentials as well as to establish an early practical contact. An additional explanation for the predominant American role in inspection is derived from the USA's economic and logistical capability to perform inspections, especially as the personnel - the number of 'observers' attached to a team has been circa four to nine - require transport over considerable distances in order to visit several bases. In the past observer teams have utilised ski-equipped aircraft, but more frequently have relied upon the ice-breakers and helicopters of the US Coastguard assigned to the inspection visit. In general, the 'observers' have been drawn from the Arms Control and Disarmament Agency, the US Navy and the State Department.

Most inspections have been conducted by the USA, but other inspections have been mounted by New Zealand during November and December 1963 - this involved two observers visiting the American McMurdo, South Pole and Byrd bases and is regarded as the first-ever inspection - by Australia and the UK in December 1963 of three American and one New Zealand station as well as by Argentina in 1965 and 1977

[42]. Naturally, these inspections occurred on a much lower scale than those conducted by the USA; in fact, during 1963 Australia, New Zealand and the UK even utilised transport provided by the USA in order to reach the American bases to be inspected. There were plans during the early 1980s for a British inspection of the new West German Filchner base, but the proposal was not implemented due to construction delays[43]. The Soviet Union, albeit possessing the capability, has not undertaken any inspections.

Perhaps, the main reason for the relative lack of interest in the performance of inspections has resulted from an appreciation of the fiscal, organisational and logistical demands of visits. In many countries, the actual resources available for Antarctic research have been limited, thereby leaving few, if any, resources for such extras as inspections. For example, the BAS' long-standing fiscal problems prior to 1982 rendered it difficult to support basic research programmes, and this caused a lack of enthusiasm for inspections, and particularly for the consequent fiscal and manpower burdens. An inspection may involve the loss of a scientist and equipment for a significant part of what is a relatively brief season; thus, Laws has observed that:

> The major constraint is on ship's time because every week that is taken out of our itinerary for that purpose (ie. inspection) is time that is not available for our own logistics and science[44].

One common feature of the inspections to date has been the conclusion that - to quote from Scully's summary of the results of the US inspection conducted between 27 January and 1 February 1980 - 'the team found no evidence of violations of either the letter or spirit of the treaty'[45]. The practice of giving prior notice of inspections, in conjunction with the relative brevity of visits, renders it debatable whether they prove as searching or revealing as they might be, and it can be argued that inspections have proved little more than token gestures designed to 'work' article VII of the treaty. The absence of reported treaty violations tends to reinforce this interpretation, since according to the US government:

> During the seven United States inspections, involving 51 station visits, there has been no evidence of any violation of either the provisions or the spirit of the Antarctic Treaty. All of the information gathered during these visits corroborates the fact that Antarctica is being used solely for peaceful purposes[46].

Undoubtedly, the last sentence is correct and reassuring, even if one is tempted to observe that such a conclusion about any inspection is predictable. Nevertheless, the apparent concern with the peaceful use of Antarctica has caused other problems to be glossed over in these general statements. For example, there is evidence that other parts of the treaty are being infringed, but not being highlighted. Sections of the 1971 inspection account indicated that at both Australian (Casey) and Soviet (Mirny) stations dogs were running free, a situation which represented 'harmful interference' to the environment, such as defined by article VII(2a) of the Agreed Measures[47]. Admittedly, this point was of less importance than the peaceful use of the continent, but the responsibility of protecting the environment and of ensuring the observance of the Agreed Measures falls within the ambit of the inspection system. Obviously, such evidence tends to qualify the credibility of the inspection procedures, at least on environmental questions.

In practice, the much-vaunted inspection and observation system of article VII has proved more apparent than real, partly because the provisions have been applied sparingly, partly because visits have been somewhat brief and superficial, and partly because those inspected have prior notice of inspection. Only one treaty power, the USA, has demonstrated effective support for the scheme, an attitude apparently more concerned with wider policy reasons extending beyond Antarctica, such as evidenced by the stress upon the principle of inspection per se and of not allowing it to fall into disuse, the frequency of visits to Soviet bases - the Soviet Union is the only country whose bases have been inspected on each of the seven US inspections - and the references to the 'precedent-setting' aspects. Other governments have attached a low priority to inspection when allocating scarce fiscal, logistical and manpower resources to Antarctic programmes, and without the impact of policy considerations this situation seems likely to continue.

Nevertheless, Antarctica has proved the site for an international experiment in inspection of arms control and other provisions, and their application by the major international powers means that the scheme possesses an inevitable utility as a precedent in spite of the practical problems. In the event, the Antarctic inspection scheme has worked - or been worked - in a selective and non-rigorous manner, and the chequered inspection of inspection in Antarctica does not augur well for its precedent-setting qualities in respect to areas or topics of greater international significance and sensitivity. In particular, it is a long step from inspecting a Soviet base in Antarctica to the inspection of Soviet territory proper. In fact, another part of the treaty (article III(1)) has partially filled the vacuum left by the relative inactivity of the inspection provisions, since the scheme for the exchange of scientists offers an alternative, less formal and possibly more effective method of ensuring the observance of the treaty's obligations, thereby highlighting the tendency of the treaty system to evolve in a pragmatic and often unforeseen fashion[48].

Although it is easy to be critical, the mere existence of the inspection provisions should not be under-estimated, since article VII represents part of the explanation for the continuing use of Antarctica for peaceful purposes only. In a very real sense, article I, V and VII contribute to each other's role in securing the stability of a whole continent, such as reflected in the perceptions of the treaty powers, which:

> Are convinced that it contributes significantly to the effectiveness of the Treaty and the realisation of its principles and objectives, the most important of which is the preservation of peace in Antarctica. They believe that the practice of inspection has also served the best way of ensuring the absence of suspicion[49].

Antarctica's Strategic Value

Over the years frequent references have been made to the strategic utility of Antarctica, but it has never proved easy to articulate this aspect, especially on account of the tendency of certain governments to identify such a value in order to justify an Antarctic presence and expenditure to sceptical politicians - these tend to be more impressed by strategic rather than by scientific rationale - and yet at the same time to deny the continent's strategic significance in order to reinforce the impact of articles I and V.

Throughout the present century Antarctica has been oft-depicted in terms of strategic considerations. For instance, the formulation of British policy towards Antarctica during 1919-20 was influenced to some extent by strategic arguments advanced against the background of the First World War, which established whale oil as a vital wartime resource and prompted the Admiralty to express fears of 'raiding operations' conducted from Antarctica in a future war against British imperial territories in the southern hemisphere, including Australia and New Zealand, on account of 'the increasing radius of submarines and aircraft'[50]. These preoccupations were revived during the Second World War, when the activities of German naval raiders in the Southern Oceans, in conjunction with Argentine expeditions to Antarctica, gave substance to the perceived threat to British territory, shipping and imperial communications around the Cape of Good Hope as well as around Cape Horn through Drake Passage. The despatch of Operation Tabarin to establish a permanent Antarctic presence was a function of such strategic considerations, which continued into the post-war period, such as on account of the escalation of international activity in Antarctica or of speculation about the possibility of discovering uranium in Antarctica. However, the post-1945 American expeditions, including Operation Highjump, proved a reflection of the strategic importance of the Arctic rather than of Antarctica, since the chief objective was to train personnel, test equipment (eg., aircraft and ice-breakers) and check techniques (eg., runway construction) in polar conditions. From this perspective, Antarctica constituted a proving-ground for the more sensitive and strategically-significant Arctic.

There has been considerable debate about the continent's strategic value at the time the Antarctic Treaty was negotiated, and thus about the extent to which it figured in the policy priorities of the various parties. Obviously, Drake Passage remained important to Argentina, Chile, the UK and the USA, but during the 1950s the main subject of discussion tended to relate to the strategic implications of the Cold War - defined in both territorial and nuclear terms - for Antarctica on account of the growing involvement there of the Soviet and American governments. Inevitably, speculation occurred about the continent's role in respect to a range of activities, including its use as a site for launching missiles, military and submarine bases, and intelligence gathering, and the resulting debate revived earlier fears that Antarctica might provide harbours or ice cover for attacks against either countries in the southern hemisphere or shipping passing round the tip of South America or of Africa. These anxieties were accentuated by an appreciation of the vulnerability of the Panama and Suez Canal routes, and particularly of the recent closure of the latter in the wake of the 1956 Suez War. In 1957 Walter Sullivan wrote of Antarctica that:

> Its vastness provides a sanctuary from which aircraft could dominate the waters that, apart from the vulnerable Panama and Suez Canals, provide the only ready links between the Atlantic and Pacific and the Atlantic and Indian Oceans[51].

The escalation of Soviet activity in Antarctica preoccupied American officials and opinion, thereby inclining them to perceive a strategic role for Antarctica. For instance, Admiral George Dufek, US Antarctic Projects Officer, pressed this aspect frequently and even prepared contingency plans for Antarctica in the event of hostilities[52]. Similarly, during the Washington Conference of 1959 a New York Times article urged that:

> It is in our interest to insure that this vast region should never be turned by the Russians into a kind of Antarctic Albania ... launching pads could be used by the USSR to blackmail the entire Southern Hemisphere from here[53].

During the 1950s one southern hemisphere government, Australia, oft-expressed concern about the actions of the Soviet Union within AAT, partly for sovereignty reasons and partly for fear of a strategic threat to Australia itself from its 'Near South'. This anxiety was articulated by Richard Casey, the foreign minister, in 1953:

> The Australian Antarctic sector is of vital importance to Australia. For strategic reasons, it is important that this area, lying as it does so close to Australia's backdoor, shall remain under Australian control[54].

These examples foster the conclusion that the strategic value of Antarctica derived less from a concern to use it for military or nuclear purposes but more from a desire to deny an advantage to a rival power[55]. As such, Antarctica possessed a negative strategic role, since its utility proved a function of what might happen rather than of what had actually happened. Recent developments in both the Antarctic and the wider international contexts meant that several governments perceived a threat to the existing <u>de facto</u> neutralisation of the continent, a change which would prove unwelcome, inconvenient and even dangerous. Against this background, the Antarctic Treaty performed an important role in the preservation of the non-militarised and non-nuclearised status of the region, and served to meet not only the policy objectives of the treaty powers but also the need identified in the UN Secretary-General's 1960 report to fill the gaps in the international system in order to prevent other regions being drawn into the Cold War. Although the Antarctic Treaty had yet to come into force in 1960, it promised to fill the Antarctic 'gap' and in a manner compatible with the UN Charter.

The continuing neutralisation of Antarctica constituted the basic <u>raison d'être</u> of the treaty; in fact, it was deemed difficult to achieve this objective without the treaty. Nevertheless, some reservations were expressed upon the subject, such as demonstrated by the criticisms arising in the Senate Relations Committee regarding the US government's failure either to stake a territorial claim in Antarctica or to prevent the Soviet Union from acquiring a voice in Antarctic affairs. One senator complained that the Soviet government had been placed in a position to veto the views of the governments, while a more extreme comment emanated from Senator Dodd, who objected to a treaty which placed 'the free world and the slave world on the same footing ... do we want to spread the disease of communism even to the penguins?'[56].

However, criticisms of the treaty proved relatively insignificant, since its conclusion was welcomed by the twelve governments - and possibly by others, including India - and the treaty's maintenance became a key policy objective for both general and specific reasons. In particular, the neutralisation of the continent served to moderate and contain - some might argue, to remove - Antarctic tensions, while also insulating the area from friction in the wider world. Naturally, most observations on the strategic value of the treaty have approached the matter from the point of view of the majority of treaty powers, which saw Antarctica mainly in terms of a potential Soviet threat linked to the wider East-West conflict. But at the same time the Soviet government interpreted the treaty in a similar manner, since 'the aggressive imperialist circles seek to redraw the map of the world and openly proclaim various regions of the world to be zones of their "vital interests"'[57]. The agreement met Soviet interests because it erected 'a secure barrier to the spread of the arms race to the region and its inclusion within the military strategic interests of the imperialist states'[58].

Obviously the most significant international relationship, that is, the Soviet-American relationship, has influenced developments in Antarctica, as in any other part of the world, albeit not in a serious military sense. In general, even low points in the wider Soviet-American conflict have failed either to spill over into Antarctica or to thwart the development of cooperation there. On the contrary, the early 1980s witnessed a rather difficult phase in the general Soviet-American relationship at the same time as the two governments were echoing each other in support of the maintenance of the Antarctic Treaty System, such as by a joint emphasis upon the benefits of the peaceful use of Antarctica in opening 'the door to the development of peaceful cooperation among States'[59].

Perhaps, the most significant perceived threat to the peace of Antarctica, at least recently, arose in 1982 as a by-product of the Anglo-Argentine War over the Falkland Islands, since this conflict served not only to focus attention upon the nearby Antarctic territories but also to foster fears that the war might spread from the Falklands and the FID to Antarctica, another area of Anglo-Argentine rivalry and interpreted by Argentina as part of one territorial claim embracing the Falklands, the FID and Antarctica[60]. Memories of past problems prompted some members of both Houses of Parliament in Britain to refer to the Antarctic implications of an escalation of the Falklands War; thus, there were repeated parliamentary and press suggestions that the issues at stake included Antarctic sovereignty, even if it proved difficult to define the precise nature of the threat to the BAT. Nevertheless, the day after the Argentine invasion of the Falklands, Lord Shackleton reminded the British government that:

> There is much more at stake than the Falkland Islands ... What is at stake and what understandably is in the

minds of the Argentinians is not just the Falkland Islands but their claim to Antarctic territory[61].

In the event, fears about the extension of the Falklands War to Antarctica proved groundless, partly because of a possible mis-reading of Argentine intentions, partly because of Argentine setbacks in the Falklands and the FID, and partly because of a general tendency to under-estimate, even to ignore, the protective qualities of the Antarctic Treaty, of which both Argentina and the UK were among the original signatories. During the 1982 War Antarctica retained its post-treaty peaceful status, and consequently its relative insulation from international disputes between its parties in other parts of the world, even if these clashes arose in a geographically-proximate area, such as the Falklands and the FID. In fact, the cooperative qualities of the treaty were highlighted by the fact that during the war itself Argentine and British representatives sat down together at the same table in connection with discussions on Antarctic marine resources and on a proposed minerals regime at Hobart (May 1982) and Wellington (June 1982) respectively. It was perhaps not surprising that some commentators began to see the Antarctic Treaty as one way out of the Anglo-Argentine impasse on the Falklands, that is, the treaty area should be extended to embrace the Falklands and the FID in order to freeze the sovereignty question and to facilitate improved relations upon other matters[62]. However, the surface attractions of such a proposal conceal a range of difficulties, including the risk of introducing a destabilising element into the treaty system, which has enough other problems at the present time.

Inevitably, the post-war re-appraisal of British policy towards the Falklands embraced Antarctica, and the 1982 Shackleton Report on the Falklands found it necessary to adopt a wider regional perspective and to 'draw attention to wider and longer-term issues in the South Atlantic and the Antarctic'[63]. The infamous "Falklands factor" provided the foundation for a change of course regarding Britain's Antarctic role in order to promote greater British visibility in the whole South Atlantic region, among other policy considerations, and this resulted in a 60% increase in the funding of the BAS and in the reprieve of HMS Endurance, which was interpreted as a visible symbol of Britain's commitment to the area[64]. The increased funding of BAS offered a clear example of the way in which political decisions on Antarctica were reflected through the level of official support for scientific research. Finally, it is worth pointing out that, while Argentina continues to be depicted as the basic strategic threat to British territory, certain commentators have identified other dangers; thus, in December 1983 Lord Buxton expressed some anxiety about Soviet intentions in the region, and especially about the nature of its ambitions regarding neighbouring territories, including the Cape of Good Hope[65].

The 1982 Falklands War was deemed to pose a significant threat to stability in Antarctica, but instead its main effect was to accelerate the emergence of Antarctica as an international issue. Similarly, another geographically-proximate problem, that is, the long-standing Argentine-Chilean dispute over the Beagle Channel, was perceived also as possessing Antarctic implications, especially as the islands at the heart of the matter - the Picton, Nueva and Lennox islands - proved of little intrinsic utility. Apart from representing another manifestation of traditional Argentine-Chilean rivalry, the dispute raised a range of prestige, resource and other considerations. For example, Argentina claimed that the islands, located in the Atlantic, were incompatible with Chile's role as a Pacific power, thereby illustrating the disagreement over rival conceptions of their regional roles, a question with Antarctic connotations. Bilateral negotiations, British arbitration and papal mediation failed to resolve the problem, and for a time at the close of the 1970s a tense and warlike situation ensued. As a result, the Beagle Channel question continued to prove an irritant to Argentine-Chilean relations during the early 1980s until November 1984, when a treaty was signed to settle the dispute[66]. Papal involvement facilitated the settlement, which granted the islands to Chile but guaranteed Argentine maritime rights in the area. The dispute had given an added edge to Argentine-Chilean rivalry in the region as a whole, thereby serving to weaken their ability to concert in support of the concept of a South American Antarctic. In addition prior to 1984 the Beagle Channel dispute, in conjunction with the Falklands question, highlighted the difficulties of resolving any sovereignty dispute involving Argentina and Chile through negotiations, and this point fostered an appreciation of the value of article IV of the Antarctic Treaty, which suspended the 'insoluble' Anglo-Argentine-Chilean dispute over Antarctic territory. In a more practical sense, the Beagle Channel dispute occasioned problems for BAS ships using the channel *en route* to Antarctica.

The emergence of greater international interest in Antarctica during the 1980s has both reflected and fostered speculation about its basic utility, and the emphasis upon the continent's resource potential has been accompanied by suggestions about a strategic importance, such as in the wake of the Falklands War or in relation to discussions about access to increasingly scarce resources. However, official assessments of these aspects have altered little, if at all, since the late 1950s on account of the treaty's continuing existence. Therefore, a recent British statement merely repeated a strategic concern 'to deny the use of Antarctica for military purposes', while Soviet policy still favours keeping the continent free of the imperialist powers[67]. Possibly the most extensive appraisals on the strategic role of Antarctica have occurred in Australia - most notably by Paul Dibb - even if the basic conclusions differ little from those emanating from other countries; thus, for Australia Antarctica was assigned a strategic non-role, but this situation might change if the treaty ended and a hostile power established bases therein. According to Dibb, the Australian Department of Defence defined the region as a 'primary strategic concern', that is, an area in which the military activities of an unfriendly power would be in a position either to attack or to threaten Australian territory and adjacent maritime areas[68]. For example, this situation might endanger the southern approaches to Australia and facilitate the exertion of a maritime blockade, although it has been argued that there are more convenient and accessible areas from which to attack Australia[69].

However, in reality these discussions have proved academic, since such threats have been removed as a consequence of the treaty's neutralisation of the continent. Antarctica remains 'of strategic importance potentially' - to quote Wyndham, an Australian diplomat - but for the time being the treaty has removed strategic threats to Australia, especially as it meant that 'political, as distinct from military solutions to any dangers are to be expected'[70]. According to the Australian government, the Antarctic Treaty:

> Has furthered Australian security interests by ensuring that the Antarctic region, which is geographically proximate to Australia, remains free from conflict and military activity and from political contention[71].

In this context, Dibb believes that Australia's interests in Antarctica, including those of a strategic nature, 'are safeguarded by the continuation of the Antarctic Treaty, not by our claims to sovereignty'[72]. The treaty's survival was significant, for otherwise 'unwelcome instability could be introduced into Australia's strategic circumstances'[73]. These factors have prompted an Australian commitment to the peaceful use of Antarctica, such as defined by the treaty's provisions for non-militarisation, a nuclear-free zone and on-site inspection. Nevertheless, certain Australian writers have drawn different conclusions, such as evidenced by the attempt to identify not only a Soviet military threat to the AAT but also the need for a defence capability in the area; thus, one writer has advocated 'a limited Antarctic warfare capability' for Australia in order to deal with threats to the undefended AAT[74].

However, the advocates of an Antarctic warfare capacity are in a minority not only in Australia but also in other countries, which follow the line mapped out by Dibb according to which the treaty's existence renders such precautions superfluous. Therefore, there is a general tendency in New Zealand to interpret Antarctica as 'a neighbour ... at the backdoor of New Zealand'[75]. At the moment, the treaty served to keep the door closed, but - to quote Barber - 'a 21st.century scenario might blast New Zealand's backdoor from its hinges'[76]. It is impossible to deal with every treaty power in this manner, but finally Argentina and Chile can be cited as further examples of countries aware of the strategic value of the peaceful use provisions of the treaty. Occasional anxiety has been expressed about the possible use of Antarctica by the Soviet Union to threaten South America, while Guyer has referred to the benefits of Antarctica as a nuclear-free zone; thus, 'we are less than a thousand kilometres from Antarctica and if, for instance, an atomic explosion occurred, it could have very concrete effects for us'[77].

Although references are often made regarding Antarctica's strategic utility, and even to the continent as a '*casus belli*', in general it is perceived to be of minimal strategic importance, a situation secured in part by articles I, V and VII of the Antarctic Treaty, which transformed the continent into a strategic irrelevance. The continent has been effectively neutralised to become a strategic non-fact, since the treaty removed Antarctica 'from the arena of strategic rivalry, saving all concerned the expense of maintaining defenses against the real or supposed aggressive designs of their adversaries'[78]. At the time the treaty was concluded the UN Secretary-General was stressing the need to:

> Aim at keeping newly-arising conflicts outside the sphere of bloc differences ... preventive action in such cases must ... aim at filling the vacuum so that it will not provoke action from any of the major parties[79].

The 1959 agreement filled the 'vacuum' in Antarctica, whose separation was confirmed from 'the orbit of present-day conflicts between power blocs', especially as the participation of both superpowers implied the existence of a Soviet-American 'strategic consensus' regarding the continent's role, or rather non-role, in the Cold War[80]. The maintenance of this neutralised status has become an important element in the policies of other signatories also, and the treaty system has worked and survived because it responds to the national interests of a rather diverse range of governments. These 'interests' tend to be of both a selfish and an altruistic, cooperative nature on account of the manner in which the treaty is perceived to represent - to quote a Chilean writer -'peace and international common sense'[81]. In turn, Antarctica appears likely to remain 'a continent for peace' as long as the treaty survives, since its breakdown, or even the withdrawal of a key signatory say on account of disagreements over resource questions, might bring discord and armaments to the region; in fact, an awareness of this danger has served to reinforce the determination of the parties to preserve the treaty system, such as to ensure that it is consolidated through resource regime agreements. Similarly, any third party adjudged likely to threaten the peace of the continent will be subject to the joint pressure of the parties either to contain its activities or to join the treaty.

Naturally, the 'continent for peace' aspect proves most beneficial for the powers actually concerned about Antarctica, such as in the guise of a claimant to territory or of a country geographically-proximate to the continent. However, in the context of the views embodied in the UN Secretary-General's Report for 1960, there has been an increased tendency upon the part of the treaty powers, and others, to refer to the benefits of Antarctica's neutralisation to the wider international community. The Antarctic Treaty can be interpreted as a pioneer in respect to responding to the aspirations expressed in the UN Charter and subsequent General Assembly resolutions in favour of conventional disarmament and the creation of nuclear-free zones. For example, it was the first treaty to give effect to the UN's advocacy in the mid-1950s of nuclear-weapon-free zones, and significantly the Washington Conference of 1959 coincided with UN resolution 1378 (XIV) in favour of disarmament under effective international control[82]. Although the negotiations were motivated primarily by other considerations rather than to fulfil the wishes of the UN, the Antarctic Treaty had the effect of implementing such principles, albeit upon a regional basis; in fact, in this sense it paved the way for the Treaty of Tlatelolco of February 1967, which created a nuclear-weapon-free zone in Latin America[83].

In addition, there has emerged a heightened appreciation of the 'regional dimension in conventional disarmament' and of the fact that 'the scope for regional initiatives is virtually unlimited'[84]. These comments have been extracted from a recent UN study on disarmament, which identified also the merits of regional disarmament agreements, such as in 'keeping regions from becoming involved in confrontations originating outside them', in accommodating the special needs of any region, in supporting and assisting efforts at global disarmament, and in acting as 'valid models for other regions'[85]. The Antarctic Treaty can be regarded as satisfying such criteria, and certainly the treaty powers have pointed to these benefits. The 1984 UN Study on the Question of Antarctica proved to be very supportive of the treaty's peaceful use provisions, a point reinforced by the 1985 UN Study on Conventional Disarmament, which referred to the fact that:

> All regional measures which have been adopted so far, including the Antarctic Treaty, the Treaty for the Prohibition of Nuclear Weapons in Latin America (ie. Tlatelolco) ... have been designed not only with regional purposes in mind but also as contributions to global security and as means to promote disarmament in a wider framework through partial, geographically-limited measures[86].

The Antarctic Treaty's significance in this respect is enhanced by its inclusion of a mutual and verifiable system of inspection[87].

In conclusion, it is desirable to point to the peaceful and disarmed experience of Antarctica since the early 1960s in order to test the practical value of the 1959 treaty. During the course of his 1983 voyage to Antarctica on *HMS Endurance* Robert Fox noted the treaty's provisions when mentioning that the ship had crossed 'the magic line of latitude 60°S ... In accordance with this (treaty), *Endurance*'s two 20-mm guns were covered with tarpaulins whenever she was in Antarctic waters, and no firing practice was allowed'[88]. In this sense, articles I, V and VII serve as 'tarpaulins', which cover the whole treaty area in the interests of the peaceful use of the continent, and the merits of such a situation are accentuated by an awareness of the alternative possibilities, such as evidenced by the 'Antarctic past'. Thus, Troyanovsky, the Soviet delegate, informed the UN First Committee in November 1984 that:

> Turning back the pages of history, we find that there was indeed a time when Antarctica was the scene of bitter international conflict, dispute and claims ... the conclusion of the Antarctic Treaty was an important and effective means of preventing disputes, friction and conflict among States ... its effectiveness and practicality has been verified and proved by its history of almost a quarter of a century[89].

NOTES

1. *The Antarctic Treaty*, Cmnd.8652, p.51.
2. John Hanessian, 'The Antarctic Treaty 1959', *International and Comparative Law Quarterly*, vol.9 (1960), pp.452-4; *The Times*, 12 Feb.1958; *New York Times*, 13 Feb.1958; *Hansard (Commons)*, vol.582, col.1033, 18 Feb.1958.
3. *New York Times*, 4 May 1958.
4. Daniels, *The Antarctic Treaty*, pp.36-38; Peter J. Beck, 'The Secret Antarctic Treaty Preparatory Negotiations of 1958-1959', unpublished manuscript, 1984. An abbreviated version of this paper appeared as Peter J. Beck, 'Preparatory

Meetings for the Antarctic Treaty, 1958-59', *Polar Record*, vol.22, no.141 (1985), pp.653-64. See also Finn Sollie, 'The Political Experiment in Antarctica' in Lewis and Smith, *Frozen Future*, pp.46-63.

5. Richard Casey, 15 Oct.1959, *The Conference on Antarctica*, p.25.

6. Heap, *Antarctic Cooperation*, p.104.

7. Vasili Kuznetsov, 15 Oct.1959, *The Conference on Antarctica*, p.23.

8. Henry Dater, 20 July 1959 quoted in Beck, *Secret Antarctic Treaty Preparatory Negotiations*.

9. G.I. Tunkin, 'An Example of International Cooperation', *International Affairs (Moscow)*, no.2 (1960), p.45.

10. Philip Jessup and Howard Taubenfeld, 'Outer Space, Antarctica and the UN', *International Organization*, vol.13, no.3 (1959), pp.363-79; Philip C. Jessup and Howard J. Taubenfeld, *Controls for Outer Space and the Antarctic Analogy* (Columbia University Press, New York, 1959).

11. Tunkin, *Example of International Cooperation*, pp.43-5.

12. Adolfo Scilingo, 15 Oct.1959, *The Conference on Antarctica*, p.31; Auburn, *Antarctic Law and Politics*, p.94.

13. Sir Esler Dening, 15 Oct.1959, *The Conference on Antarctica*, p.36.

14. Beck, *Secret Antarctic Treaty Preparatory Negotiations*.

15. Ibid.; J. Peter A. Bernhardt, 'Sovereignty in Antarctica', *California Western International Law Journal*, vol.5, no.2 (1975), pp.302-10; Alfred van der Essen, 'The Application of the Law of the Sea to the Antarctic Continent' in Vicuna, *Antarctic Resources Policy*, p.233.

16. Van der Essen, *Application of the Law of the Sea to the Antarctic*, pp.232-4.

17. Auburn, *Antarctic Law and Politics*, pp.134-5.

18. Vicuna, *Antarctic Resources Policy*, pp.8-9.

19. UNGA A/39/583 (Part I), 1984, p.23; *The United Nations Disarmament Yearbook, vol.8: 1983* (UN, New York, 1984), pp.215-6.

20. Beck, *Secret Antarctic Treaty Preparatory Negotiations*.

21. Quigg, *A Pole Apart*, pp.63-5.

22. Quoted Auburn, *Antarctic Law and Politics*, p.97.

23. *HCFAC*, Falkland Islands, Minutes of Evidence, 13 Dec.1982, pp.94-6; *cf*. UNGA A/39/583 (Part II), 1984, vol.1, pp.14-16, Argentine response, 12 July 1984.

24. *HCFAC*, Falkland Islands, Minutes of Evidence, 13 Dec.1982, p.94. Another survey based on SCAR figures over a 3-year period after 1979 comes to slightly different conclusions, that is, 588 publications for the UK, 67 for Chile and 29 for Argentina (these figures are totals, not averages):

W.A. Budd, 'Scientific Research in Antarctica and Australia's Effort', in Stuart Harris (ed.), *Australia's Antarctic Policy Options* (CRES, Canberra, 1984), p.241.

25. UNGA A/39/583 (Part II), 1984, vol.1, pp.13-17, Argentine response, 12 July 1984.

26. *Hansard (Lords)*, vol.445, col.1000, 6 Dec.1983; *HCFAC*, Falkland Islands, Minutes of Evidence, 13 Dec.1982, p.123.

27. UNGA A/39/583 (Part I), 1984, p.44; Tunkin, *Example of International Cooperation*, pp.43-4.

28. UNGA A/39/583 (Part I), 1984, p.44.

29. James Simsarian, 'Inspection Experience under the Antarctic Treaty and the International Atomic Energy Agency', *American Journal of International Law*, vol.60 (1966), pp.502 *et seq*.

30. Beck, *Secret Antarctic Treaty Preparatory Negotiations*.

31. Simsarian, *Inspection Experience under the Antarctic Treaty*, p.507; UNGA A/39/583 (Part II), 1984, vol.3, pp.111-3, US response, 29 May 1984.

32. Tunkin, *Example of International Cooperation*, p.44.

33. Simsarian, *Inspection Experience under the Antarctic Treaty*, pp.507-8; UNGA A/39/583 (Part II), 1984, vol.3, pp.110-13, US response, 29 May 1984.

34. See for example, Arms Control and Disarmament Agency, *Report of the 1971 Antarctic Inspection* (Washington, 1971); US Arms Control and Disarmament Agency, *Report of the 1975 United States Antarctic Inspection* (Washington, 1975); Albert S. Chapman, 'US Observer Team Visits Foreign Research Stations', *Antarctic Journal*, vol. XVIII, no.5 (1983), pp.287-8.

35. Simsarian, *Inspection Experience under the Antarctic Treaty*, p.507; Quigg, *A Pole Apart*, pp.153-4.

36. *New York Times*, 22 Sept.1963.

37. R. Tucker Scully, 'Inspection of Non-US Stations in Antarctica', *Antarctic Journal*, vol.XV, no.5 (1980), p.221.

38. *HCFAC*, Falkland Islands, Minutes of Evidence, 13 Dec.1982, p.96; UNGA A/39/583 (Part II), 1984, vol.3, p.111, US response, 29 May 1984.

39. Simsarian, *Inspection Experience under the Antarctic Treaty*. p.507.

40. Quoted Quigg, *A Pole Apart*, p.148.

41. UNGA A/39/583 (Part II), 1984, vol.3, p.113, US response, 29 May 1984.

42. Simsarian, *Inspection Experience under the Antarctic Treaty*, pp.507-8; *Polar Regions Atlas* (CIA, Washington, 1978), p.44.

43. *HCFAC*, Falkland Islands, Minutes of Evidence, 13 Dec.1982, p.96.

44. Ibid.

45. Scully, Inspection of Non-US Stations in Antarctica, p.222.

46. UNGA A/39/583 (Part II), 1984, vol.3, p.113, US response, 29 May 1984.

47. Arms Control and Disarmament Agency, Report of the 1971 Inspection, p.3, p.36, p.61; Auburn, Antarctic Law and Politics, pp.113-4.

48. This point is developed in the next chapter, see pp.103-7.

49. UNGA A/39/583 (Part I), 1984, p.25.

50. Secretary of State for Colonies to the Governor-Generals of Australia and New Zealand, 6 Feb.1920, CO 532/160/1959, PRO.

51. Sullivan, Antarctica in a Two-Power World, p.162.

52. Quigg, A Pole Apart, p.144.

53. New York Times, 26 Oct.1959.

54. R.G. Casey, March 1953, quoted in Erebus, 'A Limited Antarctic Warfare Capability for Australia: Part I', Pacific Defence Reporter, vol.V, no.8 (1979), p.35.

55. Sullivan, Antarctica in a Two-Power World, p.163.

56. US Congressional Record: Senate, 9 Aug.1960, pp.16058-65.

57. Y. Deporov, 'Antarctica: A Zone of Peace and Cooperation', International Affairs (Moscow), no.11 (1983), p.37.

58. Ibid.; Tunkin, Example of International Cooperation, pp.43-4.

59. UNGA A/C 1/38 PV 43, p.13, 29 Nov.1983, Yakovlev, Soviet Union.

60. Beck, Britain's Antarctic Dimension, pp.429-44; F.M. Auburn, ,The Falkland Islands Dispute and Antarctica', Marine Policy Reports, vol.5, no.3 (1982), pp.1-4.

61. Hansard (Lords), vol.428, col.1585, 3 April 1982; Hansard (Commons), vol.21, col.342, 7 April 1982.

62. Beck, Britain's Antarctic Dimension, p.440.

63. Lord Shackleton, Falkland Islands. Economic Study 1982 (HMSO, London, 1982), p.3.

64. Beck, Britain's Antarctic Dimension, pp.440-1; Peter J. Beck, 'Britain's Role in the Antarctic: Some Recent Changes in Organization', Polar Record, vol.21, no.134 (1983), pp.85-7.

65. Hansard (Lords), vol.445, cols.999-1000, 6 Dec.1983.

66. Guardian, 30 Nov.1984. See Péricles Azambuja, Antártida: História e Geopolítica (Corag, Brazil, 1982), pp.225-42.

67. Foreign and Commonwealth Office, Foreign Policy Document no.98: Antarctica: An Overview (FCO, London 1983), p.6; Deporov, Antarctica: A Zone of Peace, p.37.

68. Paul Dibb, 'Australia's Strategic Interests in Antarctica', paper delivered at CRES Workshop on Australia'a

Antarctic Policy Options, Australian National University, Canberra, March 1984, p.1. Most of this paper was published in Harris, Australia's Antarctic Policy Options, pp.129-33. See also Australian Ministry of Defence, Australian Defence (Canberra, 1976), pp.6-9.

69. F.N. Paramor, 'Sovereignty in Antarctica - A Case for Internationalization', Journal of the Australian Naval Institute, vol.6, no.1 (1980), p.12; Dibb, Australia's Strategic Interests, pp.1-3; Malcolm Booker, The Last Quarter: The Next Twenty-Five Years in Asia and the Pacific (Melbourne University Press, Melbourne, 1978), p.115. Booker represented Australia at the Washington treaty preparatory talks.

70. Richard Wyndham, quoted in Wolfrum, Antarctic Challenge, p.65; Australian Ministry of Defence, Australian Defence, p.9.

71. UNGA A/39/583 (Part II), 1984, vol.1, p.86, Australian response, 31 July 1984.

72. Dibb, Australia's Strategic Interests, p.4.

73. Ibid., p.2.

74. Erebus, 'A Limited Antarctic Warfare Capability for Australia: Part 2', Pacific Defence Reporter, vol.V, no.9 (1979), pp.53-60; Dennis Warner (ed.), 'Antarctica - The Defence Implications', Pacific Defence Reporter Yearbook 1977-78, p.156, p.159.

75. Nigel Roberts, 'New Zealand's Interests in Antarctica', New Zealand International Review, vol.VIII, no.5 (1983), pp.7-10; Laurie Barber, 'Keeping New Zealand's Back Door Closed', New Zealand International Review, vol. VII, no.3 (1982), pp.13-4.

76. Barber, Keeping New Zealand's Back Door Closed, p.14. .

77. Guyer, quoted in Wolfrum, Antarctic Challenge, p.59; Alphonse Max, 'The Antarctic - A Future Casus Belli', Review of the River Plate, 9 Dec.1977, p.943.

78. Steven J. Burton, 'New Stresses on the Antarctic Treaty: Toward International Legal Institutions Governing Antarctic Resources', Virginia Law Review, vol.65, no.3 (1979), p.476; Jonathan I. Charney, 'Future Strategies for an Antarctic Mineral Resource Regime - Can the Environment be Protected?', in Jonathan I. Charney (ed.), The New Nationalism and the Use of Common Spaces. Issues in Marine Pollution and the Exploitation of Antarctica (Allanheld & Osmun, Totowa, New Jersey, 1982), p.209.

79. Annual Report of the Secretary General on the Work of the Organization 1959-60, UNGA 15th.Session, Supplement 1A, pp.4-5.

80. Ibid.; Cisca Spencer, 'The Evolution of Antarctic Interests', in Harris, Australia's Antarctic Policy Options, p.126; cf. certain suspicions of this consensus - UNGA A 39/PV 30, p.12, Jacobs, Antigua and Barbuda, 11 Oct.1984.

81. Oscar Pinochet de la Barra, 'Evolución politico-juridica del problema antártico', *Estudios Internacional*, vol.14, no.55 (1981), p.393.
82. *United Nations Disarmament Yearbook 1982*, vol.7 (UN, New York, 1983), p.107; *United Nations Disarmament Yearbook 1983*, vol.8 (UN, New York, 1984), pp.215-6.
83. Foreign Office Briefing, *Nuclear Options in Latin America* (FCO, London, 1983).
84. Department of Disarmament Affairs, *Study on Conventional Disarmament* (UN, New York, 1985), p.34.
85. Ibid., pp.35-6.
86. UNGA A/39/583 (Part I), 1984, pp.44-6; Department of Disarmament Affairs, *Study on Conventional Disarmament*, p.36.
87. Department of Disarmament Affairs, *Study on Conventional Disarmament*, pp.36-7.
88. Robert Fox, *Antarctica and the South Atlantic: Discovery, Development and Dispute* (BBC, London, 1985), p.48, p.129.
89. UNGA A/C 1/39 PV 53, p.41, pp.43-5, 29 Nov.1984.

Chapter Five

THE ANTARCTIC TREATY: A CONTINENT FOR SCIENCE

A Frozen Time Capsule

The ice sheet is the predominant feature of Antarctica, and inevitably it has attracted a considerable scientific effort, such as upon the part of glaciologists, who have studied its form, flow and stability. These matters possess a significance extending well beyond Antarctica; for example, the ice sheet's stability represents the principal factor controlling world sea levels, whether around Britain, Australia or the USA, while the ice-covered continent constitutes a key influence upon global weather and climates. In addition, David Peel of BAS has described Antarctica as a 'frozen time capsule' in recognition of the ice sheet's role as a historical record not only of snow accumulations in Antarctica but also of climatic and pollution conditions in other parts of the world[1]. An ice core collected in Antarctica can provide data relating to a long time period, and a bore hole penetrating about 90% of the ice sheet may cover a time period of between 20,000 to 200,000 years, occasionally in excess of one million years. In this manner, scientific research can construct 'a detailed record of past environments'[2]. The results can fill gaps in existing knowledge, and, to quote a recent BAS publication:

> Where else can one find snow that fell when the Romans invaded Britain or samples of the atmosphere from before and after the advent of leaded petrol? Where else, alas, can one find nuclear weapons tests recorded for posterity in neatly stacked layers of harmless but detectable radioactivity[3].

As a historical record, an ice core can illustrate, among other things, the impact of the industrial revolution upon the atmosphere, and especially upon levels of pollution, thereby highlighting the manner in which the intrinsic merit of Antarctic science is reinforced by an applied value extending beyond the treaty area.

According to Peel the first ice core was recovered during 1950-1 by the Norwegian-British-Swedish expedition, and this provided the foundation for work on ice cores during the IGY. Over the years glaciologists have refined their techniques, such as in respect to drilling, dating and analysis, in order to yield significant amounts of information.

> By careful detective work, glaciologists have succeeded in linking the composition of ice with a wide range of important environmental features including air temperature, levels of atmospheric dust, volcanic activity, solar activity and a host of airborne pollutants[4].

Glaciologists have worked in both national and international frameworks, such as highlighted in the national case by the Scott Polar Research Institute's Glaciological and Geophysical Folio or in the international sphere by the International Antarctic Glaciological Project on a large part of the East Antarctic Ice Sheet[5]. In fact, it is difficult to define the boundary between national and international programmes, since the above-mentioned Folio was based upon collaborative research with Danish and American institutions. In this manner, research on the ice sheet highlights the manner in which the treaty provided an environment favourable to the promotion of science in Antarctica and to the conduct of research within an international framework.

A Scientific Laboratory

The US note of May 1958 stressed that the main objectives of any treaty should be to ensure the peaceful use of Antarctica as well as to facilitate scientific research there, and the acceptance of the invitations to the preparatory talks implied agreement upon these points; indeed, Ledovski, the Soviet delegate, asserted that they constituted the only proper topics for discussion[6]. Laurence Gould has described Antarctica as a scientific laboratory, while Fuchs has proved a frequent advocate of the view that the 1959 treaty transformed, or perhaps confirmed, Antarctica as a 'continent for science'[7]. In this context, it has been argued that the recent emphasis upon its resource potential should not obscure the fact that Antarctica's basic current utility derives from scientific research and that - to quote Gould - 'for many ... many years to come ... the most important export of Antarctica is going to be its scientific data'[8].

However, scientific research *per se* does not tend to be a subject of major national interest, and in the case of conflicting objectives the cause of science cannot compete with the impact of political or economic goals. In practice, Antarctic science has become inter-twined with other questions in spite of the alleged treaty separation of science and politics, such as applauded by Fuchs' concept of a continent for science:

> At last, Antarctica had become an international laboratory, a far cry from the days when plans and movements were discussed in code or cypher lest someone else should forestall the next move[9].

Fuchs' role as director of the FIDS after the late 1940s made him cognisant of the problems posed for scientific investigation by political considerations. During the pre-treaty period, national projects tended to proceed in deliberate isolation, even rivalry, with each other - the Norwegian-British-Swedish expedition represented one of the few exceptions to this rule - and scientists were interpreted basically as political instruments, who were exploited either to support and reinforce sovereignty claims or to enhance national prestige; thus, the intrinsic scientific merit of either a project or location was less important than politico-legal considerations.

Nevertheless, the scientific contribution of the pre-1959 period should not be under-estimated, for many scientists placed on-the-spot in Antarctica for sovereignty and other reasons saw themselves as engaged in a quest for knowledge, that is, a role rising above politico-legal factors and one facilitated by official fiscal support. To some extent, the scientist was able to turn the tables upon governments, and to exploit politics for the advancement of science. The IGY experience highlighted this ability to rise above politics and to push governments aside in the interests of international scientific cooperation. In turn, a general desire to continue the IGY-type scenario provided one of the key rationale for the treaty negotiations, and the role of science was emphasised throughout the preamble and main part of the resulting agreement, such as recognised by Gould, who had visited Antarctica with Byrd and proved active in the USA's IGY programmes.

> International scientific cooperation is not new. It has existed for many centuries, but the IGY did add a new and significant dimension. It demonstrated, as never before, that the international community of science is the most hopeful of examples of world cooperation and organization. Scientific cooperation in Antarctica led to the creation of the first treaty ever designed to protect a scientific programme; the Antarctic Treaty[10].

An interesting feature of the preparatory negotiations was the manner in which the evaluation of drafts on peaceful use and scientific investigation proceeded in harmony with each other.

Although the peaceful use aspect retained predominance the promotion of scientific cooperation and research proved the key principle embodied in articles II-III of the treaty; thus, the latter provided a systematic framework designed to establish a workable relationship between the scientific and political worlds in the interests of ensuring the centrality of science. According to article II, 'freedom of scientific investigation in Antarctica and cooperation toward that end, as applied during the International Geophysical Year, shall continue', a point reaffirmed by article III (1)'s emphasis upon the objective 'to promote international cooperation in scientific investigation in Antarctica'. Inevitably, the treaty framework was welcomed by scientists, who noted also the setting aside of the sovereignty dispute, the non-militarisation of the continent and the provisions for the exchange of scientific information and personnel. Some members of the scientific community expressed initial reservations about the treaty, such as on account of fears about the intervention of politicians and diplomats in questions best left in their view to scientists. But most comments were supportive, and it became commonplace for Fuchs, Gould and others to assert that 'the Antarctic Treaty is indispensable to the world of science which knows no national or other political boundaries'[11].

The Commonwealth of Science

Harry King has employed the phrase 'the Commonwealth of Science' to describe the practical nature of international scientific cooperation in Antarctica, which has served to bring together scientists and governments from a diverse range of countries, thereby enhancing the quality of the overall research contribution, promoting international understanding, and perhaps defusing, even removing, sovereignty problems[12]. In any case, the harsh, hostile and unyielding nature of the Antarctic environment, in conjunction with the size of the continent, provides a stimulus for a cooperative effort on account not only of the extent of the scientific problems to be resolved but also of the need for joint action in the event of emergencies.

The Antarctic treaty powers have employed the treaty as a framework for a range of scientific research conducted upon both a national and international basis in such spheres as the earth sciences, glaciology, atmospheric sciences, and the marine sciences, and performed by, or organised under the auspices of, such bodies as the BAS, the National Science Foundation in the USA and the Department of Ocean Development in India[13]. There exist varying levels of government involvement and control in such aspects as the organisation of research and the provision of logistical support through bases, ships and aircraft. For example, the BAS is organised as a non-political organisation, which plans and performs research programmes, provides its own logistical support and relies largely upon government funding channelled through the Natural Environmental Research Council[14] (See Figure 5.1). In certain countries, including the USA and South Africa, the government provides transport and other facilities, whereas in other cases, such as the Soviet Union, the government's role is all-embracing (See Figure 5.2). However, in practice, the situation is not as clear as this, and not even the BAS is immune from political influences, such as demonstrated by the enhanced levels of government funding provided for policy reasons in the wake of the 1982 Falklands War[15].

International scientific links are fostered through SCAR - its role will be examined in a subsequent chapter - as well as through a range of formal and informal links conducted through such bodies as the World Meteorological Organisation. In fact, international cooperation embraces not only research programmes but also logistics, such as evidenced by New Zealand's use of American support facilities or by Chilean air collaboration for BAS cartography. Naturally, scientists place emphasis upon the extent and utility of their research and cooperation, along with the desire to preserve the treaty in order to continue such activities. For example, in 1982 Laws pointed out that:

> In the scientific field there is the Scientific Committee for Antarctic Research ... there are a number of working groups in various areas of science and some of the working groups have mounted collaborative programmes. In biology, for example, there is a new programme developing called BIOMASS, the Biological Investigations of Marine Antarctic Systems and Stocks, which is concerned with krill and its consumers and the Southern Ocean ecosystem, which will produce information of great value ... There is collaboration in the Antarctic Peninsular in the project called Glaciology of the Antarctic Peninsular between a number of nations. There is, of course, very close collaboration in the physical sciences, where the geophysical location of stations as part of a network is very important. There are many other examples I could give[16].

In fact, Laws, who was giving evidence to a parliamentary committee, added that the Chilean Air Force had agreed recently to a joint project in the Antarctic Peninsular - the area of competing Anglo-Chilean claims - according to which Chile would provide the aerial contribution, the 'major cost of the exercise', and the BAS would produce the maps[17].

The BIOMASS programme represents perhaps the most significant current manifestation of international scientific cooperation, and thus of the form of collaboration encouraged

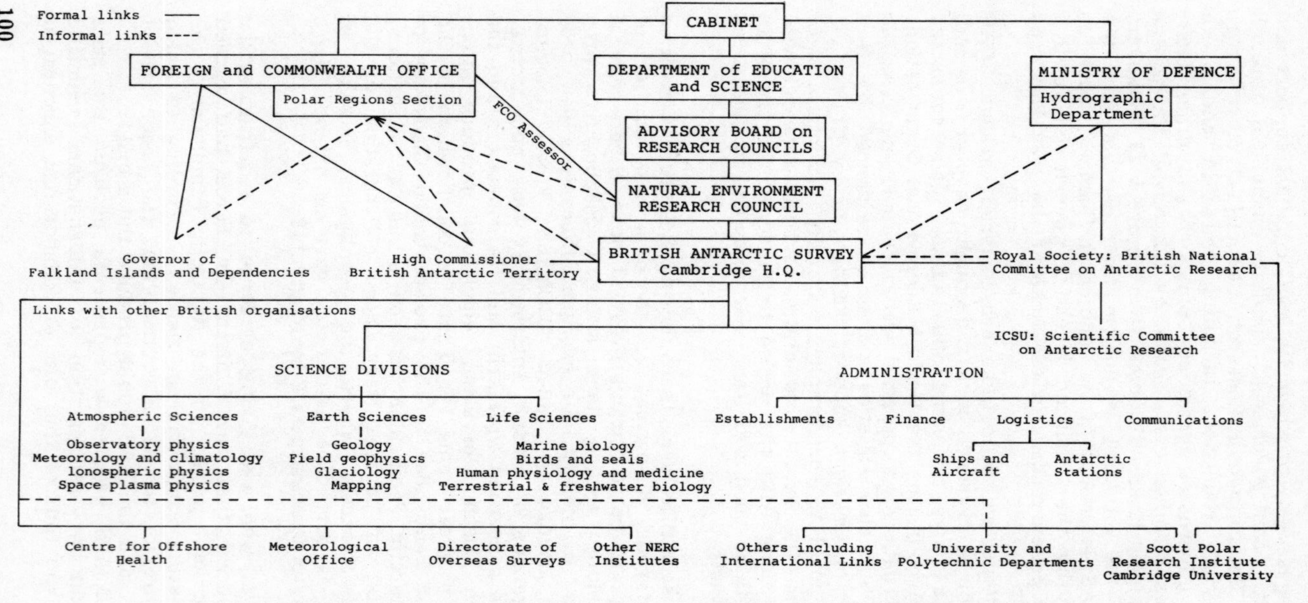

British organization in Antarctica. The distinction between formal and informal links is not always clear; come currently informal links (for example those between BAS and the universities) may become more formal as the BAS scientific programme develops. NERC: Natural Environment Research Council; ICSU: International Council of Scientific Unions. Prepared by B. L. Beck.

Fig. 5.1: Organisation of British Antarctic activities.

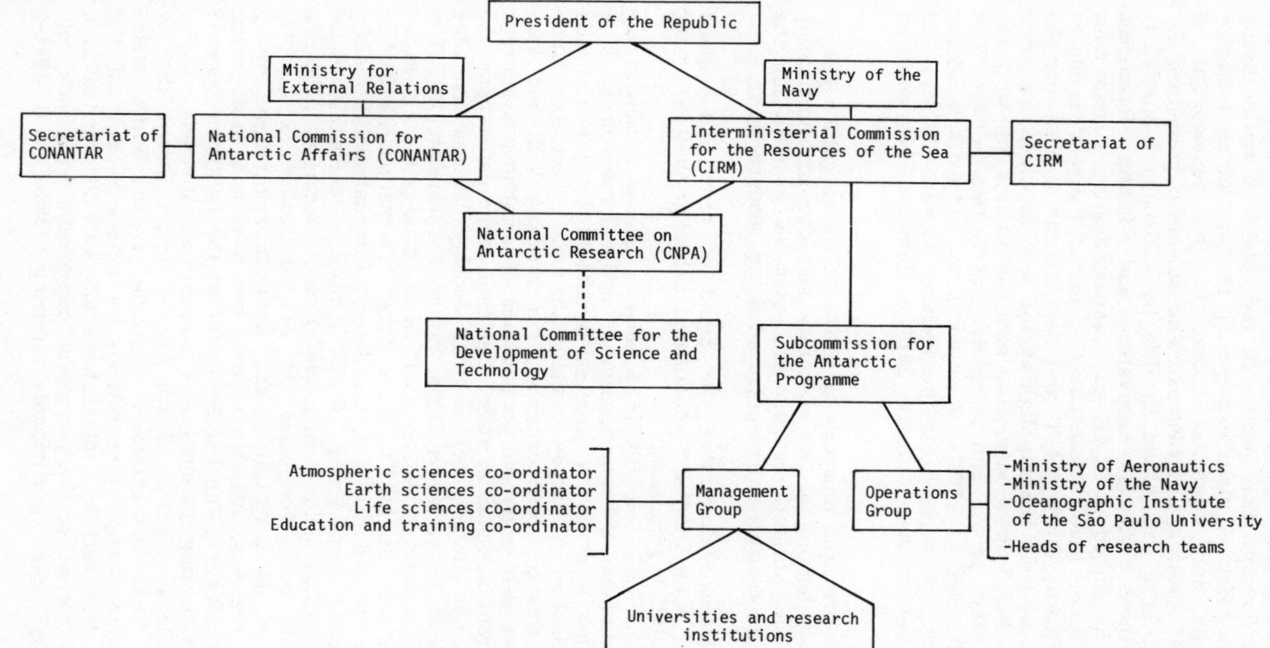

Fig. 5.2: Organisation of Brazilian Antarctic activities. Reproduced from the Brazilian response to the UN, UNGA A/39/583 (Part II), 1984, vol.2, p.9.

between scientists from different countries as a result of the Antarctic Treaty. This project in the sphere of marine living resources offers a vivid example of the continuing interplay of nations and scientific bodies in the development of Antarctic research programmes. The scientific guidelines for BIOMASS were established in 1976 by a Group of Specialists on Southern Oceans Ecosystem and Living Resources (GSSOELR) linked to SCAR and developed after a conference held at Woods Hole, Massachusetts, under the joint sponsorship of SCAR, SCOR, IABO and the FAO. In this manner the evolution of BIOMASS highlighted the way in which Antarctic research has looked outwards, such as to link up with the work of other groups and to receive inputs from outside. The GSSOELR acted as BIOMASS' mother body and established the framework for a ten-year programme between 1977-86. El Sayed, the convenor of the 1976 conference, has asserted that:

> The principal objective of BIOMASS is to gain a deeper understanding of the structure and dynamic functioning of the Antarctic marine ecosystem as a basis for the future management of potential living resources[18].

This statement illustrates the blend of pure and applied research, since BIOMASS constituted a background factor for the CCAMLR negotiations.

In addition, the BIOMASS scheme offered a method for the coordination and enhancement of national research work in the marine sciences, a process facilitated by the project's standardisation of survey methods through a 'Methods Handbook' - this provided criteria for monitoring krill and seabirds - as well as by the performance of simultaneous surveys by different nations. In turn, the data accumulated upon the topics under study, such as krill ecology, became available for analysis by an international group of specialists[19]. The BIOMASS project involved two major data-gathering expeditions known as FIBEX - the First International BIOMASS Expedition - and SIBEX - the Second International BIOMASS Expedition - respectively. FIBEX proved a ten-nation multiship expedition held during 1980-1 and concerned primarily with krill; thus, the basic aim was to produce a synoptic picture of its distribution and abundance through survey work in the West Atlantic sector, the West and East Indian Ocean sectors and the Pacific sector of the Southern Oceans. The participating nations were Argentina, Australia, Chile, France, Japan, Poland, South Africa, Soviet Union, the UK and the USA. For example, Australia, Japan, South Africa and France worked cooperatively in adjacent parts of the Indian Ocean sector, while information was documented in a standard format to enable direct comparison with data collected by other participants. During 1983-4 and 1984-5

SIBEX-1 and SIBEX II respectively continued the project and were designed to cast light upon the dynamics of the Antarctic ecosystem, including such aspects as the growth and productivity of krill, the nature and extent of any krill surplus, and the relationship between animals and the physical structure of the ocean. Therefore, the BIOMASS project provided a graphic illustration of international scientific cooperation in action upon a programme of both fundamental and applied research. However, there were occasional problems, mainly on account of fiscal and logistical difficulties. In fact, fiscal constraints resulted in the scaling-down of the ambitious objectives characteristic of the initial BIOMASS plans, and this shortage of money was largely due to the USA's relative lack of interest in krill fishing; thus, the USA performed a supportive rather than a major role in the project[20]. Australia, a participant in FIBEX, was forced to cancel its involvement in SIBEX-I due to shipping and fiscal problems, although it participated in SIBEX-II[21].

Therefore, Antarctic science programmes embrace a diverse range of disciplines and occur in both national and international frameworks. It is impossible to cover all the possibilities, but it is worth pointing to a further cooperative aspect, which derives from the manner in which the more established Antarctic powers offer a reservoir of scientific expertise of particular value to newcomers. As a result, entrants into the sphere of Antarctic research have relied extensively upon this advice on such matters as costings, the design of base stations and of research programmes, and the form of logistical support. In general, the formal commencement of Antarctic research programmes by newcomers has often been preceded by the appointment of scientists to the base stations of existing treaty powers. For example, Polish scientists participated in Soviet research schemes during the 1960s and 1970s, while at present Cuban scientists are involved on Soviet expeditions.

The Exchange of Scientific Information and Personnel

Another treaty consequence of the IGY was article III (1)'s provision for the exchange of scientific information and personnel, since the contracting parties agreed that:

> To the greatest extent feasible and practicable:
>
> a) information regarding plans for scientific programs in Antarctica shall be exchanged to permit maximum economy and efficiency of operations;
> b) scientific personnel shall be exchanged in Antarctica between expeditions and stations;
> c) scientific observations and results from Antarctica shall be exchanged and made freely available.

These provisions have been developed by recommendations emanating from the Consultative Meetings, and the position was partially codified and systematised at Oslo in 1975 through recommendation VIII-6 on the Standard Format for the Exchange of Information. In fact, the 1983 Consultative Meeting held at Canberra devoted considerable attention to the topic of the exchange of information under the treaty, and it was suggested that the requirements for effective exchanges should be considered by governments in order to prepare for a review of the question at the 1985 Consultative Meeting[22]. These arrangements have been supplemented by the exchange obligations embodied in other Antarctic agreements, including article V of the 1972 Sealing Convention and article XX of the CCAMLR.

As a result, treaty powers are obliged to perform certain functions designed to promote international cooperation in scientific investigation, such as the advance notification of research plans or the availability of research findings by the 30 November of each year. However, these points have to be satisfied only as far as is 'feasible and practicable', and such a qualification means that there exists no absolute and binding obligation, since the onus of fulfilment is left to the goodwill and efficiency of nations. Perhaps inevitably there have been problems regarding compliance, and a frequent topic of Consultative Meetings has concerned the failure of certain parties either to submit reports on their activities, such as on the number of seals killed or captured in the treaty area and on the location of mineral occurrences, or to provide information on time[23].The problems of non-submission and of unpunctuality have been recognised by the treaty powers, but hitherto there has been no real effort to tighten up procedures, such as evidenced by the inactivity upon this aspect in 1975 when the Standard Format on Exchange was being drafted. However, the problem has not disappeared and the 1983 Consultative Meeting served to identify areas for attention and for possible action at future meetings to improve 'timely exchange'. Certain points were highlighted for consideration by the bodies responsible for national Antarctic programmes, including the date by which they would ideally wish to receive exchanged information, whether their own exchanged information could be assembled one month prior to the ideal date so that the material could be transmitted through the diplomatic channels, whether some information required by recommendation VIII-6 might better be exchanged after, rather than before, the activity in question, and whether, 'as one means of more effectively implementing Article III (1c) of the Treaty', brief reports on the implementation of scientific investigations might be included in the information exchanged. National responses upon these points would be considered at the 1985 Consultative Meeting, but 'in the meantime, the Meeting agreed that it would be useful to encourage the maximum of early informal information exchange between offices responsible for national Antarctic programs'[24]. This suggestion implies that any action will be designed to advance the exchange date prior to 30 November as well as to improve punctual submission.

Although the exchange of information provisions are liable to future refinements, existing difficulties have not prevented the regular annual exchange of substantial amounts of information between the treaty powers, especially as the 'scientific' exchange under article III is supplemented by the obligations of article VII (5), which stipulates that:

> Each Contracting Party shall ... inform the other Contracting Parties ... in advance, of
> a) all expeditions to and within Antarctica, on the part of its ships or nationals ...
> b) all stations in Antarctica occupied by its nationals; and
> c) any military personnel or equipment intended to be introduced into Antarctica.

Obviously, this requirement reinforces the peaceful use aspect of the treaty, and particularly the inspection scheme, but it serves also to provide information relating to expeditions, base locations and manning levels in respect to both civilian and military personnel. In turn, such information exchanges are reinforced by another frequent and enduring cooperative device, that is, the exchange of scientists, a scheme possessing both scientific and political benefits.

The exchange programme is capable of providing the treaty powers with far more information upon the activities of other parties than any brief inspection trip, especially as the length of most exchange visits precludes the possibility of disguising any treaty evasions. In addition, the treaty powers have displayed greater enthusiasm for exchange, and the Soviet Union's involvement in the exchange of scientists contrasts vividly with its inactivity in the sphere of inspection. However, the basic objective of exchange concerns the advancement of science rather than a check upon treaty compliance, even if the intelligence role is never absent. For example, F. Michael Maish, an American environmental scientist, was attached to the Soviet Vostok station in 1969, and subsequently he wrote that:

> The US-USSR exchange of scientists is part of the implementation of article 3 of the Antarctic Treaty ... scores of Americans have been involved with the Antarctic expeditions of other nations in Antarctica[25].

Apart from scientific cooperation upon specific projects, it is clear that Maish's assignment at Vostok enabled the accumulation of a detailed appreciation of Soviet activities and modes of operation, while at the same time B.G. Lopatin, a Soviet geologist, served with the American research programme, including a nine-month stay at McMurdo station. Lopatin observed that:

> The spirit of friendly cooperation in the survey groups was very high. We discussed mutual problems, helped each other in collecting rock samples, and are now going to exchange scientific information ... Besides advantages in scientific research, the exchange program in Antarctica is very important for establishing close personal contacts and better understanding among nations[26].

Maish echoed such thoughts:

> The exchange-scientist program in Antarctica has been warmly received by the participating nations. The scientist-diplomats involved have furthered scientific exchange and harmony in Antarctica amongst the nations engaged. It seems already an axiom that man finds his warmest international relations in the coldest regions of the earth[27].

Even allowing for a certain amount of natural exaggeration upon the part of Maish and Lopatin, it is apparent that their comments typify the thoughts of many scientists about the exchange scheme, such as in respect to emphasising the fact that Antarctic science knows no political boundaries. However, it can be argued that Maish's comment throws new light upon the uneasy alliance of science and politics in the continent.

In a sense, therefore, the exchange of information and of personnel provisions have served to compensate for the relative inactivity of the inspection provisions, especially as formal exchanges have been supplemented by more informal contacts within Antarctica, such as by base visits and radio conversations, and outside, such as at scientific conferences and meetings of subject working groups.

For instance, in December 1982 Laws was asked by a parliamentary committee, 'if you do not take part in inspection very often how do you find out what is going on in the bases' (of other nations)?[28]. He responded that:

> We visit other bases quite regularly, and in fact I visited in February/March this year the Russian station at Bellingshausen, the Chilean station at Frei, the American station at Palmer, the Argentine station at San Martin, among others, and this is a regular event during the Antarctic summer[29].

In this manner, scientists from different nations have been enabled to make contact in a range of ways, and have helped not only to fulfil one of the major motivating forces of the Antarctic treaty negotiations, that is, the desire to perpetuate the IGY-type environment, but also to give substance to articles II and III of the treaty.

Science, Politics and Resource Exploration

Previous sections have highlighted the way in which the Antarctic Treaty System has provided a living framework for international scientific cooperation, such as in respect to the sharing of results and data, the coordination of research programmes and the exchange of personnel. The political benefits of such cooperative trends are difficult to quantify, but they have been significant, especially as political necessities contributed to the dedication of Antarctica to science. Maish's references to 'the scientist-diplomats' implied an appreciation of the inter-connection of science and politics, such as in terms of exerting a moderating and harmonising effect upon international relationships and significantly scientific cooperation in Antarctica - for example, between the Soviet Union and the USA or between Argentina and the UK - has proceeded in spite of their divisions in other parts of the world. Although there exists some evidence of occasional Anglo-Argentine scientific problems in the wake of the Falklands War - for instance, Fox has mentioned Foreign Office advice to BAS scientists at Signy in the South Orkneys not to contact their Argentine neighbours at Orcadas - Antarctic relationships have been insulated to some extent from the divisive factors apparent elsewhere[30]. There is also the hope that the experience of practical cooperation in Antarctica might exert significant political effects beyond the treaty area, although it remains difficult to assess the impact of Soviet-American cooperation in the sphere of Antarctic science upon their wider global relationship. In addition, Quigg has introduced a critical voice, since he has argued that the IGY experience fostered an automatic acceptance of the merits of any multi-national scientific programme, so that certain international scientific projects may be liable to criticism as manifestations of a somewhat artificial form of cooperation; thus, Quigg fears that some schemes may reflect a kind of *pro-forma* link rather than a genuine desire for scientific cooperation[31].

One problem looming on the horizon of the Antarctic Treaty System concerns the definition of 'scientific investigation' as allowed and promoted by articles II and III. In fact, like many issues, the matter was raised at the preparatory negotiations, but not really tackled at the time in spite of British concern that activities contrary to the treaty might be performed under the pretext or cover of 'research'[32]. At the time the British representatives felt unable to spell out the precise nature of any problems, but clearly the point had been raised against a background of the pre-1959 tendency to politicise Antarctic research, something of which the British government was as guilty as any other government. In the event, this problem has persisted during the post-1959 period, such as demonstrated by the sovereignty-related nature of certain 'scientific research' - this will be elaborated in the next chapter - and by the predominance of non-scientific personnel at bases operated by countries with a relatively low research output. Rightly or wrongly, Argentina has been oft-placed in this category on account of its alleged emphasis upon politico-legal considerations rather than upon the cause of science.

The recent preoccupation with Antarctica's resource potential has posed a further problem, since scientists have been subjected to increased pressure either to pronounce on the continent's resource utility or to pursue resource-related research. This problem is likely to become more acute as research programmes assume an applied character, such as demonstrated by Japan's stress upon offshore hydrocarbons or by BAS' post-1982 emphasis upon 'resource-orientated research' in the 'thrust' areas of the earth and marine sciences[33]. In practice, it is often difficult, if not impossible, to separate pure from applied research, especially as certain kinds of research in the earth and marine sciences possess a clear relevance in respect to resources; for example, the borderline between 'scientific investigation' - this is permitted and encouraged by the treaty - and resource exploration - this is subject either to the provisions of CCAMLR or to the mineral exploration moratorium - proves rather vague and confused, and has led to criticism of certain governments for using the cover of 'research' for exploration. Thus work in the earth sciences can contribute to a more accurate picture of Antarctic geology, but the results may serve also to provide a more informed assessment of the location and extent of minerals. The difficulties are accentuated by the fact that at times of fiscal stringency there is even more pressure upon scientists to demonstrate to their government paymasters the practical utility of their work, especially as politicians tend to be more impressed by the results of applied rather than of fundamental research.

However, 'relevance' is a difficult concept to apply in any sphere of activity, and there is a danger that some may be tempted to over-state the utility and immediacy of Antarctic science, especially in view of the perceived need for an Antarctic research organisation to justify its share of increasingly scarce fiscal resources and to show sceptical and often disinterested politicians that it is doing something worthwhile with taxpayers' money. In reality, any over-selling of the merits of Antarctic science does little either to promote the cause of science or to educate politicians and others about the intrinsic worth of scientific research and of international scientific cooperation in Antarctica. Nor will it serve to resolve the discrepancy between the short-term perceptions of politicians and the long-term realities of any substantial Antarctic resource benefits. In addition, the advocacy of the case for science needs to be tempered by the realism displayed by Crary, the chief scientist of the US Antarctic research programme, who has criticised the pretensions of some of his scientific colleagues:

> Looking back (from the early 1970s) at Antarctica in the past dozen years, perhaps we should ask ... Have we done too much? What was the big hurry? Must we continue to entice hundreds of scientists to the continent each year? ... Could we have done all that was really needed at half the cost? ... the trend continues up and up ... there is no hint of retreat[34].

Similarly, the alleged 'good' of science in Antarctica must be balanced against environmental factors, since even the scientific use of the continent poses environmental risks, such as through the effects of refuse and sewage around bases, of excessive disturbance in heavily-researched locations, and even the alleged visual 'pollution' caused by base structures. Admittedly, there are various safeguards in existence to regulate scientific activities, but there is evidence of non-compliance, such as highlighted recently by the environmental damage caused during 1983-4 by France's construction of an airstrip at Pointe Geologie in Adélie Land. Although the project was justified upon the grounds of enhancing air transport facilities at Dumont d'Urville base, the construction process aroused considerable criticism from environmental groups concerned about the resulting threat to the breeding grounds of several species of bird-life[35].

Some Conclusions

During the post-IGY period scientific investigation in Antarctica has continued to expand and diversify, a process facilitated, indeed fostered, by the Antarctic Treaty System, which includes a contribution from SCAR, whose role should not be under-estimated. As a result, a considerable advance in knowledge about Antarctica and its interactions with the wider world has occurred, and will continue to occur, especially as the 'new' Antarctic powers - for instance, Brazil, China and India - begin to make their own contributions. But, for scientists 'many gaps still exist'[36]. There is a tendency to advocate the idea of a 'continent for science', but this concept has been threatened by a range of political and other problems, which raise the question of whether politicians and diplomats will ever allow Antarctica to become a scientific laboratory. In any case, it has never proved easy to define 'scientific investigation' in a clear and precise manner.

In addition, there is a need to treat science in Antarctica in a more critical manner in order to correct some of the existing mis-conceptions regarding the role of Antarctic science. For example, in general the Antarctic Treaty is supposed to have terminated the national rivalries characteristic of the pre-IGY period, thereby clearing the way for the advance of science in both national and international frameworks. However, Phillip Law, a former director of Australia's Antarctic research programme, has introduced a more cautious note.

> International competition for territorial gain has now been replaced by international rivalry in science, as the various Antarctic nations strive to demonstrate their scientific competence and technical prowess in the various fields of Antarctic research[37].

Similar considerations have influenced US research - for example, an earlier quote by Dater indicated the American concern to compete with the scientific effort of the Soviet Union - while, more recently, Mrs Gandhi justified India's development in the sphere of Antarctic research partly in terms of the prestige argument; thus, she told the Indian Lower House in February 1982 that:

> In undertaking this advanced work India has now joined a select band of countries. The significance of this expedition for, and also its impact on, our younger generation will be as important as its scientific accomplishment. I hope it will imbue our younger generation with scientific temper and encourage them to take a keener interest in the oceans and their exploration. Let pride in achievement urge us forward to greater efforts[38].

In the meantime, science constitutes Antarctica's chief product and the continent remains in a relatively pristine condition. But the future will bring new pressures, such as for the exploitation of resources, and hence question marks must be raised concerning the preservation of this state of affairs. The potential resource yield of krill, fish, oil or of natural gas has been depicted as the key threat to the Antarctic environment, but in the context of the opening lines of this chapter it is worth noting the emerging interest in the sphere of iceberg utilisation for areas of water shortage, since this concern has given an added dimension to the research work of glaciologists upon such aspects as the stability of the ice sheet and icebergs. In turn, research has moved on in some instances to an examination of towing techniques in order to evaluate the feasibility of transporting icebergs to Australia, South Africa or the Middle East, thereby highlighting yet again the difficulties of insulating science from commercial and other considerations.

NOTES

1. David A. Peel, 'Antarctic Ice: The Frozen Time Capsule', New Scientist, 19 May 1983, p.476.
2. Ibid., p.483.
3. BAS, Research in the Antarctic, p.15.
4. Peel, Antarctic Ice: The Frozen Time Capsule, p.476.
5. David Drewry (ed.), Antarctica: Glaciological and Geophysical Folio (Scott Polar Research Institute, Cambridge, 1983); Uwe Radok, 'International Antarctic Glaciological Project Activities, 1981-1982', Antarctic Journal, vol.XVIII, no.2 (1983), pp.10-12; 'Ice Cores Available for Research', Antarctic Journal, vol.XIX, no.1 (1984), pp.16-17.
6. Beck, Secret Antarctic Treaty Negotiations.
7. Gould, Emergence of Antarctica, p.26; Sir Vivian Fuchs, 'Evolution of a Venture in Antarctic Science: Operation Tabarin and the British Antarctic Survey' in Lewis and Smith, Frozen Future, p.248; Law, Antarctic Odyssey, pp.267-72.
8. Gould, Emergence of Antarctica, p.29; Quigg, A Pole Apart, p.39.
9. Fuchs, Evolution of a Venture in Antarctic Science, p.238.
10. Gould, Emergence of Antarctica, p.27.
11. Ibid., p.28.
12. King, The Antarctic, p.234.
13. Ibid., pp.262-6; Quigg, A Pole Apart, pp.55-74; Department of Ocean Development, Annual Report 1983-84 (Government of India, New Delhi, 1984).
14. Beck, Britain's Role in the Antarctic: Some Recent Changes, pp.85-7.
15. Beck, Britain's Antarctic Dimension, pp.440-2.
16. HCFAC, Falkland Islands, Minutes of Evidence, 13 Dec.1982, pp.91-2.
17. Ibid., p.92.
18. SCAR/SCOR Group of Specialists in Living Resources of the Southern Ocean, Biological Investigations of Marine Antarctic Systems and Stocks (SCAR, Cambridge, 1977), vol.1.
19. Takesi Nagata, 'The Implementation of the Convention on the Conservation of Antarctic Marine Living Resources: Needs and Problems' in Vicuna, Antarctic Resources Policy, pp.126-9.

20. Quigg, A Pole Apart, pp.83-4.

21. UNGA A/39/583 (Part II), 1984, vol.1, p.51, Australian response, 31 July 1984.

22. Antarctic Treaty. Report of the Twelth Consultative Meeting: September 1983 (Dept. of Foreign Affairs, Canberra, 1984), pp.16-17.

23. Auburn, Antarctic Law and Politics, pp.102-3; Brian Roberts, 'International Cooperation for Antarctic Development: The Test for the Antarctic Treaty', Polar Record, vol.19, no.119 (1978), p.109.

24. Antarctic Treaty. Report of the Twelth Consultative Meeting, p.17.

25. F. Michael Maish, 'US-Soviet Exchange Program at Vostok' in Lewis and Smith, Frozen Future, p.344; Herman R. Friis, 'With the Japanese Antarctic Research Expedition to Antarctica, 1969-1970' in Lewis and Smith, Frozen Future, pp.353-67.

26. B.G. Lopatin, 'Soviet Exchange Scientist at McMurdo' in Lewis and Smith, Frozen Future, p.351-2.

27. Maish, US-Soviet Exchange Program at Vostok, p.349.

28. HCFAC, Falkland Islands, Minutes of Evidence, 13 Dec.1982, p.96, D. Canavan.

29. Ibid., p.96.

30. Fox, Antarctica and the South Atlantic, p.60.

31. Quigg, A Pole Apart, p.217.

32. Beck, Secret Antarctic Treaty Preparatory Negotiations.

33. Memorandum by BAS of 6 Dec.1982, HCFAC, Falkland Islands, Minutes of Evidence, p.89.

34. A.P. Crary, 'The Long Look Ahead' in Lewis and Smith, Frozen Future, pp.308-9.

35. For example, see ECO, vol.XXVI, no.2 (1984), pp.1-3.

36. James H. Zumberge, 'Potential Mineral Resource Availability and Possible Environmental Problems in Antarctica' in Charney, The New Nationalism and the Use of Common Spaces, p.116.

37. Law, Antarctic Odyssey, p.272.

38. Indian Lok Sabha Debates, vol.XXIV, cols.426-7, 19 Feb.1982; Peter J. Beck, 'India in Antarctica: Science - and Politics - on Ice', Nature, 10 Nov.1983, pp.106-7. Dater is quoted on p.64-5 of this book.

Chapter Six

THE ANTARCTIC TREATY: A CONTINENT IN SEARCH OF A SOVEREIGN

The Last Great Land Rush on Earth

The late 19th. and early 20th. centuries have been oft-described as 'the Age of Imperialism', that is, as a period during which the major powers carved up Africa and areas of the Pacific and Far East as part of a 'final surge of land hunger'[1]. However, Antarctica remained relatively untouched by the imperial process at this time, and it was not until the First World War period that any real interest was taken in the control of the southern continent, particularly by Britain, whose large territorial share from the scrambles for African and Pacific lands was evidenced by the predominance of red on pre-1914 maps. The inter-war period witnessed a developing concern upon the part of several governments to acquire Antarctic territory for a range of reasons - these included strategic, resource, prestige and imperial motives - so that by the time of the Second World War the existing pattern of claims had been revealed; thus, seven governments laid claim to the continent, or rather to sections therein, and inevitably one consequence of this process was friction and controversy, most notably between Argentina, Chile and the UK. In this manner the various national claims date back over 40 years, thereby leaving only one sector - this amounts to about 15% of the area - unclaimed. The first formal claim to part of Antarctica was advanced in fact over 75 years ago, when Britain included Graham Land in the 1908 and 1917 Letters Patent announcing British sovereignty over the so-called FID, which became subsequently the site for rival claims emanating from Argentina and Chile.

The various inter-state rivalries over Antarctic territory have been complicated by legal controversies arising out of disagreements over the most appropriate method of supporting claims in a 'new territory' not previously subject to an internationally-recognised sovereignty[2]. In an area of terra nullius, a no-man's land, international law stressed effective occupation as a key criterion of sovereignty, such as applied by the 1885 Treaty of Berlin for the partition of Africa. How far could this doctrine be applied to polar regions, where climatic and other factors rendered long-term occupation difficult or impossible? In the absence of either judicial precedent or established international law other principles were utilised to support legal claims, including discovery, the formal taking of possession by an explorer and the introduction of diluted elements of 'government', such as the issue of whaling regulations and licenses. These criteria emerged as the polar equivalent of 'effective occupation', but not all governments or jurists accepted this view, thereby adding another dimension to inter-state territorial problems. The US government refused after 1924 to recognise Antarctic territorial claims - indeed, it even suggested that the perfection of legal title was impossible in Antarctic conditions - and this non-recognition theme became a key feature of US policy, which contributed to exacerbate relations with the claimants.

Historically, Antarctica's international political role has proved mainly a function of the sovereignty dispute, that is, of the politico-legal controversy concerning its ownership, such as demonstrated by the disagreements between rival claimants or between claimants and non-claimants. The historical development of the sovereignty question has been outlined in an earlier chapter in order to highlight the way in which prior to 1959 competing Antarctic policies proved a cause of both actual and potential friction, and resulted in fears of a serious confrontation between say Argentina and Britain or the Soviet Union and the USA. Inevitably, this kind of 'diplomatic Monopoly game for Antarctic real estate', a 'game' which some feared might spill over into something more serious, has provided the most enduring source of official and academic interest in Antarctica, especially as it offered the major challenge to the negotiators of the Antarctic Treaty[3]. For example, the nature of this challenge was indicated not only by the rival positions assumed by governments upon political and legal questions but also by the claim of the US Commission to Study the Organization of Peace that during the late 1950s Antarctica was still 'in search of a sovereign'[4].

Basically, the Antarctic Treaty was designed to create a legal framework for the containment of both existing and potential politico-legal disputes in order to preserve peace and stability in the region and to promote the cause of science and IGY-type cooperation. In one respect at least the treaty provided an element of certainty in the form of an international legal answer intended to reconcile varying viewpoints, albeit only in a manner suspending rather than resolving the sovereignty problem. Certainly, for a time after the treaty came into effect, the sovereignty question subsided in terms of its significance, and some even hoped that it would disappear through the passage of time. However, in the event, the divisions between claimants, non-claimants and those refusing to recognise claims have never completely disappeared from the international political scene in Antarctica, such as evidenced by the continuing sovereignty-related activities of such claimants as Argentina, Australia and Chile or more recently by the impact of the sovereignty aspect upon the marine and mineral regime negotiations of the 1970s and early 1980s.

These conflicting legal positions, complicated by policy considerations and by controversy regarding the legal validity of supporting arguments - for instance, the role of discovery or the definition of 'effective occupation' - serve to threaten the unity of the Antarctic Treaty System as it moves forward into resource responsibilities. In any case, these divisions were sharpened after the 1970s by the emergence of a new and alternative legal approach focussed upon the common heritage principle, which tended not only to deny the validity of existing claims to _terra communis_ but also to question the international acceptability of the Antarctic Treaty System. This new legal approach, underlain by various political factors in favour of a universalist approach to such areas as Antarctica, fostered suggestions that the treaty system should be replaced by a more representative international regime, and perhaps by some UN-based organisation modelled upon the UNCLOS precedent; thus, an ISBA-type authority would assume responsibility for the global common of Antarctica. In fact, this UNCLOS link has been accentuated by the questions raised about the extent to which Antarctica can be interpreted as 'beyond the limits of national jurisdiction' according to article 1 (1.1) of the convention. Certainly, the leading critics of the Antarctic Treaty System, most notably Dr. Mahathir, the Prime Minister of Malaysia, believe that:

> Uninhabited lands ... the largest of which is the continent of Antarctica ... do not legally belong to the discoverers as much as the colonial territories do not belong to the colonial powers[5].

This recent type of challenge symbolises one aspect of the continuing debate about the precise location of sovereign authority in Antarctica, and also raises the question of whether the problem of ownership can be resolved without making the continent the object of international discord. An additional aspect concerns the ability of the treaty system in the future to accommodate varying and conflicting legal positions, a task rendered more difficult through the interposition of political factors.

Sovereignty and Article IV of the Treaty

Inevitably, the preparatory negotiations of 1958-59 focussed upon various manifestations of the sovereignty problem, and several delegations responded positively to the 1958 US note's reference to the treatment of Antarctica's legal status as 'frozen', especially as the concept was inspired in part by the Escudero proposal of 1948 and the 'gentleman's agreement' of 1955[6]. As a result, the talks moved on soon to legal questions as an essential pre-requisite of the peaceful and scientific use of the continent. For example, Daniels stressed the US government's anxiety to set aside such legal problems - 'an extremely important subject' - in order to advance upon other fronts, and this preoccupation caused him to present a draft formula in July 1958[7]. The form of words embodied therein was designed basically to formalise the IGY arrangement in a way safeguarding the legal positions of claimants, non-claimants and others.

Although certain governments remained hawkish on sovereignty - most notably, Argentina and Chile - and utilised every occasion to remind other delegates of the nature and validity of their claims, there existed a general acceptance of the concept of a freeze based upon the legal status quo, which represented a non-solution, a modus vivendi, intended to facilitate the conclusion of the treaty. The relative unanimity of Argentina, Chile and the UK was of interest in the context of the generally thorny nature of their Antarctic relationships, and this outcome reflected not only a realistic evaluation of the sovereignty problem but also a consequence of private discussions - these involved at various times representatives from Argentina, Australia, Chile, New Zealand, the UK and the USA - conducted outside of the actual preparatory negotiations. However, the Soviet delegation assumed a different stance, since Ledovski argued that the sovereignty issue went beyond the agreed brief of the talks and should be dealt with separately at some future conference, even if he took the opportunity to remind the other delegates about Soviet rights in Antarctica through prior discovery and about his government's refusal to recognise existing claims. But this dissenting view - the Soviet attitude did not change until April 1959 - failed to deter the rest of the delegates pushing the negotiations forward on sovereignty matters on the grounds that - to quote Daniels - the main objective of the talks could not be achieved 'unless some way were found to put aside the legal and political conflicts in Antarctica'[8]. Although certain semantic differences remained, Daniels' draft article submitted in November 1958 as article IV - this represented a development of an earlier draft discussed in July 1958 - was virtually identical to the version incorporated as article IV in the eventual treaty[9].

It is perhaps natural that article IV of the Antarctic Treaty has been described as 'the cornerstone of the Treaty', for it provided a form of words sufficient at least to suspend the sovereignty disputes and to clear the way for science and international cooperation[10]. Therefore, this article served to reconcile different stances on the subject, since, by agreeing to differ and to respect each other's positions for the time being, the treaty powers utilised the semantic ingenuity of article IV to bring themselves to a single point of agreement. This 'imaginative juridical accommodation' represented the fundamental act of statesmanship required from the twelve governments to secure the treaty[11].

> The statesmanship underlying the cooperation consisted of all governments concerned resisting the temptation to carry their particular view of sovereignty in the Antarctic to a logical conclusion. They denied the temptation to rivalry[12].

The sovereignty issue, the one question capable of causing a breakdown in the negotiations, had to be glossed over through a legal compromise rather than resolved, and van der Essen, one of the Belgian negotiators, described the outcome as 'an example of legal acrobatics which poorly conceal an internal contradiction'[13]. In turn, the restraints upon sovereignty in article IV can be related to articles I and V, which involved the renunciation of the exercise of military and nuclear power in Antarctica.

According to article IV (1):

> Nothing contained in the present Treaty shall be interpreted as:
> a) a renunciation by any Contracting Party of previously asserted rights or claims to territorial sovereignty in Antarctica;
> b) a renunciation or diminution by any Contracting Party of any basis of claim to territorial sovereignty in Antarctica which it may have whether as a result of its activities or those of its nationals in Antarctica, or otherwise;
> c) prejudicing the position of any Contracting Party as regards its recognition or non-recognition of any other State's right of or claim or basis of claim to territorial sovereignty in Antarctica.

In this manner, the treaty was designed to by-pass the impasse on sovereignty, and thus, it was anticipated, to obviate the possibility of a return to the international difficulties characteristic of the pre-IGY period.

The formula of article IV (1) enabled all treaty powers, whether claimants, non-claimants or those pursuing a non-recognition stance, to preserve their position and to co-exist in a pragmatic manner. A variety of descriptive expressions have been utilised to explain the effect of this article; in fact, the term 'freeze' was oft-employed in the preparatory talks, and has been repeated since, along with a range of other words and phrases, including 'suspension', 'on ice' and 'moratorium'[14]. Perhaps none of these is entirely accurate, and one recent Australian participant in the operations of the Antarctic treaty system has argued that 'the Treaty did not freeze territorial claims, it merely put them on the back burner to keep warm'[15]. Nevertheless, the concept of a freeze based upon the legal status quo proves broadly acceptable - in particular, the idea of a freeze was expressed by most of the negotiators during 1958-59 - on account of the fact that article IV pushed aside the sovereignty problem for the time being and in a way permitting each party to reserve its position on sovereignty as it stood when the treaty came into effect. In this respect, the operative date was 23 June 1961 rather than 1 December 1959, and in a sense the treaty was designed to keep the legal clock stopped at 1961 for the duration of the treaty, that is, for an indefinite period[16]. Such a formula was deemed necessary to secure the treaty, while the resulting subordination of the sovereignty issue was intended to allow for the development of other aspects of the treaty.

The impact of the legal freeze was reinforced by article IV (2)'s assertion that nothing performed after 1961 can alter the position on sovereignty of any treaty power.

> No acts or activities taking place while the present Treaty is in force shall constitute a basis for asserting, supporting or denying a claim to territorial sovereignty in Antarctica or create any rights of sovereignty in Antarctica. No new claim, or enlargement of an existing claim, to territorial sovereignty in Antarctica shall be asserted while the present Treaty is in force.

As such, this section of the treaty supports article IV (I)'s attempt to keep the clock stopped at 1961, since in theory claims can be neither improved nor worsened. According to this view, the establishment of a base station in a new location or the escalation of Antarctic research activities by a claimant could do nothing either to strengthen and extend its claim or to undermine the position of other treaty parties. Conversely, inaction or neglect would not weaken the position of any party, even if such a policy might threaten a government's eligibility for Consultative Party status (article IX (2)).

The treaty powers accepted that article IV represented merely a non-solution of a problem which could never be swept completely under the carpet. Obviously, at some future date the various issues might have to be faced, if not resolved, but it was realised that as long as the treaty survived the problem would remain either upon or just below - it has never been beyond - the horizon. In fact, an appreciation of this point has served to encourage the parties to advocate the treaty's indefinite duration, such as on account of the perceived insoluble nature of the sovereignty problem. In any case, the passage of time has exacerbated the potential problems, since certain non-claimants (the Soviet Union, the USA) have reinforced their 'rights' in Antarctica, other governments (Brazil and Peru) have announced 'rights' also, and the common heritage approach constitutes a challenge not only to existing claims but also to the whole basis of article IV.

Claimants, non-claimants and others

The continuing significance of the sovereignty question for all aspects of Antarctic affairs renders it desirable to examine the basis of existing viewpoints. At present, seven governments claim sovereignty over wedge-shaped parts of Antarctica (as shown in Figure 6.1).

Argentina

Claim: Antártida Argentina defined as 25°W-74°W (originally 68° 34'W) south of 60°S; this includes the Antarctic continent as well as such islands as the South Orkneys.

Extent: 550,000 square miles.

Date: The claim was defined during 1943-7, but allegedly the claim precedes this date; for example, a formal claim was made to the South Orkneys in 1925 and to the FID as a whole in 1937.

Basis: 'Argentine sovereignty over the territory is based on deep-rooted historical rights - maintained firmly in every circumstance by the Argentine governments - which are spiritually identified with the feelings of the entire people of the nation; on the superior geographical position of the Republic; on the geological contiguity of its land with the Antarctic territories; on the climatological influence which the neighbouring polar zones exercise on its territories; on the rights of first occupation; on the necessary diplomatic action and finally on its uninterrupted activities in the Antarctic territory itself'[17]. 'Effective and continuous occupation has gone on since 1904 (in the South Orkneys) ... our country is the only one which (in 1940) has lived there for 37 years ... Argentina's rights are not solely dependent upon the principal fact of this occupation'[18].

Australia

Claim: Australian Antarctic Territory defined as 45°E-160°E south of 60°S, excluding Adélie Land at 136°E-142°E.

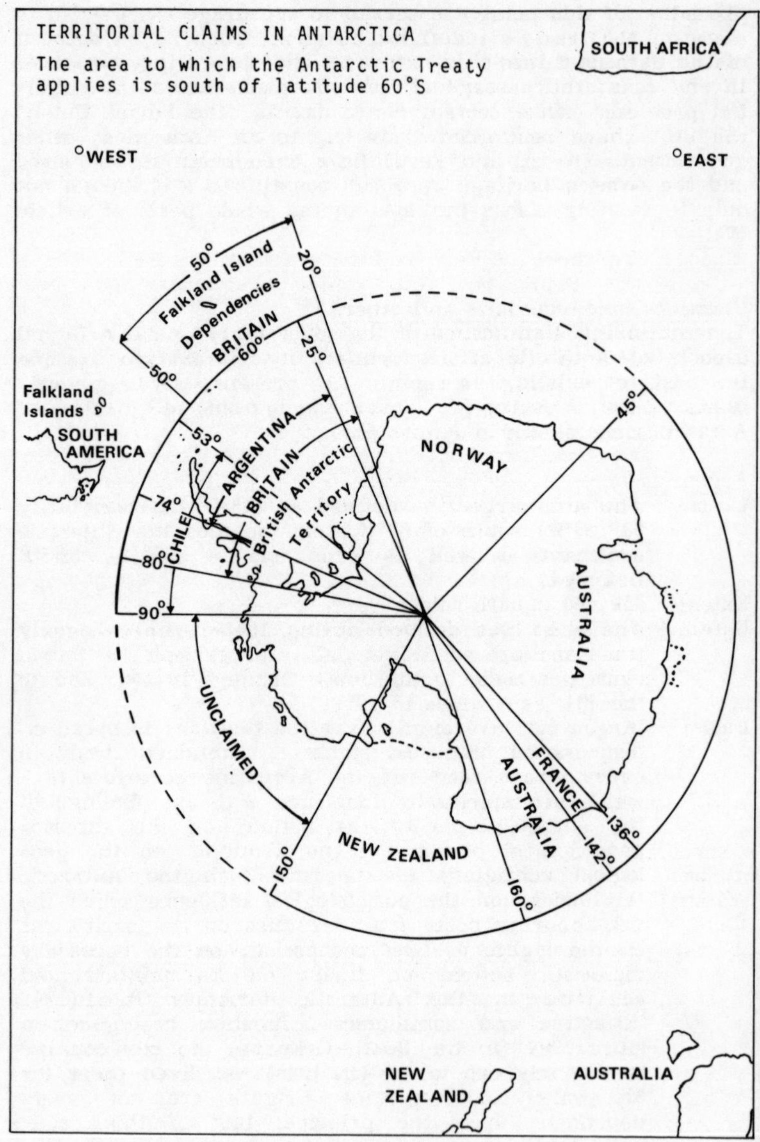

Fig. 6.1: Territorial claims in Antarctica.

Extent: 2.4 million square miles.
Date: 1933 and 1936.
Basis: 'Australia's claim to sovereignty over the Australian Antarctic Territory is based on acts of discovery and exploration by British and Australian navigators going back to the time of Captain Cook, and subsequent continuous occupation, administration and control'[19].

Chile
Claim: Territorio Chileno Antártico defined as 53°W-90°W to the South Pole (no northern boundary has been announced).
Extent: 500,000 square miles.
Date: 1940 (in 1906 it announced that the territory was to be defined).
Basis: 'Our country holds the oldest rights of sovereignty on this Territory; as established in the first place by Spain, and then later, throughout our life as a Republic, by successive acts of our Government and the uninterrupted exercise of such sovereignty'[20]. 'The boundaries of Chile in said polar region ... constitute a natural prolongation of the national soil ... (and are based on) historical data (eg. acts and discoveries by Spain) ... geographic continuity of the Chilean Antarctic as regards the southern end of the American Continent ... geographic contiguity (eg. geological links) ... scientific factors (eg. climatic and glaciological influences) ... sector theory ... different manifestations of sovereignty represented by the acts of occupation realised throughout our history ... diplomatic facts ... administrative antecedents'[21].

France
Claim: Adélie Land defined as 136°E-142°E south of 60°S.
Extent: 150,000 square miles.
Date: 1924 but not defined until 1933-8.
Basis: 'Sovereignty over Adélie Land, discovered in 1840 by Dumont d'Urville ... explored by Charcot, crossed in recent years by the French polar expeditions rests on solid foundations. The French government is proud, in addition to having indisputable historical claims, to be able to rely on a permanent occupation'[22].

New Zealand
Claim: The Ross Dependency defined as 160°E-150°W south of 60°S.
Extent: 175,000 square miles.
Date: 1923.

Basis: 'New Zealand's claim to the Ross Dependency rests on ... discovery by a British explorer (ie. Ross), certain Government actions connected with territorial rights in the Ross Sea area (eg. the issue of special postage stamps for the 1907-09 Shackleton expedition) ... annexation - Order in Council of 1923, subsequent exploration, certain acts of occupation upon the assumption of sovereignty, the exaction and receipt of revenue, in particular from individuals other than British subjects (ie. Norwegian whalers) ... paper acts of sovereignty'[23].

Norway

Claim: Dronning Maud Land defined as 20°W-45°E covering, 'that part of the mainland coast in the Antarctic extending from Falkland Islands Dependency to Australian Antarctic Territory with the land lying within this coast and the environing sea'[24]. Neither a northern nor a southern limit was defined.

Extent: 1.2 million square miles (but note problem of definition).

Date: 1939.

Basis: 'Norway's right to bring the said unclaimed land under her dominion is founded on the geographical exploration work done by Norwegians in this region, in which work they have been alone'[25].

United Kingdom

Claim: British Antarctic Territory defined as 20°W-80°W south of 60°S, and including the mainland sector centred on Graham Land, plus the South Orkneys and South Shetlands (until 1962 these were claimed as part of the Falkland Islands Dependencies).

Extent: 700,000 square miles.

Date: 1908 and 1917.

Basis: 'The root of the United Kingdom's title to the islands and territories comprising the British Antarctic Territory lies in British acts of discovery between 1819 and 1843, accompanied by formal claims in the name of the British Crown. British sovereignty over these islands and territories was formally confirmed and defined by the Crown in Letters Patent in 1908 (as amended by further Letters Patent in 1917). Since then there has been in regard to the islands and territories now comprising the British Antarctic Territory a continuous display of British sovereignty and activity appropriate to the circumstances'[26].

In this way, seven governments have advanced formal territorial claims to Antarctica, along with adjacent islands, based upon a range of criteria adjudged adequate to support legal title, such as prior discovery, taking possession and 'occupation'. Occasionally positive assertions of national sovereignty have been supplemented by efforts to deny the title of others on account of the overlapping nature of Argentine, British and Chilean claims (as shown in Figure 6.2). As a result, within the Antarctic sector lying between 20°W and 90°W, there arose an overlap of Anglo-Argentine claims for 49°(25°W-74°W), of Anglo-Argentine-Chilean claims for 21°(53°W-74°W), of Anglo-Chilean claims for 27° (53°W-80°W) and of Argentine-Chilean claims for 21° (53°W-74°W); thus, only 5° of BAT and 10° of Territorio Chileno Antártico remain undisputed. The whole of Antártida Argentina was in dispute. At one time, there were difficulties between Australia, France and the UK as well as between Norway and the UK, but these problems were resolved during the 1930s. The Australian, British and New Zealand claims were mutually recognised, since they derived from one British imperial policy, and during 1938-9 these three governments, in conjunction with France and Norway, acted to recognise each other's claims. The combined effect of these seven claims - all advanced formally by the early 1940s and still maintained - meant that only one sector of Antarctica was unclaimed, that is, the area between 90°W and 150°W, apart from the undefined hinterland of Dronning Maud Land not claimed by Norway.

In addition, other governments have indicated either their 'rights' to Antarctic territory based upon factors such as discovery and geographic proximity and/or their non-

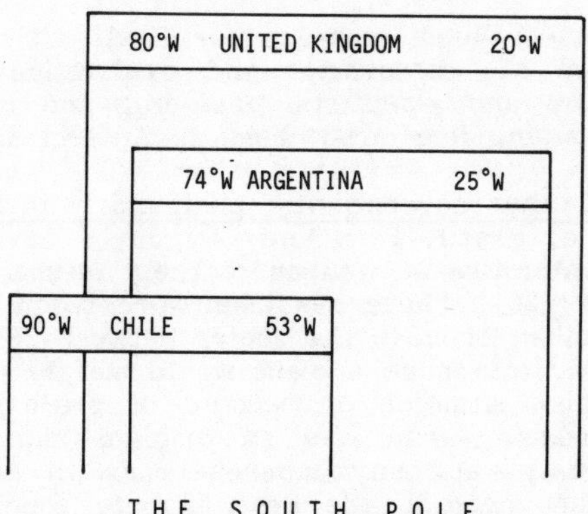

In the north, the Argentine and British claims are bounded by 60°S. The Chilean claim has no northern limit.

Fig. 6.2: The competing Antarctic claims of Argentina, Chile and the United Kingdom.

recognition of existing claims, even if such governments have yet to give substance to these alleged 'rights'. Although the US government has oft-considered becoming a claimant nation, it has merely reserved its 'rights' in Antarctica, while stating constantly that the continent was not considered to be under the sovereignty of any government.

> The United States for many years has had, and at the present time continues to have, direct and substantial rights and interests in Antarctica. Throughout a period of many years, commencing in the early eighteen-hundreds, many areas of the Antarctic region have been discovered, sighted, explored and claimed on behalf of the United States by nationals of the United States. During this period, the Government of the United States and its nationals have engaged in well-known and extensive activities in Antarctica. In view of the activities of the United States and its nationals referred to above, my Government reserves all of the rights of the United States with respect to the Antarctic region, including the right to assert a territorial claim or claims[27]... The basic United States policy towards Antarctica has remained constant for the past 60 years - the United States does not recognize any claims to territorial sovereignty in Antarctica and does not assert any claims of its own, although it reserves its basis of claim[28].

The Soviet Union has assumed a somewhat similar line towards Antarctica:

> The Soviet Union reserves for itself all of the rights based on the discoveries and explorations of Russian navigators and scientists, including the right to make corresponding territorial claims in Antarctica[29].

A number of other governments, particularly in Latin America - for instance, Brazil, Peru and Uruguay - have referred to 'rights' in Antarctica as well as to their refusal to recognise existing claims[30]. There has been speculation concerning a possible Brazilian claim to the sector between 28°W and 53°W, and it is clear that such a claim would merely exacerbate an already complex situation on account of pre-existing Anglo-Argentine claims. Japan was an original signatory to the Antarctic Treaty, and any Japanese claim in Antarctica was effectively renounced in the Peace Treaty concluded at San Francisco in 1951.

Prior to 1959 both claimants and non-claimants sought to protect their respective legal positions. As a result, claimants enacted laws, established post offices and issued stamps, performed symbolic acts such as presidential visits, and protested against any infringement of their sovereignty by other powers, whereas non-claimants ensured that their actions involved neither a recognition of any government's sovereignty - for example, the US government instructed its nationals to refrain from seeking permission to explore and to establish postal and wireless offices within territory claimed by Britain and New Zealand - nor a diminution of their 'rights'. In essence, the Antarctic Treaty was designed to accommodate these divergent politico-legal positions, since article IV was supposed to remove the pressure to continue the pre-1959-type activities.

The Legal Support for Claims

The preceding pages outline the manner in which governments have attempted to find support for their respective viewpoints on sovereignty in a variety of international legal theories and principles, which tend to be based essentially upon the traditional legal criteria employed to establish sovereignty, that is, first discovery, taking possession, and perfecting an inchoate title through effective occupation[31]. The general emphasis has been placed upon discovery reinforced by 'occupation', which has usually taken the form of various administrative activities backed by a permanent scientific presence. However, Argentina and Chile have gone further, for they have tended to employ virtually every kind of argument, including points dating back to papal awards in the 1490s and other achievements of their mother country, the inheritance through the _uti possidetis_ doctrine of rights previously accruing to Spain, and a range of geographical and scientific factors[32].

In practice, the situation is confused on account of the problems appertaining to the nature and validity of 'discovery' and 'occupation'. Apart from rival claims for the prior discovery of particular locations, doubts have been expressed about the authenticity of several alleged 'discoveries' as well as about such matters as the ability to extend claims to areas not seen or the validity of claim forms dropped from planes. In any case, discovery is regarded generally as conferring no more than an inchoate title, which needs to be perfected within a reasonable period by occupation. But what is 'reasonable' or 'occupation'? For example, was France entitled in 1924 to claim Adélie Lane as French territory, thereby perfecting a title dating back to discovery in 1840 but in an area upon which no Frenchman had yet set foot? A more significant controversy has centred upon the nature of an 'effective occupation' in the context of Antarctica's harsh climate, remoteness and lack of population. As a result, claimants have tended to rely upon a minimal control interpretation, a diluted version of occupation encouraged further by the guidelines provided by international legal judgements on such cases as those of Palmas Island (1928), Clipperton

Island (1931), East Greenland (1933) and Minquiers and Ecrehos (1957).

Naturally, these cases dealt with particular facts, which did not harmonise easily with the classifications of text-writers on international law, and hence some lawyers - for example, Triggs - regard them as 'weak' precedents for Antarctica[33]. Nevertheless, claimants have oft-cited such cases because of their general tendency to stress a flexible approach and the display and exercise of state authority sufficient bearing in mind the circumstances of the territory concerned; thus, the Palmas arbitral award stated that:

> Sovereignty cannot be exercised in fact at every moment on every point of a territory. The intermittence and discontinuity compatible with the maintenance of the right necessarily differ according as inhabited or uninhabited regions are involved[34].

By implication, it was argued that less control was required to sustain a territorial claim in the polar regions than elsewhere, so that administrative regulations, symbolic acts, including the appointment of magistrates and postmasters, and occasional visits, could provide substance for title. However, international law does not remain static, and this factor, in conjunction with developments in polar techniques, facilitated a re-evaluation of the meaning of 'effective occupation' during the late 1930s and 1940s. As a result, a permanent Antarctic presence through a scientific base and associated administrative arrangements came to be regarded as essential for the satisfaction of the effectiveness criteria, and during the 1940s governments were subject to pressures to maintain their claims in this manner, such as evidenced by Britain's Operation Tabarin and its peacetime version, the FIDS. Other claimants followed in the late 1940s and 1950s, and upon this basis such governments argued that during the pre-1959 period they had managed not only to confirm the effectiveness of their respective occupations but also to establish that 'the alleged impossibility of obtaining sovereignty by occupation of polar lands on the ground of their uninhabitability is founded on a false premiss'[35].

In the Arctic, Canada and the Soviet Union utilised the sector principle to justify territorial claims, and this precedent was followed in Antarctica by some claimants, which oft-defined claims by meridians drawn to the South Pole based either upon their mainland boundaries (eg. Argentina and Chile) or upon the coastal limits of their Antarctic territory (eg. Australia, New Zealand and the UK). In fact, Norway, anxious not to infringe its Arctic interests, decided deliberately in 1939 against the employment of this principle, thereby leaving undefined the northern and southern limits of its Antarctic claim. Although BAT represents a sector, the

British government has avoided an emphasis upon the sector theory, partly because of a desire not to be exposed to the perceived weaknesses of the principle, such as laying claims to territory within the sector neither seen nor discovered by its nationals. For Britain these intrinsic weaknesses were accentuated by the fear that criticisms of the sector principle tend also to undermine, even to contradict, the force of existing arguments based upon effective occupation. In any case, the sector theory might be interpreted not only as working to the advantage of Argentina and Chile on the grounds of geographical contiguity but also as encouraging sector claims from other southern hemisphere governments, particularly in Latin America. Consequently, Britain has regarded sector theory as not providing 'a sufficient legal root of title' such as compared to discovery or occupation[36].

During 1939 Reeves asserted that 'the sector principle as applied at least to Antarctica is now part of the accepted international legal order', but this point remains debatable on account of the fact that Britain's lack of enthusiasm for the concept has been paralleled by American and Norwegian denials of its validity in Antarctica[37]. Like many other international lawyers, Auburn has criticised the legal validity of the principle; indeed, he has argued that 'a sector is itself an admission of the failure to comply with the general standards of the law of nations'[38]. Nevertheless, Argentina and Chile have proved far from reticent in the utilisation of the sector concept, a point highlighted by the employment of arguments based upon geographical contiguity and proximity in order to advocate the existence of a South American Antarctic sector as part of their efforts to oppose British territorial ambitions. This concept, embodied in the Rio Treaty of 1947, resembled a kind of extension of the Monroe Doctrine, for it was argued that 'the countries neighbouring the sectors ... have preferential rights of sovereignty over them'[39].

However, in practice the primary mode used to acquire sovereignty in Antarctica, a so-called *terra nullius*, has been taking possession and effective occupation, coupled with the inchoate title deriving from discovery. According to Bernhardt:

> Diverse problems associated with the history of Antarctica and continuing into the present time - problems to a large degree dictated by the severe climatic conditions of the continent - have created certain exceptions to the traditional *occupatio* doctrine[40].

In general, 'possession and administration are the two essential factors that constitute an effective occupation', and in this context the claimants have pressed the case that such criteria have been fulfilled, particularly allowing for the 'exceptions' identified by Bernhardt and recognised by a series of international legal judgements, including the East Greenland case[41]. But certain governments and international lawyers have assumed a different view. For example, in 1957 the US-based Commission to Study the Organization of Peace concluded that in respect to Antarctica 'effective occupation in terms of international law has not yet taken place', a point seconded since then by such international lawyers as Bernhardt and more recently by subscribers to the common heritage principle[42]. Naturally, one can find official and legal authority to support both viewpoints, a point reflecting not only the usual legal uncertainties and controversies but also the fact that arguments in the sphere of international law are oft-influenced as much by political as by legal considerations; thus, legal criteria may be distorted or exploited to accommodate political requirements, and this tendency recalls Auburn's observation that 'the sector theory is ... more of a political than a legal principle'[43].

The Prevalence of Sovereignty Problems

The apparent simplicity of article IV was employed to conceal a rather messy and confused situation, and perhaps inevitably these sovereignty-based problems have never quite disappeared. In turn, the situation has been exacerbated not only by the political and legal uncertainties concerning claims but also by the emergence of new problems of a politico-legal nature.

In theory, claimant states are entitled by article IV (2) to maintain their respective claims, along with any prestige appertaining thereto, without either performing the usual responsibilities or incurring the costs of a sovereign power. However, in practice, certain governments have continued to act in the hawkish-type of manner characteristic of the pre-treaty period, that is, in a way implying a belief in the continuing existence of a close link between their sovereignty and the nature, extent and location of their Antarctic presences; thus, it appears that their activities, albeit of an ostensibly scientific orientation, have been interpreted by such governments as the method of recording, maintaining and strengthening their territorial claims. The two South American claimants have never really moderated their stances on sovereignty, and their assertive, overt and, at times, flamboyant attitudes have been directed at both domestic and international audiences. For instance, domestic political considerations have encouraged successive Argentine and Chilean governments to view Antarctica as a popular, even unifying, issue, and their respective populations have been presented with the prestige, resource and other benefits of the claims.

Their people have been led to believe that the national patrimony is at stake and that untold riches lies at hand in their sovereign territories to the south[44].

The Anglo-Argentine-Chilean rivalry for the same piece of Antarctic real estate serves to explain the anxiety of Argentina and Chile to establish the international visibility of their Antarctic roles.

In the international context, symbolic acts have proved significant, such as the erection of name plates announcing, 'Antártida Argentina', the issue of postage stamps depicting the extent and nature of the claim, the anxiety to stamp the passports of tourists therein and presidential visits. In 1961 President Frondizi of Argentina visited Deception Island, while this was followed in August 1973 by the visit of President Lastiri and the Argentine Cabinet to Marambio base, which was declared the temporary capital of Argentina[45]. The positive aspects of such visits, such as in respect to publicity and to the reaffirmation of sovereignty, were reinforced by other considerations, including Argentine anxiety about Brazilian intentions regarding Antarctic territory. A recent article in an Argentine popular journal pointed to its country's research, aviation, tourist and other activities in Antarctica, including the establishment of family groups at bases, the conduct of weddings and the birth of babies - 'all citizens of Argentina and the Antarctic' - therein, and even the establishment of a school[46]. The first of these Argentine Antarctic citizens, Emilio de Palma, was born at Esperanza base in January 1978, and such developments can be interpreted as convincing proof for an effective occupation of Antarctic territory. According to the article, such 'uninterrupted activity' reinforced Argentina's basic historical and legal rights:

All this contributes to Argentina's legitimate aspirations to sovereignty. Although all Antarctic claims have been temporarily suspended by virtue of the treaty, they are still pending and are a part of the genuine prestige of Argentina among the Antarctic countries[47].

This ambivalent approach upon sovereignty has been shared by Chile, which has performed a rather similar high-profile role in Antarctica, such as demonstrated in January 1977 by President Pinochet's visit to Antarctica, where he declared that Chile's claim was merely a continuation of mainland territory, or more recently during 1984 by the establishment of a Chilean 'family settlement' in Antarctica[48]. Simon Alterman of Reuters visited the Chilean base of Teniente Marsh at the tip of the Antarctic peninsula to interview the families:

> Chile, whose Antarctic claim largely overlaps those of Britain and Argentina, made a political point in February (1984) by sending the six families - 12 adults and six children aged 1 to 7 - to live for two years at this base. Thirty other people are on the base for a one-year period ... the six three-bedroom residences are pleasant and well-equipped, with carpeting, central heating, washing machines, televisions, video recorders and other electrical appliances ... "The only thing that I don't like about the house is the color", said one woman[49].

However, the principal method of recording an Antarctic interest and presence has been through science, and this point has been enhanced by the 'research activity' criterion specified for membership of the Antarctic Treaty System according to article IX (2). The continuing preoccupation of many governments with sovereignty - recent and on-going moves in respect to the development of Antarctic resource regimes have served to revive such concerns - means that a scientific role has possessed a perceived politico-legal value, especially as scientists have been appointed to perform administrative functions in Antarctica, such as magistrates or postmasters. The scientists provide an overt on-the-spot presence, and clearly several governments have viewed their research programmes at least partly through political spectacles; thus, a scientific base records a claim, upholds national interests as against other governments and prevents a possible loss of membership status through default. These linkages were highlighted in 1981 by an Australian parliamentary report:

> As long as it remains our national policy that we have sovereignty over the Australian Antarctic Territory, in international terms it is imperative that we should exercise it and can be seen to exercise it to an appropriate degree in technological terms, Our presence and our stations are evidence of our assertion of sovereignty[50].

Or, as one Australian writer has commented, 'we may agree to fold up the flag for a time, but we don't chop down the flagpole'[51].

In fact, the level of any country's politico-legal commitment to Antarctica is oft-measured in terms of expenditure upon scientific research therein, even if varying modes of organisation renders comparative surveys difficult to compile; for example, logistical support provided by the navy or air force may be costed in overall defence costs, thereby preventing an accurate assessment of Antarctic costings. Nevertheless, changing manpower and research expenditure levels can serve to indicate transformations in a government's policy towards Antarctica. During 1982-3 official funding for BAS increased by over 60% as part of the post-Falklands War enhancement of Britain's role in the South West Atlantic[52]. After some 15 years of level funding and of declining BAS research activities, the British government allocated extra money to BAS - significantly, at a time when other research organisations were subjected to fiscal constraints - since the Survey offered the only way in which a reorientation of British Antarctic policy could be expressed. In this context, during recent years many Australians have argued for a similar enhancement in their country's scientific programme; for example, during 1984 Professor David Caro, chairman of the Antarctic Research Policy Advisory Committee, repeatedly urged an injection of funds, partly for scientific reasons - 'Australia seems to have drifted to a point where little is being achieved' - and partly for sovereignty reasons[53].

> Australia should either spend a little more and do a great deal more, or if we are honest, we should abandon the area to those countries willing to work there.

Caro's advocacy prompted press interest and debate, and one editorial highlighted the perceived inter-connection between research and sovereignty.

> As claimant to six million square kilometres ... Australia should be a leader in Antarctic research ... Australia's aspirations seem even less plausible given its apparent lack of commitment to the region ... The Government should contribute more actively and visibly to the international research programme. Otherwise it might as well give up its massive territorial claims in Antarctica[54].

A further complication arises from the conflicting messages or signals emanating from claimants, since certain governments have maintained and even reinforced their Antarctic activities, while also indicating or implying a qualification of their stance upon sovereignty. Recently, this point has been made about Australia during the course of the on-going debate about the country's commitment to AAT, and similar question marks have been raised about other governments, including New Zealand and the UK. During the late 1950s the New Zealand government's preoccupation with the burdens of an Antarctic role, and especially with the costs of protecting its claim to the Ross Dependency, fostered its emergence as an advocate of an international solution for Antarctica, a proposal indicating either the surrender or scaling-down of its claim[55]. In 1972 New Zealand raised the possibility of an international solution at the Consultative Meeting, and this evidence, in conjunction with an appreciation of pre-1959 developments, has fostered doubts about the government's commitment towards the claim, even if the maintenance of the claim to the Ross Dependency remains one of New Zealand's 'principal Antarctic objectives'[56]. Some observers have detected a similar ambiguity about British intentions, but this has proved impossible to confirm. However, some have pointed to British sympathy for New Zealand's internationalisation proposals in the 1950s, while in 1977 Brian Roberts, a long-standing influence upon the formulation of British Antarctic policy, used his recent retirement from the Foreign Office to suggest that in certain circumstances it might be advisable for Britain to compromise upon claims, that is, 'to look upon itself as a non-claimant state'[57]. It is, of course, debatable as to how far these 'unofficial' comments reflect official thinking in London, although occasionally official statements have moved in this direction; for instance, in June 1982 Watts, the head of the UK delegation, informed the Wellington mineral regime negotiations that, while the British government approached the topic as a claimant, it might be prepared 'in the common interest' to employ 'certain powers at present vested in the United Kingdom ... for the general good'[58]. However, many detect a contrary strand in British policy, and have identified an assertiveness strengthened in the wake of the 1982 Falklands War by a substantial up-grading of Britain's Antarctic role and visibility[59]. The impact of the resource regime talks may have reinforced this trend, such as through the special meetings held on the subject of the minerals regime by claimant nations. As a result, any official definition of British interests in Antarctica continues to attach significance to control over BAT, and a recent statement gave priority to the 'territorial' interest, which was elaborated as 'to protect our sovereignty over BAT'[60].

As far as the other claimants are concerned, the French government has not only remained active but also developed its Antarctic presence, and the recent construction of an improved runway in Adélie Land - this prompted objections from environmentalists - was designed in part to enable France 'to step up its research through the extension of the length of time spent by the scientific teams on the ground'[61]. Norway's Antarctic role became somewhat fragmentary and marginal during the 1960s and 1970s - the Norway station in Dronning Maud Land was not permanently manned after 1960 and some questioned whether the level of Norwegian research activity satisfied the membership criteria of article IX (2). A Norwegian expedition visited Antarctica during 1984-5, and 'the intention of the Norwegian government is to follow up this expedition with new ones at regular intervals in the future', even if this expectation falls short of re-establishing a permanent scientific presence[62].

Hitherto, this section has concentrated upon the claimants, but many of the above points are relevant to non-claimants also, since those with alleged 'rights' in Antarctica have used science as an instrument designed not only to consolidate these rights but also to confirm the government's right to a say in the continent's affairs. Certainly, both the American and Soviet governments have maintained their Antarctic positions, and emerged as the two most visible governments in the sphere of Antarctic research and expenditure, while the way in which Soviet bases are located around Antarctica has prompted speculation concerning the Soviet desire for a foothold or territorial stake in every section of the continent. However, in many respects, such hypothesising can be dismissed as a rather academic and sterile exercise, since the effect of article IV of the treaty has been to permit any government, whatever its position regarding claims, to keep open policy options on sovereignty, and thus to delay making any definite decision on the matter. In fact, this quality has contributed to the ambiguity of the sovereignty positions of New Zealand and the United Kingdom, such as discussed earlier.

However, at the same time the apparent acceptance of a significant link between current research activity and sovereignty implies a certain lack of confidence in article IV, which was supposed to reduce the need for sovereignty-related activities. Admittedly, certain treaty parties have stressed this value of article IV, and the British government has oft-quoted it when faced with reports of the overt actions of Argentina and Chile within BAT; thus, article IV (2) has been identified as a reason for inaction on account of 'the protection given by the Treaty to the United Kingdom's position in the British Antarctic Territory'[63]. As a result, the strength of Britain's Antarctic claim will remain as it was in 1961, when the treaty came into effect, and this position could not be altered by post-1961 Argentine and Chilean moves. On the surface, it appears easy to take this view of article IV, according to which any activities by a treaty party will not count for sovereignty purposes; indeed, sovereignty-related activities might be interpreted as in breach with the spirit, if not the letter, of the treaty. For example, the 1982 Shackleton Report indicated:

> The need for awareness of possible threats to the Antarctic Treaty ... an example of this is Argentina's action in maintaining armed military on their bases, having pregnant Argentinian women flown there to have their Argentinian babies and thus to claim rights based on "settlement", and even at one stage declaring Marambio, one of their Antarctic bases, temporary capital of Argentina, where they held a Cabinet meeting![64].

However, in practice problems can be anticipated in the future, such as upon the occasion of the termination of the treaty or of its review, when certain governments may seek recognition of the manner in which their claims have been 'improved' since 1961, especially at the expense of other claimants. As long as governments perceive a linkage between research and sovereignty, they are likely to demand a tangible return upon their Antarctic 'investments' of time, money and manpower[65]. It might prove possible to pre-empt future problems through a Consultative Meeting recommendation or statement designed to interpret article IV (2) in a manner discounting post-1961 activities, thereby serving as a timely reminder of the original intention of the treaty negotiators. But this is easier said than done, since governments with significant post-1961 'investments' in Antarctica might hinder such a move, perhaps in conjunction with those governments which believe that any action is superfluous, particularly as long as the treaty remains in operation.

But there is another problem related to the attempt to keep the clock stopped at 1961 as far as sovereignty is concerned. This point concerns the alleged difficulty of applying static principles to a changing world; thus, it remains questionable whether rights to sovereignty, albeit asserted or reserved, can be preserved over a long period of suspension. Will it ever be possible to return easily to the status quo of 1961? A number of factors provide cause for doubt, especially as the problems arising within the Antarctic Treaty System itself will be compounded by the development of new approaches to international law. The extensive, continuous and continent-wide role performed by the American and Soviet governments may be seen as possessing legal implications, a point accentuated by the fact that they have performed more research within a particular sector than the government laying claim to that area. For instance, a claimant might experience legal as well as political difficulties when attempting to vindicate its sovereignty as against a more active - and more powerful - government, and in part the case for an enhancement of Australia's Antarctic research has been influenced by the significant level of Soviet activity and bases within AAT.

In addition, certain treaty developments, most notably the creation of resource regimes, have qualified the sovereignty of claimants, which have accepted the evolution of the treaty system in a cooperative manner somewhat different from the traditional understanding of sovereignty in international law[66]. There exists also the argument that the treaty experience of freedom of movement by scientists and others across so-called Antarctic 'boundaries' might be interpreted as serving not only to erode the force of claimant positions but also to develop a kind of regional customary law based upon an international rather than upon a national approach to the continent[67]. As a result of the development of the Antarctic Treaty System, non-claimants have become accepted by the claimants as possessing a clear right to a say in Antarctica's affairs, a point reinforced by the major research role performed by many non-claimants as well as by the changing composition of the treaty powers. In 1959 the Consultative Parties split 7:5 in favour of claimants, whereas in 1985 the split was 7:9. An awareness of such trends, in conjunction with the perceived difficulties of a reversion back to a situation based on national sovereignty, has fostered arguments that the existing situation tends to promote the de facto internationalisation of Antarctica. In any case, certain claimants might not wish to push their legal rights in Antarctica, such as for policy reasons related to support for the preservation and development of the Antarctic Treaty System as a political fact.

One sector of Antarctica, that is, the area between 90°W and 150°W, remains unclaimed, even if the US government was expected to claim this sector during the 1930s and 1940s. At present, this sector is terra nullius, but its unclaimed status has not prevented the treaty powers from acting as if it was part of the treaty area, and thus subject to the various recommendations and other agreements emanating from the Consultative Meetings. A related question concerns the attitude of the treaty powers should an outsider advance a claim to any part of Antarctica, including the unclaimed sector. In fact, the parties have considered already the nature of any response to the Antarctic activities of a third party, and in 1972 recommendation VIII-8 asserted that:

> In such circumstances, it would be advisable for Governments to consult together as provided by the Treaty, and to be ready to urge or invite as appropriate the State or States concerned to accede to the Treaty, pointing out the rights and benefits they would receive and also the responsibilities and obligations of Contracting Parties.

Although this might be dismissed as rather vague, the impact of any pressure emanating from the Antarctic treaty powers will be accentuated by the inclusion of such governments as those of India, the Soviet Union and the USA in the Antarctic Treaty System.

Sovereignty and the Operation of the Antarctic Treaty System

Clearly sovereignty problems have never disappeared from the perceptions of the treaty powers, and Heap has observed:

> Where sovereignty has been claimed, it is unlikely that any State, having claimed it, will give it up. And indeed, the more it is attacked, the less likely it is to be given up ... the same applies to those who do not

> claim sovereignty in Antarctica, and who do not recognise it[68].

Similarly, during the 1960s the sovereignty problem was implicit in the tendency of Consultative Meetings either to avoid or to refrain from pressing topics raising sovereignty issues, such as resource questions. In fact, the legal aspect surfaced occasionally, such as during discussions on conservation or on the preservation of historic monuments. But resource questions could not be avoided indefinitely, and after the late 1970s each stage in the evolution of the treaty system in the direction of marine and mineral resource management was preceded by a recognition of the varying positions upon sovereignty as embodied in article IV. Resource discussions raised the sovereignty issue in a relatively acute form since - to quote an Australian government statement -

> The right to exploit resources is traditionally an integral part of the concept of national sovereignty ... Australia and the other claimants will be looking for a role in a regime commensurate with their sovereignty status[69].

However, the successful conclusion of CCAMLR in 1980 indicated the ability of the treaty powers to reconcile the sovereignty issue - or rather article IV - with the resource management role. The mineral regime negotiations provide a greater challenge, such as evidenced by the practice of claimants to meet prior to each session of the negotiations. A recent British Foreign Office paper pointed out that:

> The divide between Claimants and non-Claimant States regarding the role to be played by States asserting sovereignty is at the heart of the negotiations for a mineral regime. It is the principal cause of the difficulties encountered in the negotiations so far[70].

Although the Antarctic Treaty attempted through article IV to push aside the sovereignty problem, this chapter has indicated that, contrary to some hopes, it has neither disappeared nor faded away. The recent introduction of resource perceptions has merely confirmed the existence of the difficulty, which is complicated further by the confusions and ambiguities surrounding article IV. In a sense, this state of affairs has proved a function of the article's quality of glossing over conflicting viewpoints, such as epitomised by Senator Gruening in 1960; thus, he commented that article IV stated 'what it did not mean and did not state what it did mean'[71].

Nevertheless, the article continues to be presented as a key provision around which the treaty structure was constructed and has evolved; thus, in 1959 it offered a convenient rug under which to sweep the sovereignty issue in order to enable progress upon other fronts, and more recently the treaty powers have come to appreciate article IV's advantages in respect to pushing the claims problem into the long-term and to promoting stability in the international politics of Antarctica. In turn, the sovereignty aspect has persisted in a range of guises - for example, the territorial chess games conducted between certain governments - but has never proved sufficient to thwart the Antarctic Treaty System's development in a range of new directions, even in those arousing legal sensitivities. Hitherto, the treaty powers have found ways of overcoming the sovereignty problem, such as through the ingenious drafting - the so-called 'bi-focal approach' - characteristic of article IV of the 1980 CCAMLR. At the same time, Auburn has warned against exaggerating the achievements of article IV of the Antarctic Treaty, since the continent's relative lack of utility has rendered it 'an illusory safeguard'[72]. From this perspective, the real test for article IV will come if and when minerals are actually found within the treaty area; in fact, already it is clear that the sovereignty issue has proved the main reason for the slow progress of the Antarctic mineral regime negotiations.

Jurisdiction

There exists a clear link between sovereignty and jurisdiction, and inevitably the Washington treaty negotiations witnessed differences of view regarding the treatment of jurisdiction in Antarctica; in turn, these divisions rendered it difficult for the Consultative Meetings to make any real progress upon the issue. As a result, jurisdiction, like sovereignty, remains one of the unresolved problems, or loose-ends, even if the treaty parties were forced to address certain aspects required to work the treaty, such as matters of jurisdiction appertaining to observers and exchange scientists[73]. Naturally, agreement could be secured for only a relatively modest provision, such as stipulated by article VIII (1):

> In order to facilitate the exercise of their functions under the present Treaty ... observers ... and scientific personnel exchanged ... shall be subject only to the jurisdiction of the Contracting Party of which they are nationals in respect of all acts or omissions occurring while they are in Antarctica for the purpose of exercising their functions.

In theory, claimants to Antarctic territory might be expected to establish their claims through the enforcement of jurisdiction over all activities in their sectors, so that what might be treated as an offence in Buenos Aires, Canberra or London would be dealt with in the same manner as in Antarctica. One Australian writer has depicted this point in a somewhat picturesque manner; thus, 'if there were parking offences in such frozen wildernesses ... they would be punished in the same way as if they were committed by a housewife in Civic Centre, Canberra'[74]. However, in practice, non-claimants and others are unprepared to recognise either the sovereignty or jurisdiction of claimants within 'their' territories, and this necessitated the low-key approach characteristic of article VIII. The situation has been influenced also by an appreciation of the realities of Antarctica, such as the point that those active in Antarctica tend to be subject to other constraints; for example, scientific personnel are subject either to the disciplinary code of their employers or to the regulations attached to their research grants. Military personnel, who predominate in the Antarctic presence of some governments, have their own codes of conduct, while the nature of Antarctica means that any other visitors cannot act in an entirely unsupervised manner.

Inevitably, the vague and incomplete nature of article VIII (1) provides scope for trouble, and several commentators have attempted to construct potential scenarios[75]. For example, what might happen if an American tourist was arrested by Argentina. From one point of view, the tourist might be subject to the law of Argentina, a claimant to sovereignty over the sector where the alleged offence occurred, whereas from another perspective the offender would be liable to the jurisdiction of the American government. In fact, Herman Phleger, the head of the US delegation at the Washington Conference, testified to the Senate Foreign Relations Committee that:

> By virtue of recognizing that there is no sovereignty over Antarctica we retain jurisdiction over our citizens who go down there and we would deny the right of the other claimants to try that citizen[76].

Phleger indicated that any infringment of this position would create 'an international controversy'. Although most jurisdictional difficulties prove a function of the varying positions on sovereignty, some writers have pointed to an added complication, which is related to the view that the development of the Antarctic Treaty System has resulted in the emergence of a kind of <u>de facto</u> collective jurisdiction exercised by the treaty powers.

Undoubtedly, as Phleger conceded, there remains room for controversy, perhaps even for conflict, and the tidying-up of the jurisdictional question constitutes one method of improving and stabilising the Antarctic Treaty System. In the meantime, article VIII (2) provides an avenue designed to alleviate inter-governmental difficulties, since:

> The Contracting Parties concerned in any case of dispute with regard to the exercise of jurisdiction in Antarctica shall immediately consult together with a view to reaching a mutually acceptable solution.

Basically, this article encourages the adoption of a pragmatic approach towards problems, thereby taking advantage not only of the treaty powers' desire to work the treaty but also of their special Antarctic relationships. In addition, article IX (e) empowers them to cover 'questions relating to the exercise of jurisdiction in Antarctica' at the regular Consultative Meetings[77]. However, at the early Meetings in the 1960s Argentina and Chile blocked such discussions, and an awareness of the sovereignty implications of jurisdiction has fostered a general reluctance upon the part of the treaty powers to press the point at Consultative Meetings[78].

The Common Heritage Principle

In the context of the legal controversies on article IV and other aspects prevalent within the Antarctic Treaty System, the recent emergence of the common heritage principle proves of interest, since it serves to reflect not only the changing nature of international law but also the political desire of certain governments to replace the Antarctic Treaty System with an international regime linked perhaps to the UN. This attempt to apply the law of common spaces to Antarctica possesses significant implications for the Antarctic scene in the sphere of international politics, such as in respect to seeking revolution rather than reform. Although there are variants of approach, in brief the advocates of the *terra communis* idea follow Honnold in arguing that exclusive sovereign rights to Antarctic territory and resources 'are barred by contemporary principles of international law ... Antarctica must be governed by an international "law of common spaces" ... a fully international regime must be established'[79].

Honnold typifies the attack launched by critics against the traditional criteria employed to support sovereignty in Antarctica; thus, he asserts that the arguments of claimants are:

> Arcane ... an unclear and unconvincing foundation for national claims ... exclusive claims in Antarctica are not only founded on outmoded legal doctrines, but also are ill-advised in the light of the world's changing political and economic realities ... The several territorial theories still invoked in support of exclusive claims in Antarctica

> have never been validly applied snd spring from a colonial era long since passed[80].

Obviously, there are differences of emphasis, but most advocates of the common heritage approach subscribe to these broad principles, and in turn such legal arguments have constituted part of the foundation for the political campaign mounted by Malaysia and other governments against the Antarctic Treaty System - this will be examined in a subsequent chapter - thereby exacerbating the problem of external accommodation[81].

The advent of the common heritage argument has complicated an already-confused legal situation, even if the treaty powers, and particularly the claimants, assert that legally the critics are on weak ground not only because of the long-standing nature of their sovereignty claims but also because of the alleged failure of outsiders to fulfil certain criteria, such as to establish a right to participate in Antarctic affairs or to deliver protests against the activities of the treaty powers[82]. Paradoxically, one of the most effective ripostes to the critics has emanated from an official of a non-claimant, albeit from a state with alleged 'rights' in Antarctica; thus, Leigh Ratiner observed that:

> The difference between the deep sea bed and Antarctica and between the moon and Antarctica is stated quite simply - territorial sovereignty; and a sovereign claim, be it valid or dubious under international law, is nonetheless the grist of the international law mill[83].

In general, outside interest in Antarctic questions has proved vague and infrequent, and even such key recent developments in the Treaty System as the conclusion of the CCAMLR in 1980 or as the decision in 1981 to commence negotiations for a mineral regime failed to evoke formal protests from non-treaty powers. Rich, a lawyer in the Australian department of Foreign Affairs, believes that, 'the Consultative Parties having acted on the basis of this consistent silence, some form of estoppel now operates against third parties'[84]. However, the continuing international debate upon Antarctica indicates that outsiders are reluctant to concede that silence should be interpreted as acquiescence.

A Tangled Situation

The debate about ownership and jurisdiction in Antarctica has excited debate over a long period, and recently a variety of alternative models have been suggested, albeit mainly in academic rather than political circles. Possible scenarios have included a national solution, centred upon the implementation of a claimant's sovereignty within each sector, a condominium either within a sector - for example, of New Zealand and the USA in the Ross Dependency - or over the whole continent as the treaty powers assert sovereignty as a collective body, a Spitsbergen-type scheme - this is modelled upon the 1920 Spitsbergen Treaty - vesting sovereignty in the treaty powers but guaranteeing third parties access to resources, an UN-based regime acting upon behalf of the international community and in conformity with the common heritage idea, or a declaration of Antarctica as a world park for environmental reasons[85].

Any solution needs to establish both its workability and its credibility in the international arena as a regime capable of representing the interests of the international community and of reconciling the contrasting legal positions of claimants, non-claimants, common heritage advocates and others. It is difficult to anticipate an easy way forward, such as to a regime better than that offered by the Antarctic Treaty System. In many respects, the legal controversies, like the academic debates about alternative regimes, can be interpreted as somewhat arid. But some perceive a way forward. For instance, Heap has pointed to the Antarctic Treaty System's attempt to build 'something new ... a positive contribution to the relationship between states' capable of embracing varying viewpoints[86]. In such circumstances, it might be prudent to work towards a pragmatic political accommodation in preference to a legal solution, particularly since the situation can be adjudged as 'ripe with potential conflict'[87]. Similarly, Dibb has suggested that certain claimants' interests in Antarctica would be promoted by the maintenance of the Antarctic Treaty rather than by the pursuit of sovereignty claims[88].

Recently, Fox has written somewhat sarcastically that:

> The logic of the claims ranges from the eccentric to the surreal, a historical pedant's dream or an international lawyer's nightmare[89].

Certainly, the legal situation in Antarctica remains 'tangled' - to quote Richard Bilder - and during the mid-1980s it seemed appropriate still for Luard to ask 'Who Owns the Antarctic?'[90]. Is Antarctica subject to the sovereignty of the claimants, is it <u>terra nullius</u>, or is it <u>terra communis</u>? Was an American Rear Admiral correct in 1967, when he asserted that 'after all we don't own the continent. Nobody does'[91]. However, neither governments nor academics have been able to agree upon an answer, and in the meantime the Antarctic Treaty, including article IV, remains in force, albeit not unchallenged. In turn, the problem of ownership and control merges into the question of the future relationship between the Antarctic Treaty System and the international community as a whole. Article IV provides a means of accommodating a variety of legal positions, including perhaps also the common heritage approach. From this perspective, the unresolved question of ownership provides the best foundation for the future stability of Antarctic politics, even if some writers claim that the treaty's prospects will be 'gloomy' as long as the differences prevail[92]. In fact, any attempt to resolve the sovereignty problem must be adjudged as likely to threaten not only the survival of the treaty but also the stability of the international politics of Antarctica. Finally, serious thought needs to be given to the position of legal principles in a dynamic world, such as suggested by Triggs:

> Traditional principles of international law may no longer be accurate guides for future government action ... in changing times ... the challenge is to promote policies which accord more with the reasonable expectations of the international community than with traditional and often inappropriate principles of international law[93].

NOTES

1. David S. Landes, The Unbound Prometheus (Cambridge University Press, Cambridge, 1969), p.241.

2. T. W. Balch, 'The Arctic and Antarctic Regions and the Law of Nations', American Journal of International Law, vol.IV, no.1 (1910), pp.273-5; L. Oppenheim, International Law: A Treatise (Longman, London, 1912), p.292; W.E. Hall, A Treatise on International Law (Oxford University Press, London, 1917), p.103; G. Skagestad and K. Traavik, 'New Problems - Old Solutions', Cooperation and Conflict, vol.9 (1974), pp.39-51.

3. Fox, Antarctica and the South Atlantic, p.79.

4. Commission to Study the Organization of Peace, Strengthening the United Nations (Harper, New York, 1957), pp.212-16.

5. UNGA A/37/PV 10, pp.17-20, Mahathir, 29 Sept. 1982.

6. Whiteman, Digest of International Law, vol.2, pp.1242-3; Plott, Development of US Antarctic Policy, p.164; Daniels, The Antarctic Treaty, pp.35-6.

7. Beck, Secret Antarctic Treaty Preparatory Negotiations; Bush, Antarctica and International Law, vol.1, pp.27-116.

8. Alfred van der Essen, 'Le problème politico-juridique de l'Antarctique et le Traité de Washington', Annales de Droit et de Sciences Politiques, vol.20, no.3 (1960), p.236.

9. Beck, Secret Antarctic Treaty Preparatory Negotiations.

10. Auburn, Antarctic Law and Politics, p.104.

11. R. Tucker Scully, 'Alternatives for Cooperation and Institutionalization in Antarctica: Outlook for the 1990s', in Vicuna, Antarctic Resources Policy, p.282.
12. Heap, Antarctic Cooperation, p.104.
13. Van der Essen, Application of the Law of the Sea to the Antarctic, p.232.
14. Ibid., p.231; Sollie, Development of the Antarctic Treaty System, p.19; Roberto E. Guyer, quoted in Wolfrum, Antarctic Challenge, p.59.
15. Keith Brennan, quoted in Quigg, A Pole Apart, p.196.
16. Some writers point incorrectly to 1959; see Oscar González-Ferrán, 'Geologic Data and its Impact on the Discussion on a regime for Mineral resources', in Vicuna, Antarctic Resources Policy, p.164.
17. Molina, Argentine Foreign Minister, to the British ambassador, 20 Feb.1953, in Bush, Antarctica and International Law, vol.1, p.699; Norberto Arduino, 'Antártida Argentina: Su Situacion Actual', Revista Argentina de Relaciones Internacionales, vol.IV, no.11 (1978), pp.42-6; Jorge A. Fraga, Introducción a la Geopolítica Antártica (Direccion Nacional del Antartico, Buenos Aires, 1979), pp.24-6.
18. Argentine government to Chile, 12 Nov.1940, in Bush, Antarctica and International Law, vol.1, p.608.
19. UNGA A/39/583 (Part II), 1984, vol.1, pp.39-40, Australian response, 31 July 1984; Australian Parliamentary Debates, House of Representatives, vol.139, cols.1949-51, 26 May 1933; Spencer, Evolution of Antarctic Interests, pp.113-18; Gillian D. Triggs, Australia's Sovereignty in Antarctica: the validity of Australia's Claim at International Law (Melbourne University, Melbourne, 1983), vols.1-2; Gillian Triggs, 'Australian Sovereignty in Antarctica: Traditional Principles of Territorial Acquisition versus a "common heritage"', in Harris, Australia's Antarctic Policy Options, pp.29-63.
20. Chilean government statement, 18 Feb.1958, in Bush, Antarctica and International Law, vol.II, pp.415-16; Oscar Pinochet de la Barra, Chilean Sovereignty in Antarctica (Editorial del Pacifico, Santiago, 1955), pp.9-59.
21. Gomez, Chilean Foreign Minister to Senate, 21 Jan. 1947, in Bush, Antarctica and International Law, vol.II, pp.334-64.
22. French government decree, 1 April 1938, in Bush, Antarctica and International Law, vol.II, pp.505-06; Pierre Charpentier, 15 Oct.1959, The Conference on Antarctica, p.30; Jean F. da Costa, L'Antarctique et le Droit International (Centre de Documentation Universitaire, Paris, 1948), pp.1-13.

23. Memorandum by Department of External Affairs, 21 Feb.1947, M 1 25/2321 Pt. II, New Zealand Archives, Wellington; Hill, *New Zealand and Antarctica*, pp.18-25; Hugh F.M. Logan, 'Cold Commitment: the Development of New Zealand's Territorial Role in Antarctica, 1920-1960', unpublished MA Thesis, University of Canterbury, Christchurch, 1979.

24. Royal decree, 14 Jan.1939, *Polar Record*, vol.3, no.18 (1939), pp.169-73; Haakon Børde, 'Norge i Antarktis', *Samtiden*, vol.86, no.10 (1977), pp.577-93.

25. Royal decree, 14 Jan.1939, *Polar Record*, vol.3, no.18 (1939), pp.169-73.

26. *HCFAC*, Falkland Islands, Minutes of Evidence, 10 Nov.1982, p.3, Memorandum by Foreign Office, 13 Oct.1982; Anon., 'The British Title to Sovereignty in the Falkland Islands Dependencies', *Polar Record*, vol.8, no.53 (1956), pp.125-51.

27. US note, 2 May 1958, in *New York Times*, 4 May 1958.

28. UNGA A/39/583 (Part II), 1984, vol.3, p.101, US response, 29 May 1984.

29. Soviet note to the US government, 2 June 1958, *Pravda*, 4 June 1958.

30. See Fraga, *Introducción a la Geopolítica Antártica*, pp.36-8; Bush, *Antarctica and International Law*, vol.II, p.356; C da Gama Pinto, 'Battle for Treasure of the last frontier on Earth', *South*, Dec.1983, p.39; Azambuja, *Antártida: Historia e Geopolítica*, pp.267-89.

31. Brownlie, *Principles of Public International Law*, pp.109 *et seq*.

32. J. Daniel, 'Conflict of Sovereignties in the Antarctic', in *1949 Yearbook of World Affairs*, vol.3 (1949), pp.262-8; Barra, *Chilean Sovereignty in Antarctica*, p.10.

33. Gillian Triggs, 'Australian Sovereignty in Antarctica: Part I', *Melbourne University Law Review*, vol.13 (1981), pp.129-39.

34. Brownlie, *Principles of Public International Law*, pp.144-6; Waldock, *Disputed Sovereignty in the Falkland Islands Dependencies*, pp.314-7; Bernhardt, *Sovereignty in Antarctica*, pp.316-32.

35. Waldock, *Disputed Sovereignty in the Falkland Islands Dependencies*, p.317.

36. Ibid., p.346.

37. J.S. Reeves, 'Antarctic Sectors', *American Journal of International Law*, vol.33 (1939), pp.519-21.

38. Auburn, *Antarctic Law and Politics*, pp.23-31; Triggs, *Australian Sovereignty in Antarctica: Part I (Melbourne Law Review)*, pp.139-42.

39. Gomez, Chilean Foreign Minister to Senate, 21 Jan.1947, in Bush, *Antarctica and International Law*, vol.II, p.357.

40. Bernhardt, Sovereignty in Antarctica, p.318.

41. Brownlie, Principles of Public International Law, pp.130-55.

42. Commission to Study the Organization of Peace, Strengthening the United Nations, p.216; Bernhardt, Sovereignty in Antarctica, p.330; Triggs, Australian Sovereignty in Antarctica: Part I (Melbourne Law Review), p.125.

43. Auburn, Antarctic Law and Politics, p.31.

44. Quigg, A Pole Apart, p.113.

45. New York Times, 11 June 1961; El Mercurio, 10 Aug.1973; Auburn, Antarctic Law and Politics, pp.59-61; Peter J. Beck, 'Argentina's Philatelic Annexation of the Falklands', History Today, vol.33; no.2 (1983), pp.39-44.

46. Anon, 'Tres Generaciones Argentinas en la Antártida', Argentina, no.13 (1981), p.13.

47. Ibid., p.13.

48. Christian Science Monitor, 28 Jan.1977.

49. Philadelphia Inquirer, 8 April 1984.

50. Australian Parliamentary Committee on Public Works, Redevelopment of Australian Antarctic Bases, p.9.

51. Warner, Antarctica - the Defence Implications, p.157.

52. Beck, Britain's Role in the Antarctic: Some Recent Changes, pp.85-7; Beck, Britain's Antarctic Dimension, pp.440-4.

53. Science Newsletter, vol.11, no.6 (1984), pp.9-10; Canberra Times, 16 May 1984; Canberra Times, 29 May 1984.

54. The West Australian, 10 Sept.1984.

55. Hill, New Zealand and Antarctica, p.30; G.W. Schroff, 'Antarctica: Politics and Resources', Seaford House Papers 1982 (1983), p.114.

56. Hill, New Zealand and Antarctica, p.98.

57. Roberts, International Cooperation for Antarctic Development, p.112.

58. Antarctic Treaty: Special Consultative Meeting on Antarctic Mineral Resources 14-25 June 1982 (Department of Foreign Affairs, Wellington, 1982), p.2, A. Watts, 14 June 1982.

59. Beck, Britain's Antarctic Dimension, pp.440-4; Fox, Antarctica and the South Atlantic, p.141.

60. Foreign Policy Document no.98: Antarctica: An Overview (Foreign and Commonwealth Office, London, 1983), p.6.

61. UNGA A/39/583 (Part II), 1984, vol.2, p.64, French response, 18 June 1984.

62. UNGA A/39/583 (Part II), 1984, vol.3, pp.28-9, Norwegian response, 20 June 1984.

63. HCFAC, Falkland Islands, Minutes of Evidence, 10 Nov.1982, Memorandum by Foreign Office, 13 Oct.1982, p.4.

64. Shackleton, Falkland Islands. Economic Study 1982, p.3.

65. HCFAC, Falkland Islands, Minutes of Evidence, 13 Dec.1982, Memorandum by P.J. Beck, 4 Dec.1982, p.111; Bernhardt, Sovereignty in Antarctica, p.315.

66. Jost Delbrück, quoted in Wolfrum, Antarctic Challenge, p.119; Gillian Triggs, 'Australian Sovereignty in Antarctica: Part II', Melbourne University Law Review, vol.13 (1982), pp.329-31.

67. Howard J. Taubenfeld, 'A Treaty for Antarctica', International Conciliation, no.531 (1961), p.288.

68. Heap, quoted in Wolfrum, Antarctic Challenge, p.58.

69. Anon, 'Antarctica in the 1980s', Australian Foreign Affairs Record, vol.52, no.1 (1981), pp.12-13.

70. Foreign Policy Document no.98: Antarctica: An Overview, p.6.

71. Antarctic Treaty Hearings before the Senate Committee on Foreign Relations, 86th. Congress, 2nd. Session, 1960, p.13.

72. Auburn, Antarctic Law and Politics, p.110.

73. Daniels, The Antarctic Treaty, p.44; Heap, Antarctic Cooperation, p.104; Sollie, Development of the Antarctic Treaty System, p.32; Auburn, Antarctic Law and Politics, p.184.

74. D. Horne, 1970, quoted in Auburn, Antarctic Law and Politics, pp.184-5.

75. Gerald S. Schatz (ed.), Science, Technology and Sovereignty in the Polar Regions (Lexington Books, Lexington, Mass., 1974), pp.215 et seq.; Charles Neider, Edge of the World (Doubleday, New York, 1961), p.77; Auburn, Antarctic Law and Politics, pp.184-204.

76. Antarctic Treaty Hearings before the Senate Committee on Foreign Relations, 1960, p.62.

77. Finn Sollie, 'Jurisdictional Problems in Relation to Antarctic Mineral Resources in Political Perspective', in Vicuna, Antarctic Resources Policy, pp.329-31.

78. Jeffrey D. Myhre, 'The Antarctic Treaty Consultative Meetings, 1961-68: A Case Study in Cooperation, Compliance and Negotiation in the International System', unpublished Ph.D. dissertation, London School of Economics, University of London, 1983, pp.124-5.

79. E. Honnold, 'Thaw in International Law? Rights in Antarctica under the Law of Common Spaces', Yale Law Journal, vol.87 (1978), pp.806-07; Bernhardt, Sovereignty in Antarctica, pp.348-9; Per Magnus Wijkman, 'Managing the Global Commons', International Organization, vol.36, no.3 (1982), pp.511-6, pp.532-4.

80. Honnold, Thaw in International Law?, pp.807-08, pp.827-8; Triggs, Australia's Sovereignty in Antarctica: the

Validity of Australia's Claim at International Law, vol.2, pp.572-642.

81. See Peter J. Beck, The International Politics of Antarctica (Croom Helm, 1986), pp.284-97 this volume.

82. Wyndham, quoted in Wolfrum, Antarctic Challenge, p.181.

83. Statement by Leigh Ratiner to Earthscan press briefing, 27 July 1977, quoted in UNGA A/39/583 (Part I), 1984, p.65.

84. Roland Rich, 'A Minerals Regime for Antarctica', International and Comparative Law Quarterly, vol.31, no.4 (1982), pp.714-5.

85. Ibid., pp.723-5; F.M. Auburn, 'A Sometime World of Men: Legal Rights in the Ross Dependency', American Journal of International Law, vol.65 (1971), p.581; Charney, Future Strategies for an Antarctic Mineral Resource Regime, pp.217-31; Peterson, Antarctica: the last great land rush on earth, pp.391 et seq.

86. Heap, quoted in Wolfrum, Antarctic Challenge, p.58.

87. Keith Brennan, 'Criteria for Access to the Resources of Antarctica: Alternatives, Procedure and Experience Applicable', in Vicuna, Antarctic Resources Policy, pp.224-7; Wyndham, quoted in Wolfrum, Antarctic Challenge, p.118.

88. Dibb, Australia's Strategic Interests, p.4.

89. Fox, Antarctica and the South Atlantic, p.76.

90. Richard B. Bilder, 'The Present Legal and Political Situation in Antarctica', in Charney, The New Nationalism and the Use of Common Spaces, p.190; Luard, Who Owns the Antarctic?, p.1175.

91. Rear Admiral Abbott, quoted in D. Ballantyne, 'When Hardy Souls Go South', Auckland Star, 18 Dec.1967.

92. Margaret Taylor, 'Latin America and the Future of the Antarctic Treaty', unpublished MA Thesis, Institute of Latin American Studies, University of London, 1984, p.45.

93. Triggs, Australian Sovereignty in Antarctica (Harris), pp. 62-3.

Chapter Seven

THE ANTARCTIC TREATY: A CONTINENT MANAGED BY THE ANTARCTIC TREATY SYSTEM

During 1981 the Twelth Consultative Meeting of the Antarctic Treaty powers held in Buenos Aires was used to mark the 20th.anniversary of the entry into force of the treaty, and in turn the occasion prompted the meeting to reflect upon the nature and achievements of 'the evolving system of obligations that had been undertaken by the Consultative Parties'[1]. These reflections emphasised the significant contributions made to international politics as well as to the cause of scientific investigation by 'the Antarctic Treaty System of continually evolving consultative procedures', which 'has produced recommendations covering a wide variety of subjects which benefit from international cooperation'. In this context, attention was focussed upon 'the System's achievements', in such spheres as conservation and international scientific cooperation, in order to provide the foundation for the assertion that 'the Antarctic Treaty System of arrangements dealing with the practical requirements for international action is the only widely accepted arrangement which exists in the area'.

This paragraph highlights the attempt by the Antarctic powers to depict the unity, effectiveness and uniqueness of the Antarctic Treaty System, which in effect has separated the management of the continent from other parts of the world. However, not all governments accept this claim, such as demonstrated by the emerging interest of the wider international community in the affairs of Antarctica. Inevitably, the resulting criticism of the treaty system - this has included attempts to advocate its replacement - has caused a closing of ranks by the treaty powers, a reinforcement of their regional consciousness and a more determined effort to expound the system's virtues to the international audience. To some extent, this development has given further encouragement to the impression regarding the exclusivity of the so-called "Antarctic club", another aspect criticised by outsiders, even if the Antarctic powers dispute this point and respond that in reality their policy serves not only to benefit

Antarctica and the wider international community but also to encourage other governments to participate in the system.

The Antarctic Treaty System

In any discussion on Antarctica the term 'Antarctic Treaty System' arises frequently as a convenient short-hand description of a range of agreements centred upon the Antarctic Treaty of 1959, while it is oft-employed by the Consultative Parties to indicate the permanent and coherent character of their framework of cooperation. Basically, the operations of the treaty are performed by the Consultative Parties acting through regular Consultative Meetings, which are held normally upon a biennial basis and are interspersed by other formal and informal contacts. These regular sessions have been supplemented by special Consultative Meetings held upon specific topics - these embrace resource and membership questions - as well as by additional agreements, such as the Agreed Measures (1964), the Sealing Convention (1972) and CCAMLR (1980). Collectively, this 'institutional structure' has attracted the term 'the Antarctic Treaty System', and thus separate conventions on sealing and marine living resources have been interpreted as new elements within the system rather than as separate parallel structures alongside the treaty, especially as the Consultative Parties performed a predominant role in the origins and completion of these agreements. In fact, the latter were designed to fill perceived gaps in the treaty and to ensure that such questions were covered within the parameters of the treaty system.

To many people, the term "system" implies an established political order, centred upon a permanent organisation and appropriate bodies. However, this strict definition does not apply to Antarctica, whose weak and non-permanent structures have encouraged claims that the Antarctic Treaty System is a mis-nomer and inappropriate to the Antarctic reality. Nevertheless, the term has acquired a general acceptability, such as evidenced by its employment not only in Consultative Meeting recommendations - for example, recommendations X-9 and XII-6 - but also in UN resolutions dealing with the continent; thus, in December 1983 the General Assembly stipulated that the UN Study on Antarctica should take account of 'all relevant factors', including 'the Antarctic Treaty System'[2]. In any case, historians of the period 1815-22 may recall the so-called "Congress System", which also lacked any permanent structure and only met periodically. As a result, there seems no reason why a certain amount of semantic licence should not be granted to the Antarctic powers, particularly on account of the term's convenience in describing a range of diverse measures (as seen in Figures 7.1 and 7.2).

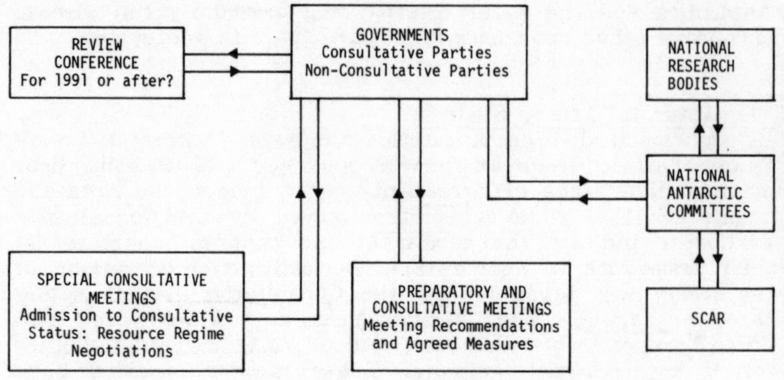

Fig. 7.1: The Antarctic Treaty Framework.

Indeed, in certain quarters the Antarctic Treaty System has been interpreted as something more substantial, such as constituting an objective international reality. Van der Essen, a participant in the treaty negotiations, has asserted that 'in one sense, the signatory powers of the Treaty gave birth to a certain legislative right over the region', that is, a form of collective continent-wide jurisdiction[3]. Similarly, Fernando Zegers, who has represented Chile at both the UN and Consultative Meetings, has oft-argued that the Antarctic Treaty System:

> Represents a subsystem integrated into the overall international system, which confirms and gives expression to the principles and purposes of the United Nations' Charter[4].
> It is a subsystem that works better than the general international system ... there is an Antarctic system ... a legal regime that has been applied with general international acceptance to the frozen continent[5].

Naturally, these views do not command universal acceptance, but it is clear that participation in the Antarctic Treaty System has fostered in the parties a perception of the system's dynamic character and benefits, a sense of pride in its operation, and a commitment to its future preservation[6]. This attitude has resulted in a will to work the system, to extend its sphere of operation, and to defend it against the rising number of critics, who approach the system with a similar sense of commitment - for instance, most critics articulate support for the common heritage principle and the equal rights of developing countries - and attack it as a privileged grouping.

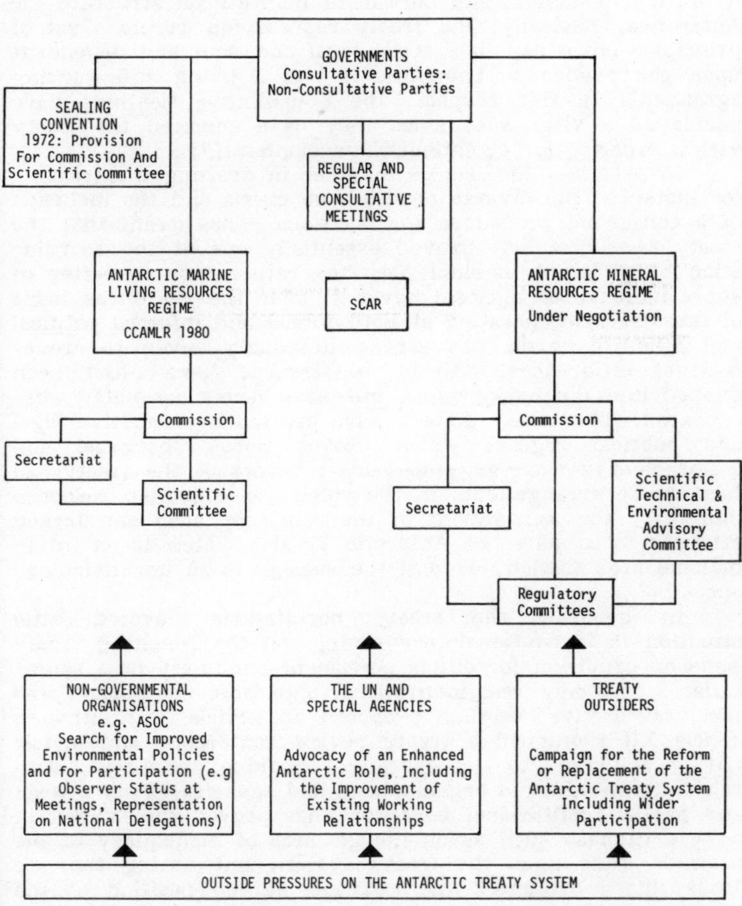

Note: (i) The institutional framework for the Minerals regime has been based upon the text of Beeby II (the final agreement might differ). (ii) There are already some linkages between the Antarctic Treaty System and outside bodies, such as UN special agencies. (iii) This figure should be used with Figure 7.1 (eg. on SCAR).

Fig. 7.2: The Antarctic Treaty System in the international context.

Antarctic Consultative Meetings

Although the Antarctic Treaty placed the continent under a form of international, or rather inter-governmental control, it failed to establish any permanent institutional structure for Antarctica. Basically, the treaty represented merely a set of principles enshrined in a static legal document and dependent upon the parties to transform it into a living and working agreement. In this respect, the Consultative Meetings have performed a vital role, since they have endowed the treaty with a capacity for evolutionary development[7].

In practice, the factors involved in drafting the treaty - for instance, the diverse positions on claims and the inclusion of a consensus procedure for decisions - has meant that the treaty mechanism has proved essentially one of the coordination of different national positions rather than a matter of supra-national management, even if over the years the habit of inter-state cooperation at both formal and informal political and scientific levels has served to qualify, even to erode, national differences. Indeed, differences have often been pushed into the background, but have never completely disappeared. The treaty powers have created a distinctive legal and political regime, which proves more substantial and comprehensive than suggested by the text of the treaty. In fact, these arrangements in the sphere of collective responsibility for the management of the continent have encouraged attempts to compare the Antarctic Treaty System to an international organisation, even if the analogy is an unsatisfactory one.

In general, the treaty negotiations devoted little attention to institutional provisions, and the resulting treaty made no provision for either permanent machinery or a secretariat. The only real institutional apparatus established was the Consultative Meeting proposed in article IX, although article XII mentioned a treaty review conference and article III(2) referred to 'co-operative working relations' with relevant international organisations and agencies. Such a weak and partial institutional framework has proved the subject of many critiques, such as on the grounds of inadequacy to the demands made upon the treaty system, but during the late 1950s this represented the maximum agreed position of the treaty parties. Initially, the preparatory negotiations of 1958-9 tended to skirt institutional aspects, except to identify the fact that some kind of administrative machinery would be required. White, a New Zealand delegate, raised the matter at an early meeting, since the appointment of observers and other provisions related to the peaceful and scientific use of the continent would depend upon support from an administrative system, which might range 'from a large organisation with many functions to the opposite extreme of almost no organisation at all'[8]. Subsequently the matter rested until the negotiations moved onto the consideration of the draft articles submitted by Daniels in November 1958, when it became clear that an ambitious interpretation of 'administrative measures' - this was defined as the creation of a permanent

Antarctic organisation and secretariat - went beyond what the majority of governments were prepared to accept. Certain claimants, including Argentina and Chile, feared that the 'creeping internationalization' inherent in a strong institutional structure would threaten their sovereignty positions, although one claimant, the United Kingdom, was more sympathetic to the idea of an ambitious interpretation and favoured - to quote its delegate to the Washington Conference - 'some organization vested with more effective and comprehensive powers than that which is now contemplated'[9].

As a result, the Antarctic treaty provided for minimal administrative arrangements, that is, for a relatively weak, decentralised and functionally-orientated structure. The absence of a central governing body means that the substance of the treaty is provided by the series of Consultative Meetings, which according to article IX(1) constitute a formal mechanism of collective responsibility - a regime for international cooperation in Antarctica - within the framework of the treaty's rules and principles. Inevitably, the regular Consulative Meetings, at which delegates act under the instructions of their respective governments, offer the most obvious evidence of the Antarctic Treaty System at work. The meetings' decisions are embodied in recommendations, and by 1983 some 138 recommendations had emanated from twelve Consultative Meetings upon a diverse range of topics, including Antarctic Telecommunications, Man's Impact on the Environment, Cooperation in Transport, Tourism, Stamps and Postal Services, the Exchange of Information, Antarctic Minerals and Antarctic Marine Resources[10]. This decision-making role has inclined some writers to claim that 'the Consultative Meetings actually exercise a type of global jurisdiction over all of Antarctica'[11]. Although it would seem an exaggeration to describe the meetings as the nucleus of a regional legislative body, they have developed to become a central and effective feature of the smooth working of the treaty system, thereby illustrating the adoption of a gradualist and evolutionary approach to international politics in respect to Antarctica. From this perspective, vague, weak articles and 'gaps' in the treaty, far from hindering international cooperation, have facilitated the pragmatic development of the system in response to changing needs and new challenges. The boundaries of the treaty system have been explored, even extended, as a result of this process. In certain instances, this trend has caused a limited amount of institution-building, such as demonstrated by the Commission and Secretariat created under the auspices of CCAMLR (1980).

Twelve sessions of the Consultative Meetings have been held since the treaty came into force in 1961, and the 13th. session is scheduled for Brussels in 1985 (as shown in Table 7.3). According to article IX(1):

Table 7.3: The Antarctic Treaty Consultative Meetings

Session	Place	Year	Date	Recommendations	
I	Canberra	1961	10-24 July	I	I-XVI
II	Buenos Aires	1962	18-28 July	II	I-X
III	Brussels	1964	2-13 June	III	I-XI
IV	Santiago	1966	3-18 November	IV	1-28
V	Paris	1968	18-29 November	V	1-9
VI	Tokyo	1970	19-31 October	VI	1-15
VII	Wellington	1972	30 October-10 November	VII	1-9
VIII	Oslo	1975	9-20 June	VIII	1-14
IX	London	1977	19 September-7 October	IX	1-6
X	Washington	1979	17 September-5 October	X	1-9
XI	Buenos Aires	1981	23 June-7 July	XI	1-3
XII	Canberra	1983	13-27 September	XII	1-8
XIII	Brussels	1985	7-18 October	XIII	1-16
XIV	Brasilia	1987			

Note: Neither South Africa nor the Soviet Union have hosted meetings.

> Representatives of the Contracting Parties named in the preamble to the present Treaty shall meet at the City of Canberra within two months after the date of entry into force of the Treaty, and thereafter at suitable intervals and places, for the purpose of exchanging information, consulting together on matters of common interest pertaining to Antarctica, and formulating and considering, and recommending to their Governments, measures in furtherance of the principles and objectives of the Treaty.

The functions of the meetings were not specified precisely, but included:

> Measures regarding ... use of Antarctica for peaceful purposes only ... facilitation of scientific research in Antarctica ... facilitation of international scientific co-operation in Antarctica ... facilitation of the exercise of the rights of inspection ... questions relating to the exercise of jurisdiction in Antarctica ... preservation and conservation of living resources in Antarctica (article IX(1)).

In reality, this selective listing covers an extensive range of topics in the spheres of politics, law, science and the environment, and such a wide brief, in association with the general emphasis upon dealing with 'matters of common interest' and 'measures in furtherance of the principles and objectives of the Treaty', has led both diplomats and academics to describe article IX(1), rather than the oft-cited article IV, as not only the most significant article but also 'the key reason responsible for the dynamic development of the treaty'[12]. In fact, the emergence of this article, which was not viewed as very important initially, has been accentuated perhaps by the uncertainties surrounding article IV. In the event, article IX has acted as a moving force, which has ensured that the treaty system has evolved rather than stagnated. Quigg has followed others in identifying it as the treaty's 'most important and innovative provision', since 'it has meant the difference between a rigid document, frozen in time and circumstance, and an evolving system with the capacity for change'[13].

Working by Consensus

The recommendations of Consultative Meetings do not become effective, and part of the Antarctic legal regime, until approved and ratified by all the Consultative Parties in accordance with articles IX(4) and XII(1). This implicit unanimity requirement imposes a positive obligation to reach agreement through consensus and the application of a spirit of international cooperation. There is no actual provision for a veto, but the consensus procedure gives rise to an effective veto, such as through either a tendency to delay the treatment of controversial issues or an appreciation of the desirability not to press points of difference to the limit. One participant, Heap, has observed that:

> The ultimate power of an Antarctic treaty State lies in refusing to take part in a consensus under which its freedom would be restricted. It cannot alter the *status quo* in its favour by refusing a consensus; the *status quo* can only be changed if all the parties agree that it should be changed[14].

In effect, there exists a kind of double veto available to the treaty powers, firstly, at the Consultative Meeting, and then, secondly, at the stage of ratification.

One of the serious perceived defects of the Antarctic Treaty System concerns the length of time - this tends to be at least six to eight years - required to complete negotiations upon relatively complex and significant issues; thus, a new topic can be raised at one meeting in order to secure its inclusion on the agenda of the next Consultative Meeting, the second meeting may examine or shelve the matter, the third meeting may take the subject further in the form of a recommendation, while about two years or more may be required to secure the approval of all the Consultative Parties before coming into effect. One of the participants has conceded that:

> This leads to a slow progression of decisions; to, successively, a decision to look at a problem, a decision to adopt tentative guidelines for voluntary regulation, to a decision to draft something more binding and then, finally, to adopt a binding agreement[15].

There has been a tendency also for the treaty system to avoid controversial issues upon which agreement seemed questionable, such as evidenced by the evasion of resource questions during the 1960s and early 1970s. However, in the event, the possibility of either paralysis or stagnation has never proved serious, partly because a way has been found of by-passing such problems through the introduction of interim guidelines pending a more permanent arrangement. In any case, difficulties can be either avoided or minimised by adequate prior consultations and information, since experience has indicated the risks of springing new ideas at Consultative Meetings, where instructions restrict the discretion of delegates.

Obviously, a consensus procedure provides one part of the explanation regarding the cautious development of the Antarctic Treaty System, for the result of any particular negotiation will represent the lowest common denominator of views. Nevertheless, even a government with a conservative policy on most aspects - the Soviet Union has acquired this reputation - can be encouraged through skilful diplomacy to up-grade its views in favour of a compromise settlement. At the same time, the procedure's weakness proves a strength, since Consultative Meeting recommendations reflect an agreed and realistic solution likely to be implemented by all parties. The treaty system has worked and developed, albeit slowly, rather than stagnated, and this advance through consensus contrasts favourably with the majority voting procedure of the UN Assembly, which encourages approval of unworkable and unheeded resolutions.

Consultative Meetings: Development and Problems

One influence upon the working of the Antarctic Treaty System has been the absence of a permanent institutional structure. The Antarctic Treaty reflected the rejection of an ambitious interpretation of 'joint administrative arrangements', and therefore failed to make provision for either a permanent Antarctic secretariat and bureaucracy, an archive or an executive organisational authority. This situation occurred in spite of the secretarial functions implicit in the treaty's functions, such as in regard to the exchange of information, inspection, notification of expeditions and the deposit of ratifications. But the most extensive secretarial demands and costs arise from the preparation, conduct and operation of Consultative Meetings, especially in the light of the rules of procedure adopted at the first meeting held in 1961 at Canberra. Henceforth, Consultative Meetings would be held in turn within each member country by alphabetical order, and the secretarial functions would be rotated similarly under the responsibility of the host government. Recommendation I-XIV stipulated the role of the host government to include the preparation of a provisional agenda, consideration of the date, the provision of additional information as required and of facilities for the simultaneous translation of discussions into English, French, Russian and Spanish, and the circulation of the final report, recommendations and other agreements. In practice, the host government has to identify the issues for discussion, such as through diplomatic contact with other parties or through links with SCAR on scientific matters, and to arrange a preparatory meeting to prepare the agenda and to annotate items in sufficient detail to facilitate effective discussion at the actual Consultative Meeting[16].

As a result, practical considerations meant that the secretarial function could not be ignored, a point accentuated during the early Consultative Meetings when Australia proposed the establishment of an Antarctic secretariat based in Canberra. The basic case for such an institution has always rested upon the demands and extent of the secretarial functions to be performed, since the present method imposes a heavy fiscal, administrative and manpower burden upon the host country, a point exacerbated by the fact that certain Consultative Parties are relatively small states - indeed, some are developing countries - and that the secretarial burden is not shared equally between parties, since Consultative Meetings have not been held in either South Africa or the Soviet Union for political reasons. The administrative burden has been accentuated by the developing responsibilities and increasing membership of the Antarctic Treaty System. During 1983 there were indications that Belgium, which was scheduled to host the next Consultative Meeting, might be unable to fulfil its obligations for fiscal and other reasons. In the event, the problem was alleviated by the decision of the 1983 Consultative Meeting to the effect that Australia - this hosted the 1983 meeting - should continue to perform an informal secretarial role until the next Preparatory Meeting[17].

In addition, the present practice carries the risks and costs of discontinuity of administrative experience as well as of the absence of a formal institutional memory, thereby causing problems in the preparation of meetings, the provision of adequate documentation, the slowness of meetings, and the codification of recommendations. Such problems have hampered progress, although the relative continuity of personnel in certain Antarctic delegations - for instance, of

Norway, the United Kingdom and the USA - has moderated the extent of the difficulty; in fact, one participant, Finn Sollie of Norway, has testified to:

> The easy informality and the dedication ... that prevails within the group. This no doubt has contributed greatly to a quiet effectiveness in the work within the Antarctic Treaty System that may be lacking in other and larger international groups ... It has been in a sense a "secret weapon" that has offset the weaknesses of lack of support from a permanent secretariat and of central administrative services[18].

However, whenever the matter has been debated, most opposition has centred upon the grounds of expense, the absence of a need and the fear of an interfering bureacracy[19]. Possibly, these arguments possess some justification, although it might be argued that the assertion about the superfluous nature of a bureaucracy represents a front for policy reasons. For example, certain claimants have indicated an anxiety about the consequences for their sovereignty claims, while it has been suggested that US opposition emanated from concern about the presence of a Soviet representative on the Antarctic secretariat[20]. In the meantime, the Antarctic Treaty System will continue to be characterised by a weak institutional framework, even if recent developments - most notably, the extension of the system's responsibilities and membership - may compel a re-examination of the case for institutional development, particularly in the light of the experience of working CCAMLR, which occasioned the establishment of permanent bodies, including a secretariat, based in Hobart. Therefore, part of the system now possesses a permanent Commission and secretariat, and any benefits of this procedure may encourage its spread to the system as a whole, such as in the context of the appraisal of the operation of the Antarctic Treaty System initiated at the 1983 Consultative Meeting.

The divergence of views regarding the merits of a secretariat and other institutional developments has been paralleled by the existence of different schools of thought concerning the preferred mode of development of Consultative Meetings[21]. Basically two main attitudes can be distinguished. On the one hand, the 'passive' school interpreted the meetings as a kind of fire-fighting mechanism designed to respond to urgent problems upon a pragmatic and ad hoc basis, whereas, on the other hand, the 'active' view favoured a more continuous and visible problem-solving role intended in part to pre-empt anticipated difficulties. To some extent, the 1961 Consultative Meeting cleared the way for the emergence, and continued primacy, of the 'active' school of thought, since the session was utilised to examine a range of topics, including scientific exchange, conservation of flora and fauna, preservation of historic sites and emergency procedures, with a view to action. Obviously, this trend was not welcomed in all quarters, such as implied by van der Essen's observation that:

> From the very beginning, perhaps ill-advisedly, these meetings took on a role which definitely went beyond the express provisions of 1959 ... Thus, these consultative meetings have imperceptibly come to be a form of legislative body for Antarctica[22].

One of the obvious by-products of the 'active' approach has been the attempt to employ the treaty system to explore the boundaries of the treaty, and this trend, in conjunction with an appreciation of the perceived advantages of working together in Antarctica, has served to widen the system's limits, albeit in a cautious and gradualist manner on account of the constraints imposed by the consensus procedure. Inevitably, advocates of the 'active' view, among others, have criticised the apparent slowness of Consultative Meeting decision-making; for instance, the 1972 Sealing Convention represented the result of some six to eight years of discussions and took a further six years to become effective through ratification. Similarly, an Antarctic minerals regime was raised first in 1970, but was not really pursued until the late 1970s and is still an on-going topic for debate. Although it is easy to dismiss such delays as a function of the consensus procedure, they can be treated as a reflection of the institutional weaknesses of the treaty, such as in respect to the absence of a secretariat, the need to seek expert scientific advice from outside bodies, most notably from SCAR, and the relative slowness of parties in approving recommendations[23].

Nevertheless, the Consultative Parties have in general attempted to move forward in conformity with the 'active' school of thought, that is, to deal with emerging problems of a political, scientific, economic and environmental nature before they became serious. Heap has remarked that 'the driving force was fear of the chaos that might engulf the system. The price to be paid for maintaining order was a series of exercises in foresight'[24]. In turn, this has contributed a dynamic quality to the system's operations.

> The Antarctic Treaty itself and the system that has been developed under it constitute a remarkable exercise in prudent forethought ... which ... has given rise to a number of "firsts", among which are: the Agreed Measures ... the first international agreement to prohibit the killing of any native mammal or native bird in Antarctica without a permit ... the Convention for ... Seals, the first ... international agreement to regulate

> the utilization of a living resource before any industry has developed to exploit it ... (CCAMLR), the first international agreement to require that regulation of the utilization of target species shall have regard to the effect that utilization has on the ecosystem as a whole ... the system has shown itself capable of dynamic development ... the record elsewhere shows few examples of prudent international action to pre-empt the undesirable effects of what can be foreseen ... the record shows that this is not the case in Antarctica[25].

The key initial moves were in the spheres of conservation and environmental protection, such as recognised by Heap, but more recently the Consultative Parties have moved on to resource-related questions, albeit with a continuing environmental emphasis, which was indicated by the ecosystem approach of CCAMLR. In addition, the criticism of slowness has been partially answered during the marine and mineral resource negotiations by the identification of a problem and the adoption of voluntary interim guidelines pending the formal conclusion of the negotiations[26].

Another significant development concerns the introduction of the device of a Special Consultative Meeting. These meetings have been held occasionally since 1977 in order to deal with a specific issue, arising normally out of either admission to Consultative Party status or resource regime questions (as shown in Table 7.4). Although some of these meetings have occurred at the same time as, or just prior to, the regular Consultative Meeting, the special session should be viewed as a distinctive event, which is supportive of the operations and evolution of the Antarctic Treaty System. The contribution of Special Consultative Meetings will be considered at the appropriate place in subsequent chapters. Other techniques have been evolved to deal with matters in need of common action as well as of either expert guidance or links with outside bodies. For example, meetings of experts have been held on Antarctic communications (eg.1962) and Antarctic minerals (1973 and 1979), while such a device offers a way of drawing upon outside experts in bodies like the World Meteorological Organisation (WMO) and the International Telecommunications Union (ITU)[27]. In fact, article III (2) actively encourages 'the establishment of co-operative working relations' with specialised agencies of the UN and other relevant international organisations, and this has fostered a range of formal and informal links between the Antarctic Treaty System and such bodies as the WMO, ITU, the UN Food and Agriculture Organization (FAO), and the Scientific Committee on Oceanic Research (SCOR)[28]. The 1983 WMO Congress held in Geneva considered meteorological research and observation programmes in Antarctica, and advocated the continuation of them as well as of its working group on

Table 7.4: The Antarctic Treaty Special Consultative Meetings

Number	Subject	Place	Year	Date
First	Admission of Poland to Consultative Status	London	1977	25-29 July
Second	Negotiation of Antarctic Marine Living Resources Convention		1978-1980	
		i) Canberra	1978	27 Feb.-16 March
		ii) Buenos Aires	1978	17-28 July
		iii) Canberra	1980	5-6 May
		Informal sessions occurred at Washington (Sept. 1978), Berne (March 1979) and Washington (June-July and Sept.-Oct. 1979). The Conference met in Canberra from 7-20 May 1980.		
Third	Admission of West Germany to Consultative Status	Buenos Aires	1981	3 March
Fourth	Negotiation of Antarctic Minerals Regime (in progress)		1982-	still in progress
		i) Wellington	1982	14-25 June
		ii) Wellington	1983	17-28 January
		iii) Bonn	1983	11-22 July
		iv) Washington	1984	18-27 January
		v) Tokyo	1984	22-31 May
		vi) Rio de Janeiro	1985	26 Feb.-8 March
		vii) Paris	1985	23 Sept.-4 October
		viii) Hobart	1986	14-25 April
Fifth	Admission of Brazil and India to Consultative Status	Canberra	1983	12 September
Sixth	Admission of China and Uruguay to Consultative Status	Brussels	1985	7 October

Antarctic meteorology. The recommendations of the WMO are brought to the attention of the Consultative Meetings through government delegations, while recommendations of the Antarctic Treaty System are passed onto the WMO through the representatives of the treaty powers. This type of working relationship serves not only to coordinate meteorological research and observations in Antarctica but also to ensure that Antarctic meteorology is treated as a meaningful part of the WMO programmes and conducted within the framework of the Antarctic Treaty System. Significantly, the 1983 Antarctic Consultative Meeting produced recommendation XII-1, which urged treaty powers to support the work of the WMO.

SCAR

Like the Antarctic Treaty, SCAR - initially, this was entitled the Special Committee on Antarctic Research, but soon 'Special' was replaced by 'Scientific' - owes its origins to the IGY period and, since its foundation in 1958, has developed the functions of planning and coordinating post-IGY Antarctic research projects in a manner relevant to the Antarctic Treaty System. SCAR is a scientific committee of UNESCO'S International Council of Scientific Unions (ICSU), and, according to its constitution,

> Is a scientific committee of ICSU charged with the initiation, promotion, and coordination of scientific activity in the Antarctic, with a view to framing and reviewing scientific programmes of circum-polar scope and significance.

SCAR represents a body organised essentially in an autonomous manner, albeit linked to the ICSU, and its scientific expertise in Antarctic research means that it has acted as a necessary supplement to the Antarctic Treaty System; indeed, it functions as an unofficial scientific arm of the system, since SCAR may either suggest scientific aspects in need of the attention of the Consultative Meetings or respond to requests for scientific advice from the treaty powers. It provides a link between the Consultative Parties and national scientific committees, which are responsible for national research programmes, while also offering a framework for the international coordination of such projects.

SCAR is composed of permanent delegates nominated by each national Antarctic research committee, along with delegates from ICSU (1 delegate), ICSU-affiliated scientific unions (3 representatives) and the WMO (1 delegate). An Executive Committee meets once a year, a general meeting assembles every other year, while a small part-time secretariat is based upon the Scott Polar Research Institute at Cambridge. This 'simple and cheap structure' is supported by a number of working groups based on such disciplines as biology, geology, and meteorology, as well as by *ad hoc* groups of specialists for the study of multi-disciplinary or special programmes, including sea ice, seals and climate research[29]. SCAR programmes are based upon the recommendations of these groups, and in this manner they serve not only to reflect and coordinate national activities but also to influence national schemes in the light of the overall framework agreed to by SCAR. Naturally, individual programmes will tend to be influenced by national needs and interests, but in many instances the views of SCAR and its working groups will be respected, or at least considered[30].

As a result, SCAR provides a permanent focus and machinery for Antarctic research as well as a driving force for international cooperation. Although it can be interpreted as both a part of and a prop for the treaty system, SCAR represents a non-governmental organisation anxious to avoid matters of international politics and lacking any formal connection to the Antarctic Treaty System; indeed, its guidelines instruct SCAR to 'abstain from involvement in political and juridical matters'. The precise nature of SCAR's role was discussed at the first Consultative Meeting held in 1961, when a range of views were advanced regarding the formal position of SCAR *vis à vis* the Antarctic Treaty System and led to recommendation I-IV favouring an independent, non-governmental scientific advisory body. In addition, SCAR's area of concern is bounded by the Antarctic Convergence (plus other areas, such as Tristan da Cunha) rather than the more limited treaty area defined by 60° South. In the event, SCAR has developed an effective working relationship with the system upon the basis of a subtle politico-scientific interaction; thus, the Consultative Meetings seek expert advice from SCAR as a means of facilitating the process of management of Antarctica. For instance, SCAR has advised upon guidelines for the creation of Specially Protected Areas (SPAs), Sites of Special Scientific Interest (SSSIs) and the regulation of pelagic sealing. More recently, it has performed a significant role in the progress of resource regime discussions, especially as a result of the *ad hoc* groups set up to formulate scientific recommendations in response to the requests made by the Consultative Parties, that is, the Group of Specialists on Southern Ocean Ecosystems and their Living Resources and the Group of Specialists on Antarctic Environmental Implications of Possible Mineral Exploration and Exploitation[31]. SCAR's value was recognised by the 1983 Consultative Meeting, which made several calls upon its services; for instance, recommendation XII-2 invited SCAR to consider issues related to the increased use of satellite communications and to the adequacy of Antarctic telecommunications systems in the context of the enhancement of research activities in the region. This examination would enable SCAR to suggest improvements to the Consultative Parties. Recommendation XII-3 indicated to governments that:

> Through their National Committees, they invited the Scientific Committee on Antarctic Research (SCAR) to offer:
> i) scientific advice regarding the definition of categories of research and logistic activity in Antarctica which might reasonably be expected to have a significant impact on the environment; and
> ii) bearing in mind the discussion at this meeting, ... such advice as seems to SCAR to be relevant to the elaboration of assessment procedures which may be applied by the relevant agencies of the Consultative Parties, on an experimental basis, with regard to research and logistic activity.

In turn, recommendation XII-5 noted SCAR's intention to review all SSSIs at its 1984 meeting and to present the results to the 1985 Antarctic Consultative Meeting. Such examples epitomise the vital role of SCAR in the effective operations of the Antarctic Treaty System, while also indicating the manner in which the linkage is conducted through National Antarctic Committees rather than directly. The resulting two-way exchange of requests and expert advice has been reinforced by the inclusion of some SCAR participants in national delegations to Consultative Meetings.

Zumberge, the president of SCAR affiliated to the University of Southern California, has described the committee's basic philosophy, as follows:

> SCAR has been active in planning and coordinating Antarctic research since the end of the IGY and during the intervening years we have managed to keep SCAR clear of involvement in the international politics of Antarctica. We accomplish this mainly by concentrating on science and leaving the politics to the Consultative Parties[32].

In Antarctica it has never proved easy to differentiate politics from science, but SCAR has succeeded in its quest to be identified as a scientific body relatively immune from political pressures. Scientists from nations characterised by diverse political philosophies, even from nations having no diplomatic relations with each other, have come together within SCAR in the cause of scientific cooperation, thereby reinforcing the effectiveness of national scientific programmes, enhancing the status of Antarctic science in the perceptions of governments, and facilitating the informed and smooth development of the Antarctic Treaty System. SCAR guarantees the existence of an expert scientific input into the system, and it has come to perform this crucial role in spite of its non-governmental and advisory character and of its limited budget. In fact, recently some observers have suggested that lack of money might threaten the quality of SCAR's future contribution to the treaty system, and this anxiety has prompted claims that Consultative Parties need to enhance funding levels through their national Antarctic committees in order to either maintain or improve the existing level of scientific support[33]. This problem was discussed at the 1983 Consultative Meeting, and recommendation XII-8 served to urge increased funding for SCAR; thus:

> The Representatives ... recognising that SCAR ... comprises a unique assemblage of knowledge and expertise in Antarctic scientific fields; noting with appreciation the advice provided to the Antarctic Treaty Consultative Parties by SCAR in response to various requests; ... being aware also that the assistance requested of SCAR by the Consultative Parties imposes additional demands on scarce resources; Recommend to their Governments:
>
> That they consider in the light of its expertise and past assistance any requests that may be made by their national committees for additional funding to meet costs to SCAR of responding to requests for advice by the Antarctic Treaty Consultative Parties.

A further problem derives from the delays inherent in the SCAR-Consultative Meeting relationship, which compounds other difficulties, such as those emanating from the consensus procedure. Obviously, there are weaknesses in respect to SCAR's role in the treaty system, even if the mechanism is perceived generally as 'satisfactory', particularly regarding the perpetuation of the IGY pattern of international scientific cooperation[34].

Dispute Settlement

The provisions regarding jurisdiction allow for the possibility of dispute, and a mode of dispute settlement is specified also in regard to the interpretation and application of the treaty. In the event of dispute, the parties involved:

> Shall consult among themselves with a view to having the dispute resolved by negotiation, inquiry, mediation, conciliation, arbitration, judicial settlement or other peaceful means of their own choice (article XI (1)) ... Any dispute of this character not so resolved shall, with the consent ... of all parties, be referred to the International Court of Justice for settlement (article XI (2)).

This procedure is not binding, and these relatively weak provisions fell far short of the negotiating position of certain governments, which, like the USA, favoured compulsory arbitration by the International Court; indeed, such a scheme was included in the draft treaty articles[35]. However, this proposal met with opposition from Argentina, Chile and the Soviet Union, and was not included in the final treaty, whose dispute procedures outlined in article XI have been described by Hayton as 'very weak, permissive' and as adding little to the pre-existing position[36]. Auburn and Burton have identified potential points of difficulty, such as in respect to the resolution of disputes arising out of the interpretation of article IV[37].

However, in the event, no serious disputes have occurred regarding the interpretation of the treaty, and hence any inadequacies have remained below the surface. Although this state of affairs might be treated as indicative of an actual lack of controversy, it has been suggested that the Consultative Parties have held back on problem areas in order to avoid serious disputes and to promote the cooperative working relationship of the Antarctic Treaty System.

The Amendment and Review of the Treaty

Any amendments or modifications of the Antarctic Treaty require 'the unanimous agreement' of the Consultative Parties, and such changes only 'enter into force when the depositary Government has received notice from all such Contracting Parties that they have ratified it' (article XII (1)). This provision applies also to the alterations emerging from the treaty review conference allowable under article XII (2). Obviously, the implicit veto of this procedure serves to restrict the rapid development of the treaty system, since it proves difficult to proceed faster than the pace of the slower parties. However, hitherto neither modifications nor amendments have been proposed to the text of the treaty by the parties.

As a result, more interest has been shown in the review provisions, since article XII (2) states that:

> If after the expiration of thirty years from the date of entry into force of the present Treaty, any of the Contracting Parties whose representatives are entitled to participate in the meetings provided for under article IX so requests by a communication addressed to the depositary Government, a Conference of all the Contracting Parties shall be held as soon as practicable to review the operation of the treaty.

Therefore, a review conference may be called during or after 1991, but only at the request of the Consultative Parties. Neither the acceding states nor outsiders can call for a review. It is difficult to assess the basic objective of any conference, since article XII merely utilises the phrase 'to review the operation of the treaty', and this implies that the latter is intended to continue, albeit subject to 'any modification or amendment to the present Treaty ... approved at such a Conference' (article XII (2)). The presumption is that the drafters of the treaty saw 30 years as a suitable period to judge the effectiveness of the treaty, although initial drafts of article XII - these originated from article XI of Daniels' proposals advanced in November 1958 - referred to a 'meeting' after ten years[38]. Subsequent negotiations resulted in some re-writing of this provision, such as to increase the period to 30 years and to mention a review 'conference'.

However, the evolving nature of the Antarctic Treaty System, in conjunction with the determination of the Consultative Parties to retain their primacy in the management of the continent, encourages the view that a review conference will prove both superfluous and dangerous. The example of the Consultative Meetings - this includes the resource regime discussions - indicates that the Consultative Parties can achieve their interests through the normal operation and development of the treaty system, particularly as no textual amendments to the treaty have been introduced. Hitherto, the existing mechanisms and procedures have met the interests and need of the parties, thereby enabling the continued development of the treaty system, such as in the light of the periodic 'reviews' conducted at each Consultative Meeting. In addition, there exists a fear that a review conference might raise more problems and controversies than it resolves, a risk accentuated by increased outside interest in Antarctic affairs. There is little evidence to indicate that the treaty parties feel that they might benefit from a review conference, although the position of individual governments might change under the impact of future events, which might include the discovery of exploitable minerals.

It is of relevance to note that the unanimous conclusion of the participants in an Antarctic seminar held in October 1982 - and most of the speakers were involved in the policy-making process - was that:

> It is very unlikely that the Antarctic Treaty will be reviewed in 1991 ... none of the Consultative Parties would have reason to request such a review, since the cooperation which has taken place under this instrument has been to the mutual benefit of all of them and of the international community as a whole[39].

Sir Vivian Fuchs, a former director of BAS, adjudged it to be 'inconceivable' for any party to contemplate either review or termination of the treaty, and the British government has oft-stressed its support of this approach, such as illustrated in November 1982 by Mrs. Thatcher's parliamentary reply:

> We are satisfied with the operation of the Antarctic Treaty to date and will continue to support it ... We have no plans to call for a review of its terms in 1991[40].

However, Tucker Scully, an American government representative, has suggested the need to anticipate the possibility of a review assessment in 1991, since the Antarctic Treaty may be affected by what Auburn has described as 'a fundamental change in the situation'; thus, certain alterations in international political circumstances might undermine or threaten the treaty's survival[41]. To some extent, this argument has been encouraged by the growing UN-based interest in Antarctica, and especially by the imponderables deriving from the determination of certain governments to replace the Antarctic Treaty; in fact, the outcome of this initiative might serve to pre-empt any moves provided for in article XII. Already the involvement of the UN has prompted a fairly close and searching review of all aspects of the Antarctic Treaty System, and this has been associated with modifications regarding the enhanced involvement of acceding states and publicity. On the other hand, since 1959 the treaty has demonstrated its capacity to survive a range of international crises, including disputes, even wars, between its parties - for example, it has survived serious rifts in East-West relations as well as the effects of the Beagle Channel and Falklands disputes - and this has fostered the view that it will prevail into the 1990s and beyond[42].

One of the interesting features of the review procedure concerns the manner in which article XII (2) allows for majority approval of any modification or amendment - this must include 'a majority of those whose representatives are entitled to participate in the meetings provided for under article IX', that is, the Consultative Parties - which will enter into force when all the Contracting Parties have ratified it.

> If any such modification or amendment has not entered into force ... within a period of two years after the date of its communication to all the Contracting Parties, any Contracting Party may at any time after the expiration of that period give notice to the depositary Government of its withdrawal from the present Treaty; and such withdrawal shall take effect two years after the receipt of the notice by the depositary Government.

In this manner, the treaty provides for either its termination or the withdrawal of parties only through amendment and review, although it appears that, if a review conference is summoned, the treaty system will survive, since the majority of parties will support its continuation and ratify any changes. In any case, the termination of any party's involvement would not occur before 1995 upon the assumption that the conference met in 1991, that the ratification period expired in 1993, and that withdrawal was effected two years later.

The arrangements for the implementation of the results of any review conference are based upon those applicable to Consultative Meeting recommendations. The most significant difference between the two situations arises from the consensus procedure employed at Consultative Meetings and the provision for majority decision-making at a review conference. Certain commentators have been encouraged by this change to argue mistakenly that after 1991 the treaty system will adopt the majority principle for Consultative Meetings[43]. An even more common misconception about the Antarctic Treaty concerns its duration, since this aspect has been confused with the time period specified for review.

The Duration of the Treaty

The year 1991 is depicted frequently as a critical date for Antarctica; indeed, many commentators, including those who should know better, have interpreted this year as one in which the whole treaty system will fall apart on account of its alleged 30-year duration after coming into effect in June 1961. Numerous politicians and diplomats have argued this point, and even Malcolm Booker, an Australian diplomat active in the treaty negotiations in the late 1950s, has written that 'the treaty expires in 1991'[44]. Parliamentary debates in Britain have been littered with the same mistake, such as evidenced - by Lord Cledwyn in December 1983, when he observed that:

> The Treaty has a life of 30 years and therefore comes up for re-negotiation in a few years' time. I hope that it will be re-negotiated in the same spirit of goodwill which animated the present signatories[45].

This quote was taken from a House of Lords debate, which was characterised by a number of other confused references to the 'renewability' and 're-negotiation' of the treaty[46]. A similar mis-understanding has been shown by some polar experts, including John Bechervaise, who has referred to the importance of 1991.

> As the initial period of the Antarctic treaty proceeds through its last decade ... it would seem certain that

> none of the great nations will be prepared to ... depart from any Antarctic territory when the term of the present treaty expires ... only by one means may ultimate strife and despoilation (sic) be avoided ... Extend the treaty for 50 years[47].

The Times newspaper has not been immune from this type of error either, and in January 1983 an editorial referred to Antarctica, 'whose Treaty is to be renewed in six years' time'; thus, The Times committed a double mistake in respect not only to the matter of renewal but also to the irrelevance of the year 1989, even in the sphere of treaty review[48]. Possibly, one of the most significant illustrations concerns an article written by Paul Daniels about ten years after his prominent role in the treaty negotiations of 1958-9; in fact, it is possible that this assertion has fostered subsequent errors, thereby giving the 30-year duration period credibility through repetition.

> Already more than 10 years have elapsed since the Treaty was signed on December 1 1959. The Treaty is to remain in effect for 30 years from the date of its entry into force on June 23 1961. Four years can be added to that period because of the procedures provided for withdrawal and possible termination. Accordingly, the Treaty is safe until 1995. But the future of the treaty should be considered in broader terms than merely references to its stated duration. What is more important is that the broad principles embodied in the Treaty, if not the treaty itself, continue on indefinitely. This will not happen automatically[49].

The general tendency to associate the treaty with a life-span of only 30 years arises from a mis-interpretation of the treaty, and particularly from a mis-reading of article XII (2)'s provisions for a review conference 'after the expiration of thirty years from the date of entry into force of the present Treaty'. This review period has been oft-confused with treaty duration, thereby causing 1991 to be interpreted as a crucial date. It seems probable that few people have actually read the terms of the treaty itself, but instead have followed the line assumed by the above-mentioned quotations, especially as Daniels and Booker were actually involved in drafting the treaty and presumably knew what it was meant to do.

However, in reality, the position is somewhat different from the impression created by these quotations, such as indicated by Sorzano, the US delegate, to the UN First Committee in 1983.

> We have heard that the Treaty is static and due to expire in 1991 ... the facts point in a different direction. The treaty is of unlimited duration[50].

The Treaty includes no mention of any time limit or 'stated duration', and it can last indefinitely without any need for renewal or re-negotiation. Significantly, the preamble employs the word 'forever' in regard to the treaty's objectives; thus, 'it is in the interests of mankind that Antarctica shall continue forever to be used exclusively for peaceful purposes'. During the treaty negotiations discussions about time periods ranged between ten years and an indefinite limit, but it appears that some governments, including Argentina, Chile and France, feared that the actual specification of an indefinite limit would undermine the strength of their sovereignty claims[51]. In a sense, the Antarctic Treaty System has been perceived by many governments as 'a temporary regime' - to quote one American participant - albeit one endowed with certain permanent qualities[52]. Although the intentions of some parties remain a matter of conjecture, there is evidence that most parties regard the treaty as a long-term obligation, which extends into the indefinite future, on account of an appreciation of the national and international benefits accruing from the preservation of the treaty system, such as in respect to international scientific cooperation, the freeze on sovereignty and the continent's demilitarised status.

The British government has oft-stated the fact that:

> The Antarctic Treaty does not have a date of termination ... the Antarctic Treaty remains in force indefinitely. We are satisfied with the operation of the Antarctic treaty to date and will continue to support it[53].

The UN debates have occasioned similar assertions of long-term support for the treaty system from other parties, such as typified by Yakovlev in 1983:

> The Soviet Union has consistently favoured and continues to favour the maintenance of the Antarctic Treaty and the strengthening of the international legal regime which is established in it[54].

Obviously, the support of the contracting parties will contribute to the treaty's indefinite duration, but Sorzano has suggested another factor; thus, 'the Treaty is of unlimited duration and includes built-in mechanisms to ensure its evolution and adaptation to emerging circumstances'[55].

Publicity and Information about the Antarctic Treaty System

Even today, it proves difficult to formulate a comprehensive and informed view of the background negotiations for the Antarctic Treaty, especially as those involved therein appear determined to preserve the secrecy of the discussions, such as agreed at the time[56]. In fact, during the preparatory talks of 1958-9 the twelve governments devoted considerable attention to the publicity, or rather its absence, of their proceedings, and the very first session of 13 June 1958 provided the basic guidelines in favour of the policy that 'there should be a minimum of publicity'[57]. Consequently the delegations were reluctant to release very much information for public consumption and an awareness, that certain journalists - most notably Walter Sullivan of the New York Times - were rather too well-informed, resulted in the progressive up-grading of documents from 'For Official Use Only' through 'Confidential' to 'Secret'. Inevitably, it was decided that the projected conference for the conclusion of the treaty would meet in private, with the exception of the opening plenary session, while conference rule of procedure number 37, by specifying that conference records would be available only 'to delegations', was intended to exclude public access to documents.

This experience of secrecy helped to set the tone for the conduct of both regular and special Consultative Meetings, since according to rules of procedure adopted in 1961 they are conducted in secret, so that only the opening speeches, recommendations and a brief report on the proceedings are published; thus, 'the opening plenary session shall be held in public; other sessions shall be held in private unless the meeting shall determine otherwise' (rule 7)[58]. Obviously, meaningful international negotiations require some degree of confidentiality, such as to facilitate the reconciliation of divergent positions, and traditionally this has been the way in which diplomatic negotiations have been conducted. As a result, the decision-making procedures of the Antarctic Treaty System conform to usual international practice in respect to the formulation of 'open agreements secretly arrived at'; in fact, it might be argued that the consensus procedures of the system place a premium upon secrecy in the interests of moving towards an agreed position[59]. Nevertheless, the secret methods of the treaty system have attracted increased criticism not only from outside governments but also from academics - this point is written in part from experience - concerned about the difficulties of obtaining an informed view of developments.

Whether the practice of general secrecy is justifiable must be debatable, since certain topics discussed at Consultative Meetings appear unworthy of such exalted treatment. In fact, there was a heated exchange on this aspect at the Antarctic seminar held at the Australian National University, Canberra, in 1984, when Auburn's critique of the practice of secrecy throughout the treaty system excited a sharp response from Ian Nicholson, a member of the Australian Department of Foreign Affairs[60]. The latter claimed that:

> We certainly try not to be ... there is no secrecy in the approach to the provision of information about the issues involved. Information is made available, indeed, actively made available, to the public, and debate is encouraged ... There is a problem in making available as much information as might be wished on the negotiations themselves because of the sensitivities of some countries.

In practice, the Australian government has proved more forthcoming than most - certainly, it responds to researchers more readily than most - but in general the members of the Antarctic Treaty System have a poor record in the promotion of public knowledge and debate about Antarctic questions. The resulting void has been filled in part by the work of environmental groups, which have proved active in advancing their approach on Antarctica and creating public interest in Antarctica. The Antarctic Treaty System has failed in respect to public relations, and the dismal level of press coverage of Antarctic matters reflects this collective failure. For example, readers of the British press, especially of The Times, could be forgiven for thinking that nothing had happened in Antarctica during the past decade or so[61].

Although Nicholson offered a line of defence to Auburn, his references to 'the sensitivities of some countries' admitted by implication the existence of a publicity problem, which explains the lack of information about Consultative Meetings and resource regime negotiations. In particular, since 1982 the Antarctic minerals regime talks have been conducted in strict secrecy, punctuated only by the usual terse communiqué or by the occasional leak, such as of the Beeby draft treaty. This situation is detrimental to informed public and academic debate, and inevitably has attracted considerable criticism during the course of the post-1983 UN debates on Antarctica, since this feature can be easily related to the alleged exclusivity and elitism of the 'Antarctic club'. In 1983 Jacobs, speaking for Antigua and Barbuda, pointed out that:

> Each of these regular meetings, as is the case of other special meetings ... was secret and held behind closed doors in secret session. Not only other nations but even their own people were denied any knowledge of the decisions taken by those 14 (sic) countries ... In our view the world has a right to know about those meetings and about the decisions that are made[62].

The Malaysian government, like others, joined Jacobs in the complaint about 'closed-door meetings', especially on the minerals negotiations, while also stressing that between

1961-83 not even the acceding states were allowed to attend Consultative Meetings[63]. Naturally, such charges have been refuted by the Consultative Parties on the grounds that the critics mis-represent the actual situation, which merely conforms to normal diplomatic negotiating procedures. In November 1983, Heap, the British delegate, told the UN that:

> The Treaty has been charged with excessive secrecy with its pejorative overtones ... This charge does not bear serious examination. What is important is that the results of those negotiations are made freely available. Nothing could be further from the truth than the assertion of (Jacobs, quoted above) ... that our own people were denied any knowledge of the decisions made by the Consultative Parties. The United Kingdom has published as Parliamentary White Papers all the recommendations of all the consultative meetings ... the charge of secrecy is false[64].

To some extent, this view is correct, but cannot disguise the basic paucity of information available about the workings of the Antarctic Treaty System.

Therefore, a perceived problem exists regarding the subject of publicity and secrecy of the Antarctic Treaty System, since the treaty powers have continued to prove rather unforthcoming about their activities, especially about the on-going mineral regime negotiations. In July 1984 a British Foreign Office parliamentary answer - presumably, this was either drafted or approved by Heap - typified the minimal information released upon this subject, such as in respect to the recent session of talks held at Tokyo in May 1984.

> The negotiations in Tokyo provided a further opportunity to carry on the work of earlier meetings at Wellington, Bonn and Washington towards the elaboration of a practical Antarctic minerals regime[65].

Obviously, such answers need to be concise, but this reply epitomised the reluctance to reveal any 'hard' information on either issues, problems or the degree of progress. In fact, the most useful source of evidence on the negotiations has been the series of occasional newspapers, entitled *Eco*, published by a number of non-governmental organisations centred upon Friends of the Earth International. *Ecos* have been produced for most sessions of the minerals regime negotiations, thereby highlighting the manner in which non-governmental organisations have filled the information vacuum regarding the operation of the Antarctic Treaty System, albeit with a message not always sympathetic to the treaty powers.

During the early 1980s the emerging critique about secrecy was reinforced by signs of unrest among the acceding states regarding their marginal involvement in the treaty system, such as in respect to the receipt of information and the decisions of Consultative Meetings. In this context, it proved difficult for the Consultative Parties to ignore the problem, and since 1983 the defensive speeches delivered at the UN have been supplemented by action. The 1983 Consultative Meeting, led by Chile, considered the operation of the Antarctic Treaty System, and this occurred in the presence of observers from the acceding states. In addition, this discussion resulted in recommendation XII-6, which was designed to reinforce this trend towards a more open system. Thus:

> The Representatives, ... Desiring to involve the Contracting Parties to the Antarctic treaty which are not Consultative Parties more closely with the Antarctic Treaty System; Conscious of the value of increasing public knowledge of the achievements and operation of the Antarctic Treaty System;
> Recalling Article III, paragraph 2 of the Antarctic Treaty ... Recommend.

This preamble indicated signs of change, for it provided the background for a series of recommendations designed not only to provide more information but also to reinforce the existing levels of 'co-operative working relations' with the UN and other international organisations conducted under the auspices of article III (2). In future, the host government would send copies of the Final Report and recommendations of Consultative Meetings to the UN and non-Consultative Parties, while the latter would receive also documents of that meeting. The host government was assigned responsibility for up-dating the 'Handbook of the Antarctic Treaty' - this represented a revised title for the existing handbook of recommendations - while the Australian government, as host of the 1983 Meeting, was asked to expand the existing handbook through sections on the history and background of the treaty. An attempt would also be made to improve public availability of meeting documents not only for future sessions but also for past meetings, while the US government, the depositary government, was invited 'to examine the question of information about the Antarctic Treaty System ... with a view to identifying and cataloguing publicly available information about the System'. Recommendation XII-6 provided also for the operation of the treaty system to be placed on the agenda of the 1985 Consultative Meeting, thereby holding out the prospect of further developments in this area.

Therefore, the matter of publicity and secrecy remains an on-going topic for debate, which has been prompted to a large extent by outside criticism. It appears that the Chilean government introduced the discussion at the 1983 Consultative Meeting in terms of the view that such criticism was due more to poor public relations by the treaty system and parties rather than to poor performance. Certainly, recommendation XII-6, in conjunction with the enhanced involvement in the system by acceding states, represents an attempt to deal with the problem, while serving also as an implicit admission of guilt regarding the validity of criticism on the subject. In fact, certain governments, including the Soviet government, are reputed to have observed at the 1983 Meeting that any response would merely give credibility to the critics[66]. In the meantime, it is of interest to note the manner in which the UN's involvement in Antarctica, and especially the 1984 Study, has promoted the objectives embodied in recommendation XII-6, since the post-1983 UN episode has served not only to provide an unprecedented amount of information on Antarctic matters but also to educate the wider international community regarding the nature and significance of a continent, which was perceived previously by most governments - to quote, Gbeho of Ghana - as 'remote, obscure and forbidding'[67]. Perhaps, this achievement might prove the most enduring legacy of the UN debates about Antarctica. Nevertheless, the UN's discussions will work primarily at the official level, and hence an additional public relations effort is required to educate public opinion on areas beyond where questions have been customarily asked. Recently, Stuart Harris emphasised the need, at least in Australia, for an improved community understanding of Antarctic questions.

> Greater public understanding ... is not only essential for determining priorities among objectives and facilitating a clearer assessment of policy options, but also for gaining public support for an increased commitment to Antarctica that is probably involved under any (policy) option but withdrawal[68].

The general desire of the Antarctic powers to preserve the treaty system gives greater force to such advice.

Conclusion

The Antarctic Treaty represented the product of contrasting viewpoints, and this situation gave rise to a relatively weak institutional framework. However, since 1959 the treaty system has evolved in a flexible and pragmatic manner designed to accommodate new needs and problems. This process of organic growth has extended recently into the sphere of resources, and such developments have proceeded under the auspices of article IX, whose potential has resulted in its emergence as a key article. The most notable effect has been the active decision-making role assumed by the

Consultative Meetings, which have provided the institutional substance for the Antarctic Treaty System.

Question marks remain about the future stability and international acceptability of the Antarctic Treaty System, but basically the treaty parties have developed their own perceptions regarding its merits. The recent UN debates have helped to bring such thoughts out into the open in order to defend the system against the critics; thus, individually and collectively, the treaty parties have extolled the merits of the system, which has been depicted as preferable to any alternative. Speaking on behalf of the Consultative Parties in November 1983, Richard Woolcott asserted that:

> The Treaty System has proved to be a remarkably successful, practical and dynamic arrangement and every effort should be made to preserve and maintain it ... it is unrealistic to think that ... a new or better legal regime for Antarctica could be agreed upon[69].

Although this approach reflected an appreciation of the national policy value of the system, the commitment has arisen in part from an intangible factor described as the 'Antarctic spirit', which has influenced the perceptions of participating governments. Guyer believes that 'the Antarctic spirit does not only exist but is a powerful instrument of progress of Antarctic affairs'[70]. This collective spirit has survived policy differences and international crises, such as in East-West relations or the 1982 Falklands War, while there exists evidence that the system exerts a similar 'conversion' effect upon individuals as a result of a close and continuing relationship[71].

The Antarctic Treaty System has developed in a relevant and effective manner, and by the early 1980s could be regarded as a well-established feature of the international political system. In this respect, it can be compared to other regional groupings, such as the Organization of American States, the Organization of African Unity, and the European Economic Community. Nevertheless, the system possesses its weak-points in need of reform, including slow and cumbersome working procedures at Consultative Meetings, the infrequency of such meetings, the burden of the secretarial function, and the problem of publicity and secrecy. There exists no easy answer to such problems, especially as any response to one aspect may aggravate another area; for example, the attempt of recommendation XII-6 to enhance public knowledge about the treaty system will serve only to accentuate the secretarial burden imposed upon the host and depositary governments. The recent emphasis upon publicity, in conjunction with the admission of acceding states as observers to Consultative Meetings, will facilitate a more informed appreciation of the actual working practices of the Antarctic Treaty System, which remain shrouded in secrecy. In 1983 Jeffrey Myhre suggested a way forward for theoretical and practical study on the negotiating processes of the system, and this tentative beginning highlighted the need for more work on this aspect, especially on the more recent period[72]. Myhre was also forced to admit that, even for the early 1960s, the research problem is compounded by the 'incomplete' nature of evidence.

> This makes analysis more difficult than would otherwise be the case. The crucial move or offer just is not recorded. The only way around it is to muddle through on what the record does offer[73].

In practice, the record offers very little, although recommendation XII-6 promises an improvement in the future as long as certain governments' obsession for secrecy can be overcome.

In the meantime, the operation of the Antarctic Treaty System has become a major topic for discussion in both the UN and the Consultative Meetings, and it is possible that institutional changes might result, especially regarding the secretarial function. At the 1983 Consultative Meeting:

> It was agreed that the establishment of a more permanent infrastructure to undertake these tasks (ie. secretarial) would be premature at the present time, but that the matter, together with the question of frequency of meetings, should be discussed further[74].

In addition, the completion of the on-going minerals regime negotiations will provide permanent institutions, thereby paralleling those established for CCAMLR. There is also the view that this achievement will consolidate, perhaps even complete, the Antarctic Treaty System. These institutional developments will be accompanied by greater participation in the system; in fact, an extended membership will reinforce the case for an enhanced organisational framework, even if this might involve the loss of the existing advantages deriving from the relatively compact nature of the system. This concern led to South African reservations about the admission of acceding states to Consultative Meetings. The Indian government, a recent addition, provides an appropriate concluding comment for this chapter, albeit from a pro-system viewpoint.

> The Antarctic Treaty System... is an evolving institution whose structural and organizational framework is conceived in a flexible manner ... which is gradually evolving further, taking into account the legitimate concerns of all ... It would be unrealistic and counter-

> productive to think of a new regime in the present situation ... The Antarctic Treaty System is an open system ... and should be broadened by the accession of more States. The evolving Treaty system should be made more open and responsive to the viewpoints of all states[75].

This assertion demonstrates also the way in which any debate about the merits of the Antarctic Treaty System merges imperceptibly into the question of participation, which has proved the prime focus of the international community's recent interest in Antarctica.

NOTES

1. The Antarctic Treaty, Cmnd.8652, p.51.
2. Resolution 38/77; UNGA A/38/646, Report of the First Committee, 12 Dec.1983.
3. A. van der Essen, 'L'Antarctique et le droit de la mer', Revue iranienne des relations internationales, no.5-6 (1975-76), p.89.
4. Zegers, 13 Sept.1983, Antarctic Treaty: Report of the Twelth Consultative Meeting, p.66.
5. UNGA A/C 1/39 PV 50, pp.51-2, 28 Nov.1984; UNGA A/C 1/38 PV 42, pp.28-9, 28 Nov.1983.
6. Scully, Alternatives for Cooperation and Institutionalization in Antarctica, p.293.
7. Ibid., pp.291-3.
8. Beck, Secret Antarctic Treaty Preparatory Negotiations.
9. Sir Esler Dening, 15 Oct.1959, The Conference on Antarctica, p.36; F.M. Auburn, 'The Antarctic Environment', Yearbook of World Affairs 1981 (Stevens, London, 1981), p.249.
10. Antarctic Treaty: Handbook. This gives the text of the Consultative Meeting recommendations.
11. Van der Essen, Application of the Law of the Sea to the Antarctic, pp.234-5.
12. Ibid., p.234; Finn Sollie, 'Jurisdictional Problems in Relation to Antarctic mineral resources in political perspective', in Vicuna, Antarctic Resources Policy, p.329.
13. Quigg, A Pole Apart, p.150.
14. UNGA A/C 1/39 PV 52, p.26, 29 Nov.1984.
15. UNGA A/C 1/39 PV 52, p.26, 29 Nov.1984, Heap.
16. Scully, Alternatives for Cooperation and Institutionalization in Antarctica, pp.285-6.
17. Antarctic Treaty: Report of the Twelth Consultative Meeting, p.14. The Preparatory Meeting took place in April 1985.
18. Sollie, Development of the Antarctic Treaty System, pp.22-3.

19. Myhre, The Antarctic Treaty Consultative Meetings, 1961-68, pp.121-2; Roberts, International Cooperation for Antarctic Development, p.118.

20. Quigg, A Pole Apart, p.158. According to Myhre, the Australian proposal for a secretariat was supported by New Zealand, South Africa and the UK, while opposition came from Argentina, Belgium, Chile, France, the Soviet Union and the USA: see Myhre, The Antarctic Treaty Consultative Meetings, 1961-68, p.121.

21. Heap, Antarctic Cooperation, pp.106-07.

22. Van der Essen, Application of the Law of the Sea to the Antarctic, p.235.

23. F.M. Auburn, 'Consultative Status under the Antarctic Treaty', International and Comparative Law Quarterly, vol.28 (1979), p.518; John Brook, 'Australia's Policies towards Antarctica', in Harris, Australia's Antarctic Policy Options, pp.261-2.

24. Heap, Antarctic Cooperation, p.107.

25. UNGA A/C 1/38 PV 44, pp.18-20, 29 Nov.1983, Heap.

26. Scully, Alternatives for Cooperation and Institutionalization in Antarctica, pp.285-6.

27. Ibid.; Roberts, International Cooperation for Antarctic Development, p.118.

28. UNGA A/39/583 (Part I), 1984, p.24, pp.86-9.

29. Tore Gjelsvik, 'Scientific Research and Cooperation in Antarctica', in Wolfrum, Antarctic Challenge, p.43. See Polar Record for regular SCAR Bulletins, including details of membership and organisation.

30. Gotthilf Hempel, 'Antarctic Research in the Federal Republic of Germany', in Wolfrum, Antarctic Challenge, pp.137-42.

31. Gjelsvik, Scientific Research and Cooperation in Antarctica, pp.45-51.

32. J.H. Zumberge, quoted, Ibid., pp.50-51; Heap, Antarctic Cooperation, p.106; Zumberge, Potential Mineral Resources Availability in Antarctica, p.149; Myhre, The Antarctic Treaty Consultative Meetings, 1961-68, pp.113-4.

33. Gjelsvik, Scientific Research and Cooperation in Antarctica, p.51.

34. UNGA A/39/583 (Part I), 1984, p.47.

35. Beck, Secret Antarctic Treaty Preparatory Negotiations; Sollie, Jurisdictional Problems in relation to Antarctic mineral resources, pp.329-30.

36. Robert D. Hayton, 'The Antarctic Settlement of 1959', American Journal of International Law, vol.54 (1960), p.364; Christopher Beeby, The Antarctic Treaty (New Zealand Institute of International Affairs, Wellington, 1972), p.15.

37. Burton, New Stresses on the Antarctic Treaty, p.467, p.478; Auburn, Antarctic Law and Politics, pp.140-1.

38. Beck, Secret Antarctic Treaty Preparatory Negotiations.

39. Vicuna, Antarctic Resources Policy, p.10; Brennan, Criteria for Access to the Resources of Antarctica, p.226; Scully, Alternatives for Cooperation and Institutionalization in Antarctica, pp.292-3.

40. Hansard (Commons), vol.31, col.55, 8 Nov.1982; Fuchs, Antarctica: Its History and Development, p.18.

41. Scully, Alternatives for Cooperation and Institutionalization in Antarctica, p.281; Auburn, Antarctic Law and Politics, p.144.

42. For example, during the early 1960s it was suggested that any Soviet breach of the treaty would release the USA from its obligations: see US Congressional Record: Senate, 8 Aug.1960, p.15981.

43. Fox, Antarctica and the South Atlantic, p.16.

44. Booker, The Last Quarter, p.116.

45. Hansard (Lords), vol.445, col.1003, 16 Dec.1983.

46. See Hansard (Lords), vol.445, col.1024, col.1049, 16 Dec.1983.

47. Bechervaise, Imperative Need for a Pax Antarctica, p.28.

48. The Times, 10 Jan.1983.

49. Daniels, The Antarctic Treaty, pp.44-5.

50. UNGA A/C 1/38 PV 45, p.7, 30 Nov.1983; UNGA A/C 1/39 PV 50, p.31, 28 Nov.1984, Woolcott; Foreign Policy Document no.98: Antarctica: An Overview, p.3.

51. Auburn, Antarctic Law and Politics, p.143; Sollie, The Political Experiment in Antarctica, p.62.

52. Bernhardt, Sovereignty in Antarctica, pp.310-1.

53. Hansard (Commons), vol.22, col.156, 23 April 1982; Hansard (Commons), vol.25, col.54, 8 June 1982; Hansard (Commons), vol.31, col.55, 8 Nov.1982.

54. UNGA A/C 1/38 PV 43, p.16, 29 Nov.1983. See also Wyndham, quoted, Wolfrum, Antarctic Challenge, p.65; Brook, Australia's Policies towards Antarctica, pp.261-3.

55. UNGA A/C 1/38 PV 45, p.6, 30 Nov.1983.

56. Beck, Secret Antarctic Treaty Preparatory Negotiations.

57. Ibid.

58. Myhre, The Antarctic Treaty Consultative Meetings, 1961-68, pp.106-10.

59. UNGA A/C 1/38 PV 42, p.44, 28 Nov.1983, Harland, New Zealand.

60. Ian Nicholson, 'Comments', in Harris, Australia's Antarctic Policy Options, p.303. In my experience, Australian diplomats have been more forthcoming than most of their counterparts.

61. In Britain The Guardian has included occasional items, whereas The Times has ignored the UN episode. The fullest reporting was reserved for the relatively trivial

(politically) rescue of the Brabant Island expedition in March 1985; thus, the simultaneous mineral talks in Rio de Janeiro were ignored.

62. UNGA A/C 1/38 PV 42, pp.6-7, 28 Nov.1983. Note that the Consultative Parties numbered 16 after September 1983.

63. UNGA A/C 1/38 PV 42, p.19, 28 Nov.1983.

64. UNGA A/C 1/38 PV 44, pp.24-5, 29 Nov.1983.

65. Hansard (Commons), vol.65, col.113, 30 July 1984. However, see the following for slight elaboration: Foreign Policy Document no.98: Antarctica: An Overview, p.6.

66. Certain points in this section might be regarded as undermining my critique of system secrecy, but such evidence has proved difficult to obtain. Note also that the 1983 discussion on documents was developed in part from a debate at the 1981 Consultative Meeting.

67. UNGA A/C 1/39 PV 53, p.47, 29 Nov.1984.

68. Stuart Harris, 'A Review of Australia's Antarctic Policy Options', in Harris, Australia's Antarctic Policy Options, p.28.

69. UNGA A/C 1/38 PV 42, p.24, 28 Nov.1983.

70. Guyer, quoted, in Wolfrum, Antarctic Challenge, p.54.

71. Quigg, A Pole Apart, p.155.

72. Myhre, The Antarctic Treaty Consultative Meetings, 1961-68, pp.206 et seq.

73. Ibid., p.206.

74. Antarctic Treaty: Report of the Twelth Consultative Meeting, p.14.

75. UNGA A/C 1/39 PV 53, pp.6-7, 29 Nov.1984, Verma.

Chapter Eight

THE ANTARCTIC TREATY: A CONTINENT FOR LIMITED PARTICIPATION IN AN OPEN TREATY SYSTEM

At the beginning of 1985 32 governments were signatories of the Antarctic Treaty; thus, 16 act as Consultative Parties, which possess a decision-making role at Consultative Meetings, while a further 16 governments are acceding parties, or non-Consultative Parties, which accept the principles of the treaty but perform a more limited contribution towards the operation of the Antarctic Treaty System. The Antarctic Treaty had twelve original signatories, and, after a slow start, it has attracted a further 20 governments, of which the most significant developments have occurred during the past decade. As a result, about 20 per cent of the UN's membership - this stood at 159 states at the beginning of 1985 - participate in the Antarctic Treaty System, although the quality of this proportion is accentuated by the composition of the treaty's signatories, which include the world's most powerful and influential governments, including China, India, the Soviet Union, the USA and most EEC countries. At the same time, the heterogeneous nature of the system's membership is reflected by the inclusion of developed and developing nations, of Eastern and Western bloc governments, as well as of representatives from every continent, albeit with a weak African involvement.

The Current Debate on Participation

The emergence of Antarctica as an international political problem has been characterised during the early 1980s by debate and controversy about the level of participation in the decision-making procedures of the Antarctic Treaty System. The post-1983 UN debates have typified this point, such as evidenced by the critique of the Malaysian government.

> We believe that the major deficiency of the current system is that decisions are made exclusively by the Consultative Parties. Is this privileged status acceptable

> to the international community today, and why should they not be accountable to the international community?[1].

This approach attracted support from other delegations, including Ghana, whose primary concern was 'to ensure the establishment of broader international cooperation and participation of all nations in the control and exploitation of the resources of the region for the benefit of all'[2]. The developing world has tended to depict the Antarctic Treaty System as a kind of 'rich man's club', which is not only incompatible with the present-day international system but also inimical to the interests of the international community. The alleged need for a more equitable and representative system of international management for Antarctica has been influenced by emerging political, legal and economic concepts - for example, the common heritage principle - and, in this context, Gbeho, the Ghanaian delegate, urged the Consultative Parties to 'recognize and bow to the winds of change sweeping over that continent'[3]. As during 1983, in November 1984 the UN attack upon the Antarctic Treaty System was initiated by Jacobs of Antigua and Barbuda, who stressed that:

> The world has vastly changed since the Antarctic Treaty was signed in 1959. There are now 159 Member States of the United Nations, most of which are developing countries. In 1959 they had neither the opportunity nor the sovereign competence to participate in events in Antarctica. It is not only unfair, it is unjust to suggest that we should abide by decisions made without our involvement ... It is in the interests of global peace and stability to address the democratization of Antarctica now[4].

In a sense, the international debate about the future of Antarctica, and especially of the Antarctic Treaty System, has assumed the form of a confrontation between elitist and democratic perspectives of control, even if the treaty powers have taken pains to refute the accusations emanating from Malaysia and other governments. Sorzano, the US delegate, responded at the UN in the following terms:

> We have heard that the Treaty is an exclusive club. The facts, however, indicate otherwise. The Antarctic treaty is an open multilateral Treaty ... this openness has led to heterogeneous and truly representative membership representing East and West, North and South, developed and developing, and - if, I may say so - non-aligned and aligned as well ... the nature and accomplishments of the Antarctic Treaty System ... stand as a remarkable achievement in multilateral international cooperation

> and as a monument to the principles and objectives of the United Nations Charter[5].

Significantly, the Soviet government has adopted the same approach, as has India, a leading member of the Non-Aligned Movement, which has asserted that 'the Antarctic Treaty System is not an exclusive body ... the Antarctic Treaty System is an open system which is gradually evolving further'[6]. India's acquisition of Consultative Party status in 1983 appeared to offer vivid proof for this claim, which derived substance also from the manner in which the parties have been encouraging other governments to accede to the treaty, such as evidenced by the UN speech of Woolcott delivered in his capacity as chairman of the Consultative Parties in New York. Thus,

> We renew our invitation to those countries which continue to seek further information on Antarctica and which have a genuine interest in Antarctica to consider joining the Treaty and working within its system. The charges of exclusivity and secretiveness are false[7].

Therefore, the participation question is relevant also to the international acceptability of the Antarctic Treaty System, such as in regard to raising the question of <u>cui bono</u>? Varying views exist relating to the treaty system's benefits to the wider community of powers, and certain critics have utilised the participation aspect as the foundation of their campaign to either replace or reform the Antarctic Treaty System. In the meantime, the latter has continued to develop not only in the institutional sense - this was discussed in the previous chapter - but also in the sphere of wider participation, which may serve to enhance its stability and its prospects of international acceptance. Several governments have become acceding or Consultative Parties during the recent period, and this process is adjudged likely to continue, and even to gather pace, especially as the implementation of CCAMLR and the on-going minerals regime discussions are attracting additional governments to the affairs of Antarctica.

Participation and the Treaty Negotiations

Participation remains, and will continue to be, a topic of debate, just as considerable time had to be devoted to the topic during the 1958-9 treaty negotiations. At that time, the basic point at stake was whether the treaty should be confined, at least initially, to the 12 governments represented at the preparatory talks. On the one hand, most delegations favoured a treaty negotiated and worked only by the 12 governments which possessed the requisite Antarctic experience. Guyer, the Argentine representative, asserted that this case rested upon 'an apolitical standard based upon actual scientific participation in the Antarctic program of the IGY', while his Chilean counterpart stressed the primacy of 'the householders in the area'[8]. Some concern was articulated - most notably by the claimant governments - about the danger that governments, lacking in Antarctic expertise and involvement, might employ participation to countermand the 'informed' political and scientific interests of the 12 governments. In fact, participation was interpreted as 'a fundamental question' by Chile, which emphasised the unacceptability of any wider international involvement. However, this general desire to limit participation was tempered by an appreciation that they might be criticised for the creation of an Antarctic monopoly; thus, the basic preference was for a first stage of limited participation in drafting, concluding and working the treaty, which would be succeeded by a second stage characterised by an open door approach towards further accessions.

On the other hand, Ledovski, the Soviet delegate at the preparatory talks, followed his government's note of 2 June 1958 and advocated wider participation in the negotiation and operation of the treaty. He criticised the more limited approach, and during July-August 1958 Ledovski argued that:

> The twelve countries represented here should not alone be allowed to decide the future of Antarctica ... All humanity was interested in the future of the area[9].

Although other delegations doubted Soviet sincerity in pressing for wider participation, this argument became a prominent and consistent part of what other representatives perceived as the obstructive attitude of the Soviet government. However, pending the availablity of more evidence, it proves difficult to conclude whether the issue was being pressed by Ledovski for either tactical or policy reasons, perhaps related to the wider Cold War context. In the event, the dispute served not only to divide the Soviet from other delegations but also to delay the progress of the preparatory negotiations until _circa_ March-April 1959, when the Soviet delegation acquiesced in the majority line. As a result, the Antarctic Treaty was based upon a limited, even restrictive, concept of participation, such as reflected by the predominant role performed by the original 12 signatories in the operation of the Antarctic Treaty System.

Membership of the Antarctic Treaty System

The Antarctic Treaty was characterised by limited participation, since certain criteria had to be satisfied for the attainment of Consultative Party status. This procedure was designed to prevent the treaty system being swamped by the views of governments uninformed about Antarctic practicalities, although it served also to ensure the continued predominance of the original twelve signatories on account of the inevitably select nature of a grouping based upon specialised criteria. In effect, the Antarctic Treaty created two stages of membership, that is, a first tier of Consultative Parties and a second tier of acceding states, or non-Consultative Parties; in turn, this type of hierarchical structure has been perpetuated in CCAMLR.

Any state, which is either a member of the UN or invited by the Consultative Parties, may accede to the treaty (article XIII (1-2)) in the sense of accepting its principles and objectives - for example, the promotion of international scientific cooperation and of Antarctica as a zone of peace - as well as its obligations. A relatively large number of governments have taken this route since 1961 - by the close of 1984, 20 governments had acceded - and four governments, Cuba, Finland, Hungary and Sweden, joined the system in this capacity during 1984 (as shown in Table 8.1). Accession provides a means of indicating an interest in Antarctic matters, but without the extensive fiscal and material commitment required of Consultative status. In fact, the rate of accession has gained pace in parallel with the perceived increase in Antarctica's international significance, which has encouraged not only a desire on the part of certain governments for some kind of stake in its affairs but also an attempt by the Consultative Parties to widen participation as a means of enhancing international acceptance of the treaty system (as shown in Table 8.2). In particular, the act of accession implies a recognition of the international legal validity of the Antarctic Treaty System in preference to any alternative regime, such as advocated recently by the Malaysian government and others. In September 1983 a joint statement issued by the acceding states indicated their 'interest in the development of the Antarctic System and ... willingness to contribute to the maintenance and further development of the principles and objectives of the Antarctic Treaty'[10]. For example, East Germany, which acceded in 1974, has pointed out that:

> With its affiliation to the Antarctic Treaty, the German Democratic Republic underscores its view that the Treaty is one of the most effective international conventions of contemporary international law and that it has proven its worth[11].

The fact of Finland's accession was accentuated by the way in which it occurred at the time of the UN debates on Antarctica.

Table 8.1: The Antartic Treaty Parties

A) CONSULTATIVE PARTIES — 18 governments

Original Treaty Signatories and Consultative Parties		Date of Ratification of Antarctic Treaty
Argentina		23 June 1961
Australia		23 June 1961
Belgium		26 July 1960
Chile		23 June 1961
France		16 September 1960
Japan		4 August 1960
New Zealand		1 November 1960
Norway		24 August 1960
South Africa		21 June 1960
Soviet Union		2 November 1960
United Kingdom		31 May 1960
USA		18 August 1960
Additional Consultative Parties	**Date of Acceptance**	**Date of Accession**
Brazil	12 September 1983	16 May 1975
China	7 October 1985	8 June 1983
Germany, West	3 March 1981	5 February 1979
India	12 September 1983	19 August 1983
Poland	29 July 1977	8 June 1961
Uruguay	7 October 1985	11 January 1980

B) NON-CONSULTATIVE PARTIES/ACCEDING STATES — 14 governments

	Date of Accession
Bulgaria	11 September 1978
Cuba	16 August 1984
Czechoslovakia	14 June 1962
Denmark	20 May 1965
Finland	15 May 1984
Germany, East	17 November 1974*
Hungary	27 January 1984
Italy	18 March 1981
Netherlands	30 March 1967
Papua & New Guinea	16 March 1981
Peru	10 April 1981
Romania	15 September 1971
Spain	31 March 1982
Sweden	24 April 1984

*Although this date is given in the <u>Antarctic Treaty Handbook</u> as well as in several other sources, another date (19 November 1974) is quoted elsewhere, such as in the British Treaty Series List (1975), Cmnd.6174 (HMSO, London, 1975), p.3.

Table 8.2: Additions to Treaty Membership

a) By Time Period:

Period	Additional Consultative Parties	Additional Acceding Parties
1961-1977	1	7
1978-1980	0	3
1981-1983	3	6
1984-1985	2	4

b) By Year

Year	Consultative Parties	Acceding Parties
1961		Poland
1962		Czechoslovakia
1963		
1964		
1965		Denmark
1966		
1967		Netherlands
1968		
1969		
1970		
1971		Romania
1972		
1973		
1974		East Germany
1975		Brazil
1976		
1977	Poland	
1978		Bulgaria
1979		West Germany
1980		Uruguay
1981	West Germany	Papua & New Guinea, Italy, Peru
1982		Spain
1983	Brazil, India	China, India
1984		Hungary, Sweden, Finland, Cuba
1985	China, Uruguay	

> The Government of Finland believes that by acceding to this Treaty it can best contribute to the strengthening and development of the present Treaty System[12].

Sweden acceded at the same period, and the 'decisive consideration leading to this step were the Swedish government's strong support of the basic principles of the Antarctic Treaty'[13].

Accession confers few rights, and traditionally the immediate benefits were not very substantial. However, recent changes have been introduced to enhance the attractions of accession, and in 1983 acceding states were allowed to attend Consulative Meetings for the first time, albeit only as observers. This concession did not extend to the minerals regime negotiations, since Special Consultative Meetings are subject to separate rules of procedure, but in May 1984 the Consultative Parties agreed to extend observer status to acceding states with effect from the next session scheduled for Rio de Janeiro in 1985[14]. In turn, this increased level of participation in the operation of the Antarctic Treaty System was paralleled by a decision to keep acceding states more informed than in the past about Antarctic matters, such as in respect to the distribution of documents. These moves were welcomed by the acceding states as a way 'to a more meaningful and substantive participation of non-Consultative Parties, which would undoubtedly contribute to strengthening the system'[15].

In fact, the developments during 1983-4 were prompted in part by pressure from the acceding states - for example, from China, Denmark, Italy, Netherlands, Peru and Spain - in favour of a more active role and - to quote the Romanian government - of the view that:

> All States parties to this instrument and other States so wishing and displaying interest in the problems relating to international cooperation in the region should be invited to participate in future meetings of representatives of the Contracting Parties ... the Romanian government believes that a greater openness on the part of the Consultative Parties ... would help to reduce speculation about the future use of the region, stimulate the non-consultative parties' interest (if they were assured of a specific role), and create conditions more likely to enable other States to accede to the Antarctic Treaty[16].

Thus, not all the criticisms regarding the closed nature of Consultative Meetings have come from outside the treaty system, and other acceding states, including China and East Germany, have publicised their complaints[17]. From this perspective, the Consultative Parties appreciated that the more visible participation of acceding states in the working of the Antarctic Treaty System would improve its stability, while also providing public relations' benefits, such as in regard to undermining the force of the exclusivity argument. However, there is evidence that certain Consultative Parties, including Argentina, Brazil, South Africa and the Soviet Union, believed that any concessions to the acceding states would merely give credibility to the criticism, and perhaps even open up a Pandora's box of problems.

For certain governments, the attractions of accession have been related to its role as an intermediate, preparatory stage en route to the more significant decision-making function inherent in Consultative status. For example, Poland acceded in 1961 - this occurred after its failure to become one of the original signatories - and advanced to Consultative status in 1977, for West Germany the respective dates were 1979 and 1981, for Brazil 1975 and 1983, while for India the two stages were separated by the space of only a few weeks (August and September 1983). Several acceding states appear poised to advance to Consultative status sooner rather than later, such as on account of an escalation of their activities in Antarctica. During 1984 Woolcott, as chairman of the Consultative Parties in New York, informed the UN First Committee that 'a number of non-Consultative Parties, including China, have signalled their wish to move to consultative status as this activity increases'[18]. China's advance would appear imminent, since its first Antarctic expedition of 1984-5 constructed a research station on King George Island in the South Shetlands[19]. Similarly, Spain's desire to perform 'more extensive future exploratory and scientific activities in the Antarctic' has prompted the assertion that 'once these future activities have been completed, Spain would like to become a Consultative Party to the Treaty'[20]. Other acceding states, including Italy, the Netherlands, Peru and Uruguay, have either expressed a desire to work towards Consultative status or announced an enhancement of their Antarctic research activities[21]. In addition, most acceding states have scientific personnel attached to the programmes conducted by the Consultative Parties, such as demonstrated by the presence of Cuban and Czech scientists on Soviet expeditions or of Chinese scientists on Argentine, Australian, Chilean and New Zealand programmes.

Consultative Party Status

The first tier of membership, Consultative Party status, is restricted to the original twelve signatories of the treaty and to any other governments which are accepted by the Consultative Parties as fulfilling the membership criteria. By 1983 four governments, Brazil, India, Poland and West Germany, had been added to the initial grouping of twelve parties (see Tables 8.1 and 8.2). Initially, this form of membership was confined to the twelve parties, which

> Shall be entitled to appoint representatives to participate in the meetings ... during such time as that Contracting Party demonstrates its interest in Antarctica by conducting substantial research activity there, such as the establishment of a scientific station or the despatch of a scientific expedition (article IX (2)).

In fact, this clause implies that a significant decline or cessation of research activity in Antarctica might render a party ineligible for participation in the Consultative Meetings, even if to date this step has not been implemented in spite of evidence that certain states - Belgium and Norway have been oft-cited in this connection - have conducted relatively little recent Antarctic research[22]. The evidence on Norway proves inconclusive, for there have been occasional research programmes and base stations and 'the intention of the Norwegian Government is to follow up this expedition (ie. of 1984-5) with new ones at regular intervals in the future'[23]. This recent enhancement of Norwegian activity can be interpreted in part as a response to criticisms of inactivity, although the position of Belgium has attracted most attention in this regard, such as evidenced by the recent UN debates. For instance, Bhurgari of Pakistan attacked the privileged role of the Consultative Parties, and especially the fact:

> That some of the original twelve countries - Belgium, for example - have virtually ceased all Antarctic activity, but nonetheless retain their consultative status under the treaty[24].

As a result, the treaty system appears guilty of double standards on membership, since the research test is applied to new members but not to the original signatories, which retain their decision-making role regardless of the level of their recent Antarctic activities. Certainly, the situation appears to undermine the Consultative Parties' case regarding the need for an informed background for such a status, since Belgium's 'background' can be interpreted as rather insubstantial. Nevertheless, the Belgian government has defended its role and interests in Antarctica, albeit primarily in historical rather than in contemporary terms. Dever told the UN in 1983 that:

> Eighty years ago Adrien de Gerlache de Gomery conducted the first Belgian expedition to Antarctica. Many Belgians have since followed in his footsteps ... Our contributions have been made in many areas where

> Antarctica offers many scientific opportunities ... Belgium continues to have great interest in the sixth continent. We will continue to play our role there[25].

In reality, Belgium's post-1959 role in Antarctica has proved somewhat inconsistent and marginal - its response to the UN Study in 1984 concentrated primarily upon the scientific and practical contribution of Gomery's Belgica expedition of 1897-9 - and during the 1970s and 1980s has assumed the form only of the participation of individuals in other countries' expeditions[26]. In May 1983 a parliamentary reply admitted that 'for budgetary reasons our country does not actually perform any activity in Antarctica', and hence Belgium's contribution has concentrated upon the diplomatic sphere in respect to representation at Consultative and other meetings[27]. The Belgian government has rationalised its retention of this status in spite of research inactivity in terms of article IX (1); thus, 'the Contracting Parties which are mentioned in its preamble (which is the case of Belgium) participate without conditions in all Consultative Meetings'[28].

The whole concept of 'substantial research activity' specified in article IX is clouded in doubt, partly because the treaty negotiators had failed to agree upon anything more precise and partly because of the difficulties of distinguishing scientific research from other activities, such as resource exploration and exploitation. An added problem surrounds the extent of activity required to be adjudged 'substantial', for the treaty lacked absolute criteria and suggested merely a few possibilities, such as the establishment of a scientific base or the despatch of an expedition. Obviously, this situation leaves room for debate and uncertainty, and Vicuna has argued that:

> It is certainly not the case that any research whatsoever is sufficient reason for granting this special responsibility, but rather only those research efforts whose significance clearly demonstrates the presence of the necessary qualifications[29].

However, there are perhaps advantages deriving from imprecision on membership requirements, since this permits the interposition of discretionary, pragmatic and policy considerations, especially as applications for promotion to Consultative status are vetted by the existing holders of that status.

Admissions to Consultative Status

Perhaps, the most meaningful guidance upon the subject of membership derives from what might be described as the Antarctic Treaty System's case law, that is, the example of the four additions to Consultative Party status. The first addition did not occur until 1977, when Poland's long-standing pursuit of this status was satisfied. Poland had applied for admission to the treaty negotiations in April 1959, a request justified in terms of its historical involvement in Antarctica as well as of its recent takeover of a Soviet Antarctic base. But the request proved unsuccessful, and in 1961 Poland merely acceded to the treaty; indeed, this represented the first such accession. In the event, Consultative status proved the result less of a long campaign but more of a recognition of the level of Poland's Antarctic activities in the sphere of marine research - this was evidenced by the expedition of 1975-6 - and of its establishment (February 1977) of a permanent base station, the Arctowski base, in the South Shetlands. These achievements were stressed in the note of 2 March 1977 sent by the Polish government to the Consultative Parties in order to seek admission to consultative status[30]. In turn, the request was considered, and approved, at a Special Consultative Meeting held in July 1977.

The episode in 1977 established a procedural precedent, according to which an applicant first notifies the American government, the treaty depositary, of its interest, then supplies supporting material for circulation to the Consultative Parties, and within twelve months a special Consultative Meeting has to be called to consider the application[31]. The establishment of a permanent base, the Georg von Neumayer station in Atka Bay, in conjunction with a series of Antarctic research expeditions commenced in 1975-6, cleared the way for the implementation of the 1977 precedent and for the admission of West Germany as a Consultative Party at a special Consultative Meeting held in March 1981[32]. Like Poland, West Germany had taken a close interest in the Antarctic Treaty negotiations - its concern was displayed in exchanges with the US government - but political and other factors led the Bonn government not to take the matter further[33].

At this point, it is of interest to examine the nature of West Germany's interest in Antarctica, such as reflected not only in its accession to the treaty in 1979 and application of 7 October 1980 for consultative status but also in the establishment of the Georg von Neumayer station in February 1981[34].

> The main motives for these steps by the Federal Republic of Germany were:
> a) In view of the great importance of Antarctica to the environment and to research, the FRG wanted to contribute its scientific capabilities to a system which envisages the free exchange and accessibility of research findings to the benefit of all mankind;

> b) considering the geostrategic significance of Antarctica, it wanted to support a system which keeps the continent free from military activities and nuclear explosions;
> c) conscious of Antarctica's importance to the northern hemisphere too, it wanted to preserve the unique natural environment of the continent, support the measures already taken to this end and contribute towards advancing them;
> d) it was willing to assume its share of responsibility for determining the political and economic affairs of the continent[35].

Of course, this official version might encourage one to overlook other factors, such as a desire for a more active role in Antarctic decision-making or an interest in the mineral marine resources of Antarctica for economic purposes.

The Polish and West German episodes indicated that the basic test of 'substantial research activity' was the establishment of a permanent Antarctic presence, and thus both Special Consultative Meetings adopted the same practice of noting the establishment of 'a permanent scientific station' as a demonstration of an 'interest in Antarctica in accordance with Article IX, paragraph 2 of the Treaty', of checking that any activities were in accordance with article X of the Treaty - this involved an inspection in the case of Poland - and of acknowledging that the government concerned 'has fulfilled the requirements established in Article IX, paragraph 2 of the Antarctic Treaty ... and has the right to appoint representatives in order to participate in the Consultative Meetings'[36]. However, this precedent was partially undermined in September 1983, when Brazil and India were admitted, albeit having satisfied a lesser standard of activity than that apparently applied in 1977 and 1981. Brazil possessed a track record of interest and research in Antarctica, but prior to September 1983 there had been only one 'exploratory' expedition during 1982-3[37]. However, plans existed for an ongoing research programme, including another Antarctic expedition in 1983-4.

> Concomitantly to these preparations, the Brazilian Government began a series of diplomatic contacts with the Consultative Parties with a view to obtaining full participation in the Twelth Antarctic Consultative Meeting ... A comprehensive document was prepared containing a detailed description of activities carried out in 1982/1983 and of the projects planned for the following austral summer ... on 12 September 1983, the Fifth Special Consultative Meeting acknowledged that Brazil, together with India, had fulfilled the requirements established in article IX, paragraph 2, of the Antarctic Treaty[38].

India had entered Antarctic research more recently, but its admission had been preceded by a more active role, such as evidenced by the expeditions of 1981-2 and of 1982-3, the establishment of an unmanned monitoring station and plans for a permanent base.

> Ever since the first Indian expedition returned from Antarctica, the Government of India had been considering the implications of joining the Antarctic Treaty ... India's decision to join the treaty was based on the following considerations:
> a) that India will be able to exchange scientific information with other members of the Treaty and thereby enhance its analytical capabilities;
> b) that if elected, India would be able to participate in the meetings of the Consultative Committee and in doing so be able to project effectively its own views as well as those of the non-aligned countries;
> c) that India would be able to participate in the ongoing discussions on the resources of Antarctica and ensure that any regime that is set up is in harmony with the overall policies and objectives pursued by India; ... In September 1983 ... the representatives of the Consultative Parties acknowledged by consensus that India fulfilled the requirements established in article IX, paragraph 2, of the Antarctic Treaty[39].

Although the Special Consultative Meeting held in September 1983 conformed to previous practice in respect to the treatment of admission to consultative status as a non-automatic process - checks were made regarding adherence to articles IX (2) and X - Brazil and India were interpreted as having fulfilled article IX (2) in spite of the fact that neither country had established a permanent scientific station. Admittedly, both applicants possessed plans for future expeditions and bases, but by September 1983 Brazil and India had merely despatched one and two expeditions respectively, even if there existed an all-the-year-round unmanned weather station established by the first Indian expedition.

In a sense, the resulting award of consultative status to Brazil and India implied a lower standard of performance to satisfy the criteria of 'substantial research activity' - indeed, Auburn has argued that the episode effected 'a major reduction in the immediate outlay for achieving consultative status' - while also suggesting the intervention of other considerations[40]. The device of a Special Consultative Meeting perpetuates the ability of the Consultative Parties not only to maintain a check on the composition of Consultative Meetings but also to exercise a measure of discretion and pragmatism for policy and other reasons. In September 1983, 'policy and other reasons' proved as significant as the usual criteria, although there was evidence that both Brazil and India intended in the near future to perform a more substantial research role. In the event, India established a permanent research station, named Dakshin Gangotri - this was promised in the Indian government's statement at the 1983 Consultative Meeting - during the 1983-4 season, that is, rather earlier than the date oft-cited previously[41]. Similarly, Brazil established an Antarctic base in the South Shetlands during the same season - the base was entitled Comandante Ferraz - with plans for permanent occupation with effect from 1985-6[42]. Therefore, there was the promise of, 'substantial research activity', and it is probable that this point, in conjunction with policy factors, facilitated the promotion of the two governments. However, secrecy renders it difficult to make any precise comments.

Naturally, in 1983 the Consultative Parties welcomed the chance to extend participation at a time of increased criticism of the privileged and exclusive nature of the Antarctic Treaty System. As a result, the simultaneous admission to Consultative Party status of two significant governments would serve not only to undermine the justification for such criticism but also to strengthen the treaty system. In particular, India, a leading member of the non-aligned movement, was adjudged to be a positive asset on account not only of its recent activities in Antarctica - these had occasioned anxieties amongst the treaty powers regarding Indian intentions - but also of the belief that membership would contain any problems likely to emanate from India, which had close links with the developing world and had proved at one time an advocate of a UN role in Antarctica[43]. From this perspective, the addition of India represented a considerable coup for the treaty powers, since it reduced the chances of India either leading or supporting the anti-treaty campaign initiated by Malaysia. Conversely, India perceived membership to be advantageous, since it would enable a more effective way of pressing Indian and Third World interests in Antarctica. The importance of Indian entry was accentuated by the simultaneous admission to consultative status of Brazil, a major force in Latin America, as well as by the recent accession of China, which was indicating an eventual desire to emulate Brazil and India.

In this respect, the approval procedure for Consultative Parties implies a check not only upon the matter of a meaningful research contribution but also upon the admission's effect regarding the stability of the Antarctic Treaty System within the context of international politics[44]. Obviously, additional Consultative Parties drawn from the ranks of the more powerful and influential powers will strengthen the Antarctic Treaty System, even if some fear the dangers of over-expansion. In the event, the admission of Poland, West Germany, Brazil and India has consolidated the system, particularly as these governments have become active campaigners on behalf of the Antarctic Treaty, while accepting also - to quote the Brazilian government - 'the decisions and Recommendations which, in furtherance of those (treaty) principles, have been adopted over a period of more than twenty years'[45]. The 1977 Special Consultative Meeting noted the desire to urge future applicants for Consultative Party status to make a declaration of intent to approve all previous Recommendations, a form of words less strong than advocated by such parties as the US government[46]. In the event, there have been no problems, and applicants have stressed their willingness to approve the relevant recommendations; for example, this point was stressed in a West German note sent to the depositary government on 17 February 1981, that is, prior to the Special Consultative Meeting. Nevertheless, there exists the view that it might prove beneficial to admit even governments, which are otherwise qualified but are adjudged likely to cause problems, on the grounds that admission might either neutralise and contain them or convert them to a more cooperative attitude. In fact, India excited such speculation in 1983, such as in terms of the suggestion that entry might enable it to transform or destroy the treaty system from within. At the close of 1983, the author discussed India's intentions, as follows:

> Of course, it might be argued that India intends to exploit entry in order to destroy the Antarctic club from within, or to exacerbate the existing internal divisions. Only time will tell[47].

In the event, India has emerged as an effective participant in the system and as a supporter for its retention, even if there are signs of concern about certain aspects, such as the practice of secrecy. Certainly, India's advocacy on behalf of the treaty system has served to disarm the impact of the criticism from the developing world, while also hindering Malaysian efforts to secure more effective support from the Non-Aligned Movement against the treaty[48].

The apparent trend in 1983 towards liberalising the admission of new Consultative Parties on account of the interposition of policy considerations encourages one to look again at previous admissions, which appeared to conform to a substantial research commitment. For example, in 1977 the initiation of marine resources regime negotiations meant that, for policy reasons, the active cooperation of Poland was deemed desirable because of its interest and research activities in this sphere. Similarly, the entry of West Germany, whose research included a geological emphasis, occurred at a time when the treaty system was moving towards formal discussions on a minerals regime. As such, policy and resource-related considerations can be interpreted as either supplementing or supplanting the scientific criteria favoured by the drafters of the treaty, especially as this trend reflects the evolution of the treaty system, such as its extension into resource management. In addition, there exists the suspicion that other factors are relevant, including East-West and Latin American relations. For instance, did West German entry counter-balance that of Poland or was Brazil's admission the result of an attempt to maintain a strong Latin American position within an expanding treaty system?

The Price of Entry to Consultative Meetings

The practice of Special Consultative Meetings, the need to interpret the criteria required to satisfy article IX (2), and the intervention of policy factors, provide scope for a subjective approach towards applications for consultative status. In addition, the confused conclusions emanating from a study of admissions since 1977, in conjunction with the secrecy of meetings, mean that an element of uncertainty continues to characterise any discussion on this aspect.

Nevertheless, certain observations can be advanced on membership, and, in the context of the criticism regarding the 'closed' nature of the Antarctic Treaty System, one of the most significant comments concerns the relatively high entrance fee. Although a liberalisation of the qualifications can be detected, Consultative Party status can be acquired only by a limited number of governments because of the level of scientific and logistical costs involved. As a result, this status is 'still beyond the contemplation of all but the most determined and technologically advanced of the developing countries'[49]. In fact, the example of Belgium highlights the burden even for a developed country, although such demands have not hindered the decisions of the Dutch, Italian and Spanish governments to enhance their Antarctic research activities. Obviously, it proves difficult to quantify the precise costs of entrance, but Poland's application has been estimated to have involved prior costs of three million dollars, whereas in West Germany 'the Ministry of Science and Technology put more than 110 millions dollar worth of equipment at the disposal of the Alfred Wegener Institute' for Antarctic research[50]. The Indian government's budget for Antarctica during 1983-4 was 58,500,000 rupees[51]. In any case, the extent of the initial costs is accentuated by the continuing expenditure required to maintain an Antarctic presence, and India's Antarctic budget for 1984-5 was 65,700,000 rupees. In this manner, the high entrance fee, even for the lower 1983-type criteria, acts as a significant and continuing restriction, especially as Antarctic research programmes assume also a sound scientific and logistical infrastructure. Certainly, Mrs Gandhi interpreted India's Antarctic role as both emerging from and confirming her country's high level of scientific expertise[52].

Although the select nature of the grouping of Consultative Parties can be viewed as a realistic recognition of the necessity for an informed and practical basis for the work of Consultative Meetings, many outsiders have used the UN debates to complain about the inequitable, closed and unrepresentative treaty system. Naturally, the Consultative Parties have refuted charges of elitism, while pointing to the realism of current practice. Vicuna, who has argued for the strict and rigorous application of article IX (2), has provided a typical rationale:

> Participation in Antarctic activities has to be selective, involving only those who have the backing of a solid professional capability. We cannot run the risk of failure in activities carried out in Antarctica because the damage which such a failure might entail could well be of catastrophic proportions. Having this solid background is entailed in the 1959 Treaty provisions regarding eligibility for Consultative Party status[53].

The UN debates have been characterised by a concerted effort by the treaty powers to defend this type of position, such as demonstrated by Kuroda of Japan:

> Any claim that the Antarctic Treaty was the "exclusive" club of the consultative parties could only be made from a lack of awareness of the difficulties of maintaining scientific research activities under such severe geophysical conditions[54].

Against this background, the admission of governments not active in Antarctica to Consultative Meetings has been perceived by the Consultative Parties to pose problems, since the consensus procedure would permit any inexperienced government to thwart their wishes. According to Heap:

> The existing Antarctic Treaty System whereby binding decisions are taken by those who are going to be affected by them is right ... a decision by those who will not be affected by the consequences of those decisions is a bid to exercise power without responsibility. My government could not accept this[55].

Heap feared that this would prove 'a recipe for chaos'. This Consultative Party-orientated rationale implies not only the Antarctic inadequacies of outsiders but also the fact that the system is 'open' to any government prepared and able to fulfil the requirements of article IX (2); thus, other governments are blamed for their failure to demonstrate any real or substantial interest in Antarctica, although Vicuna was perhaps rather optimistic in suggesting that other governments should have 'no difficulty in qualifying as Consultative Parties'[56]. The relatively recent admission of four Consultative Parties lends some credence to the 'open' view of the system, but other observers have proved less certain. In theory, no government is excluded from Consultative Party status, but in practice a large part of the international community will be incapable of qualification for this role.

To some extent, the perceived problem has been alleviated by the admission of acceding governments to observer status at Consultative Meetings, for accession offers a no-cost method of partial participation. In addition, in 1983 the Consultative Meeting considered the possibility of allowing the attendance of observers from appropriate international organisations[57]. However, other proposals have been advanced, such as that of Pinto, a Sri Lankan diplomat, in favour of the presence at Consultative Meetings of an equal number of representatives from non-treaty powers; thus, these representatives could be appointed upon a geographical basis upon a three year rotational scheme[58]. The Bangladesh government has floated the idea that developing countries might participate in Consultative Meetings upon either a regional basis or through affiliation with an existing Consultative Party[59]. However, such proposals have evoked little response from the Consultative Parties, which regard them as superfluous and unrealistic.

Withdrawals

Hitherto, the Antarctic Treaty System has tended to increase in membership, and the general perception is that this trend will continue. No Consultative Parties have either withdrawn or been excluded, and as a result little attention has been devoted to the subject in spite of the fact that the withdrawal of a major signatory, such as the Soviet Union or the USA, would exert a damaging effect upon the operation and international credibility of the system. According to the treaty, withdrawals can occur as a consequence of the treaty review conference or of the non-ratification of amendments within two years (article XII (1)b)[60]. It is difficult to predict other causes of withdrawal, but possible scenarios include a breakdown in the minerals regime negotiations or a conflict over sovereignty. There is also the possibility of a fundamental change in the Antarctic situation, such as caused by the exploitation of oil, since this might prompt action upon the part of those governments favouring a status quo interpretation of the Antarctic Treaty. According to Scully:

> If a State chose, it could argue at any time that circumstances had so changed since the treaty had been negotiated that it had the right under general international law to withdraw[61].

However, at present the treaty powers appear to favour not only the continued evolution of the treaty system but also its indefinite duration, and therefore withdrawal has been interpreted as a remote possibility.

The Participation of South Africa

One of the by-products of the recent international debate about the Antarctic Treaty System has been the enhanced intrusion of political considerations, and during 1983 Caribbean and African governments combined to introduce a new dimension into the discussion in the form of an attack upon the participation of South Africa, a founder member of the system. This element permitted not only a further development of the anti-treaty argument but also an aspect capable of attracting the support of other governments more concerned to condemn South Africa than to consider the future interests of Antarctica. The topic was originated, it appears, by Antigua and Barbuda in mid-1983 at meetings of CARICOM and the OECS, was developed subsequently through diplomatic contacts, and then pressed at the UN at the close of 1983[62]. At this time, Jacobs, told the UN First Committee that 'we demand its immediate expulsion from membership in the Consultative Group', and Sierra Leone, acting on behalf of the African group, attempted to include this point in the proposed UN resolution[63]. But the matter was not pressed, however, delegates realising that to do so would threaten the adoption by consensus of the demand for an UN Study, which represented the immediate priority.

The South African aspect proved more prominent at the 1984 UN debate, which followed on from the usual condemnation of South African politics at the meeting of non-aligned governments in New York between 1-5 October 1984[64]. In the First Committee Jacobs reaffirmed the approach adopted the previous year.

> South Africa's participation in Antarctica is totally unacceptable to my delegation and to my country. The international community has constantly condemned the racist policies of South Africa. South Africa has been forced to vacate its seat in the United Nations. Every decent and respectable organisation has shunned South Africa like the plague. Why has South Africa been allowed to participate with the other Consultative Parties?[65].

This provided the foundation for the repetition of Antigua and Barbuda's demand for South Africa's exclusion from the treaty system as well as for its condemnation of the hypocrisy of the Soviet and other governments in sitting down with South Africa at the same time as they criticised apartheid.

This approach was supported by several other delegations, so that South African participation in the Antarctic Treaty System became one of the key themes in the UN debates. During 1982-3 the Malaysian government had failed to stress this point, but by 1984 the South African aspect was incorporated into its policy framework, such as demonstrated by its response for the UN Study:

> The Malaysian Government believes that South Africa, an international outlaw because of its apartheid policies, cannot be involved in the management of Antarctica[66].

Gbeho, the Ghanaian delegate, commented that:

> It is a sorry spectacle indeed to see what odd bedfellows the Antarctic Treaty has made of some Member States and racist South Africa[67].

In addition, for several governments, including Ghana and Nigeria, the presence of South Africa was exacerbated by the absence of any other African representation in the treaty system[68].

During the UN debates since 1983 comments by the Consultative Parties about South Africa were conspicuous by their absence, presumably on account of a deliberate desire to play down a difficult problem. Nevertheless, the Consultative Parties have appreciated the position, such as articulated by Cisca Spencer, an Australian diplomat,

> South Africa is perhaps the country most directly affected by the Third World's current interest in Antarctica ... South Africa's presence in the treaty ... is likely to be a continuing problem[69].

However, there is evidence that this relative public silence has been qualified by diplomatic activity, and in November 1984 Gbeho admitted that:

> In the consultations that have been held since the debate last year, most of the Treaty Powers have indicated to us that they wish to separate this issue from apartheid. They have even accused us of naïveté since South Africa's geographic position and scientific potential make it a natural party to the Treaty[70].

Obviously, the South African aspect has further politicised and polarised the Antarctic debate, and there is a danger that the emotive and myopic manner in which many governments approach the topic will damage the quality of discussion, and thus the eventual outcome. In many respects, the campaign might be deemed irrelevant and inappropriate to

Antarctic realities, particularly in the context of South Africa's geographical proximity to Antarctica, Antarctic research programmes in the atmospheric, biological, earth and ocean sciences, the SANAE base in Antarctica, and involvement as 'an active Consultative Party' in the responsible operation of the treaty over a period of almost 25 years alongside a range of other governments, including the Soviet Union and (since 1983) India[71]. In the meantime, South African participation in the treaty system has been placed on the international agenda, and, to repeat Spencer, promises to cause continuing difficulties. Hitherto, the ability of South Africa to work with other governments within the Antarctic system in spite of apartheid has highlighted the ability of the treaty powers to cooperate through the accommodation of divergent positions. Now the South African problem has aggravated the Antarctic Treaty System's task of internal and external accommodation, while also adding a further element to the participation debate. The presence of South Africa has encouraged outsiders to attack the system in general, and it is possible that this may delay extended participation in the Antarctic Treaty on account of a reluctance to accede to an agreement including South Africa.

Conclusion

The participation question has become closely inter-connected with the wider debate about the acceptability of the Antarctic Treaty System, and therefore will retain international interest. Although wider participation may defuse criticism and consolidate the system, the hierarchical and selective nature of its membership renders it liable for attack upon the grounds of exclusivity at the decision-making level. In the meantime, was Meissner, the East German representative, correct in stating that the interests of Antarctica and of the international community would be best served by 'not revision but accession to the Treaty by other states interested in the Antarctic'?[72]. Recently acceding states have performed a more active role in the treaty system, such as in the form of observer status at Consultative Meetings, but even some acceding states have expressed reservations about participation; in fact, certain acceding states will resolve the problem through promotion to consultative status, albeit at a high price. Also, the level of participation is relevant to the matter of the optimum size of the Antarctic grouping; thus, under-expansion exposes the system to criticism for exclusivity, whereas over-expansion through extended participation may exacerbate the search for consensus and internal accommodation.

In the near future the basic debate will be between two main viewpoints. On the one hand, the Malaysian government argues that:

> The present machinery for Antarctica has not kept pace with current international realities. The Antarctic Treaty system with its two-tiered membership is unacceptable because of its exclusivity, its unaccountability, and its secrecy. Membership as Consultative Parties requires the ability to meet stringent qualifications established by the original Consultative Parties themselves, which can only be met by rich and scientifically-developed countries. The Consultative Parties are not, and do not regard themselves as accountable to the international community[73].

By contrast, Woolcott believes that:

> The essential question is this: how are ... activities in this large and very special part of the world to be best regulated? Should this be achieved by attempting to introduce some new international agreement ... or is it not better to develop the existing, sound Antarctic treaty System, which has been tested and which has proved to be both open and flexible? For the members of the Treaty, the answer to these questions is unanimous and clear ... We renew our invitation to those countries which have an interest in Antarctica to consider joining the Treaty[74].

The attitude of such governments as Malaysia makes it debatable whether Woolcott's invitation will elicit any response, especially as not every government accepts this perception of the open and successful nature of the Antarctic Treaty System.

NOTES

1. UNGA A/C 1/39 PV 50, p.12, 28 Nov.1984, Zain.
2. UNGA A/C 1/38 PV 43, p.20, 29 Nov.1983.
3. UNGA A/C 1/39 PV 53, pp.53-5, 29 Nov.1984; UNGA A/C 1/38 PV 43, p.21, 29 Nov.1983, Gbeho.
4. UNGA A/C 1/39 PV 50, p.6, 28 Nov.1984.
5. UNGA A/C 1/38 PV 45, p.6, 30 Nov.1983.
6. UNGA A/C 1/39 PV 53, p.6, 29 Nov.1984, Verma.
7. UNGA A/C 1/39 PV 50, pp.33-5, 28 Nov.1984.
8. Beck, _Secret Antarctic Treaty Preparatory Negotiations_.
9. Ibid.; Kuznetsov, 15 Oct.1959, _The Conference on Antarctica_, pp.21-2.
10. Statement of Non-Consultative Parties, 27 Sept. 1983, _Antarctic Treaty: Report of the Twelth Consultative Meeting_, p.122.
11. UNGA A/39/583(Part II), 1984, vol.2, p.68, 12 June 1984, East German response.

12. UNGA A/39/583(Part II), 1984, vol.2, p.48, 28 Aug.1984, Finland's response.

13. UNGA A/39/583(Part II), 1984, vol.3, p.77, 14 June 1984, Swedish response.

14. Antarctic Treaty: Report of the Twelth Consultative Meeting, pp.14-5.

15. Statement of Non-Consultative Parties, 27 Sept. 1983, Antarctic Treaty: Report of the Twelth Consultative Meeting, p.122.

16. UNGA A/39/583(Part II), 1984, vol.3, p.50, 28 May 1984, Romanian response.

17. UNGA A/C 1/39 PV 52, p.6, 29 Nov.1984, Suess, East Germany; UNGA A/C 1/38 PV 42, p.38, 28 Nov.1983, Meissner, East Germany; UNGA A/C 1/38 PV 42, p.46, 28 Nov.1983, Qian Jiadong, China.

18. UNGA A/C 1/39 PV 50, p.32, 28 Nov.1984.

19. Peking Evening News, 13 Oct.1984; Daily Telegraph, 29 Sept.1984; Guardian, 2 Jan.1985; Anon., 'First Chinese Expedition to Antarctica', Antarctic, vol.10, no.7 (1984), p.264.

20. UNGA A/39/583(Part II), 1984, vol.3, p.70, 13 June 1984, Spain's response.

21. UNGA A/C 1/39 PV 52, pp.18-20, 29 Nov.1984, Treves, Italy; UNGA A/C 1/39, PV 55, p.7, 30 Nov.1984, Engels, Netherlands; UNGA A/C 1/39 PV 52, p.56, 29 Nov. 1984, Blanco, Uruguay; Jose F. Torres Muga, Peru, 13 Sept. 1983, Antarctic Treaty: Report of the Twelth Consultative Meeting, p.113.

22. Auburn, Consultative Status under the Antarctic Treaty, pp.514-9.

23. UNGA A/39/583(Part II), 1984, vol.3, pp.28-9, 20 June 1984, Norwegian response.

24. UNGA A/C 1/38 PV 44, p.9, 29 Nov.1983.

25. UNGA A/C 1/38 PV 45, p.22, 30 Nov.1983; UNGA A/39/583(Part II), 1984, vol.1, pp.93-101, 27 Aug.1984, Belgian response.

26. UNGA A/39/583(Part II), 1984, vol.1, p.96, 27 Aug.1984, Belgian response; Fox, Antarctica and the South Atlantic, p.96.

27. Questions et Réponses - Chambre - 29 May 1984 (30), Belgium, no.159 du 9 Mai 1984. See p.157 for rumours regarding the difficulties of hosting the 1985 Consultative Meeting.

28. Ibid; Questions et Réponses - Chambre - 15 May 1984(28), Belgium, no.143 du 20 Avril 1984. However, while this manuscript was in press, the Belgium government decided (Summer 1985) to support financially a 5-year Antarctic research programme performed by Belgian universities.

29. Vicuna, Antarctic Resources Policy, p.3.

30. Auburn, Antarctic Law and Politics, pp.149-53; Antarctic Treaty: Handbook, pp.6601-2, p.6701.

31. Antarctic Treaty: Handbook, pp.6601-2, p.6701; Auburn, Antarctic Law and Politics, pp.147-51.

32. Antarctic Treaty: Handbook, pp.6702-3; Hempel, Antarctic Research in the Federal Republic of Germany, pp.133-42.

33. Beck, Secret Antarctic Treaty Preparatory Negotiations.

34. The original intention had been to establish a station on the Filchner-Ronne Ice Shelf, but heavy pack ice forced alternative plans.

35. UNGA A/39/583(Part II), 1984, vol.2, p.73, 1 June 1984, West German response.

36. Antarctic Treaty: Handbook, pp.6701-3. There were British plans to inspect the German base on the Filchner Ice Shelf, but the change of programme ruled out this inspection; see p.78.

37. Jefferson Simoes, 'Brazilian Antarctic Research Programme', Polar Record, vol.22, no.138(1984), pp.325-6; UNGA A/39/583(Part II), 1984, vol.2, p.6, 18 July 1984, Brazilian response.

38. UNGA A/39/583(Part II), 1984, vol.2, p.6, 18 July 1984, Brazilian response.

39. UNGA A/39/583(Part II), 1984, vol.2, pp.87-8, 16 July 1984, Indian response; Department of Ocean Development, India, Annual Report 1983-84, pp.1-32.

40. Francis Auburn, 'The Antarctic Minerals Regime: sovereignty, exploration, institutions and environment', in Harris, Australia's Antarctic Policy Options, p.279.

41. S.Z. Qasim, 13 Sept.1983, Antarctic Treaty: Report of the Twelth Consultative Meeting, pp.73-8; Peter J. Beck, 'Antarctica's Indian Summer', Contemporary Review, vol.243, no.1415(1983), p.298.

42. UNGA A/39/583(Part II), 1984, vol.2, pp.6-7, 18 July 1984, Brazilian response.

43. Beck, Antarctica's Indian Summer, pp.297-9; Francis Auburn, 'Antarctic Minerals and the Third World', Fram: Journal of Polar Studies, vol.1, no.1(1984), pp.217-9.

44. Francisco Orrego Vicuna, 'The application of the law of sea and the exclusive economic zone to the Antarctic continent', in Vicuna, Antarctic Resources Policy, p.250.

45. Marcos C. de Azambuja, 13 Sept.1983, Antarctic Treaty: Report of the Twelth Consultative Meeting, p.63.

46. Auburn, Consultative Status under the Antarctic Treaty, pp.518-9; Antarctic Treaty: Handbook, p.6601.

47. Beck, Antarctica's Indian Summer, p.299.

48. UNGA A/C 1/39 PV 53, pp.3-7, 29 Nov.1984, Verma. In 1984 India assumed a stronger pro-treaty line than during the previous year: UNGA A/C 1/38 PV 44, pp.3-5, 29 Nov.1983, Verma.

49. Auburn, The Antarctic Minerals Regime, p.279.

50. Auburn, Antarctic Law and Politics, pp.152-3; Hempel, Antarctic Research in the Federal Republic of Germany, p.140.

51. Department of Ocean Development, India, Annual Report 1983-84, p.62. The approximate equivalent was £4 million.

52. See p.110, where Mrs Gandhi referred to a 'select band of countries'.

53. Vicuna, Antarctica Resources Policy, p.3; Vicuna, Application of the law of the sea and the EEZ to the Antarctic continent, p.250.

54. UNGA A/C 1/38 PV 44, p.12, 29 Nov.1983.

55. UNGA A/C 1/39 PV 52, pp.26-7, 29 Nov.1984.

56. Vicuna, Antarctic Resources Policy, p.10.

57. Antarctic Treaty: Report of the Twelth Consultative Meeting, p.16.

58. Pinto, quoted, in Wolfrum, Antarctic Challenge, p.168.

59. UNGA A/C 1/38 PV 46, p.10, 30 Nov.1983, Wasiuddin.

60. Auburn, Antarctic Law and Politics, pp.143-5.

61. Quoted, in Auburn, Antarctic Law and Politics, p.144.

62. Peter J. Beck, 'Antarctica: A Case for the UN?', The World Today, vol.40, no.4 (1984), pp.166-70; Barbara Mitchell, Frozen Stakes: The Future of Antarctic Minerals (IIED, London, 1983), pp.43-4.

63. UNGA A/C 1/38 PV 42, p.7, 28 Nov.1983; Peter J. Beck, 'The United Nations and Antarctica', Polar Record, vol.22, no. 137 (1984), p.141.

64. UNGA A/39/560 S/16773, 9 Oct.1984, pp.12-14.

65. UNGA A/C 1/39 PV 50, pp.7-10, 28 Nov.1984.

66. UNGA A/39/583 (Part II), 1984, vol.2, p.110, 1 June 1984, Malaysian response.

67. UNGA A/C 1/39 PV 53, p.52, 29 Nov.1984.

68. UNGA A/C 1/39 PV 53, pp.18-20, 29 Nov.1984, Mgbokwere, Nigeria; UNGA A/39/583 (Part I), 1984, pp.35-6.

69. Spencer, The Evolution of Antarctic Interests, p.125.

70. UNGA A/C 1/39 PV 53, p.52, 29 Nov.1984.

71. UNGA A/39/583 (Part II), 1984, vol.3, pp.63-9, 30 May 1984, South African response.

72. UNGA A/C 1/38 PV 42, p.39, 28 Nov.1983.

73. UNGA A/39/583 (Part II), 1984, vol.2, p.110, 1 June 1984, Malaysian response.

74. UNGA A/C 1/39 PV 50, pp.33-5, 28 Nov.1984.

Chapter Nine

THE ANTARCTIC TREATY: A CONTINENT FOR THE MANAGEMENT OF LIVING MARINE RESOURCES IN AN ENVIRONMENTAL FRAMEWORK

Antarctica as a treasure island

It is clear that resources, or at least the prospect of resources, have served in the past as a major cause of interest in Antarctica - for example, the attractions of whaling stimulated British interest in the continent during the early years of this century - and, in turn, the region's resource potential explains much of the contemporary interest therein, especially upon the part of the developing world. In fact, this resource emphasis has offered one method of overcoming governmental and public disinterest in Antarctica, since the political, economic, scientific and environmental implications have fostered widespread interest and debate, such as upon the part of governments, international organisations and non-governmental organisations.

Certain marine resources, including fish and krill, are exploited on a limited scale already in the seas around Antarctica, but most of the current interest in marine and mineral resources is based upon supposed rather than upon actual resources. Inevitably, speculation has oft-encouraged a somewhat exaggerated vision of the possibilities in respect to the quantities of krill, fish, oil and natural gas likely to be available for exploitation. A recent press article typified this trend, for it was headlined by the phrase, 'Gold Rush for South Pole Wealth', while many speakers at such international forums as the UN have tended to adopt a similar approach and to depict the continent as a kind of treasure trove ripe for exploitation[1]. This interest in Antarctic resources has developed against a background of the growing perception of a global scramble for access to increasingly scarce products, including an awareness of the manner in which access to food stocks and hydrocarbons will prove a significant element of power in the international arena[2]. In addition, during the 1970s there was an appreciation that the total world fish catch might be reaching a plateau at around 70 million tons per annum, and such considerations in conjunction with regional shortages, fostered attention upon the search for alternative catching areas and types of marine resource. In fact, the FAO believes that the south-west Atlantic and Indian Oceans offer scope for increasing the world catch, although several countries have interpreted Antarctic Oceans as another possibility[3]. The problem has been accentuated by the extension of national offshore boundaries to 200 miles, and especially by the manner in which the Law of the Sea Convention encouraged the creation of 200-mile "exclusive economic zones" (EEZs) and deprived some high seas fishing fleets of their traditional fishing grounds. In the sphere of minerals, the 1973 oil crisis exerted a similar effect in terms of focussing attention upon Antarctica, although this aspect will be developed in the next chapter.

In practice, Antarctic resource realities may prove to be somewhat at variance with the grandiose visions advanced in certain quarters. Although it is possible to refer to the possibilities of krill - indeed, the 1982 Shackleton Report mentioned opinions that the total krill catch might equal the current world fish catch - or to follow the 1974 US Geological Survey's report regarding the vast estimated amounts of Antarctic oil and natural gas, the current position is far different, and most Antarctic experts have adopted a cautious, if not pessimistic, note when assessing the continent's resource prospects. Kuroda of Japan reminded the UN in 1983 that 'there has not yet been sufficient investigation to determine whether the region is in fact endowed with abundant natural resources'[4]. In turn, this lack of information has been compounded by other problems, including those posed by climate, distance, technological requirements and environmental protection; thus, any talk of resource exploitation should be related to the long-term, and even then relatively little actual exploitation might either occur or prove possible. As a result, the primacy of scientific data as an Antarctic export is unlikely to be challenged until at least the early years of the next century, and expressions of optimism about Antarctic resource prospects need to be qualified by reminders about the salutary lesson experienced some two centuries ago by Yves-Joseph de Kerguelen. In 1772 he discovered the islands known now as the Kerguelen Islands, which he suspected to 'form the central mass of the Antarctic continent' and felt promised 'all the crops of the Mother Country ... wool, minerals, diamonds, rubies and precious stones and marble will be found'[5]. A return visit the following year forced him to appreciate the reality of a barren territory, which he re-named "Land of Desolation"[6].

In certain respects, Antarctica might prove another land of desolation. In the long term, resources might be exploited in considerable quantities, thereby qualifying such an image, but realism demands a more cautious line towards the future, especially as a less ambitious vision of the resource potential will soften any disappointment if such hopes are not fulfilled.

Recently, the Consultative Parties have advocated a realistic approach towards the resources question, even if this has not prevented their increased emphasis upon resource-related research, such as evidenced by the BIOMASS programme. The line of separation between pure and applied research is far from clear, but many research schemes have adopted an applied emphasis, thereby providing an informed foundation for the attempt of the Consultative Parties to establish management regimes for both marine and mineral resources. Negotiations commenced on both topics during the 1970s, and in 1980 CCAMLR was signed and came into effect in 1982. The minerals regime question was treated as less urgent, and it was not until the early 1980s that discussions were initiated; in fact, these negotiations are still proceeding.

This chapter will concentrate upon living marine resources - the minerals question will be reserved for the next chapter - with emphasis upon the effects of the question for the development of the Antarctic Treaty System in particular and of the international system in general. Although there are similarities in the marine and mineral resource topics, such as in respect to sovereignty and environmental problems, the Consultative Parties have treated them separately, even if in practice CCAMLR has come to be treated as a possible precedent for an Antarctic minerals regime, and has proved part of any evaluation of the mineral negotiations.

Resources and the Antarctic Treaty

The recent emphasis upon resource regime negotiations highlights the fact that matters of economic use of resources had not been covered in the 1959 treaty, or so it has been argued. In any case, during the late 1950s resource aspects were not a prime policy factor, especially as compared to strategic, diplomatic and scientific considerations. In addition, the sovereignty implications - for instance, who owned any fish or minerals exploited? - meant that any attempt to cover resources during 1958-9 might have ruled out the prospect of the Antarctic Treaty, and this view is encouraged by the general reluctance of the parties to raise resource problems during the first decade of the Consultative Meetings[7].

In the event, the Antarctic Treaty proved relatively silent on the subject of resources, mainly because of an appreciation of the need to avoid divisive issues related to the ownership of resources. Nevertheless, the list of Consultative Party responsibilities, as contained in article IX (1f), did mention measures regarding the 'preservation and conservation of living resources in Antarctica', and the non-exhaustive nature of this list meant that other resource responsibilities could be interpreted as implicit within the wide scope of article IX (1). However, Zegers, a Chilean official, has pointed to the manner in which the treaty restricted some spheres of sovereign action, such as in respect to prohibitions on the military use of Antarctica, and has gone on to argue that by implication 'the topic of resources became the object to a certain extent of a political and legal moratorium'[8]. In practice, the Consultative Parties found it difficult to ignore resource questions, and the occasional pressures of the 1960s were succeeded in the 1970s by a greater sense of urgency regarding the need for action. The resulting exchanges revealed an appreciation not only of the resource gaps in the Antarctic Treaty but also of the prudence of arrangements linked to the treaty system in order to deal with the resource problem in a manner acceptable to both the treaty parties and the wider international community. The task of resource management was perceived also in terms of the evolving responsibilities of the Antarctic Treaty System, and especially of its abilities to pre-empt problems through prior action.

In certain quarters, the development of Antarctic resource regimes has been greeted with criticism. For example, the advent of such regimes has been interpreted by the conservation movement as a threat to Antarctica's fragile environment, while others have argued that resource matters are too important to be left to the Consultative Parties and should be decided by a more representative international regime. In this manner, the debate about resources has proved important in acting as a catalyst to draw attention to the basic problems facing the Antarctic System, thereby serving also to transform the affairs of Antarctica into a more significant international issue.

The Antarctic Ecosystem

The area of coverage for the CCAMLR is defined by the Antarctic Convergence, whose biological role arises out of the manner in which its frontal conditions provide areas of high productivity and act as a major biotic boundary for phytoplankton, zooplankton, fishes and birds. Here the warmer water flowing south from the Indian, Pacific and Atlantic Oceans and rich in such nutrients as nitrogen and silicates encounters the cold Antarctic waters, and the conditions prove favourable for the development of phytoplankton, the first link in the rather short and simple food chain supporting the extensive biological life of the Southern Ocean. Phytoplankton are microscopic floating plants, which grow in the Antarctic summer's sunlight and provide the food for organisms known as zooplankton, of which krill is the most significant variety[9]. The name "krill" was given by Norwegian whalers to the euphausid shrimp, whose main species - *Euphausia superba* and *Euphausia frigida* - are found with a circum-polar distribution to the south of the Antarctic Convergence. In summer dense swarms of krill near the surface impart a reddish appearance to the oceans, while krill constitute the basic food for all higher forms of life in the Antarctic ecosystem (as shown in Figure 9.1). Traditionally penguins, seals and whales have been depicted as typical forms of life in the Southern Oceans, but increasingly krill has emerged as the central area of focus, that is, as the key linking organism, rich in protein and with a major resource potential[10].

Although krill tends to have a circum-polar distribution, there appear to be areas of concentration, such as around South Georgia and the South Orkneys in the South Atlantic Ocean. In theory, the occurrence of dense concentrations near the surface facilitates catching, especially as some super swarms have been estimated to comprise circa five to ten million tons of krill, but in practice the variable distribution of krill, in conjunction with a basic lack of information on many aspects, has hampered both stock assessment and commercial exploitation. Inevitably, national and international research programmes - most notably the BIOMASS project - have attempted to fill the gaps in knowledge, but relatively little is known still about such matters as growth rates, longevity and swarming potential[11].

Japan and the Soviet Union have caught krill since the 1960s, and they were joined during the 1970s by other countries, including Bulgaria, Chile, East Germany, Poland, South Korea and West Germany. Some of the catching has been research-orientated, and the total krill catch has only reached a half million tons, which has been derived mainly from the Atlantic and Indian Ocean sectors of the Southern Ocean[12]. Most krill have been caught by the Soviet Union, with Japan, Bulgaria, East Germany and Poland accounting

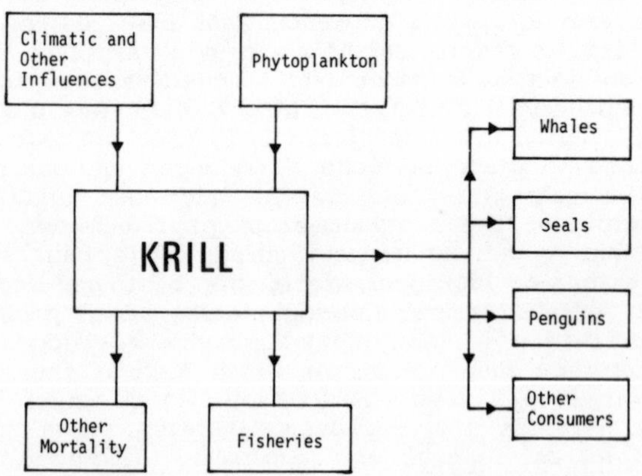

Fig. 9.1: Krill in the Antarctic Ecosystem.

for lesser amounts. The swarming characteristics of krill have enabled occasional high catch rates of up to 40 tons per hour, but it has not proved easy to locate actual krill concentrations. A more difficult question surrounds the potential total krill catch, since a wide range of sustainable catch figures have been suggested, such as of 50 million, 70 million, 100 million - this proved a favoured figure after a 1974 FAO Conference in Rome - 150 million or 170 million tons per annum[13]. Such estimates have been encouraged not only by the alleged surplus of krill consequent upon the decline of whale stocks but also by the apparent abundance of krill, even if there exists a similar range of estimates regarding the krill biomass[14].

As a result, a number of question marks surround any discussion of krill's resource value. Ecosystem models are still in their infancy, and hence 'all predictions are qualified by uncertainties'[15]. Much of the debate has centred upon the alleged existence of a krill surplus caused by declining whale stocks, but inadequate information, different approaches, and the argument that other species, including seals, have absorbed the surplus have caused controversy and doubt. The problem has been exacerbated by the fact that krill performs a crucial role in the Antarctic ecosystem, and its diminution would exert serious effects upon all parts of the food chain, perhaps even reversing the recent recoveries of whale and seal stocks. High catch figures have been criticised as either logistically unreal or environmentally irresponsible, and certain experts have proposed relatively low catch figures of four to five million tons per annum, while pointing to the need for estimates based upon ecosystem criteria rather than upon traditional maximum sustainable yield criteria. This background of uncertainty and disagreement necessitated a cautious approach to krill harvesting and management, such as through a regime capable of responding not only to the dynamic and interactive nature of changes within the ecosystem but also to political, economic, scientific and environmental factors[16].

Obviously, any discussion of the krill catch needs to be related to market possibilities and technological aspects. There exists still a search for acceptable methods of utilising krill for human and animal consumption, and a variety of products, including whole boiled krill, krill mince, krill sticks, krill paste and protein concentrate, have been tried with varying degrees of acceptance[17]. An initial problem concerning high fluoride levels has been resolved through processing changes, but a continuing difficulty concerns the need to overcome a strong, distinct taste and smell. The prospects for harvesting are influenced also by the significance not only of careful catching methods to avoid crushing krill but also of rapid processing to prevent deterioration. Further constraints derive from the capital and fuel cost requirements of long-distance fleets and of catching/processing technology, and their impact is accentuated by the relatively short catching season of some three to seven months. Although krill catching has increased rapidly during the past decade or so, and is expected to increase further, the future resource value of krill remains a subject of debate. It is unlikely that some of the more optimistic catch figures will be approached, but even a catch towards the lower end of the estimates, such as five million tons, would make Antarctic krill one of the world's major fishing resources. In this context, Everson has observed that:

> Until quite recently the name Antarctica conjured up images to the layman on the one hand of heroic exploration and on the other of the ruthless slaughter of whales. Over the past few years an additional dimension has been introduced, that of krill[18].

Although there exist still significant gaps in knowledge regarding fish in the Southern Ocean, such as in regard to their numbers, types and natural history, about 100 species of fish have been identified there out of a world total of over 20,000 fish species. Overall, it has been suggested that fish constitute a small, albeit important, part of the Antarctic marine ecosystem. The major group, Nototheniiformes, tend to be large-headed and demersal, that is, to live at significant depths. Fish types include Antarctic herring, cod and toothfish, but similarities of name conceal basic differences, since fish in Southern Oceans are characterised by high endemism on account of the physical and climatic isolation of their environment, which includes the need to adapt their physiology to low water temperatures[19].

Only about twelve or so species of fish might possess a commercial potential, such as Antarctic cod and herring, but exploitation has been hampered by distance, climate and the apparent absence of dense shoals. In addition, Antarctic stocks seem vulnerable to over-exploitation because of the slow growth and longevity rates of fish, such as evidenced by the examples of fishing around South Georgia (1969-70) and the Kerguelen Islands (1971-4). In these cases, high initial catches were followed within a year or so by a rapid decline - a Southern Ocean fish catch of 431,900 tons for 1969-70 plunged to 13,500 tons for 1972-3 - thereby indicating that stocks had been reduced below the sustainable yield figure. Nevertheless, the late 1970s witnessed a resumption of activity led by the Soviet Union, but also including East Germany, Japan and Poland, and catch figures fluctuated between the levels of 115,000-268,000 tons[20]. It remains debatable whether these figures can be improved or even maintained, although the fishing interest will persist as part of the global preoccupation for alternative fishing grounds.

Similarly, squid have attracted the interest of Spain and other nations, but little is known about either their numbers or distribution, since both research and catching have proved difficult[21].

Historically, whales constituted the primary resource of Antarctic oceans, and during the early twentieth century the region, including the sub-Antarctic islands, emerged as the dominant world whaling ground responsible for about 60-70 per cent of the world's catch. In this manner, whaling fostered political, economic and scientific interest in Antarctica, and proved a major factor in serving not only to undermine the continent's isolation from the mainstream of international affairs but also to promote scientific research on whales and related aspects[22]. Whaling stocks have been severely depleted - some suggest that the current biomass is 16 per cent of the former level - and inevitably a link has been drawn between this trend and stocks of krill, the primary food of whales; indeed, the daily consumption of a blue whale, the largest of the dozen or so species found in the region, may reach four tons per day. This has prompted speculation about both the existence and amount of the krill surplus available for other predators, including man. Another imponderable concerns future whaling catches, such as in the context of environmental concern and of the International Whaling Commission's attempts to establish a moratorium on whaling with effect from 1985-6[23]. Japan and the Soviet Union remain the only countries still whaling in Antarctica.

Sealing was another important Antarctic activity during the eighteenth and nineteenth centuries - fur and oil were the main attractions - but such exploitation halted during the early years of this century. The Weddell and Crabeater seals tend to be the most abundant species, and their functional areas are the fast and pack ice respectively. Crabeater seals live almost solely on krill, whereas other seals eat fish and squid also and, in the case of leopard seals, even penguins. The termination of commercial sealing, in association with other factors such as the krill surplus, has contributed to an increase in the seal population; indeed, some refer to a population explosion, and Llano estimates a total biomass of 17 million seals[24]. In practice, it proves difficult to quantify the seal population, although seals constitute a significant biomass performing a key role in the marine ecosystem of Antarctica. In spite of the recovery of stocks, commercial sealing is adjudged unlikely, partly because of public opposition to sealing and partly because of lack of demand for sealing products. In any case, exploitation will have to be conducted within the parameters of the Sealing Convention, which prohibits the killing of Ross, elephant and fur seals and imposes annual restrictions upon the catch of Crabeater, leopard and Weddell seals.

Birds provide the other major dimension to the extensive and rich ecosystem, although only a relatively few species - about 40 species - are found with a coastal and insular distribution. The austral summer witnesses the convergence upon Antarctica of a range of seabirds, mainly penguins, albatrosses, petrels and skuas, and, while the species may be few, the bird numbers are substantial, possibly in excess of about 180 million birds[25]. Consequently, birds comprise a substantial part of the ecosystem, and tend, like other elements, to be characterised by a circum-polar distribution, that is, to be confined to the coastal margins, the pack ice and the sub-Antarctic islands. Although birds are eaten, such as by leopard seals, they are primarily consumers of krill, fish and squid, and this explains their significance in the ecosystem. Paradoxically, perhaps more is known about birds than any other part of the ecosystem, and yet they figure rarely in discussions about resource exploitation, even if penguins have been utilised for oil in the past. In fact, scientists might argue that the level of research on birds illustrates that scientific work has possessed a pure rather than an applied emphasis.

The Agreed Measures

From one perspective, it is possible to treat the 1980 CCAMLR as the logical culmination of the Consultative Parties' long-standing preoccupation with environmental questions, for it seems possible to trace a progressive and evolving pattern of development. However, there is at the same time a danger of giving undue precision to a set of events, which need to be interpreted as disparate and fortuitous measures[26].

During the early 1960s the Antarctic Treaty System demonstrated a clear concern for environmental protection, especially because the parties viewed conservation as one aspect of their responsibilities, such as specified in article IX (1f) of the treaty. In addition, this role accorded with the personal interests of those involved in Consultative Meetings, and Brian Roberts of the UK has been oft-cited in this connection. This sense of responsibility pervaded the system's work during its first decade, and was articulated in 1970 by recommendation VI-4, which identified the vulnerability of the Antarctic environment and the scientific value of 'its uncontaminated and undisturbed condition', stressed 'an increasingly urgent need to protect the environment from human interference', and advocated that 'the Consultative Parties should assume responsibility for the protection of the environment and the wise use of the Treaty Area'. In this context, the first Consultative Meeting of 1961 had indicated the 'urgent need for the protection of living resources against man' as well as the importance of agreed measures, developed with the advice of SCAR, on protection and conservation (recommendation I-VIII). The next Consultative Meeting proposed that voluntary rules of conduct should be submitted to its successor (recommendation II-II), thereby clearing the way for the 1964 Consultative Meeting to adopt the Agreed Measures for the Conservation of Antarctic Fauna and Flora (hereafter, the Agreed Measures) in recommendation III-VIII[27].

The Agreed Measures' preamble stressed the need to protect, study and promote 'the rational use of these fauna and flora' through the consideration of the treaty area as 'a Special Conservation Area'. The measures were outlined in 14 articles, which served to limit the right to kill or capture native mammals and birds (article VI), to minimise coastal pollution and 'harmful interference', such as through disturbances to fauna by aircraft, vehicles or explosives (article VII), and to enable the establishment of 'areas of outstanding scientific interest' as Specially Protected Areas (SPAs) in order to preserve their unique natural ecological system (article VIII). Each party was obliged by article III to take appropriate action to implement the Agreed Measures, which were adopted to 'further international collaboration within the framework of the Antarctic Treaty', a linkage enhanced by the way in which the area of application coincided with 'the area to which the Antarctic Treaty is applicable' (article I). As a result, the Agreed Measures represented a significant development of the Antarctic Treaty System, albeit in a narrow manner, since there was no attempt to deal with the problem through an international agreement open to all powers. However, article X referred to outsiders and to the need for everyone active in Antarctica to conform to the Measures; thus, each party undertook to exert 'appropriate efforts ... to the end that no one engages in any activity in the Treaty Area contrary to the principles and purposes of these Agreed Measures'.

In this context, the 1966 Consultative Meeting designated 15 SPAs (recommendation IV-1-15) and scheduled two seal species, Ross and fur seals, specially protected species (recommendation IV-16-17). Obviously SCAR performed an important advisory role in such matters, and in 1972 a new category of SPA, entitled a Site of Special Scientific Interest (SSSI), was instituted by recommendation VII-3 in order to establish areas upon scientific rather than conservation criteria. SCAR advised upon criteria and sites, and subsequent additions, revisions and terminations of SPAs and SSSIs have occurred in consultation with SCAR[28]. However, these developments were parallelled by the relatively slow ratification of the Agreed Measures by the Consultative Parties. By 1972 only eight parties had accepted the relevant recommendation, and, while this delay can be interpreted as qualifying the initial urgency of the search for environmental protection, the main reason arose from the need for certain governments, especially the non-claimants to enact special legislation. Whereas claimants could implement the Agreed Measures as an aspect of their sovereignty, non-claimants were faced with the difficulty of imposing legal restraints upon their nationals in territory beyond the national borders and regarded as not belonging to any state. But the problem was not insuperable, such as demonstrated by the passage in 1978 of the Antarctic Conservation Act by the US government. The Agreed Measures did not take general effect until 1983, when they became a binding obligation, even if they had been treated as interim guide lines since 1964, such as evidenced by the creation of SPAs (recommendation III-IX).

The Sealing Convention

In 1966 the Consultative Parties designated two types of seals as protected species, a step prompted not only by advice from SCAR but also by fears that a resumption of sealing - there had been an experimental sealing voyage by the *Polarhav* during 1964-5 - might threaten the twentieth century recovery of seal stocks. In fact, already in 1964 recommendation III-XI had supported the regulation of sealing at the national level, and the 1966 Consultative Meeting continued this process through the recommendation (IV-21) of interim guidelines designed to balance conservation, scientific and economic considerations in the context of a recognition that 'the seal stocks are a resource of potential value'. The basic aim was to guard against any depletion of stocks through over-exploitation in case commercial sealing resumed. The 1968 Meeting, helped by the advice of SCAR on guidelines for the regulation of sealing, decided to proceed through means of a convention separate from the Antarctic Treaty (recommendation V-8), since this approach would serve not only to enable the participation of other governments but also to overcome the delays consequent upon the Agreed Measures-type approach through a meeting recommendation. The ambivalent position of the proposed convention *vis à vis* the Antarctic Treaty System was demonstrated during 1970, when the matter was discussed by a working group at the time of the Consultative Meeting, albeit acting outside the treaty framework. The agreement was finalised at a special conference held in London in February 1972, which prepared the way for the convention to be opened for signature on 1 June 1972. All the Consultative Parties signed in 1972, but the Convention for the Conservation of Antarctic Seals did not come into effect until 11 March 1978, that is, one month after the date of the seventh ratification (article 13).

The Sealing Convention established a series of safeguards, including a permissible catch, restrictions on killing and capture, the designation of protected species, closed seasons and seal reserves, and these provisions were to be reinforced by the development and exchange of information, with the help of SCAR, on matters appertaining to stocks and the ecological system (articles 3-5). In this manner, the Consultative Parties gave further substance to their conception of the system's responsibilities for the Antarctic environment, and the force of this point was highlighted by the fact that the convention was introduced before the commencement of exploitation. In fact, no sealing has occurred to date, such as on account not only of commercial factors but also, it is argued, of the deterrent effect of the sealing regulations. Therefore, the Sealing Convention appears to perform a preventive rather than a regulatory role, particularly as article 6 provides for an institutional framework of a commission and supporting scientific advisory committee only 'after commercial sealing has begun'; thus, at present the Antarctic sealing regime constitutes no more than a mere paper framework, albeit one capable of establishment in the event of commercial sealing.

Although the Sealing Convention was concluded outside of the treaty framework, the similar composition of the contracting parties of both agreements tended to erode the artificial legal barrier erected between them. In any case, the Consultative Parties will effectively control the operation of any sealing regime, such as in respect to the issue of sealing permits and approval of the accession of other governments, while article 1 of the convention reinforced this over-lap; thus, this article adopted 60°South as the boundary of the convention's area of application, while also reaffirming article IV of the Antarctic Treaty, partly because certain functions exercised by the commission - for example, the issue of permits - might be interpreted as undermining the sovereignty positions of certain governments. Article 12 provides for the accession of other states, which are 'invited to accede ... with the consent of the Contracting Parties', but this attempt to involve outsiders cannot disguise the fact that, in reality, the separate Sealing Convention should be treated as part of the Antarctic Treaty System. Its conclusion offered a further insight into the way in which the Consultative Parties perceived their treaty responsibilities, particularly in the environmental sphere, and it is clear that such a convention would have proved difficult to achieve but for the existence of the Antarctic Treaty System.

The Agreed Measures, a kind of mini-convention, and the Sealing Convention demonstrated the concern of the Consultative Parties to develop and consolidate the treaty system, while also offering a foundation and precedent for subsequent measures, such as in regard to the identification of a problem, the drafting of interim guidelines, the advisory role of SCAR and the conclusion of a detailed set of measures in advance of an actual need. These early achievements provided the basis for the more substantial matter of the establishment of an Antarctic marine resources regime, which became the subject for negotiations during the late 1970s and offered another avenue for the evolution of the treaty system. The 1980 CCAMLR resulted from this process and was followed in 1982 by the creation of an institutional framework to give effect to its objectives.

The Environmental Context

Although CCAMLR can be interpreted as yet another chapter in the development of the Antarctic Treaty System's role regarding marine resources, it is advisable to consider also other developments, which have proved a significant part of the background to the creation of an Antarctic marine resources regime. These influences include the pressures in favour of exploitation, the impact of international environmental law and the activities of the conservation movement upon both a national and international basis.

International environmental law is relatively new, and its emergence during the 1970s was symbolised by the 1972 Stockholm Declaration of the UN Conference on the Human Environment[29]. Although this branch of the law is still in the process of development - some would argue that it is merely embryonic - it has been argued that certain broad environmental norms are relevant to Antarctica, thereby serving to qualify the authority of the Consultative Parties. For example, article 21 of the Stockholm Declaration states 'the responsibility to ensure that activities within their jurisdiction or control do not cause damage to the environment of other states or of areas beyond the limits of national jurisdiction', and this obligation can be taken to apply to Antarctica from the point of view of both claimants and others. Against this background, environmentalists have assumed a more visible role, particularly in respect to an attempt to prevent the exploitation of Antarctica, such as through the establishment of resource development moratoria or the advocacy of the world park concept for Antarctica. During 1972 a World Conference on National Parks held at Grand Teton National Park, Wyoming, passed a resolution in favour of 'the establishment of Antarctica as a World Park, under United Nations auspices'[30]. Keith Suter has pressed this view that Antarctica 'should be preserved as a natural wilderness' as part of his campaign for the internationalisation of the continent; thus, the Antarctic Treaty System should be replaced by a regime vesting control in the UN 'as a part of the common heritage of mankind'[31]. Therefore, a range of non-governmental organisations in various parts of the globe have performed an active role in the campaign to protect Antarctica from exploitation, since - to quote from the Friends of the Earth organisation based in New Zealand - 'there can be no justification for the exploitation of

Antarctica'[32]. Most environmental groups view the Consultative Parties with some suspicion, since they are depicted as being concerned to 'guard their assumed prerogatives over the region', to develop Antarctica's resource potential, and to be half-hearted about environmental protection[33]. For example, attempts have been made to identify the non-enforcement of the Agreed Measures, such as in regard to 'harmful interference' to the environment through the operation of base stations. Since 1982 the problems appertaining to the construction of a French airstrip near D'Urville base at Point Geologie in Adélie Land have given rise to an environmental cause célèbre on account of the damage caused to birds and other aspects[34]. The activities appeared to constitute a clear breach of the Agreed Measures, even if neither France nor the other Consultative Parties took any real notice of the arguments advanced on the subject by the environmental lobby. For example, the French government justified the airstrip in terms of article II of the Antarctic Treaty, which encouraged scientific research and activities designed to facilitate this work; thus, the airstrip was presented as an essential factor in the enhancement of French research.

Although certain Consultative Parties have proved sympathetic to the conservationist cause, there has been general irritation with the demands for an alternative regime or for such absolutes as no exploitation. These demands have been dismissed as lacking not only a grasp of political, economic and scientific realities but also confidence in the ability of the Antarctic Treaty System to manage any resource exploitation in a responsible manner. The implicit gulf existing between the environmental lobby on the one hand and the Antarctic Treaty System on the other hand has been refuted by the Consultative Parties, which have argued that, in the real world, environmental and exploitation interests need to be, and can be, synthesised. The parties have argued that environmental philosophies have underlain the operation of the treaty system under the encouragement of article IX's emphasis upon conservation, such as manifested by the Agreed Measures, the Sealing Convention and the various recommendations concerned with 'Man's Impact on the Antarctic Environment'. As a result, environmental impact assessment has become an essential part of the management function in spite of the difficulties caused by the dynamic nature of the environmental-development relationship[35]. To some extent, recommendation VIII-13 of 1975 highlighted these aspects, for it stressed the Consultative Parties' conception of 'their responsibility for the wise use and protection of the Antarctic environment' in conformity with 'the interests of mankind'. It was stipulated that no action liable to modify the Antarctic environment should be undertaken unless:

> Appropriate steps have been taken to foresee the probable modifications and to exercise appropriate controls with respect to the harmful environmental effects such uses of the Antarctic Treaty Area may have.

Any changes would be monitored upon a continuous basis, while the world community would be informed of any significant consequences arising from man's activities in Antarctica. At the same Consultative Meeting, another recommendation (VIII-11) reaffirmed this anxiety 'to minimise the impact of man on the Antarctic environment' through the implementation of a Code of Conduct for Antarctic expeditions and station activities, which had been drafted with the advice of SCAR. In turn, the Consultative Parties believe that 'their special responsibility for the protection of the environment' can be reconciled with 'the wise use of the Treaty Area' (recommendation X-8), and during the late 1970s the negotiation of the CCAMLR was designed to give substance to this assertion.

The Negotiation of CCAMLR

The 1975 Consultative Meeting's environmental preoccupations were complemented by its formal placement of the topic of Antarctic Marine Living Resources on the agenda, a step prompted by evidence of over-fishing in the early 1970s, by growing interest in krill harvesting and by memories of the over-exploitation of whales and seals in the past. In this context, recommendation VIII-10 recognised the need for action on marine resources and developed the informal mention of the topic at the 1972 Consultative Meeting. There was also a belief that, if the Antarctic Treaty System failed to deal with the management of marine resources, this might be regarded as an abrogation of responsibility, thereby tempting intervention by the international community, which was engaged already on the UNCLOS discussions[36]. As a result, the late 1970s witnessed a series of negotiations designed to establish an Antarctic marine resources regime; indeed, the perceived importance and urgency of the topic explains the rapid evolution of the project, which overtook the pre-existing discussions regarding a minerals regime. The continuing absence of a regime posed the danger that the Antarctic Treaty System might be overtaken by events, such as upon the part either of intervention by the international community or of over-exploitation of krill and other marine resources. The discussions were under-pinned by a meaningful scientific input from SCAR, especially as recommendation VIII-10 had identified the preliminary need for an enhancement of marine research in order to provide an informed foundation for the negotiations. In this respect, the most significant parallel development was the BIOMASS programme, which was focussed essentially upon the position of krill in the Antarctic ecosystem.

The first substantive moves were taken by the 1977 Consultative Meeting, which called for 'a definitive regime' for the conservation of Antarctic marine living resources to be concluded before the close of 1978 and provided a set of interim guidelines pending such an agreement (recommendation IX-2). Scientific considerations proved influential at an early stage, for such scientists as Laws, the director of BAS, convinced the Consultative Parties that the effective protection of the Antarctic ecosystem demanded a regime area bounded by the Antarctic Convergence rather than by the Antarctic Treaty area, which had been the initial intention. Laws established that the exploitation of krill would exert effects throughout the ecosystem, whose variable boundaries extended beyond 60°South, and consequently recommendation IX-2 stated that 'the regime should extend north of 60°South latitude where this is necessary for the effective conservation of species of the Antarctic ecosystem'. In this manner, the Consultative Parties accepted responsibility for the search for an ecosystem-based regime designed to regulate the use of marine living resources 'within the framework of the Antarctic Treaty' (recommendation VIII-10).

Recommendation IX-2 provided that the draft regime would be negotiated through the device of a Special Consultative Meeting, and this took the form of a series of formal and informal sessions, which began at Canberra in February 1978 and met also at Buenos Aires, Washington and Berne as well as at Canberra again (see Table 7.4)[37]. The sessions were attended by 13 Consultative Parties, since Poland achieved this status prior to the commencement of the negotiations; in fact, Poland's admission was influenced in part by the impending marine resources regime discussions on account of its research and fishing interest in this topic. The initial plan had been to complete the regime by the end of 1978, but a series of difficulties, such as over the terms and participation, hindered progress, so that at times the prospects for agreement looked bleak. During 1978-9 a series of informal sessions and diplomatic exchanges proved necessary to get the negotiations back on track again, and eventually a final session of the Special Consultative Meeting prepared the way for an international conference held at Canberra between 7-20 May 1980[38]. CCAMLR was signed on 20 May 1980[39].

The negotiations occurred in secret, and in a manner serving not only to preserve the dominant role of the Consultative Parties but also to insulate the negotiations from interference by the international community; thus, the draft conventions were neither published nor made available to the UN and other outside parties. No opportunity was made available for outsiders to make an input to the negotiations, although non-governmental organisations secured representation on the US delegation.

The Convention on the Conservation of Antarctic Marine Living Resources

A favoured descriptive terminology for recent Antarctic negotiations has proved that of the need for internal and external accommodations, since the requirement for consensus within the Antarctic Treaty System is paralleled by the need for international acceptance of the system. Internally, the interests of conservationist (*eg*. Australia, the UK and the USA) and of fishing (*eg*. Japan and the Soviet Union) nations had to be reconciled, such as demonstrated by CCAMLR's preamble emphasis upon 'the importance of safeguarding the environment and protecting the integrity of the ecosystem of the seas surrounding Antarctica' in the context of 'the increased interest in the possibilities offered by the utilisation of these resources'. This point was highlighted by article II (2); thus, 'for the purposes of this Convention, the term "conservation" includes rational use', which meant that any harvesting had to be in conformity with certain conservation principles including:

> Prevention of decrease in the size of any harvested population to levels below those which ensure its stable recruitment ... maintenance of the ecological relationships between harvested, dependent and related populations of Antarctic marine resources and the restoration of depleted populations ... prevention of changes or minimisation of the risk of changes in the marine ecosystem which are not potentially reversible over two or three decades.

This conservationist approach was emphasised by the coverage of the Antarctic marine ecosystem - 'the complex of relationships of Antarctic marine living resources with each other and with their physical environment' (article I (3)) - as well as by the extension of protection not only to an exploited resource but also to the marine species connected through the food chain. The stress upon the ecosystem was encouraged also by an appreciation of the problems associated with previous fisheries management schemes based upon target species and operated in ignorance of fishing's effects upon other species in the food chain. As a result, article I (1) utilised the Antarctic Convergence as the boundary for CCAMLR, even if this resulted in a variable line fluctuating between 45°South and 60°South (article I (4)).

Inevitably, the negotiations raised the usual sovereignty problems, a problem exacerbated by the manner in which the regime's area included sub-Antarctic islands - for instance,

South Georgia, Bouvet Island and Heard Island - outside of the Antarctic Treaty area. A further complication derived from the need to cover marine resources and yet to respect the Antarctic Treaty's exclusion of the high seas. Although the negotiators attempted to avoid legal controversy, the problem could not be glossed over, since questions of coastal state jurisdiction over marine resources for either conservation or fishing purposes drew attention to underlying sovereignty considerations. Progress upon this aspect was secured through what has been described as the "bi-focal" approach, which obscured the differing legal positions of the Consultative Parties. In a sense, this 'constructive ambiguity' represented merely another application of the drafting ingenuity characteristic of the Antarctic Treaty negotiations. Article IV of CCAMLR repeated the wording of article IV of the 1959 Treaty, but with the addition of a phrase referring to the right 'to exercise coastal state jurisdiction under international law within the area to which the convention applies' (article IV (2b)). This form of wording enables both claimants and non-claimants to interpret the same language differently, such as indicated by the bi-focal description. As a result, claimants can interpret the article's references to 'claims to territorial sovereignty' and 'coastal state jurisdiction' as constituting no threat to their Antarctic claims, whereas the position is acceptable also to non-claimants, which can take such phrases to refer to the sub-Antarctic islands included within the convention area and under the sovereignty of such governments as Australia, Norway or France. Wyndham, an Australian diplomat, has pointed out that 'this was the "bi-focal" approach. You interpret it in your way, and I interpret it in mine'[40]. Like article IV of the Antarctic Treaty, article IV of CCAMLR represented essentially a non-solution, based upon forebearance and intended to side-step legal controversy.

Nevertheless, at one stage, a sovereignty-related matter - the question of French rights over the marine resources of the Kerguelen and Crozet Islands - caused serious problems and negotiating delays, even if in reality it was relatively trivial in the context of the CCAMLR talks as a whole. The problem arose out of the extension of the convention area into the zone north of 60°South, and illustrated the dispute potential of Antarctic and sub-Antarctic sovereignty questions. Eventually, the matter was resolved though a statement inserted in the Final Act of the 1980 Canberra conference in order to recognise French jurisdiction over 'the waters adjacent to Kerguelen and Crozet'; in effect, the French government was allowed to choose which existing conservation measures would remain in force once CCAMLR came into force. Then:

> After the Convention has come into force, it would be open to France either to agree that the waters should be included in the area of application of any specific conservation measures under consideration or to indicate that they should be excluded.

This concession to French sensitivities on sovereignty also enabled the implementation of tighter controls over fishing around the islands, which were attracting exploitation already.

The growth of international interest in Antarctica meant that the position of the proposed regime in the international community was an important consideration, and focussed attention upon such issues as participation and the convention's relation to the Antarctic Treaty System. Once again, problems ensued, and the question of participation provided an additional cause of delay in the negotiations. The Consultative Parties aspired to universality for the proposed regime, and this led to an attempt to reconcile their prime responsibilities with the interests of all mankind, such as by treating their responsible management of the Antarctic environment as a kind of trust and by establishing an ability to deal with new problems within the framework of the Antarctic Treaty System[41]. Although the resulting convention would be a separate legal instrument and create new institutions independent of the Consultative Meetings, there was a conscious attempt to secure inter-connections between CCAMLR and the Antarctic Treaty, thereby reinforcing the treaty system, preserving the authority of the Consultative Parties, and contributing to 'the developing law of the Antarctic under the Antarctic Treaty as a basis'[42]. Therefore, the convention was drafted so that every signatory, whether or not an existing Antarctic treaty power, accepted through articles III-V 'the principles and purposes of that (Antarctic) Treaty' and agreed to be 'bound by the obligations contained in articles I and V of the Antarctic Treaty'. In effect, non-signatories of the Antarctic Treaty had to underwrite its basic principles and rules as the price of their involvement in CCAMLR. Article V of CCAMLR involves an explicit acknowledgement of 'the special obligations and responsibilities of the Antarctic Treaty Consultative Parties ... for the Antarctic Treaty area', since it was deemed desirable that newcomers should observe the existing Antarctic framework. Two British participants in the negotiations have written that:

> It is not unreasonable to expect states to adhere to a regime such as the Antarctic Treaty System in order to avoid serious irregularities from developing between themselves and those states which have bound themselves to it[43].

Like the Antarctic Treaty, CCAMLR established a two-stage process of involvement, that is, a first stage of accession by interested states (article XXIX), followed by a second stage of participation in decision-making by the contracting parties, which were defined as the participants at the 1980 Canberra Conference - this embraced the 13 existing Consultative Parties, plus East and West Germany - and other states 'engaged in research or harvesting activities in relation to marine living resources' (article VII (2)). This formula preserved the primacy of the Consultative Parties, while enabling the active involvement of outsiders becoming more interested in Antarctica. Such a status is open also to regional economic organisations, although this provision gave rise to negotiating difficulties, mainly on account of Soviet opposition. However, eventually the matter was resolved, since the EEC was responsible for the fishing policy of several Consultative Parties. Inevitably, the provisions for limited active participation, in conjunction with the secret and closed nature of the negotiations, prompted some critical comments, such as from Barnes:

> It is unclear on what basis the Parties felt they had the right to negotiate in secret a treaty regarding high seas resources and then to present the document for the rest of the world to endorse as a *fait accompli*[44].

Although certain outsiders were awarded observer status at the Canberra conference in May 1980 - these included the EEC, FAO and the International Whaling Commission - the Consultative Parties appeared guilty of assuming a somewhat arrogant attitude when dealing with a subject possessing significant implications for the wider world. As such, this debate raised the usual problem of securing external recognition for the work of the Antarctic Treaty System.

CCAMLR's objectives are to be secured through an institutional framework based upon a Commission for the Conservation of Antarctic Marine Living Resources and a Scientific Committee. Executive authority is vested in the Commission, which is an inter-governmental body composed of one representative from each of the Contracting Parties and of the acceding states engaged in marine research or harvesting (article VII (2)). Regional economic organisations acceding to CCAMLR are entitled to representation also. The Commission's functions are fairly broad, for it is instructed in article IX 'to give effect to the objectives and principles of this Convention', such as by the encouragement of research and data collection on marine resources or by the formulation, adoption and supervision of conservation measures. The list of functions excludes the allocation of catch totals in order to avoid sovereignty complications. The Commission's headquarters have been established at Hobart in Tasmania,

Australia, and it is required to meet annually, and additionally, as required. In most instances decisions will be taken by majority decision, but 'matters of substance' must secure consensus, such as like the procedure operated for Consultative Meetings (article XII). In turn, the Commission, lacking its own powers of enforcement, has to act through the convention's parties to implement decisions, except in the case of matters concerning non-parties, whose attention would be drawn to any activity undertaken by its nationals contrary to the objectives of CCAMLR (article X).

Obviously, much of the Commission's work will be related to scientific considerations, and this supportive role will be performed by a Scientific Committee, 'a consultative body to the Commission' (article XIV), based also at Hobart. Each member of the Commission is entitled to appoint a representative, although provision is made for the presence of other experts and for *ad hoc* advice. A range of functions are defined and are centred upon the committee's role as 'a forum for consultation and cooperation' concerning scientific data and information on aspects appertaining to conservation and exploitation. For example, it can formulate proposals for the guidance of national and international marine research, thereby qualifying the absence of its own research capability. Perhaps, the key functions relate to the transmission of reports and recommendations to the Commission either upon topics as requested or upon its own initiative.

A significant provision concerns the existence of an Executive Secretary and Secretariat (article XVII), since this represents an innovatory element within the Antarctic Treaty System. This institutional and administrative framework will be financed by a budget, which will be shared equally between the Commission members for 5 years, that is, until 1987, when account will be taken also of a member's harvesting levels (article XIX).

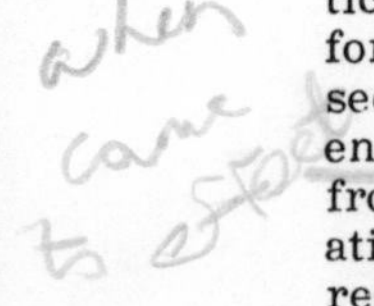
It is difficult to assess how the Convention, and particularly its institutional structure, will function in practice, for the regime is still in the process of development. Having secured the requisite number of ratifications, CCAMLR entered into force on 7 April 1982, that is, within five years from the time of the effective commencement of the negotiations[45]. In fact, the underlying desire to operate the regime as soon as possible meant that the signatories had met in Hobart during September 1981 in order to ensure the rapid creation of the institutional framework once the convention came into force. As a result, the first formal meeting of the signatories was held at Hobart between 25 May and 11 June 1982, and this enabled the establishment of the Commission and the associated administrative arrangements, such as the appointment of an Executive Secretary. Various procedural problems prevented the creation of the Scientific Committee, but an informal scientific session occurred between 7-10 June

at which a number of points were emphasised, including the need for a sound foundation of knowledge for resource management, the areas for marine research, suitable management goals, the role of ecosystem models and the value of a data base. In general, the regime meetings have concentrated so far upon procedural and information questions, including the actual establishment of the Scientific Committee after the difficulties experienced in 1982. Conservation groups have complained about the relative inactivity of the Commission in 1983 and 1984 regarding the setting of fishing quotas and moratoria, especially in the context of evidence about the over-exploitation of fin-fish[46].

These developments have given some substance to the criticisms directed at CCAMLR at the time of its signature, when Barnes attacked it as 'a flawed instrument', which was 'far from ideal'[47]. Obviously, conservationists were bound to express reservations about any agreement for the exploitation of Antarctica, but CCAMLR was criticised for its weaknesses in the sphere of conservation; thus, the need for consensus on important questions permitted fishing nations to thwart conservation measures, while this problem was accentuated by the system of flag-state enforcement, according to which measures were enforced by member states. For example, will a fishing nation implement conservation measures liable to hamper its harvesting activities? Will fishing nations, which will be paying a greater share of the budget after 1987, use their monetary power to influence the Commission's deliberations? Although CCAMLR was negotiated in a manner designed to reconcile fishing (eg. Japan and the Soviet Union) and conservationist (eg. Australia, New Zealand, the UK and the USA) nations, most commentators have tended to interpret it from one of the two viewpoints rather than as a total package. As a result, the possible clash of fishing and conservation interests has figured prominently in most appraisals, particularly as any problems may be aggravated by the lack of an obligatory disputes procedure. It is easy to identify such problems, but this point needs to be balanced against an appreciation of the way in which the Antarctic Treaty System has been characterised by the search for consensus between divergent viewpoints in the interests of a cooperative working relationship; thus, predictions of discord may prove both premature and unduly pessimistic.

The future development of the marine resources regime will depend upon a range of imponderables, such as the interaction of fishing and conservation interests or the contribution of marine research[48]. There is also the matter of CCAMLR's attractions to outsiders, especially in the light of the way in which the early 1980s witnessed a growing tendency to question the rights of the Consultative Parties to control Antarctica. Not every outsider has been impressed by the argument that CCAMLR represented the interests of all mankind, even if there has been an attempt by the parties to develop cooperative relations with appropriate bodies, such as demonstrated by the attendance of observers from FAO and the IWC, among other organisations, at the sessions of the Commission and Scientific Committee.

Conclusion

Lagoni has argued that 'the establishment of the Commission opened up a new era in the international relations concerning Antarctica', an opinion encouraged by the fact that the convention managed not only to accommodate varying attitudes within the Antarctic Treaty System but also to provide a meaningful point of contact between the system and the international community[49]. This wider significance has been emphasised by Zegers, who viewed CCAMLR as 'a vitally important political event and it has an effect on the Antarctic system itself and the problems associated with mineral resources'[50]. The convention partially filled the resource management gap left by the Antarctic Treaty, thereby demonstrating the treaty system's capacity to develop a regime designed to reconcile both exploitation and conservation interests (see Figure 7.2). Although environmental groups have proved critical on several aspects, CCAMLR should be interpreted as part of a continuing series of conservation measures - these have included the Agreed Measures and the Sealing Convention - intended to minimise man's impact on the fragile Antarctic environment. This aspect was highlighted by CCAMLR's ecosystem approach, which represented a unique and innovatory feature as compared to traditional fisheries management schemes[51]. Recently, Fox has remarked that 'it took twenty-one years before CCAMLR was ratified and brought into effect', a point which reflected rather unfavourably on the Antarctic Treaty System at work[52]. However, this comment proved both unfair and incorrect, for the convention came into effect within five years of the initiation of negotiations on account of not only of the perceived urgency of the problem but also of the vision of the Consultative Parties, which demanded action before marine stocks became seriously depleted.

The vision of the Antarctic powers, in conjunction with the example of a flexible and imaginative approach to the negotiations, has encouraged attempts to interpret CCAMLR as a significant achievement for the Antarctic Treaty System, thereby enhancing the prospects for the successful outcome of the Antarctic minerals regime negotiations. In addition, the convention has been viewed as a model instrument for the protection of ecosystems in other parts of the world, such as 'a model for the use of a common good ... for the conservation and utilization of living resources on the high seas'[53]. According to Lagoni:

> The Convention provides a sophisticated model of co-operation with agreed legal principles for the conservation and utilization of the living resources, and an inter-governmental body, which also may develop binding rules for the allocation of these resources for its members[54].

CCAMLR can be treated also as a regional fisheries agreement in conformity with the Law of the Sea Convention, and especially with such articles as 118 and 311. In 1984 the UN Study noted that:

> In accordance with modern international law, States have a duty to co-operate with each other in taking necessary measures for the conservation and management of living resources of the high seas. Those provisions of general international law were recently confirmed in the 1982 UNCLOS ... the various measures taken by the Consultative Parties for the conservation of Antarctic living resources have evidently aimed at fulfilling this goal ... The Convention can be characterised as a regional agreement for the conservation and management of the living resources. It fits neatly into this general requirement of international law. At the same time, the Convention differs from other fishery agreements[55].

From this perspective, CCAMLR has resolved the Antarctic part of a global problem, albeit in a unique manner appropriate to the nature of the Antarctic ecosystem as well as to international law. The convention allows for the participation of interested outsiders, whether governments or international organisations, and represents a measure capable of broadening and strengthening the Antarctic Treaty System through greater international recognition and involvement.

Although the living marine resource wealth of Antarctica remains of speculative value, the existence of CCAMLR confirms that resource issues have become an integral part not only of the operation of the treaty system but also of its future role in international politics. The convention may not be perfect, but it must be considered - to quote John Rowland, an Australian diplomat involved in its negotiation - 'better than nothing'[56]. In fact, it must be rated as far more significant than this from both the Antarctic and global points of view, especially as the convention possesses the capability to evolve in the light of changing circumstances, such as of fresh knowledge in the spheres of either the marine sciences or environmental impact. In the meantime, the flexibility characteristic of the Antarctic Treaty System appears the preferable future policy for CCAMLR. According to Vicuna:

> Pending science's answer and until such time as the development of these resources becomes a real possibility, the only thing which is clear is the need for a prudent and gradual policy which would be open to review and study. Neither paralysis nor rapid development would seem to be advisable at this point[57].

In turn, this advice would appear relevant to the on-going negotiations designed to establish an Antarctic minerals regime in parallel to the marine resources institutional framework.

NOTES

1. _Sunday Times_, 13 Feb.1983.
2. Bruce Russett, 'Security and the Resources Scramble: Will 1984 be like 1914?', _International Affairs_, vol.58, no.1 (1981-2), p.42, p.57; Peterson, _Antarctica: the last great land rush on earth_, p.377.
3. Foreign and Commonwealth Office Background Brief, _World Fisheries_ (FCO, London, 1984), pp.1-2.
4. UNGA A/C 1/38 PV 44, p.12, 28 Nov.1983, Kuroda.
5. Quoted in, Ian Cameron, _Antarctica: the Last Continent_ (Little Brown, Boston, 1974), p.33.
6. It was not until the 1890s that any real interest was shown in the offshore resources of the Kerguelen Islands.
7. Beck, _Secret Antarctic Treaty Preparatory Negotiations_; Sollie, _Jurisdictional Problems in Relation to Antarctic mineral resources_, p.318; Myhre, _The Antarctic Treaty Consultative Meetings 1961-68_, pp.111 _et seq_.
8. Fernando Zegers, 'The Canberra Convention: objectives and political aspects of its negotiation', in Vicuna, _Antarctic Resources Policy_, p.149.
9. Llano, _Ecology of the Southern Ocean Region_, pp.358-9; Inigo Everson, _The Living Resources of the Southern Ocean_ (FAO, Rome, 1977); Richard Laws, 'Antarctica: A Convergence of Life', _New Scientist_, 1 Sept.1983, pp.608-16; Knox, _Living Resources of the Southern Ocean_, pp.28-34.
10. Everson, _The Living Resources of the Southern Ocean_, pp.129-37; Shackleton, _Falkland Islands. Economic Study 1982_, p.78.
11. UNGA A/39/583 (Part II), 1984, vol.1, p.58, 31 July 1984, Australian response.
12. Krill catch: 1973-4 22,343 tons; 1979-80 477,025 tons; 1981-2 529,505 tons (based on FAO figures).
13. Knox, _Living Resources of the Southern Ocean_, p.33, p.53; Nagata, _The Implementation of CCAMLR_, p.125; Zumberge, _Potential Mineral Resources Available_, p.121.
14. Knox, _Living Resources of the Southern Ocean_, p.32.

15. D.L. Powell, 'Scientific and economic considerations relating to the conservation of marine living resources in Antarctica', in Vicuna, Antarctic Resources Policy, p.114.
16. Nagata, The Implementation of CCAMLR, p.126.
17. Quigg, A Pole Apart, pp.85-7.
18. Everson, The Living Resources of the Southern Ocean, p.1.
19. Llano, Ecology of the Southern Ocean Region, pp.361-2.
20. Knox, Living Resources of the Southern Ocean, pp.38-9; Sahrhage, Present Knowledge of Living Marine Resources in the Antarctic, pp.76-80.
21. Sahrhage, Present Knowledge of Living Marine Resources in the Antarctic, p.80.
22. Beck, Securing the Dominant Place in the Wan Antarctic Sun, pp.453-6.
23. Patricia W. Birnie, 'International Protection of Whales', in Yearbook of World Affairs 1983 (Stevens, London, 1983), pp. 248-61; G.P. Donovan, 'Thirty-Sixth Annual Meeting of the International Whaling Commission, June 1984', Polar Record, vol.22, no.139 (1985), pp.421-5.
24. Llano, Ecology of the Southern Ocean Region, pp.365-6.
25. Lovering and Prescott, Last of Lands, pp.37-40; Knox, Living Resources of the Southern Ocean, p.40.
26. Bilder, Present Legal and Political Situation in Antarctica, pp.175-80.
27. Auburn, The Antarctic Environment, pp.252-62; Boleslaw A. Boczek, 'The Protection of the Antarctic Ecosystem: A Study in International Environmental Law', Ocean Development and International Law Journal, vol.13, no.3 (1983), pp.367-72.
28. Boczek, Protection of the Antarctic Ecosystem, pp.371-2. See recommendation XII-5 of 1983.
29. Bilder, Present Legal and Political Situation in Antarctica, pp.193-6; Boczek, Protection of the Antarctic Ecosystem, pp.388-9.
30. Greenpeace International, The Future of the Antarctic: Background for a Second UN Debate (Greenpeace, Lewes, 1984), appendix 7.
31. K.D. Suter, World Law and the Last Wilderness (Friends of the Earth, Sydney, 1979), p.48.
32. Quoted in, Barney Brewster, Antarctica: Wilderness at Risk (Reed, Wellington, 1982), p.ix.
33. James N. Barnes, Let's Save Antarctica (Greenhouse, Richmond, Australia, 1982), pp.9-20; J. Barnes, 'Non-governmental Organizations: increasing the global perspective', Marine Policy, vol.8, no.2 (1984), pp.171-85.
34. Greenpeace International, The Future of the Antarctic, pp.10-12.

35. M.W. Holdgate, 'Environmental Factors in the development of Antarctica', in Vicuna, Antarctic Resources Policy, pp.86-98. See recommendations VI-4, VII-1, VIII-11, IX-5, X-4-6 and XII-4.

36. Roberts, International Cooperation for Antarctic Development, pp.113-5.

37. James N. Barnes, 'The Emerging Convention on the Conservation of Antarctic Marine Living Resources: An Attempt to Meet the New Realities of Resource Exploitation in the Southern Ocean', in Charney, The New Nationalism and the Use of Common Spaces, pp.247-55, pp.281-2.

38. Ibid.; Wyndham, quoted in Wolfrum, Antarctic Challenge, p.118; John Rowland, quoted in Harris, Australia's Antarctic Policy Options, p.357.

39. Antarctic Treaty: Handbook, pp.9501-15; Ronald F. Frank, 'The Convention on the Conservation of Antarctic Marine Living Resources', Ocean Development and International Law Journal, vol.13, no.3 (1983), pp.300-12.

40. Wyndham, quoted in Wolfrum, Antarctic Challenge, p.115.

41. Scully, Alternatives for Cooperation and Institutionalization in Antarctica, pp.286-91; Rainer Lagoni, 'Convention on the Conservation of Marine Living Resources: A Model for the Use of a Common Good' in Wolfrum, Antarctic Challenge, pp.105-8.

42. Wyndham, quoted in Wolfrum, Antarctic Challenge, p.118; Francisco Orrego Vicuna, 'The definition of a regime on Antarctic mineral resources', in Vicuna, Antarctic Resources Policy, p.211.

43. David M. Edwards and John A. Heap, 'Convention on the Conservation of Antarctic Marine Living Resources: A Commentary', Polar Record, vol.20, no.127 (1981), p.360.

44. Barnes, The Emerging CCAMLR, p.247.

45. By June 1984 CCAMLR had been ratified by all of the original twelve Consultative Parties, plus Poland, West Germany and East Germany, that is, the 15 governments represented at Canberra. Accessions came from the EEC, Spain and Sweden.

46. See Eco, vol.XXV, nos.1-3 (1983); Eco, vol.XXIX, nos.1-3 (1984)

47. Barnes, The Emerging CCAMLR, p.260, p.268.

48. Josyane Couratier, 'The Regime for the Conservation of Antarctica's living resources', in Vicuna, Antarctic Resource Policy, pp.147-8.

49. Lagoni, Convention on the Conservation of Marine Living Resources, p.104.

50. Zegers, The Canberra Convention, p.151.

51. UNGA A/39/583 (Part I), 1984, pp.58-9.

52. Fox, Antarctica and the South Atlantic, p.173.

53. Lagoni, Convention on the Conservation of Marine Living Resources, p.105.

54. Ibid. p.107.
55. UNGA A/39/583 (Part I), 1984, p.54, p.58.
56. Rowland, quoted in Harris, Australia's Antarctic Policy Options, p.357.
57. Vicuna, Antarctic Resources Policy, p.4.

Chapter Ten

THE ANTARCTIC TREATY: A CONTINENT IN SEARCH OF A MINERALS REGIME

On their return journey from the South Pole in 1912 Captain Scott and his companions continued to perform scientific observations and work, and on 8 February one of his party, Edward Wilson, made the following diary entry:

> Camped under ... cliffs of Mount Buckley .. coal seams at all heights in the sandstone cliffs and lumps of weathered coal with fossils ...As we travelled along the cliff on the 9th. we saw one or two seams of ... really black coal[1].

Although Huntford criticised Scott for 'grotesque misjudgement' in stopping to collect geological samples - 'geology cost him six or seven miles, and when time was against him' - this episode at Mount Buckley does possess a contemporary significance for the manner in which it illuminates not only the inter-connection of exploration, research and mineral resources but also the long-running debate about the mineral wealth of Antarctica[2].

The Emergence of the Minerals Question

Many of the early explorers reported mineral occurrences, such as in the above-mentioned example concerning coal, and their evidence has provided a basis for the claim that Antarctica should be regarded as a major source for minerals. Over the years the focus of attention has changed; for example, during the late 1940s uranium proved a major source of speculation, whereas more recently oil and natural gas have moved to the forefront. To some extent, this supposed mineral potential has proved the root cause of international interest in Antarctica, and there is general agreement that the minerals question constitutes the most significant issue confronting the Antarctic Treaty System. In turn, it is suggested that the ability to resolve this problem provides the key test for the system's survival.

During the 1970s the Consultative Parties realised that increased interest in the exploration and exploitation of Antarctic minerals was stimulating pressures both within and outside the treaty system, thereby introducing another factor into the international politics and law of Antarctica at a period of debate about the international acceptability of the existing treaty arrangements. From this perspective, the political and legal implications of the question became interpreted as a threat to stability, perhaps even to the survival of the Antarctic Treaty, although the Consultative Parties believed that the issue could be settled within its framework, and in a manner consolidating - some say, completing - the treaty system, such as through the creation of an institutional framework for mineral resources to complement the Marine Living Resources regime established already by CCAMLR.

The Prospect for Minerals in Antarctica

Over the years many reports have been filed regarding the occurrence of minerals in Antarctica. The list is long, and includes iron in the Prince Charles Mountains, titanium, copper, uranium, gold, coal and graphite in East Antarctica, tin, copper, lead, zinc, molybdenum and coal in the Transantarctic Mountains, and molybdenum, copper, silver, gold, zinc, iron, nickel, cobalt, and chromium in the Antarctic Peninsula[3]. On paper, this listing looks impressive - this impression has been accentuated by the frequent reproduction of maps indicating the location of such occurrences - but in reality the whole issue is clouded in doubt, since an occurrence represents merely a trace rather than evidence of the existence of a deposit worthy and capable of exploitation. There are a few exceptions, since the coal found in the Transantarctic Mountains is known to be part of a substantial deposit, which amounts possibly to the world's largest coal reserve. However, an informed discussion about most occurrences is handicapped by a lack of knowledge, especially as the ice sheet hinders an effective understanding of Antarctic geology. The early random sightings of minerals by such explorers as Scott and Mawson have been followed by a more substantial and systematic scientific effort, which has provided an improved, albeit still imperfect, appreciation of Antarctica's geological framework, including its tectonic-stratigraphical correlation with other continents as part of the former super-continent of Gondwanaland. In fact, the implied links with other mineral-bearing continents has reinforced the impact of the reported mineral occurrences, thereby stimulating speculation also about offshore resources, such as oil and natural gas, as well as about manganese nodules - these may contain copper and nickel - on the deep ocean floor.

Each year brings additional increments of information on the geology of the Antarctic continent and offshore areas, even if - to quote, Tore Gjelsvik -

> The geological research on the continent has so far provided little evidence to support the overoptimistic notion of tremendous riches in Antarctica, so often presented in newspapers[4].

In fact, a realistic appreciation of the current position requires a reference to the process of mineral exploitation, which can be divided into four main stages, subject to the usual proviso concerning the fact that each stage cannot always be clearly defined[5]. The first stage involves research of an exploratory character designed to survey the geological structures of a large area for scientific purposes, even if the results facilitate also an assessment of resource possibilities, thereby leading into the next stage of commercial exploration of the more promising structures. The discovery of actual deposits provides the basis for the third stage of exploratory drilling intended to determine the existence, quantity and quality of specific deposits. Finally, commercial exploitation occurs of deposits, which are suitable also from technological, economic and other viewpoints. It appears that the negotiating text utilised for the Antarctic minerals regime discussions is based upon a three-stage variant of this classification, namely, prospecting, exploration and exploitation.

The past decade or so has witnessed a surge of geological and geophysical research in Antarctica, such as through aeromagnetic and seismic surveys, but the primary role of this work has been directed towards the determination of the broad picture of Antarctic geology rather than towards the identification of mineral deposits. As a result, Antarctica tends to be at the first stage of the exploitation process, although in certain areas, including the Ross and Weddell Seas, activity might be described as being of a second stage character. In addition, each stage imposes its own technical and fiscal demands, and in general it proves more expensive and time-consuming to pass through any stage as compared to its predecessor. Antarctica poses its own special problems, and it has been suggested that the costs and duration of each stage there will be up to five and ten times greater as compared to other parts of the world[6].

Although surveys have been conducted in East Antarctica by Australia, France and the Soviet Union, the relatively wide, shallow and accessible continental shelf of West Antarctica has been treated as the better hydrocarbon prospect, such as evidenced by American, Japanese, Norwegian, Soviet and West German work in the Amundsen-Bellingshausen, Ross and Weddell Sea areas[7]. These studies of the continental margins have established the presence of several sedimentary basins, which are an important precondition for hydrocarbons, although further investigation is required before an informed evaluation of the resource prospects becomes possible[8]. Two members of the Soviet department of Antarctic Geology and Mineral Resources have stressed this point:

> Only very preliminary answers to these questions can be given at present due to the reconnaisance state of Antarctic geologic exploration and, in particular, meagre evidence directly related to mineral occurrences[9].

It is reasonable to assume that minerals exist in and around Antarctica, such as in the light of mineral occurrences, scientific research and the Gondwanaland hypothesis, even if current discussions on the subject are qualified by the low state of knowledge, so that 'the geologists are chewing on the same scanty information over and over again'[10]. As a result, one can neither assume that exploitable minerals exist nor assert that they do not exist. In the context of the existing preoccupation with oil and natural gas, it is worth stressing that no exploitable deposits have been found yet of either resource, but this has failed to diminish optimism regarding their eventual discovery, especially as the oft-quoted US Geological Survey Report of 1974 has inspired educated and speculative estimates. This report referred to a possible yield from Antarctica of 45 billion barrels of oil and 115 trillion cubic feet of natural gas, but these figures represented merely statistical estimates underlain by minimal exploration information[11]. In the event, these figures acquired unjustified credibility through repetition, partly because of the appeal of such vast amounts and partly because of the promise of recent drillings by the USS Glomar Challenger, whose drillings in the Ross and Weddell Seas as part of the US Deep Sea Drilling Project indicated traces of gas, ethane and ethylene and implied a hydrocarbons potential[12]. Speculation has continued, and in February 1979 a representative of Gulf Oil suggested that the oil potential of the Ross and Weddell Seas should be at least 50 billion barrels[13].

However, the geological promise of Antarctica in regard to minerals is qualified by a series of other factors, which mean that, even if deposits exist, there is no guarantee of exploitation. On land, the existence and depth of the ice sheet constitutes a severe obstacle to mining, along with other influences, such as the climate, distance from markets, lack of infrastructure, high energy, transport and personnel costs, and technological considerations. As a result, the extensive coal deposits of the Transantarctic Mountains possess no economic value, especially as their relatively low grade and the availability of coal in more accessible parts of the world compound the deterrent effect of Antarctic conditions. Similarly, a range of geographical, economic, technological, environmental and other factors hinder offshore exploitation. For example, drilling platforms and oil tankers will have to cope with difficulties arising from the presence of pack ice and ice bergs as well as from the depth of water, while the water temperatures may expose the limitations of divers in supporting such offshore operations[14]. Although smaller icebergs can be towed or nudged away by ships and others split by explosives, drills will need to be capable of dis-engagement to deal with large bergs. However, it is believed that the special technological demands of Antarctica can be met, particularly in the context of developments in the North Sea and the Arctic[15]. Unless it proves feasible to exploit any minerals, Antarctic will possess no real resource value, and inevitably optimistic estimates have been countered by the relative pessimism of many experts, such as Zumberge.

> All who have dealt with this matter have come to the same conclusion: no mineral deposits likely to be of economic value in the foreseeable future are known in Antarctica.
> This statement is not to say that Antarctica has no mineral resources, but rather, if they exist, they have no economic significance today or in the near-term future[16].

In this context, it is difficult to quantify the extent of commercial interest in Antarctic minerals. On the one hand, there is evidence of prospecting applications submitted to the New Zealand, UK and US governments, and recently Luard, having pointed to enhanced research activity in the earth sciences and mentioned such companies as British Petroleum (BP), argued that 'all this activity would not be taking place in the absence of a real possibility of major oil and gas finds'[17]. Barbara Mitchell's recent book cited the interest of the Gulf and Exxon companies in the region, and claimed that 'B.P. is watching Antarctic developments closely'[18]. On the other hand, the oil companies have displayed little public interest in Antarctica, and have proved evasive about the nature and extent of their interest, if any. But it must be presumed that most oil companies are fully conscious and informed of Antarctic developments, and are keeping open their options there, while pursuing exploration in more accessible areas. Barnes' contacts with such companies prompted two conclusions:

> The first is that the Antarctic is just about the last place on earth that they ever want to go to exploit minerals of any sort. For all sorts of reasons, but one

> of them is cost. And second, they don't really want to volunteer to close off any options[19].

Heap, a British diplomat, has specifically denied the Luard-type assertion, for:

> British oil companies do not view the prospects of Antarctic oil as anything more than speculative, as indeed are the prospects in all sorts of other areas on which they, nevertheless, keep a watching eye[20].

This 'watching eye' seems to have developed into something more substantial than the situation implied by Heap, since papers delivered by BP staff indicate an informed and interested attitude towards Antartic minerals. For example, a paper presented by T.J. Sanderson of BP Petroleum Development (Overseas) to the Pacific Science Congress at Dunedin in 1983 displayed a clear grasp of both the problems and the potential.

> In the Ross Sea the iceberg risk and the great water depth mean that the existing technology must be extrapolated by a factor of about 10 (as compared to Alaska) ... this could be achieved, though not easily or cheaply.
> It is not yet known what reserves, if any, exist in Antarctica. For production to be economic, they would have to be huge, and alternative less hostile sources scarce ... No exploratory wells have yet been drilled[21].

Sanderson pointed out also the environmental constraints:

> The Antarctic is a sensitive area environmentally. It is likely that standards for safety and pollution would be even higher than the already high standards applying in the Arctic. Such standards, which might for instance involve even deeper pipeline burial, are expensive to achieve[22].

In this manner, the economic viability of any minerals might be undermined by environmental factors, such as an appreciation of the consequences of oil spillages and blowouts as well as of man's sketchy knowledge of environmental impact questions. In any case, the Consultative Parties' emphasis upon their conservation responsibilities, which led to Antarctica's designation as a 'Special Conservation Area' by the Agreed Measures, introduces a further cause for caution in any discussion of mineral wealth, especially as the environmental organisations have proved active as pressure groups during Antarctic resource discussions[23].

According to Zumberge, 'it is self-evident that for Antarctica one can only speak in terms of speculative mineral resources'[24]. In the short-term, Antarctica's mineral resource value is minimal, while a variety of economic, technical, environmental and other factors, in conjunction with alternative stocks in other parts of the world, mean that even the long-term prospects are of a dubious nature[25]. Obviously, the situation might change on account of either a major resource find in Antarctica - for instance, of oil or of a high-value metal - or of external pressures, such as of another 1973-type oil crisis. In certain circumstances, the impact of international political considerations might over-ride constraining factors, and result in a 'political grab for control of real or metaphysical resources in Antarctica'[26]. This policy is more likely to characterise a nation lacking its own assured supplies of oil, such as Japan. In the meantime, interest and speculation about minerals will prove an enduring feature of the Antarctic scene, since the uncertainties appear to be incapable of preventing international perceptions of the continent's treasure trove qualities, particularly as the attempt to create an Antarctic minerals regime has fuelled discussion on the subject.

Towards the Minerals Regime Negotiations

The CCAMLR episode highlighted the fact that the Antarctic Treaty provided neither machinery nor rules for the regulation of resource exploitation, even if the Antarctic Treaty System served to provide a linking framework within which to deal with such topics as the management of marine living resources. At present, negotiations are proceeding to establish an Antarctic minerals regime designed not only to manage mineral exploration and exploitation in a responsible manner but also to fill the perceived treaty gap on this topic. In the event, there were different schools of thought on this subject, since some believed that mineral exploitation was inconsistent with the treaty's emphasis upon the cause of science and the protection of the environment, whereas others interpreted exploitation as a 'peaceful purpose' permitted by article I of the treaty.

Several observers have criticised the search for a minerals regime on the grounds that Antarctica's resource prospects provide no cause for urgency, and the fact that the Consultative Parties have pursued the subject in a determined manner during the early 1980s has fostered comment to the effect that perhaps the prospects were much better than indicated in their public pronouncements. However, the Consultative Parties were aware of other pressures to move forward on this matter, and these included the enhanced international interest in Antarctic minerals, the receipt of prospecting applications and the anxieties of environmental organisations. In any case, the Consultative Parties believed that one of the key qualities of the Antarctic Treaty System derives from an ability to deal with topics in advance of actual difficulties through 'an exercise in prudent forethought'[27]. It was realised that an agreed minerals regime would be easier to conclude before any minerals were discovered in exploitable quantities, thereby raising the political stakes in the discussions and perhaps even encouraging unilateral rather than multilateral action. Inaction might encourage criticism of the treaty system's capacity to manage the continent, while also leaving a political and legal vacuum which might be filled by an alternative management scheme linked to an outside body like the UN. This neurotic fear was accentuated by the activities of the UNCLOS discussions as well as by the emerging critique of the Antarctic Treaty System.

The right to exploit and control resources has proved an integral part of the concept of national sovereignty, and the sovereignty implications of the minerals question were partly responsible for the evasion of the issue during both the treaty negotiations and the early Consultative Meetings. The finite and non-renewable nature of minerals imparted an extra edge to this aspect as compared to living marine resources, and not surprisingly in 1970, when New Zealand and the UK made the first attempt to raise the subject of minerals at a Consultative Meeting, the mere mention of the topic evoked 'a horrified silence' upon the part of the other delegations, even if a member of the American State department regarded it as a 'most important' item[28]. However, a sense of Antarctic realities persuaded most Consultative Parties that action was required, and gave them 'the courage to think about the unthinkable'[29].

The first serious discussion occurred at the 1972 Consultative Meeting held in Wellington, and this resulted in recommendation VII-6 in order to identify the need for careful study of the topic of mineral resources in the context of both the 'protection of the environment' and 'the wise use of resources'; in fact, the latter phrase served not only to imply development but also to prompt concern about a possible conflict with the environmental objective[30]. As a result, 'Antarctic Mineral Resources' now became a regular agenda topic at Consultative Meetings, and a series of recommendations - VIII-14 (1975), IX-1 (1977), X-1 (1979) and XI-1 (1981) - clarified the thinking of the Consultative Parties on the subject, reflected the softening of divergent viewpoints, stressed the need for collective action, and established not only a series of principles intended to define the framework of 'a regime for Antarctic mineral resources' but also the usual interim guidelines pending a definitive agreement. These moves were justified in terms of the provisions of the Antarctic Treaty regarding the creation of 'a regime for international cooperation', and implicitly of articles I and IX, which encouraged actions of a 'peaceful' nature and 'in furtherance of the principles and objectives of the Treaty'. In addition, these developments were supported and reinforced by a continuing specialist input upon scientific, environmental and related matters, such as from SCAR, including its geology working group, and from informal meetings of experts, such as that held at the Nansen Foundation in May-June 1973[31].

The 1975 Consultative Meeting proposed that the matter should be proceeded with through the convention of a special preparatory meeting on mineral resources and the establishment of a SCAR-based group to advise on relevant scientific programmes and environmental impacts (recommendation VIII-14). Between 28 June and 10 July 1976 the special preparatory meeting assembled in Paris, and enunciated four basic principles for the proposed regime, that is:

> The Consultative Parties will continue to play an active and responsible role ... the Antarctic Treaty must be maintained in its entirety ... protection of the unique Antarctic environment and of its dependent ecosystems should be a basic consideration ... the Consultative Parties ... should not prejudice the interests of all mankind in Antarctica.

In the meantime, a SCAR group of experts on the Environmental Impact Assessment of Mineral Resource Exploration and Exploitation in Antarctica (EAMREA group) met under the chairmanship of Dr. Martin Holdgate (UK) in September 1977 to provide guidance on environmental, scientific and technical aspects related to the exploitation of minerals[32]. Against this background, the 1977 Consultative Meeting produced recommendation IX-1, which endorsed the four principles from the Paris meeting, noted the EAMREA report and the need to continue such expert discussions, urged a moratorium on the exploration and exploitation of minerals until an agreed regime was adopted, and stressed 'that the provisions of article IV of the Antarctic Treaty shall not be affected by the regime'.

In this manner, the Consultative Parties accepted the need for a regime, thereby indicating that even the Soviet government - this was reputed to possess reservations on the case for a regime, allegedly for environmental reasons but reportedly because of its technological deficiencies to take advantage of a regime - accepted the general view. This meeting was followed by 'intensified consultation' between the Consultative Parties within and outside the Consultative Meetings, and was paralleled by expert scientific discussions, which offered yet another excellent example of the interchange of political and scientific perspectives within the Antarctic Treaty System. During March 1979 the environmental implications - for instance, the hazards of oil spills -

were debated at a workshop in Bellagio, while between 25-29 June 1979 another group of experts, as provided for in recommendation IX-1, assembled at Washington 'as part of the Preparatory Meeting to the Tenth Consultative Meeting' to draft guidelines for the 1979 Consultative Meeting upon such aspects as minimising environmental impacts[33]. This expert report provided the foundation for the 1979 Consultative Meeting, which pressed for 'the early conclusion and entry into force' of the Marine Living Resources regime (recommendation X-2) at the same time as it recognised 'the importance ... (and) the necessity for progress towards the timely adoption of an agreed regime concerning Antarctic mineral resources' (recommendation X-1). Consultations would continue 'to develop a common understanding of the general purposes of the regime and to identify the specific elements of the regime needed to ensure achievement of those purposes', while, in line with the expert advice, it was stipulated that there should be provision for the assessment of environmental impacts and of the acceptability of mineral resource activities. Further research was encouraged on such matters through SCAR and national Antarctic committees, and in 1980 a new group of specialists on Antarctic Environmental Implications of Possible Mineral Exploration and Exploitation (AEIMEE) was founded to advise SCAR, such as demonstrated by its report on petroleum and environmental hazards.

In 1977 recommendation IX-1's mention of article IV of the Antarctic Treaty drew attention to the politico-legal aspects of the topic, and the 1979 Consultative Meeting benefitted also from the work of another working group, chaired by Norman Wulf (USA), which concluded that a regime should be able to accommodate the varying positions of the Consultative Parties on sovereignty. In some respects, this provided one of the key obstacles to agreement, but there existed a confident belief that any difficulties could be surmounted, a view accentuated by the steady progress of the marine resources regime negotiations.

By 1979 formal and informal discussions had been proceeding for nearly a decade, albeit with no sense of urgency for most of the 1970s, such as evidenced by the way in which the marine regime question acquired greater priority circa 1976-7 and in effect overtook the minerals talks. But by 1979-80 the search for a minerals regime assumed a more urgent character, and the 1979 Consultative Meeting's anxiety for progress resulted in the call for a special meeting on the subject in 1980. This acceleration was encouraged by a range of factors, including growing international interest in Antarctic minerals, and was facilitated in 1980 by the conclusion of the CCAMLR negotiations. A special meeting held at Washington in December 1980 proved both a cause and effect of this new sense of purpose and urgency on minerals, and here the Consultative Parties displayed a readiness to discuss the actual form of the regime, thereby highlighting points of difficulty[34]. Busby (USA), the chairman, reminded the other parties of the need not only for internal accommodation between the Consultative Parties but also for external accommodation between them and the international community, and subsequently these phrases became essential constituents of any discussion on the Antarctic Treaty System[35].

Against this background of informed and detailed discussion at both the political and scientific levels, the 1981 Consultative Meeting held at Buenos Aires felt able to refine and codify the existing points of agreement as the foundation for the convention of a Special Consultative Meeting designed to draft a minerals regime and bring the negotiations to a conclusion (recommendation XI-1). This procedure was based upon the precedent of the method employed for the successful CCAMLR discussions. The Consultative Parties agreed that 'a regime on Antarctic mineral resources should be concluded as a matter of urgency' and should be based upon the five previously-agreed principles, that is, the four points emerging from the Paris meeting in 1976 plus the safeguard for article IV introduced in recommendation IX-1. This ensured that the regime would serve to preserve not only the primacy of the Consultative Parties but also the significance of the Antarctic Treaty System, such as on account of a belief that this approach would be beneficial for the Antarctic environment as well as for the interests of all mankind. The sovereignty question loomed large in the forthcoming negotiations, and recommendation XI-1 included a lengthy elaboration to clarify the nature of the difficulty.

> Any agreement that may be reached on a regime for mineral exploration and exploitation in Antarctica elaborated by the Consultative Parties should be acceptable and be without prejudice to those States which have previously asserted rights of or claims to territorial sovereignty in Antarctica as well as to those States which neither recognize such rights of or claims to territorial sovereignty in Antarctica nor, under the provisions of the Antarctic Treaty, assert such rights or claims.

Environmental aspects were identified as another priority area, which would be considered in the light of the reports of experts and of SCAR's definition of relevant research programmes.

The Consultative Parties were particularly aware of the external pressures upon the treaty system, and of the resulting need for international acceptability of a regime, which should be designed not only to enable the adherence of other governments, albeit 'bound by the basic provisions of the Antarctic Treaty and by the relevant Recommendations adopted by the Consultative Parties' (recommendation XI-1), but also to include 'provisions for cooperative arrangements between the regime and other relevant international organizations' The relevance of the international political context was reaffirmed by the recommendation's reference to the ongoing UNCLOS discussions - the Consultative Parties admitted that they were 'mindful of the negotiations that are taking place in the Third United Nations Conference on the Law of the Sea' - and this caused the assertion that the area of the regime's application should be confined to the Antarctic continent and its adjacent offshore areas 'but without encroachment on the deep seabed'.

The development of the Consultative Parties' discussions during the period 1975-81 had been distinguished by an evolving pattern in respect to the employment of words and phrases, such as evidenced by the gradual move towards resource-related expressions or by elaboration of the mode of external accommodation. In turn, the 1981 Consultative Meeting marked the culmination of what might be described as the preparatory stage of the Antarctic minerals regime negotiations, that is, a stage designed to identify goals and principles for the draft agreement to be drawn up by the Fourth Special Consultative Meeting. Obviously, many question marks remained, but the Consultative Parties were now on course towards a minerals regime in order to complement the recently-agreed Marine Resources regime and to 'further strengthen the Antarctic Treaty framework' (recommendation XI-1). Although expert advice indicated that exploitation was not imminent, a series of pressures from within and outside the treaty system had combined to impart a sense of urgency to the topic. The various external pressures fostered an enhanced appreciation of the international political ramifications of the discussions, even if the Consultative Parties opted predictably for a limited multilateral approach within the parameters of the Antarctic Treaty System rather than for an alternative method based upon a more universalist strategy[36]. The choice of this limited scheme tended, however, to place greater pressure upon the Consultative Parties for internal accommodation, that is, to reconcile divergent national positions as one method of presenting a united front _vis à vis_ the international community.

A Voluntary Moratorium

Pending the conclusion of an agreed regime, the Consulative Parties accepted a series of interim guidelines on minerals, including a voluntary moratorium on exploration and exploitation; thus, the parties agreed to urge their nationals, as well as those from outsiders, to refrain from such activities (recommendation IX-1). This voluntary restraint lacked the force of an injunction, but evidence has been advanced that the Consultative Parties have implemented this recommendation as policy, such as the reported refusal by the US government in July 1978 of Gulf Oil's request to undertake seismic studies in Antarctica. However, certain commentators have cast doubt regarding the alleged forebearance of the Consultative Parties, since some have been accused of exploring for minerals under the guise of scientific research. On the surface, such activities have been interpreted as a clear example of the type of scientific work actively encouraged by the Antarctic Treaty, whereas in reality the research was in contravention of the moratorium applied through recommendation IX-1. For example, since 1980 the Japanese National Oil Corporation's vessel, the Hakurei Maru, has been working in the Ross Sea, and, in the face of accusations that the ship was engaged in an oil survey project, the Japanese government responded that it was a scientific survey in conformity with both the treaty and recommendations[37]. Other parties, including France, the Soviet Union and West Germany, have faced similar criticism, and the problem re-emerged in 1984 when the USS S.P. Lee's proposed geophysical drilling work in Antarctica as part of the US Geological Survey's Operation Deep Sweep encountered comments that the work was concerned more with oil exploration than with the cause of science[38].

In many respects, these controversies have proved as much a function of the vagueness of the boundary between scientific research and resource exploration as of resource-related pressures; indeed, a previous chapter highlighted the difficulty, if not the impossibility, of defining such a boundary. This problem seems likely to persist, since many nations involved in Antarctic have moved increasingly towards applied, even resource-related research, partly under domestic fiscal pressures to show a real return on funding - politicians have not generally regarded scientific data as a 'real return' - and partly under the expectation of securing industrial support for Antarctic research, which has often struggled for money. As long ago as October 1970 an American presidential directive identified 'the prediction and assessment of resources' as a research role, while in 1978 Talboys, the New Zealand Foreign Minister, articulated a 'concern that the research programmes of some countries were leaning progressively further in the direction of exploration for mineral resources'[39]. More recently, BAS announced that part of its increased post-1982 funding would be employed for 'resource-oriented research' in the life and earth sciences, thereby facilitating 'an appraisal of the offshore hydrocarbon and terrestrial potential of British Antarctic Territory'[40].

Nevertheless, on paper, the moratorium remains in effect, and will remain so until a minerals regime has been concluded. In the meantime, the situation has caused problems, which can only get worse.

> It has become apparent that voluntary restraint and timely progress are linked. Unless there is indeed a regime in the near future it will be difficult to support a continuation of the moratorium. This self-imposed difficulty is made worse by the exploration activities of Consultative Parties contrary to the interim moratorium. Should the Hakurei Maru delineate promising sedimentary formations in a specific area the negotiations could collapse under the pressure of sovereignty claims and other interests[41].

In turn, environmental groups hope that the voluntary restraint can be transformed into a more permanent arrangement, such as expressed through their desire to make Antarctica a world park on account of a belief that:

> The entire Treaty area is a "Special Conservation Zone", which is closed to minerals activity, and have called for the entire region to be formally protected as an international wildlife sanctuary and science preserve[42].

However, the difficulties of maintaining the voluntary moratorium, in conjunction with the desire of certain Consultative Parties to keep open their mineral resource opportunities in Antarctica, do not augur well for the 'natural option' favoured by environmentalists.

One other problem concerns the position of non-parties and the moratorium, especially in the light of the apprehension caused among the Consultative Parties when India, a non-party, began to assume an interest in Antarctica during the early 1980s. In the event, no problems ensued, and India joined the Antarctic Treaty System in 1983, thereby reaffirming Bilder's dismissal of difficulties.

> Other considerations, such as a lack of immediate interest in conducting Antarctic resource activities, a general habit of deference to the Treaty regime, and a political reluctance to incur possible adverse attitudes or actions by the Treaty Parties, are very likely to result in non-Parties respecting the moratorium[43].

The Work of the Fourth Special Consultative Meeting

Since the 1981 Buenos Aires Consultative Meeting the momentum of the minerals règime negotiations has been maintained through the various sets of formal and informal exchanges conducted between the Consultative Parties as part of the Fourth Special Consultative Meeting. The meeting opened at

Wellington in June 1982, and further sessions have been held at Wellington and Bonn in 1983, Washington and Tokyo in 1984 and Rio de Janeiro in 1985 (see Table 7.4). Further sessions are still required. The process has been dominated by the Consultative Parties, which were reinforced in mid-course during 1983 by the addition of Brazil and India as new Consultative Parties. Another important change occurred in respect to acceding parties, since at Tokyo it was agreed to admit them as observers to the minerals regime negotiations with effect from the session scheduled for Rio in early 1985; in fact, Beeby (New Zealand), the chairman of the regime negotiations, attempted to involve the non-Consultative Parties before the Rio meeting, since he gave a briefing of the Tokyo session, including copies of the negotiating text, to local diplomatic representatives of acceding governments at the close of the discussions. Although the award of observer status to acceding parties was a natural consequence of developments in the Antarctic Treaty System regarding an enhancement of this status, this step served to qualify the closed nature of the negotiations, which have been conducted in considerable secrecy. In this context, another interesting trend has been the inclusion of non-governmental representatives on national delegations from Australia, New Zealand and the USA - this has been a traditional feature of US delegations to Consultative and other meetings - since this has served also to undermine the impact of secrecy, while also enabling a committed environmental input to the negotiations.

Obviously, it is easy to criticise the Consultative Parties for secrecy - this has proved a constant theme of many speakers at the UN - but it needs to be remembered that such procedures are not only the norm for diplomacy but also the essential requirement for the reconciliation of divergent positions. Nevertheless, secrecy, in conjunction with the apparent reluctance of the Consultative Parties to release much information on the sessions, render it difficult to comment upon either the nature of the proposed regime, the pace of the negotiations or the likely conclusion date for the Fourth Special Consultative Meeting. In the event, occasional leaks have occurred, partly because of the close attentions of environmental groups, and in 1983 the initial negotiating text was leaked to the press and other interested bodies. This draft proposal, the Beeby draft, was produced by Christopher Beeby, in his capacity as chairman, after the two sessions held at Wellington during 1982-3. Basically, these sessions had served to stake out the various positions of Consultative Parties on the subject, and upon this foundation Beeby produced a text of 36 articles which was accepted as the basis for negotiations at the Bonn and Washington meetings (1983-4)[44]. The first real discussion of the central issues underlying the proposed regime occurred at Bonn and Washington and, in this context, Beeby produced a revised version, "Beeby II", which was circulated to Consultative Parties in March 1984 and provided the negotiating text for the Tokyo and Rio de Janeiro sessions[45].

Since 1982 the Consultative Parties have advanced gradually towards the conclusion of an agreed minerals regime for Antarctica designed to give effect to recommendation XI-1.

> The principal purpose of those negotiations is to ensure that unregulated minerals activity, which could prove environmentally harmful, which could adversely affect other users of the continent and which could lead to renewed contention, does not take place. What the Consultative Parties are seeking to negotiate therefore is an arrangement which will lay down the ground rules for any future activity and established mechanisms to ensure that the Antarctic environment is stringently protected and that potential conflict is avoided. We regard it as important to negotiate such a regime now, before any pressures to exploit possible resources might develop in the future. Any minerals agreement concluded now will, in our view, further the interests of all mankind and will be open to all nations[46].

The lapse of time since 1982 and the number of meetings held already testify to the difficulties of the negotiators in search of an agreed regime; indeed, some commentators have suggested that the episode might end in failure on account of an inability to achieve internal accommodation, a failure which might threaten also the survival of the Antarctic Treaty System. There has been a tendency to regard the process of external accommodation as the most difficult task for the Consultative Parties, thereby overlooking the multiplicity of internal differences to be overcome, such as mentioned by the Australian government.

> Accommodations need to be made between the interests of claimant and non-claimant states, between the Consultative Parties as a whole and other states, between pro-conservation and pro-development interest groups, and between industrialised and developing states. The divergent economic and management perceptions of Eastern European and Western Consultative Parties will also need to be bridged[47].

Obviously, the durability and effectiveness of any minerals regime will prove dependent upon the ability of the Consultative Parties to achieve a consensus between their respective viewpoints in an agreement capable also of responding to changing conditions[48].

The Matter of Sovereignty

The British government, a party actively involved in the negotiations, has pointed to the basic problem of sovereignty as the primary cause of delay and difficulty.

> The negotiations for a minerals regime are proving tough-going. This was expected. The divide between Claimant and non-Claimant States regarding the role to be played by States asserting sovereignty is at the heart of the negotiations for a minerals regime. It is the principal cause of the difficulties encountered in the negotiations so far[49].

Although the Antarctic Treaty has served to contain the sovereignty problem, the matter has never completely disappeared. Most Consultative Parties, whether claimants or non-claimants, attach considerable significance to the preservation of their respective legal positions, at least in public, and the jurisdictional implications of resource management imparted an extra edge to policy, and at a time when such events as the 1982 Falklands War were sharpening political perceptions towards Antarctic claims. The position was accentuated by the perceived monetary and strategic utility of mineral resources as well as by their finite and non-renewable nature.

Traditionally, the regulation of mineral activities has assumed the clear identification of ownership for the purpose of control over exploration and management and the distribution of resource benefits. However, Antarctica lacks a clear legal framework, and the disputed nature of its ownership has been complicated recently by the emergence of an alternative approach centred upon the common heritage principle[50]. Within the ranks of the Consultative Parties, there existed two basic opening positions, which were diametrically opposed to each other.

> On the one hand, those States asserting sovereignty in Antarctica start from the position that there can be no exploitation of minerals in their areas which is not wholly regulated by them. On the other hand, those States that do not recognize such assertions of sovereignty start from the position that their nationals are free to go to Antarctica to search for and exploit minerals and that no other State has the right to regulate, in any sense, the activities of their nationals ... For all practical purposes, there could be virtually no mineral activity, even prospecting, which would not give rise to the high probability of a dispute[51].

If either side attempted to press their legal stance to its logical conclusion, there could be no basis for an agreed regime, even if, as recommendation XI-1 recognised in its identification of the need for the parties to take account of article IV of the Antarctic Treaty, a regime could not be negotiated in a legal vacuum. Therefore, the regime had to be embedded into the existing Antarctic legal framework, whatever the nature of the difficulties to be surmounted.

One writer, Rich, has suggested that the claims problem should be viewed as an asset rather than as a divisive element, since 'the claims could then become the tool with which to fashion a minerals regime'[52]. Although this approach has not commended itself to non-claimants, the negotiators have been forced to appreciate, to quote Arthur Watts, a British Foreign Office legal adviser, that:

> The sovereignty claims made by a number of states are very real. They are a fact of political life and they will not go away ... They have got to be taken into account in any solution that we may reach in negotiating a minerals regime: the solution must in some substantial way recognise the position of those States which assert sovereignty in Antarctica[53].

He conceded that it would be possible to draft a regime upon the assumption that no territorial rights existed in Antarctica, but 'such a regime is most unlikely to be acceptable to some of the states participating in the negotiations'. In this respect, one of the most significant developments has been the practice of the seven claimant states to meet together in secret prior to each session of the minerals talks in order to discuss their collective position and to arrive at a mutually acceptable negotiating strategy. This 'exclusive cabal' first met in Canberra during May 1982 prior to the opening session of the Special Consultative Meeting in June, and the practice appears to have been repeated for subsequent sessions[54]. This represented a new trend, which served not only to contrast with the marine regime negotiations but also to highlight the sovereignty implications of the minerals regime proposals. Heap has admitted that, 'the claimants do call meetings ... It would be surprising if they did not seek common positions ... the claimants discuss interests which they have in common'[55]. Although other Consultative Parties know about such meetings, it must be presumed that they are not privy to the decisions deriving from a development which has accentuated the impact of rival sovereignty positions, thereby posing a threat to the unity of the Antarctic Treaty System.

Nevertheless, there exists a general confidence that the problem can be resolved, an opinion encouraged by the example of the negotiating achievements typified by article IV of the Antarctic Treaty and by the bi-focal approach of CCAMLR. Admittedly, the minerals regime raises more complex problems, such as in respect to the authorisation of exploration and exploitation in areas subject to territorial claims or to the distribution of fees and royalties, but the Antarctic Treaty System's record of success over the years through the resolution of difficulties in a pragmatic and imaginative manner has encouraged confidence in the eventual success of the Special Consultative Meeting. In 1979 a working group of political and legal experts advised the Consultative Parties that:

> There was an exchange of views on the differing positions on sovereignty in Antarctica. While these differences are fundamental, all participants believed that accommodation of these differences could be found, considering the positive experience of nearly two decades under the Antarctic Treaty[56].

It appears likely that an act of creative imagination, an act of 'jurisdictional ambiguity', will enable agreement upon a draft designed to reflect a political and legal modus vivendi[57].

Although the claimants will seek some recognition of their special status, it has been suggested that yet another reaffirmation of article IV, in conjunction with non-claimant participation in the management of mineral resources, will tend to undermine the position of claimants. In fact, Auburn believes that 'the regime would be likely to mark the practical end of claims to sovereignty', since

> Even the most rudimentary form of licensing and decision-making must be regarded as having a considerable impact on sovereignty ... once this has been achieved in a stable form continuing indefinitely, there will be no apparent difference in Antarctic system entitlements between claimants and non-claimants[58].

Significantly, Ian Nicholson, a diplomat from Australia, one of the more sovereignty-conscious governments, supported this view:

> I agree with Auburn's conclusion that sovereignty will probably be weakened as a result of the conclusion of a minerals regime, but it will not be spent. This is because those claiming sovereignty will have agreed to whatever regime is to govern any minerals exploitation activity that might take place[59].

This debate recalls the previous discussion about sovereignty in chapter 6, according to which the interests of claimants might be served best through the maintenance of the Antarctic Treaty System rather than through the emphasis of sovereignty, a point implicitly recognised by Nicholson, when he suggested that 'the route Australia must take in preserving its interests, which the treaty already does, is the strengthening of the treaty'; thus, the achievement of an Antarctic minerals regime will prove a vital part of this 'strengthening' process[60].

Against this background, it appears appropriate to examine the likely format of the minerals regime, albeit in the knowledge that the text of the agreement remains under discussion and has yet to be finalised. Beeby's drafts established an institutional framework based upon a Commission, an Advisory Committee on technical, scientific and environmental matters, a series of Regulatory Committees on mineral activities and a Secretariat. The central Antarctic Mineral Resources Commission, composed of the Contracting Parties, will act as the ultimate political body, such as in respect to the establishment of rules and guidelines for the regime area and the designation of areas to be opened up for minerals activity. For every general area made open, a Regulatory Committee would be created to draft, monitor and enforce a management scheme, while a Scientific, Technical and Environmental Advisory Committee, composed of experts from each member of the Commission and receiving views from interested organisations, will support the work of both the Commission and Regulatory Committees. The whole framework will be supported administratively by a Secretariat.

The key aspect in respect to internal accommodation is the composition and role of a regulatory committee, which will be small and contain normally no more than eight representatives. Each committee would consist of the sponsoring state for the exploration application, any claimant to that area, three other claimants chosen by the first claimant, plus additional non-claimants chosen by the Chairman of the Commission. These complicated arrangements, which have attempted also to ensure American and Soviet representation on each committee, were drafted to ensure a balance between claimants and non-claimants, while avoiding awkward decisions about the ownership of resources. Although this format has been criticised for favouring the claimants, a point accentuated by the power of the Regulatory Committees, there is also the argument made by Auburn and Nicholson concerning the way in which the regime will qualify the position of claimants. Obviously, further refinements may occur before an agreed draft is concluded, but the complex ingenuity of the Beeby scheme provides yet another example of the effort to develop the Antarctic Treaty System through points of difficulty by the employment of jurisdictional ambiguity, that is, to set aside and obscure such thorny aspects as the ownership of resources in the interests of consensus.

The Penguins Are Watching

Sir Peter Scott, the son of the first Briton to reach the South Pole, has acted as a public focus for the critique of the minerals regime negotiations.

> All this for perhaps 3 or 5 years' supply of oil for the world ... How can this short-term gain really be worth the terrible risks to the last great pristine wilderness on earth? This would be an ultimate desecration, for the sake of marginal and short-term profit[61].

Scott's admonitions have attracted more British media interest than have the actual minerals regime negotiations, and have performed an important part of the public relations campaign conducted by conservation groups, such as reflected in the regular lobbying of negotiating sessions. For example, during 1983 at the time of the Bonn session, six members of Greenpeace, dressed in penguin outfits and accompanied by 15 stuffed and some 150 inflatable penguins, attempted to remind delegates about the environmental dangers of resource exploitation in Antarctica[62]. The rather motley collection of penguins assembled in front of Bonn's Science centre symbolised the opposition of conservation groups to mineral activities, and typified their public relations effort at each session. 'The penguins are watching', the delegates were told, but whether they felt threatened by the penguin invasion of Bonn was debatable, since the Consultative Parties were preoccupied mainly with political and legal questions.

Naturally, environmentalists were bound to oppose the mere fact of a minerals regime, since this implied development and a threat to the Antarctic environment. The recent example of oil rig incidents concerning the Alexander Kielland and Ocean Ranger rigs in the North Sea and off Newfoundland respectively accentuated the anxieties, such as by displaying environmental deficiencies and problems[63]. The environmentalist's advocacy of a no-mining and "do without" strategy derived from an unwillingness to compromise Antarctica's wilderness value, and inevitably they attacked the Beeby drafts, which were motivated primarily by the need to resolve the sovereignty problem; thus, it was argued that this objective was achieved at the expense of other considerations, including environmental protection[64]. Critics were not reassured by the inclusion of articles related to the importance of the Antarctic environment, since the employment of such terms as 'acceptable' in respect to judging environmental impact failed to provide a secure level of protection. The Consultative Parties have pointed to their responsible management of the continent, especially in the sphere of environmental matters, and they have responded to criticism in terms of references to the environmental provisions for the proposed regime; thus, any area of Antarctica will remain closed to activity except in respect to sections opened up as the result of a considered decision by the Commission, which would be fully apprised of environmental impacts.

This debate about a conflict of interest between mineral exploitation and environmental groups recalls the fishing/ conservation controversy about CCAMLR. However, it proves difficult to evaluate the degree of environmental protection until the regime becomes operative, but informed commentators have tended to sympathise with the fears of conservationists. For instance, Charney has argued that:

> Even those nations which are most sensitive to environmental issues are ready to displace that interest when it conflicts with the more traditional economic, political and military interests[65].

Evidence regarding inaction by the Consultative Parties in response to infringements of the Agreed Measures - most notably, the French airstrip controversy - has inclined Auburn to anticipate weak environmental provisions, especially as political, economic and other factors have always assumed priority over environmental interests[66]. In any case, it would appear that the concept of a world park for Antarctica has been overtaken by events, and particularly by the progress of resource regime negotiations, and, in this context, some conservationists have adopted a more realistic attitude, that is, to accept the likelihood of development and to press for strict environmental controls over any activity[67]. In turn, conservation groups have suggested that an Antarctic Environmental Protection Agency should be added to the institutional framework proposed by Beeby in order to provide a more meaningful environmental input to decision-making[68].

The Minerals Regime and the International Community

The Consultative Parties have attached considerable significance to the task of external accommodation with the international community as a whole in order not only to secure general acceptance for the regime but also to pre-empt any attempt to establish an alternative management framework centred perhaps upon the UN. During the late 1970s the Consultative Parties stressed the need for any regime to take account of 'the interests of all mankind' - no effort has ever been made to define the precise nature of these 'interests' - and in 1977 Brian Roberts, a key participant in the system since the early 1960s, emphasised the fact that 'however much the signatories of the Treaty may disagree with this view, it is a political reality which we cannot afford to ignore'[69]. In 1982 Beeby reaffirmed this requirement:

> The interests of the international community at large, and in particular of the developing world, will need to be taken into account in the negotiation of a mineral regime and in advance of United Nations debates about it[70].

This external aspect has raised a range of problems, especially as most of the developing world tends to interpret Antarctica from a common heritage and developmental perspective, thereby further complicating the sovereignty question. Naturally, the UN debates on Antarctica during 1983 and 1984 devoted considerable attention to the minerals question, and served to highlight the polarisation of views on the subject. Although the Consultative Parties defended the proposed minerals regime in terms of both the global and Antarctic benefits, a number of governments assumed a critical stance, such as demonstated by Malaysia:

> We are told by the Treaty Consultative Parties that Antarctic mineral exploration will not be technologically feasible and commercially viable until the next century. Yet they themselves are none the less pursuing seriously and secretly an exclusive minerals regime ... We should well ask whether any group of countries should confer upon itself the moral or legal right to self-elected determination or management of Antarctica ... the manner and speed in which this negotiation is undertaken has quite naturally engendered suspicion, especially when the United Nations is only beginning to discuss Antarctica as a whole[71].

In this way, the minerals question has become an integral part of the campaign to replace the Antarctic Treaty System with an allegedly more representative regime; indeed, the minerals topic appears to have acted as the catalyst for the emergence of this campaign. Most developing countries have followed the Malaysian line, although Antigua and Barbuda has proposed reform of the treaty system, including a more democratic approach towards the minerals regime. In November 1984 the Antiguan representative advocated a regime under the umbrella of the treaty, including institutions based upon an equal number of Consultative Parties and of outsiders as well as upon a system of international taxation and revenue sharing; thus, any revenue would be utilised for the maintenance of the Antarctic environment and for loans and grants to the developing nations[72].

However, the Consultative Parties have not been attracted by the prospect of either alternative or parallel mechanisms, and the negotiations have been conducted upon the basis that the external accommodation process would be achieved within the parameters of the Antarctic Treaty

System. It was argued that this approach was not incompatible with the interests of the international community, particularly as working relationships with interested international organisations would be encouraged and as other governments would be able to accede to the regime. Similarly the regime area has been defined in order to avoid any encroachment upon the deep seabed, and thus upon UNCLOS' area of concern. Nevertheless, many aspects remain under discussion, and some outsiders have expressed reservations about the way in which Beeby's scheme allows merely eight governments - those represented on any Regulatory Committee - considerable power over minerals activities.

Ice as a Mineral Resource and its wider value

Antarctic ice in its various forms represents a mineral, albeit a renewable one, which has become interpreted as perhaps one of the most promising resources from an economic point of view, particularly as it actually exists and is available in large quantities and as no other part of the world can rival Antarctica's supply. However, there has been no effort to cover such aspects as the exploitation of icebergs in the ongoing minerals regime negotiations, and thus it remains an unregulated area and awaits consideration by the treaty system. Nevertheless, this represents an appropriate place in the book to conduct a brief appraisal of ice's utility.

Within Antarctica ice is employed already at base stations as a source of fresh water or for the storage of perishables, while airstrips have been constructed from compressed ice. The scientific utility of ice is considerable, such as evidenced by the research work on ice cores and the stability of the ice sheet. These roles will continue, and may even develop, such as to support mineral activity; for example, in the Arctic, artificial ice islands and platforms have been utilised for drilling and other equipment, and a recent paper by Sanderson - this was quoted previously - has suggested the application of the Arctic precedent to Antarctica[73]. From time to time, attempts have been made to revive Richard Byrd's proposal to the effect that Antarctica should be used as a vast natural deep freeze for surplus and emergency food stocks, but logistical and transport problems have contributed to reduce the scheme's attractions. Similar objections have been advanced against the suggestion that radioactive waste should be disposed of in the Antarctic ice sheet, although at present this activity is banned anyway by article V of the Antarctic Treaty. As a result, only limited use is made of ice within Antarctica, and future development seems unlikely, except in the case of tourism. Ice in its various forms constitutes an essential element of the Antarctic landscape and wilderness value, and thereby proves a key part of the continent's tourist appeal[74].

Tourism represents an existing, albeit limited, activity, which has taken the form primarily of visits by cruise ships, such as by the Lindblad Explorer, or of tourist overflights operated by QANTAS and Air New Zealand until their termination after the DC 10 crash on Mount Erebus in 1979 with the loss of 257 lives. In this context, the potential and nature of Antarctic tourism has attracted increased study, while a concern about the environmental and other problems - these include the difficulties of search and rescue, such as highlighted by the Erebus crash - persuaded the Consultative Parties to introduce a series of measures - recommendations IV-27, VI-7, VII-4, VIII-9, and X-8 - designed to regulate tourism in order to ensure not only the interests of Antarctica but also the safety of tourists. The Twelth Consultative Meeting in 1983 'discussed the implications of the increase of tourism ... in Antarctica', but problems of jurisdiction and responsibility resulted in the withdrawal of the draft recommendation which had been tabled; thus, the matter will be followed up at the 1985 Meeting[75].

Most contemporary discussions of ice's resource value have concentrated upon its export role, that is, a resource for use outside Antarctica, such as through the towing of icebergs to areas of water shortage in Australia, the Middle East or South America. As long ago as the 1770s Captain Cook referred to the employment of pieces of ice from the Southern Ocean to yield several tons of fresh water, even if the 'most expeditious' character of the melting process was qualified by its tedium. The concept of iceberg utilisation was discussed occasionally during the 1960s and 1970s, and acquired some degree of respectability after the conference held on the subject at Iowa State University, USA, in October 1977 - significantly, it was supported by Middle East funding - and further theoretical studies on such aspects as towing techniques and difficulties[76]. The resulting discussions have identified the potential, including vast quantities of fresh water, and the problems, such as the environmental and climatic effects, shipping hazards, processing costs and ownership of icebergs. In fact, one recent study estimated the initial costs for iceberg utilisation in Saudi Arabia to be in the order of $16-80 billion.

> According to researchers this would, in the long term, result in relatively low costs for water ... because of the massive amount of water transported. However, the initial investment for facilities, dredging and port modification would be so great that it is believed there are few nations that could even contemplate such expenditure[77].

In 1983 an Australian paper suggested that Perth could be supplied with water from an iceberg towed from Antarctica far more cheaply (Australian $0.66 cu.metre) than supplies either pumped from the Ord River (A$9.40 cu.m.) or secured through desalination (A$1.70 cu.m.)[78]. However, such costings exceed current figures (A$0.12 cu.m.), and the study concluded that the existence of a range of technological, economic and other problems rendered it 'unlikely that icebergs will be harvested for fresh water in the near future'. Therefore, the resource value of icebergs, like that of other Antarctic minerals, lies in the long term, if then, even if the escalating global demand for fresh water will keep the subject under serious consideration. In this respect, regulatory action by the Consultative Parties might prove necessary.

Conclusion

The Antarctic minerals regime negotiations appear to have reached a relatively advanced stage, and this feature tends to undermine the utility of the numerous attempts to suggest alternative ways of resolving the topic[79]. These suggestions, whether by governments or academics, have been overtaken by events, even if it can be argued that any discussion of ideal regimes offers a basis for an informed evaluation of the actual regime when it emerges. In the meantime, the relative secrecy of the negotiations, in conjunction with the continuing development of several aspects of the proposed regime, renders detailed comment impossible, if not unwise.

The actual task facing the Consultative Parties in mid-1982, when they commenced the detailed discussions for a minerals regime, was a formidable one, especially as the search for internal and external accommodation was exacerbated by a range of uncertainties.

> The Consultative Parties are negotiating towards a minerals regime against a background of five uncertainties - that is, to say, virtually complete ignorance as to what minerals there are, where they are, when they will be exploited, who will do it and whether, indeed, it will ever happen[80].

To some extent, it is tempting to compare the minerals regime talks with the preceding marine resource negotiations, but at the same time it is prudent to remember that 'the two conventions, on marine living resources and on minerals, deal with similar but far from identical problems'[81]. The anxiety to develop and reinforce the Antarctic Treaty System has provided one of the fundamental motives for the minerals negotiations, which have been perceived by both the Consultative Parties and outsiders as of crucial importance; indeed, Antarctic minerals have proved the central issue in the emerging international debate about the future of Antarctica.

In 1982 Beeby referred to the 'intellectual challenge' confronting the Consultative Parties, which would need to exercise 'imaginative ingenuity' in order to resolve 'irreconcilable' political, legal and environmental positions[82]. Subsequently, the Beeby drafts were intended to provide the basis for a sound and agreed way forward, and it seems that the regime has every chance of coming into operation, albeit in a modified form to Beeby II, sooner rather than later[83]. For example, Sollie, a Norwegian closely involved in the treaty system, has stated that the 'indications are that full agreement may soon be reached'[84]. At one time, the year of 1986 was oft-depicted as the most likely date for the advent of the minerals regime, but the continuing discussions imply that this deadline might not be met.

Nevertheless, a regime should be in place before any actual exploitation occurs, if any Antarctic minerals are ever exploited. In the context of several optimistic, albeit ill-informed, assessments of the continent's minerals potential, it is desirable to conclude with a sense of reality, such as to recall Gould's comment in 1960 to the effect that he 'would not give a nickel for all the riches of Antarctica'[85]. The 1974 US Geological Survey Report has been oft-cited on account of its optimistic estimates of Antarctica's oil and gas potential, but it is helpful to consider another section of the report, which observed that 'the probability that mineral deposits exist in Antarctica seems to be high ... but the crucial factor is whether they can be found'[86]. Even if minerals can be found, a range of technological, economic, environmental and other obstacles diminish the prospects of actual exploitation, such as recognised by the 1984 UN Study after an appraisal of existing research; thus, 'Antarctic mineral deposits and occurrences are not likely to be exploited in the near future'[87]. As a result, Antarctica, the so-called 'last continent' and the site of the last great land rush on earth, possesses little immediate utility from the point of view of minerals; in fact, its minerals would appear to be 'the resource of last resort'[88]. However, conditions may change, and - to quote Zumberge - 'the status of Antarctica as a target for future mineral exploration must be viewed in light of changing world politics and international developments'[89].

NOTES

1. H.G.R. King (ed.), Edward Wilson, Diary of the Terra Nova Expedition to the Antarctic 1910-1912 (Blandford, London, 1972), p.241.

2. Huntford, Scott and Amundsen, p.241.

3. Tore Gjelsvik, 'The Mineral Resources of Antarctica: progress in their identification', in Vicuna, Antarctic

Resources Policy, p.62; Mitchell, *Frozen Stakes*, pp.7-21; Zumberge, *Potential Mineral Resource Availability*, pp.123-30; UNGA A/39/583 (Part I), 1984, pp.89-103.

4. Gjelsvik, *Scientific Research and Cooperation in Antarctica*, p.48.

5. Egil Bergsager, 'Basic conditions for the exploration and exploitation of mineral resources in Antarctica: options and precedents', in Vicuna, *Antarctic Resources Policy*, pp.169-70.

6. E.F. Roots, 'Resource development in polar regions: comments on technology', in Vicuna, *Antarctic Resources Policy*, p.299; T.J.O. Sanderson, 'Offshore Oil Development in Polar Regions', paper presented to Pacific Science Congress, Dunedin, 1983, in Australian Government, *Antarctica: Appendices to Australian Contribution in Response to the Request from the Secretary-General of the United Nations* (Australian Government, Canberra, 1984), vol.I, p.142.

7. Gjelsvik, *The Mineral Resources of Antarctica*, pp.63-76; Franz Tessensohn, 'Present Knowledge of Non-Living Resources in the Antarctic, Possibilities for their Exploitation and Scientific Perspectives', in Wolfrum, *Antarctic Challenge*, pp.194-204.

8. P.D. Rowley, A.B. Ford, P.L. Williams and D.E. Pride, ,Metallogenic Provinces of Antarctica', in R.L. Oliver, P.R. James and J.B. Jago (eds.), *Antarctic Earth Sciences* (Cambridge University Press, Cambridge, 1983), p.414.

9. G.I. Kameneva and G.E. Grikurov, 'A Metallogenic Reconnaissance of Antarctic Major Structural Provinces', in Oliver, *Antarctic Earth Sciences*, p.420; J.C. Behrendt, 'Geophysical and Geological Studies Relevant to Assessment of the Petroleum Resources of Antarctica', in Oliver, *Antarctic Earth Sciences*, pp.423-7.

10. Gjelsvik, *The Mineral Resources of Antarctica*, p.62.

11. N.A. Wright and P.L. Williams (ed.), *Mineral Resources of Antarctica* (US Geological Survey, circular 705, Washington, 1974).

12. Gjelsvik, *The Mineral Resources of Antarctica*, pp.68-74; Behrendt, *Geophysical and Geological Studies Relevant to Assessment of Petroleum Resources of Antarctica*, pp.426-7.

13. Mitchell, *Frozen Stakes*, p.9.

14. Fox, *Antarctica and the South Atlantic*, p.95.

15. Roots, *Resource development in polar regions*, pp.297-315; Sanderson, *Offshore Oil Development in Polar Regions*, pp. 139-42; *HCFAC*, Falkland Islands, Minutes of Evidence, 13 Dec.1982, pp.107-8.

16. Zumberge, *Potential Mineral Resource Availability*, p.124.

17. Luard, *Who Owns the Antarctic?*, p.1183; *Eco*, vol.XIX, no.1 (1982), p.1, p.4.

18. Mitchell, Frozen Stakes, p.17. Note that Britoil sponsored the 'Whither Antarctica?' conference held in London, April 1985.

19. James Barnes, quoted in Wolfrum, Antarctic Challenge, p.179.

20. UNGA A/39/C 1 PV 52, p.31, 29 Nov.1984.

21. Sanderson, Offshore Oil Development in Polar Regions, p.142.

22. Ibid.

23. Mitchell, Frozen Stakes, pp.22-4; Brewster, Antarctica's Wilderness at Risk, pp.87-104; Holdgate, Environmental factors in the development of Antarctica, pp.77-99.

24. Zumberge, Potential Mineral Resource Availability, p.125.

25. Giulio Pontecorvo, 'The Economics of the Resources of Antarctica', in Charney, The New Nationalism and the Use of Common Spaces, pp.155-64.

26. Ibid., p.163; Sollie, Jurisdictional Problems in Relation to Antarctic Mineral Resources, pp.322-3.

27. UNGA A/38/C 1 PV 44, p.18, 29 Nov.1983, Heap; Sollie, quoted in Wolfrum, Antarctic Challenge, p.224.

28. John Heap, 'Meeting on Antarctic Mineral Resources, Wellington, New Zealand, 17-28 January 1983', Polar Record, vol.21, no.134 (1983), p.501; Auburn, Consultative Status under the Antarctic Treaty, p.517.

29. Heap, Meeting on Antarctic Mineral Resources, p.501.

30. Beeby, The Antarctic Treaty, pp.18-9; Sollie, Development of the Antarctic Treaty System, p.35.

31. Bush, Antarctica and International Law, vol.I, pp.283-92.

32. Antarctic Treaty: Handbook, pp.9601-07; Holdgate, Environmental factors in the development of Antarctica, p.79.

33. Antarctic Treaty: Handbook, pp.9618-26; Lucía Ramírez Aranda, 'El SCAR y el Desarrollo de la Cooperacion en Materia Cientifica', in Francisco Orrego Vicuna, Maria Teresa Infante Caffi and Pilar Armanet Armanet (eds.), Politica Antarctica de Chile (University of Chile, Santiago, 1984), pp.142-5.

34. Mitchell, Frozen Stakes, pp.50-1.

35. C.D. Beeby, 'An overview of the problems which should be addressed in the preparation of a regime governing the mineral resources of Antarctica', in Vicuna, Antarctic Resources Policy, p.194.

36. Charney, Future Strategies for an Antarctic Mineral Resources Regime, pp.225-9.

37. Auburn, Antarctic Minerals and the Third World, p.205.

38. Eco, vol.XXVI, no.2 (1984), pp.4-5.

39. Quigg, A Pole Apart, p.88; B.E. Talboys, 'New Zealand and the Antarctic Treaty', New Zealand Foreign Affairs Review, vol. 28, nos.3-4 (1978), p.32.

40. HCFAC, Falkland Islands, Minutes of Evidence, 13 Dec.1982, p.89.

41. Auburn, Antarctic Minerals and the Third World, pp.206-07.

42. Antarctica Briefing: no.5 Status of Antarctic Minerals Negotiations (The Antarctica Project, Washington DC, 1984), p.1; Geoff Mosley, 'The Natural Option: the Case for an Antarctic World Park', in Harris, Australia's Antarctic Policy Options, p.32.

43. Bilder, Present Legal and Political Situation in Antarctica, p.188.

44. Eco, vol.XXIII, no.1 (1983), pp.1-16; Eco, vol.XXVII, nos.1-3 (1984).

45. Foreign Policy Document no.98: Antarctica: An Overview, p.6; Heap, Meeting on Antarctic Mineral Resources, pp.501-02; Ian Nicholson, quoted in Harris, Australia's Antarctic Policy Options, p.303.

46. UNGA A/39/C 1 PV 55, pp.11-12, 30 Nov.1984, Sorzano, USA; UNGA A/38/C 1 PV 45, p.7, 29 Nov.1983, Sorzano.

47. UNGA A/39/583 (Part II), 1984, vol.1, p.84, Australian response 31 July 1984.

48. Brennan, Criteria for Access to the Resources of Antarctica, pp.218-9; Vicuna, Antarctic Resources Policy, pp.7-8.

49. Foreign Policy Document no.98: Antarctica: An Overview, p.6; Auburn, Antarctic Minerals and the Third World, pp.207-09.

50. Mitchell, Frozen Stakes, pp.91-7; Honnold, Thaw in International Law?, p.807; Stephen A. Zorn, 'Antarctic Minerals: a common heritage approach', Resources Policy, vol.10, no.1 (1984), pp.15-18.

51. UNGA A/38/C 1 PV 44, p.21, 29 Nov.1983, Heap.

52. Rich, A Minerals Regime for Antarctica, p.725.

53. Watts, quoted in Wolfrum, Antarctic Challenge, p.221; Charney, Future Strategies for an Antarctic Mineral Resources Regime, pp.227-8.

54. Eco, vol.XX, no.1 (1982), p.1.

55. Heap, quoted in Wolfrum, Antarctic Challenge, p.62.

56. Bush, Antarctica and International Law, vol.I, p.390.

57. Heap, Antarctic Cooperation, pp.106-07; Mitchell, Frozen Stakes, pp.114-24; Auburn, The Antarctic Minerals Regime, p.279.

58. Auburn, Antarctic Minerals and the Third World, p.219; Auburn, The Antarctic Minerals Regime, p.273.

59. Nicholson, quoted in Harris, Australia's Antarctic Policy Options, p.300.

60. Ibid., p.301.

61. Telegram, 17 Jan.1984, Eco, vol.XXVI, no.2 (1984), p.2.

62. Beck, Antarctica's Indian Summer, p.297.

63. Auburn, Antarctic Minerals and the Third World, pp.213-5; Mitchell, Frozen Stakes, p.73. These incidents occurred in 1980 and 1982 respectively.

64. Auburn, Antarctic Minerals and the Third World, pp.211-2.

65. Charney, Future Strategies for an Antarctic Mineral Resources Regime, pp.207-08; Auburn, The Antarctic Minerals Regime, p.274.

66. Auburn, Antarctic Minerals and the Third World, p.219.

67. Lyn Goldsworthy, 'World Park on Ice', Chain Reaction, no.37 (1984), p.40; see letters, Chain Reaction, no.38 (1984), pp.41-3; Annette Horsler, quoted in Harris, Australia's Antarctic Policy Options, pp.327-38.

68. Eco, vol. XXVII, no.3 (1984); Antarctica Briefing: no.6 An Antarctic Environmental Protection Agency (The Antarctic Project, Washington DC, 1984), pp.1-2.

69. Roberts, International Cooperation for Antarctic Development, p.111.

70. Beeby, Problems which should be addressed in the preparation of a regime governing the mineral resources of Antarctica, p.197; Guyer, Antarctica's role in International Relations, p.277.

71. UNGA A/38/C 1 PV 42, p.19, 28 Nov.1983, Zainal Abidin.

72. UNGA A/39/C 1 PV 50, pp.6-7, 28 Nov.1984, Jacobs.

73. Sanderson, Offshore Oil Development in Polar Regions, pp.135-42.

74. Rosamunde J. Reich, 'The Development of Antarctic Tourism', Polar Record, vol.20, no.126 (1980), pp.203-14; Patricia J. Scharlin, Antarctic Tourism - Trends and Impact (NSF, Washington, 1979); Rosamunde J. Codling (née Reich), 'Sea-borne Tourism in the Antarctic: an evaluation', Polar Record, vol.21, no.130 (1982), pp.3-9.

75. Antarctic Treaty: Report of thc Twelth Consultative Meeting, pp.11-12.

76. A.A. Husseiny (ed.), Iceberg Utilization. Proceedings of the First International Conference on Iceberg Utilization at Iowa State University October 1977 (Pergamon, New York, 1978).

77. UNGA A/39/583 (Part I), 1984, pp.102-03.

78. Australian Antarctic Division, 'The Utilisation of Antarctic Ice', in Australian Government, Antarctica:

Appendices to Australian Contribution, vol.2, pp.186-203; Canberra Times, 29 Sept.1983.

79. For example, see Mitchell, Frozen Stakes, pp.57 et seq.

80. UNGA A/39/C 1 PV 52, p.31, 29 Nov.1984, Heap.

81. Nicholson, quoted in Harris, Australia's Antarctic Policy Options, p.300.

82. Beeby, Overview of Problems which should be addressed in the preparation of a regime governing the mineral resources of Antarctica, p.191, pp.194-5.

83. Brennan, Criteria for Access to the Resources of Antarctica, p.217.

84. Sollie, Development of the Antarctic Treaty System, p.36.

85. Gould, quoted in Auburn, Antarctic Law and Politics, p.241, and Guyer, in Wolfrum, Antarctic Challenge, p.56.

86. Wright, Mineral Resources of Antarctica, p.1.

87. UNGA A/39/583 (Part I), 1984, p.96.

88. UNGA A/39/C 1 PV 52, p.31, 29 Nov.1984, Heap.

89. Zumberge, Potential Mineral Resource Availability, p.124.

Chapter Eleven

THE ANTARCTIC TREATY: A CONTINENT AND ITS PLACE IN THE INTERNATIONAL COMMUNITY

In February 1947 Admiral Richard Byrd used a flight over the South Pole - this was made as part of Operation Highjump (1946-7) - to drop 'a cardboard box containing multi-colored little flags of the United Nations' as an 'obvious symbolism' of his desire for international harmony in Antarctica, perhaps achieved under the umbrella of the UN[1]. However, neither this gesture nor subsequent inter-governmental exchanges conducted during the late 1940s regarding an international solution for Antarctica resulted in any real UN role, and it was not until the close of 1983 that the UN performed any substantial action in respect to the region. On 15 December 1983 the UN General Assembly, acting upon the basis of debates in the First Committee, adopted a draft resolution on 'The Question of Antarctica', which requested the Secretary-General to prepare a study 'on all aspects of Antarctica', thereby providing the basis not only for debate in the 1984 Assembly session but also for attempts to modify the relationship between the Antarctic Treaty System and the international community[2]. The impact of this episode was reinforced by the wider framework of Antarctic developments during the early 1980s, since the moves at the UN in New York provided a new dimension to the search for external accommodation with governments and international organisations upon the part of the Antarctic Treaty System as a whole and of the proposed minerals regime in particular.

The UN's non-role in Antarctica after 1945

One of the more surprising features of post-1945 Antarctic history was the failure of the UN to become involved in a meaningful manner in the affairs of a continent oft-identified as a suitable case for treatment by the UN. In fact, its early years witnessed a number of calls for intervention, partly because of a concern about international friction in Antarctica and partly because of the initial enthusiasm for the new international organisation. For instance, during April 1947 the

New York Times advocated a UN trusteeship for Antarctica, which should 'be held in trust for the peoples of all the world', and possibly this reference inspired the petitions submitted to the UN Trusteeship Council in December 1947 in order to suggest that polar trusteeship regimes should be created under the aegis of the UN[3]. In the event, the matter was not pursued, especially as the link between the Arctic and the Antarctic caused difficulties at a time of East-West sensitivities about the strategic value of the former, although this abortive episode could not prevent subsequent speculation about the feasibility of applying articles 75-85 of the UN Charter, that is, the trusteeship articles, to Antarctica in spite of its lack of population.

In the same year, Antarctica attracted the interest of the American-based Commission to Study the Organization of Peace, whose Fifth Report (1947) recommended that, 'an international regime for the Antarctic continent should be established, with direct administration by the United Nations', an approach reiterated with greater 'urgency' by the same body a decade later to the effect that 'Antarctica is a continent in search of a sovereign. The United Nations ought to establish its sovereignty there'[4]. The internationalist cause was pressed also by a number of prominent individuals, including in 1948 Julian Huxley, the first director-general of UNESCO; thus, he urged that UNESCO should organise an International Antarctic Research Institute, while a year later Edward Shackleton, then a MP - he is now Lord Shackleton - and, of course, the son of the famous explorer, returned to the trusteeship theme[5].

> The Antarctic ... is being left to direct negotiation between the governments concerned. And yet there is no problem in the world which the United Nations is better suited to handle ... The Antarctic should be administered internationally, and the United Nations should be the body to do it.

Shackleton, recalling recent debates about UN trusteeship, dismissed as a mere 'academic quibble' the argument that the Charter applied only to people not penguins, but such demands that 'ultimately the Antarctic should become United Nations territory' fell upon barren ground, for the governments actually involved there preferred a more direct approach, such as evidenced by their relatively cool response to the US proposals advanced during 1948-9 in favour of an international solution for the Antarctic question[6]. As a result, after 1945 the UN steered clear, or rather it was steered clear, of the region's affairs mainly because of the desire of the Antarctic powers to retain direct control over events.

This experience was repeated during the late 1950s, when Arthur Lall, representing India, made two attempts to place 'The Question of Antarctica' upon the General Assembly's agenda.

> It would be appropriate and timely now for all nations to agree and affirm that the area will be utilized entirely for peaceful purposes and for the welfare of the whole world ... this subject is of great importance to the international community as a whole and not merely for certain countries ... the United Nations should call upon all States to utilize this territory solely for peaceful purposes ... the Government of India are of the view that the action proposed can only be taken by the world community as a whole[7].

However, in November 1956 the first Indian request was withdrawn allegedly because of 'a heavy agenda and the exploration of Antarctica was still proceeding', but possibly also because of diplomatic pressure from the Antarctic powers[8]. In turn, the revival of the proposal in 1958 was overtaken by the preparatory negotiations for the 1959 Antarctic Treaty, that is, an agreement providing for the peaceful use of the continent, albeit placed under the control of a limited multilateral grouping of twelve governments rather than under the whole international community acting through the UN. Nevertheless, the treaty included a number of references to the UN, such as indicated by the preamble's stress upon the desire to 'further the purposes and principles embodied in the Charter of the United Nations' and upon the fact that the peaceful use of Antarctica was 'in the interest of all mankind'. In addition article III (2) advocated cooperative working relationships with UN agencies and other international organisations, and article X stipulated that each party undertook 'to exert appropriate efforts, consistent with the Charter of the United Nations, to the end that no one engages in any activity in Antarctica contrary to the principles and purposes of the treaty'. But such references failed to disguise the fact that in reality the treaty assigned the UN a virtual non-role in the affairs of about ten per cent of the world's land surface, thereby continuing and regularising the situation prevalent since 1945. The UN was effectively pushed aside by the treaty, in spite of evidence that certain signatories were either sympathetic or supportive of an UN role in Antarctica; for instance, the USA had floated the idea of a UN solution during the late 1940s and in 1956 Walter Nash, the prime minister of New Zealand, a claimant, proposed a trusteeship in order to make Antarctica a 'world territory under the control of the UN'[9]. It appears that New Zealand repeated this view during the treaty negotiations, where the proposal evoked little general support, except perhaps from the

UK[10]. The strong opposition from most claimants persuaded New Zealand to recognise that it was unrealistic to press for the fulfilment of Nash's 1956 proposal, particularly as both Argentina and Chile proved rather hawkish on sovereignty; thus, the Chilean representative asserted that the UN had no cause for intervention, since Chilean Antarctic Territory 'does not have the character of a colonial possession but is part of its metropolitan territory'[11].

The US note of May 1958 - this served to initiate the treaty preparatory negotiations - had stressed already the wider international political context, and during the resulting discussions the representatives showed an awareness of the dangers emanating from the relatively exclusive nature of their grouping, which was liable to be perceived as arrogating to the twelve governments sole rights to Antarctic decision-making. According to Heap, a British diplomat, 'nothing in the Treaty supports such an acquisitive view of the motives of the twelve', even if there existed a selfish element in their respective policies[12]. However, the negotiators attempted at the same time to consider the wider perspective, such as the need to take account of, or at least to give this impression, the interests of the international community; thus, the Consultative Parties presented the results of the treaty as some kind of internationalisation method in the 'interest of all mankind', while its limited approach was qualified by the ability of other governments to accede to the treaty. Such window-dressing obscured the manner in which the treaty fell short of the UN role in Antarctica favoured in certain quarters, a point accentuated by the fact that the negotiating process of 1958-9 resulted in a marked diminution of the functions initially envisaged for the UN. Even a relatively minor role, such as in acting as the treaty depositary, was removed from the early treaty drafts.

Like any other international agreement, the Antarctic Treaty binds only the contracting parties, and considerable debate has occurred appertaining to its status and acceptability in the sphere of international politics and law[13]. Naturally, the Consultative Parties have advocated its general validity, such as in respect to its consistency with the UN Charter and with the 'interest of all mankind'; thus, the non-militarised status and scientific orientation of Antarctica have been presented as treaty consequences of universal relevance. Upon this basis, the Consultative Parties have developed article X to justify the view that:

> The Antarctic Treaty places a special responsibility on the Contracting Parties to exert appropriate efforts, consistent with the Charter of the United Nations, to the end that no one engages in any activity in the Antarctic Treaty area contrary to the principles and purposes of the Treaty (recommendation VIII-8)[14].

Their Antarctic role could be interpreted as fitting in with the peacekeeping role of the United Nations, and an earlier part of this book highlighted the manner in which the treaty fulfilled the UN Secretary-General's desire - this was articulated in his 1960 report - to remove 'newly-arising conflicts outside the sphere of bloc differences ... through ... their strict localization'[15]. From this perspective, the 1959 treaty had served not only to fill the power vacuum in Antarctica but also to insulate the continent from East-West complications, even if the Secretary-General's 1960 report failed to acknowledge this point in a specific manner. However, subsequently, UN publications have identified the wider relevance of the Antarctic Treaty, particularly in the sphere of regional disarmament measures[16].

After 1959 the Consultative Parties developed a clear conception of their Antarctic responsibilities in the global context, and in 1961, when they assembled for the First Consultative Meeting, the US embassy in Canberra reported that:

> The 64 delegates from the 12 signatory countries are calling this first Meeting on the Antarctica treaty the Polar United Nations[17].

This encouraged a belief that outsiders, lacking any appreciation of Antarctic realities, would be unable to perform any meaningful role in the region's affairs, an approach facilitated by the fact that during the early decade or so of the Antarctic Treaty System non-treaty powers posed relatively few problems, and appeared by implication to assume a deferential role towards the Consultative Parties[18]. Hitherto, India had proved one of the few other governments, outside the ranks of the twelve Consultative Parties, to display any real interest in Antarctica, and it was tempting to assume that India's post-1959 failure to revive the 1956 and 1958 attempts to place Antarctica upon the agenda of the UN signified acceptance of the Antarctic Treaty, such as in respect to meeting the policy objective in favour of the peaceful use of the continent. To some extent, this interpretation was encouraged by an Indian article published in 1961, when Ahluwalia praised the treaty as a contribution to disarmament and world peace[19]. But this support was qualified by her mention of an Indian preference for 'full internationalisation', a view developed more fully in 1974 by another academic, Jain, who identified 'glaring drawbacks' in the 1959 treaty and asserted that Antarctica 'should be controlled by the UN in conformity with the wider community expectations'[20]. The absence of government statements on Antarctica during this period renders it difficult to evaluate how far Ahluwalia and Jain reflected official Indian thinking.

In any case, the fiscal, logistical and other burdens of Antarctic activities have helped to mitigate the impact of third parties upon the continent's affairs, even if this has not prevented certain governments from developing an Antarctic presence; in fact, emerging third party activity, such as upon the part of Brazil, prompted a discussion of the subject at the 1972 Consultative Meeting in order to prepare the way for the 1975 Meeting to pass recommendation VIII-8. It was agreed that, in the event of activity in the treaty area by non-parties:

> It would be advisable for Governments to consult together as provided for by the Treaty and to be ready to urge or invite as appropriate the State or States concerned to accede to the Treaty, pointing out the rights and benefits they would receive and also the responsibilities of Contracting Parties.

In general, most outsiders becoming more active in Antarctica have acceded to the treaty, such as evidenced by the example of Brazil in 1975, even if the intentions of India gave the Consultative Parties some cause for concern between 1981-3, that is, prior to its accession to the treaty.

As a result, the Consultative Parties adopted the view that the continent's affairs should be managed only within the parameters of the Antarctic Treaty System. Additional responsibilities could be absorbed through the pragmatic evolution of the system, and inevitably the Consultative Parties assumed an unenthusiastic and negative, even hostile, attitude towards outside intervention, whether by governments or international organisations, in Antarctic questions. In general the Consultative Parties have remained anxious to preserve the UN's non-role in the region, and this attitude led the 1964 Consultative Meeting to decide against any action upon a British proposal to clarify the treaty system's relationship with international organisations[21]. Similarly, the 1972 Consultative Meeting failed to respond positively to New Zealand's revival of the UN trusteeship proposal[22].

Outside Pressure During the 1970s

In fact, the early 1970s witnessed a series of efforts by the Consultative Parties to block various initiatives perceived as a threat to their conception of Antarctic management. For instance, in January 1971 the Secretary-General advised the Committee on Natural Resources of the UN Economic and Social Council (ECOSOC) that:

> Any world-wide assessment of natural resources would be incomplete if the resources-related information now being gathered in Antarctica, and the relevant data that will

> undoubtedly come to light in the future, were missing altogether or not taken fully into account during the Committee's deliberations about natural resources on a global scale[23].

It appears that the Argentine government, among others, acted to contain any ECOSOC intervention in the Consultative Parties' sphere of influence, although the UN was informed that such matters were under consideration already, such as by SCAR[24]. A similar story of outside interest and Consultative Party opposition characterised two other episodes, which involved the United Nations Environment Program (UNEP) and the United Nations Development Program (UNDP). During February 1975 the UNEP proposed UN involvement in the environmental protection of Antarctica, such as in respect to the establishment of guidelines in the event of resource exploration and exploitation, and it would appear that this move was prompted not only by emerging international perceptions of Antarctica's resource potential but also by the 1972 UN Environment Conference at Stockholm, which fostered the development of international environmental law. The Consultative Parties, which had oft-expressed their prime responsibilities for the Antarctic environment, utilised their influence upon the UNEP Governing Council - eight were represented thereupon - to foil any action; thus, the Consultative Parties pointed out the lack of need for UNEP intervention, and in effect employed the 1975 Consultative Meeting to highlight the capacity of the Antarctic Treaty System to protect the environment without outside help, such as demonstrated by recommendations VIII-11 and VIII-13[25].

Whereas the UNEP had approached Antarctica from the environmental point of view of resources, the UNDP was more interested in the fishing potential of Antarctic oceans, such as indicated in 1976 by its approval of $202,000 for a Southern Oceans Fisheries Survey Program to be executed by the FAO. One of the outstanding results of this project was Inigo Everson's survey of The Living Resources of the Southern Ocean, but in 1979 the FAO decided not to implement a proposed $45 million ten-year programme on the exploration, exploitation and utilisation of living resources south of 45°S[26]. The ostensible reason was the FAO desire to give primacy to the development of the offshore economic zones of Third World nations, but diplomatic pressure from the Consultative Parties has been oft-mentioned as the main cause, especially as the BIOMASS programme was presented as already performing the projected function of the FAO programme[27]. Therefore, both the UNEP and UNDP initiatives were contained by the Consultative Parties, partly through the exercise of diplomatic and other forms of pressure and partly through the argument that the activities of the Antarctic Treaty System rendered superfluous any external intervention[28]. In turn, the FAO Fisheries Committee's decision to desist from parallel activities has been interpreted as an implicit international recognition of the competence of the Antarctic Treaty System in resource-related and other areas.

The FAO discussions reflected another key trend of the 1970s, that is, the growing interest of developing nations in Antarctica's resource potential, an interest which led into the advocacy of a more equitable approach towards decision-making and the distribution of resource benefits. Guinea employed the FAO in 1976 to press the case for an alternative international regime beyond the Antarctic Treaty, thereby encouraging governments to question the validity of the existing Antarctic arrangements, which permitted minimal inputs from the outside world. There was also a brief discussion at the 1976 Non-Aligned Conference held at Colombo, where the Sri Lankan delegation drew attention to the importance of reconciling the management and utilisation of the resources south of 45°S with the interests of the international community. Argentina, a Consultative Party represented there, secured the topic's deletion from the conference resolutions, but the episode symbolised the manner in which the validity of the Antarctic Treaty, the lynchpin of the Antarctic system, was being questioned by developing countries, such as in terms of its presentation as a product of the colonial era and of their pre-independence days. It was argued that the treaty, having been concluded without their participation, was being undermined by changing politico-legal concepts centred upon the New International Economic Order (NIEO) and the common heritage principle.

Neither international politics nor international law remain static, and the emergence of the developing nations - the so-called Group of 77 - served not only to increase the membership of the UN but also to foster the rise of new concepts to challenge traditional doctrines, such as typified in 1974 by the UN's support for a NIEO[29]. The basic philosophy of NIEO derived from the 'injustice' of the 'widening gap between the developed and developing countries', which arose in part from colonialism.

> All States are juridically equal and, as equal members of the international community, have the right to participate fully and effectively in the international decision-making process in the solution of world ... problems ... and to share equitably in the benefits resulting therefrom.

Antarctica became depicted as a suitable problem, which required treatment through the active and equal participation of the developing countries in the formulation and application of all decisions, an approach further encouraged by the fact that the Antarctic Treaty could be interpreted as one of the 'remaining vestiges of ... colonial domination' responsible for the gulf between the developed and developing countries. In turn, the political impact of the NIEO was underlain by the common heritage principle, which resulted in efforts to identify Antarctica as a common space, or global common, in order to reinforce the case against the Antarctic Treaty System, and especially against the pretensions of the Consultative Parties to manage resources.

The rise of the common heritage concept possessed significant implications not only for the international acceptability of the Antarctic Treaty System but also for the validity of individual sovereignty claims, since the argument that Antarctica must be terra communis involved an implicit denial of the traditional legal approaches based upon discovery, taking possession and effective occupation. These points were discussed in chapter six, where Honnold was quoted as an advocate of the view that a new international regime should replace the 'stalemated' Antarctic Treaty, while Barnes has claimed that 'it is questionable whether the theoretical underpinnings of claims to national sovereignty will continue to be viable in the new international climate'[30]. The common heritage idea provided outsiders with a legal rationale for intervention in Antarctica, particularly as the concept harmonised with the NIEO philosophy and was given substance by international developments regarding the law of the sea and outer space. During the years following its signature the Antarctic Treaty was oft-discussed as a precedent for international agreement upon outer space, whereas by the 1970s the application of the common heritage idea to outer space reversed the process, and caused commentators to advocate the transformation of Antarctica in the light of the 1967 Outer Space Treaty or subsequently of the 1979 Moon Treaty[31]. In fact, the Outer Space Treaty contained certain similarities to the Antarctic Treaty, including provisions for non-militarisation, freedom of scientific research, exchange of information and inspection, but there existed significant variations; thus, article I stipulated that outer space should be regulated 'for the benefit and in the interests of all countries ... and shall be the province of all mankind', and this common heritage approach led into article II's provision that outer space 'is not subject to national appropriation by claims of sovereignty'[32]. Subsequently, the 1979 Moon Treaty declared that 'the moon and its natural resources are the common heritage of mankind' (article II), and included rules for the orderly and safe development of resources and the equitable sharing of benefits.

The Impact of the UNCLOS Episode upon Antarctica

Naturally, outer space has proved one area of inspiration for the attempt of developing countries to transform Antarctica's political and legal position, but the most significant influence upon international perceptions towards Antarctica has been the UNCLOS episode, which culminated during 1982 with a Convention, according to which article 136 stated that 'the area and its resources are the common heritage of mankind'. This project commenced in 1967, when the UN General Assembly first discussed the common heritage concept with regard to the sea-bed and ocean floor, thereby providing the basis for the adoption in 1970 of a Declaration of Principles; thus, 'the sea-bed and ocean floor ... beyond the limits of national jurisdiction ... as well as the resources of the area, are the common heritage of mankind ... (and ... shall not be subject to appropriation by States'. In this manner, resolution 2749 spelled out the underlying philosophy of the UNCLOS negotiations, which served not only to preoccupy the international community during the 1970s but also to encourage occasional UN initiatives - for example, by ECOSOC, the UNEP and the UNDP - in respect to Antarctica. The changing political and legal considerations and the sense of idealism underlying these moves came together also in a key speech delivered in October 1975 to the General Assembly by Shirley Amerasinghe, the Sri Lankan president of the UNCLOS.

> There are still areas of the planet where opportunities remain for constructive and peaceful cooperation on the part of the international community for the common good of all rather than the benefit of a few. Such an area is the Antarctic Continent ... Antarctica is an area where the now widely accepted ideas and concepts relating to international economic cooperation, with their special stress on the principle of equitable sharing of the world's resources, can find ample scope for application, given the cooperation and goodwill of those who have so far been active in this area[33].

Although Amerasinghe expressed the hope that 'a new initiative' for Antarctica 'will not create a flutter in any dovecotes', it was apparent that the Consultative Parties were becoming not only aware of the challenge to the Antarctic Treaty System but also more anxious about the consequences, even if the actual impact of the threat was qualified by the relative incoherence and debatable international acceptability of the common heritage concept[34]. The latter's increased visibility did not mean the displacement of existing legal notions, especially as the Consultative Parties argued that Antarctica was subject already to a legal regime prior to the emergence of the common heritage principle; thus, this feature differentiated Antarctica sharply from the deep sea-bed or outer space[35]. It was felt that the critics misunderstood the nature of the Antarctic Treaty System, partly because ideological prejudices caused them to overlook

Antarctic realities; for example, in 1977 one American official complained that the common heritage concept was:

> A banner which cloaks a neo-imperialist ethic that large numbers of countries which collectively form a political unit in the United Nations should be given functional sovereignty over two-thirds of the earth's surface because they asked for it as a kind of symbolic compensation for prior decades of Western imperialism[36].

In general, the critics of the Antarctic Treaty System spoke a similar language, but failed to come together in a coherent and consistent campaign, such as demonstrated by the occasional statements of the Algerian, Guinean, Libyan and Sri Lankan governments. One of the more significant opinions came from Christopher Pinto, a Sri Lankan diplomat involved in the UNCLOS talks, who echoed Amerasinghe and spoke in 1977 of the need for any Antarctic regime to take account of the interests of the international community in order to:

> Secure optimum benefits for mankind as a whole, and in particular for the developing countries, in accordance with appropriate global international arrangements, and within the framework of the new international economic order[37].

In 1978 he predicted that 'the Antarctic is ripe for conflict', and in this context Pinto urged UN action 'to reconcile the interests of the world community with the interests of individual countries' as well as to perform 'a comprehensive study of the economic potential of Antarctica'[38]. He proposed that UN action should comprise the creation of a committee of the Consultative Parties and fifteen other states to advise the General Assembly. During September 1979 Alvaro de Soto, a Peruvian diplomat and UNCLOS spokesman for the Group of 77, launched a strong attack upon the secretive and exclusive Antarctic Treaty System, which he likened to a form of 'international apartheid' in an overt attempt to apply the language of the NIEO.

> The silence of the (international) community regarding the Treaty can hardly be understood as a form of acquiescence. Nor is it possible to say that there is any statute of limitation in respect of the options open to the rest of mankind ... a comprehensive political debate on the question of Antarctica is inevitable ... and may well be desirable[39].

Although these statements possess a contemporary relevance, they need to be viewed in proportion, since at the time the interests of the international community in general, and of the developing countries in particular, in respect to Antarctica were pressed neither vigorously nor consistently, and the oft-cited but relatively isolated exhortations of Pinto and others made relatively little headway against the Antarctic system. In part, this resulted from the preoccupation of most developing nations with the on-going UNCLOS negotiations, since there existed a fear that the introduction of the Antarctic issue would serve not only to complicate the discussions but also to threaten the prospects of success; for example, certain Consultative Parties might have withdrawn from the talks rather than compromise their legal rights to Antarctica. The anxiety that 'Antarctica could blow the Conference right out of the water' encouraged the UNCLOS negotiators to steer clear of Antarctica and reduced the level of governmental pressure against the Antarctic Treaty System[40]. In addition, Amerasinghe's replacement as a member of the Sri Lankan UN delegation, left a void in the sense that most critics during the late 1970s lacked his status and respect, while the much-quoted comments of Pinto and de Soto were made essentially in their personal capacities under the umbrella of the environmental movement, that is, during the course of press conferences arranged by the International Institute for the Environment and Development (IIED) and by Earthscan. Quigg has proved critical also of the quality of the arguments advanced against the treaty system - 'non-treaty powers can surely marshal better arguments' - but such developments encouraged the Consultative Parties to assume a more defensive attitude regarding the system's merits, a trend highlighted by the speech used by Ted Rowlands, the British minister of state at the Foreign Office, to open the 1977 Consultative Meeting[41].

> Whether we like it or not, one of the tests of the obligations imposed on us ... is whether the decisions we reach are acceptable to the wider world community. The test of that acceptability will largely depend on the clarity with which we are seen to be serving the long-term interests of the Antarctic and the world community rather than short-term illusions of national advantage[42].

It is easy to dismiss such statements as mere rhetoric designed to appease critics, but the British government, like some of the other Consultative Parties, was developing a realistic appreciation of the need not only to consider the interests of the international community but also to promote a more positive picture regarding the benefits of the existing Antarctic framework. However, an ability to pose the problem of external accommodation was no guarantee of success in establishing the merits of the treaty system, and during 1977

Brian Roberts pointed out that in the future the Consultative Parties 'will no longer be able to make effective decisions about the peaceful development of the Antarctic without steadily growing opposition'[43]. In this context, he observed that certain changes would be required if the Consultative Parties were 'to be recognised by the United Nations as responsible trustees acting on behalf of a much wider group of nations'. Roberts' emphasis upon the dangers of procrastination followed Rowlands' warning at the 1977 Consultative Meeting.

> The world will not give us long to see if we can pass these tests. If we fail them, the obligation to come up with answers to Antarctic problems will inevitably devolve on the wider community[44].

In the event, no real attempt was made by the Consultative Parties to examine how the interests of the international community might be fulfilled, and vague phrases - most notably, 'the interests of mankind' - were employed regularly in recommendations to gloss over this difficult problem. Indeed, in 1977, that is, the year in which Rowlands and Roberts made the above-cited remarks, a British Foreign Office briefing paper highlighted the view that wider interests would have to be satisfied within the treaty framework rather than through an international solution.

> If the Antarctic were brought under the control of a world-wide agency, possibly within the United Nations, it would be far more difficult to achieve the level of cooperation that has been possible within the Antarctic Treaty framework ... an Antarctic authority could prove even harder to set up than a Sea-bed Authority. An ill-functioning international arrangement might tempt countries active in the Antarctic to act unilaterally with possible risks for the environment and with damaging effects for Antarctic scientific cooperation. The vast investments required to exploit Antarctic resources would be made in the medium term only if clear cut and stable régimes were seen to be operating[45].

By implication, the interests of the international community could be met only within the Antarctic Treaty System - the marine resource negotiations of 1977-80 emphasised this point - since any international regime would bring instability, thereby harming both Antarctic and global interests. In any case, the common heritage principle was viewed with little enthusiasm by the Consultative Parties in terms of its relevance to Antarctica, although there is evidence that one claimant, Norway, was more sympathetic to the principle[46].

During the 1970s the UNCLOS negotiations helped to alleviate the strength of the pressure exerted against the Antarctic Treaty System by the global commons lobby, even if the Consultative Parties conceded that eventually the challenge would have to be confronted. For example, in 1979 a working group on Antarctic minerals stated that 'representatives were mindful of the developments likely to result from the Third UN Conference on the Law of the Sea', a sentiment embodied in recommendation XI-1 (1981), which stipulated also that the minerals regime area would include the offshore part of Antarctica 'but without encroachment on the deep seabed'[47]. Although this form of words was designed to avoid overlapping areas of jurisdiction, the conclusion of the UNCLOS talks gave claimants cause for concern, since article 1 (1) of the Convention indicated its application to the seabed and ocean floor 'beyond the limits of national jurisdiction'. From the perspective of the advocates of the common heritage principle, this phrase could be interpreted as including Antarctica and its coastal shelf, thereby permitting the ISBA to adopt an ambitious view of its area of responsibility[48]. The Antarctic implications of UNCLOS have been oft-discussed in terms of the convention's embodiment of the common heritage principle as a customary rule of international law in maritime zones, although the Consultative Parties feared also that the agreement would raise a new dimension to the sovereignty question, since the declaration of 200 mile EEZs might cause controversy. On the one hand, the claimants could regard an EEZ as an attribute of sovereignty which had to be announced in order to preserve the credibility of their claims, whereas on the other hand non-claimants could treat an EEZ as an extension of a claim in breach of the freeze imposed by article IV of the Antarctic Treaty. Another view argued that the absence of a generally-recognised sovereignty in Antarctica ruled out the possibility of coastal state jurisdiction. Such matters have aroused intense speculation, but as yet there have occurred no serious difficulties[49]. However, at one time, there appeared the possibility of complications arising out of the Australian government's declaration of a 200 mile EEZ around its territories, including the AAT. However, this proclamation of 20 September 1979 was followed soon by another, dated 31 October 1979, which exempted AAT from this provision[50]. In this manner, the Australian government asserted its legal rights regarding the AAT, but decided against their exercise in the interests of Antarctic cooperation. These examples illustrate certain aspects of the debate regarding the Antarctic implications of the UNCLOS negotiations, but there is also a need to remember that certain Consultative Parties, including the UK, the USA and West Germany, have assumed a critical stance to the Law of the Sea Convention *per se*, and have refused to sign it.

Malaysia and the Campaign against the Antarctic Treaty System

Against this background, it was perhaps inevitable that the UNCLOS signing ceremony held at Montego Bay, Jamaica, during December 1982 inspired some delegates to urge that:

> It is time now to focus our attention on another area of common interest ... I refer to Antarctica, where immense potentialities exist for the benefit of all mankind[51].

This statement emanated from the Malaysian delegate, Ghazali Shafie, and developed a point made the previous day by the Tanzanian representative regarding the 'unfortunate' omission of Antarctica from the Convention. On the surface, these assertions reflected the commitment of developing countries to the further implementation of the common heritage principle, but some cynics among the Consultative Parties suggested that the international lawyers and others involved for a long time in the UNCLOS negotiations were seeking merely another source of employment for their time and energy. Possibly, there was some truth in this comment, but it failed to do justice to the motives of the Malaysian government, which emerged during 1982-3 as the leading advocate of an UNCLOS-inspired, UN-based alternative to the Antarctic Treaty System. In fact, the Malaysian government, and expecially the prime minister, Dr. Mahathir Mohamad, provided something which the critical lobby had lacked hitherto, that is, leadership consistency and strength of pressure, and a clear sense of purpose. Until this period, the priority of the Antarctic problem had been low for developing countries, and it proved easy for the Consultative Parties to question the strength of the critical lobby[52]. However, the early 1980s witnessed a growth of interest, such as demonstrated after 1981 by India's expeditions and, it is reported, in 1982 by a note sent by Mrs Gandhi to 25 neighbouring heads of government on the subject of the Third World's role in Antarctica; thus, developing countries might operate either within or outside the Antarctic Treaty System in order to secure change[53]. In the event, India decided to sign the Antarctic Treaty as the most appropriate way to advance the interests of India and of the developing countries, whereas the Malaysian government decided to act from outside through a well-orchestrated campaign to make other governments and international organisations aware of their case, or rather of the case presented by Malaysia on behalf of the international community. This campaign served to give Malaysia, and particularly Dr Mahathir, greater international visibility as well as to associate it with an altruistic concern for global issues, even if some commentators questioned the sincerity of Mahathir's motives in pushing the Antarctic problem. However, his support for the common heritage concept harmonised with the thinking of the Group of 77, including the desire to move on from UNCLOS to other perceived problem areas, while the campaign might be interpreted in part as a consequence of Mahathir's philosophical and radical approach to politics, such as demonstrated within Malaysia by the adoption of 'new ideas and new approaches in the task of nation-building'[54]. The precise motivations for Malaysian policy towards Antarctica await further study.

In fact, Malaysia's first real move on the subject occurred a few months prior to the UNCLOS signing ceremony, for Mahathir launched his campaign on 29 September 1982 in a speech delivered to the UN General Assembly. He ranged over various topics relating to the gulf between rich and poor nations and to the consequent need to protect the interests of developing nations.

> Henceforth all the unclaimed wealth of this earth must be regarded as the common heritage of all the nations ... Now that we have reached agreement on the law of the sea the United Nations must convene a meeting in order to define the problem of uninhabited lands ... It is now time that the United Nations focussed its attention on these areas, the largest of which is the continent of Antarctica[55].

Although the Antarctic Treaty possessed 'some merit', he dismissed it as:

> An agreement between a select group of countries and does not reflect the true feelings of the Members of the United Nations or their just claims. A new international agreement is required so these historical episodes are not made into facts to substantiate claims.

During 1983 the most significant moves occurred between 7-12 March at the Seventh Non-Aligned Summit Meeting held at New Delhi, where Mahathir secured the backing of the non-aligned movement for at least part of his policy. His speech delivered on 8 March sought both an alternative to the Antarctic Treaty and a UN study of the Antarctic question:

> So that we may have a truly universal cooperation on Antarctica under the umbrella of the United Nations similar to the Convention on the Law of the Sea. The United Nations must address itself to the issue and re-examine the potentials for a more universal framework of international cooperation on Antarctica[56].

However, the Economic Declaration issued at the close of the Summit Meeting scaled down these demands, for the Heads of State and Government 'considered that the United Nations should undertake a comprehensive study on Antarctica' and merely noted rather than condemned the Antarctic Treaty[57]. It appears that behind-the-scenes lobbying by Argentina, the only Consultative Party represented at the Summit, had contributed to this situation. Nevertheless, the non-aligned movement - 99 governments were represented at New Delhi - had been mobilised in support of the Malaysian initiative, and this episode fostered increased international visibility for Antarctic matters, especially as Malaysian ministers endeavoured henceforth to keep the topic to the forefront of the international community's attention. Mahathir's speeches returned constantly to the UN-Antarctic theme, and his meetings with other governments were utilised either to secure declarations of support, such as from Sri Lanka (April 1983) or from Turkey (May and September 1983) or to promote a wider understanding of his objectives, such as characterised by his visits to Yugoslavia (May 1983) and South Korea (August 1983).

In this manner, Antarctica emerged as a more significant perceived international issue, even for governments which had taken no previous interest in the continent. For example, certain African and Caribbean governments assumed a close interest in the topic, and the government of Antigua and Barbuda became Malaysia's leading supporter. As a result, Antarctica was discussed at both the OECS and CARICOM meetings held in May and June 1983 respectively. Lester Bird, Antigua's deputy prime minister, told the OECS that:

> What is sad about this connivance (the treaty system) between eastern and western industrialised nations is that a handful of Third World countries are active participants with them to exclude other Third World countries[58].

Although there was the usual stress upon the iniquities of the Antarctic Treaty System, the Antiguan government introduced a further dimension to the international debate on Antarctica on account of Bird's complaint that 'what is monstrous is that South Africa is an accepted partner in these deliberations'. Inevitably, the addition of the South African apartheid issue attracted other governments, particularly those from Africa, whose activities were coordinated in part through their diplomatic representatives in London.

The momentum of the campaign to involve the UN was maintained during mid-1983, and its perceived strength proved sufficient to cause the Consultative Parties considerable anxiety about the potential threat to the Antarctic Treaty system, thereby prompting some Consultative Parties to exert diplomatic pressure upon the critics in order to contain the consequences of the campaign. Obviously, the nature and details of these moves remain unclear, but there is evidence to suggest that they included British pressure upon Antigua and Barbuda - for example, Howe, the foreign minister, discussed the matter in London with Vere Bird, Antigua's prime minister - as well as action by the Australian, Soviet and US governments upon other Caribbean nations[59]. These individual and clandestine efforts were paralleled by a collective note handed to the Malaysian representative at the UN by the Australian government, which was acting on behalf of the Consultative Parties and had been coordinating their views. This note, dated 29 July 1983, highlighted the Consultative Parties' views regarding the merits of the treaty system and emphasised their solidarity in opposing the Malaysian initiative.

> The revision or replacement of the Treaty which Malaysia is now proposing would undermine this system of international law and order in Antarctica with very serious consequences for international peace and cooperation ... the Consultative Parties to the Antarctic Treaty object unanimously to the Malaysian initiative, and to any attempt to revise or replace the Treaty[60].

Although some feel that the Consultative Parties have shown an exaggerated concern, verging perhaps upon neurosis and fear, about the UN aspect, it is worth noting the unity displayed by them towards outsiders, including the manner in which the episode brought together such groups of governments as the Soviet Union and the USA or Argentina and Britain, which were not enjoying the most harmonious relationships in other parts of the world[61].

In September 1983 the Consultative Parties attempted to reinforce their position through the addition of two more Consultative Parties, Brazil and India, whose promotion served not only to strengthen the treaty system but also to undermine the potential power of the critical campaign; thus, such considerations overrode the fact that neither country had fulfilled the traditional requirements of this status[62]. In particular, India's international stature, including its chairmanship of the Non-Aligned Movement, meant that its participation in the treaty system represented not only a considerable coup for the Consultative Parties but also a significant transformation in the situation, even if some suspected that India might attempt to weaken the system from within[63]. The inclusion of acceding states as observers at the Consultative Meeting of September 1983 constituted another response - this move was designed to defuse criticism about the closed and exclusive nature of the system - as did the meeting's discussions about publicity and information. Naturally, the session provided an opportunity for an exchange of views about the UN initiative, and resulted in a statement in which the 'Consultative Parties unanimously reaffirmed their commitment to the Antarctic Treaty and expressed their concern' about Malaysian and other proposals[64]. Basically, the Consultative Parties were opposed still to any universalist solution for Antarctica, partly because of their belief in the merits of the Antarctic Treaty System and partly because of more specific reasons; thus, any attempt to apply common heritage principles to Antarctica proved unwelcome because of existing sovereignty claims and of the Antarctic Treaty regime. Such pre-existing legal arrangement differentiated Antarctica from outer space and the deep seabed, and Vicuna has stressed that 'the concept of the common heritage cannot be extended beyond the specific regimes which have accepted it'[65]. These legal arguments have reinforced, perhaps been employed to rationalise, political considerations relating to the desire of the Consultative Parties to preserve the Antarctic Treaty System and their primacy in the management of the continent; in addition, it was feared that any alternative regime would pose 'great risks of a political kind to continued peace in Antarctica'[66].

But the individual and collective efforts made during 1983 by the Consultative Parties failed to deter Malaysia and its supporters. On 11 August 1983 Malaysia and Antigua and Barbuda sent a note to the UN Secretary-General on the subject of Antarctica, and in September their advocacy, in conjunction with the support of such governments as Algeria, Pakistan and Singapore, resulted in the placement of Antarctica on the agenda of the forthcoming General Assembly[67]. A few days later the Malaysian foreign ministry utilised Malaysian television and a news conference held in Kuala Lumpur to indicate the primacy - 'it is another major issue for us' - attached to the topic by the government[68]. Naturally, the Consultative Parties were unhappy about the trend of events, and the UN General Committee's debate on the Assembly agenda was employed to express their 'serious reservations' on the matter[69]. This attitude was repeated at greater length in a series of notes sent to the UN Secretary-General by Richard Woolcott, the Australian chairman of the New York working group of the Consultative Parties; thus, the notes stressed the political, scientific and environmental benefits deriving from the existence and preservation of the Antarctic Treaty System.

> The Treaty serves the international community well ... Revision or replacement of the Treaty which is now being suggested by Malaysia and Antigua and Barbuda would undermine this system of international law and order in Antarctica with very serious consequences for international peace and cooperation ... Every effort should be made to preserve and maintain it[70].

The UN Discusses Antarctica for the First Time in 1983

These events provided the background to the UN's first real involvement in the 'Question of Antarctica', which was taken up by the Assembly's First Committee and discussed at five sessions held in November 1983. The choice of the First Committee implied a general perception that the topic was primarily of political rather than of legal and economic significance; in fact, the Law of the Sea negotiations had commenced in a similar manner.

Although the First Committee devoted nearly nine hours to the topic and heard from 41 delegates, the sessions were characterised by the repetition of a few themes, grouped essentially around two main viewpoints; thus, the single-minded emphasis of the Antarctic Treaty powers upon the merits of the treaty system was matched by the manner in which the critics tended to echo each other, albeit with occasional differences of stress. To some extent, this polarisation of views had been encouraged by preceding exchanges within each camp, for the interchanges of the treaty powers in Canberra and New York were paralleled by those of the developing countries during the course of the meeting of non-aligned states held in New York between 4-7 October 1983[71]. Certain delegations, including those from Antigua and Barbuda, Australia, Argentina, Chile, Malaysia and New Zealand, had outlined their basic positions during the course of speeches delivered to the General Assembly itself during late September and early October, and hence the statements made in the First Committee served merely to repeat familiar attitudes, albeit at greater length, particularly as the general tendency was to follow the UN practice of stating positions rather than to engage in meaningful debate[72].

The relative predictability of the UN events recalled Keith Brennan's comment made in 1982, when he anticipated that the critics would direct their attack mainly at the closed and privileged nature of a group of Consultative Parties intent on 'monopolising the resources of Antarctica'[73]. This line characterised the opening speeches delivered by the Antiguan and Malaysian delegations, and their joint attack upon the treaty system placed the Consultative Parties on the defensive from the start[74]. Jacobs of Antigua and Barbuda asserted the importance of upholding the common heritage principle, such as applied in the recent UNCLOS negotiations, especially in the context of the narrow basis of Antarctic decision-making and of the alleged failure of the Consultative Parties to consider Third World interests. This theme was developed by Zainal Abidin (Malaysia), who pointed to the 'democratisation of decision-making on the international scene' and to the fact that 'the world of 1959, when the Antarctic Treaty was first formulated, is different from that of 1983'[75]. Inevitably, he focussed attention upon the closed nature of the treaty system, such as to its 'exclusivity', its enhancement of the interests of 'the privileged few', and its secrecy. The approach mapped out by Jacobs and Zainal Abidin was followed by other speakers from the developing world, including Algeria, Bangladesh, Bhutan, Egypt, Ghana, Jamaica, Libya, Pakistan, Philippines, Sierra Leone, Sri Lanka, Sudan, Tunisia, Yugoslavia and Zambia. The main thrust of the critics was in favour of an UN Study on Antarctica as a first step by the international community, since this demand was in conformity with the Non-Aligned Summit Declaration of March. However, there was some disagreement about the ultimate objective. The Malaysian delegation stated that:

> It is time for the United Nations to address itself to considering further internationalist modalities to deal with the question of Antarctica ... it is time that a proper and representative international regime beyond the Antarctic Treaty be explored within the framework of the United Nations[76].

This advocacy of a new international regime for Antarctica in place of the 1959 Treaty was seconded by other speakers, such as from Pakistan, but Antigua and Barbuda, while oft-quoted in the same breath as Malaysia, implied a more limited aim; thus, Jacobs commented that 'my delegation does not seek to tear up the Antarctic Treaty', thereby indicating his government's desire for 'new perceptions' and reform within rather than outside the Antarctic Treaty System[77]. Nevertheless, Antigua's desire to open up the system was qualified by its demand for South Africa's 'immediate expulsion from membership in the Consultative Group'[78]. Inevitably, this demand was endorsed by several other delegates mainly for reasons having little to do with Antarctic conditions, and this overt political intrusion into the continent's affairs was highlighted by the attempt made by Sierra Leone, acting on behalf of African governments, to include the South African point in the proposed resolution of the First Committee[79].

In response to this critique the Treaty parties assumed both a positive and a negative attitude, such as demonstrated by the emphasis upon the merits of the treaty system and the rebuttal of specific criticisms. In fact, the relative unanimity shown by the Treaty powers offered an interesting insight into not only the cooperative tendencies of the system but also the manner in which the external challenge had reinforced pre-existing levels of unity. Speakers focussed upon their respective country's historical involvement and expertise in Antarctica as well as upon their proven concern for its responsible management, while also attempting, like Harland (New Zealand), Sorzano (USA) and Heap (UK), to correct the distorted picture of the Antarctic system allegedly held by the critics. For example, Heap admitted that 'if there is a leitmotif to my statement, it is that misconceptions abound', so that insufficient credit was given for the way in which the treaty system constituted 'a remarkable exercise in prudent forethought ... capable of dynamic development' based upon 'political forebearance and accommodation'[80]. Yakovlev, the Soviet delegate, pointed to the open nature of the system, such as evidenced by the recent admission of Brazil and India as Consultative Parties, and urged other governments to adhere to the treaty[81]. The anxiety to defend the on-going minerals regime talks encouraged delegates to play down the prospects of resource exploitation, and Kuroda (Japan) criticised the worrying tendency of some governments to regard Antarctica as 'a kind of treasure island' soon to yield its resources[82]. In the light of the speculation surrounding India's recent entry to the treaty system, it is worth noting that Verma, its First Committee delegate, adopted a relatively low-key role as compared to the representatives of the other Consultative Parties, while Mrs Gandhi's speech to the Assembly on 28 September was significant for its omission of any mention of Antarctica[83].

After their failure to prevent UN intervention, the Consultative Parties acted to control the nature of any resolution, and Woolcott (Australia) remarked that the draft placed before the First Committee proved:

> The product of a long and very delicate set of negotiations between its sponsors, on the one hand, and the members of the Antarctic Treaty, on the other, in which I, as Chairman of the Group, was closely involved[84].

This search for consensus between the treaty powers and the critics meant that Sierra Leone was persuaded not to press for the inclusion of a South African reference in the draft resolution, which was carried without a vote in both the First Committee and the General Assembly on 30 November and 15 December 1983 respectively[85]. As a result, the UN Secretary-General was requested to prepare for the next Assembly 'a comprehensive, factual and objective study on all aspects of Antarctica, taking fully into account the Antarctic Treaty System and other relevant factors'. The views of member states were to be solicited for the guidance of the Secretary-General. This resolution, 38/77, represented the UN's first meaningful move in regard to Antarctica, and provided a possible foundation for its future role in the region. Although changing international conditions encouraged the adoption of different perspectives towards Antarctica, it is clear that without the determined efforts of the Malaysian government the UN reference would not have occurred in 1983. The First Committee's debates were characterised by a polarisation of views, but such divisions should not obscure the fact that the episode had brought together the Antarctic Treaty System and the UN for an exchange of opinions, a point accentuated by the achievement of a consensus resolution. Whether the UN Study would enable the maintenance of this dialogue was debatable, especially as both sides anticipated that the report would support their respective viewpoints; in turn, the appearance of the Study would allow Sierra Leone and other governments to return again to the South African aspect[86]. The debates had compelled also the wider international community not only to consider Antarctica but also to take sides; thus, the general support of several developing countries for the critique of the Antarctic Treaty System was paralleled by the decision of Finland and Sweden to accede to the treaty in the near future in order to express their belief in its merits.

The 1984 UN Study on Antarctica

The UN Study was prepared at speed in 1984, and was based upon a range of source material, including published articles and books - the choice was often somewhat eccentric - and responses submitted by member governments and interested organisations. This involved processing vast quantities of information - for example, Australia's 159 page response was accompanied by two large volumes of appendices - and naturally time constraints rendered it difficult to feed everything into the Study, particularly as several responses were either delayed or not received in time. In the event, preparation and translation difficulties meant that the Study appeared late, that is, only a few days prior to the scheduled debate[87].

The UN Study comprised 116 pages, and provided a concise, sound account of relevant political, legal, scientific and geographical matters, while the balanced approach, in conjunction with the absence of a concluding chapter, highlighted the factual nature of a report designed to permit member governments to draw their own conclusions. The British representative, Heap, observed that it had sailed between 'the Scylla and Charybdis of differing political viewpoints', although it was clear that governments would read what they wanted into the Study[88]. However, in many places, the Study implied an opinion, such as conceding the merits of the Antarctic Treaty System. For example, it recognised the manner in which the conclusion of the Antarctic Treaty during the late 1950s served to avoid a possible 'confrontation on a world-wide scale ... in the area' and then to maintain, 'two and a half decades of peace in Antarctica'; in addition, the treaty system had ensured that 'human activities in Antarctica ... are being carried out in accordance with the strict rules and regulations imposed on such activities by the Antarctic Treaty Consultative Parties'[89].

As a result, the Study found it difficult to remain 'factual and objective', and certain polar experts might also disagree with the assertion that 'the first definite sighting of Antarctica was made on 28 January 1820 ... by von Bellingshausen'[90].

In the meantime, the heightened international significance of Antarctica was evidenced by the frequent references to the topic in the General Assembly speeches delivered during September and October 1984, since it was not a subject - to quote Howe, the British foreign minister - 'much visited by Foreign Ministers'[91]. These Assembly statements reaffirmed the differences revealed in 1983, for the clear determination of the Australian, British and New Zealand governments to preserve the Antarctic Treaty System contrasted with the critical stance of Malaysia and Antigua and Barbuda. In turn, this sparring in the Assembly provided the background for the eventual appearance of the UN Study as well as for the First Committee's discussions between 28-30 November 1984, which followed the 1983 precedent in the sense that the five sessions were employed largely for 'general statements of well-known views' rather than for a meaningful debate on detailed issues[92]. Once again, the critique was led by Antigua and Barbuda and Malaysia, although the former's anxiety to reform and democratise the Antarctic Treaty System contrasted with the latter's preference for an alternative international regime[93]. Most other developing nations followed these guidelines, and placed special emphasis upon participation - most notably, the system's exclusivity and inclusion of South Africa - and the management of resources in the context of the common heritage principle and of the UNCLOS and outer space precedents. Such attitudes emanated from the delegations of Bangladesh, Cameroon, Cape Verde, Egypt, Nigeria, Pakistan, Philippines, Sri Lanka and Zambia, but perhaps the strongest attack upon the Antarctic status quo was launched by Gbeho of Ghana, who argued that 'Ghana cannot and will not continue to accept the present situation'; thus, he reserved his government's right to oppose any minerals regime drafted for the region by an 'exclusive and selfish' group, which needed to 'recognise and bow to the winds of change sweeping over that continent'[94].

Woolcott, the Australian chairman of the Consultative Parties in New York, opened the defence, which resembled the 1983 format in the sense of combining both positive and negative arguments[95]. Delegates from the treaty powers developed these aspects with varying degrees of emphasis, but considerable attention was devoted to the manner in which the treaty system preserved Antarctica as a zone of peace characterised by international cooperation. The 'open' nature of participation was pressed in order to disarm the exclusivity argument, and interested governments were urged to follow the four states which had acceded to the treaty in 1984.

References to the position of South Africa were conspicuous by their absence.

In this manner, speakers tended to adopt a committed approach either for or against the Antarctic Treaty System, although the critical contribution of Antigua and Barbuda proved of interest on account not only of its desire to work for reform rather than revolution but also of the attempt to go beyond the general arguments employed by other delegations. Therefore, Jacobs proposed the creation of a parallel minerals authority for Antarctica, which would be composed of an equal number of representatives from both the treaty powers and non-signatories; in addition, its management role would involve the implementation of a system of international taxation on production, the proceeds of which would be utilised for 'maintaining' the Antarctic environment and for loans to developing countries[96].

Sorzano (USA) suggested that there existed 'no justification for the presumption of a dichotomy between the Antarctic Treaty System and the UN system', and in this vein some delegates stressed the desirability of dialogue and consensus[97]. However, others from the treaty powers implied the risk of confrontation, such as in consequence of their unanimous refusal to countenance either replacement or parallel mechanisms for Antarctica; in fact, the Argentine and Chilean representatives went further, and indicated their respective governments' refusal to participate in any other regime[98]. Nevertheless, in general the UN discussions remained on a relatively low-key level, and appeared to attract less official and media interest than in 1983, especially as the late appearance of the UN Study induced a general reluctance to press matters too far pending a considered evaluation of its contents. In 1984 the prime Malaysian objective was the creation of a special UN committee, which would be composed of representatives drawn from both the treaty powers and the outsiders and would be instructed to consider specific items in order to advise the UN upon an agreed way forward from the Study[99]. But the proposal - this gave some substance to ideas floated in the past, such as by Pinto in the late 1970s and Brennan in 1982 - evoked only limited support from the critics, and significantly it was not endorsed by the meeting of non-aligned governments held in New York between 1-5 October 1984 under India's chairmanship. The project attracted the outright opposition of the treaty powers, which expressed - to quote, Woolcott - 'a strong preference to complete consideration of this item in a constructive manner at this year's session' and were not attracted by the implications of Malaysia's suggestion that the UN's involvement was only at an 'early stage'[100].

In the event, protracted and difficult behind-the-scenes negotiations between Woolcott and Zain - one journalist argued that these were intended to seek a compromise and to 'avert a bitterly divisive brawl in the United Nations over Antarctica' - resulted in the production of a relatively mild resolution acceptable to all factions; thus, it merely thanked the Secretary-General for the Study and placed the topic upon the agenda of the 1985 Assembly[101]. Woolcott, speaking for the Consultative Parties, asserted that the UN initiative had gone too far already and he urged the Malaysian government to re-consider the position, perhaps even to accede to the treaty. On the other hand, Zain found it difficult to conceal his dissatisfaction with the outcome, which marked no real advance upon the 1983 resolution.

> The draft resolution ... is the best that we could come up with in the end ... what the draft resolution has done, in essence, is to postpone such in-depth discussion and any decisions we may wish to make to the 40th.Session of the General Assembly[102].

The resolution was adopted without a vote by the First Committee on 30 November 1984, and subsequently approved by the Assembly on 20 December[103]. Although Antarctica remained on the UN agenda, the result was interpreted as a 'semi-defeat' for the Malaysian campaign and as a 'significant reverse for developing countries'[104]. Woolcott welcomed the outcome as an 'excellent result' for the Consultative Parties, although whether one press correspondent was correct to describe, 'the Antarctic compromise as good as a victory' for the treaty system remains a matter for speculation, particularly as Malaysia and its supporters have not accepted the failure of the UN initiative[105].

Some Developments in 1985

Although the most significant events regarding the Antarctic Treaty System and the international community will not occur until the close of 1985, that is, the Consultative Meeting and the third phase of the UN discussions, the year commenced with an interesting development relevant to this issue. Between 7-13 January 1985 a Workshop on the Antarctic Treaty System was held at Beardmore Camp on the Bowden Neve in the Transantarctic Mountains[106]. The meeting was organised by the US Polar Research Board and involved some sixty delegates drawn from Consultative Parties, acceding states, outsiders (Korea, Malaysia, Sierra Leone and Tunisia) and non-governmental organisations. The episode provided an informal method of facilitating international understanding and dialogue about Antarctica and the treaty system, and the convenience of the on-the-spot location enabled participants to visit the Amundsen-Scott South Polar station. In many respects, the exercise provided another point of contact between the Antarctic Treaty System and the international community, although the format of discussions encouraged the view that the workshop was basically a public relations effort on behalf of the treaty powers. Hatherton observed that the phrase 'common heritage' recurred continuously, particularly in the light of the attempt to allow poorer states an Antarctic role; thus, various proposals were advanced regarding joint occupation of base stations or an international station for scientists from developing nations, 'which may raise productive ripples'[107].

To some extent, this process of dialogue was continued in April 1985 by a Whither Antarctica? conference held in London, where participants assembled from both treaty powers, including Chile, Norway and the UK, and the critics, such as demonstrated by the presence of Zain, who presented the Malaysian case at the UN in 1984[108]. Although most contributions proved predictable, the paper presented by Zain showed further evidence of movement in the Malaysian position, while implying that the 1985 UN debates will be employed for a further critique of the treaty system. Zain, who displayed a clear appreciation of Antarctic realities - these were defined to include the determination of the treaty powers to preserve the Antarctic system - in the international context, concentrated upon the manner in which a few governments exercised control over the continent[109].

> The current regime of the Antarctic Treaty System ... a system of self-conferred rights which are exclusive, total and unaccountable, is seriously flawed and unjustified and it should be remedied ... they (the non-treaty powers) have an open mind. They are conscious of the legal and practical realities. They are not wedded to any particular structure for an acceptable regime. They believe that there should first be agreement on the objectives and the general characteristics of a regime, on the basis of which an acceptable structure should be worked out[110].

This evidence of a more open and conciliatory approach by the Malaysian government (even if Zain claimed to be speaking in a personal capacity) was designed to enable progress towards the establishment of a 'forum where the interested participants would be on an equal footing ... examine in depth all the outstanding issues and consider ways and means in which these differences can be reconciled'[111]. By implication, Malaysia will attempt to press again the proposal for an ad hoc UN committee to consider such 'serious questions' as rights in Antarctica, accountability, the notion of involvement, the minerals issue, and the accommodation of the views of the non-treaty powers regarding the treaty system's deficiencies. However, the comments of participants involved in the policy formulation of Consultative Parties - for example, these included Heap (UK), Vicuna (Chile) and Anderson (Norway) - tended to reaffirm their governments' antipathy towards any parallel or alternative Antarctic mechanisms; in turn, this resulted in strong opposition to the UN Committee proposal, which was viewed as a method by which the international community as a whole would be placed in a position to dismantle the Antarctic Treaty System.

Conclusion

During 1982, when UN intervention was coming closer, albeit still on the horizon, many realised that the relatively calm Antarctic situation was under threat. For instance, Brennan feared that this 'atmosphere is soon to be shattered. The (mineral) discussions will find themselves at the centre of a raging tornado when the debate on Antarctica is taken up in the United Nations'[112]. Two sessions of the UN have discussed Antarctica already, but hitherto the 'tornado' has been contained by the treaty powers, even if the continuing UN involvement brings the risk of complications; thus, the discussions at New York may go off in a range of directions, such as mentioned by Zain, who told the London seminar of the danger that the UN initiative might become 'an unguided missile'[113].

In the meantime, various question marks exist regarding Antarctica's future. For example, will the treaty powers retain their unity against the critics? Will the divisions in the ranks of the critics, such as between the Antiguan and Malaysian approaches, widen or be bridged? Will the Malaysian initiative result in a special UN committee or prove a damp squib? These questions lead into the basic point regarding the nature of the UN's future role in Antarctica. The uncertainties are reinforced by the relative fluidity of Antarctic politics, such as caused by alterations in membership - it appears likely that China will become a Consultative Party in 1985 - while the impact of future developments upon the international stability of Antarctica is equally debatable, since the position is complicated by the divergent interpretations advanced on the subject by the respective factions. On the one hand, the Consultative Parties argue that any change in the present arrangements will destabilise the situation.

> It is unrealistic to think that in the present state of world affairs a new or better legal regime could be agreed upon. Revision could open the way to an arms race in the region and might lead to new territorial claims. It will not serve the interests of any country, or group of countries, if Antarctica became an area of international conflict and discord[114].

The Consultative Parties do 'not accept the presumption that the Antarctic Treaty system is somehow a "problem" in need of revision or replacement', and Hayden (Australia) reminded the General Assembly in 1983 that 'the UN was created to solve problems, not to create new ones'[115]. On the other hand, the critical outsiders believe that Antarctica, as an international problem, requires a new approach to remedy the perceived deficiencies of the treaty system; in turn, these changes would 'ensure that the Antarctic continent is to be used for peaceful purposes and not degenerate into a new hotbed of tension and discord'[116].

Although the current international debate about Antarctica is characterised by several novel features, including the emphasis upon democratisation and the common heritage principle, the episode can be interpreted also as merely another chapter in the long-running debate of whether Antarctica should be governed through a limited or universal model[117]. In the event, the limited approach has remained predominant in respect to both the pre-1959 and post-1959 periods, and at present the Antarctic Treaty System appears well-established, a point accentuated by the combined power and influence of the participants as well as by the forthcoming conclusion of the minerals regime negotiations. But the challenge from outside cannot be ignored, especially as the post-1983 UN phase represents the most serious threat yet to the survival of the treaty system. Prediction is difficult, even if this has not prevented commentators hypothesising about a vast number of possibilities, often in a manner divorced from an appreciation of either Antarctic or international realities. However, one possible and realistic scenario during the 1980s and 1990s might comprise an enhanced UN role in the affairs of Antarctica, albeit acting within the parameters defined by the Antarctic Treaty System, which will survive and develop through additional functions and increased participation. This interpretation is encouraged by the treaty system's historical evolution, which has established an ability to accommodate changing conditions in a manner involving no real waiver in the responsibilities of the Consultative Parties. In any case, it is difficult to develop universal solutions in a world of national states, which are motivated by selfish rather than by altruistic interests. A universal international organisation for Antarctica may not necessarily constitute the best way of fulfilling and protecting the international community's interests in the region, and Charney, among others, has suggested that a more limited regime like the Antarctic Treaty System can satisfy global interests more effectively[118]. In fact, claimant governments continue to believe that territorial sovereignty possesses a relevance, such as in respect to providing for the better regulation of the continent; for example, Heap informed the 1985 London conference that one should not be deceived by contemporary rhetoric regarding the alleged merits of international regimes, since these tended to be characterised by diffuseness in decision-making[119].

At present, the prospects for the fulfillment of Malaysian objectives appear somewhat dim, although even if the UN initiative ends in failure the episode will not have been futile. Already the discussions since 1983 have reaffirmed the limits of internationalisation in Antarctica, while a more significant development has proved the consolidation of the unity of the Antarctic Treaty System. Both Vicuna and Beeby have pointed out that 'it can confidently be said that the importance attached to the system by the Treaty parties is greater today than at any other time before'; thus, this unintended consequence of the challenge to the treaty system further diminished the critics' chances of success[120]. In addition, the recent UN involvement has provided the first real point of contact between the Antarctic Treaty System and the international community acting through the UN, thereby offering a foundation for some kind of continuing working relationship, especially as the UN debates have revealed perhaps more similarities than differences. For instance there existed widespread support for the non-militarised status of Antarctica as well as for other aspects, including international scientific cooperation and environmental protection[121]. These points of agreement might prove the basis for a synthesis designed to provide a way forward during the late 1980s for the Antarctic Treaty System, albeit in a manner acceptable also to such outsiders as Malaysia and Antigua and Barbuda; in fact, treaty powers have oft-suggested that the difficulty might be resolved in part by the transformation of outsiders to treaty insiders.

The various UN-related events since 1983 have served also to provide an invaluable amount of information about all aspects of Antarctic affairs, such as highlighted by the 1984 UN Study and the accompanying national responses, which offered insights into government policies and activities. To some extent, this feature has promoted the objectives of the 1983 Consultative Meeting recommendation XII-6, which was designed to increase public knowledge about the achievements and operations of the Antarctic Treaty System. In turn, the UN episode has helped to educate the wider international community regarding the nature and significance of Antarctica, which was perceived previously by most governments - to quote, Gbeho of Ghana - as 'remote, obscure and forbidding'[122]. Antarctic politics, law and science have become more visible, and from this point of view the continent will never be quite the same again.

NOTES

1. Rose, <u>Assault on Eternity: Byrd and Antarctica</u>, p.219.

2. UNGA A/38 PV 97, pp.30-31, 15 Dec.1983; UNGA A/38/C 1 PV 46, p.13, 30 Nov.1983.

3. New York Times, 16 April 1947; United Nations: Resolutions Adopted by the Trusteeship Council 1947-1948, resolution 22 (11), p.13, 11 Dec.1947.

4. Report of the Commission to Study the Organization of Peace, Security and Disarmament under the United Nations (New York, 1947), p.22; Commission to Study the Organization of Peace, Strengthening the United Nations, p.212, p.216.

5. Hanessian, The Antarctic Treaty, pp.448-9; Edward Shackleton, 'The New Continent', United Nations World, vol.1, no.10 (1949) pp.380-2. Note also T.E.M. McKitterick, 'The Validity of Territorial and Other Claims in Polar Regions', Journal of Comparative Legislation and International Law, vol.21 (1939), p.97.

6. See above pp.38-40.

7. UNGA A/3852, p.5, 15 July 1958; UNGA A/3118, p.1, 17 Feb.1956 UNGA A/3118/Add.2, p.2, 16 Oct.1956.

8. UNGA vol. XI A (4), p.7, 14 Nov.1956; Joel Larus, 'India Claims a Role in Antarctica', The Round Table, no.289 (1984), p.53.

9. Hanessian, The Antarctic Treaty, p.450.

10. Beck, Secret Antarctic Treaty Preparatory Negotiations.

11. Ibid.

12. Heap, Antarctic Cooperation, pp.104-105.

13. Auburn, Antarctic Law and Politics, p.118; Guyer, Antarctica's Role in International Relations, p.278; Rüdiger Wolfrum, 'The Use of Antarctic Non-Living Resources: The Search for a Trustee?', in Wolfrum, Antarctic Challenge, p.162; Pinto, quoted in Wolfrum, Antarctic Challenge, p.165.

14. See Roberts, International Cooperation for Antarctic Development, p.117.

15. Annual Report of the Secretary-General on the Work of the Organization 1959-1960, UNGA 15th.Session, Supplement 1A, p.4.

16. See above pp.87-9.

17. Note dated 14 July 1961, quoted in Myhre, The Antarctic Treaty Consultative Meetings, 1961-68. p.122, note 35.

18. Bilder, Present Legal and Political Situation in Antarctica, p.188; Guyer, Antarctica's Role in International Relations, p.278.

19. Ahluwalia, The Antarctic Treaty, p.483; Hanessian, The Antarctic Treaty, p.462.

20. Subash C. Jain, 'Antarctica: Geopolitics and International Law', Indian Yearbook of International Affairs, vol.17 (1974), p.271, pp.277-8.

21. Myhre, The Antarctic Treaty Consultative Meetings, 1961-68, pp.17-18, p.171.

22. Quigg, A Pole Apart, p.165.

23. UNGA E/C 7/5, annex, p.3, 25 January 1971; Schroff, Antarctica: Politics and Resources, p.117.

24. Schroff, Antarctica: Politics and Resources, p.117.

25. Auburn, Antarctic Law and Politics, pp.124-5; Gregory P. Wilson, 'Antarctica, the Southern Ocean and the Law of the Sea', JAG Journal, vol.XXX (1978), p.61; Barbara Mitchell and Lee Kimball, 'Conflict over the Cold Continent', Foreign Policy (1979), p.133.

26. Barbara Mitchell and Richard Sandbrook, The Management of the Southern Ocean (IIED, London, 1980), pp.28-9; Auburn, Antarctic Law and Politics, pp.127-8.

27. UNGA A/39/583 (Part I), 1984, pp.56-7.

28. Wyndham, quoted in Wolfrum, Antarctic Challenge, p.116; Barbara Mitchell, 'The Politics of Antarctica', Environment, vol.22, no.1 (1980), pp.19-20.

29. D.H.N. Johnson, 'The New International Economic Order (1)', Yearbook of World Affairs 1983 (Stevens, London, 1983), p.204, pp.213-7; Rudolf Illing, quoted in Wolfrum, Antarctic Challenge, pp.109-111.

30. Honnold, Thaw in International Law?, pp.807-08, pp.824-8; Barnes, The Emerging CCAMLR, pp.272-3.

31. New York Times, 4 Dec.1959; Honnold, Thaw in International Law?, pp.846-7; Triggs, Australia's Sovereignty in Antarctica: the Validity of Australia's Claim at International Law, pp.593-611.

32. Brownlie, Principles of Public International Law, p.267; Burton, New Stresses on the Antarctic Treaty, pp.498-509.

33. UNGA A/30/PV 2380, pp.13-15, 8 Oct.1975.

34. Bilder, Present Legal and Political Situation in Antarctica, pp.192-3.

35. Leigh Ratiner, Earthscan Press Briefing, 27 July 1977, quoted UNGA A/39/583 (Part I), 1984, p.65.

36. Quoted in Financial Times, 5 Sept.1977 (Leigh Ratiner).

37. Pinto, 25 July 1977, quoted Mitchell, The Politics of Antarctica, pp.20-21.

38. M.C.W. Pinto, 'The International Community and Antarctica', University of Miami Law Review, vol.33, no.2 (1978), p.480-5.

39. De Soto, 14 Sept.1979, quoted in Mitchell, The Politics of Antarctica, p.39.

40. Quoted, in D. Shapley, 'Antarctic Problems: Tiny Krill to Usher in New Resource Era', Science, 196 (1977), p.505.

41. Quigg, A Pole Apart, p.170.

42. Final Report of the Ninth Antarctic Treaty Consultative Meeting (HMSO, London, 1977), p.25, 19 Sept.1977.

43. Roberts, International Cooperation for Antarctic Development, p.112, p.119 (note that this article published in 1978 was based upon a paper given in 1977).

44. Final Report of Ninth Consultative Meeting, p.25.

45. International Interests in Antarctica (FCO, London, 1977), p.5.

46. Note that treaty parties may support the common heritage principle in other regions: see Francisco Orrego Vicuna, 'The Antarctic Treaty System: A Viable Alternative for the Regulation of Resource Orientated Activities', paper delivered at the Whither Antarctica? Conference, London, 12 April 1985, p.156; Sollie, Jurisdictional Problems in relation to Antarctic mineral resources, p.325, p.335 (note 24).

47. Bush, Antarctica and International Law, vol.I, pp.390-1.

48. Vicuna, The Definition of a Regime on Antarctic mineral resources, p.212; Brennan, Criteria for Access to the Resources of Antarctica, pp.219-27; Pinto, quoted in Wolfrum, Antarctic Challenge, pp.166-7.

49. The debate over Antarctica and UNCLOS has prompted a vast literature, but note Scharnhorst Müller, 'The Impact of UNCLOS III on the Antarctic Regime', in Wolfrum, Antarctic Challenge, pp.169-76; Ralph L. Harry, 'The Antarctic Regime and the Law of the Sea Convention: An Australian View', Virginia Journal of International Law, vol.21, no.4 (1981), pp.727-44.

50. Bush, Antarctica and International Law, vol.II, pp.202-09.

51. UN A/CONF.62/PV 192, p.12, 9 Dec.1982; UN A/CONF.62/PV 187, pp.81-2, 7 Dec.1982.

52. Pinto, The International Community and Antarctica, p.485; Peterson, Antarctica: the last great land rush on earth, pp.401-02.

53. Keith Suter, 'Preventing a land grab in Antarctica', National Outlook, March 1984, p.10.

54. Roger Kershaw, 'Anglo-Malaysian Relations: old roles versus new rules', International Affairs, vol.59, no.4 (1983), pp. 629-48; Stuart Drummond, 'Mahathir's Malaysia', The World Today, vol.39, nos.7/8 (1983), pp.304-311.

55. UNGA A/37/PV 10, pp.17-20, 29 Sept.1982.

56. Mahathir, 8 March 1983, Foreign Affairs Malaysia, vol.16, no.1 (1983), pp.7-8.

57. UNGA A/38/132 S/15675, p.98, paragraphs 122-3.

58. Pinto, Battle for the Treasure of the last frontier on earth, p.38.

59. Ibid. This point is based primarily on private information.

60. Note to Malaysia, 29 July 1983 supplied by the Malaysian High Commission in London.

61. Auburn, Antarctic Minerals and the Third World, p.204.

62. See above pp.196-7.
63. Beck, Antarctica's Indian Summer, p.299.
64. Antarctic Treaty: Report of the Twelth Consultative Meeting, p.12; Canberra Times, 29 Sept.1983.
65. Vicuna, The Antarctic Treaty System, p.156; Watts, quoted in Wolfrum, Antarctic Challenge, p.222.
66. Watts, quoted in Wolfrum, Antarctic Challenge, p.222.
67. UNGA A/38/193, p.1, letter of 11 August 1983; UNGA A/BUR/38/SR.2, pp.3-10, 21 Sept.1983.
68. New Straits Times, 23 Sept.1983; Malaysian Digest, 15 Oct.1983.
69. UNGA A/BUR/38/SR.2, p.7, 21 Sept.1983, Sir John Thomson (UK).
70. UNGA A/38/439, pp.1-2, letter of 19 Sept.1983.
71. UNGA A/38/495, S/16035, p.4, p.24, letter of 10 Oct.1983.
72. Beck, The United Nations and Antarctica, pp.140-1.
73. Brennan, Criteria for Access to the Resources of Antarctica, p.225.
74. UNGA A/C 1/38 PV 42, pp.7-23, 28 Nov.1983.
75. UNGA A/C 1/38 PV 42, p.22, 28 Nov.1983.
76. Ibid, p.20, p.23.
77. Ibid, p.10.
78. Ibid, p.7.
79. UNGA A/C 1/38 L 84, 30 Nov.1983.
80. UNGA A/C 1/38 PV 44, pp.16-18, 29 Nov.1983.
81. UNGA A/C 1/38 PV 43, p.16, 29 Nov.1983.
82. UNGA A/C 1/38 PV 44, p.12, 29 Nov.1983.
83. Ibid, pp.3-5.
84. UNGA A/C 1/38 PV 46, p.11, 30 Nov.1983.
85. UNGA A/38/PV 97, pp.30-31, 15 Dec.1983; UNGA A/38/646, pp.1-3 12 Dec.1983; UNGA A/C 1/38 PV 46, p.13, 30 Nov.1983; UNGA A/C 1/38/L.80, pp.1-2, 28 Nov.1983.
86. For a contemporary assessment of the position, see Beck, The United Nations and Antarctica, pp.142-3.
87. UNGA A/39/583 (Part I), 1984. The responses were published in three volumes (these have been quoted earlier in the book): UNGA A/39/583 (Part II), 1984, vols.1-3.
88. UNGA A/C 1/39 PV 52, pp.18-20, 29 Nov.1984.
89. UNGA A/39/583 (Part I), 1984, p.21, p.44, p.49.
90. Ibid, p.80; Rubin, Who Discovered Antarctica?, pp.508-509.
91. UNGA A/39/PV 9, p.31, 26 Sept.1984.
92. UNGA A/C 1/39 PV 50, p.16, 28 Nov.1984, Zain (Malaysia).
93. Ibid, pp.2-30.
94. UNGA A/C 1/39 PV 53, p.51, pp.53-5, 29 Nov.1984.
95. UNGA A/C 1/39 PV 50, pp.28-35, 28 Nov.1984.
96. Ibid, pp.6-7.

97. UNGA A/C 1/39 PV 53, p.62, 29 Nov.1984.

98. Ibid, p.16, Beauge (Argentina); UNGA A/C 1/39 PV 50, p.57, 28 Nov.1984, Zegers (Chile).

99. UNGA A/C 1/39, PV 50, pp.8-10, 28 Nov.1984; UNGA A/39/583 (Part II), 1984, pp.107-111, Malaysian response, 31 May 1984.

100. UNGA A/C 1/39 PV 50, pp.8-10, pp.33-5.

101. Canberra Times, 1 Dec.1984; UNGA A/C 1/39 PV 55, pp.13-17, 30 Nov.1984.

102. UNGA A/C 1/39 PV 55, p.17, 30 Nov.1984; Zain, comment at Whither Antarctica? Conference, London, 12 April 1985.

103. UNGA A/C 1/39 PV 55, pp.17-20, 30 Nov.1984; UNGA A/C 1/39 L.83, pp.1-2, 30 Nov.1984; UNGA A/39/756, pp.1-3, 10 Dec. 1984.

104. Sydney Morning Herald, 3 Dec.1984; The Guardian, 4 Dec.1984.

105. Canberra Times, 1 Dec.1984; West Australian, 3 Dec.1984.

106. T. Hatherton, 'The Beardmore Workshop- A Participant's View', Antarctic, vol.10, no.8 (1985), pp.283-5; Anon., 'Antarctic Talks Near South Pole', Antarctic, vol.10, no.7 (1984), pp.251-2; Anon., 'Workshop on the Antarctic Treaty System', Polar Record, vol.22, no.139 (1985), p.451.

107. Hatherton, The Beardmore Workshop, p.285.

108. The conference was organised by the British Institute of International and Comparative Law, London. Most of the papers are available in typescript, and may be published.

109. Zain-Azraai, 'Antarctica: The Claims of "Expertise" vs. "interest" ', paper delivered at Whither Antarctica? Conference, London, 12 April 1985, pp.1-3.

110. Ibid, pp.8-9.

111. Ibid, p.12.

112. Brennan, Criteria for Access to the Resources of Antarctica, p.225.

113. Zain, comment at Whither Antarctica? Conference, London, 12 April 1985.

114. Note to Malaysia, 29 July 1983.

115. UNGA A/C 1/38 PV 45, p.4, 30 Nov.1983, Sorzano (USA); UNGA A/38/PV 17, pp.79-80, 4 Oct.1983, Hayden (Australia).

116. Mahathir to Non-Aligned Summit Meeting, New Delhi, 8 March 1983, Foreign Affairs Malaysia, vol.16, no.1 (1983), p.7.

117. Vicuna, The Antarctic Treaty System, pp.144-58.

118. Charney, The New Nationalism and the Use of Common Spaces, p.3.

119. John A.Heap, 'Current and Future Problems arising from Activities in Antarctica', paper delivered at Whither Antarctica? Conference, London, 11 April 1985.

120. Vicuna, The Antarctic Treaty System, p.158, p.161 (note 26).

121. See also Gillian Triggs, 'Antarctica: A Jurisdictional Vacuum or The Common Heritage of Mankind?', paper delivered at Whither Antarctica? Conference, London, 11 April 1985, pp.104-105.

122. UNGA A/C 1/39 PV 53, p.47, 29 Nov.1984; Rich, A Minerals Regime for Antarctica, p.714-5.

PART FOUR

THE ANTARCTIC FUTURE

Chapter Twelve

ANTARCTICA IN THE 1980s AND 1990s

On 1 December 1984 the Consultative Parties celebrated the 25th. anniversary of the conclusion of the Antarctic Treaty, and it proved rather ironic that the previous week witnessed another significant phase of the international debate upon the future of Antarctica, and especially of the efforts of certain governments to replace the Antarctic Treaty by an alternative UN-centred regime. In this manner, the 1984 UN discussions gave further substance to the observation of Engels, the Dutch representative, that 'after decades as a peaceful scientific backwater, Antarctica has recently emerged to command international and public attention'[1]. The outcome of this development remains uncertain, although the Antarctic Treaty System seems likely to survive, albeit in a way permitting a more meaningful input from outsiders acting through the UN. In many respects, the episode has consolidated the unity of the Antarctic Treaty System, whose durability is further confirmed by the fact that the year 1986 marks its 25th. year of operation, since the 1959 treaty did not become effective until June 1961.

The early 1980s have demonstrated an increased tendency by governments and international bodies to refer to Antarctica not only as an international problem but also as a potential crisis point in the late 1980s or in 1991, when many believe that the 1959 treaty expires; indeed, some even depict the continent as 'a future casus belli'[2]. This trend at the government and media level has been paralleled by greater interest upon the part of academics in the spheres of international politics and of international law, a development accentuated by the manner in which traditionally Antarctic affairs have been ignored by practitioners in these subject areas. Significantly, the 1985 Whither Antarctica? Conference held at London was organised by the British Institute of International and Comparative Law, thereby highlighting the fact that academics have begun to realise the need to bring Antarctica into the mainstream of study, partly because of its intrinsic importance and interest and partly because of its relevance to a range of other topics, including sovereignty and ownership, resource management, scientific research and cooperation, environmental protection, outer space and the deep seabed. Antarctica is oft-interpreted as a unique region with its own specific problems, that is, as an international oddity or 'a Pole apart', but the post-1983 UN debate has helped to place the continent in the wider international context and to stress the consequent need to consider it as an integrated part of the global political framework; in fact, this interpretation represents a natural development of the view taken by such scientists as David Drewry, director of the Scott Polar Research Institute, to the effect that 'Antarctica forms a unique yet integral part of the environmental systems of planet earth'[3]. As a result, Heap has pointed out that, 'most problems are merely Antarctic examples of problems we find elsewhere', such as in respect to the regulation of activities, the enforcement of regulations, the management of resources, sovereignty and environmental protection[4]. For example, the recent resource regime negotiations have shown that the continent proves another site for what O'Riordan has described as the controversy between the technocentric and ecocentric perspectives, that is, whether to exploit resources regardless of the environmental impact or to conserve; indeed, the role of environmental groups in Antarctica has constituted both a cause and reflection of international concern about the region, while the role of such non-governmental organisations in Antarctic politics offers interesting opportunities for study[5]. In fact, research on Antarctic questions provides an invaluable dimension to numerous aspects of study in international politics, law, history and science, whose academic contribution is enhanced by the inter-disciplinary nature of Antarctic topics.

The recent escalation of international interest in the southern continent has encouraged some commentators, conscious of the length of the UNCLOS negotiations, to anticipate a similar period of debate about Antarctica in the wake of the 1983 UN reference, which has been interpreted as 'only the first shot in a long war which could last for years'[6]. However, the apparent novelty of this episode is qualified by the fact that, in reality, the on-going international debate represents merely a further chapter in the long-running story of Antarctica's role in international relations, a saga which covers a longer period of time - this was argued in the early part of this book - than is often presumed. As the 20th century has progressed, Antarctica has become less of a 'frontier' region and has assumed a higher international profile as its affairs have been integrated more directly into not only the policies of an increasing number of governments but also the operation of the international political system. Naturally, this trend has undermined the attempt of scientists to preserve Antarctica as 'a continent for science' insulated from political complications, but a study of the 'Antarctic past' establishes that this Fuchs-type vision proved as difficult to achieve during the early decades of this century as during the 1970s and early 1980s. A few years ago one prominent polar scientist, Zumberge, conceded that 'the idea that Antarctica can be held forever as a scientific laboratory is losing ground', even if scientific and geographical information remain the chief 'exports' from Antarctica[7].

It is always difficult to conclude a book dealing with contemporary problems, since the on-going and fluid nature of such questions means that any observations are liable to be overtaken by the development of events. However, academic, media and official interest is increasing, and seems likely to gain pace as the decade progresses, in the affairs of Antarctica, even if its perceived significance will never rival that of such areas as the Middle East and Central America or even that of the Arctic, where the Antarctic-type equation of 'frontier' and resource problems 'has caused the political temperature there to rise a few degrees'[8]. Nevertheless, the continent's future international role should not be underestimated, partly because of its vast size, partly because of the involvement of the major international actors, and partly because the early 1980s have highlighted already the conflict possibilities of other oft-forgotten and seemingly unimportant parts of the world, such as the Falkland Islands and Grenada. In this context, the 1982 Falklands War excited some speculation regarding the implications for Antarctica; for instance, there existed suggestions that the Argentine invasion of the Falklands was motivated in part by its Antarctic ambitions so that the war might spread from the Falklands and South Georgia to disputed Anglo-Argentine territory in Antarctica[9].

By June 1986 the Antarctic Treaty will have been operational for 25 years, and the agreement remains still the central fact of Antarctica's international political, legal and scientific life and forms the nucleus of a well-established system of cooperative international relationships capable of indefinite duration into the next decade and beyond. Many governments, including the most influential members of the international community, take the system's preservation for granted on account both of its merits and of the fact that - to quote Scully of the USA - 'if it ain't broke, don't fix it'[10]. As a result, Antarctica represents one of the few international issues uniting the Soviet and American governments in a common cause, a feature characteristic of the recent UN discussions. During November 1983, the Soviet delegation stressed:

> The significance of the Treaty and the system of international cooperation based on it, it is obvious that the Treaty is an extremely important international treaty,

> whose role and significance should not be underestimated ... the Soviet Union has consistently favoured and continues to favour the maintenance of the Antarctic Treaty and the strengthening of the international legal regime which is established in it[11].

This was followed one day later by the American statement, which focussed upon the utility and preservation of the treaty; thus, Sorzano stated that:

> I have dwelt upon the nature and accomplishments of the Antarctic Treaty system in some detail because they stand as a remarkable achievement in multilateral international co-operation and as a monument to the principles and objectives of the United Nations Charter ... the United States will firmly resist any effort to weaken, undermine or replace that system[12].

Basically the Antarctic Treaty System is valued on account of its proven ability to harmonise the divergent interests of a number of governments, including claimants and non-claimants, eastern and western bloc countries as well as developed and developing governments. The recent emphasis upon the problem of external accommodation with the international community has tended to obscure the system's achievements in the sphere of the difficult and demanding task of internal accommodation. This success has been facilitated by the determination of the parties to preserve the perceived benefits of the treaty's existence, which countermand any disadvantages, such as those affecting claimants as a consequence of the freeze on sovereignty. Perhaps, the key treaty advantage concerns the indefinite maintenance of the continent as a zone of peace in a troubled world, such as emphasised by Brian Roberts, one of the system's architects and exponents.

> Some degree of international order evolved out of chaos; harmony has replaced discord; many apparently insoluble problems have been resolved one after another ... without any significant sacrifice of national autonomy and to the common advantage of all[13].

At the UN since 1983 both Soviet and American delegates admitted their mutual support for Antarctica's treaty separation from the East-West problem, including the associated nuclear rivalry.

> There are no arms races, there is no nuclear escalation in the Antarctic. It is a zone of peace and a nuclear-free zone[14].

This American assertion was seconded by delegates from the other treaty powers, including the Soviet Union, which interpreted the Antarctic Treaty as:

> A new stage in the evolution of international relations. For the first time in history not only individual territories but an entire continent was declared to be a zone of peace and international cooperation[15].

Obviously, an arms control agreement was easier to secure in Antarctica than would have been the case in more sensitive regions, but the extent of the treaty's achievements should not be under-rated, since during the late 1950s the fear of international conflict over Antarctica was a very real one. In turn, the Antarctic Treaty has served not only to insulate the continent from conflict situations in other parts of the world, including the 1982 Falklands War, but also to ensure its preservation as a strategic irrelevance.

Without the treaty, the international position might be transformed, so that, for example, Australia's 'Near South' would become a strategic fact again. In this vein, Deporov feared that the treaty's revision or replacement 'could damage the regime of exclusive peaceful use of Antarctica ... have an adverse effect on the international situation ... turn Antarctica from a zone of peace and fruitful cooperation into a zone of friction and dangerous international conflict'[16]. In the power vacuum caused by the demise of the treaty system, there might occur a scramble for influence, territory and resources in Antarctica - Peterson's 'last great land rush on earth' - thereby returning to the bad old days of the 1940s and 1950s. However, the very success of the treaty's peaceful use provisions renders it easy to forget the tensions and dangers of the 'Antarctic past', and recently Guyer, who was involved also in the 1958-9 negotiations, claimed that to imagine the continent without the treaty would become a 'true science fiction process'; thus, otherwise, 'it would be the scene of serious confrontation'[17]. The treaty parties have pressed these arguments, such as demonstrated by the joint note sent to the Malaysian government on 29 July 1983, and this explains their support for the treaty system's preservation; for instance, in 1984 a British Foreign Office paper stressed that:

> Although it has come under some criticism in recent years, the Antarctic Treaty has worked effectively and this seems likely to ensure its preservation ... other States cannot seek to act as arbiters of the obligations of those within the system without risking the release of the tensions that the system has been designed to keep in check[18].

In any case, the Antarctic Treaty was a product of its time, that is, of a period when internationalism was viewed with considerable favour, and clearly its most beneficial provisions would prove very difficult, if not impossible, to secure in today's world.

The commitment of the treaty parties to the political aspects of the system has been paralleled by the support of the scientific community, which has followed Fuchs in regarding the treaty as 'an outstanding success' in the scientific and environmental spheres[19]. The scientists' appreciation of the post-IGY advance of the frontiers of knowledge in a cooperative framework was typified by the comment of Richard Laws, the director of BAS, that 'it would be difficult to find another part of the world where international cooperation is better'[20]. The 1984 UN Study reaffirmed the political, scientific and environmental achievements of the treaty system, even if certain commentators, particularly those involved in the environment movement, have questioned such conclusions. Nevertheless, the UN Study drew attention to the 'cooperative spirit' prevalent in Antarctica as a consequence of the interaction of political and scientific factors.

> Frequently the wish had been expressed that the same spontaneous friendships based on shared goals and the same close cooperation founded on free scientific inquiry could exist without inhibition elsewhere in the world[21].

Upon this basis, the Antarctic Treaty System's regional role has been oft-interpreted as possessing a wider significance partly because its Antarctic contribution satisfies also various international interests, such as in respect to peace, environmental protection and the applied nature of scientific research, and partly because of its precedent-setting qualities. As a result, the Antarctic Treaty has tended to become interpreted more as 'a model for international cooperation' rather than as 'a kind of oddity in the field of international relations'. Antarctica became the first area subject to arms control and free of nuclear weapons, and the 1959 treaty represented - to quote the UN Study - 'one of the most significant post-war contributions toward averting nuclear weapons proliferation and halting the nuclear arms race'[22]. Although this precedent has been applied to other problems, it has become apparent that different situations are never quite analogous, and recently Bloomfield gave only qualified support for the creation of a conflict-free zone in the Arctic based upon the Antarctic example; thus, he concluded that 'Arctic political cooperation will not be as easy as it was in 1959 in the Antarctic'[23]. Therefore, the chief imitative possibilities of the Antarctic Treaty derive essentially from its component parts, such as of peaceful use, inspection, scientific cooperation and the exchange of information, rather than from its character as a package. For example, certain features were applied in the 1967 Outer Space Treaty, although the recent period has witnessed a reverse linkage according to which attempts have been made to apply other agreements - most notably the convention on the Law of the Sea - as precedents upon which to model future changes in Antarctica, such as highlighted by the emphasis upon the common heritage principle.

Although it lacks still an extensive institutional framework, the Antarctic Treaty System has demonstrated over the years an ability to respond in a pragmatic, flexible and responsible manner towards the accommodation of emerging problems in the light of a range of political, legal, scientific, environmental and other realities. The treaty system has worked, has survived, has adapted, has permitted the co-existence of varying national viewpoints, has extended its sphere of competence, and has attracted additional participants. This process of development has been facilitated by forethought and prudence, such as to deal with topics before they become problems, as well as by forebearance, including the willingness of Consultative Parties not to press their legal positions to the limit. To some extent, this evolution has been encouraged by the underlying fear of Consultative Parties about renewed conflict in the event of the failure of the system; thus, in the face of each new situation, they have opted for action rather than inaction, since the latter course might create a power vacuum and prove a recipe for international instability[24]. During the 1960s the Agreed Measures were drafted to deal with the treaty's shortcomings in the sphere of environmental protection, and subsequently perceived deficiencies in respect to living resources led to the 1972 Seals Convention and the 1980 CCAMLR. The treaty "gap" on mineral resources is now in the process of coverage, and this task is oft-depicted as the crucial test for the Antarctic Treaty System, since the negotiating process raises a series of complex problems in the spheres of both internal and external accommodation. The minerals question has been exacerbated by the speculation about Antarctica's untold wealth in regard to oil and natural gas, particularly as this aspect has proved a prime cause of contemporary interest in the region. However, the negotiations for an Antarctic minerals regime are already a good way along the road to an agreement, partly because the Consultative Parties are anxious to prove to the outside world their ability to accommodate even the most demanding Antarctic problems. In April 1985 Arthur Watts, one of the British negotiators, pointed out that, while the talks are still in mid-course and the 'end is not immediately in sight', there existed 'a growing measure of consensus', which fostered hopes of a successful outcome perhaps even within 'a couple of years' or so[25]. Nevertheless, the establishment of an Antarctic minerals regime will not alter the relatively dismal prospects for the actual exploitation of minerals in and around the continent; in fact, a regime might prove a hypothetical solution to a hypothetical problem, and Larminie, who works for British Petroleum and possesses considerable Arctic expertise, reminded the 1985 Whither Antarctica? Conference that the oil industry - he claimed to have discussed the subject with the seven major companies - holds a rather jaundiced and pessimistic view of Antarctica[26]. In addition, the conclusion of an Antarctic minerals regime will represent a further institutional development of the Antarctic Treaty System (Figure 7.2), and certain commentators interpret this regime as the final piece in the Antarctic jigsaw puzzle in the sense that it will 'complete' the system, even if others suggest the need for further additions, such as either to accommodate tourism, Antarctic environmental protection, and iceberg exploitation, or to provide a Secretariat for the whole system[27].

In 1978 Zegers, who presented the Chilean case on Antarctica at the UN during both 1983 and 1984, used an article to urge the view that:

> Antarctica is not, nor can be considered as, res nullius or a zone located outside the activity and juridical regulation of man. There exists on the continent a valid and operative juridical system of advanced maturity ... there exists a real Antarctic System, which integrates perfectly with the general international system, conforms to the principles and objectives of the United Nations and has proven its efficiency in both time and space[28].

As a result, it was 'through the Antarctic System, and in close cooperation with it, that the solution to the question of utilization of the resources of the area should be found'; indeed, he stressed that the answer to any Antarctic question should be found only within the principles and parameters of this system. Zegers' arguments typify the case utilised by the Consultative Parties to justify their special position in regard to the management of the region, although recent UN-related developments highlight the fact that several treaty outsiders remain sceptical about this rationale, and especially about the Consultative Parties' frequent assertions that their role was conducted in 'the interests of all mankind'. During the 1960s there appeared to exist general international acquiescence in the Antarctic Treaty System and, while this feature could be attributed to its successful operation, in reality there was general international apathy and ignorance about the continent. Most governments ignored the vast southern territory, even India - this had displayed some interest during the late 1950s - but this situation began to alter during the 1970s as resource questions came together with emerging legal principles, such as that concerning the common heritage of mankind, to promote international concern about Antarctica's future, especially upon the part of the developing countries. This interest encouraged some governments to become active in Antarctica and to join the treaty system, whereas other governments assumed a more critical approach in favour of a reformed or replacement regime. As a result, the question of external accommodation emerged as a major preoccupation for the Consultative Parties, such as to establish that the interests of the 159 members of the UN could be represented adequately by the 32 treaty powers. Although some argue that 'time has run out for ... the treaty parties', the Antarctic Treaty System seems likely to survive, so that any UN role will need to be conducted within the confines of the system, whose future international contribution will be enhanced through various refinements such as in respect to an improved public relations effort, less secrecy, or quicker decision-making procedures[29].

Although most attention has been devoted to the international level, that is, to the Antarctic Treaty System, it should be remembered that there are also difficulties at the national level, since within any one participating country there exist varying, even conflicting, perceptions regarding Antarctica, such as those deriving from politicians and diplomats, scientists, industrialists, environmentalists and others. Several treaty powers have experienced some difficulty in the clarification of national interests in Antarctica, a point evidenced by the ambiguous and vague nature of their policies; indeed, it has been suggested that certain governments, such as Australia, Norway and the USA, lack either clearly structured guidelines or even a policy[30]. To some extent, this feature has resulted from the fact that Antarctica has not been interpreted as a prime policy interest, and claimants have been criticised for a failure to provide the fiscal commitment required to match their territorial assertions. Although Australia, New Zealand and Norway have attracted most criticism, the British government was exposed also to this accusation prior to its enhancement of Antarctic expenditure in 1982, even if this proved a reflection of Falklands rather than of Antarctic priorities. In any case, the existence of the Antarctic Treaty positively encourages the adoption of a vague and non-committal attitude, such as to permit claimants to keep open their sovereignty options without the need for any activity. Although the UN episode has compelled treaty governments to re-examine their respective positions, it is clear that many Antarctic policies are in a state of disarray and comprise little more than a series of goals and interests unsupported by an adequate commitment, such as in terms of research activity or expenditure.

Naturally, the 'Antarctic future' will be influenced by both the 'Antarctic past' and the 'Antarctic present'. In this context, the Antarctic Treaty System will continue, even if the future is clouded by various imponderables, including those relating to the minerals regime negotiations and to the role of the international community in the continent's affairs. In the meantime, an extract from the diary of Peter Scott, the son of Captain Robert Scott, offers an appropriate concluding comment.

> Goodbye to the Antarctic ... There is no denying its tremendous appeal. Cold and inhospitable it may be, but oh the exquisite beauty of it - and the challenge that is still there[31].

NOTES

1. UNGA A/C 1/39 PV 55, p.6, 30 Nov.1984.
2. Mahathir, 8 March 1983, Foreign Affairs Malaysia, vol.16, no.1(1983), pp.7-8; Max, The Antarctic - A Future Casus Belli, pp.943-5.
3. D.J. Drewry, 'The Antarctic Physical Environment', paper delivered at Whither Antarctica? Conference, London, 11 April 1985, p.1.
4. Heap, Current and Future Problems arising from Activities in Antarctica.
5. Bruce Davis, 'Australia and Antarctica: aspects of policy process', in Harris, Australia's Antarctic Policy Options, p.344; T. O'Riordan, Environmentalism (Pion, London, 1976), pp.1-12.
6. Luard, Who Owns the Antarctic?, p.1175; UNGA A/C 1/39 PV 50, pp.8-10, 28 Nov.1984, Zain (Malaysia).
7. Zumberge, Potential Mineral Resource Availability, pp.115-47.
8. Clive Archer and David Scrivener, 'Frozen Frontiers and resource wrangles: conflict and cooperation in Northern Waters', International Affairs, vol.59, no.1(1982-3), p.76; Bloomfield, The Arctic: Last Unmanaged Frontier, pp.87 et seq.
9. Lord Shackleton, 'Why the Falklands Matter', The Times, 22 April 1985.
10. Scully, Alternatives for Cooperation and Institutionalization in Antarctica, p.293.
11. UNGA A/C 1/38 PV 43, p.16, 29 Nov.1983, Yakovlev.
12. UNGA A/C 1/38 PV 45, pp.7-8, 30 Nov.1983.
13. Roberts, International Cooperation for Antarctic Development, p.107.
14. UNGA A/C 1/38 PV 45, p.5, 30 Nov.1983, Sorzano.
15. UNGA A/C 1/38 PV 43, p.13, 29 Nov.1983, Yakovlev.
16. Deporov, Antarctica: A Zone of Peace, pp.36-7.

17. Guyer, Antarctica's Role in International Relations, p.273.

18. British Foreign Office Background Brief, Antarctic Treaty: 25th.Anniversary (FCO, London, 1984), p.5.

19. Fuchs, Antarctica: Its History and Development, p.18.

20. HCFAC, Falkland Islands, Minutes of Evidence, 13 Dec.1982, p.91.

21. UNGA A/39/583 (Part I), 1984, p.26. See also p.21, p.44, p.49.

22. Ibid, p.46.

23. Bloomfield, The Arctic: Last Unmanaged Frontier, p.103.

24. Heap, quoted in Wolfrum, Antarctic Challenge, p.39.

25. A.D. Watts, 'Antarctic Mineral Resources: Negotiations for a Mineral Resources Regime', paper delivered at Whither Antarctica? Conference, London, 11 April 1985, p.19 and comments.

26. F.G. Larminie, 'Mineral Resources: Commercial Prospects for Antarctic Minerals', paper delivered at Whither Antarctica? Conference, London, 11 April 1985.

27. For example, see Ian Nicholson, quoted in Harris, Australia's Antarctic Policy Options, p.301.

28. Fernando Zegers Santa Cruz, 'The Antarctic System and the Utilization of Resources', University of Miami Law Review, vol.33, no.2(1978), pp.431-3, p.471.

29. Honnold, Thaw in International Law?, p.859.

30. For example, see Auburn, United States Antarctic Policy, pp.35-6. Note the forthcoming book on national policies: Carlos Moneta (ed.), Antartida, 1981-1991: Hacia un Nuevo Orden Antartico? (Buenos Aires, in press for 1985-6). The author contributed a chapter on Britain and Antarctica.

31. Miranda Weston-Smith (ed.), Peter Scott. Travel Diaries of a Naturalist: I(Collins, London, 1983), p.246.

SELECT BIBLIOGRAPHY

It would prove difficult to provide an adequate bibliography for this book, even if a large number of pages were made available for this purpose. The existence of specialised polar bibliographies, in conjunction with the long booklists in secondary works, has encouraged the employment of extra pages for text rather than for books. Thus, a select bibliography only has been included in order to highlight titles capable of providing in toto a wide-ranging and balanced perspective upon Antarctic developments, even if certain individual books offer neither objective nor completely accurate coverage, such as on account of a national or journalistic approach. Specialist articles have been excluded, but the extensive footnotes in this book will guide readers to specialist material.

Antarctic Treaty: Handbook of Measures in Furtherance of the Principles and Objectives of the Antarctic Treaty, 3rd.edn (Department of Foreign Affairs, Canberra, 1983)

Auburn, F.M. Antarctic Law and Politics (Hurst, London, 1982)

Azambuja, P. Antártida: História e Geopolitica (Corag, Brazil, 1982)

Barnes, J.N. Let's Save Antarctica (Greenhouse, Richmond, Australia, 1982)

Beeby, C. The Antarctic Treaty (New Zealand Institute of International Affairs, Wellington, 1972)

Bonner, W.N. and Walton, D.W.H. (eds) Key Environments: Antarctica (Pergamon, Oxford, 1985)

Brewster, B. Antarctica: Wilderness at Risk (Reed, Wellington, 1982)

Brownlie, I. Principles of Public International Law, 3rd.edn (Oxford University Press, Oxford, 1979)

Bush, W.M. (ed) Antarctica and International Law: A Collection of Inter-State and National Documents, vols.1-2 (Oceana, New York, 1982) A third volume is in press

Center for Ocean Management Studies, Antarctic Politics and Marine Resources: Critical Choices for the 1980s (COMS, University of Rhode Island, Kingston, 1985)

Central Intelligence Agency, Polar Regions Atlas (CIA, Washington, 1978)

Charney, J.I. (ed) The New Nationalism and the Use of Common Spaces. Issues in Marine Pollution and the Exploitation of Antarctica (Allanheld and Osmun, Totowa, New Jersey, 1982)

The Conference on Antarctica 1959 (US Government, Washington, 1960)

Debenham, F. Antarctica: The Story of a Continent (Macmillan, New York, 1961)

Everson, I. The Living Resources of the Southern Ocean (FAO, Rome, 1977)

Fox, R. Antarctica and the South Atlantic: Discovery, Development and Dispute (BBC, London, 1985)

Fraga, J.A. Introduccion a la Geopolítica Antártica (Direccion Nacional del Antartico, Buenos Aires, 1983) This is the latest edition of the 1979 version cited in this book

----- La Argentina y el Atlántico Sur (Pleamar, Buenos Aires, 1983)

Fuchs, V. Of Ice and Men: The Story of the British Antarctic Survey (Anthony Nelson, Oswestry, 1982)

Greenpeace International, The Future of the Antarctic: Background to a Second UN Debate (Greenpeace, Lewes, 1984)

Harris, S. (ed) Australia's Antarctic Policy Options (CRES, Canberra, 1984)

Hill, J. New Zealand and Antarctica (New Zealand Govenment, Wellington, 1983)

Honnywill, E. The Challenge of Antarctica (Anthony Nelson, Oswestry, 1984)

Hunter Christie, E.W. The Antarctic Problem (Allen and Unwin, London, 1951)

King, H.G.R. The Antarctic (Blandford, London, 1969)

Lewis, R.S. and Smith, P.M. (eds) Frozen Future: A Prophetic Report from Antarctica (Quadrangle, New York, 1973)

Lovering, J.F. and Prescott, J.R.V. Last of Lands ... Antarctica (Melbourne University Press, Melbourne, 1979)

Mitchell, B. Frozen Stakes: The Future of Antarctic Minerals (IIED, London, 1983)

Moneta, C. (ed) Antartida, 1981-1991: Hacia un Nuevo Orden Antartico? (Buenos Aires, in press)

Myhre, J.D. 'The Antarctic Treaty Consultative Meetings 1961-68: A case study in cooperation, compliance and negotiation in the international system', unpublished Ph.D thesis, University of London, 1983

Oliver, R.L., Jones, P.R. and Jago, J.B. (eds) Antarctic Earth Sciences: Fourth International Symposium (Cambridge University Press, Cambridge, 1983)
Quigg, P.W. A Pole Apart: The Emerging Issue of Antarctica (McGraw Hill, New York, 1983)
Schatz, G.S. (ed) Science, Technology and Sovereignty in the Polar Regions (Lexington, Books, Lexington, Mass., 1974)
Splettstoesser, J.F. (ed) Mineral Resource Potential of Antarctica (University of Texas Press, Austin, in press)
Sugden, D. Arctic and Antarctic: a modern geographical synthesis (Blackwell, Oxford, 1982)
United Nations, Report on the Question of Antarctica (UNGA A/39/583: Part I United Nations, New York, 1984)
Vicuna, F.O. (ed) Antarctic Resources Policy: Scientific, Legal and Political Issues (Cambridge University Press, Cambridge, 1983)
------ Caffi, M.T.I. and Armanet, P.A. (eds) Politica Antartica de Chile (University of Chile, Santiago, 1984)
Whither Antarctica?: The Regulation of Activities in the Region, Conference Papers (British Institute of International and Comparative Law, London, 1985)
Wolfrum, R. (ed) Antarctic Challenge: Conflicting Interests, Cooperation, Environmental Protection, Economic Development (Duncker and Humblot, Berlin, 1984)

The chief bibliographical aids are Antarctic Bibliography of the Library of Congress Science Technology Division (US Government Printing Office, Washington) - these have been published periodically since 1951 and volume 13 appeared in 1984 - Current Antarctic Literature (monthly compilations eventually cumulated in Antarctic Bibliography) and Recent Polar and Glaciological Literature (published three times per year, Scott Polar Research Institute, University of Cambridge). The majority of citations are scientific, while international political and legal items tend to be listed under 'Political Geography', a practice highlighting the backwardness of Antarctica in the sphere of international politics and international law.

Although certain international political and legal journals have begun to devote more space to polar matters, the most useful journals are Antarctic (New Zealand Antarctic Society, Wellington), Antarctic Journal (National Science Foundation, Washington), ECO (Friends of the Earth International), Fram: Journal of Polar Studies (Polaris Publications, Bangor, Maine) and Polar Record (Scott Polar Research Institute, University of Cambridge). Mention should be made also of BAS Club Newsletter (BAS Club, BAS, Cambridge), whose academic value has been enhanced under the editorial direction of David Wynn-Williams.

INDEX

Acheson, Dean 37
Adélie Lane 24, 29, 109, 119, 121, 125, 132, 223
Agreed Measures for Conservation of Antarctic Fauna and Flora 61, 69, 79, 149, 159, 218-20, 223, 232, 243, 259, 315
Ahluwalia, K 274
Algeria 280, 288, 290
Alterman, Simon 129
Amerasinghe, Shirley 279, 281
Amundsen, Roald 25, 47
Antarctica 8-14, 24, 61, 95, 238, 318
  Antarctic Convergence 11-12, 68, 163, 213, 225, 226
  discovery 23-4, 40, 116, 123, 125
  environmental protection see environmental interests
  historical dimension 21-3, 40, 54-6, 62, 89, 113-14, 285, 298, 310-11, 314
  International Geophysical Year (IGY) see International Geophysical Year
  international political role 5, 22, 41, 54, 56, 65, 68, 74, 85,
Antarctica (continued)
  international political role (continued) 114-15, 141-2, 151, 164, 176, 183-5, 187, 205-6, 225, 228, 232-4, 238, 244, 248-9, 270-99, 310-12
  international problem 3, 15, 40-1, 52, 54, 62, 85, 115, 128-35, 148, 176-9, 210-13, 297-9, 309-18
  legal claims and sovereignty 9, 27-8, 39-40, 46, 48, 52-4, 55, 62, 65, 66, 68-9, 70, 85, 97, 98, 110, 113-42, 158, 212, 220, 221, 226-8, 245, 247-8, 254-8, 264, 278-80, 283, 288, 298, 310, 312, 316
  marine ecosystem 11-12, 67, 68, 102-3, 212-18, 225-6, 232
  resources see Resources, Marine Resources, Mineral Resources
  scientific utility 95-8 see science
  strategic and military role 26, 32-3, 37-8, 40-1, 50-2, 64-5, 66-7, 69-73, 80-9,

Antarctica (continued)
strategic and military role (continued) 196, 212, 254, 274, 312-14
subject for study 5-7, 15, 309-11
Antarctic Treaty 4, 8, 21, 22, 34, 39, 55, 61, 64, 66, 69, 82, 84, 89, 96, 141, 176, 212, 246, 272, 309, 311, 314
article I 69, 71, 72-3, 76, 80, 87, 89, 117, 228, 244, 245
article II 53, 98-107, 223
article III 53, 79, 98, 103, 104, 105, 107, 152, 160, 175, 272
article IV 53, 85, 115-19, 124, 128, 133-7, 139, 141-2, 155, 165, 221, 227, 246, 248, 255-6, 283
article V 69, 73, 76, 80, 87, 89, 117, 228, 261
article VI 67-9,
article VII 73-80, 87, 89, 105
article VIII 137-9
article IX 67, 77, 130, 132, 139, 152-6, 166, 176, 193-4, 196-202, 212, 218, 245
article X 196, 272, 273
article XI 165-6
article XII 152, 155, 166-70, 202
dispute settlement 165-6
duration 6, 67, 87, 118, 119, 169-71, 202-3, 311-12
internationalisation 39-41, 48, 62, 65, 115, 131-2, 134-5, 139, 184-5, 222, 270-99
origins 50-3, 61-4, 67-8, 73, 82, 88, 96-8, 107-8, 114-16, 118, 137, 152-3, 166, 167,
Antarctic Treaty (continued)
origins (continued) 171-2, 185-6, 194-5, 212, 272-3, 314
review provisions 134, 150, 152, 166-7, 202
treaty provisions
preamble 67, 69, 97, 171, 272
Antarctic Treaty System 148-51
see Marine Resources, Mineral Resources
Consultative Meetings 69, 104, 134, 149-66, 167, 172-7, 178, 188-90, 195-202, 212-13, 218-26, 251
Consultative Parties 150, 151, 160-1, 167, 183, 185-202, 205-6, 239, 248, 287, 295, 309
development 4, 6, 55, 61, 66, 88, 109, 115, 134, 141, 148-67, 176-9, 183, 198-200, 212-13, 219-26, 228-9, 230, 231-4, 238-9, 244-9, 253, 255-7, 259-61, 263-4, 270-99, 309-18
participation 4, 66-7, 130, 151, 178-9, 183-206, 228, 293
publicity and information 171-6, 177, 184-5, 191-2, 252
third parties 88, 135, 140-1, 148, 151, 201-2, 206, 219, 220-1, 225, 228-9, 231-2, 233, 249, 251-3, 263, 270-99, 316
Antigua and Barbuda 173, 184, 203, 260, 286-90, 293-4, 297, 299
Arctic 7, 31, 40, 50, 65, 81, 126, 242, 243, 261, 271, 311, 314

Argentina 30, 31-5, 41, 49, 55, 65, 71-2, 75-6, 77, 80-1, 85, 87, 102, 106-7, 113-14, 116, 119-20, 125, 126-7, 128-9, 133, 139, 152, 166, 171, 188, 192, 273, 277, 286, 287, 289, 294, 311
Anglo-Argentine rivalry 3, 21, 30-6, 54, 83-5, 107, 123, 129, 287
Auburn, Francis M. 7, 51, 53, 127, 128, 137, 166, 168, 172-3, 197, 256-7
Australia 13, 25, 28, 29-30, 36, 46, 49, 50, 54, 62, 63, 75, 77, 79, 80, 82, 86-7, 95, 102-3, 116, 119-21, 123, 126, 130-1, 134, 136, 138, 140, 157, 173, 175, 188, 192, 226, 230, 240, 252, 253, 256-7, 262, 283, 287, 289, 292-3, 297, 313, 317
Australian Antarctic Territory (AAT) 29, 82, 86, 119, 283

Bangladesh 202, 290, 293
BANZARE expedition 28, 29
Barber, Laurie 87
Barnes, James 229, 231, 242, 278
Beagle Channel Dispute 85, 168
Bechervaise, John 169
Beckett, W.E. 32
Beeby, Christopher 15, 151, 173, 252, 257, 259, 264, 299
Belgium 25, 49, 157, 188, 193-4, 200, 207 notes 27-8
Bellingshausen, Fabian von 23, 40, 293
Berkner, Lloyd 47
Bernhardt, J.P.A. 127-8
Bertrand, Kenneth J. 23
Bhurgari 193
Bhutan 290
Bi-focalism 137, 227, 255
Bilder, Richard 141, 251
BIOMASS project 99, 102-3, 212, 214, 224, 276
Bird, Lester 286
Bird, Vere 287
Birds in Antarctica 214, 218
Bloomfield, Lincoln 314
Bondi, Sir Hermann 14
Booker, Malcolm 169, 170
Borchgrevink, Carsten 25
Bouvet Island 227
Bowman, Isaiah 7
Bransfield, Edward 23, 28
Brazil 101, 109, 119, 124, 129, 161, 188, 190, 192, 196-200, 252, 275, 287
Brennan, Keith 289, 294, 297
Britain 18, 21, 22-3, 25, 26-36, 38, 41, 48, 49, 54-6, 62, 64-6, 68, 71-2, 75-6, 77, 80-1, 83-5, 95-7, 100, 102, 107-8, 113-14, 116, 120, 122-4, 126-7, 131, 132-3, 136, 153, 168, 171, 174, 188, 226, 242, 245, 254-5, 275, 281, 283, 287, 290, 293, 296, 313, 317
British Antarctic Survey (BAS) 13-14, 23, 32, 72, 78, 84-5, 95, 99-100, 107-8, 131, 250, 314
British Antarctic Territory (BAT) 60, 83, 122, 126, 132, 133, 250
British Petroleum (BP) 242-3, 316
Bruce, William 25
Bulgaria 189, 190, 214
Burton, S. 166
Busby 247
Buxton, Lord 72, 84
Byrd, Richard E. 10, 27, 30, 37, 47, 261, 270

Cameroons 293
Canada 126
Cape Verde 293
Caribbean Common Market (CARICOM) 4, 203, 286
Caro, David 131
Casey, Richard 63, 82
Challenger, HMS 25
Charcot, Jean-Baptiste 25, 121
Charney, Jonathan 259, 298
Chile 21, 23, 30, 31-7, 39, 41, 49, 54, 55, 65, 68, 71-2, 75-6, 81, 85, 87, 99, 102, 106, 113-14, 116, 120-1, 123, 125, 126-7, 129-30, 133, 139, 153, 166, 171, 175-6, 186, 188-92, 214, 273, 289, 294, 296-7
China 15, 109, 161, 183, 188, 190, 191-2, 198, 297
Cledwyn, Lord 169
Clifford, Sir Miles 35
Clipperton Island Case 31, 125
Cold War 21-2, 40, 52, 54, 62, 64, 70, 81-2, 87, 186, 200
Commission to Study the Organization of Peace 114, 127, 271
Common Heritage Principle 16, 23, 115, 119, 128, 139-42, 150, 184, 222, 254, 260, 277-9, 282-5, 288, 289, 293, 296, 298, 315, 317
Consultative Parties and Meetings, see Antarctic Treaty System
Convention for the Conservation of Antarctic Marine Living Resources (CCAMLR) 12, 61, 68, 69, 102, 104, 108, 136-7, 140, 149, 151, 153, 158, 160, 161, 178, 187, 213-34, 239, 244, 247-8, 259, 315
Cook, James 24, 120, 262
Crary, Albert 109
Crozet Islands 227
Cuba 103, 167, 189, 190, 192
Czechoslovakia 189, 190, 192

Dalrymple, Alexander 24
Daniels, Paul C. 62, 63, 73, 116, 152, 167, 170
Darlington, Jennie 38
Dater, Henry 64, 110
Debenham, Frank 10
Demilitarisation and Arms Control 65, 69, 73-6, 77, 79, 80-9, 273, 312-14
Denmark 77, 96, 189, 190, 191
Deporov, Y. 313
Developing Countries 150, 183-4, 276-8, 259-61, 280, 285
see also Third World
Dever, E. 193
Dibb, Paul 86-7, 141
Discovery Investigations 22, 27, 47
Dodd, Senator 82
Donoso-La Rosa Declaration 34
Drewry, David 310
Drygalski, Erich von 25
Dufek, George 81
Dulles, John F. 50
D'Urville, Dumont 24, 121

Earthscan 281
East Germany (German Democratic Republic) 187, 189, 190, 191, 205, 214, 216, 229
see Germany
Eastern Greenland Case 31, 126, 127
ECOs 174
Effective Occupation 27, 29, 30, 31-3, 36, 46, 54-5, 113-15, 125-8, 278
Egypt 290, 293

Ellsworth, Lincoln 27, 30, 37, 47
El Sayed, S.Z. 102
Endurance, HMS 84, 89
Engels 309
Environmental Interests 132, 141, 151, 173, 213, 222-4, 231, 232, 243, 244, 251-2, 258-9, 260, 310, 314
  Environmental Protection 66, 109-10, 159, 215, 218-24, 231, 232, 246, 248, 258-9, 310-11, 316
  International Environmental Law 222, 233, 276
  Specially Protected Areas (SPAs) 163-4, 219
Erebus, Mount 8, 262
Escudero Declaration 39, 55, 116
Essen, Alfred van der 117, 150, 158
European Economic Community (EEC) 177, 183, 229
Everson, Inigo 216, 276
Exclusive Economic Zone (EEZ) 69, 211, 283
Exxon 242

Falkland Islands 30, 34-5, 85, 100
  Falklands War (1982) 3, 83-5, 99, 107, 131, 132, 168, 177, 254, 311, 313, 317
Falkland Islands Dependencies (FID) 26, 30, 31, 32, 33-4, 68, 83-4, 100, 119-20, 122
Falkland Islands Dependencies Survey (FIDS) 23, 32-3, 35-6, 41, 126
Filchner, Wilhelm 25, 78
Finland 187, 189, 190, 191, 292
Fish 214, 216-17, 224
Fox, Robert 89, 107, 141, 232
France 24, 25, 29, 36, 41, 49, 54, 75-6, 102, 109, 120-1, 123, 125, 132, 171, 188, 223, 227-8, 240, 250, 259
Friends of the Earth 4, 174, 223
Frondizi, President 129
Fuchs, Sir Vivian 7, 15, 49, 53, 96-8, 168, 311, 314

Gandhi, Mrs Indira 13, 110, 200, 284, 291
Gbeho 176, 184, 204, 293, 299
Gentleman's Agreement (1955) 47, 50, 51-2, 55, 116
Gerlache, Adrien de 25, 193
Germany 25, 27, 30, 32, 80 _see_ East Germany, West Germany
Ghana 176, 184, 204, 290, 293, 299
Ghazali Shafie 284
Gjelsvik, Tore 240
Gondwanaland Thesis 12-13, 239, 241
Gould, Laurence M. 96, 97-8, 264
Greenpeace International 4, 258
Gruening, Senator 136
Guinea 277, 280
Gulf Oil 241, 242, 250
Guyer, Roberto E. 5, 52, 54, 87, 177, 186, 313

Hambro, Edvard 5
Harland 290
Harris, Stuart 176
Hatherton, Trevor 296
Hayden, William 297
Hayton, Robert 166
Heap, John 52, 135, 141, 155, 159, 174, 201, 243, 255, 273, 290, 292, 297, 298, 309

Heard Island 227
Hedgpeth, J.W. 11
Highjump, Operation 37, 70, 81, 270
Hillary, Edmund 49
Holdgate, Martin 246
Honnold, E. 139-40, 278
Hope Bay Incident 35, 52
Howe, Sir Geoffrey 287, 293
Hughes, Charles 31, 114
Hungary 187, 189, 190
Huntford, Roland 26, 238
Huxley, Julian 271

Icebergs and Ice shelves 9, 25, 28, 67-8, 110-11, 242, 261-3, 316
India 13, 32, 35, 51-2, 82, 99, 109, 110, 161, 178-9, 183, 185, 188, 190, 192, 196-9, 200, 251, 252, 272, 274-5, 284, 287, 291, 294, 316
Inspection in Antarctica 73-80, 106
International Antarctic Glaciological Project 96, 99
International Council of Scientific Unions (ICSU) 47, 100, 162
International Court 34, 35, 52, 165-6
International Environmental Law
see Environmental Interests
International Geographical Congress (1895) 25
International Geophysical Cooperation Year 50
International Geophysical Year (IGY) 21, 41, 46-55, 61-2, 67, 97-8, 103, 107, 162
International Institute for Environment and Development (IIED) 281
International Sea-Bed Authority (ISBA) 69, 115, 282, 310
International Telecommunications Union (ITU) 160
International Whaling Commission (IWC) 217, 229, 232
Iowa State University 262
Italy 189, 190, 191, 192, 200

Jacobs, Lloydstone 173, 184, 203, 289-90, 294
Jain, Subash C. 274
Jamaica 284, 290
Japan 25, 27, 49, 75-6, 102, 108, 124, 188, 201, 211, 214, 216-17, 226, 240, 244, 250, 291
Jurisdiction 137-9

Kennedy, President John 76
Kerguelen, Yves-Joseph de 211
Kerguelen Islands 211, 216, 227
Khrushchev, N. 64
King, H.G.R. 98
Krill 99, 102-3, 213-16, 224
Kuroda 201, 211, 291
Kuznetsov 64

Lagoni, Rainer 232
Lall, Arthur 272
Larminie, F.G. 316
Lastiri, President 129
Law, Phillip 46, 47, 110
Laws, Richard 72, 78, 99, 106, 225, 314
Ledovski, Andrei 63, 96, 116, 186
Libya 280, 290
Lindblad Tours 262
Llano, George 11, 217
Lopatin, B.G. 105-6
Luard, Evan 141, 242-3

McIver, George 25
Macmillan, Harold 62
Mahathir, Dr. 115, 284-6
Maish, F. Michael 105-7

Malaysia 4, 115, 140, 173, 183-4, 187, 198, 204, 205-6, 260, 284-97, 298-9, 313
Marguerite Bay 38
Marine Resources and Regime Negotiations 84, 151, 160, 212-34, 247, 263-4
Maury, Matthew 24
Mawson, Douglas 10, 25, 28, 29, 50, 239
Meissner 205
Menzies, Robert 62
Mineral Resources and Regime Negotiations 6, 12-13, 15, 41, 61, 84, 132, 136-7, 140, 151, 159-60, 161, 173-4, 178, 212-13, 232-4, 238-64, 283, 293, 315
Minquiers and Ecrehos Case 126
Mitchell, Barbara 242
Moon Treaty
see Outer Space
Myhre, Jeffrey 178

Nash, Sir W. 62, 272
National Science Foundation (NSF) 71, 99
Nehru, President 52
Netherlands 189, 190, 191, 192, 200, 309
New International Economic Order (NIEO) 4, 277-80
New York Times 81, 172, 271
New Zealand 28, 29, 36, 49, 54, 62, 70, 74-6, 77, 80, 87, 99, 116, 120-1, 123, 126, 131-2, 133, 141, 152, 188, 192, 242, 245, 250, 252, 272, 275, 289, 290, 293, 317
Nicholson, Ian 173, 256-7
Nigeria 204, 293
Non-Aligned Movement 4, 185, 199, 203, 277, 285-6, 287, 290
Non-Governmental Organisations (NGOs) 4, 151, 173, 174, 210, 222-4, 226, 244, 252, 295, 310
Nordenskjold, Otto 25
Norway 25, 27, 30, 32, 40, 48, 49, 54, 68, 96, 97, 120, 122, 126, 132, 188, 193, 240, 282, 296-7, 317
Nuclear Weapons 52, 64, 66, 69-73, 81-9, 312, 314
Nukey Poo 70

Oates, Titus 26
Organization of African Unity (OAU) 177
Organization of American States (OAS) 177
Organization of Eastern Caribbean States (OECS) 4, 203, 286
O'Riordan, T. 310
Outer Space and Moon Treaties 7, 65, 140, 278, 279, 288, 310, 315

Pakistan 193, 288, 290, 293
Palmas Island Case 31, 125-6
Palmer, Nathaniel 23
Papua and New Guinea 189, 190
Peary, Admiral 25
Peel, David 95-6
Peru 119, 124, 189, 190, 191, 192, 280
Peterson 313
Philippines 290, 293
Phleger, Herman 138
Pinochet, President 129
Pinto, C. 202, 280, 281, 294
Poland 75, 77, 102-3, 161, 188, 190, 192, 195, 198-200, 214, 216, 225
Polarhav Voyages 220
Puerto Montt, Act of 35

Quigg, Philip W. 26, 56, 107, 155, 281

Ratiner, Leigh 140, 279
Reeves, J.S. 127
Resources in Antarctica 70, 88, 108-11, 130, 134, 136, 150-1, 156, 159-60, 163, 199-200, 210-12, 222-3
  see Marine Resources, Mineral Resources
Review Conference 67, 150, 152, 166-9, 202
Rich, Roland 140, 255
Rio Treaty 36, 127
Roberts, Brian 64, 132, 218, 259, 282, 312
Romania 189, 190, 191
Ronne, Finn 38
Roosevelt, President F.D. 27
Ross, James Clark 24, 122
  Ross Dependency 29, 30, 121-2, 131
Rowland, John 233
Rowlands, Red 281-2
Rusk, Dean 76-7
Rymill, John 28

Sanderson, T.J. 243, 261
Saudi Arabia 262
Science in Antarctica
  continent for science 7, 52-3, 66-7, 95-111, 310
  politics and science 7, 15, 28-9, 32-3, 35-6, 37, 41, 46, 48, 49-50, 52, 55, 65, 70-3, 80, 96-8, 105-9, 128-35, 163, 164-5, 246
  research 13-14, 41, 46-7, 49, 50, 62, 162-5, 193-202, 212, 218, 230, 234, 238-44, 250, 310-11, 314
  Scientific Committee on Antarctic Research (SCAR) 50-1, 99, 100, 102, 109, 150-1, 157, 159, 162-5, 218-21, 224, 246-8, 276
  Sites of Special Scientific Interest (SSSIs) 163-4, 219
  Special Committee for Oceanic Research (SCOR) 102, 160
Scott, Peter 258, 318
Scott Polar Research Institute 96, 100, 162, 310
Scott, Robert F. 14, 25-6, 28, 47, 238, 239, 318
Scott, R. Tucker 76-7, 78, 168, 202, 311
Sealing 214, 217, 224
  Sealing Convention (1972) 104, 149, 151, 159, 217, 220-2, 223, 232, 315
Sector Principle 126-7
Shackleton, Edward (Lord) 23, 56, 83, 271
  Shackleton Report (1982) 84, 133, 211
Shackleton, Ernest 25, 122
Shirase 25
Sierra Leone 203, 290, 291, 292, 295
Singapore 288
Sollie, Finn 158, 264
Sorzano 170-1, 184, 290, 294, 312
Soto, Alvaro de 280, 281
South Africa 15, 49, 72, 75-6, 99, 102, 154, 157, 178, 188, 192, 203-5, 286, 290, 291-2, 293-4
South American Antarctic 34-5, 36, 85, 127
South Georgia 216, 227, 311
South Korea 214, 286, 295
Soviet Union (USSR) 22, 38-9, 40, 41, 46, 49-51, 54-5, 62-5, 66, 68, 71,

Soviet Union (USSR) (continued) 72, 73-6, 78-9, 81-3, 84, 86-7, 89, 99, 102-3, 105-6, 107, 116, 124, 126, 133, 134, 154-6, 157, 158, 166, 171, 176, 183, 185, 186, 188, 192, 202, 214, 216-17, 226, 229, 240-1, 246, 250, 257, 287, 291, 311-13
Spain 189, 190, 191, 192, 200, 217
Spencer, Cisca 204-5
Spitsbergen Treaty 141
Spotswood, Christopher 25
Sri Lanka 202, 277, 279, 280-1, 286, 290, 293
Stockholm Declaration (1972) 222, 276
Sudan 290
Suez Crisis (1956) 81
Sullivan, Walter L. 81, 172
Suter, Keith 3, 222
Sweden 25, 48, 96, 97, 187, 189, 190, 191, 292

Tabarin, Operation 31-3, 54, 80, 126
Talboys, B.E. 250
Tanzania 284
Thatcher, Margaret 168
Third World 198, 204, 276, 286
Times, The 169, 173
Tlatelolco, Treaty of 88-9
Tourism 261-2, 316
Triggs, Gillian 126, 142
Troyanovsky 89
Tunisia 290, 295
Turkey 286
Tyree, Admiral 70

United Kingdom
  see Britain
United Nations (UN) 4-5, 15-16, 39, 51, 62, 67, 82, 87-9, 115, 139, 141, 149, 150, 151, 156, 160, 170-1, 173-6, 177-8, 183-5, 192, 193, 198, 201, 203-5, 210-11, 222, 225, 245, 249, 252, 259-60, 270-99, 309-18
  Conference on Human Environment 222, 276
  Development Program (UNDP) 276, 279
  Economic and Social Council (ECOSOC) 275-6, 279
  Environmental Program (UNEP) 276, 279
  Food and Agriculture Organization (FAO) 102, 160, 215, 229, 232, 276-7
  Law of the Sea Conference and Convention (UNCLOS) 4, 5, 16, 69, 115, 140, 211, 224, 235, 245, 249, 261, 278-86, 288, 289, 310, 315
  Study on Antarctica (1984) 5, 15, 73, 88, 149, 176, 193, 203-4, 233, 264, 270, 289, 290, 291-5, 299, 314
UNESCO 162, 271
United States of America (USA) 21, 23, 24, 27, 30, 31, 35, 36, 41, 49-56, 62-5, 70, 71, 73-80, 81-3, 95-6, 99, 102-3, 105-6, 107, 114, 116, 124-5, 133, 134-5, 138-9, 141, 158, 166, 171, 175, 183, 184, 188, 202, 220, 226, 240, 242, 252, 257, 271, 274, 283, 287, 290, 311-12, 317
  Antarctic Service (USAS) 27, 30-1
  Arms Control and Disarmament Agency 76, 77
  Deep Sea Drilling Project 241

United States of America
(USA) (continued)
Geological Survey 211,
241, 250, 264
Uruguay 15, 124, 161, 188,
190, 192

Verma 291
Vicuna, Francisco Orrego
7, 194, 201, 233-4, 288,
297, 299
Videla, President 33
Vinson Massif 8

Washington Conference
(1959) 64, 70, 81, 88
Watts, Arthur 132, 255, 315
West Germany (German
Federal Republic) 75-6,
77-8, 161, 188, 190,
192, 195-6, 198-200,
214, 229, 240, 250, 283
see Germany
Whale Oil 26-7
Whaling 26-7, 40, 210, 214,
216-17, 224
Whither Antarctica
Conference? (1985) 296,
298, 309, 316
Wilkes, Charles 24, 28, 30
Wilkins, Sir Hubert 27
Wilson, Edward 238
Windmill, Operation 37
Woolcott, Richard 177, 185,
192, 206, 288, 291, 293,
294-5
Workshop on Antarctic
Treaty System (1985)
295
World Meteorological
Organization (WMO) 99,
160, 162-3
World Park in Antarctica
141, 222, 251
Wulf, Norman 247
Wyndham, Richard 21, 86,
227

Yakovlev 171, 291
Yugoslavia 286, 290

Zain, Ambassador 294,
296-7
Zainal Abidin 289
Zambia 290, 293
Zegers 23, 150, 212, 232,
316
Zumberge, J.H. 164, 242,
243, 264, 311

D1348331